Hindsight Is 2020

Nancy —
Thanks so much for
ordering my book. I hope you
find it inspirational. I hope you
In friendship;

Hindsight Is 2020

Torah Lessons from a Turbulent Time

RABBI MARGIE CELLA

BOLD
STORY
PRESS

CHEVY CHASE, MD

Bold Story Press, Chevy Chase, MD 20815
www.boldstorypress.com

First edition: November 2023

Library of Congress Control Number: 2023913233

ISBN: 978-1-954805-54-5 (paperback)
ISBN: 978-1-954805-55-2 (e-book)

Text and cover design by KP Design
Author photo by Rudy Gray

Printed in the United States of America
10   9   8   7   6   5   4   3   2   1

For my husband, Raymond,
without whose support
none of this would have been possible.

TABLE OF CONTENTS

---

* The time period covered by these writings, from March, 2020, through March, 2021, coincided with the years 5780-5781 on the Hebrew calendar, neither of which was a leap year. As a result, several weeks saw a doubling of *parshiyot*. Therefore, during these weeks, I wrote two entries each day, as I needed to cover two *parshiyot* in seven days' time.

† Sometimes the weekly cycle of Torah reading was interrupted by a holiday which fell on Shabbat (chol hamoed Pesach, Shavuot, Rosh Hashanah, chol hamoed Sukkot). As a result, I had a period of two weeks to write the commentaries for one *parashah*.

BOOK 2

Book of Bereshit (Genesis)

Book of Shemot (Exodus)

* The time period covered by these writings, from March, 2020, through March, 2021, coincided with the years 5780-5781 on the Hebrew calendar, neither of which was a leap year. As a result, several weeks saw a doubling of *parshiyot*. Therefore, during these weeks, I wrote 2 entries each day, as I needed to cover 2 *parshiyot* in 7 days' time.

† Sometimes the weekly cycle of Torah reading was interrupted by a holiday which fell on Shabbat (chol hamoed Pesach, Shavuot, Rosh Hashanah, chol hamoed Sukkot). As a result, I had a period of 2 weeks to write the commentaries for one *parashah*.

‡ This *parashah,* the last of the Book of Deuteronomy, and thus of the entire Torah, is never read on a Shabbat morning, only on the holiday of Simchat Torah. Nevertheless, it was important to include writings on this *parashah,* to complete the annual cycle of Torah readings.

INTRODUCTION

On Wednesday, March 11, 2020, the world shut down . . .

The World Health Organization officially declared that the global emergence of the COVID-19 virus had reached pandemic status. Schools and businesses were shuttered as all non-essential workers were told to stay home. Houses of worship across the country were forced to shut their doors.

How was this possible? Hadn't we celebrated the joyous holiday of Purim just the day before?

Members of the clergy of all faiths and denominations scrambled to answer the unthinkable: How could they meet the spiritual needs of their congregants who were now denied the opportunity to come together for prayer, study, and worship?

My husband and I are long-time members of the North Shore Jewish Center, a Conservative congregation of approximately four hundred member families located in Port Jefferson Station, on the north shore of Long Island, about fifty-five miles east of Manhattan in New York. Our synagogue, like others all across the country, was forced to close its doors as the coronavirus spread unchecked.

A few days later, I was one of several congregants to receive an email from the congregation's rabbi, Aaron Benson. Each of us served the congregation in some educational or leadership capacity. Now he was asking for our help. Was there some contribution that we could make to help sustain congregants during this time of isolation?

I knew that I wanted to do something educational because that is both my love and my strength. Exactly what form that would take I wasn't quite sure yet, but an idea began to germinate in my mind.

I am a lover of text; study of our sacred scriptures has been a major component of my Jewish observance for over thirty-five years. Indeed, just two months earlier, on January 5, I had joined the tens of thousands of people worldwide who embarked on the newest seven-and-a-half-year cycle of Daf Yomi, the commitment to study one page of the Babylonian Talmud each day. Even as I decided to embark on this project, I still harbored a long-held personal pet peeve. As important as I believe the study of the Talmud to be, I am bothered by the large numbers of people who would endeavor to learn Gemara without having first studied our most fundamental text, the Torah, in detail. This is the sacred text which preceded all the others. To use an analogy from mathematics, studying Talmud without having first studied Torah is like studying calculus without having first studied algebra, geometry, and trigonometry.

My thought was to embark on a project of daily Torah study based on the model of Daf Yomi. Since each Torah portion is divided into seven aliyot, I reasoned that this lended itself quite naturally to studying one aliyah each day, thus completing the entire parashah by the end of the week. Calling my project Parashat Shevui (A Parashah per Week), I proposed to write a daily Torah commentary designed to be emailed out to the members of the congregation. Since we were, at that time, only about a week away from the beginning of the book of Vayikra (Leviticus), that would be the most logical place to start.

And so it was that on March 22, 2020, just ten months after my ordination at the Jewish Theological Seminary of America, I embarked on this project. Each day, I sat with my laptop surrounded by three of my favorite Torah commentaries. I studied what others had written and synthesized what I had read into one single interpretation and message to share with congregants. Keeping in mind that the project's intent was to sustain the congregation through a period of isolation unlike anything that any of us had ever experienced in our lifetimes, I often—though not always—related my message to the coronavirus. As time went on, I often found myself relating my daily commentaries to the political and social events of the day. Thus, Parashat Shavui became not only a study of the Torah, but also a diary of sorts, a reflection of the turbulent time during which it was written.

When I began writing in March 2020, I had no idea how far I would go. No one knew how long we would be in isolation. Initially, many of us thought it would just be a few months. Never having lived through a global pandemic before, we couldn't possibly imagine the length of time that COVID-19 would be with us or the number of victims that it would claim. In May, I completed the book of Vayikra and moved on to Bamidbar. By July 2020, the synagogue opened again for Shabbat morning services, though only eleven socially distanced people were permitted to be in attendance. Still, I continued my writing. I completed a second book and moved on to the book of Devarim. Gradually, our number of attendees increased to twenty-five. Summer became autumn; in October, I completed a third book. I turned to the beginning of the Torah, and the book of Bereshit. In November, we saw a surge of the coronavirus that shuttered the synagogue's doors once again. As I continued to write, I realized that I had invested so much in this project that I needed to see it through to completion of all five books. In January 2021, I began the fifth and final book of the Torah, Shemot. The synagogue opened again for good in March 2021, and on March 13, I wrote my three hundred seventy-eighth entry on the last aliyah of parashat Pekudei, completing the cycle of the entire Torah.

A few weeks later on March 25, I reflected on my year of writing when I taught at the pre-Pesach Siyyum Bechor. It was only at that point that I fully realized the uniqueness of the project I had undertaken and decided that what I had could be the basis of a book. Before it would be ready for publication, however, I had a good deal of work to do. For one thing, each entry would need to be edited. Additionally, since my original pieces had just been intended as congregational emails, I had not cited any of the sources I had quoted and would need to go back and find them. Finally, all those individual entries would need to be combined into one large document. It would be another year and a half before I completed those finishing touches.

My original texts all included a copy of the biblical text of that day's portion in both Hebrew and English. The intent was for the reader to read the actual text first before reading my commentary. Including those texts in this book, however, would have created a volume of over one thousand pages. Therefore, in the interest of space, I had to remove them. Keeping in mind that my words were meant to be read and studied in conjunction with the Torah text, I suggest that the reader refer to a copy of the Chumash, or a Hebrew or English bible, to study the accompanying biblical verses to each day's entry.

The entries appear in the order in which they were written, and each contains the date on which it was originally written. Therefore, my commentary begins with the book of Vayikra (Leviticus) rather than the book of Bereshit (Genesis). The reader can choose to read the entries from beginning to end in the order in which I wrote them—this will surely give the best reflection of the time between 2020-2021. On the other hand, if you are interested in reading what I wrote on a specific date, you may do that, as well, by referring to the calendar dates in the Table of Contents. Or you may choose to study the entries as they correspond to the weekly Torah reading.

Those who are looking for scholarly work may be disappointed. My goal was to write a Torah commentary that would be accessible to readers of various levels. Still, I believe that there is something here for anyone with a genuine interest in Torah study.

Some may question the many references to COVID-19. Three years on, even as we continue to be plagued by the seemingly endless parade of variants, our lives have largely returned to what they were before March 2020. Yet, the fact remains that the time spent in isolation during the pandemic provided a unique opportunity for introspection. Like it or not, each of our lives was profoundly affected by the events of that year. We do ourselves a disservice to put the pandemic in the rearview mirror without retaining the lessons that it taught us. Indeed, COVID-19 was the phenomenon that allowed me to write this book.

In a similar vein, the political and social upheavals of that tumultuous time are reflected in these pages, as well. These, too, must not be forgotten. Our world has been forever changed by the events of that year. In this book, my responses to these events are filtered through the lens of Torah values.

I believe, therefore, that the book you are holding is something truly unique: a Torah commentary and a social commentary combined into one document. A memoir and a historical record of the events that framed a turbulent year. May we never lose sight of the lessons it taught us about the fragility of our lives:

Hindsight is 2020.

—Rabbi Margie Cella
January 2023

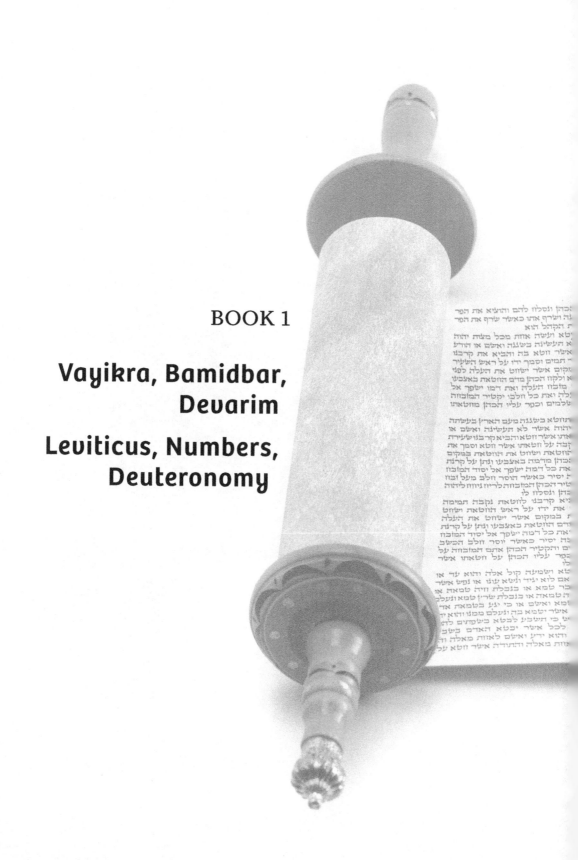

BOOK 1

Vayikra, Bamidbar, Devarim

Leviticus, Numbers, Deuteronomy

ואת כל החלב אשר על הקרב ואת שתי הכלית
ואת החלב אשר עלהן אשר על הכסלים ואת
היתרת על הכבד על הכליות יסירנה והקטירם
הכהן המזבחה לחם אשה לריח ניחח כל חלב
כל חלב וכל דם לא תאכלו בכל מושבתיכם

וידבר יהוה אל משה לאמר דבר אל בני ישראל
לאמר נפש כי תחטא בשגגה מכל מצות יהוה
אשר לא תעשינה ועשה מאחת מהנה אם הכהן
המשיח יחטא לאשמת העם והקריב על חטאתו
אשר חטא פר בן בקר תמים ליהוה לחטאת
והביא את הפר אל פתח אהל מועד לפני יהוה
וסמך את ידו על ראש הפר ושחט את הפר לפני
יהוה ולקח הכהן המשיח מדם הפר והביא אתו
אל אהל מועד וטבל הכהן את אצבעו בדם והזה
מן הדם שבע פעמים לפני יהוה את פני פרכת
הקדש ונתן הכהן מן הדם על קרנות מזבח קטרת
הסמים לפני יהוה אשר באהל מועד ואת כל דם
הפר ישפך אל יסוד מזבח העלה אשר פתח אהל
מועד ואת כל חלב פר החטאת ירים ממנו את
החלב המכסה על הקרב ואת כל החלב אשר על
הקרב ואת שתי הכלית ואת החלב אשר עליהן
אשר על הכסלים ואת היתרת על הכבד על
הכליות יסירנה כאשר יורם משור זבח השלמים
והקטירם הכהן על מזבח העלה ואת עור הפר ואת
כל בשרו על ראשו ועל כרעיו וקרבו ופרשו
והוציא את כל הפר אל מחוץ למחנה אל מקום
טהור אל שפך הדשן ושרף אתו על עצים באש
על שפך הדשן ישרף

ואם כל עדת ישראל ישגו ונעלם דבר מעיני
הקהל ועשו אחת מכל מצות יהוה אשר לא
תעשינה ואשמו ונודעה החטאת אשר חטאו עליה
והקריבו הקהל פר בן בקר לחטאת והביאו אתו
לפני אהל מועד וסמכו זקני העדה את ידיהם על
ראש הפר לפני יהוה ושחט את הפר לפני יהוה
והביא הכהן המשיח מדם הפר אל אהל מועד
וטבל הכהן אצבעו מן הדם והזה שבע פעמים
לפני יהוה את פני הפרכת ומן הדם יתן על קרנת
המזבח אשר לפני יהוה אשר באהל מועד ואת כל
הדם ישפך אל יסוד מזבח העלה אשר פתח אהל
מועד ואת כל חלבו ירים ממנו והקטיר המזבחה
ועשה לפר כאשר עשה לפר החטאת כן יעשה לו

BOOK OF VAYIKRA
Parashat Vayikra

FIRST ALIYAH: LEVITICUS 1:1–13
SUNDAY, MARCH 22, 2020

The Little Aleph that Could

Today, we begin the study of the Torah with the book of *Vayikra*. In this first *aliyah,* I would like to focus on just the first word of the text, *Vayikra,* and He [God] called. In the Torah, this word is written with the final letter, an *aleph,* smaller than the others. Whoa! What's that all about?

Since nothing in the Torah is deemed as accidental, the rabbis go to great lengths to explain the letter's diminutive size. A *midrash* is told by the medieval commentator R. Yaakov ben Raash, also known as the Ba'al haTurim: Moses, being both great and humble, had a disagreement with God when writing down the Torah.[1] He wanted to write the word as *vayikar,* without the *aleph* on the end. In this form, the relationship implied is much more casual and *one-sided,* such as in God speaking to someone in a dream, as He did with the non-Jewish prophet Balaam (see Numbers 22-24). Moses intended to put himself on the same level as Balaam! God disagreed with him. The word *vayikra,* with the *aleph* on the end, implies a closer, more intimate relationship of *two-sided* communication. By calling out to Moses, God's desire was for him to enter the completed *mishkan* (tabernacle) and into communion with the Divine. God told Moses to write the *aleph.* Moses deferred to God but said that he would do so only if he could write it smaller than all the other letters. So, they compromised . . .

That little *aleph* causes us to stop and pause and look harder in order to be able to see it. It requires a conscious effort on our part. That small *aleph,* like the still small voice of God, calls out to each and every one of us to enter into communion with the Divine through the tent of Torah. God will meet us there.

As we embark on this study of the Torah, I encourage you to read the text each day—in Hebrew if you can, in English if you're more comfortable with that. And let it speak to you. Ask questions, seek out answers. No matter what level we ourselves may think we're at, God elevates us to the level of a partner. But we must answer the call.

SECOND ALIYAH: LEVITICUS 1:14–2:6
MONDAY, MARCH 23, 2020

Opening the Lines of Communication

Here in the book of Leviticus we learn about the requirements for the various types of sacrifices: who brings them, what they bring, how the item is sacrificed. The second half of this *aliyah* lays out the specifics of the meal offering, which is given freely, usually as an expression of gratitude to God. Since it was comprised of cakes or wafers made from fine flour and oil, rather than an animal sacrifice, it was the type of sacrifice offered most frequently by the person of lesser means.

What is noticeable here is the unusual Hebrew word used to denote the person who brings this sacrifice. Instead of the more common *adam* or *ish*, the word used here is *nefesh* [1:1]. This word is more frequently translated as "soul," that part of our being which is separate from our physical self, that is the essence of who we are, and that we hope lives on after death. Frequently throughout the book of Leviticus it is used to refer to the one who brings a sacrifice, as we see here. Why?

For our ancestors, sacrifices were offered as an opportunity to draw close to God. Though this concept may seem strange to our modern sensitivities, the desire to connect with the Divine is no less important to us today when we have replaced sacrifices with prayer.

Prayer may come in the form of the prescribed prayers we find in the *siddur*, or personal thoughts and feelings. At times, you may feel more comfortable with the former, other times with the latter or sometimes you may want to combine the two. The method isn't important. What is important is finding the time to reach out to God to find that closeness. Allow your *neshama* to commune with its Creator. In these trying times, we all need to feel the nourishment provided to our souls that comes with opening these lines of communication.

What's That Buzz?

In the beginning of today's reading, we are still receiving instructions about the meal offering: "If your offering is a meal offering **in a pan [***marcheshet***]**, it shall be made of choice flour in oil." [2:7]

This word, *marcheshet,* translated as "in a pan," is an unusual word that appears only this one time in the entire *Tanakh*. Rashi, our most famous medieval commentator, says that, because this pan was deep, the oil in it was also deep and thus the pan would not be burned by the fire. Therefore, "the meal offerings made in it were creeping [elastic] . . . seeming to move . . ."[2]

Ibn Ezra, a Spanish commentator who was a little later than Rashi, in describing this word *marcheshet*, which he translates as "braised" or "fried," says that this kind of cooking is very noisy, connecting it to the word *rachash* in this verse from Psalms: "My heart is **astir** [abuzz—*rachash*] with gracious words; I speak my poem to a king; my tongue is the pen of an expert scribe." [*Psalm 45:2*]

If we look at these ideas in the context of the *neshama* reaching out for a connection to the Divine that I discussed yesterday, they take on new meaning. Our relationships with God should be elastic and flexible; like the meal offering, they should move, change, when touched by the situations we encounter in our daily lives. When we are sad or anxious, as I'm sure many of us are now, we need to be able to pour out our hearts to God. Often when I pray with patients in the hospital, I ask that God give them the strength to deal with whatever lies ahead. None of us really knows what the future will bring, but we can look to God for strength and sustenance.

On the other hand, there may be times (and God-willing there will be many more of these to come) when our hearts will be abuzz, eager to rejoice in our relationship with God. May God sustain us all in these difficult days and bring us to a happier time, a time of rejoicing.

FOURTH ALIYAH: LEVITICUS 3:1–17
WEDNESDAY, MARCH 25, 2020

God is on the Guest List

This section of *Vayikra* is the first place in which we read about the *zevach shlachim*, translated here as "sacrifice of well-being" [3:1] or in other places as a "peace offering." We see several things about this sacrifice from our reading:

- the animal sacrificed could be a cow, a sheep, or a goat [3:1, 6, 12]
- the one who brought the offering participated in the slaughter of the animal [3:2, 8, 13]
- the blood of the animal was not consumed; rather, the priests dashed it on the altar [3:2, 8, 13]
- only specific parts of the animal (the fat, the kidneys, and the "protuberance" on the liver) were burned on the altar. This was designated as God's portion [3:3-4, 9, 14-15].

What we will learn later is that only certain parts of the animal (the breast and right shoulder) were designated for the priests. The rest of the animal was designated for the one who brought it, along with his family and any guests he chose to invite.

Sacrificing animals seems strange and cruel to our modern way of thinking, and that is really another discussion for another time.

The point I want to make here is that these sacrifices were offered in times of gratitude and happiness. They were joyous occasions when the entire extended family and their guests sat down together for a giant celebratory meal, often accompanied by wine. The word *shlamim* [3:3] really means "whole" or "complete." These joyous family celebrations included God on the guest list.

This year, many of us are scrambling to figure out what to do about our *Pesach* seders. In a time that dictates social distancing, we are saddened to think that we can only sit down to the table with the members of our immediate households, that our usual guest list of twenty to thirty people will this year perhaps be only two to four. The question, "How is this night different from all other nights?" takes on a new and bittersweet meaning. But let us remember that even though our guest lists may be small this year, God is still on the list. We can still celebrate the deliverance from Egypt as we pray for a deliverance from COVID-19.

May we all be blessed with the possibility afforded us this year to share our seders in the intimacy of our relationship with the Divine.

Every Day is Like—Yom Kippur?

In this reading, we again encounter the use of the word *nefesh* to refer to a person [4:2]. Here the person has committed some transgression that will require him/her to bring a sacrifice. The Hebrew phrase is *ki techeta*, translated as "if a soul will sin." In fact, the word *ki* doesn't always mean "if." Often, it translates as "when." I believe that is the case here—not if, but when. When a soul will sin. The implication is that falling short of God's expectations is inevitable. Not only that but the sin committed here also occurred without the soul being aware of it. It reminds me of that line in the *al chet* prayer that we recite on Yom Kippur listing all the sins of which we may have been guilty in the previous year: "for the sins that we have committed both knowingly and unknowingly."

But what exactly is a *chet?* Though the word is usually translated as "sin," I prefer to think of it as falling short of expectations, of disappointing the other party.

The point is this, we *do* fall short of what God expects of us, sometimes without even being aware that we are doing so. We can't help ourselves. And when we do, it puts a strain on the relationship between us and the Divine. The *nefesh* that longs to be close to God now must work to repair the damage it has caused.

For our ancestors, the way back was through sacrifice, through a sin offering. Even the priests—including the high priest, the *Cohen Gadol*—had to bring an offering when they sinned. For us today, the way back is through *teshuvah,* acknowledging our guilt, asking God's forgiveness, and working to make ourselves better.

Sounds like Yom Kippur, you say? In fact, the weekday morning *Amidah* includes the following two *brachot:*

> Our Father, bring us back to Your Torah. Our King, draw us near
> to Your service. Lead us back to You, truly repentant. Praised are
> You, Lord who welcomes repentance.

> Forgive us, our Father, for we have sinned; pardon us, our King, for
> we have transgressed, for You forgive and pardon. Praised are You,
> gracious and forgiving Lord.

So, just as our ancestors did not have to wait until Yom Kippur to bring their sin offerings, we also do not have to wait to repair our relationship with the Divine. Six days a week we can do *teshuvah*, and on the seventh day our *nefesh* can draw near once again to the God with whom we have reconciled.

SIXTH ALIYAH: LEVITICUS 4:27–5:10
FRIDAY, MARCH 27, 2020

Don't Put Off Until Tomorrow What You Can Do Today

The second half of today's reading, beginning with chapter five, outlines the circumstances which obligate a person (again, *nefesh*) to bring a female sheep or goat as a sin offering: failing to testify after witnessing something, touching anything or anyone that is unclean, uttering an oath and not fulfilling it [5:1-6]. Reading further, we see that if (s)he does not have the means to bring either of these animals, (s)he is to bring two turtledoves or two pigeons [5:7]. Still later, we read that if (s)he cannot even afford the two birds, (s)he is to bring a tenth of an ephah of choice flour [5:10].

The nineteenth century commentator Solomon Kimhi said that if a person does not have the financial means to bring an animal, ". . . he is not to borrow the money or work at his trade to acquire it. In fact, even if he has a sheep but does not have the money for travel expenses [since the sacrifice had to be offered at the Temple in Jerusalem], he is to bring a less expensive offering."[3] God does not expect us to go beyond what we can afford in order to perform a *mitzvah*; the seder plate that costs $10 serves the same function as the seder plate that costs $500, as long as both have the six spots allotted for the six required items.

Writing six hundred years earlier in the thirteenth century, Hizkuni said that there is an additional explanation, saying that the priority should be to observe a *mitzvah* at its proper time, even if waiting would allow one to fulfill it at greater expense.[3] In other words, we should not put off observing a *mitzvah*, even if it means that doing it now will be under simpler, less-than-ideal circumstances.

When I read this, I thought of *Pesach* Sheni, or second Passover. This event, described in the book of Numbers (9:5-13) originated on the first anniversary of the original Passover as our ancestors wandered the desert. A number of men who had become unclean through contact with a dead body were excluded from observing the *Pesach* offering and came to complain to Moses. As a result, God decreed that from then on anyone who found himself unable to observe *Pesach*, either because of a state of impurity or absence due to a long journey, could observe Passover one month later. This is the ultimate second chance. But God also stipulated that any person who could observe Passover at its prescribed time in the month of Nisan—who was not unclean or on a journey but nevertheless neglected to observe it at its appointed time—was guilty of sin and was to be cut off from the nation.

So, why was I thinking about this? Several weeks ago, it became clear that *Pesach* would be a very different experience for all of us this year, that we would not be able to hold the large gatherings so many of us are accustomed to. As such, a number of rabbis in an online discussion group that I participate in suggested that perhaps this would be a situation that justified observing *Pesach* Sheni. The thought of Passover in May does sound tempting. After much debating back and forth, however, everyone agreed that the bottom line was that there is no justification for postponing the seders. Yes, we must make adjustments. No, they will not be as festive and joyous as the seders we have become accustomed to. But, so long as we are here and able to celebrate the holiday in a timely, albeit reduced fashion, we have every reason to do so.

May we all be blessed to have meaningful seders in these very trying times.

SEVENTH ALIYAH: LEVITICUS 5:11–26
WRITTEN FOR SHABBAT, SATURDAY, MARCH 28, 2020

Visiting the Lost and Found

During my first semester studying in Rabbinical School at the Jewish Theological Seminary, after having just retired from a thirty-year teaching career only three months earlier, I often felt overwhelmed by the magnitude of all of the major life changes I had experienced that year, as well as by a five-hour round-trip daily commute to Manhattan via the Long Island Rail Road and the New York City Subway System (not to mention all of the awesome learning I was experiencing). One night, lost in thought on my way home, I got off the train at the last stop only to realize as the train pulled away that I had left my backpack behind. It contained my iPad that had all my class notes on it, as well as my *tallit* and *tefilin*. I was devastated. Calls to the MTA (Metropolitan Transportation Authority) brought the discouraging news that I would have to wait at least three to four days before I could even inquire at the railroad's lost and found about the bag—about which they were not very optimistic that I would get it back. Those few days seemed endless. When I finally was able to go and ask, I was relieved not only to retrieve the backpack, but to find that only some wire phone and iPad chargers had been stolen. All of the important things were still there.

In discussing the sin offerings in today's reading, we find here a list containing a number of sins that are defined as "a trespass against the Lord" and yet in reality are distinctly sins that have human victims [5:21-22]: deceiving someone, robbery, defrauding someone, finding something lost and lying about it, and swearing falsely about having committed any of these transgressions.

The rabbis of the Talmud went to great lengths to define the parameters of the *mitzvah* of returning a lost object, including the answers to some of the following questions: To what extremes must a person go in order to find the owner? At what point may one take ownership of it? Are we equally obligated to return the lost property of both our friend and our enemy?

As a fitting end to our first week of studying Torah together, I would like to quote from my teacher, Rabbi Danny Nevins, [now former] Dean of the JTS Rabbinical School, who wrote in his commentary "The Jewish Lost and Found" on *Parashat* Ki Tetzei in August 2010:

> ". . . What is the most valuable property of the Jewish people? Is
> it not the Torah itself, which is called "the inheritance of Jacob's
> congregation" (Deut. 33:5)? The Torah, which belongs to all of us,
> is nevertheless a lost inheritance for most Jews . . . The Hasidic
> author Sefat Emet said that every day a heavenly voice announces
> that a valuable lost object—the Torah—has been found and is
> waiting to be claimed . . . On Shabbat, the Jewish soul remembers
> that it is missing something, and it goes to seek . . . the Torah and
> study it . . ."[4]

In these days when we are denied the possibility of hearing the Torah portion chanted and studying it together on Shabbat morning, may we each find the opportunity to reclaim our lost heritage by studying on our own.

I hope that you have found some meaning in these words of Torah I have shared with you this week. May we continue to nourish our souls by reclaiming that which may have been lost to us.

Parashat Tzav

FIRST ALIYAH: LEVITICUS 6:1–11
SUNDAY, MARCH 29, 2020

Keeping the Home Fire Burning

In this section, we read about the laws of the burnt offering, which was to be totally consumed on the altar. What caught my attention is the fact that in the first six verses of this reading, we are told *three times* [6:2, 5-6] that the fire on the sacrificial altar was to be a *perpetual fire, never to be extinguished*. This commandment, repeated three times in close proximity, appears nowhere else in the entire *Tanakh*. Surely there is a message there.

Was it really meant to be perpetual? Rashbam (grandson of Rashi) says that what is meant is that the fire burned by night and day alike.[1] The Ramban says that the meaning was that the fire should not be allowed to go out at all.[2] The Tur says that "this fire must be kept going on a year-round basis."[3] Chizkuni not only says that the implication is that the fire should be kept burning every day, even on Shabbat, he also says that even while the people of Israel traveled through the desert, they were required to take precautions to ensure that this flame be kept going.[4] Pirkei de Rabbi Eliezer cites a *midrash* which states that this fire began the year after we left Egypt, and burned continually for **one hundred sixteen years,** thirty-nine years in the wilderness and an additional seventy-seven in Eretz Israel![5]

So, indeed we are to believe that this was a perpetual fire, maintained through years of traveling in the desert and beyond. Why is it important that we hold this belief?

Abarbanel makes a beautiful comparison between these three mentions of the perpetual fire and the three daily services, *shacharit* (morning),

15

minchah (afternoon), and *maariv* (evening). He says that "... the love of God that impels one to pray burns like a flame."[6]

This means that for us today the responsibility to keep the flame burning rests with us. The fire that leads us to reach out to God in prayer should burn in our hearts perpetually. And reaching out to God in prayer is so important to sustaining our daily existence, quite possibly more so now than ever before.

SECOND ALIYAH: LEVITICUS 6:12–7:10
MONDAY, MARCH 30, 2020

Not Just Holy—Most Holy

The phrase *kodesh kodeshim hi (it is most holy)* is used to describe either the various types of sacrifices or those who offer them on the altar (i.e., the priests, Aaron and his descendants). It appears twelve times in the *Tanakh*, all but one of them in the Torah. Of these, ten are found in the book of Leviticus with four of them appearing in today's reading [6:18, 22; 7:1,6]. The first two refer to the sin offering, and the third and fourth to the guilt offering.

All of this tells us how much God values our repentance, our *teshuvah*. Indeed, the fifteenth century commentator Abarbanel says that the guilt offering, like the sin offering, is called "most holy" because it honors those who have sinned and then repented. This, he says, is a higher level of spirituality than one who is completely righteous.[7] Sin causes a rift in our relationship with the Divine. For our biblical ancestors, the way to repair that rift was through the offering of a sacrifice. For us today, prayer—sincere, honest heart-felt prayer—is the way back to God. And we need to remember that this prayer is most holy. Yes, a life of *mitzvot* is important, but it is only meaningful when it is part of an open and honest relationship with God that involves ongoing communication.

God is Here, God is There, God is Truly Everywhere

This passage talks about the laws of the sacrifice of well-being as well as the elevation offering. I would like to look at the *tenufah*, the wave offering (which is sometimes referred to as an elevation offering). Both translations are accepted, as both actions were part of the priests' actions as they presented this offering: they both waved it and elevated it, as explained in these two Talmudic texts:

> How does one perform this waving? He places the two loaves on top of the two lambs and places his two hands below the loaves and the lambs, extends the offerings to each of the four directions and brings them back, then raises and lowers them . . . [*BT Menachot 61A:7*]*

> . . . the two lambs are waved in the following manner: The priest places his two hands below the lambs, extends them to each of the four directions and brings them back, then raises and lowers them . . . He extends the lambs and brings them back in order to dedicate them to He to Whom the four directions belong. He raises and lowers them in order to dedicate them to He to Whom the heavens and the earth belong. [*BT Menachot 62A:14*]

The sacrifice is waved in all four directions—east, south, west, and north—then lifted up and lowered down. In doing so, the priest acknowledges the One who is responsible for all our blessings, and Whose presence fills the world all around us and above us and below us.

Does this sound familiar? Indeed, the text of Menachot goes on to explain that one should perform the same actions with a *lulav* on *Sukkot*, and for the same reasons. [*BT Menachot 62A:16*]

This beautiful, ancient ritual that we still perform in the same way today on the Festival of Sukkot is not just a meaningless exercise of hocus-pocus. Rather, like the wave offering, it is meant to acknowledge the transcendent and yet present God with gratitude for all the blessings that we have received.

May we be privileged to wave our *lulavim* together once more this coming October. That would truly be a joyous celebration.

* See note page 609

FOURTH ALIYAH: LEVITICUS 8:1–13
WEDNESDAY, APRIL 1, 2020

I'll Meet You Halfway

Now that we have learned all the laws of the various types of sacrifices, we read in today's *aliyah* how Moses anointed Aaron and his sons to serve as the priests who would serve the religious needs of the community, bringing the various sacrifices to the altar to be offered to God on behalf of the people. After ritually washing his brother to serve as high priest, Moses adorns him in his priestly garments in preparation for his holy task.

Okay, so are you ready for a little Trivial Pursuit, category Torah? Here's the question: How many verses are there in the Torah? Answer: Well, that depends.

According to the Masoretic text of the Torah, the sum of the verses of the Torah is 5,845.[8]

But according to the Talmud, there are 5,888 verses. [BT *Kiddushin 30A:14*]

How can there be such a discrepancy? According to R. Yehudah Epstein, there are eight verses from the Torah that are quoted in the Psalms [therefore making them not really "new" verses] and thirty-five such verses in the books of Chronicles. 8+35=43, and adding forty-three to the original 5,845, we get a total of 5,888![9]

Further, half of 5,888 yields 2,944.

So, why do I ask about this? Because the Masoretic text of the Torah contains this comment on verse 8 of today's reading: "Half of the Torah in verses."[10] That would mean that this verse is the 2,944th verse of the Torah, the end of the first half. Also, this verse and the next verse [8:9] together are the middle of the Torah in verses. When we think of the middle of something, we think of a climax of sorts, an apex. And what do we find being described in these two verses?

Moses is placing on his brother Aaron the two most important parts of the garments of the High Priest: the breastplate containing the Urim and Thummim, and the headdress that contains the words, "Holy to God." The Urim and Thummim were used to discern the will of God, and the headdress served to remind God that the people were holy.

So, in a way, we could say that the center of the Torah represents the place where the Divine and the human come together in the most holy of relationships.

Today, we have no high priest to intercede on our behalf. Today, each one of us is called upon to remind God that we are holy, and, as such, we daily seek Divine guidance to help us navigate the world and all the confusing circumstances that present themselves to us.

Time to De-Sin?

Now that we have learned the laws of all the sacrifices, it is time for Aaron and his sons to be consecrated for the sacred task they have been chosen by God to fulfill for the nation, serving as the priests who will offer up all the people's sacrifices on the altar. As a first step, a bull is brought as a sin offering. The priests must cleanse themselves of their own sins before they can offer the sacrifices for anyone else. Why a bull? Remember that it was Aaron who helped the nation build the golden calf. Through the offering of this bull, he will be reminded that it is his job to help lead the people *to,* not *away from* God. Not even the *Cohen Gadol,* the high priest, is above sinning. This *par hachatat,* bull of sin offering, is mentioned twice in verse 14. Notice the word *chet,* "sin," embedded in this phrase.

But it was not only the priests who needed to be consecrated. We see in verse 15 that the blood from the bull was used to "cleanse" the altar. The altar itself on which the sacrifices would be offered needed to be consecrated before it could serve its sacred purpose. Let's examine the word *vayecheta,* translated here as "cleanse." Notice that this word, too, has the root word *chet,* "sin," contained in it, meaning that it is closely related to the concept of sin! (For those who understand biblical Hebrew verb forms, this is the *pi'el* form of the verb.) This verb literally means to "de-sin." In other words, remove sin.

Personally, I love that there is this connection between the words. The message for us today? If we wish to approach God for a closer relationship, we need to "de-sin" ourselves—find the areas of our lives in which we are falling short, or missing the mark, and work to change them.

This is a very difficult time for us all, for ourselves, our families, our congregations, our country, and the world. May we take advantage of the time and opportunity that has been granted to us to slow down, examine our lives, "de-sin," and experience a renewed and deepened closeness to our Creator.

SIXTH ALIYAH: LEVITICUS 8:22–29
FRIDAY, APRIL 3, 2020

He Who Hesitates

Today's reading continues the description of the ceremony in which Moses ordains his brother Aaron and his sons to serve as the priests who would oversee the sacrifices and the religious life of the nation. Moses slaughters the ram of ordination then smears its blood on three parts of Aaron's body: his right earlobe, his right thumb, and his right big toe. Ibn Ezra explains that the thumb and the big toe are the prominent digits on their respective limbs, and as such represent the essence of action, which must now be subjugated to the will of God; the ear "is a reminder to hear that which is commanded" by God.[11] The priests must be the exemplars of holy behavior to the rest of the people.

There is an unusual trope note on the first word of verse 23, *vayishchat* (and he slaughtered), which resembles a lightning bolt. This note, called a *shalshelet*, consists of three cycles of about five notes up and five more back down. There is no mistaking it when you hear it; the repeated up and down quivering implies some hesitation taking place in the narrative. There are only four places where this note is found in the entire Torah (three times in Genesis, and this one time here in Leviticus). These are the three characters in Genesis who appear to hesitate:

- Lot and his wife were reluctant to follow the angel's instructions and leave the city of Sodom before God destroyed it because of the immorality of its inhabitants. [*Genesis 19:16*]

- Abraham's servant Eliezer asked God to make his mission to find a wife for Isaac successful; some believe that he secretly hoped that Isaac would marry his own daughter. [*Genesis 24:12*]

- When Potiphar's wife tried to seduce Joseph, he refused her advances; but apparently, he had been seriously tempted by her. [*Genesis 39:8*]

So, what then, you may be wondering, is the hesitation in our situation? Moses is anointing his brother Aaron to serve as the High Priest. After everything that he himself has done for the nation, including receiving the Torah from God and disseminating it to the people, it would be natural for him to experience some element of jealousy here. Why, he might have wondered, had God chosen Aaron as High Priest and not himself? And yet, when God instructed Moses to anoint his brother as the High Priest, he did so, despite any personal misgivings he might have had.

So, the message is this: when God asks us to do something, whatever it is, do it without hesitation.

Torah trivia with a message.

SEVENTH ALIYAH: LEVITICUS 8:30–36
WRITTEN FOR SHABBAT, SATURDAY, APRIL 4, 2020

Sheltering in Place

After finally completing the process of the ordination of Aaron and his sons, Moses instructs them that they are to remain at the entrance to the tent of meeting (Tabernacle) for seven days before their ordination is complete. In verse 35, he commands them that they remain at the entrance to the Tabernacle "day and night for seven days . . ." in order that they may not die. Now that they have been purified, they must not directly encounter the outside world; they cannot risk coming into contact with any impure thing. Abarbanel says that Moses ". . . may have been hinting to them here that leaving the sacred enclosure to bring fire from outside it would entail death . . ."[12] In other words, Moses instructs the *cohenim* to shelter in place! Though their confinement was only for seven days, the analogy to our current situation is unmistakable: leaving the confines of the Tabernacle could possibly expose them to something dangerous and lethal, something that could cause their death.

The last verse of the *parashah* tells us that they did indeed comply with God's wishes as they were transmitted to them through Moses (at least for now, as we shall see a decidedly different incident in the next *parashah*).

Today, we have all been ordered to shelter in place. Indeed, going into the outside world could potentially expose us to something very dangerous, possibly leading even to death. This instruction has been enjoined upon us by our political leaders, but also by our religious authorities.

Shabbat is here. We cannot go to synagogue to hear the Torah reading or the rabbi's sermon, or the cantor's beautiful davening. But we *can* daven at home, study the *parashah* alone or with family members, enjoy the company of our loved ones, and use the time to draw closer to God. Let us take advantage of this most auspicious opportunity which has been offered to us in these days of uncertainty and worry.

Parashat Shemini

FIRST ALIYAH: LEVITICUS 9:1–16
SUNDAY, APRIL 5, 2020

Who Knows Eight? I Know Eight . . .

This *parashah*, Shemini, which means "eighth" is the only *parashah* that includes a number in the name. The opening verse tells us that the action takes place on the eighth day. We may wonder, "eighth day of what?" We need to look back to the end of the last *parashah*, Tzav, for the answer. It left off with the story of the ordination of Aaron and his sons as the priests of the nation. After all the sacrifices had been completed, Moses instructed them to remain inside the door of the Tent of Meeting for seven days. So, our *parashah* opens on the eighth day of the ordination process. In terms of the calendar, most commentators believe that the actual date was the first of Nisan. The Baal HaTurim even uses some gematria (Hebrew numerology in which each letter is assigned a numerical value) to prove this.[1] He says that the phrase *hashmini kara Moses*, "[on] the eighth [day] Moses called," has a gematria of 1,061.

And the phrase *hayah bayom rosh chodesh Nisan*, "(it) was on the first day of Nisan," also has a gematria of 1,061!

Michael Carasik points out that the first of Nisan is considered by some to be the date of the creation of the world, and, he says, "the inauguration of the Tabernacle is considered a new stage of creation."[2]

The number eight is significant in our tradition. While seven may be the number that represents completeness, wholeness, eight is the number that stands for continuity. Probably the most well-known eight in Judaism is that a baby boy is circumcised on his eighth day of life and brought into the covenant. In much the same way, the priests here begin to serve in their holy capacity on the eighth day of the ordination ceremony.

Probably the second most well-known eight in our tradition is the eight days of Chanukah. The eighth day of the holiday celebrates the idea that the one cruse of holy oil that should have lasted only one day lasted instead for eight days—until new oil could be made. It also celebrates the unlikely victory of the Maccabees over the Syrians, and the rededication of the Temple that took eight days, just like the original dedication in Solomon's time. Both elements of the story assured our survival as a people.

Probably the next most well-known eight in our tradition is the eight strings of *tzitzit* on each corner of a tallit. The *tzitzit* remind us of the commandments of God, the observance of which is the foundation of our religious lives.

Other eights in Judaism include: the *Cohen Gadol,* High Priest, wore eight garments when serving in his ritual capacity; animals in biblical times had to remain with their mother eight days before they could be offered as a sacrifice; following the holiday of Sukkot, we have the one-day holiday of Shemini Atzeret, the Eighth Day of Assembly; and, finally, and perhaps most timely and relevant for those of us living in the diaspora, the holiday of *Pesach* is eight days long.

As we enter this eight-day celebration, which will be far different this year than any other year that any of us can remember, may our commitment to our relationship with God be renewed. May we all find a new strength to guide us through our new reality and beyond.

SECOND ALIYAH: LEVITICUS 9:17–23
MONDAY, APRIL 6, 2020

Live Long and Prosper[3]

Now that Aaron and his sons have been initiated, the altar and the Tabernacle itself must be initiated as the ritual center of the nation. After offering several more sacrifices, we are told that Aaron "lifted his hands toward the people and blessed them." [9:22] What was this blessing? Rashi says that this was what we know today as the priestly blessing, the *birkat Cohenim,* found in the book of Numbers:[4]

> (24) The LORD bless you and protect you! (25) The LORD deal kindly and graciously with you! (26) The LORD bestow His favor upon you and grant you peace! [Numbers 6:24-26]

Indeed, this is the blessing chanted by the *Cohenim* on every holiday. During this mystical experience, those of us in the congregation avert our eyes and/or cover our heads with our *tallitot*. We do not look upon the hands of the *cohenim* as they extend God's blessing to us. This ancient ritual has been handed down to us over the centuries. According to Rashi and other commentators, this incident in our *parashah* at the dedication of the Tabernacle was the very first time that the *cohenim* blessed us in this fashion.

Today, this blessing is incorporated into the blessing that parents give to their children on Friday nights and other special occasions. Rabbis also use these words to give their blessings on special occasions. If you have ever been on the receiving end of such a blessing, it can be a truly awesome experience.

We can only begin to imagine how it must have felt for the nation of Israel, poised at the entrance of the Tabernacle, waiting for the presence of God to come and fill the space, to be the first recipients of this blessing.

THIRD ALIYAH: LEVITICUS 9:24–10:11
SUNDAY, APRIL 12, 2020

Curb Your Enthusiasm[5]

Today's reading contains perhaps one of the most discussed and disturbing incidents in the Torah. After the construction and dedication of the Tabernacle, and seven days of ordination of Aaron and his four sons to the priesthood, and all the sacrifices, the entire nation now gathered expectantly, waiting for the presence of God to fill the holy space. In what was surely an awe-inspiring moment, fire came forth from God and consumed the parts of the sacrifice that were on the altar. This happened in the first verse of the reading: "**Fire came forth from before the LORD and consumed** the burnt offering and the fat parts on the altar . . ." [9:24]

The next two verses go on to describe how Nadav and Avihu, Aaron's two oldest sons, were so carried away with the moment that they put "alien fire" in their incense pans to offer to God. However, something went horribly wrong, and, using exactly the same language as the first verse, the Torah tells us that they, too, were consumed by the fire that came forth from God! "**And fire came forth from the LORD and consumed** them . . ." [10:2]

This leaves us with many questions, the biggest and most obvious of which is "Why?" What did they do wrong? How could God punish them for being over-zealous? And why this day and time of all times?

These questions and many more have been debated by the rabbis and commentators for centuries. Many different explanations have been offered as suggestions for the reason why God took their lives at all, and especially in such a shocking way. Here are some of them:

- Plain and simple, they were disobedient. They brought alien fire that God had not commanded.
- They were drunk. A priest should never be drunk when administering sacrifices. [*Rashi*][6]
- They had refused to have children, thus spurning the primary commandment given by God, *pru ur'vu* (be fruitful and multiply). [*BT Yevamot 64A:2*]
- They showed disrespect for Moses and Aaron. Walking behind them one day, they said to each other, "When will these two old men die so that we can take over?" [*BT Sanhedrin 52A:11*]
- They made a halachic decision in the presence of Moses regarding the sacrifices. [*Rashi*[7] *and BT Eruvin 63A:15* and *Yoma 53A:20*]
- They acted on impulse, seeking the advice of no one—not Moses, not Aaron, not even each other.

The Baal HaTurim, citing the word *otam* (them) spelled here with a *vav* (whose numerical value is six), says that they actually were guilty of all six of these infractions![8]

Rashbam says that they brought their firepans at the exact same moment that the fire came forth from God to consume the sacrifices on the altar, and simply got caught in the middle—literally the line of fire.[9] The support for this argument is that the language is identical.

Even if any or all of these were so, we may still say, "isn't God's reaction here a bit extreme?" We struggle to make sense of this story to this day. Perhaps the best answer is to acknowledge the fact that, since the sages themselves have offered so many varied and contradictory explanations, we know that they, too, struggled to reconcile this story with the image that they had of a just and loving God. If the greatest minds from the Talmudic period until today have not been able to sufficiently explain the rationale for God's actions here, then we, like them, must continue to wrestle with the text.

Perhaps, then, like the *Haggadah* that we just read this past week, that is the real point: to cause us to pause and to take note—and to ask the questions—even though there may be no satisfactory answers.

FOURTH ALIYAH: LEVITICUS 10:12–15
MONDAY, APRIL 13, 2020

Holier Than Thou

In this very short reading, Moses gives instructions to Aaron about how he and his two remaining sons, Eleazar and Itamar are to behave in the aftermath of the deaths of Nadav and Avihu, beginning with the very first verse: "Moses spoke to Aaron and to his **remaining** sons, Eleazar and Ithamar: Take the meal offering that **is left over** from [*Adonai's*] offerings by fire and eat it unleavened beside the altar, for it is most holy." [10:12]

We see here that the same Hebrew word, *notar*, is used to describe both Aaron's remaining sons, and the meal offering that is left over.

In a very chilling moment, we realize the comparison: Elazar and Itamar are the sons who were spared by the consuming fire of God, just as the part of the offering that the priests are now instructed to eat is also the part that was spared by the consuming fire of God. Following this analogy, we see that the meal offering is declared by Moses to be most holy. By inference, then, Aaron, the nation, and we the readers all know that Elazar and Itamar (and their descendants) are also most holy to God. Their priesthood has been confirmed for all time.

FIFTH ALIYAH: LEVITICUS 10:16–20
TUESDAY, APRIL 14, 2020

The Heart of the Matter

Okay, so first off, a little more Torah trivia. In *Parashat* Tzav, we had the middle *verse* of the Torah; in the first verse of today's reading, we have the *middle two words* of the Torah: "Then Moses inquired about the goat of sin offering, and it had already been burned! He was angry with Eleazar and Ithamar, Aaron's remaining sons . . ." [10:16]

The two middle words of this verse are *darosh darash* ([he] surely sought). Since the sefer Torah is written without vowels, they appear identical in the scroll, thereby setting up a kind of mirror image in the middle of the scroll. The Hebrew root ד-ר-ש can sometimes mean "to teach" or "to preach," as in someone giving a *drashah*. Here, however, it has another meaning: "to ask" or more precisely, "to demand." The first word, *darosh,* is an infinitive construct form of the verb, making the verb emphatic, as in the word "surely." The second word, *darash,* is a simple past tense form of the verb "he asked" or "he demanded." This two-word phrase has sometimes been translated as "[he] diligently sought" or "[he] inquired insistently." Most translations, unfortunately, ignore the emphasis of the first word altogether, simply translating the phrase as "[he] inquired" or "[he] asked."

The early eighteenth century commentator Or HaChaim has a different translation.[13] He says that the phrase indicates that Moses *kept on asking.* He goes on to explain that Moses had not yet decided what the *halakha* was regarding the three sacrificial goats he was inquiring about, that the repetition of the words is an indication that there were two possible halachic rulings that could have been made in this case.

This reminds me of how our Law Committee (CJLS, Committee on Jewish Law and Standards, the deciding halachic body for Conservative Judaism) functions today. Sometimes there are two different ways of interpreting *halacha. Tshuvot* are presented, discussed, and voted on. A majority opinion is recognized as the accepted ruling, but sometimes a minority opinion receives enough votes and support to be recognized as also acceptable. This is clearly an oversimplification of the process, but my point is that *halachah* is an ever-evolving process, beginning with Moses and continuing to our day. May it continue to be a vibrant force, leading us to ask, to learn, to study, and to continue to commit ourselves to lives of *mitzvot* as proud Conservative Jews.

SIXTH ALIYAH: LEVITICUS 11:1–32
FRIDAY, APRIL 17, 2020

To Your Health!

This chapter of the book of Leviticus is one of two places in the Torah where we find the laws concerning which animals we may and may not eat:

- Beasts (or land animals) must have hooves that are cleft all the way through and must chew their cud (digest their food partially, regurgitate it, then digest it further) [11:3]

- Just in case we have any doubts, we are told which are the only four animals that do only one of these things and not the other: the camel, the daman, and the hare (chew their cud but don't have split hooves), and the pig (has split hooves, but does not chew its cud). These are *not* to be eaten [11:4-7].

• Water animals must have both fins and scales [11:9-10].

• Birds are not defined by their characteristics, rather we are given a list of the birds we cannot eat: the eagle, vulture, black vulture, kite, falcons, ravens, ostrich, nighthawk, seagull, hawks, little owl, cormorant, great owl, white owl, pelican, bustard, stork, herons, hoopoe, bat [11:13-20].

• Winged swarming things may not be eaten, except for locusts, bald locusts, crickets, grasshoppers [11:22-23].

• Among other "swarming things," moles, mice, lizards, geckos, crocodiles, chameleons are not allowed [11:29-30].

The other place in the Torah where we find these instructions is in the fourteenth chapter of Deuteronomy. There is one major noticeable difference between the two lists: the text in Deuteronomy includes the prohibition on boiling a kid in its mother's milk (from which the rabbis extrapolate the separation of meat and dairy). Interestingly, our text here in Leviticus does not include this prohibition.

Practically since these texts were first given, scholars and laypeople alike have debated the rationale for them, with no definitive answer. The Torah text does not give us the reason(s) for the observance of these laws.

What we do know is that observing the laws of kashrut infuses our tables with a sense of holiness. When we make a conscious decision to *not* eat something because the laws of kashrut forbid it, we are acknowledging our identity as Jews, and our relationship with the Divine. God calls us to be holy because God is holy. And making conscious decisions about what we do and do not eat, and how we eat, is part of a life of holiness. For centuries, it has been suggested by many people that we are forbidden to eat certain animals for sanitary reasons, and just as many people have disproven that theory.

The laws of kashrut may not be designed to improve our *physical* health; it could be argued, however, that they are designed to improve our *spiritual* health.

Let Me Take You Higher[11]

Okay, one more bit of Torah trivia. We've seen the middle verse of the Torah and the middle words of the Torah. Now we have the ultimate middle: the middle *letter* of the Torah. The word *gachon* in verse 42 appears in the Torah scroll with the letter *vav* written larger than the others. The reason given for this is that this letter is the middle letter of the Torah. So, we have officially reached the point where it is better to call a right-handed person than a left-handed person for *hagbah*, raising the Torah!

On another note, I want to point out verse 45: "For I the LORD am He who **brought you up** from the land of Egypt to be your God: you shall be holy, for I am holy." [11:45] Usually, when God talks about bringing us out of Egypt, the verb that is used is *ha-motzi* (yes, just like the blessing over bread). God says that God brought us forth out of Egypt. Here, however, the verb is *ha-ma-aleh*, who brought you *up* from Egypt. This is the same verb from which we get the word *aliyah* that is used to refer both to being called up to the Torah and to moving to *Eretz Israel*. What is implied in all these cases is a *spiritual* elevation. Leaving Egypt is a spiritual elevation to a closer relationship with God. We have just finished celebrating the holiday of *Pesach*, commemorating our liberation from Egypt. Though we are all going through some very difficult times right now, I hope that the uncharacteristic celebration of Passover has brought you up closer to God and that you will continue to be sustained by that relationship in the days and weeks to come.

Parashat Tazria

FIRST ALIYAH: LEVITICUS 12:1–13:5
SUNDAY, APRIL 19, 2020

Postpartum Blues

Here we read about the laws referring to a woman who has given birth:

- For a son, she is "unclean" for seven days, followed by another thirty-three days of purification [12:2, 4].
- For a daughter, she is "unclean" for fourteen days, followed by another sixty-six days of purification [12:5].
- At the end of her time of purification, she brings a burnt offering, and then a sin offering [12: 6].

At first read, we may find several things here that are offensive to our way of thinking. Therefore, we surely need to examine this a little more deeply.

- The translation "unclean" of the word *tameh*, used to describe the woman's postpartum status, carries a very negative connotation; a better translation is "impure." In ancient Israel, a state of impurity resulted from close contact with death; we know that the instance of death in childbirth was much greater then than it is today, so the experience of giving birth was most assuredly perceived as having a brush with death. The Baal HaTurim points out that these seven days of impurity can be compared to the seven days of *shiva* following the death of a close family loved one.[1]

31

- Purification following the birth of a girl takes twice as long as purification for a boy. Or perhaps a better way to look at it: the initial period of impurity for a boy ends at seven days so that his mother can attend his *bris* (circumcision) on the eighth day [12:3]. This is, of course, a commandment that had already been established from the time of Abraham. There is no such requirement for a girl, thus allowing the new mother more time alone with her daughter.

- Quoting the Baal HaTurim, "*Chasam Sofer* suggests that the term 'male child' in this context may not refer to gender but to a person of accomplishment . . . one who engages in procreative activity with modesty . . . will be rewarded with creative and accomplished children [whether male or female] who will leave their mark on the world."[2]

- Regarding the offerings that the new mother is required to bring: the burnt offering, the purpose of which is to draw closer to God and express gratitude, precedes the sin offering.

- Why a sin offering? According to Ramban, the rabbis understood this in the context of things she might have angrily said during childbirth, such as swearing that (and here I paraphrase a little) she would never let her husband near her again.[3] Perhaps the rabbis understood more than we give them credit for!

SECOND ALIYAH: LEVITICUS 13:6–17
SUNDAY, APRIL 19, 2020

Quarantine-while[4]

Now we learn about a skin disease, *tsara'at*, most often translated as "leprosy," although it is generally not considered to be what we call leprosy today. We do not know exactly what this skin affliction was but what we *do* know is that it was highly contagious. A person who was suspected of having this condition had to be examined by the priest. If the priest determined that the person had this condition, (s)he was declared unclean. If the priest suspected that the person *might* have this condition but couldn't be sure, (s)he would be isolated (i.e., quarantined) for seven days then reexamined. If the results were still inconclusive, a second seven-day isolation period could be imposed. If the infection had turned white, the person was declared clean. If two weeks passed and the rash cleared up, the person was declared clean.

Regarding this quarantine, Rashi says that the priest should confine the afflicted person to one house and that (s)he should not appear until the end of the seven days.[5] Several commentators actually use the word "quarantined" to describe this isolation.

Keeping in mind the idea that a state of being "unclean" resulted from some experience of being exposed to a brush with death; it's very difficult to escape the obvious correlation to what we have been experiencing of late with COVID-19. The maximum isolation period of fourteen days to determine whether the disease is present or not equates *exactly* to the fourteen days of self-quarantine required of anyone who suspects that they have been exposed to or are exhibiting symptoms of coronavirus (i.e., a potential brush with death).

The ancient people may not have understood everything about sickness, but it certainly seems that they had a good handle on avoiding its transmission. We would do well to follow their lead.

THIRD ALIYAH: LEVITICUS 13:18–23
MONDAY, APRIL 20, 2020

To Quarantine or Not to Quarantine

Now that we have learned about this mystery skin disease, *tzara'at*, the Torah goes on to address several other situations of skin afflictions which might possibly be confused with it. Instructions are given for the priest to be able to determine if *tzara'at* is present or not. This first of these is a scar that results from an injury. Again, the person must present him/herself to the priest for examination. If there is clear evidence of *tzara'at* the priest declares the afflicted person unclean. If the evidence is inconclusive, again a seven-day isolation is ordered. At the end of this quarantine, if the infection has spread, (s)he is declared unclean. If it has not spread, it is then declared to be only a scar. Did (s)he have the infection? If so, does (s)he no longer have it? Again, we see that extreme caution is being exercised here when it comes to this highly infectious disease. Sounds familiar, no?

FOURTH ALIYAH: LEVITICUS 13:24–28
MONDAY, APRIL 20, 2020

Testing, Testing . . .

The situation addressed here is a scar from a burn that begins to display possible symptoms of *tzara'at*. Again, if there are clear symptoms, the individual is declared unclean. If it is questionable, the individual is isolated for seven days before being reexamined by the priest. At that time, if the symptoms have spread, (s)he is declared unclean; if not, it is declared to be just a scar from the burn.

Again, we see that the Torah is being overly cautious in addressing every possible situation that could be perceived as *tzara'at*. Equating this to our situation today, the one thing that we do know is that there is still much we don't know about COVID-19. The symptoms and their severity are as varied as its victims. We do keep hearing, however, that the key to solving the mystery is testing, testing, and more testing. Kind of like the priests here, leaving no stone unturned and examining (testing) every possibility.

FIFTH ALIYAH: LEVITICUS 13:29–39
TUESDAY, APRIL 21, 2020

See Me, Feel Me, Touch Me, Heal Me[6]

This section continues to deal with various types of infections that occur either on the scalp or in beards. The word used here is *netek* "scall" [13:30], defined in modern dictionaries as "a scaly eruption of the skin or scalp." Again, we are not quite sure exactly what this is. Some suggest it is dandruff, some suggest acne, or something else. In any event, the same procedure applies: upon examination by the priest, if it is definitively determined to be *netek*, the individual is declared unclean. If it is suspicious but not confirmed, the individual is isolated for seven days before being reexamined by the priest. If it has not spread, the individual must shave him/herself and wait seven more days for a reexamination to determine if the scall has spread or not. If not, (s)he is clean; if yes, but there is only black hair in it, still unclean; if yes, but yellow hair in it, unclean.

The word *v'hitgalach* (he will shave himself) [13:33] appears in the Torah scroll with the *gimel* (whose numerical value is three) written larger than the other letters. According to the Baal HaTurim, the reason for this is that there are three categories of people who are required to do a complete shaving of their heads and bodies: the Levites, as part of their purification process for serving in the Tabernacle [Numbers 8:5-7]; the *metzora,* the leper, as part of his/her cleansing process once (s)he has been declared clean [Leviticus 14:8-9]; the *nazir,* the one who takes a Nazirite vow, after his/her vow has been either unintentionally broken [Numbers 6:9] or completed [Numbers 6:18], as part of his/her cleansing process.[7]

So, there seems to be a connection between shaving and purification/ cleansing. To reunite with God, it seems one needs to totally renounce concerns about one's physical appearance. Or could there possibly be a different interpretation?

Did you ever notice that when you look at someone who has no hair, either because they have shaved it or lost it for one reason or another, you tend to concentrate more on the person's face? In other words, you are really seeing the individual on a deeper level. So, in a way, the person who needs to be purified/cleansed to reunite with God must really feel as if (s)he is exposing him/herself to God, making him/herself vulnerable, saying, "Look at me. See me. See me for who I am."

Perhaps, accompanied by shaving or not, we all need to feel this way before God at one time or another. Perhaps you already have.

SIXTH ALIYAH: LEVITICUS 13:40–54
TUESDAY, APRIL 21, 2020

Every Breath You Take[8]

Today's reading deals with the person who is fully or partially bald through natural means (i.e., not shaved) who may possibly show signs of skin affliction. The process he undergoes to determine whether he is clean or not is similar to the others we have already encountered.

What caught my attention here is the requirement made of the person who is declared unclean, leprous. Among other things, he must "cover over his upper lip; and he shall call out, 'Unclean! Unclean!'" [13:45]. What exactly is meant by covering over his upper lip? The Baal HaTurim says that he should "cover his mouth that none should smell his breath for his breath is harmful."[9] Ibn Ezra says, "he shall 'cover' it with his garment . . . to keep his breath from harming others by spreading the disease." Further, he goes on to explain that the reason he must call out "Unclean! Unclean!" is ". . . so that people can take care to avoid him."[10] The Bekhor Shor says that the reason he says this is so that those who see him will beg God to show him mercy.[10]

Once again, the parallel to today's situation with COVID-19 is unmistakable. Covering the lip was the biblical equivalent of wearing a mask. Today's medical experts say that the main reason for wearing a mask is not to protect yourself from others, but rather to protect others from you. Additionally, today's social distancing is the equivalent of shouting "unclean" to warn others to stay away.

Finally, we see in the Torah passage that the afflicted person is to dwell "apart . . . outside the camp." This was for the protection of others—just as the person infected by coronavirus must be quarantined for the protection of others.

Though over three thousand years have passed since the words of the Torah were first written down, they still bear relevance today.

TAZRIA SEVENTH ALIYAH: LEVITICUS 13:55–59
WEDNESDAY, APRIL 22, 2020

Cleanliness is Godliness

This passage is about an article of clothing that was thought to have been infected with *tzara'at*; the treatment calls for the item to be washed. If the stain remains, the garment is unclean and must be burned. If it fades, then that part that is stained is cut out of the garment; if a stain reappears, the garment is burned. But what if the stain disappears? In this case, the garment is washed a second time and then declared clean. Why a second washing if the item is clean?

Rashi and Onkelos both explain that the first washing is actual laundering, designed to get the stain out, whereas the second washing is ritual immersion for the sake of spiritual purity.[11]

Washing for spiritual purity is a much more prevalent concept in our tradition than many realize.

• Every time we have a *shabbat* or *yom tov* meal, we wash our hands before reciting *ha-motzi* over the challah. Our hands should be physically clean before we do this.

• Many people who have kosher homes have the practice of *toveling* (immersing in a *mikvah* or natural body of water) dishes and cooking utensils before introducing them into their kitchen. The dishes should be clean before this is done.

- Women who observe the laws of *niddah* (family purity) immerse themselves in a *mikvah* once a month seven days after the completion of their menstruation. They must bathe completely before doing this.

There is one more, though, which was the first one that came to my mind when I read Rashi's comment, in which he said that the scholar Onkelos (first and second century CE) always translated the words for "washing" in this passage as ritual immersion. I said to myself, "of course Onkelos would translate it that way!" (Onkelos was well known as a Roman convert to Judaism who was the author of Targum Onkelos, an Aramaic translation of the Torah.) One who chooses to convert to Judaism is also required to ritually immerse in a *mikvah* three times: once to mark the entry into a new life as a part of the Jewish people, and twice to thank God for having brought him/her to this defining moment. Those of us who have experienced it can attest to the fact that it truly is a spiritually transforming experience.

Parashat Metzora

FIRST ALIYAH: LEVITICUS 14:1–12
WEDNESDAY, APRIL 22, 2020

This One's for the Birds

This section talks about the ritual for cleansing someone who had been afflicted with leprosy and quarantined outside the camp. Part of the ritual involves "two live clean birds." One of these is slaughtered and the other is eventually set free into the desert [14:4–6]. The commentators make much of these birds; what is meant by a "live clean bird?" For several, the answer is based on the idea that leprosy was thought to result from any one of a list of sinful, malicious acts, not least of which was gossiping, or slandering speech. (Indeed, the incident of Miriam becoming leprous [Numbers 12:10–15] is attributed by many to her gossiping about Moses and his wife, Tziporah—whose name, by the way, means "a bird").

The Talmud says that since, ". . . He acted by speaking malicious speech with an act of chatter; therefore . . . he is to bring an offering of birds, who chirp and chatter all the time." [BT Arakhin 16B:3]

If you have spent much time outside lately, you know exactly what is being described here. Since the beginning of our isolation period for the coronavirus, I have developed the practice of going outside on my back deck (weather permitting) to daven the *shacharit* service in the morning. Since my husband recently installed two bird feeders in our backyard, most mornings my davening is accompanied by plenty of chattering. Indeed, Ramban says that, after careful analysis of the sources, he feels that the word *tzipor* refers specifically to birds that wake early in the morning to sing and chirp. He also says that the birds must be free flying. He further narrows it down and says that the sages understood that the bird referred to here was specifically a swallow, the Hebrew word for which, *dror*, also means freedom.[1] These are the kinds of birds involved in cleansing the leper. Why? For one thing, to remind him/her of the sin that (s)he committed. Additionally, according to the Bekhor Shor, "the dead bird symbolizes the deadness of leprosy, setting the live bird free symbolizes the leper's return to freedom of movement."[2]

And, finally, the Baal HaTurim says that the slaughtered bird indicates the hope that the leprosy will never return, while the living bird which is sent away is a reminder that it has the possibility of returning; just as, if the now healed leper returns to his/her sinful ways, so, too, will the leprosy return to his/her body.[3]

So, go outside and listen to the birds around us. They have much to teach us. Who knew we could learn so much from the chattering of the birds in the morning?

SECOND ALIYAH: LEVITICUS 14:13–20
THURSDAY APRIL 23

Leprosy of the Soul

Today's reading continues to describe in very precise detail the purification procedure for the leper who has been healed. This ceremony included several sacrifices: the priest was to take some of the blood of the lamb which was slaughtered as a guilt offering and place it on the right ear, right thumb, and right big toe of the individual being purified [14:14]. You may recall that Moses did the same thing to Aaron and his sons as part of their ordination process. Ibn Ezra says that, since the thumb and big toe are the most prominent parts of the hand and the foot, respectively, they therefore represent the essence of action.[4] Thus, this strange ritual comes to remind the individual of the need to subjugate his/her actions to the commandments of God.

The inclusion of the ear comes to remind the individual to hear (listen to) that which (s)he has been commanded. The ear carries a great deal of significance. Remember that the rabbis thought that the most common sin which was a root cause of leprosy was gossip. When we think of someone gossiping, we tend to think, naturally, of the mouth. However, for gossip to be effective, both a *listener,* as well as a *speaker,* are required, for if the slanderous statements fall on deaf ears, they lose their effectiveness. At the very least, the one who listens to and believes gossip is just as guilty as the one who spreads it.

Contrasting with this verse, we have the following verse from the book of Exodus, which was spoken by Moses to the people of Israel shortly after they experienced the miracle of the parting of the Red Sea:

> He said, "If you will heed the LORD your God diligently, doing what is upright in His sight, giving ear to His commandments and keeping all His laws, *then I will not bring upon you any of the diseases that I brought upon the Egyptians, for I the LORD am your healer.*" [italics mine] [*Exodus 15:26*]

This would indeed support the idea that sin is the cause of disease. We, of course, do not believe that today. But there can be no doubt that it is a root cause of inner, spiritual sickness, that prevents us from drawing close to God. As Ibn Ezra describes it, "sin is the leprosy of the soul."[4]

THIRD ALIYAH: LEVITICUS 14:21–32
THURSDAY, APRIL 23, 2020

He's a New Man

Today we read about the leper who has been healed but does not have the financial means to bring the required three animals that must be sacrificed to affect purification. A provision is made: two of the animals may be replaced with birds, but the guilt offering must still be a lamb so that there will be sufficient blood for the ritual of placing it on the individual's right ear, thumb, and big toe" [14:21-25] (apparently, that was a very important part of the ritual, as has been previously mentioned).

Unfortunately, sometimes there are those of means who say to themselves, "there is a way to become cleansed with lesser means. I will simply say that I do not have the means and bring a smaller sacrifice." The following story from the Zohar, quoted in Kav HaYashar, addresses just this issue:

> . . . A wealthy man once brought two young pigeons, a poor man's sacrifice, to a *Cohen* . . . But the *Cohen* said to him, "This sacrifice is not fitting for you," whereupon the man returned home sullenly. "Why are you so sullen?" his brothers inquired? "Because the *Cohen* would not offer up my sacrifice of two pigeons," he explained. "He acted properly," they told him, "for that is the sacrifice of a poor man, as it is written, 'And if he is too

poor, etc.' . . . Instead, you must offer up an ox." The man thought to himself, "If the Torah requires a person to sacrifice an ox to atone for the mere thought of sin, how much more is required for an actual sin! I vow that I will never again entertain thoughts of sin!" So, how did he conduct himself from then on? All day long he engaged in business, then at night he would sleep a little bit and call over his brothers to study Torah with him. They began to refer to him as "Yehudah the new man." [*Parashas Vayikra* 9a][5]

If I could hazard a guess, I would imagine that part of his new, changed life involved providing the lambs for the healed lepers who were too destitute to be able to afford even one lamb for their purification.

FOURTH ALIYAH: LEVITICUS 14:33–53
FRIDAY, APRIL 24, 2020

The Cohen Knows Best

This section describes the purification ritual for a house that is deemed to have contracted some form of "leprosy" in it. The ritual is almost identical to that for a person deemed leprous, including the two birds, one of which is slaughtered, and one of which is set free.

So, what should a person do if (s)he suspects that his/her house has contracted leprosy? "The owner of the house shall come and tell the priest, saying, 'Something like a plague has appeared upon my house'" [14:35]. So, first and foremost, the priest needs to be informed. Why? The *cohenim* were the only ones authorized by God to rule on cases of leprosy, be they in people, objects, or houses. Yet, the wording of the statement made by the homeowner to the priest seems a little strange and awkward. For someone who is not a priest to say definitively, "there is leprosy in my house" is presumptuous; he is ruling on something over which he has no authority to do so. (The modern-day version is the patient telling the doctor what his/her diagnosis is, or, better yet, the congregant telling the rabbi what the halachic ruling should be on something.)

Mishnah Negaim takes this explanation even a step further:

Even if he is a learned sage and knows that it is definitely a nega, he may not speak with certainty saying, "A plague has appeared upon my house," but rather, "Something like a plague has appeared upon my house." [*Mishnah Negaim 12:5*][6]

The Baal HaTurim explains this as follows: there may be a situation where the homeowner is a sage, a learned man, who knows more than a priest, who is perhaps new and inexperienced at ruling on infections. In this case, rather than assume the responsibility of making the diagnosis himself, the sage instructs the *cohen* on what to say. If he sees an infection, he tells the priest, "Say 'it is impure.'" and the priest says it is impure. Otherwise, the sage tells the priest, "Say 'it is pure.'" and the priest says it is pure.[7] In other words, rather than make the ruling himself and risk embarrassing the priest, the sage effectively tells the priest what to say so that he himself is the one making the ruling. What a great lesson in humility! The sage, as learned as he might be, must be sure to preserve the dignity of the young priest.

Perhaps there's a lesson here that we all can learn.

FIFTH ALIYAH: LEVITICUS 14:54–15:15
FRIDAY, APRIL 24, 2020

Don't Spit on Me

Today's reading deals with any man who has an unnatural discharge from his "member." Not only is this man deemed unclean, but so is anyone/anything that comes into contact with him. While much of what we read in this *parashah* seems quite extreme to our modern sensibilities, I was struck by the following: "If one with a discharge spits on one who is clean, the latter shall wash his clothes, bathe in water, and remain unclean until evening." [15:8] About this, Rashi says, ". . . spittle makes one unclean through carrying as well as through touch."[8] Ibn Ezra says, "even his saliva is dangerous."[9] Baruch A. Levine says, "spittle was considered to carry infection and disease."[8]

Considering what we know today about germs, and specifically about COVID-19, all of this makes amazing sense. Why are we told to cover our sneezes and coughs and to wear masks? Because we know that droplets spread germs and disease! This is a very real, physical reminder of how contagious our germs can be.

But on a deeper level, let's look at it this way: the rabbis believed that physical sickness was the external manifestation of some internal spiritual sickness. When we are spiritually sick inside, we expose those around us to that sickness; if they are not strong internally, they are vulnerable to being affected by us.

Therefore, we are responsible for maintaining a healthy relationship with God not only for ourselves, but also for the benefit of all those with whom we come into contact.

SIXTH ALIYAH: LEVITICUS 15:16–28
WRITTEN FOR SHABBAT, SATURDAY, APRIL 25, 2020

Choose Life

This text tells us that both a man who has a "natural" discharge of semen and a woman who has a "natural" discharge of menstrual blood are classified as unclean for a period of seven days. It is from these verses that the laws of *niddah*, family purity, are derived. Each month, a woman remains impure for the duration of her menstruation and counts seven days of uncleanness after that before she can have sexual relations with her husband again. Today, to complete her period of impurity, a woman immerses in the *mikvah*, though that is not required in this text.

According to the text, the man who has a discharge is required to bring a sacrifice of two turtledoves or two pigeons at the end of his seven-day period of impurity. No such requirement is made of a woman at the end of her seven-day period of impurity. Why not? What's the difference? The reason, according to Ramban, is that for the woman, menstruation is a natural biological function, not a disease that requires healing.[10]

Okay, if that's the case, then why is she considered unclean? Abarbanel asks even more questions: Why is the man unclean after having relations with her [15:18]? Since he was fulfilling a *mitzvah* by doing so, he must not "withhold from . . . her food, her clothing, or her conjugal rights." [Exodus 21:10] If these bodily emissions (menstrual blood and semen) are sources of uncleanness, why is that not also true of urine and excrement, bodily emissions that we would naturally consider to be disgusting? Furthermore, if blood is a source of uncleanness, why does that not include other blood, such as from a nosebleed or a cut?[10]

The answer, it would seem, is somehow related to procreation or, more accurately, the lack thereof. Both menstrual blood and seminal discharge were thought to be symbols of lost opportunities to create new life. The implication, therefore, is that they were brushes with death, and association with death was the real source of impurity.

In these trying days of COVID-19, we are surrounded by so much death. There is almost no one who hasn't known someone who fell victim to this devastating disease. It's very hard to not be brought down by that, particularly for the healthcare workers dealing with this on the front lines.

The Torah calls upon us to choose life [Deuteronomy 30:19]. Find ways to celebrate life for yourself and others. Reach out to others. Give support and accept support. That is the best response that we can give right now.

SEVENTH ALIYAH: LEVITICUS 15:29–33
WRITTEN FOR SHABBAT, SATURDAY, APRIL 25, 2020

Pure as the Driven Snow—Not!

This short section summarizes the laws of impurity brought about by vaginal or seminal emissions, both unnatural and natural.

First, let me point out that the woman described here, who is required to bring two birds as a sacrifice at the end of her impurity after a period of vaginal bleeding [15:29] suffered from an "unnatural" (i.e., non-menstrual) bleeding. This contrasts with the woman discussed in the previous reading whose menstrual blood was viewed as a natural bodily function.

More importantly, we read further: "You shall put the Israelites on guard against their uncleanness, lest they die through their uncleanness by defiling My Tabernacle which is among them." [15:31]

The real problem, as I've mentioned before, is the internal impurity that we cannot see, that is associated with the external impurity. If this internal impurity is not addressed, it will have the opportunity to fester and grow, affecting the entire community. Baruch Levine says, "it is not the condition of impurity per se that evokes God's punishment, but the failure to rectify that condition so as to restore a state of purity."[11] Failure to address the impurities in our lives is damaging not only to us personally, but to others around us, and ultimately to the life of the whole community.

Most of us have a lot more time on our hands these days. Let us use that time productively to improve our lives and the lives of others. Let us endeavor to make the world around us a better place.

Parashat Acharei Mot

FIRST ALIYAH: LEVITICUS 16:1–17
SUNDAY, APRIL 26, 2020

Every Day is Like Yom Kippur

Now that we have learned all the laws of purity and impurity, God gives the instructions for the annual purification of the sanctuary that took place on Yom Kippur. Only the *cohen gadol,* the High Priest (in this case, Aaron) was permitted to enter the innermost part of the sanctuary, the Holy of Holies, to make expiation for the people. First, Aaron had to offer a bull on behalf of himself and his family [16:6]. Then, to secure expiation for the nation, two goats were brought forward. After casting lots, one of these goats was designated "for the Lord;" this goat would be sacrificed. The other goat was designated "for Azazel" [16:7-10]. Exactly what is meant by Azazel has been widely debated. Generally, most rabbis believe that it is the name of a rugged mountain or a desolate place in the desert. What is important for us to note is that, like the second bird in the ritual for purifying a leprous person or house, this goat was kept alive and released into the desert, symbolizing the carrying away of the sins of the people.

The Baal HaTurim points out that the word *l'Azazel* (for Azazel) is mentioned three times in this passage. He explains that these correspond to the three types of sin which God forgives, as denoted in the thirteen attributes of God which are included multiple times in our Yom Kippur liturgy:[1]

> . . . "The LORD! The LORD! A God compassionate and gracious,
> slow to anger, abounding in kindness and faithfulness, (7)
> extending kindness to the thousandth generation, forgiving
> iniquity, transgression, and sin; [*Exodus 34:6-7*]

Let's extend this analogy even further. Today, we no longer have a goat to send to Azazel, carrying away our sins, but we do have this line from the *Unetana Tokef* prayer from Yom Kippur:

> But repentance, prayer, and righteousness [*tzedakah*] have the
> power to transform the harshness of our destiny.

God has given us three ways to make expiation for our sins today. I hope that we will all be able to come together on Yom Kippur this year to hear the cantor sing this beautiful, awe-inspiring prayer.

But in the meantime, we don't have to wait until Yom Kippur to start practicing these three things.

SECOND ALIYAH: LEVITICUS 16:18–24
SUNDAY, APRIL 26, 2020

Could Today be the Last Day of the Rest of Your Life?

This short section continues the narrative of the goat that is to be sent out to the wilderness, to Azazel. Aaron placed both of his hands on the head of the goat and confessed the sins of the people, thereby transferring them to the goat [16:21]. The Torah is no more specific than this, however. So, we may wonder, what exactly did Aaron say during this ritual? The Talmud fills in the gaps:

> MISHNA: The Yom Kippur service continues: The High Priest
> comes over to the scapegoat, places both his hands upon it, and
> confesses. And he would say as follows: Please, God, Your people,
> the house of Israel, have sinned, and done wrong, and rebelled
> before You. Please, God, grant atonement, please, for the sins, and
> for the wrongs, and for the rebellions that they have sinned, and
> done wrong, and rebelled before You, Your people, the house of
> Israel, as it is written in the Torah of Moses, Your servant, saying:
> "For on this day atonement shall be made for you to cleanse you
> of all your sins; before the Lord you shall be purified" (Leviticus
> 16:30). [*BT Yoma 66A:10*]

Aaron uses the word "please" exactly three times in this speech, imploring God on behalf of the people. With the sins of the people now placed onto its head, the goat was sent out into the wilderness, but not by Aaron. Instead, it was sent out at the hand of "a designated man." What exactly did this mean, and who was this man? The rabbis say that he was designated from the day before, and that he was not a *cohen.* One might think that this task was an awesome responsibility, and therefore it would have been a great honor to be chosen to carry it out. However, Chizkuni quotes a *midrash* which says something quite different:

> . . . the word *iti,* which could be translated as "whose time had come," this is someone who was destined to die before this year is out. This would account for the fact that it was noticed that the man who had been entrusted with this task never lived out that year. We must assume that in those days people used astrology to determine who was not destined to live out the year.[2]

It doesn't sound like this was a task people were anxious to be chosen for. And yet, this man knew something many of us wish we could know—that his death was near. Therefore, he could prepare for it. In Pirkei Avot 2:10, we read that Rabbi Eliezer said: ". . . Repent one day before your death."

"How can I do that if I don't know when I am going to die?" you might ask. But that, after all, is exactly the point. The Talmud explains this statement: "one should repent today lest he die tomorrow; and by following this advice one will spend his entire life in a state of repentance . . ." [*BT Shabbat 153A:5*]

Today would probably be a good day to start.

THIRD ALIYAH: LEVITICUS 16:25–34
MONDAY, APRIL 27, 2020

This is the Day the Lord has Made

This is the section that tells us definitively that the day we are talking about, the tenth day of the seventh month, is Yom Kippur. The seventh month of the year is Tishrei, and the tenth of Tishrei is the date of the Day of Atonement. The Torah text tells us *t'anu at nafshotechem* (afflict your souls [practice self-denial]) on that day [16:29].

What exactly does it mean to afflict one's soul? Traditionally, according to the rabbis, what is usually implied is fasting, which, of course, we know we practice on this day. So, where do we find this idea specifically mentioned? And what about the other restrictions we practice? These are found in the following Mishna: "[On] Yom HaKippurim it is forbidden to eat, to drink, to wash, to anoint oneself, to put on sandals, or to have intercourse . . ." [Mishna Yoma 8:1].

Additionally, the phrase *ki vayom hazeh* (on *this* day) [16:30] appears here as one of only seven occurrences in the entire *Tanakh* (whereas, according to the Masorah, "on *that* day" appears more than two hundred times)[3]. Ralbag explains that it is meant to tell us that "'this day' shall make atonement for you, whether the Temple is standing or not, and the rituals can be performed."[3] The Temple has not stood in Jerusalem for over two thousand years, and the performance of the rituals defined in our text ceased taking place long ago. Nevertheless, *this* day, Yom Kippur, provides atonement for us today no less than it did for the nation of Israel on the first Day of Atonement described here in the Torah text.

FOURTH ALIYAH: LEVITICUS 17:1–7
MONDAY, APRIL 27, 2020

Beware of Goat Demons

In this short section, the people of Israel are warned about making their own sacrifices outside of the Tabernacle instead of bringing them to the priests to offer them on their behalf. Apparently, the message is that God takes this very seriously. We are told that the person who offers such a sacrifice will be cut off from among his people [17:4]. We might think that this is rather harsh. Baruch A. Levine explains that the words *dam shafach* (shed blood) found here are usually used to refer to murder, intentional homicide.[4]

First and foremost, we must understand that the animals being sacrificed were not being used for food—that is another conversation. These were animals that were being improperly sacrificed, sometimes to other deities (note the goat-demons in 17:7), by people who were not authorized to offer them. Taking the animals' lives in this way was thought to be a first step towards desensitizing an individual to the taking of a life; the fear was that this desensitization, if left unchecked, could make it that much easier for someone to take a human life.

Additionally, the word used to describe the actions of someone who offers a sacrifice to the goat-demons is *zonim, stray*, as in committing adultery [17:7]. The relationship between Israel and God is often portrayed in our scriptures as a marriage: we, Israel, are the bride and God the groom. When we are tempted to stray after other gods, that is equated with being an unfaithful wife. When infidelity occurs in a marriage, divorce is often the ultimate consequence. So, here, we see that God, a jealous husband, says that He will "divorce" us if we are unfaithful.

Of course, none of us are making sacrifices to goat-demons today (at least, no one that I am aware of!), or to any other gods, for that matter. Nevertheless, if there are things in our lives that take precedence over our relationship to God, the ultimate consequence is no less serious or harmful.

And that is why every day needs to be a day of atonement.

FIFTH ALIYAH: LEVITICUS 17:8–18:5
TUESDAY, APRIL 28, 2020

Hey, I'm Walking Here![5]

The first part of this reading continues the instructions on the topic of shedding blood of animals. Even animals that are killed for food must have their blood drained out on the ground and covered over. Blood is equated with life, and we are enjoined to not treat it lightly.

The last section [18:1-5] is the first reading of the *minchah* service on Yom Kippur afternoon. These five verses have much to tell us. The phrase, *"Ani Adonai Eloheichem,"* ("I the Lord am your God") reminiscent of the beginning of the Ten Commandments at Sinai, appears twice, and additionally one time in slightly shortened form, *"Ani Adonai"* ("I am the Lord"). The message is clear: these commandments, no less than the original ten, originate directly from God.

Additionally, God's laws, which we are commanded to obey, are compared to the laws of Egypt and Canaan, that we are commanded *not* to obey. In both cases, forms of the Hebrew verb *halach* (to walk) are used: *telechu* [18:3] and *lalechet* [18:4], both translated here as "follow." "Walking" is a commonly used metaphor for living a life of adherence to the *mitzvot* as it is a verb of action, implying constant movement.

As I sit here writing this, I am preparing to go out for one of my two daily walks with my husband; depending on the weather, we often see others out walking, as well. Everyone is polite and friendly (more so than in pre-COVID times) and respectful (we make sure we have our masks with us!). Walking gets us out of the house so that we don't go stir crazy but it is, of course, also good for our health, both mental and physical. If you, like us, have been walking more lately, then you can really appreciate this metaphor.

Finally, we see the phrase *vachai bahem* (you shall live by them) [18:5]. That, after all, is the message: living a life according to the *mitzvot* brings *life*—both physical and mental. It's good for you!

So, get out there and walk both literally (if you can) and metaphorically!

SIXTH ALIYAH: LEVITICUS 18:6–21
TUESDAY, APRIL 28, 2020

Forbidden Unions, Forbidden Sacrifices

This section, which is also traditionally the second Torah reading for the minchah service on Yom Kippur afternoon, outlines which sexual relationships were forbidden. The primary motivation for human beings to engage in sex was procreation. Therefore, these restrictions are all placed upon the man since the commandment to be fruitful and multiply is, according to rabbinic tradition, an obligation enjoined only upon men, not women. Additionally, the custom was to marry within one's tribe, and even more specifically within one's extended family. Therefore, the Torah specifies which relatives are forbidden for a man to marry: mother, father's wife, sister (by father and/or mother), granddaughter, aunt (father's or mother's sister), daughter-in-law, and finally brother's wife [18:6-16]. This last one has an exception. Since the obligation to have offspring was incumbent on a man, if a man died without having children, then his brother was obligated to marry his widow and the child they had together was considered to be the heir of the deceased man [Deuteronomy 25:5-10]. An entire tractate of the Talmud, Yevamot, deals with the laws regarding this practice.

Next, the Torah lists some other things that are forbidden: marrying both a woman and her daughter, or two women who are sisters [18:17-20]. A man may not have sexual relations with a woman who is menstruating—this commandment governs the relationship that *is* permitted to him, that with his own wife. It is interesting to note that this is immediately followed by the restriction on having sexual relations with one's neighbor's wife; the apparent assumption is that this would be particularly tempting during those monthly times when his wife was off limits.

Finally, the section ends with a warning not to offer any of one's children up as a sacrifice to Molech (or any other foreign god, for that matter). At first glance, one might wonder what this verse is doing in this section with all these forbidden sexual relationships. I believe it is related to the idea that we are to consider ourselves to be in a marriage relationship to God. God had demanded "only" animal sacrifices and to go beyond that and offer a human sacrifice, particularly of one's child, was, in God's eyes, not only murder, but the ultimate form of infidelity and unfaithfulness. Were there any doubt of this in our minds, we are reminded yet again at the beginning [18:6] and the end [18:21] of this section from Whom all these commandments originate: "I am the Lord."

SEVENTH ALIYAH: LEVITICUS 18:22–30
WEDNESDAY, APRIL 29, 2020

Outside of Our Comfort Zone

This short section is the third part of the traditional Torah reading for the *minchah* service on the afternoon of Yom Kippur. It finishes out the section on prohibited sexual relations with mention of two specific prohibitions. The first of these is one of the most controversial verses in the Torah, stating that a man is not to "lie with a male as one lies with a woman" because it is abhorrent [18:22]. For centuries, this verse has been used as justification for declaring homosexuality to be sinful. Probably no other verse in the Torah has caused more pain to more people than this one. Levine notes that there are two specific incidents of homosexuality in the Bible: the men of Sodom who demanded that Lot hand over to them the "man" [angel] who had come to his house so they could have sex with him [Genesis 19]; and a similar incident that ends tragically with a young woman's savage murder and dismemberment [Judges 19].[6] Levine says that both depictions are clear evidence of xenophobia in the biblical writers since both are meant to show the depravity of the other nations surrounding Israel. Both stories describe incidents of a violent sexual encounter which are to be condemned regardless of whether they occur between people of the same or opposite genders. There is no explicit mention in the *Tanakh* of a loving relationship between two members of the same sex (though many believe that that was indeed the nature of the relationship between David and Jonathan, son of King Saul). This sensitive topic is one which is far too broad for me to properly address here. However, it should be stated clearly that Conservative Judaism today not only legitimizes same sex relationships, but it also allows same sex marriage, and ordains members of the LGBTQ+ community as rabbis. (The issue of lesbian relationships is not specifically addressed in the Torah, but these are equally legitimized today, as well.)

This controversial verse is followed immediately by a commandment prohibiting bestiality [18:23].

Ibn Ezra explains that, since the primary reason for having sex was procreation, the Torah is here prohibiting sexual relationships that could not possibly produce children, and that that is really the true offense here.[7] This is a classic example, in my opinion, of putting one's foot in one's mouth, or trying so hard to make something better that one does the opposite and makes it worse. While it may be factually true that neither of these relationships can produce children, it is incomprehensible to compare a loving relationship between two men to bestiality. This attitude does not even begin to take into consideration the human emotional toll it exacts on those whose relationships do not conform to the "traditional" heterosexual mold.

These verses still give us much to think about today. They make us uncomfortable. And each of us needs to question what the text says and implies and how we feel about that.

I encourage you to find access to and read the texts on homosexuality that have been approved by the Committee on Jewish Laws and Standards of the Conservative movement. Wrestle with the texts and decide for yourself where you stand on the issues.

Parashat Kedoshim

FIRST ALIYAH: LEVITICUS 19:1–14
WEDNESDAY, APRIL 29, 2020

Holiness is Godliness

ParashahParashat Kedoshim is a rabbi's delight in terms of giving a sermon; it is chock full of *mitzvot*, so there are plenty of things that can be addressed. Indeed, right here in the first *aliyah*, many believe that there is a mini repetition of the Ten Commandments.

The *parashah* opens with Moses gathering all the people together, just as they were gathered at Mt. Sinai; this alone indicates how important the following instructions will be. God begins by instructing us that we should be ḳedoshim (holy). Why? Because God is *kadosh* (holy) [19:2]. We are to emulate God. According to Sforno, we humans are to try to be as much like God as possible, since [God] created us "in our image, after our likeness"[1] [Genesis 1:26].

So, being "holy" means behaving like God. And how, exactly, does one do that? That is exactly what the rest of the *parashah* comes to tell us, listing *mitzvah* after *mitzvah*, most of which govern our relationship with others.

The *mitzvot* that appear in this first *aliyah* are:

- Revere mother and father (Note that here the order is reversed from the Ten Commandments, where we are enjoined to *honor* father and mother. Much explanation has been given to this, but I prefer the simple explanation of the Bekhor Shor: the reversal of the order of the parents here simply indicates that both are of equal status.")[2] [19: 3]
- Keep the sabbath. [19:3]
- Do not worship idols. [19: 4]

- When you gather your harvest, you shall leave the "gleanings" (the parts that are dropped). [19: 9] These are to be left for the poor, so that they can gather them themselves without having to beg, thus affording them some sense of dignity.
- Same thing for your vineyard—leave the fallen fruit for the poor and the stranger. [19:10]
- Don't steal or be deceitful with your fellow human beings. [19:11]
- Do not swear falsely by God's name. If you do something wrong, don't drag God into it. [19:12]
- Don't defraud your fellow, and don't commit robbery. [19:13]
- If someone works for you for a day, you must pay him/her on that day. (Chances are, s/he's depending on that money.) [19:13]
- Do not insult the deaf. [19:14]
- Do not place a stumbling block before the blind. (This is interpreted both literally, and figuratively, meaning don't give improper advice to someone for the purpose of misleading him/her.) [19:14]

Whew! And all of that in just this first *aliyah*! Through it all, we are reminded again and again Whom we are emulating by behaving in this way. The phrase, "I the Lord am your God," appears ten times in *parashat* Kedoshim, four of them right here in this first *aliyah*. Additionally, the shortened phrase, "I am the Lord," also appears ten times in *parashat* Kedoshim, twice right here in this first *aliyah*.

All these *mitzvot* listed here are designed to preserve the dignity of our fellow human beings, for, in doing so, we recognize that they, no more or less than we ourselves, have been created in the image of God.

In these difficult days of COVID-19, we need to remember this more than ever.

So, to end this discussion, and in light of the commandment regarding our treatment of the deaf, I was touched by this story that appeared on MSNBC yesterday morning:[3]

> . . . Anchor Stephanie Ruhle broke down, Tuesday, while talking about a deaf grocery clerk who is unable to read lips with many of his store's customers now wearing protective masks due to the coronavirus.
>
> In the heart-wrenching sequence, Ruhle . . . told the story of Matthew Simmons, who, in addition to his job as a teacher at a school for the deaf, works at a Trader Joe's in Vancouver, WA. Simmons ordinarily reads lips, but can no longer do so, with so many of the store's patrons now masked. So, to compensate,

Simmons now wears a shirt which asks customers to tap him on the shoulder if they need help. He then asks them to write their request on a whiteboard he carries around.

Ruhle began breaking down as she read one customer's message to Simmons.

"It must be hard with everyone wearing masks," the customer wrote. "Thanks for your help."

The broadcast threw to commercial, with Ruhle tearfully adding her own salute to a much-deserving Matthew Simmons.

"I want to say thank you to Matthew," she said, "and all the heroes out there."

Nothing more needs to be said.

SECOND ALIYAH: LEVITICUS 19:15–22
THURSDAY, APRIL 30, 2020

No Idle Bystanders Allowed

This section includes more *mitzvot* that we are commanded to observe as a part of making ourselves holy. Several of them are recognizable. I would like to comment on two of them in greater detail:

Lo ta'amod al dam re'echa, meaning literally, "do not stand idly by the blood of your neighbor" [19:16]. The commentators have debated the meaning of this verse. There are numerous interpretations:

- You literally may not stand by and do nothing when you witness someone else who is in danger, even if it may mean placing yourself in harm's way.
- If you hear someone threatening the life of someone else, you must report what you have heard so that the third party can defend him/herself.
- You may not inflict violence on another person, either on your own or with others.
- More figuratively, if you hear someone being slandered, and you know that what you are hearing is untrue, you must speak up in defense of that person.
- If you have testimony that could be offered in defense of someone in a legal matter, you may not withhold it.

- You may not conduct your life in a way that endangers others or threatens their well-being.

All of these, in my opinion, are valid explanations of this verse. And all of them carry one central theme which is summed up in the second commandment I want to point out: *v'ahavta l'reacha kamocha*, literally "love your neighbor as yourself" [19:18]. Here the commandment is stated positively; Hillel famously stated it in the negative: "What is hateful to you do not do to your neighbor" [*BT Shabbat 31A:6*]. Rabbi Akiva said that this is "a central principle of the Torah." Stated this way, the commandment is perhaps a little easier to concretely observe by doing certain things and refraining from others in our relationship with our fellow human beings. Legislating what to feel internally is perhaps a little more difficult. After all, only God knows what we truly feel in our hearts.

In any event, both these commandments are immediately followed by the reminder, "I am the Lord." Observance of these *mitzvot* should be based on the acknowledgement that both we and our fellow human beings have been created in the image of God.

THIRD ALIYAH: LEVITICUS 19:23–32
THURSDAY, APRIL 30, 2020

Uncircumcised Trees, Tattoos, and Ghosts

This section continues its list of *mitzvot* whose observance makes us holy. Some of these are very familiar to us. They seem to be put together in a random kind of order. We see:

- The fruit of newly planted trees is forbidden for the first three years [19:23]. When visiting Israel today, markings can be seen in the orchards and vineyards designating trees that are in their first, second, or third year of planting. Interestingly, the phrase used to indicate that the fruit of these young trees is forbidden to us is *va'araltem orlato*, literally that the trees are "uncircumcised" or "blocked off" from use.

- Eating anything with its blood in it is forbidden [19:26]. In this context, this commandment is believed to refer specifically to distancing oneself from non-Jewish ritual practices which sometimes involved the use of blood.

• Practicing divination or soothsaying is forbidden [19:26]. Specifically, we are not to look for omens (either in the stars, the clouds, etc.) to determine what day will be either good or bad for embarking on something new. We are to rely on God, not natural phenomena which were created by God.

• Rounding off the corners of your beard is forbidden [19:27]. The reason for this is to distinguish oneself from non-Jewish priests who did this, and from people in other cultures who did this to mourn the dead. It is from this commandment that the ultra-Orthodox derive the idea of *peyes*, sidelocks, since they do not cut their beards at the corners. The word *tashchit* [19: 27], is associated in the Talmud with a razor; from here, we derive the practice observed by many Jewish men (especially male rabbis) of not shaving their beards.

• Making gashes in your skin as a sign of mourning is forbidden [19:28]. Many non-Jews practiced this in biblical times. We, on the other hand, are enjoined not to make markings in our flesh.

• Making permanent marks (i.e., tattoos) on your body is forbidden [19:28]. This, too, was a common mourning practice of non-Jews. Often, the name of the deceased was tattooed into their skin. This Torah prohibition still applies today (sorry, folks!). Nevertheless, it is not correct to say that one who has tattoo(s) is not permitted to be buried in a Jewish cemetery.

• Making your daughter into a prostitute is forbidden [19:29]. Hopefully, this needs no more explanation.

• We are reminded once again of the obligation to observe the Shabbat and to respect God's sanctuary [19:30]. The previous several verses directed us away from religious practices of other nations; this directs us towards proper worship of our God. Notice again that the phrase, "I am the Lord your God," appears three times in this section, and the shortened phrase "I am the Lord" appears twice.

- Turning to ghosts or familiar spirits is forbidden [19:31]. Instead of trying to ascertain the future by communicating with the dead, either on one's own or through a medium, we are to rely only on God. Additionally, we should leave the dead in peace. When King Saul had the witch of Endor conjure up the spirit of the dead prophet Samuel, it didn't turn out well. Samuel was angry at being summoned back from the grave, and delivered the news that Saul would be joining him in the afterlife the very next day! [1 Samuel 28:1-20].

- Finally, you must show respect for the elderly [19:32]. If there are any earthly beings we should turn to for advice, it is those who have experienced life. It struck me that this commandment follows right on the heels of the prohibition of conjuring up the ghosts of the dead. How many of us have a question that we wished that we had asked our mother, father, grandparent or someone else before they died? Perhaps we are being reminded here to turn to these people in our lives to seek their counsel while they are still with us rather than after they are gone.

Again, all these commandments that govern our interpersonal relationships are reflective of what our relationships with God should be. We must first be able to have strong relationships with those whom we can see before we can have a strong relationship with the One whom we cannot.

FOURTH ALIYAH: LEVITICUS 19:33–37
FRIDAY, MAY 1, 2020

You Know What It Feels Like . . .

The primary *mitzvah* of this *aliyah* is that you must love the stranger as yourself. This *mitzvah* is mentioned thirty-six times in the Torah, more times than any other commandment.! The rationale for observing this commandment? Empathy! "You all were strangers in the land of Egypt," God tells us. You know what it feels like to be a stranger. You know that pain. Therefore, you should be loath to inflict it on someone else.

Baruch A. Levine explains that the phrase *lo tonu otah* (you shall not wrong him) "usually connotes economic exploitation, the deprivation of property, or denial of legal rights."[4] All of these are things which God commands us *not* to do. The fact that this commandment originates with God is once again brought home to us by the occurrence of the phrase, "I am the Lord your God," twice in this very short passage, along with the shortened phrase, "I am the Lord," once. Rashi points out that the word *Eloheichem* (your God) is in the plural form here, meaning that "I am the God of both of you; your God and his God, too."[5] Finally, the word *gerim* (strangers) also is often used to refer to converts. The Baal HaTurim comments that, "whoever perverts judgment against a convert is considered as if he perverted judgment against God."[6]

All these commandments have taken on a particular urgency for us Jews living today in a society which is becoming increasingly more xenophobic. When we witness strangers in our country being deprived of basic human rights and dignity, it is incumbent upon us to speak out. For just as surely as we were strangers in Egypt, so, too, do almost all of us trace our heritage back to someone (or several people) who came to the shores or the borders of the United States as a stranger.

Remember: you know what it's like to be a stranger.

FIFTH ALIYAH: LEVITICUS 20:1–7
FRIDAY, MAY 1, 2020

Keep Your Eyes Wide Open

This section reiterates in no uncertain terms the prohibition of offering one's children as a sacrifice to Molech. Two things are different here: the commandment applies not only to the people of Israel, but also to the stranger who lives with them. The penalty for violating the commandment is given: one who is found guilty of this offense is to be stoned by the rest of the people. If the people fail to do so, God will cut that person and his family off from the nation. Further, ". . . if the people of the land should **shut their eyes** to that man when he gives of his offspring to Molech, and should not put him to death" [20:4]. The phrase *haleym yalimu,* translated here as "shut their eyes," refers to the people who are aware that this individual is involved in sacrificing to Molech and have refused/neglected to carry out the punishment of stoning. But I think that the Hebrew is even stronger than that. Both of these words come from the same root *ayin-lamed-mem,*. The first word, *haleym,* is the infinitive absolute form of the verb, which tends to add emphasis (as in "surely"), and the second word, *yalimu,* is a third person masculine plural imperfect form of the verb. The basic meaning of this verb is "to conceal." So, this phrase might better be translated as, "surely conceal their eyes from that man." Concealment implies covering something up. In other words, they have now made themselves complicit with his sin, even if it is something that they themselves might not think of doing. Rashi says that the repetition of the verb in the Hebrew means that "if they shut their eyes to one thing, they will end up shutting their eyes to many things."[7]

This is the reason that God considers their part in this sin so egregious as the effect of the sin is multiplied and spreads in the community. Once again, the section finishes with the reminder that we are to be holy because, "I am the Lord your God."

Now, I don't think any of us know someone today who is involved in worshipping idols through human sacrifice. However, the point is this: when a situation exists that is dangerous to the welfare of the community, we cannot be a part of it, nor can we turn a blind eye to it. We must address it. That applies in the synagogue community, as well as the larger society around us.

SIXTH ALIYAH: LEVITICUS 20:8–22
WRITTEN FOR SHABBAT, SATURDAY, MAY 2, 2020

Strong Consequences for Indiscretions

This section reiterates several of the commandments that we encountered earlier in the *parashah*. Now, however, the consequences of each act are given. Most times, these consequences are rather severe.

As explained in the Talmud, some are punishable by death for both parties:

> . . . If a person steals, it is possible that he might return his stolen property and be made straight. if a person robs from another, it is possible that he might return his robbed property and be made straight. However, one who has sexual relations with a married woman with her consent and thereby renders her forbidden to her husband is banished from the world and passes away. There is no way for him to rectify the situation and achieve atonement, because a married woman who willingly has sexual relations with another man is permanently forbidden to her husband. [*BT Chagigah 9B:14*]

The woman's husband would have to divorce her, whether she had been a willing participant or not. As Rashi explains, a thief can repent and make restitution, but a man who has sexual relations with another man's wife will be denied the possibility of repentance since the sin that he has committed is irreversible.

Again, this may all sound very harsh to us today. What message can we take from this? We need to approach *all* the *mitzvot*, not just the ones listed here, with seriousness. Flaunting them has consequences. In the last verse of this section, God reminds us to observe all the laws and commandments, for if we do not, "The land [itself] will spew you out" [20:22].

SEVENTH ALIYAH: LEVITICUS 20:23–27
WRITTEN FOR SHABBAT, SATURDAY, MAY 2, 2020

Making Clear Distinctions

So, we have finally arrived at the final *aliyah* of *Parashat* Kedoshim. These five verses tie everything together. The *parashah* ends as it began: God tells us to be holy because God is holy. (The final verse here, verse 27, seems unrelated to the rest of the text, and many believe that it is out of place.)

But what exactly does the word *kadosh* (holy) mean? It has been translated as unique, apart, separate. The Hebrew verb that means "to separate" is *hey-vav-dalet-lamed* -and God uses it four times in this short reading:

- *hivdalti* (I have separated) you from the other nations [20:24].
- *v'hivdaltem* (you shall separate) the clean animals from the unclean and the clean birds from the unclean [20:25].
- *hivdalti* (I have separated) [certain animals] as unclean [20:25].
- *va'avdel* (I have separated) you from other peoples for myself [20:26].

The message then is that a life of holiness is a life of separation: we separate holy days from ordinary days (and each Shabbat or holiday ends with the ceremony of *Havdalah* (separation)). We separate what we can and cannot eat. We separate those with whom we can and cannot have relationships. We separate ourselves from the practices of other religions. And when we make all these separations, we are conscious of the fact that we do this because God asks it of us. God began the act of creation by separating light from darkness, then separating the waters above from the waters below, then the dry land from the water, etc. All of creation consisted of acts of separation, making order out of the *tohu va-vohu*, the primordial chaos.

God continues the acts of creation by calling on us to make separations in our lives, to make order out of the chaos of our being, thereby separating ourselves for a closer relationship with the Divine. This is what it means to live a life of holiness.

These past couple of months we have all been called upon to make physical separations between ourselves and others by masking, by social distancing at least six feet, by sheltering in place. This we must do for the sake of ourselves as well as those around us. In our new reality, this, too, is part of living a life of holiness.

Parashat Emor

The Big Kahuna

In this *parashah*, God gives instructions that apply only to the priests, the *cohenim*, beginning with matters of death and matters of marriage.

We must remember that impurity in biblical times was associated with death, and we previously learned that *any* person who came into contact with a dead body was considered to have rendered him/herself impure. Remember as well that since the *cohenim* served in the Tabernacle, in the holiest of places within the camp, and offered the sacrifices on behalf of the people, they needed to be extra stringent regarding their purity, or holiness. A priest who became impure was unable to serve in the Tabernacle until he had undergone a cleansing ritual, including immersion. The soonest he would be able to return to the *mishkan* would be the next day.

Therefore, God instructs Moses to tell the priests that they may not allow themselves to become impure through caring for the body of a deceased relative, except for a very specific list: mother, father, son, daughter, brother, (virgin unmarried) sister. These are what we might call his immediate "blood" relatives. For these relatives, the priest may defile himself [21:3]. Rashi says that he not only may do so, but he must do so. We may wonder about the specification of a sister only if she is an unmarried virgin. This is because a woman, once married, was considered to be part of her husband's family, and therefore, he and/or his family members would see to her burial.

However, this explanation should bring up another question: though not a "blood" relative, why was his wife not included on the list? Should we really think that a husband should not see to his wife's burial, even if he

65

were a *cohen*? The answer the rabbis offer is in the description of the relatives for whom the priest must defile himself: *l'yishero hakarov eilav* (the relatives who are closest to him) [21:2]. Rashi, Ibn Ezra, and others say that this phrase refers to his wife, for, after all, to whom would he be closer than his wife?

In any event, this is the reason why, to this day, *cohenim* do not go into a funeral home or a cemetery or any place where a funeral is being held except for these categories of relatives. We are all technically unclean, and the priests do not offer sacrifices on our behalf any more since the Temple is no longer standing in Jerusalem. Yet still today, most *cohenim* are careful to observe these restrictions.

The *cohenim* are also given instructions regarding marriage: a priest may only marry a virgin [2:13]. Therefore, this would logically exclude a widow, divorcee or prostitute, or a victim of rape. Again, though we may bristle at reading this, we need to remember that the whole idea was the purity of the priestly clan and their offspring. Among the Orthodox, this is still strictly guarded until today. The Conservative movement is not quite as strict. If a *cohen* does marry someone who falls into one of the "restricted" categories, he gives up his *cahuna*, his status as a priest, and any sons who may result from this marriage will not be considered *cohenim*.

It is difficult for us to look back at an ancient society through the lens of the twenty-first century. Many Conservative Jews are uncomfortable with these descriptions of a separate group within the nation. With the lack of a Temple in Jerusalem, the title of *cohen* is largely symbolic today. Even so, many synagogues still observe the practice of offering the first *aliyah* to a *cohen*, as well as having the *cohenim* offer the priestly benediction to the congregation on each of the major holidays. We still accord them the respect of their *cahuna*.

SECOND ALIYAH: LEVITICUS 21:16–22:16
MONDAY, MAY 4, 2020

I May Not Be Perfect, But I'm Trying . . .

This section outlines the physical conditions that would disqualify a priest from serving in the Tabernacle. God demands perfection in every way from those who are responsible for the religious lives of the nation. To be sure, it is difficult to read this passage from a twenty-first century vantage point. Putting aside our feelings of discomfort over the discussion of disqualifying "defects" for the moment, let's look at the list. As pointed out in the JPS Commentary on Leviticus, there is a distinct correlation between seven of the things listed here and the seven things that would disqualify an animal from being used as a sacrifice (these are mentioned in the following three verses, which appear in the beginning of the next *aliyah*):1

(22) Anything blind, or injured, or maimed, or with a wen, boil-scar, or scurvy—such you shall not offer to the LORD; you shall not put any of them on the altar as offerings by fire to the LORD. (23) You may, however, present as a freewill offering an ox or a sheep with a limb extended or contracted, but it will not be accepted for a vow. (24) You shall not offer to the LORD anything [with its testes] bruised or crushed or torn or cut. You shall have no such practices in your own land . . . [22:22-24]

Here are the comparisons:

- Blindness in priests [21:18]; blindness in animals [22:22]
- A broken arm or leg in a priest [21:19]; an injured or maimed animal [22:22]
- Scurvy in a priest [21:20]; scurvy in an animal [22:22]
- A boil-scar in a priest [21:20]; a boil or a scar in an animal [22:22]
- A limb too short or too long in a priest [21:18]; a limb extended or contracted in an animal [22:23]
- Crushed testes in a priest [21:20]; crushed, bruised, torn, or cut testes in an animal [22:24]
- A growth in the eye of a priest [21:20]; a wen (cyst) in the eye of an animal [22:22]

In addition, there are three other things that would disqualify a priest but have no equivalent restrictions for a sacrificial animal: lameness [21:18], a hunched back [21:20], dwarfism [21:20].

The similarity of the two lists is, indeed, striking. So, going on the premise that nothing in the Torah is coincidental, we could ask ourselves what, if anything, is the message here? What are we to learn from the fact that the same things which disqualify a sacrifice also disqualify the one who sacrifices it?

Certainly, Aaron and his descendants knew and understood that God demanded perfection from them because they were the ones who offered the sacrifices on behalf of the people and they were the ones through whom expiation for sins was achieved. They were obligated to treat their responsibility with great seriousness.

THIRD ALIYAH: LEVITICUS 22:17–33
TUESDAY, MAY 5, 2020

Do I Hear Dueling Banjos?[2]

Today's section finishes up the instructions regarding the sacrifices. The first type of sacrifice mentioned is the burnt offering [22:18]. We are told that, "it must be a male without blemish, from cattle or sheep or goats." Here, the disqualifying defects are not specified. It is regarding the next type of sacrifice, the sacrifice of well-being, that we see the explicit list of disqualifying defects that was discussed in the previous *aliyah*. Interestingly, though, it only says that it must be "from the herd or the flock . . . without blemish." The one disqualifying characteristic that does not appear in this detailed list is gender—the animal presented for this sacrifice apparently may be female! (So, who says we never are included in anything, ladies? I say this, of course, with my tongue planted firmly in my cheek!)

On a more serious note, let's look at the concluding verses of this reading. Four more times we see the words, "I am the Lord." We conclude this section with a very strong reminder of who authored these commandments, what is expected of us, and why. In exchange for our miraculous deliverance from Egypt, God expects that we will observe the commandments to maintain a relationship of holiness with God. God brought (brings) us out of Egypt to be our God.

We are reminded of this daily as we recite the third paragraph of the Shema:

I the LORD am your God, who brought you out of the land of
Egypt to be your God: I, the LORD your God. [*Numbers 15:41*]

The *Haggadah* also reminds us that each of us is to see ourselves as if we were there in Egypt, and therefore we are encouraged to ask ourselves what in our lives constitutes a form of suffering from which God has delivered us. Or perhaps that we still need deliverance from? It could be physical suffering or emotional suffering (either of these could potentially have more truth today than ever before). Perhaps you are still waiting for the deliverance to come . . .

God delivers us because God desires to have a relationship with us. That is no longer accomplished through sacrifices, as it was for our biblical ancestors. Rather, we are called upon to open the communication with genuine, honest, unblemished prayer. I pray that we may all experience the healing presence of the Divine in our lives.

Sacred Times

Beginning with this section, God tells Moses to outline for the nation the calendar of sacred days throughout the year. This is one of three places in the Torah to do so. Because we have just learned about the sacrifices, this list delineates the sacrifices that are required on each of the holy days. God's instructions begin with the following words: "These are My fixed times, the fixed times of the LORD, which you shall proclaim as sacred occasions" [23:2]. There is a great deal being said in this one sentence. To begin with, these days are referred to as "the fixed times of the Lord." We shall see that, in almost all cases, the exact date on the Hebrew calendar is stated for each holiday. The phrase, "of the Lord" means that God has declared them to be holy days. This is only the first part of the statement, however. We are told that we, too, need to "proclaim them as sacred occasions." It is a two-part effort: God says that these days are holy, but if we do not acknowledge them and commit ourselves to celebrating them as God has commanded, they become just ordinary days to us. We miss out on a precious opportunity to celebrate them and experience the joy that doing so can bring into our lives.

Next, God reminds us that the primary holy day occurs once every seven days: Shabbat. It is a day on which no work shall be done, "throughout your settlements" [23:3]. This phrase tells us that the most important part of Shabbat observance is not what takes place in the synagogue, but what takes place at home. Setting the day aside to refrain from our weekday activities and spend time communing with God and with our families and renewing our souls is what the day should be all about. This is especially important to remember now when we are unable to join in the synagogue for communal worship.

The year begins with the month of Nisan, making *Pesach* the first holiday of the year [23:5-17]. It is fitting that this should come first because, after all, without Passover, the other holidays would not exist—had we not been liberated from Egypt, we never would have been able to celebrate any of the holidays. To borrow a phrase, we could say that *Pesach* is "the reason for the season(s)."

Next, we read about the part of the year we are in right now. We are told to begin counting starting with "the day after the sabbath" [23:15]. Here the word sabbath refers to the first day of *Pesach*, whether it was indeed Shabbat or not. So, the count, which lasts fifty days, begins on the second night of *Pesach*. This is the first day on which the *omer*, the sheaf of the wave offering, is given which is why we refer to this time as "the counting of the *omer*." Each evening during the *ma'ariv* service, we announce the official day of the count.

The fiftieth day is the next holy day, which today we call *Shavuot*. This is the day on which we commemorate the giving of the Torah at Sinai. Unlike *Pesach* and the other holidays that we will see mentioned in the upcoming readings, *Shavuot* is not given an exact date on the Hebrew calendar; its timing is only delineated *relative to Pesach*. That is because both these days are really bookends of one holiday: we were liberated from Egypt to be able to receive the Torah at Sinai. We cannot have one without the other.

For modern Conservative Jews, *Shavuot* has become one of the most misunderstood, least observed holidays of the year, which is unfortunate. It is a day for studying Torah and eating dairy foods. Commit yourself to learning something new this year, find some time to study, either with yourself or others. Remember, we all stood together at Sinai. We all have Torah to give and Torah to receive.

The final verse of this *aliyah* talks about the *mitzvah* of leaving the edges and the gleanings of your field for the poor. [23:22] One might think it is out of place here, in the middle of the discussion of the calendar. However, I think it is in exactly in the right spot, right after the mention of *Shavuot*. Why? What do you think?

FIFTH ALIYAH: LEVITICUS 23:23–32
THURSDAY, MAY 7, 2020

The Sounds of the Shofar

The setting of the calendar continues. The date for Rosh Hashanah is established as the first day of the seventh month, *Tishrei*. We are told that it is a day to be commemorated by *teruah*, loud blasts [23:24]. This, of course, is referring to the blowing of the shofar, one of the primary *mitzvot* of the day. A great deal has been written about the symbolism of the shofar. Baruch Levine says that, in ancient Israel, the sounding of horns was usually, "a method of assembling the people before moving on to a new location or of mustering troops for battle."[3] How does this apply to us today? It can be said that Rosh Hashanah, the beginning of the ten-day period leading up to Yom Kippur, the Day of Atonement, is a day when we are being mustered for a spiritual battle. We are called to spend the next week and a half doing battle with ourselves, and with that part of our nature which has caused us to sin and further distanced us from God. Therefore, metaphorically speaking, we are preparing to move on to a new location in our relationship with God, acknowledging our sins and short-comings, seeking God's forgiveness, and moving to a renewed and closer relationship with God.

Much symbolism has been attributed to the sounds of the notes themselves. The three notes that we hear are: *tekiah*, one long blast; *shevarim*, three shorter blasts; and *teruah* (the same word you saw above), nine staccato blasts.

Ideally, each of the three notes should last for the same amount of time, the duration of the one long blast of the *tekiah* equals the duration of the three short blasts of the *shevarim*, which is in turn equivalent to the nine staccato blasts of the *teruah*. It has been said that the *tekiah*, with its long, single sound, is the sound of triumph. The broken sounds of the *shevarim* and the *teruah* are the sounds of crying—wailing and sobbing, respectively.

The machzor lists the shofar blasts that are sounded on Rosh Hashanah this way:

tekiah shevarim-teruah tekiah (two times)
tekiah shevarim tekiah (five times)
tekiah shevarim tekiah gedolah

On each line, either the *shevarim* or the *teruah*, or the combination of the two, is surrounded by a *tekiah* before and a *tekiah* after. Ramban says that the *tekiah* represents God's mercy, that, even as we cry out to God, God surrounds us with mercy.[4] What a beautiful, comforting thought.

I think that this carries a strong message for us, not just on the High Holidays, but all year long—in our sorrow, when we are broken and crying, God surrounds us with mercy and healing. Just as we need to hear the message of the shofar on Rosh Hashanah, I know that there are many of us who need to hear this message today as our hearts are heavy dealing with the loss of loved ones, friends, and acquaintances. If you are dealing with sorrow and brokenness right now, I pray that you may feel the mercy of God's healing.

Please Don't Go

This *aliyah* defines the last holidays of the year, Sukkot, which begins on the fifteenth day of the seventh month (Tishrei) and lasts for seven days, and Shemini Atzeret, which falls on the twenty-second of Tishrei. We are told that the two central *mitzvot* of Sukkot are: "take the product of hadar trees [etrog], branches of palm trees, boughs of leafy trees [myrtle], and willows of the brook [this is the lulav and etrog which we wave during services]" and "live in booths [sukkot] seven days." [23:40]

Depending on the calendar, the holiday of Sukkot falls either in late September or October, a time of year when it can sometimes get a little chilly. I'm sure that many of us have wondered while sitting in the *sukkah* on a cold October night, why God couldn't have set the time for the observance of this holiday for a warmer time of the year. The reason for us to dwell in the succah is given: "in order that future generations may know that I made the Israelite people live in booths when I brought them out of the land of Egypt" [23:43]. Thus, the reason we do this is the same reason that is given for the observance of the Passover seder: our children will think that we are crazy and ask us why we are doing this when we could be inside our nice warm homes. They might not be so inclined to ask that question if it were warm outside and it might appear that the *sukkah* is there to provide shade from the sun. Just as we do at the *Pesach* seder, we will tell them that this is what God did for us when God brought us out of Egypt.

That, in turn, brings us to the very misunderstood holiday of Shemini Atzeret, literally the Eighth day of Assembly. Due to its name, many people mistakenly think that it is the Eighth day of Sukkot; however, the text clearly indicates that Sukkot is a seven-day holiday and that this is a separate holiday unto itself. Some think that the word *atzeret* means "gathering" or "assembling," however, several commentators have pointed out that it is really derived from the verb *ayin-tzadee-resh* (to detain); God is detaining us for one more day. This explanation reminds me of one of my favorite *midrashim*. It is said that the seventy nations of the world joined in the celebration of Sukkot. This is compared to a king who made a great feast that was attended by many people. At the end of the feast, when everyone else was returning home, the king turned to his children and said to them [paraphrasing], "Please don't go yet. Stay with me for one more day." [*BT Sukkah 55B*:10] So, too, when the rest of the nations left Jerusalem after the seven days of Sukkot, God desired that we would stay for just one more day. If you've ever thrown a big holiday celebration that kept you so busy that you didn't get enough time to spend time with those closest to you before they had to leave for home, you can understand how this would feel.

The Bechor Shor explains this beautifully. He says that God lets us go after *Pesach* because God knows that we will be back in fifty days for Shavuot. After Shavuot, God lets us go because we promise to be back after the summer for the High Holidays and Sukkot. But after Sukkot, we will not be back until *Pesach* in the springtime, and so God desires our presence for one more day.[5] God is reluctant to let us go. What a beautiful sentiment!

I like to take this one step further: Shemini Atzeret is one of the four times during the year when we recite Yizkor in memory of all the loved ones we have lost. So, as we stand to recite the Yizkor prayers, in a very real way, it is as if we are saying to those we are remembering, "Please, stay with me for just a little longer."

I think that this year, especially, if we are privileged to be able to spend Shemini Atzeret together in person, this poignant message will be felt more than ever.

SEVENTH ALIYAH: LEVITICUS 24:1–23
WRITTEN FOR SHABBAT, SATURDAY, MAY 9, 2020

You Shall Have One Standard

This last section of Emor includes a disturbing story of a man whose mother was an Israelite and father an Egyptian "going out" into the camp and fighting with a man who was an Israelite. During the fight, the man of mixed parentage blasphemed by using the name of God which is not to be pronounced. Ultimately, it was decided that his punishment was to be stoned by the rest of the community. The commentators went to great lengths to try to justify this; some say that his father was the Egyptian whom Moses had killed because he saw him beating an Israelite slave [Exodus 2:12]. Still, it doesn't quite sit well with us. Why are we told about this individual's parentage? And what difference does it make? Are we to believe that it was his Egyptian "blood" that caused him to commit this egregious sin? In fact, had the Israelite man been the one to blaspheme, he would have received the same punishment. How do we know this?

God commands: "You shall have one standard for stranger and citizen alike: for I the LORD am your God" [24:22]. We are to exact the same penalty for both Israelite and stranger living among us and are not to be partial in our judgement. In the phrase, "I am the Lord your God," the word "your" is plural. God has created both us and the stranger.

So, why tell us about the man's parents? After all, since his mother was an Israelite, shouldn't that make him an Israelite? Certainly, he would be by today's standards. The explanation that is given is that his mother was from the tribe of Dan. This man, therefore, wanted to claim his inheritance through his mother's father's family. The tribe, however, rejected this idea, and rejected him. He was not treated as an equal. Perhaps this was what caused his anger and thus caused him to lash out. The results, as we see, were disastrous, not only for him, but for those who had to carry out his sentence.

This is one of those stories in our Torah that we struggle with. This interpretation should give us pause. Do we also sometimes reject people because they don't have the right "pedigree?" Do we refuse to accept them because of who—or what—their parents were? Or because they think differently than us?

In these turbulent times, there are so many things that cause divisions in our world. Now, more than ever, we need to come together instead of allowing our differences to drive us apart.

Parashat Behar

FIRST ALIYAH: LEVITICUS 25:1–13
SUNDAY, MAY 10, 2020

Gifts from God

In this section, we learn about some *mitzvot* that apply only in the land of Israel. Just as we are commanded to rest and take a day off once a week by observing the Shabbat, so, too, does God command that the land itself needs to rest. When the people enter the land, they are to set aside every seventh year as a "Shabbat" for the land. No planting or harvesting is to be done during this year. Not only that but whatever produce grows of its own accord during this year is to be shared by all people, rich and poor alike, as well as all animals, the ones you own and the wild ones, as well. In a very real sense, everyone becomes a gleaner. We are all on equal footing, having to go out and gather our food. Just as Shabbat is a great equalizer, raising us all spiritually to the level of royalty, giving us the opportunity to rest from our daily routine, so, too, is the sabbatical, *shmitah* year is a great equalizer, causing us all to realize that, ultimately, we are dependent on God for our sustenance.

The message that God wishes to convey to us is that, after all, we do not own the land—none of us, neither rich nor poor. We are all tenant farmers, dependent on God for the success of our crop. Rashi says that what God is forbidding us to do is "treat it [the land] as if you owned it."[1]

God's commandment regarding the land mirrors God's commandment regarding the counting of the *omer*: "And from . . . —the day after the sabbath—you shall count off seven weeks. They must be complete: You must count until the day after the seventh week—fifty days; . . ." [25:15-16] And, "You shall count off seven weeks of years—seven times seven years—so that the period of seven weeks of years gives you a total of forty-nine years" [25:8].

Just as the period following *Pesach* consists of seven complete cycles of seven days, leading up to the fiftieth day, which is Shavuot, so, too, the yearly calendar includes seven complete cycles of seven years, leading up to the fiftieth year, called the Jubilee year. This, too, is a year when planting and harvesting are prohibited, when everyone must depend on gleaning from what the land produced on its own for their sustenance. Consequently, there were at the time of the Jubilee Year two consecutive years, the forty-ninth and fiftieth years, when nothing was planted.

Practically speaking, once the nation was settled in the land of Israel, most farmers planted extra during the sixth year of every cycle. After all, there had to be enough for themselves and the community for the seventh year, as well as most of the first year of the next cycle, until the harvest came in. In the forty eighth year, there had to be enough for the forty-ninth year, the fiftieth year, and most of the first year of the next cycle. Many of the wealthy farmers stockpiled a great deal in their houses in preparation for this long period without planting. And yet even this produce became communal property since the poor needed to be sustained during these off years, as well. In a practice called "removal of the produce," the wealthy people would share what they had with their relatives and neighbors, then bring the rest to the doorway and say, "Let everyone who needs come and take." (Sounds like the words of the *Haggadah:* let all who are hungry come and eat.")

Living in the land that God promised to us required (and still requires to this day) acknowledging that the gifts we receive from God are not just for our benefit alone, but for the benefit of the whole community.

SECOND ALIYAH: LEVITICUS 25:14–18
SUNDAY, MAY 10, 2020

Do Not Wrong One Another

Though this reading is very short, we are told twice in these five verses not to wrong one another. The first instance is in the context of selling something to your neighbor [25:14]. When selling land, the price must be prorated based on the time left until the next Jubilee year, since the land will revert to its original owner at that time. So, why do we need to hear this command again [25:17], so soon after the first one? Here, we are not given a specific context. Rashi says that this second commandment "refers to wronging one another by speech."[2] The implication is that we are not to demean anyone or give them advice that is more beneficial to ourselves than to them. This second commandment is followed by the now-familiar statement, "I am the Lord your God," where the word "your" is in the plural. Sforno says this comes to remind us that God is the Lord to both you and the other, the buyer and the seller, the one who would belittle or take advantage of someone else, as well as his/her victim.[2] Over and over again, we are reminded that none of us is more important than anyone else, nor are our needs more important than anyone else's.

This commandment has taken on a new meaning in this time of COVID-19. Certainly, none of us is happy having to be socially distant from friends and relatives or having to wear masks in public. But we do these things out of concern both for our own health and safety, as well as that of others around us, even people we don't know. Each of us is equally important in the eyes of God. Do not wrong one another.

THIRD ALIYAH: LEVITICUS 25:19–24
MONDAY, MAY 11, 2020

Strangers in a Strange Land

This is another short reading. It begins with God assuring the people that their crops in the sixth year will produce enough to sustain them for three years, as I explained in yesterday's readings. God promises to provide for the needs of the people providing that they treat the land properly—it cannot be sold beyond reclaim; meaning, no sale is to be made permanent. Every transaction requires that both buyer and seller acknowledge that it reverts to the original owner at the Jubilee year. Once again, God reminds us that the land does not belong to us. What caught my attention is the term that is used to describe the people of Israel who live on and farm the land: **strangers** residing with me [God] in the land. In other words, resident aliens. This word, gerim (strangers) appears four other times in the Torah, all of them containing the same identical phrase:

> You shall not wrong a stranger or oppress him, for you were **strangers** in the land of Egypt. [*Exodus 22:20*]

> You shall not oppress a stranger, for you know the feelings of the stranger, having yourselves been **strangers** in the land of Egypt. [*Exodus 23:9*]

The stranger who resides with you shall be to you as one of your citizens; you shall love him as yourself, for you were **strangers** in the land of Egypt: I the LORD am your God. [*Leviticus 19:34*]

You too must befriend the stranger, for you were **strangers** in the land of Egypt. [*Deuteronomy 10:19*]

God's message is loud and clear, driving home the point that we are never to forget that we were slaves in Egypt. Yet here in our verse, God tells us that we are now slaves to God. We have, it seems, exchanged one master for another. To be sure, there is a vast difference between the two. Pharaoh treated us cruelly and expected us to work for his benefit alone. God granted us freedom from Egypt; the laws that God now expects us to follow are not only for God's benefit, they are for our *own* benefit, as well as that of others around us. Though God often tells us what the consequence of not obeying the *mitzvot* is, nevertheless we have been granted free will to live by them or not.

And yet God tells us to always remember that we are still strangers in the land, and our history has proven that we have, indeed, been exiled from that land multiple times, and the results have been disastrous for us every time. And that is why it is so important that our modern State of Israel continues to exist. We should all continue to pray for God's protection of the land.

FOURTH ALIYAH: LEVITICUS 25:25–28
MONDAY, MAY 11, 2020

We All Were Gleaners

Here we learn what is to happen when someone in the land of Israel falls on hard times. The very end of the last reading commanded that we are to provide for the redemption of the land. This reading explains: if someone falls into poverty, he is permitted to sell part of the land that he holds. The Mishneh Torah elaborates on this:

One must not sell his house or his hereditary field, even though they will revert after some time, unless he has become poor, as it is written: "When your brother is reduced to poverty and has to sell part of his property" [25:25]. But one is not permitted to sell it and put the money into his pocket or into business, or spend it on furniture, slaves, and cattle; he may sell it only for food provisions. Nevertheless, if he sold it at any rate, the sale is valid. [*Mishneh Torah, Sabbatical Year and the Jubilee 11:3*][3]

Thus, we see that selling one's land was not a decision to be made lightly, and, indeed, could only be done if one needed to provide food for one's family.

Now, the laws of the Jubilee year dictate that the land will revert to its original owner at that time. But what if it's early in the forty-nine-year cycle? If the individual has sold part of his land holdings, he now has limited his capacity to grow crops and provide for his family, thus increasing his poverty. Having to wait thirty or forty years could produce an untenable situation for him and his family.

One possibility is that a relative who has the means to do so may redeem his land for him (i.e., buy it back) [25:25]. Alternatively, if the individual's financial situation improves and he has the means to buy his land back himself, he may do so [25:26]. In either case, the sale must be conducted in a manner which is totally fair to both buyer and seller. The *halachah* determined that at least two years had to have elapsed since the sale; this was to protect the buyer from a seller who might change his mind once the transaction was completed. The *halachah* also determined that if either a relative or the man himself came to redeem (buy back) the land at any time after two years, the purchaser did not have a right to refuse. The price paid at the time of the buy-back required prorating according to where in the forty-nine-year cycle it occurred [25:27]. This protected both buyer and seller from being taken advantage of by the other.

The bottom line here is that everything must be done to help an impoverished individual get back on his feet—not just through donations, but through providing him with the means to earn a living and provide for his family. All of this must be done in a manner that protects the individual's dignity.

At this most extraordinary time when so many people around us find themselves unemployed and struggling, it is truly inspiring to see how many have stepped up to help, donating time and money to help those in need.

We need to remember the lesson of the seventh *(shmitah)* year: we all become gleaners, we are all equal in the eyes of God. And God demands that we treat each other as equals and maintain the dignity of all.

FIFTH ALIYAH: LEVITICUS 25:29–38
TUESDAY, MAY 12, 2020

Your God is My God

In this passage, we learn the laws about selling a house in a walled city as opposed to an open field, and the laws about selling a house that belongs to a member of the tribe of Levi. Since they were responsible for taking care of the *mishkan* and later the Temple, the Levites did not own any land of their own, for they would have been too busy to maintain it. Therefore, property was provided for them by the other tribes.

At the very end of the passage, we find the laws concerning a relative who finds himself so impoverished that he has sold all his land and sold himself to you as a servant. God's instructions are to let him live with you "by your side" as a *ger toshav* (resident alien) [25:35]. (This is the singular form of the term that we studied in yesterday's reading.) In other words, we are to let him live with us as an equal, and we must remember that our fortunes could just as easily slip away, and we could find ourselves in the same dire straits. Allowing him to live with us, alongside us, maintains his dignity as a human being.

Additionally, Ramban and others take the words *vachai imach* literally, translating them as "he shall live with you." From here is derived a basis for the positive commandment to save a life when faced with the opportunity to do so.[4] *Pikuach nefesh* (saving a life) is, indeed, one of the primary commandments in Judaism and it is so important that it supersedes the observance of Shabbat.

God further commands that we are not to charge the impoverished person interest (either simple or compound). The passage then ends with the familiar reminder, "I am the Lord your God" [25:38]. Since the word "your" is in the plural, we are reminded here that God is God to both you and your impoverished relative. We are also reminded once again that God took us out of Egypt (where we all were strangers) to bring us to this land, to be stewards of this land, and to live an ethical and moral life based on the observance of the *mitzvot*.

Do Not Rule Ruthlessly Over Each Other

This section further elaborates the laws regarding the impoverished relative who finds himself living with you. He is not to be treated as a slave, rather a hired laborer [25:39-40]. In other words, you must pay him wages. Additionally, just as the land reverts to its original owner during the Jubilee year, so, too, the relative who works for you goes free in the Jubilee year. God gives the rationale for this: the impoverished Israelite, just like the wealthier relative who he finds himself serving, was freed from Egypt by God; God is the only master any of us should have. None of us should be a slave to anyone [25:40].

God also instructs the wealthier relative for whom his impoverished kinsman is working: "you shall not rule over him ruthlessly" [25:43]. Some of the commentators wonder what exactly does this word "ruthlessly" mean? Maimonides explains it this way:

> It is forbidden to work a Hebrew slave ruthlessly. What is meant
> by ruthless work? It is work that has no definite time or limit,
> or needless work designed only to keep the slave working and
> occupied . . . The master should not tell the Hebrew slave: "Pluck
> weeds under the vines until I arrive," because he has not given
> him a time limit. He should rather tell him Pluck weeds until a
> certain hour or up to a certain place. Nor should he say to him:
> "Dig up this place," when he does not need it. It is even forbidden
> to tell him to prepare a glass of hot or cold water for him if he
> does not need it . . . [T]he Hebrew slave is to do for the master
> only what is time-marked and needed. [*Mishneh Torah, Slaves 1:6*][5]

So, the slave is not to be given "busy work." Rather, his assigned tasks should be productive and necessary in nature. For to do otherwise would be demeaning to the servant.

Noting the use of the word *befarech* (ruthlessly), Baruch Levine notes the comparison with the following verses from the book of Exodus:[6]

> The Egyptians **ruthlessly** imposed upon the Israelites . . . the
> various labors that they made them perform. **Ruthlessly,** they
> made life bitter for them with harsh labor at mortar and bricks
> and with all sorts of tasks in the field. [*Exodus1:13-14*]

This commandment is so strong that it is repeated once again at the end of this reading in [25:46] and will show up once more in the next reading [25:53]. Indeed, these two instances in the book of Exodus and three in the book of Leviticus are the only five occurrences of the word *befarech* in the entire *Tanakh.* Therefore, it is a logical conclusion that they are connected.

The Egyptian taskmasters treated the Israelite slaves "ruthlessly." We are reminded again and again in these passages that God freed us from the tyranny of Egypt so that we could serve God. Possibly the worst insult we could inflict on God is to use our freedom to mimic the reprehensible behavior of our former captors. Rather, God commands us to turn completely away from such behavior so that we treat our fellow Jews (and, by extraction, our fellow human beings) with honesty, integrity, and respect.

SEVENTH ALIYAH: LEVITICUS 25:47–26:2
WEDNESDAY, MAY 13, 2020

What Day Is It?

Today's instructions apply in the case of someone who has become so impoverished that he is forced to sell himself as a servant. In this case, rather than sell himself to a relative, he sells himself to a *ger toshav* (resident alien). We have seen this term before. In this context, it is believed to refer to either a convert or a non-Jew living amongst the nation of Israel. The latter case would be considered the worst form of debasement for an Israelite to suffer. In any event, he still has the right to be redeemed by a kinsman, or by himself if his fortune reverses (but not quite sure how that happens if he is working as a servant to someone else). In any event, just as before, if he is not redeemed, he will go free in the Jubilee year.

The section finishes with a strong reminder of Who issued these commandments. Twice more we have the statement, "I am the Lord your God," and the section finishes with the shorter version "I am the Lord."

God states unequivocally that the reason that we should not allow either ourselves or anyone else to become a servant or slave to anyone else is that we already have a master: the One who gave us our freedom from the slavery of Egypt [25:55]. The Or haChaim explains that this statement, coming at the end of the section on the cycle of years, comes to tell us that our allegiance to God supersedes our allegiance to any human master.[7] And how do we know this? Our obligation to any human master has a fifty-year time limit on it, ending in the Jubilee year. Our obligation to God, on the other hand, does not end during the Jubilee year or any other time—it is a life-long obligation.

As a final summary of the instructions regarding the sacred times that God has laid out for us in the last several chapters, God says to us, "you shall keep my sabbaths." The word "sabbaths" here refers to the weekly Shabbat, but also to all the other appointed festivals, which are referred to as well as sabbaths in the text, and to the *shmittah* year, the last year in every seven-year cycle, and the Jubilee year, as these are also referred to as sabbaths.

For the last several months, many of us have found that while staying home, not going out to work or shop or visit others, one can easily lose track of time. Often, we must stop and ask ourselves what day it is or check the calendar as one day fades into the next. For some of us, it seems as if time moves very slowly, and for others, just the opposite.

Being a Jew means setting aside sacred times, some on a weekly basis, some on an annual basis, and sometimes every seven years, and infusing them all with spiritual significance. Doing so keeps us conscious of our relationship to God, as well as our relationship to the Land of Israel.

Parashat Bechukotai

FIRST ALIYAH: LEVITICUS 26:3–5
WEDNESDAY, MAY 13, 2020

Yesterday, Today, and Tomorrow

This very short *aliyah* consists of just three verses, and three is the number that comes up several times.

In the first verse [26:3], there are three verbs: *walking* in God's statutes, as I have mentioned previously, implies being on a journey with God. The parameters of the journey are defined by God's laws. God wants us to both *keep* [observe] and *do* the *mitzvot,* the commandments. What's the difference? *Keeping* the commandments means studying them and *doing* them is just that—acting on them. Blind obedience is not the preferred way to fulfill God's requirements. Studying Torah to better understand the whys and wherefores is a better way to go. When the observance of *mitzvot* takes on meaning for us, then we can honestly say that we are *walking* in them. They truly become a way of life. And this, of course, is God's ideal for us.

In the second verse, [26:4] three things are listed that will happen if we do all three things that God asked of us in verse 3, and all of them have to do with giving: God will *give* the rain, and as a result, the land will *give* its produce, and the trees will *give* their fruit.

God makes three more promises in the final verse [26:5]: between your crops and your vineyard, you will always have produce to deal with (note the first two verbs are the same here), you will always have what to eat, and you will live in safety and security.

The significance of the number three implies the aspects of time: past, present, future. We received the teachings of Judaism from those who came before us, we observe them today, and we pass them on by our example to the next generation. God's laws are eternal. But so, too, are God's promises.

SECOND ALIYAH: LEVITICUS 26:6–9
THURSDAY, MAY 14, 2020

Strength in Numbers

The first verse in this section may sound familiar to you from the Prayer for Peace that is recited in many congregations on Shabbat morning: I will bring peace to the land, And you shall lie down, and no one shall terrify you. I will rid the land of vicious beasts and it shall not be ravaged by war [Leviticus 26:6].

This short four-verse section continues God's promises for an idyllic future in the land premised on the continued adherence of the nation to the commandments put forth by God. The people will live in peace, undisturbed by enemies, neither human nor animal. Our enemies will be naturally afraid of us. The ratios are not the same, they are increasing (5:100 = 1:20 and 100:1000 = 1:100). What's up with that? Does the Torah have a problem with fractions, as was true of so many of the students in my math classrooms? Rashi explains it this way:

> FIVE [OF YOU SHALL PURSUE] A HUNDRED AND A HUNDRED . . . TEN THOUSAND—But is this the right proportion? Surely, it should have stated only "and a hundred of you shall pursue two thousand (and not ten thousand)!? But the explanation is: a few who fulfill the commandments of the Torah cannot compare with the many who fulfill the commandments of the Torah (i.e., the greater the group of those loyal to the Torah, the greater is the morale and, under God's blessing, the physical strength of each individual belonging to the group) [*Sifra, Bechukotai, Chapter 2:4*].[1]

Now, we may not be comfortable taking this in its literal meaning of physical war, but what if we take it metaphorically? It is much easier to live a life of Torah observance when we are surrounded by like-minded people. More than that, living an ethical life can be contagious.

This may be hard to believe in our world today, surrounded by growing partisanship and prejudice. It is also sometimes hard to feel the strength of others when we are living lives of isolation. It is more important than ever that we find opportunities to study, to spend time in prayer communing with the Divine, and reaching out to others to both give and receive support. There is strength in numbers.

THIRD ALIYAH: LEVITICUS 26:10–46
THURSDAY, MAY 14, 2020

Walking it Back

This very long section begins with the final description of what God will bring about if the people are obedient to the *mitzvot* [26:10-13]. One of the most beautiful images in this section is God's promise, "I will walk among you," Just as the verb "walk" is used to describe our journey with God, God now uses it reciprocally. Thus, we have the image of walking together with God, side by side, no social distancing required! The last words of this section are the now-familiar reminder, "I am the Lord your God."

The next section is called the *Tochecha* (the curses) [26:14-41]. God issues a very stern warning of what will happen to the people and the land if they do not obey. It is interesting to note that nowhere in this very long section is the name of God mentioned at all. This is very unusual indeed, as we have now become so accustomed to seeing the familiar phrases in which God self identifies as our God repeated frequently throughout the book of Leviticus. It is noteworthy that, in the final section, where God promises to remember the covenant with Israel [26:42-46], we do see the phrase, "I am the Lord your God," once more, and also the shortened version "I am the Lord." Thus, in a very real way, we see that the *Tochecha* represents God's abandonment of the people.

The reason for this abandonment is given: "if you walk with me in hostility" (notice the verb "walk") [26:21]. This phrase has variously been translated by commentators as "if you walk occasionally with me" (Rashi),[2] "if you walk with me only by chance" (Rashbam),[3] and "if you behave casually with me" (Baal haTurim).[4] All of these imply not taking our relationship with God seriously. If you have ever been involved in a relationship with another person who treated you this way, you know how difficult and frustrating that can be; one can only imagine how God reacts to the callousness of the entire nation. In this section, you should note several things that are the exact opposites of the blessings previously promised by God:

You shall flee though none pursues [26:17] . . .
. . . Your land shall not yield its produce, nor shall the trees of the
land yield their fruit [26:20].
I will loose wild beasts against you . . . [26:22].
. . . though you eat, you shall not be satisfied [26:26].
I will make the land desolate . . . [26:32].
I will unsheathe the sword against you . . . . [26:33].
. . . they shall fall though none pursues. With no one pursuing,
they shall stumble over one another as before the sword. You shall
not be able to stand your ground before your enemies. [26:37]

Additionally, there are many more punishments which God promises to
bring about.

Finally, in the last section, God promises to not abandon us altogether:
"Then will I remember My covenant with Jacob; I will remember also My
covenant with Isaac, and also My covenant with Abraham; and I will
remember the land." [26:42] Notice the unusual order of the names of the
patriarchs here. Instead of the usual Abraham, Isaac and Jacob, the names
are given in reverse order. It is as if God is saying that God has taken it
too far and needs to walk it back (a similar sentiment is expressed by God
after the flood).

This is one of those passages we wrestle with. What does it say about
free will if God is going to bring about all this punishment for disobedience?
And what does it mean to say that God remembers the covenant, and relents,
returning to the people and the land? Does God indeed have feelings? And
can God change God's mind (something which occurs several times in the
Torah)? If so, perhaps it is a little easier for us to understand what we are
told in the Creation story in Genesis, that we, human beings, were created
in the image of God.

FOURTH ALIYAH: LEVITICUS 27:1–15
FRIDAY, MAY 15, 2020

Make a Pledge

This section may require a little explanation. The first part [27:1-6] dis-
cusses vows, or better, pledges made by individuals to give to the sanctuary
as an offering of silver. This was a way of providing for the necessary funds
involved in the running of the *mishkan* and later the Temple. (Think Kol

Nidre pledge, or any other donation you make to the synagogue.) The measure of valuation used here was "the equivalent for a human being" [27:2]. The pledge that an individual made was the value of one's life, according to the following system set up by gender and age categories: [27:3-7]

AGE	MALE	FEMALE
20–60 years	50 shekels	30 shekels
5–20 years	20 shekels	10 shekels
5 months–5 years	5 shekels	3 shekels
Over 60 years	15 shekels	10 shekels

There are several things that we notice here, the most glaring of which is that women are valued less than men (we need to remember that it was a different, patriarchal society in a different time and a different place). Additionally, a woman's value relative to a man's changes depending on the age category, being highest in the oldest category. Here's the relevant idea behind this valuation system: no one in society was valued more than anyone else in the same gender and age category. In other words, a wealthy fifty-year-old woman had the same value as a poor fifty-year-old woman, and a twenty-one-year-old man had the same value as a fifty-nine-year-old man. In the eyes of God, we are all equally valuable, equally important, despite our social status or physical condition or capabilities.

Another interesting point is made here by the Baal HaTurim.[5] The *Tochecha* section which immediately preceded this reading that I talked about in the last section contains forty-five curses. In the book of Deuteronomy, there is a longer *Tochecha* section which contains ninety-eight curses. Adding forty-five and ninety-eight gives us a total of one hundred forty-three. If we add up all the numbers in the two columns of valuations above, we also get a sum of one hundred forty-three. The message, he says, is that making these pledges to the sanctuary was meant to atone for the ninety-eight curses that would be brought upon us by failing to take our relationships with God seriously.

The bottom line is that then, like today, the sanctuary was dependent on the financial pledges made by the people. Everyone shared equally in this responsibility, as everyone benefited from it equally. In these financially difficult times, our synagogues are experiencing the effects of a depressed economy no less than we as individuals are, while still being there for us, albeit through Zoom, providing opportunities to "meet," to learn, to sing together. Indeed, many congregations have been seeing more people participating in the weekly Zoom Shabbat services than they did before we had to close our buildings. We still have been able to celebrate holidays and life cycle events—bar/bat mitzvah ceremonies and shiva minyanim. If you have the means to contribute to your synagogue's maintenance, it is important that you do so. And at that unknown future time when we will be able to return to the physical buildings and worship together again face to face, it will be just as important to do so then, as well.

FIFTH ALIYAH: LEVITICUS 27:16–21
FRIDAY, MAY 15, 2020

Consecrated to God

In this *aliyah*, the land itself is consecrated, set aside as a donation to the sanctuary; the value was determined based on the size of the field (its seed requirement) [27:16]. In this case, however, the individual did have the right to redeem, or buy back, the land, if he was able, but for more than its assessed value. He had to add one-fifth of its value [27:19]. For those of you who are mathematically inclined, you are probably figuring that this means that one would have to add on twenty percent of the assessed value of the field, right? No! The way this really worked was that one had to actually add twenty-five percent so that, in the end, the new amount was one hundred twenty percent of the original assessment! (If the assessed value was $100, for example, the amount needed to redeem the land would be that amount plus $25, making the new total $125. The assessed value is eighty percent of the amount that is required to be paid, so it can be said that one-fifth, or twenty percent, has been added. (Sounds convoluted, I know, but that's the way they did it.) In any event, with the arrival of the Jubilee year, the land would revert to him, anyway. If the land was sold to a third party before he had the chance to redeem it, he was no longer able to redeem it [27:20]. In this case, when the Jubilee arrived, the new owner could no longer keep it, but it could not return to the original owner, either. In that situation, "the land shall be holy to the LORD, as land proscribed; it becomes the priest's holding" [27:21]. Once the land had been consecrated to the sanctuary, it attained a status of holiness in perpetuity.

We follow this same idea with ritual objects. Once something has been used for a holy purpose, rather than just throwing it away, it should be repurposed for some other holy usage. An example is the lulav and etrog; after Sukkot, the etrog can be made into jam, or into a drink (etrog flavored vodka, anyone?). The lulav is saved until *Pesach* to be used for sweeping up the crumbs of *chametz* during the search on *Erev Pesach*.

This is also the reason why we Jews do not throw away *siddurim* or *chumashim*, or any other holy books. If nothing else can be done, we bury them.

In much the same way, we ourselves are considered holy by God, each and every one of us. We, as a Jewish community, have an obligation to remember that each of our members is equally important in the eyes of God, and therefore can be no less so in our eyes as a congregation and as a people.

SIXTH ALIYAH: LEVITICUS 27:22–28
WRITTEN FOR SHABBAT, SATURDAY, MAY 16, 2020

Consecrated to God

These last two short sections, I must admit, presented a challenge. If an individual were consecrating land "that he purchased, which is not land of his holding" [27:22] the priest would help determine the assessment, prorated according to the proximity to the Jubilee year. When the Jubilee year came, the land reverted to the one from whom he originally purchased it. [27:25] So, in a way, the land never fully belonged to him in the first place, and therefore he could not really consecrate it. Regarding animals, the same verse says that "a firstling of animals, however, which—as a firstling—is the LORD's, cannot be consecrated by anybody; whether ox or sheep, it is the LORD's." God reminds the people that the firstborn of every animal belongs to God from birth; they are inherently consecrated, meaning that you don't really own them, they are already dedicated to God. This is derived from the following verses:

> "Consecrate to Me every firstborn; man and beast, the first issue
> of every womb among the Israelites is Mine." [*Exodus 13:2*]
> ". . . every firstborn is Mine: at the time that I smote every
> firstborn in the land of Egypt, I consecrated every firstborn in
> Israel, man and beast, to Myself . . ." [*Numbers 3:13*]

Now, you may have noticed that these verses mention that the firstborn of both humans and animals are consecrated to God. Since our verse in Leviticus is only talking about animals, I want to save the discussion about human firstborn for another time. Let's talk about the animals.

As these verses make clear, for the person who owned animals, every firstborn from one of his female animals was consecrated to God from birth.

Therefore, the farmer did not really own them. He was not free to do with them as he pleased and they had to be sacrificed.

Now, we don't sacrifice animals anymore today (thankfully), and most of us do not raise farm animals. But are there things that we "have" that were given to us by God that don't necessarily "belong" to us, but we are called to be stewards of? Some of you may be thinking of children. True, but again, I'm not having that discussion today. The one thing that we all have that was given to us by God is our *nefesh*, our soul. Another would be our health. These have been entrusted to us by God, and therefore we are obligated to be good stewards, of them. Caring for our soul means providing it with spiritual nourishment, finding time for prayer and study, for communicating with God, for nurturing the relationship that we have with God.

And our health? It used to be that we would say that taking care of our health meant avoiding things like smoking, drugs, drinking or eating to excess—in general not harming our bodies. All still true. But these days, caring for our bodies also means wearing a mask, washing your hands, being socially distant. If there is anything that these last five months have shown us, it is just how fragile our health can be, and how easily it can be taken from us. Remember, you owe your life to your Creator: "it is the LORD's."

SEVENTH ALIYAH: LEVITICUS 27:29–34
WRITTEN FOR SHABBAT, SATURDAY, MAY 16, 2020

Can I Count on You?

In this section, we see mention of the tithe. Eery member of the nation was required to tithe (i.e., consecrate to God) ten percent of his crop and ten percent of his animals. All tithes from the crops are holy to the Lord [27:30]. The same is true of the animals [27:32]. So, ten percent of the flock or herd belongs to God. Therefore, if you are a farmer and you have one hundred animals, ten of them would be consecrated to God. But which ten? How do you decide? Maybe you look at the animals and choose the ten poorest looking of the bunch. After all, they're going to be sacrificed, so why should you choose the good ones? On the other hand, what if you say to yourself that you really want to demonstrate your love for God, so you look for the ten choicest ones in the bunch. Or maybe you don't want your choice to be too obvious either way, so you choose ten "ordinary" animals, or, better yet, you choose ten animals at random. What's right? The answer is: none of these! We are not permitted to look at good vs. bad [27:33].

So, how was the decision to be made? "All tithes of the herd or flock—of all that passes under the shepherd's staff, every tenth one—shall be holy to the LORD" [27:32]. So, what does it mean to say that the animals pass under the shepherd's staff? Several commentators explain that the animals were put into a pen that had a narrow gate allowing only one animal through at a time. The shepherd held his staff, which had been dipped in red dye, over the animals as they passed through the gate, and counted: one, two, three . . . When he got to ten, he marked the animal with the dye on his staff; this animal was then consecrated as part of the tithe. The farmer was not allowed to influence this in any way by prodding the animals to move faster. Thus, the choice was not his in any way.

Additionally, the farmer was not allowed to make a substitution for the animals that are chosen according to this random method [27:33]. One may not substitute a good one for a bad one, or a bad one for a good one. Whichever animals are the last in each cycle of ten are the ones consecrated. But have you ever been in a situation like this, counting something, and suddenly you get distracted and find that you have lost count? Was that eight or nine? Nine or ten? What do you do now? The Sifra on Bechukotai, chapter thirteen, debates this idea at length. What if we skipped a number and called the ninth the tenth, the tenth the eleventh, and the eleventh the twelveth? What if we mixed up the numbers and called the ninth the tenth, and the tenth the ninth, and then the eleventh the tenth? What if . . . ? Several other variations are considered. At this point, if you're not a math person, your head is probably spinning. Bottom line: the tenth is always consecrated, whether we counted it correctly or not: "If he does make substitution for it, then it and its substitute shall both be holy: it cannot be redeemed" [27;33]. So, if you called the ninth the tenth by mistake, then the ninth is also consecrated since it was the substitution for the tenth. And if you called the ninth the eighth, the tenth the ninth, and the eleventh the tenth, then the eleventh would be consecrated, since it was the substitution for the tenth. But if you called the ninth the tenth, the tenth the ninth, and the eleventh the tenth, the ninth would be consecrated since it is the substitution for the tenth, but the eleventh would not, since the ninth has already been designated as the sacrifice, and there can only be one substitution.

Did you follow all of that? Why all these nit-picky details? Again, they come to make us realize that the choice is not ours. And yet we are the ones who make the designation. If we make a mistake, it could end up in two animals being designated instead of one, in which case we are consecrating more than ten percent of our animals.

The animals go through the gate randomly, but we make the designation.

If you are a farmer raising animals, you have no idea which of your animals will be the ones to be consecrated to God. Therefore, you must treat each of them as if they could potentially be the ones you "lose." Broadening this idea, we should never get too attached to our possessions as we could lose any of them at a moment's notice. In the end, everything we own is in the hands of God.

With this *Aliyah*, we have concluded the study of the book of *Vayikra*, Leviticus.

$$חֲזַק חֲזַק וְנִתְחַזֵּק!$$

BOOK OF BAMIDBAR
Parashat Bamidbar

FIRST ALIYAH: NUMBERS 1:1–19
SUNDAY, MAY 17, 2020

Say My Name

Dear _____ (insert your name here),

Welcome to the study of the book and the *parasha Bamidbar.* Now that the *mishkan* (tabernacle) has been completed and dedicated, and the priests have also been dedicated, and all the laws of sacrifice, and the purity laws have been given, the nation of Israel is finally ready to move on from Mt. Sinai and journey to the promised land. As with any important juncture like this, God orders a census to be taken of all the men aged twenty and up. The last time that a census was taken was after the incident with the golden calf [Exodus 30:12-15]. At that time, God gave the instructions that each man was to bring a half *shekel* that was to be designated for the sanctuary. After everyone had given their half *shekel*, the total amount of *shekalim* could then be counted and doubled to give the count of the men. Based on this incident, we have a tradition of not counting Jews by number. Since God promised to make Abraham's descendants as many as the stars in the sky or the grains of sand on the seashore, it should be an impossible task to complete.

But I think there is more to it than that. In today's reading, one word seems to predominate: name(s). The census was taken by listing the names of each man. Ramban says that "each one was to say his name when he was recorded."[1] To help Aaron and Moses with this task, one man is "designated by name" [1:17] from each tribe to secure the names of all the men from his tribe; these twelve men are listed by name [1:5-15]. The point is this: to God, we are not just a number; God knows each of us by name. A number is impersonal; a name is intimate.

Certainly, nothing in recent memory has brought this idea home to us more than the current COVID-19 crisis. The current statistics as I write this are over 88,000 deaths in the United States alone. That number is almost unfathomable. Yet, if you knew someone (or more than one. Let's face it, who among us doesn't?) who lost their lives to this pandemic, then they have a name—or names. It has meaning to us. It is real. We understand it.

When I was growing up, my mother z"l, was uncomfortable talking about "delicate subjects." When it came time to tell me the facts of life, she handed me a book that had been written by a Lutheran minister. The book was written for a parent to read to their child, but, as I said, Mom was uncomfortable doing so. Instead, she handed me the book, and said, "Here. Read this." So, I opened the book, and began reading. The opening line read: "Dear _____ (insert child's name here)." I had to put my own name into the book. I literally had to make the story of life my own.

Hence, the opening line of this entry. God knows you by your name. As we begin this study of a new book, I invite you to insert your name into the story and make it your own. Let us journey together to the promised land. And let us bring with us the memories of all whom we have lost.

SECOND ALIYAH: NUMBERS 1:20–54
MONDAY, MAY 18, 2020

The Numbers Don't Lie

This *aliyah* gives us the results of the census. The total for each tribe (except Levi) is given. Moses was instructed not to include the members of the tribe of Levi in the census because they were put in charge of caring for the tabernacle and its furnishings [1:50-53]. Yet there were still twelve tribes whose members were included in the census because there is no tribe of Joseph. Joseph is replaced by two half tribes named for his sons, Ephraim and Manasseh.

As we read through these verses that tally the number of men in each tribe, we are soon struck with the realization that the same wording tends to repeat itself over and over again: "of the descendants of . . . the registration of the clans of their ancestral house, as listed by name, head by head, all males aged twenty years and over, all who were able to bear arms—" This is one of several places in the Torah where we see this phenomenon occur. We ask ourselves why. Why do we need to read the same phrase again and again? Couldn't the Torah have just given the phrase one time and then listed the numbers for each of the twelve tribes? The answer, I think, is related to what I talked about yesterday: God has ordered the census because God cares about every one of us equally. Similarly, none of the tribes is any more (or less) important to God than the others. Each is given the same amount of attention.

Still, there are a few places where there are very subtle differences in the wording. As usual, since nothing in the Torah is assumed to be coincidental, the commentators look for meaning in these exceptions:

- The sons of Reuven are the first ones to be mentioned, so the Hebrew is simply *the sons* [descendants]. (The *lamed* which appears on the front of this word in most of the other cases is missing.) Since this is the first tribe listed, and the wording is just being introduced, the commentators don't make much of this. [1:20]

- The same thing happens in describing the descendants of Naphtali. The *lamed* is missing, making the word just *sons* [descendants]. According to the Masorah, this comes to tell us that, unlike all the other tribes that had both sons and daughters, the tribe of Naphtali had *only* sons. The Baal HaTurim, on the other hand, infers the opposite. He says that the tribe of Naphtali had more women than men![2] [1:22]

- An extra word, *pedudav* (their enrollment) is added into the description of the descendants of Simeon. The Masorah says that this is because the tribe of Simeon lost 37,100 men in the incident with the Midianite woman named Zimri (Numbers, chapter 25). [1:22]

One other interesting coincidence occurs here: the total number of men counted in the census is 603,550. The results of the previous census, which took place after the golden calf, are identical: "a half-shekel a head, half a shekel by the sanctuary weight, for each one who was entered in the records, from the age of twenty years up, 603,550 men." [*Exodus 38:26*]

The two censuses were a year apart, yet the number has remained the same! What should we make of that? An interesting question to ponder.

Tefilin and the Tabernacle

As the nation of Israel prepares to move on from Mt. Sinai, God gives instructions on what the camp should look like: the tabernacle is to be at the center with three tribes (Judah, Issachar, Zebulun) along its east side, three (Reuven, Shimon, Gad) on the south side, three (Benjamin, Ephraim, Menashe) on the west, and three (Asher, Dan, Naphtali) on the north. As the tribes are listed in the description, once again the name of each of their chieftains is stated, as is the total count of the men aged twenty and up. We will learn later that the camp began their journey on the twentieth day of the second month [10:11]; the original census had been ordered by God on the first day of the month, yet the counts remain the same. According to Ibn Ezra, this shows that not a single man had died in the camp during those twenty days, which is amazing considering the size of the nation.[3]

As you read through the description, look at this picture to get a visual of what the camp looked like. The camp was set up this way for security purposes. Not only did the camp look like this when they were stationary, but they also marched in this formation with the tabernacle containing the ark and the holy of holies always in the middle. The members of the tribe of Levi who were not included in the census because they were charged with caring for the tabernacle and its furnishings, marched on the east and west sides,

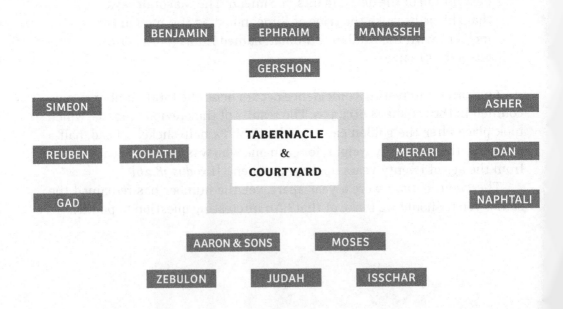

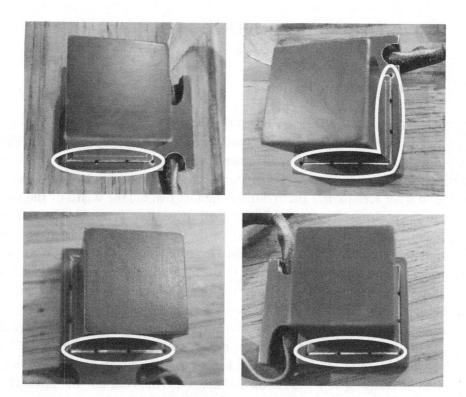

between the tabernacle and the other tribes. The largest division, Judah, was on the east and marched first. The next division, Reuven, was positioned on the south and marched second. Ephraim on the west marched third, and Dan on the north side marched last.

About two years ago, I was teaching a class on *tefilin*. The *halachah* lays out very specific guidelines on how the *tefilin* are to be constructed, and there is tremendous symbolism to be found in this beautiful *mitzvah*. I realized that when I look at the *batim*, the boxes, particularly the box for the *yad*, or hand, *tefilin*, I see a mini representation of the Israelite camp. The *halachah* requires that the boxes, which must be perfectly square, are to be sewn together using exactly three stitches of equal length on each of the four sides of the box. Above are some photos I took of my *tefilin* so you can see exactly what I am referring to.

Notice that each stitch ends in the same hole that the next one begins. The stitches are necessarily strong in order to hold the two pieces of leather together. The *bayit*, like the *aron kodesh*, the holy ark which housed the two sets of tablets of the Ten Commandments, and eventually the whole Torah, also houses words of Torah. So, every morning I am reminded of the nation united in one purpose, all tribes being equal and united in purpose, moving forward to advance and protect the Torah as we journey together.

FOURTH ALIYAH: NUMBERS 3:1–13
WEDNESDAY, MAY 20, 2020

Sorting Out the Pedigrees

In this section, the Levites are officially designated by God to be the ones responsible for caring for the sanctuary and its furnishings [3:6-10]. This sacred responsibility was originally supposed to be the job of all the firstborn in the entire nation from every tribe. Sforno says that this was the justification that God used for sparing them during the last plague, the death of the first-born, in Egypt. In exchange for sparing their lives, they were to be designated for serving God in the sanctuary. Therefore, they were expected to be at a higher spiritual level than the rest of the nation. However, they forfeited this right and privilege by participating with the rest of the nation in the sin of the golden calf. According to Sforno, God says, "I rejected the firstborn not because I changed, but because they did."[4] The Levites, however, did not worship the golden calf. Therefore, God says, "I hereby take the Levites from among the Israelites in place of all the firstborn, the first issue of the womb among the Israelites: the Levites shall be Mine" [3:12]. God told Moses that the Levites were now to be assigned (literally "given") to Aaron and his sons (the *cohenim*, the priests) to assist them by maintaining the tabernacle and all its furnishings.

This would be a good opportunity to explain the difference between *cohenim* and *leviim*. Most people know that, when *aliyot* are assigned during the Torah reading, traditionally the first goes to a *cohen*, and the second to a *levi*. I find, however, that many people don't fully understand how these two categories differ, and why.

A *levi* (plural *Leviim*) is any descendant of Levi, the third son of our patriarch Jacob, thus making him a member of the tribe of Levi. These are the people we have been learning about today. Both Moses and Aaron (since they were brothers) were members of the tribe of Levi, as their father Amram (as well as their mother, Yocheved) was a member of this tribe; hence, they were *Leviim*.

Aaron was further chosen to serve as the first *cohen gadol*, High Priest, and his sons and all future descendants to be the *cohenim*, priests. They were responsible for offering all the sacrifices and leading the religious life of the nation. So, they were a chosen group within (i.e., a subset of) the *Leviim*. Thus, every *cohen* is also a *levi*, but not vice versa. *Cohenim* is a smaller, more specified group. Therefore, a *cohen* is a higher pedigree. That means that a *cohen* can take the *levi aliyah* (in addition to the *cohen aliyah*) if there is no *levi* present. However, if there is no *cohen* present, the *levi aliyah* is moved up to the first position, and the second *aliyah* then goes to an *Israel* (the rest of us common folk). I hope that this helps clear up some of the confusion.

Support the Volunteers

Here we read of the accounting of the Levites according to God's command to Moses. Several things are different about this count from the census previously taken of the other tribes.

To begin with, verse 15 says that all the males from age one month and up are to be recorded; for the other tribes, it was age twenty years and up. That's a big difference! For the other tribes, the men being counted were those who could serve as fighting men in the army; the Levites, since they were charged with maintaining the tabernacle and its furnishings, were exempt from military service, so that explains why the twenty-year parameter wasn't used. But why one month? God commanded that the firstborn males were to be redeemed from the age of one month [Numbers 18:16]. Since, as we learned in the last *aliyah*, the Levites were taking the place of the firstborn, they had to also be counted from the age of one month.

Secondly, unlike the other tribes, whose members were recorded by *name*, as we talked about in the first *aliyah* this week, the Levites were recorded by clans [3:15]. Each of these clans was assigned specific items they were charged with maintaining. Each was also assigned a specific spot in the camp, somewhere in between the other tribes and the courtyard of the tabernacle [3;23, 29, 35, 38]. Here is the picture of the encampment again with those places highlighted:

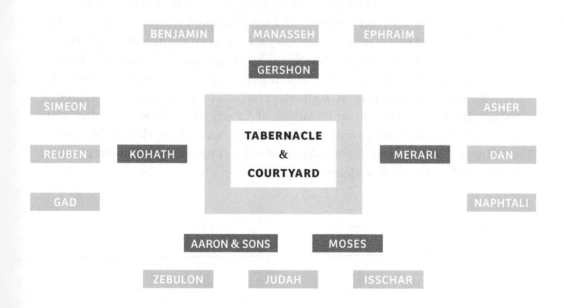

Finally, let's look at the counts that are given for the 3 clans of the Levite tribe:

CLAN	COUNT	SOURCE
Gershonites	7,500	Verse 22
Kohathites	8,600	Verse 28
Merarites	6,200	Verse 34
TOTAL	22,300	

But the total number of Levites that were recorded was 22,000 [14:39]! What's up with that? Several commentators, including Rashi, Ibn Ezra, and Rashbam say that three hundred of the Levites counted were *themselves* firstborn.[5] Remember, the Levites were appointed to take the place of the firstborn. But a firstborn cannot take the place of another firstborn, so these three hundred had to be deducted from the count.

Finally, we read that the Levites were appointed to attend to the duties of the sanctuary, "on behalf of the Israelites" [14:38]. Because the Levites are taking care of maintaining the sanctuary, the rest of the people were free to own land, make a livelihood, and come to the sanctuary to worship. In a way, the Levites can be compared to our modern-day Boards of Trustees, who give countless hours of their time to work on behalf of all the members of their congregations, assuring that the synagogues continue to function and to provide the services that we all are able to benefit from. If you have ever spent any time serving on the board of a synagogue or its auxiliary organizations, you know what I am referring to. I, myself, spent nineteen years on the Board of Trustees of my local synagogue. The amount of time put in by these volunteers can sometimes be a thankless job. I can only imagine that during these difficult days when we can't even gather in our synagogue buildings, their jobs are made even more difficult. They deserve our thanks and appreciation. Drop an email to the president or to any other board member you know, tell them how much you appreciate them and all the time they devote to the smooth operation of your synagogue. I'm sure they don't hear it often enough and would surely appreciate it.

Reconciling the Numbers

Now that God has said that the Levites will take the place of the firstborn
of the rest of the nation, and Moses has taken a tally of the Levites (22,000,
remember?), God instructs Moses to record the names of all the firstborn
[3:40]. Moses does so, and of course, wouldn't you know it, there is a problem: there are 22,273 firstborn [3:44] who need to be redeemed! What to
do about the excess two hundred seventy-three? Are they just out of luck?
God's answer is that Moses is to collect from each of them the five shekels
of silver, which was then to be given to Aaron and his sons as a redemption
price [3:47-48]. Indeed, we are told that Moses collected 1,365 (five times
two hundred seventy-three) shekalim and gave them to Aaron. This sum is
referred to as the "redemption money" [3:49-50]. The word *pidyom* is sometimes written with a final *nun* instead of a *mem: pidyon.*

What we have read about here has today become the standard procedure for a ceremony we call *Pidyon HaBen*, the Redemption of the Firstborn.
This is required for any boy who is the firstborn child of two parents, neither of whom is descended from a family of *Leviim* (and neither, therefore
a family of *Cohenim*). Our first grandson had one of these ceremonies. It is
supposed to take place when the child is thirty-one days old (just past thirty
days), but, in actual practice, can be after that; even an adult male who finds
that his parents never redeemed him can redeem himself. As part of the
ceremony, the parents give five silver dollars to someone who is a *Cohen*, a
descendant of Aaron. In doing so, we fulfill a commandment as well as perform a ceremony that goes back to biblical times. This is a ceremony that is
not performed all that often as a child must fit the exact criteria to require
redemption. Nevertheless, it is clearly part of our tradition, and it is rooted
in the Torah.

A question that may arise regarding today's reading, however, is how
did Moses decide which two hundred seventy-three of the firstborn males
would be the ones who had to pay the five shekels? One could see that this
might cause some problems in the camp! A Talmudic passage imagines how
this happened:

> ...and as for the redemption of the two hundred seventy-three
> of the firstborn of the children of Israel who are in excess over the
> number of the Levites...you shall take five shekels per head"...
> It can be explained that Moses said: How shall I do this for the

Jews? If I say to one of the firstborns: Give me money for your redemption and you may leave, as you are among the two hundred seventy-three extra firstborns, he will say to me: A Levite already redeemed me; what is the reason you think that I am among those who were not redeemed? [*BT Sanhedrin 17A:7*]

Thus, the matter was decided by lottery. Why did the rabbis go to such great lengths to come up with this explanation? They needed to make sure that Moses would not seem partial or indeed that he had anything to do with the decision at all. When things were decided by choosing lots, the decision was solely in the hands of God and who would dare to argue with that?

On the other hand, if we were to attempt to do something like this with our synagogue finances today, I imagine there would be a *lot* of complaining!

SEVENTH ALIYAH: NUMBERS 4:1–20
WRITTEN FOR SHABBAT, SATURDAY, MAY 23, 2020

The Original Dangerous Job

I love to travel (at least I used to! I'm looking forward to the time that we can do so again.). However, I hate packing! Even for one night! It's such a chore and I always leave it to the last minute, even when I went to Israel for three months during my third year of Rabbinical School. I'm sure many of you can probably relate to that. So, imagine what it must be like to have to pack up everything you own because your entire community is moving, and having to do it multiple times over thirty-eight years. That is exactly what the nation of Israel had to do after leaving Egypt. At this point in the story, they are getting ready to leave Mt. Sinai, so this will be the first of many times that all the people have to pack up all their belongings. The camp will travel in the formation that we discussed two times this week. That means that, in addition to everything else, the *mishkan*, the tabernacle, must also be dismantled and packed up for traveling, along with all its furnishings.

Think about any time that you had to pack up your household for moving. What did you do with anything that was fragile and valuable? No doubt, you took the time to wrap it very carefully, making sure it was well protected against breakage. Now just imagine that, in addition to everything else, you had to consider the fact that anyone who touched or even looked at this precious item would die instantly. Now you understand better exactly what the people were dealing with here. The Kohathites, one of the clans of the Levites, were assigned the task of caring for the most sacred objects in the tabernacle; this would naturally include the ark and the holy of holies. But no one, not even the priests, were permitted to look upon the ark or touch it under penalty of death. What to do? We read that "Aaron and his sons shall go in and take down the screening curtain and cover the Ark of the Pact with it" [4:5]. As the curtain was taken down, it immediately was placed on top of the ark, shielding it from view. Two additional coverings were placed on it for extra security [4:6]. All the other sacred objects were carefully wrapped in different colored cloths by the priests. Then, and only then, were the Kohathites permitted to come in and do their jobs.

In giving the instructions to Moses and Aaron, God told them no less than three times that they should do all of these things for the protection of the Kohathites so that they do not die. God knew that their service to God sometimes put them in danger. Indeed, they are called *la'tzavah* (to service) [4:3]. The Hebrew word, however, really means "to the army."

In these last several months, we have seen many people whose lives have been endangered by the jobs and the responsibilities they have. For their own protection, they themselves must be wrapped up carefully in PPE, gowns, masks, and face shields. The medical personnel, first responders of all types, even grocery store workers and many more are serving both God and humanity in the fight against the coronavirus. May they receive the protection of God no less than the Kohathites did while carrying out their sacred tasks.

Parashat Naso

FIRST ALIYAH: NUMBERS 4:21–37
SUNDAY, MAY 24, 2020

This Job Has Your Name On It

Here we learn about the assigned tasks of the other two clans of Levites regarding the service of the *mishkan*. The Gershonites were responsible for carrying the curtains and coverings [4:21-18]. The Merarites were responsible for carrying everything else regarding the physical structure of the Tabernacle: planks, posts, sockets, pegs, etc. [4:29-33]. So precise was this operation that each man was assigned a specific item that was his own responsibility to care for [4:32]. Some commentators (Ramban, Abarbanel) even feel that the items were marked with the name of the person who was charged with packing it up, carrying it, and setting it up again every time that the camp moved.[1] Broken down to that level, some men might have perceived their tasks as boring or menial. Imagine that one says, "I am responsible for these five tent pegs," and another says, "I am charged with caring for these five sockets." This required, therefore, that each man take his job seriously because if any piece was out of place, missing, or damaged, everyone would know exactly who was to blame.

Perhaps there's another way to look at it. The Tabernacle, the holy residence of God within the camp, was maintained simply *because* each person knew his responsibility, and *they all worked together* to make that happen.

Today, there is no longer a specific earthly dwelling place for the *Shekinah,* the presence of God. God's presence is brought into the world today only when we Jews, and, indeed, we humans, can recognize that each of us has our part to play, and that we must work in cooperation with one another to make that happen.

SECOND ALIYAH: NUMBERS 4:38–49
TUESDAY, MAY 25, 2020

Levites by the Numbers

In this section, we find the totals of the Levites in each clan between the ages of thirty and fifty years old, and therefore were eligible for service in the Tabernacle. Those numbers appear in the second column below. For comparison, the total numbers for each clan (these came from last week's *parashah*, *Bamidbar*) are in the third column. Comparing the two columns, we get the percentages that appear in the last column (in other words, these numbers represent the percentage of the total males in the clan eligible for service).

CLAN	30–50 YEARS	1 MONTH & UP	PERCENTAGES
Kohathites	2,750	8,600	32%
Gershonites	2,630	7,500	35%
Merarites	3,200	6,200	51.6%

So, we notice that for both the Kohathites and the Gershonites, the fraction of the men who were able to serve in the Tabernacle was approximately one-third (one was slightly below, one slightly above). In stark contrast to this, we see that, for the Merarites, more than half of their men were in an age category that made them available to serve in the *mishkan*. Abarbanel says that the reason for this is that they were responsible for transporting the heaviest items in the construction of the *mishkan*. In a way, their job was more important than the Merarites since they were carrying the things that formed the very structure, the foundation of the Tabernacle and their kinsman were carrying the coverings for that foundation.[1] So, it is almost as if God is providing the labor needed for the safe transport of the Tabernacle.

On the other hand, the group with the smallest percentage was the Kohathites whose job was described differently than that of the other clans. The responsibilities of the Gershonites and Merarites were twofold (service and porterage): to carry the items that they were assigned when the camp was in motion, and to guard those items when the nation was camped. The responsibility of the Kohathites, however, only involved carrying the holy items while the camp was in motion. When the nation was camped, they could not guard these items, since they could not look at them under penalty of death. These items were guarded by the priests when the people were not traveling. Furthermore, the Kohathites were instructed to carry the ark by placing its poles on their shoulders. According to some of the sages, the holiness of the ark magically upheld the strength of those who were charged with carrying it, lightening their load.

Finally, summarizing all these assignments to the various tribes, each person received his assignment from God through Moses [4:49]. Ramban says that "no Levite was permitted to do another's task or even help him."[2] Think about that for a moment: that would mean that if even one man was sick or incapacitated, the tabernacle could not be packed up for travel, and the camp could not move forward. This was a well-oiled machine, to be sure, but even it required some Divine oversight to assure its success. No one was to lose sight of the function of the *mishkan*, or of its most important Inhabitant.

THIRD ALIYAH: NUMBERS 5:1–10
THURSDAY, MAY 28, 2020

Homecoming

The first part of this reading speaks about God's requirement that any person who was in a state of impurity be put outside the camp even as the people traveled in the desert [5:1-4]. This may sound rather harsh. Let's look at it this way: God had agreed to dwell among the people in the holy of holies inside the *mishkan*. In return, God demanded that the holy presence, the *Shekinah*, be protected from impurity. Put into terms that we can relate to, the *Shekinah* had no immunity to impurity; therefore, bringing impurity into the camp endangered the holy presence, which would therefore depart from the *mishkan* at that point.

Following this, we have an interesting verse [5:6], which talks about wronging one's fellow human being by committing a trespass against God. According to the Baal HaTurim, this verse is talking about mistreating a convert. He says, "Whoever perverts judgment against a convert is considered as if he perverted judgment against Heaven." Elaborating on this, he goes on to say, "One who steals from a convert profanes God's holy name in the eyes of the convert who has come to take refuge under His wing." Continuing, he quotes Sforno, "The person who steals from a convert is guilty of committing a trespass against God."[3]

Clearly, the Baal HaTurim valued those who had made the difficult choice to leave their religion to cast their lot with the Jewish people. At the time in which he lived, such a choice would most likely have resulted in a complete schism from the family and culture in which one had been born. To then also be rejected or discriminated against by the very people one had chosen to join is unconscionable.

Today, as the number of people making this choice has increased dramatically in the Jewish world, the choice is not always so controversial as it once was (though for many it still is). Yet, I can't name any convert I know who hasn't experienced some discrimination from fellow Jews at one time or another. Though the congregation in which I am a member has always welcomed me from the very beginning, I would be lying if I told you that I had never heard the word *shiksa* used to describe me.

As we learn in the biblical story of Ruth that we read on the holiday of Shavuot, choosing to become a part of the Jewish people is something to be celebrated and applauded. Jews by Choice, myself among them, often describe the feeling after going to the *mikvah* as one of "coming home." We need to welcome them with open arms.

One of the most famous converts to Judaism was the Ger Tzedek; the story of the supreme sacrifice he made to join the Jewish people can be found online.[4] I would like to quote the last paragraph of this article:

> . . . perhaps the best way to remember the Ger Tzedek is by one of his teachings. He is reported to have taught:
>
> . . . when God offered the Torah to the nations of the world and they refused to accept it, there were individuals among them who were prepared to receive the Law; from them descended converts whose souls were present at Mount Sinai . . .
>
> I am one of those souls who stood at Sinai.

As we prepare to celebrate *Shavuot*, the holiday which marks the time that we all stood together at Sinai to receive the Torah, I celebrate my fellow brothers and sisters, anyone whose Hebrew name is *Ploni(t) ben (or bat) Avraham v'Sarah*. May you be blessed to find your home under the wings of the *Shekinah*. And I say to you all, welcome home!

Birkat Cohenim

This very long passage includes the description of the *sotah* ritual, to which a woman was subjected if she was suspected of adultery by her husband. This bizarre ceremony involved bringing her to the priest and forcing her to drink water with dirt and ink mixed in. If her body reacted, she was deemed guilty, and if not, she was deemed not guilty. There is much that could be said about this. Again, it is one of the biblical passages that disturbs our modern sensitivities.

Next, we learn about the Nazirite, either a man or woman who takes a vow to consecrate themselves temporarily to God, abstaining from all wine and alcohol, and not cutting their hair.

Neither one of these, however, though they make up the bulk of the reading, is what I want to concentrate on. Instead, I want to focus on a very short passage that comes at the end of the reading where God gives the instructions to Moses regarding how Aaron and his sons, the priests, are to administer God's blessing to the people [6:22-27]. This blessing, given by the priests for the first time here at the dedication of the *mishkan*, is still the same benediction given by the *cohenim* today:

> The LORD bless you and protect you!
> The LORD deal kindly and graciously with you!
> The LORD bestow His favor upon you and grant you peace!

We are most familiar with this blessing from the High Holiday services. In many synagogues, the *cohenim* offer this blessing to the congregation towards the end of services. Some congregations also have the *cohenim* give this blessing on the other holidays, as well. In addition, it is included at the end of every *amidah* and chanted out loud by the cantor or *shaliach tzibur* (whoever is leading the *davening*). The words are also often recited as part of any rabbinic blessing. The words are iconic; the English version appears in the liturgy of many Christian denominations, as well.

So, exactly why do these words speak to us so strongly? As Sarna explains in Hebrew, they have a perfect poetic structure: the first line has three words, the second five, and the last seven. The introduction in the first line has seven syllables, as does the conclusion in the last line. Each line consists of two Divine actions: blessing and protecting, shining (countenance) and being gracious, bestowing (favor) and granting (peace).

The "you" that is the object of all these divine actions is always written in the singular. Therefore, even though the blessing is given to the entire congregation at once, each one of us should feel as though we are the specific recipient of God's blessings.[5]

The last verse of the passage [6:27] makes it very clear that the *cohenim* are merely God's agents in administering the blessing—the blessing comes only from God.

For me, the words describe a beautiful reciprocal relationship between us and God. The very first word, *v'yevarechecha* (may He (God) bless you) (or He *will* bless you), lays the foundation for the entire three lines. God begins with the promise to bless us. For our part, we Jews begin each ritual act with a blessing. We recite a blessing before putting on a *tallit* and also *tefilin*, before eating, before lighting *shabbat* or holiday candles, when doing something for the first time, or the first time in a long time, before going to sleep, and when waking in the morning, when exiting the bathroom, when seeing a rainbow, or escaping danger, and on and on. Indeed, in the Talmud we learn the following:

> It is taught in a *baraita* that Rabbi Meir would say: A person is obligated to recite one hundred blessings every day, as it is stated in the verse: "And now, Israel, what (*ma*) does the Lord your God require of you" [Deuteronomy 10:12]. Rabbi Meir interprets the verse as though it said one hundred (*me'a*), rather than *ma*.
> [BT Menachot 43B:15]

One hundred blessings a day keeps our relationship with God always in our consciousness and fosters a sense of humility and gratitude. We bless God, and God promises to bless us.

The second action, *v'yishmerecha*, is variously translated as "may God 'keep' you" or "protect" you (or God will keep you or protect you). The verb *shomer* really means to "guard" or "watch over." It is the same word that is used by God in commanding us to "keep" the Sabbath, and to "keep" the commandments. We keep, protect God's *mitzvot*, and God keeps—protects—us.

In the next two lines, there is one word that appears twice, *panav* (his [God's] face). Though we may desire to see the face of the Divine, we are not permitted to do so (that is why we avert our eyes or cover our heads with a *tallit* during the blessing of the *cohenim*). Nevertheless, God promises to turn God's face towards us with kindness and graciousness. I was reminded of this promise early this morning as I stood on my outside deck davening the *shacharit* service. Facing east, I closed my eyes and felt the warming sun on my face. As I turned to God in prayer, I felt that God's face was turned towards me, as well.

The promises from God that are given in these three short lines are forthcoming based on this reciprocal relationship. Finally, the promises conclude with the familiar word, *shalom* (peace). Remember, this is an individual, personal blessing. Establishing this communion with God allows us the opportunity to experience an inner peace, a sense of well-being that we all so desperately need.

I pray that we may all be the grateful recipients of God's blessings, and that we may look to the strength that comes from that inner peace to help sustain us, especially through the difficult, trying times we find ourselves in right now.

FIFTH ALIYAH: NUMBERS 7:1–41
TUESDAY, JUNE 2, 2020

"I Can't Breathe!"

Now that the *mishkan* was all set up and dedicated, the chieftains of the twelve tribes (remember these were the men who had assisted with the census) came forward and brought their gifts to the tabernacle, beginning with six large carts and twelve oxen to pull them. These were given to the Levites to use in transporting the parts of the tabernacle when the nation traveled; two of the carts (with four oxen) went to the Gershonites (remember that their job was to carry the coverings of the tabernacle), and the remaining four carts (and eight oxen) went to the Merarites (they carried the poles and sockets—all the things which formed the structure of the tabernacle). The Kohathites, who were transporting all the sacred objects, received none of these as they were commanded to carry their precious cargo on their shoulders.

Next, we come to the beginning of a very long section that is a Torah reader's delight: you get to read a lot of Torah without having to prepare a lot of text. You'll see what I mean shortly.

Each chieftain came to present the gifts that the members of his tribe were offering. However, God instructed Moses from the outset that each chieftain should bring his gifts on a different day. For twelve consecutive days, one tribe each day would bring their gifts. The first person to bring his gifts was Nachshon ben Aminadav from the tribe of Judah. Unlike all the other eleven who come after him, his name is given without the title *chieftain* or *prince.* Some say that this was so that he would not come to lord it over the others that he was chosen first.

The commentator Or HaChaim explains it this way in his commentary:

> . . . The Torah omitted the word *nasi* (prince) although this title
> is used in connection with all the other princes when they are
> introduced as offering their respective gifts. The reason for this
> is that Nachshon was on a spiritually sufficiently high level to
> have qualified as the first one to bring this offering even if he
> had not been the prince of his tribe. The status of most of the
> other princes was due only to their having been elected as princes
> of their respective tribes. The Torah also wanted us to know
> that Nachshon did not think of himself in terms of his title, his
> position, but considered himself as "one of the people."[6]

So, Nachshon was a humble man. Additionally, Or HaChaim and others say that there is a reason for him being placed in the primary spot. It goes back to the day that the nation of Israel stood at the shores of the Red Sea with their Egyptian pursuers beating down behind them. Moses told the people to move forward, but they were paralyzed with fear. The Talmud tells us what happened: ". . . this tribe said: I am not going into the sea first, and that tribe said: I am not going into the sea first. Then, in jumped the prince of Judah, Nahshon ben Amminadab, and descended into the sea first, accompanied by his entire tribe . . ." [*BT Sotah 37A:3*]

Nachshon was the first one to step into the sea though the water had not yet parted. The *midrash* says that he stepped into the water and nothing happened. He continued further up to his ankles—still nothing happened. Then to his knees—still nothing happened. Then to his waist—still nothing. Then to his shoulders—still nothing. All this time, he was still able to breathe. When he continued to the point where his nostrils touched the water, the waters finally parted for it was at that moment that it became apparent to God and all the people that he had faith that God would keep him and the nation alive. And for this he was rewarded with the opportunity to be the first to bring his gifts to the Tabernacle.

We all face situations in our life that seem to have no way out. Sometimes, we must plunge forward with faith that God will sustain us and keep us alive and provide is with a lifeline.

On the other hand, as I write this, our country is in turmoil over the death of George Floyd, yet one more black man for whom, unlike Nachshon, when he said, "I can't breathe" had his cries unanswered. For him, there was no salvation at the last minute.

We as Jews have a responsibility to be part of the solution. Our history tells us all too well how easy it is to become the victims of hatred and bigotry. We must speak against injustice in any form. We talked about our mission of *tikkun olam*, repairing the world.

Our world right now seems more broken than ever. Each of us must ask ourselves what we can do to fix what is broken. And, like Nachshon, we need to be humble, and we need to have the courage to move forward though the odds against us may be strong.

Remember, according to the story, if Nachshon had not taken that first courageous step, no one else would have been ready to do so. Yet, when he did—they walked right with him.

SIXTH ALIYAH: NUMBERS 7:42–71
WEDNESDAY, JUNE 3, 2020

Hmmmm . . . Those Gifts Sound Familiar

So, if you have looked at the Torah text, by now you may have figured out why I said that this *parashah* is not only the longest *parashah* of the year, but also a Torah reader's delight. Between the last part of the fifth *aliyah* and this *aliyah*—a total of sixty verses—we have read about the gifts that were presented at the dedication of the tabernacle by the chieftains of the first ten of the twelve tribes. (The remaining two will be in the next *aliyah*.) No doubt you saw how repetitive it is. Except for the name of the chieftain and the name of his tribe, the six verses that describe the gifts are virtually the same because *they each brought exactly the same gifts:* one silver bowl weighing one hundred thirty shekels, one silver basin of seventy shekels, one gold ladle of ten shekels, filled with incense, one bull, one ram, and one lamb for a burnt offering, one goat for a sin offering, and two oxen, five rams, five he-goats, and five yearling lambs for his sacrifice of well-being.

Abarbanel says that the chieftains had all agreed in advance to bring identical offerings. Knowing how often sibling rivalry between brothers causes pride or jealousy to interfere with filial relationships, they were being extra cautious to prevent that from occurring here.[7] If that is true, then surely that showed that they had learned a lesson from the experience of their ancestor Joseph and his brothers.

Okay, then, you may be wondering why must we read this same identical list twelve times over. Why couldn't the Torah just give the list for Nachshon and tell us that all the others gave the same gifts? The Bekhor Shor says that it was "so that each would have his day in the sun."[8] Ramban says that "the Holy One wished to provide equal honor to all of them"[8] and that "each tribe brought exactly the same things in the same amount, but each had its own independent reason for doing so . . ."

The Baal HaTurim who, like me, finds symbolism in numbers, points to the fact that each of the twelve chieftains' names is mentioned in both the first and the last of the six verses describing his gifts. The twenty-four names, he says, allude to twenty-four hours. Each chieftain was given his own twenty-four-hour time period when his tribe's gifts were celebrated.[9]

The six verses allotted to each chieftain are, he says, an allusion to the six workdays of the week. Normally, the laws of Shabbat would preclude anyone from bringing gifts on that day. Yet on the seventh day, Elisha ben Amihud from the tribe of Ephraim brought his gifts. Chizkuni explains it this way: "this day was a Sabbath; permission was granted to not interrupt this string of sacrifices of which G-d had told Moses that they should be offered on consecutive days."[10]

God cared so much for the dignity and honor of each of the chieftains that for this occasion, the laws of Shabbat were suspended!

All of this tells us that God values each of us equally. The gifts that each of us has to bring are equally important in the eyes of God. None of us has the right to devalue another individual or what (s)he has to give. Neither do any of us have the right to devalue *ourselves*. Each one of us is created in the image of God; denying the importance of another is to deny the presence of God in that individual.

Unfortunately, this is a truth ignored by far too many people in our country today.

SEVENTH ALIYAH: NUMBERS 7:72–89
THURSDAY, JUNE 4, 2020

Do You Hear What I Hear?

This reading begins with the gifts of the chieftains of the last two tribes, identical, of course, to those brought by each of the first ten. Following this, the totals of all the gifts from all the chieftains was totaled up. The numbers are obvious: twelve of every item they each brought one of (silver basins, ladles, etc.), twenty-four of every item they each brought two of (bulls), sixty of every item they each brought five of (rams, he-goats, lambs). Yet every single item is tallied up. Once again, it is important to acknowledge the contributions of every one of them. God values them all.

The reading (and the *parashah*) concludes with one single verse [7:89] describing the very intimate relationship that existed between Moses and God. Moses was able to enter the tabernacle at any time and hear the Voice of God emanating from between the two cherubim that were on the covering of the ark which housed the tablets. The word *medaber*, used to describe the Voice, is an unusual verb form. Here it has been translated as "addressing him [Moses]." Most commentators, however, translate it as "speaking to Himself."[11] This would imply that, inside the holy of holies, in the innermost part of the sanctuary, God was in communication with Godself. This Voice could not be heard outside the walls of the tent and Moses was the only person who was able to enter the tent and hear it. Moses first heard this Voice at the burning bush, giving him his commission to lead the nation out of slavery in Egypt. He next heard it on top of Mt. Sinai when the people were too frightened to hear God's voice but sent Moses as their representative instead. No one before or since has had the privilege of being able to communicate with the Divine at will. This was not only reflective of the special relationship that Moses and God shared, in a way it was also a reward to Moses for all that he endured in leading the nation.

Today, if any one of us claimed to hear the Voice of God we would most likely be considered to be a little crazy. But I think the Voice of God is all around us, we just don't take the time to hear it. I am reminded of one of my favorite Psalms, number 29. It is part of the Kabbalat Shabbat service on Friday night. On Shabbat morning, before the pandemic, we used to sing it a second time, albeit using a different tune, as the sefer Torah was carried around in procession before being put back in the ark:

(1) A psalm of David. Ascribe to the LORD, O divine beings, ascribe to the LORD glory and strength.

(2) Ascribe to the LORD the glory of His name; bow down to the LORD, majestic in holiness.

(3) The voice of the LORD is over the waters; the God of glory thunders, the LORD, over the mighty waters.

(4) The voice of the LORD is power; the voice of the LORD is majesty;

(5) the voice of the LORD breaks cedars; the LORD shatters the cedars of Lebanon.

(6) He makes Lebanon skip like a calf, Sirion, like a young wild ox.

(7) The voice of the LORD kindles flames of fire;

(8) the voice of the LORD convulses the wilderness; the LORD convulses the wilderness of Kadesh;

(9) the voice of the LORD causes hinds to calve, and strips forests bare; while in His temple all say "Glory!"

(10) The LORD sat enthroned at the Flood; the LORD sits enthroned, king forever.

(11) May the LORD grant strength to His people; may the LORD bestow on His people wellbeing. [*Psalm 29*]

The Voice of God is clearly the theme of this Psalm—it is mentioned no less than seven times in eleven verses!

Have you ever stood on the beach and listened to the crashing of the waves? Or heard the roar of a waterfall? Have you been fortunate enough to hear the sound of glaciers calving? Have you felt the ground shake because of an earthquake? Or because a large tree fell? All of these and more, I think, represent the mighty, powerful Voice of God.

On the other hand, have you ever felt a soft breeze on your face? Or stood in the desert, especially at night, and heard absolute silence? These, I think, are the soft, gentle Voice of God.

Have you seen an animal giving birth? Or a woman? Or been with someone when they took their last breaths? These represent the awesome, transcendent Voice of God.

I could add so much to this list, and so could each of you. But that's the point. We may not hear words per se, but we are nevertheless surrounded by the Voice of God. We just need to listen.

This has been a devastating week for our entire country. May you be privileged to feel the comforting Voice of God as we enter Shabbat.

Parashat Behaalotecha

FIRST ALIYAH: NUMBERS 8:1–14
SUNDAY, JUNE 7, 2020

A Genuine Hands-On Experience

This *parashah* begins with a short mention of the lights that Aaron was to light inside the *mishkan*—the lights of the *menorah*. It is interesting to note that these lights did not serve the purpose of illumination. As the Baal HaTurim points out, God has no need for the light. Rather, the function was to show Israel and the rest of the nations around them that God did indeed dwell among them.[1]

The balance of this *aliyah* [8:5-14] is descriptive of the ceremony that took place to officially designate the Levites in place of the firstborn for service in the *mishkan*. It was not quite as elaborate as the ceremony for consecrating the *cohenim*—no blood—the Levites were not allowed inside the *mishkan*. Their job was to be threefold: guarding the pieces of the *mishkan*, transporting the pieces of the *mishkan*, and leading the worship in the *mishkan* through singing.

The ceremony involved cleansing them, shaving them, and washing their clothes before bringing them to the *mishkan*, where the entire nation was assembled; two bulls were sacrificed, and the entire nation laid their hands upon the Levites [8:10]. According to Hizkuni, during this part of the ceremony, each firstborn among the nation of Israel stood behind and laid his hands upon the specific Levite that was designated as his replacement.[2] In this way, the firstborn fully appreciated the magnitude of what was happening. This ceremony of laying on of hands, which was one of conveying authority, has been duplicated ever since in many cultures. For us in the Conservative movement, it has become part of the ceremony of ordination.

These two pictures are my favorite photos from my ordination ceremony in May 2019, one with Rabbi Aaron Benson (top) and one with Rabbi Moshe Edelman (below), my two mentors. I cannot even begin to describe to you what I felt in my head and my heart at these moments. It was truly one of the most profound experiences of my life.

Finally, the Levites are referred to as an elevation offering three times in this section [8:11, 13, 15]. Rashi says that these are for the Kohathites, the Gershonites, and the Merarites, the three designated clans of Levites who will serve in the *mishkan*.[3] They have become the sacrifice of the rest of the nation; they have set them apart, and God has claimed them as God's own [8:15]. Their service will elevate the spirituality of the people in their relationship to God.

Today, since the Temple is no longer standing, the *Leviim* no longer serve as they once did. Today, we each become our own sacrifice, we each must work at raising up our level of spirituality. Like the Kohathites, may you be lifted and carried by the words of the Torah, and may you sing sweetly and freely in praise of God.

SECOND ALIYAH: NUMBERS 8:15–26
MONDAY, JUNE 8, 2020

Mandatory Retirement

This section continues to describe the designation of the Levites for the service of God in the *mishkan*. God states once again that they are taking the place of the firstborn of the nation, who all belong to God since God saved them from the Angel of Death in Egypt during the last plague. Verse 19 is interesting. When reading the verse in the Hebrew, we can't help but notice that the term *bnei Israel* (Israelites) occurs five times (only four of them appear in the English translation). Normally, after the first mention, any subsequent references replace the specific designated term with an object pronoun (them, their, etc.). So, this verse calls for an explanation. Rashi says that the five mentions of *bnei Israel* reflect God's love for them. Like a parent who is so enamored of their child that they can't help but repeat their name over and over, so does God display love for "the children of Israel." So strongly does God love the people that God gives them (us) the Torah—the five books of the Torah, alluded to by these five repetitions.[4]

The Baal HaTur says that the five repetitions are representative of the five categories of people in Israel: *Cohenim, Leviim,* Israelites, converts, and freed slaves, all equally valued in the eyes of the Divine.[5] He also quotes *Minchat Shai*, whose explanation is that the *Cohenin* (Aaron and his sons) and the *Leviim* are each mentioned once in the verse along with the five mentions of Israelites. He says that these are an allusion to the seven *aliyot* of the Shabbat Torah reading.[6]

The Bekhor Shor also points to the explanation of the rationale for designating the Levites to replace the firstborn. He says that the firstborn men of the nation were not necessarily sons or even grandsons of firstborn men.[7]

Therefore, they would not necessarily be trained from birth in the service of the tabernacle. The Levites, on the other hand, being born into a tribe and thus surrounded by others who also serve, would naturally be trained from birth. It would be in their blood, literally.

Finally, in the last three verses [8:24-26], God expresses God's love for the Levites by designating a mandatory retirement age: they may not begin serving until age twenty-five, and at age fifty, they are no longer permitted to serve in the physical labor of transporting the tabernacle. They are, however, still permitted to take part in the guarding of the *mishkan* and in the leading of the worship in song. They are rewarded for their years of service by being freed from the responsibility of manual labor, but they are still valued.

THIRD ALIYAH: NUMBERS 9:1–14
TUESDAY, JUNE 9, 2020

Life is Full of Second Chances

Today's passage is about second chances.

God instructed Moses to tell the nation to observe the *Pesach* offering on the fourteenth day of the first month in commemoration of the night that they left Egypt. The people did so. However, since the laws of purity and impurity had been given by this point, there was a group of men who were unable to participate in the ritual due to the fact that they had contracted impurity through contact with a corpse. Not wanting to be excluded, they appealed to Moses, who then looked to God for an answer for them. God's response was to provide *Pesach Sheni,* a Second Passover, to be observed exactly one month later on the fourteenth day of the second month (Iyyar) by anyone who was unable to do so on the proscribed date. In other words, God gave them a second chance.

What we see here, first of all, is God amending *halachah* in response to a genuine need. If anyone is unable to observe *Pesach* on the fourteenth of Nisan because they are unclean or on a journey, they are permitted to do so exactly one month later (eventually, the *halachah* came to also include situations of danger as justification for delaying the observance of the *Pesach* sacrifice.) This *halachic* ruling is still valid today, though not often observed; many people are not even aware of its existence.

However, God also gives a very strong warning: anyone who is capable of offering the *Pesach* sacrifice at the appointed time (i.e., is not unclean or on a journey or in danger) and fails to do so will be cut off from the nation. That is a rather severe penalty, not to be taken lightly. We don't get to decide when or how to observe the *mitzvot*; they are not our laws; they are God's laws.

There was a great deal of discussion about this idea a few months ago as we all pondered the strange circumstances of observing *Pesach* in a time of pandemic. No one wanted to have small private seders or to have to use Zoom to see their family members. Some people even felt that since the COVID-19 pandemic meant that we are living in dangerous times, that was enough justification to delay the observance of the holiday. In the end, we all had to admit that there was not a strong enough rationale for delaying the celebration.

Now, here we are in June, almost two months past *Pesach*, and one month after what would have been the date for *Pesach* Sheni. With the powers of hindsight, we see that our situation in May was not much different than it had been in April, so we were right in our decision to not delay the observance of the *mitzvah*. This is a very important concept for us. It says in the *Mechilta*, "If a commandment comes your way, do not delay, for by procrastinating you may end up not performing the *mitzvah* at all."[8] If circumstances exist that truly prevent us from observing *mitzvot*, God provides us with a second chance. We may not, however, endeavor to make those determinations ourselves, for to do so implies that we know and understand more than God. That, I think, is the reason why the person who fails to observe *Pesach* in a timely manner is cut off from his/her people.

If this year has taught us anything, it is that our worlds can change in the blink of an eye. None of us knows what the future holds. When the opportunity to observe a *mitzvah* presents itself, do it. Don't delay. It may not present itself again.

FOURTH ALIYAH: NUMBERS 9:15–10:10
WEDNESDAY, JUNE 10, 2020

Listen . . .

The first nine verses of this reading describe the signals sent by God to the nation to let them know when they should break camp and travel, and when they should make camp and stay in place. God led the people in a cloud by day and fire at night. If the cloud rested on the *mishkan*, they knew to stay in place. If the cloud moved, they knew they had to follow it. This was the case for the entire time that they spent in the desert.

Another signal sent to the people, described by the rest of the verses here, was the blowing of two silver trumpets. There are three mentions of *teruah* (a short blast) which signal the people to begin to march [10:5-6]. These short blasts are to be used for setting the people in motion. The word *teruah* is the same word used on Rosh Hashanah when the shofar is blown. Rashi says that "the actual signal for setting the camp in motion was a long blast [*tekiah*], a sequence of short blasts [*teruah*], and another long blast [*tekiah*]."[9] The words in the brackets are the actual words used by Rashi in his comment; the words and their sequence should sound familiar as it is the same sequence of signals given to the shofar blower on Rosh Hashanah.

Just as these blasts were a signal to the nation that it was time to move on, so too is the sound of the shofar on the High Holidays a signal to us that it is time to move on. Time to examine our lives, seek God's forgiveness, and move on. Ramban says that the short blasts allude to God's aspect of justice, while the long blasts allude to God's aspect of mercy.[9] I have written about these blasts previously. The long wailing blast is reminiscent of a person crying out to God, pleading for divine mercy; the short staccato blasts are reminiscent of the broken spirit of the one who seeks God's forgiveness.

Remember, the people did not decide when it was time to move on and when to stay in place. God made those decisions, and when they did move, they did not decide where to go but they followed the cloud that represented the divine presence. They followed God. The nation and God were on a journey together. By following the cloud, they demonstrated their complete faith in God to lead them on the right path.

We, too, are on a journey with God. We no longer have a cloud or a pillar of fire to lead us. Instead, we are guided by the words of the *Torah* and of all the sages who have interpreted it for us. We need to be in touch with those words through prayer and study to know when it is time to move and where to go when we do. And when we do this, we answer the call of the shofar.

Open your ears and your heart and listen.

FIFTH ALIYAH: NUMBERS 10:11–34
THURSDAY, JUNE 11, 2020

Marching Orders

In this *Aliyah*, we read about the nation finally setting out from the wilderness of Sinai after staying there for almost a year. The marching orders are described in detail. First, the tribes of Judah, Zebulun, and Issachar followed by the clans of Gershon and Merari. Next, the tribes of Reuven, Gad, and Simeon. After that, the clan of Kohath. Next, the tribes of Ephraim, Menasseh, and Benjamin. And, finally, the tribes of Dan, Asher, and Naphtali.

As soon as the first three tribes set out, Aaron and his sons went into the *mishkan* to wrap up the ark and the other holy objects. Once they had done that, the Gershonites and Merarites dismantled the tent and prepared it for transport. They were followed by the next group of three tribes. Then the Kohathites advanced carrying the sacred objects, followed by the third group of three tribes, and then the final group of three tribes. By advancing this way, the ark was in the most protected position possible with six tribes in front of it and six behind. Not only that but because there were three tribes separating the Gershonites and the Merarites (the Levites who carried the structural parts of the *mishkan*) from the Kohathites, that by the time the Kohathites arrived at the new location with the ark, the tent had already been reassembled [10:21]. Therefore, the *cohenim* could immediately replace the sacred objects in their designated places. Ibn Ezra says, "as soon as the Kohathites arrived, the priests would bring the Ark into the Tabernacle and put it in place."[10] The *kavod* (honor) of the ark demanded that it never be just hanging around waiting. It was either in its assigned place or in transport. Both options placed it squarely at the center of the nation. Since the ark was the dwelling place of God inside the *mishkan*, a clear message was sent to the people that God and the Torah were the center of their existence.

We, too, need to keep God at the center of our lives. We don't have an ark in which to contain the Divine presence; instead, we must transport it within ourselves, in our hearts and minds. And we must guard it and protect it. And when it is time to move to a new place, even if only metaphorically, we must allow it to guide us on the journey.

SIXTH ALIYAH: NUMBERS 10:35–11:29
FRIDAY, JUNE 12, 2020

The Seven Books of the Torah

Today, I would like to concentrate on the first two verses of this *aliyah*, which are familiar to us from the Torah service. I will copy them here, together with the last two verses of yesterday's reading:

(33) They marched from the mountain of the LORD a distance of three days. The Ark of the Covenant of the LORD traveled in

front of them on that three days' journey to seek out a resting place for them; (34) and the LORD's cloud kept above them by day, as they moved on from camp (35) When the Ark was to set out, Mosesould say: Advance, O LORD! May Your enemies be scattered, And may Your foes flee before You! (36) And when it halted, he would say: Return, O LORD, You who are Israel's myriads of thousands!

The first thing that should jump out at us is that that the ark travelled ahead of the nation by a journey of a full three days in order to seek out a new place for the people to settle [10:33]. Wait a minute! Didn't we just learn in the elaborate description of the nation's travels in yesterday's reading about how the ark travelled in the midst of the people? How can this be? The commentators (Rashi and others) explain that this was a second ark; it was not the ark that contained the presence of God. It was the ark that contained the shards of the first set of tablets that Moses had broken when he discovered the people worshipping the golden calf. Though they were broken, the fragments were still considered holy as they had contained the original set of the Ten Commandments. This ark preceded the nation in all their travels. Now, let us go to the first two verses of today's reading [10:35-36]. As I said at the outset, these are familiar to us from the Torah service. The first is sung as we open the ark in the sanctuary to remove the Sefer Torah, and the second is sung at the end of the Torah service as the scroll is replaced in the ark. In between is the time when we study the words of the Torah.

Whenever we study the Torah in the synagogue, we reenact the journeys of the nation, led by the ark containing the broken tablets and the cloud representing the presence of God. These two verses literally surround every public reading of the Torah.

There is something else that should catch your eye if you look at the two verses written in the Hebrew: just before verse 35, there is an inverted letter *nun* (נ), and there is another just after verse 36. They are not part of any word and are just there. They appear in the Torah scroll as well as the printed editions of the text. Since nothing in the Torah is considered superfluous, the commentators try to rationalize their existence. The most well-known of these explanations comes from the Talmud:

> ...the signs are there because this portion is considered a book unto itself ... "With wisdom, she built her house, she carved its seven pillars" (Proverbs 9:1), these are the seven books of the Torah? According to whose opinion? It is according to the opinion of Rabbi Yehuda HaNasi, as by his count there are seven books

of the Torah: Genesis; Exodus; Leviticus; Numbers until: "And when the Ark traveled;" the portion: "And when the Ark traveled," which is considered its own book; the remainder of Numbers; and Deuteronomy. [*BT Shabbat 116A:2-3*]

According to this explanation, we have not five, but seven books of the Torah, since the book of Numbers is divided into three separate books. These two verses, 35-36, constitute an entire book all by themselves! All of Numbers up to this point is another book, and the rest of Numbers after this point is another book; adding in the other four books that we already know gives us a total of seven. Why would the rabbis go to such great lengths to come up with this explanation? Because seven is the perfect number, the number of completeness, the number of days in the week, the number of patriarchs and matriarchs combined. So, of course, the Torah itself must also be perfect!

A nice story. It doesn't change much, but it's something to think about the next time you witness the Torah being taken out of the ark.

I think it is also important to remember which tablets were in that ark that led the nation: the broken ones! They were broken due to human error. Nevertheless, they went ahead to show us the way to our next destination. We, like those tablets, are "broken" and imperfect yet God still travels on the journey with us, showing us the way to our next destination.

SEVENTH ALIYAH: NUMBERS 11:30–12:16
WRITTEN FOR SHABBAT, SATURDAY, JUNE 13, 2020

Opening the Line of Communication

In the last part of this section, [12:1-11], we have the story of Aaron and Miriam speaking against their brother Moses "because of the Cushite woman he married." Much has been made of this story, particularly this past week, given the recent demonstrations for an end to racism is this country. There is a tradition that the word *Cushite*, which is left untranslated, implies that Tzippora was dark-skinned (black) (Rashbam and others). There are many who say that it means instead that she was a beautiful woman, without commentary on her complexion (Rashi, Ibn Ezra, Baal HaTurim).[11, 12] Additionally, we do not know exactly what it was that Miriam and Aaron said to each other. The New JPS translation of verse 1 is not exactly accurate. The Old JPS translation is more accurate: "And Miriam and Aaron spoke against Moses because of the Cushite woman whom he had married; for he had married a Cushite woman."

This version reiterates the reason for their discussion but does not put specific words in their mouths. What has been suggested by more than one commentator (Rashi, Hizkuni, Ibn Ezra) is that, due to his close relationship with God, Moses had abandoned his marital responsibilities; his relationship with the Divine had replaced his relationship with his wife, whom he had abandoned. Tzippora had confided this to Miriam, who now shared her concern over the situation with Aaron.[13]

In any event, we see as the story unfolds that God reproves Aaron and Miriam for challenging Moses' authority [12:2]. Miriam is punished by being stricken with something that resembles leprosy and her skin turns white and flaky [12:10]. Upon seeing this, Aaron turns to Moses and pleads with him to intercede with God on her behalf. Moses' response is simple but expressive, "O God, pray heal her!" [12:13]

Here is Moses, a man who claimed he had a speech impediment, yet who has carried on lengthy conversations, not only with Pharaoh, his brother, and the nation, but regularly communicates with God as well, that when his brother asks him to pray to God for their sister, this simple prayer is all that he says. It consists of five short words, only eleven letters, that have a beautiful symmetry in the Hebrew. He doesn't plead with God, he doesn't pour his heart out, he doesn't defend his sister, he simply says, "oh God, pray heal her." We don't know what this inflection was or if there was any passion underlying his petition. I would like to think that imploring God on behalf of his sister hit a little too close to home, and that possibly he found it difficult to find more words to use to entreat God's healing for Miriam. Nevertheless, I think that the simplicity of the prayer is its beauty.

Many times, when I have found myself in hospital chaplaincy situations, people of various faiths, but most especially Jews, have asked, "Rabbi, how do I pray? I don't know how." It is not something that we Jews do naturally, and many people have difficulty opening the conversation. I would tell you to look at the example of Moses and just say what's in your heart. Don't worry about how elegant the words may or may not be. The important thing is to open the lines of communication. You may find it awkward at first if you're not used to it. It's okay. As long as the emotion is sincere, that's really all that matters. And the next time it might be a little easier. Just sharing with God your thoughts, fears, hopes, etc. can be very cathartic. If Moses didn't need to be elegant and loquacious in his prayer, then neither do you. But you do have to start the conversation.

Parashat Shelach Lecha

FIRST ALIYAH: NUMBERS 13:1–20
SUNDAY, JUNE 14, 2020

Send in the Spies

The people of Israel find themselves poised at the edge of the land of Canaan, the land that God promised to give them. God described it to them as a land flowing with milk and honey, a good land. Before they venture into the land, a decision is made to organize a reconnaissance mission. God tells Moses to send men into the land to spy it out; he is to choose one chieftain from each tribe. The twelve men chosen are listed by tribe and name and are not the same chieftains we met before. Except for two of them, we will quickly forget their names because we will not hear them again.

Interestingly, God does not just tell Moses to "send" the twelve men. If that were the case, the Hebrew would just say *sh'lach*. Instead, the Hebrew says *sh'lach-lecha*, which literally means "send for yourself." Thus, this is not really a command from God. Instead, God says, in essence, "I don't need this. I know that the land is good. I've told you that it is. But if you need this, then do it for yourself."

The verb that is used twice in this passage [13:2, 17] to define the mission of the spies is *latur*, translated here as "to scout." It really means, "to look for something." What exactly are they looking for? Moses outlines the kind of information they should seek: information about the people of the land (strong or weak, few or many?), the country (good or bad?), the towns (open or fortified?), the soil (rich or poor, wooded or not?). Finally, Moses tells them to be sure to bring back some of the fruit of the land. It was the time of the first ripe grapes [13:20] and Moses knew that they would find something good to bring back.

129

Was Moses assuming that they would also come back with a positive report?

Again, exactly what were they looking for? If they trusted God, Who had already performed so many miracles for them in freeing them from Egypt and bringing them through the waters of the Red Sea, they shouldn't have felt the need to spy out the land. Does the fact that they are willing to undertake the mission indicate a reluctance? Are they looking for excuses to not go into the land? It certainly would seem that despite everything they have witnessed, they are still afraid to trust God.

And what is Moses' role in all of this? Is he complicit? Since God has made it clear that Moses is sending them himself, it seems that he is.

We end the reading on a hopeful, positive note: the first grapes of the season are ripe. But still, we are right to have a sense of foreboding.

SECOND ALIYAH: NUMBERS 13:21–14:7
MONDAY, JUNE 15, 2020

A Lot Can Happen in Forty Days

Here we read what happened when the twelve spies went in to spy out the land (again, that word *latur* is used six times in this passage). Due to the foreshadowing at the end of the last reading, we expected them to find some grapes in the land, and Moses had instructed them to bring back some produce. Here we learn that the grapes were so large that it took two of the spies to carry back one cluster on a frame on their shoulders; this image has been recreated in the logo of the Israeli Ministry of Tourism.

Rashi says that actually there were two frames, each containing two long poles, with a man carrying each end of each pole, giving a total of eight men. One man carried a pomegranate and one a fig. Thus, ten of the spies came back bearing fruit. We may think that sounds like a great thing. On the contrary, Rashi says that their motivation was to show the enormity of the fruit, as evidence that the people of the land must be equally enormous. The only two spies who came back empty handed were Joshua and Caleb—the same two who were the only spies to advocate for going up and taking the land according to God's promise [13:30]. The ten who came back bearing fruit also bore tales of people who were giants compared to them, people whom they would not be able to overtake [13:31-33]. The results, we see, are disastrous: all the people cry out to Moses and Aaron, bemoaning the fact that they left Egypt [14:1-4]. Even as the brothers fall to the ground, Joshua and Caleb still try to persuade the nation that they will be successful in conquering the land. We know that this is not going to end well.

An interesting tidbit here is the amount of time that the spies spent scouting out the land: forty days [13:25]. There are a number of other things in the Tanakh that take place over the course of forty days (and forty nights):

- The flood at the time of Noah. [*Genesis 7:4, 12, 17, 8:6*]
- Moses was on Mt. Sinai receiving the first set of tablets.
  [*Exodus 24:18, Deuteronomy 9:9, 11*]
- Moses was on Mt. Sinai receiving the second set of tablets.
  [*Exodus 34:28, Deuteronomy 9:18, 25, 10:10*]
- Goliath taunted the people of Israel. [*1 Samuel 17:16*]
- Elijah went into the mountain of Horeb to seek the presence of
  God [*1 Kings 19:8*]
- Jonah prophesied to the people of Ninevah to repent so that
  their city would not be destroyed.

Forty is thus generally used in the Bible as a nice round number to indicate a long period of time. So, here we are being told that the reconnaissance mission was not a short, hasty one and the spies had plenty of time to see what was really happening in the land. Still, in all, it seems that ten of them didn't see what Moses had hoped that they would see, or what God had wanted them to see. Yet two of them did. Clearly, they all witnessed the same things but did not, however, perceive them the same way.

Meanwhile, the rest of the nation no doubt was growing restless waiting for them to return with their report. The last time that the nation lost patience waiting for someone to return from a forty-day mission they found themselves building a golden calf. Have they truly learned their lesson?

We shall see soon enough the devastating consequences of this spy mission.

THIRD ALIYAH: NUMBERS 14:8–25
TUESDAY, JUNE 16, 2020

Changing God's Mind

Today's reading picks up where yesterday's left off. Joshua and Caleb continue to try to convince the nation that they will be able to go in and take possession of the land, and even as they do so, the people prepare to stone them, picking up their ammunition from the ground [14:10]. Before they can carry through, however, the presence of the Lord appears, clearly angered. Speaking to Moses, God says that God is prepared to strike them with a plague and disown them and then build a new nation starting with Moses [14:12]. Moses' response is to reason with God: if God destroys the nation, he says, the rest of the nations will hear of it and say that God was unable to succeed in bringing the people into the land, and therefore just slew them [14:15-16]. That's not exactly the kind of reputation that God would want to establish in the world!

Believe it or not, this is not the first time we have seen this scenario. Let us go back to Sinai. It is the end of the first forty-day period, God has just given Moses the tablets containing the Ten Commandments. Before Moses descends, the following exchange takes place:

> (7) The LORD spoke to Moses "Hurry down, for your people, whom you brought out of the land of Egypt, have acted basely. (8) They have been quick to turn aside from the way that I enjoined upon them. They have made themselves a molten calf and bowed low to it and sacrificed to it, saying: 'This is your god, O Israel, who brought you out of the land of Egypt!'" (9) The LORD further said to Moses, "I see that this is a stiff-necked people. (10) Now, let Me be, that My anger may blaze forth against them and that I may destroy them, and make of you a great nation." (11) But Moses implored the LORD his God, saying, "Let not Your anger, O Lord, blaze forth against Your people, whom You delivered from the land of Egypt with great power and with a mighty hand. (12) Let not the Egyptians say, 'It was with evil intent that He delivered them, only to kill them off in the mountains and annihilate them from the face of the earth.' Turn from Your blazing anger, and renounce the plan to punish Your people. (13) Remember Your servants, Abraham, Isaac, and Israel, how You swore to them by Your Self and said to them: I will make your offspring as numerous as the stars of heaven, and I will give to your offspring this whole land of which I spoke, to possess forever." (14) And the LORD renounced the punishment He had planned to bring upon His people. [*Exodus 32:7-14*]

The same exact situation occurred here: God was angry with the people, threatened to destroy the nation and start over again with Moses, who then pleaded with God, saying that the Egyptians would say that God only brought them out into the desert to slay them. As in our passage, Moses asked God to forgive the nation, and God did.

In our passage, Moses also asks God to forgive the nation, reminding the Divine of God's long-suffering nature [14:18-19]. God's response is familiar to us, as it appears in our Yom Kippur liturgy: And the LORD said, "I pardon, as you have asked" [14:20].

There is, however, a major penalty: except for Caleb and Joshua, none of the men of Israel who were alive at that moment would live to enter the land of Canaan. That meant that the journey from Mt. Sinai to Canaan, which should have taken three days, would now last another thirty-eight years, making it a total of forty years from Egypt to Canaan, one for each day that the spies were in the land. It also meant that Moses himself, since he was complicit in the mission, was also subject to the punishment and he would not be able to enter the land!

These stories raise interesting theological questions for many people. Can God react in anger? Can God be reasoned with? Most importantly, can God change God's mind (i.e., can God repent?). According to both stories, the answer would seem to be a resounding yes! This idea is difficult for some people to grapple with. Isn't God perfect?

Naturally, God does not have human, physical form. Nevertheless, we are told in Genesis that we, human beings, are created in the image of God. So, when we behave in all these ways, we emulate our Creator—albeit, not in a positive way—nevertheless, we are apparently behaving as God sometimes behaves.

The important lesson I take from these stories is that, yes, we can let God know that we disagree with God and we can argue, try to reason with God. There is no guarantee that we will be heard, but we have the right to do that. And sometimes, we can convince God to change God's mind. And when we can't, then we must be willing to accept that reality, as well.

Most importantly, we can—and should—have an intimate relationship with God based on open communication and understanding.

FOURTH ALIYAH: NUMBERS 14:26–15:7
WEDNESDAY, JUNE 17, 2020

He Who Hesitates is Lost

In today's reading, God elaborates on the punishment the nation will endure for listening to the ten spies who brought a bad report and refused to go up and take the land. The ten spies who brought the negative report and caused an uproar in the camp lost their lives immediately in a plague [14:36-38] and only Joshua and Caleb survive. As for the rest of the men of the nation, their carcasses drop in the desert over the next forty years. This applies only to the men between the ages of twenty and sixty, all those men who were painstakingly counted by name in the censuses at the beginning of the book of Numbers [14:29, 30, 32]. Why only these men? To begin with, it was presumed that anyone who was over the age of sixty would die of natural causes over the next forty years (a logical assumption, even by today's standards). Second, anyone below the age of twenty was considered to be in that younger generation who would be privileged to enter the land [14:31, 33].

So, what was it about those twenty- to forty-year-olds? These were the men who constituted the standing army of the nation. Therefore, these were the men who had specifically refused to go and fight (i.e., the ones who were guilty of the sin of murmuring against God and refusing to go in to claim the land). Therefore, these are the men whom God says will be punished with death. But they were not all killed immediately, as the spies were. Why not? Well, think about it: if that had happened, that would have left the nation bereft of an army just when they have been condemned to wander in the desert for forty years and would have been left defenseless.

The *midrash* [*YT Taanit 4:6*] explains that the spies first came back and gave their report on the eighth of Av. That night, as the date changed to the ninth of Av, the people wept and bemoaned their fate. God's response was to tell them, "You wept needlessly that night, and I will therefore establish for you a true tragedy over which there will be weeping in future generations" [*BT Taanit 29A:7*]. This sounds like some parents who sometimes say to a child whom they think is demonstrating excessive childhood anguish, "You want to cry? I'll give you something to cry about!" In any event, beginning that year and for the next forty years, every male who had turned sixty during the previous year would pass away on the ninth of Av (Tisha b'Av). Thus, by the end of forty years, the entire standing army involved in the incident with the spies would have died in the wilderness, replaced by a new standing army, ready to go in and claim the land of their inheritance.

Now, a question for parents: did you ever discipline your child for not doing what you wanted them to do, only to have them say, "Okay, okay, I was wrong. I'll do it now!" And what was your reaction? Did you think, or even actually say, "Too late! You should have done it when I asked!" That is exactly what happened here. Early the next morning, a group of the people said that they were willing to go up into the land, after all; Moses warned them not to do it. The ark was not even leading them. Surely, they would not succeed [24:40-42]. Nevertheless, they went up and were sorely defeated by the people of the land. Why? Because God had not sanctioned this mission.

When we are presented with an opportunity to do the right thing, whatever that may be, we need to do it instead of putting it off as the circumstances tomorrow will surely never be exactly the same as they are today. And none of us can presume to know the future. We cannot allow ourselves to be paralyzed by the fear of doing what we know to be the right thing that is expected of us. The consequences could be devastating, both for ourselves and for others.

FIFTH ALIYAH: NUMBERS 15:8–16
THURSDAY, JUNE 18, 2020

We Are All Equal

This short section talks about animals that will be brought as sacrifices. The important message is expressed in the last three verses: "You and the stranger shall be alike before the Lord" [15:15]. The "stranger" here refers to the person who chooses to convert to Judaism. Though we may sometimes look at converts as not being "authentically Jewish," God says otherwise. There is a beautiful *midrash* that speaks to this idea:

> Why was the law given in the desert? To teach us that just as
> the desert is free to all men, so the words of the law are free to
> all who desire to learn them. Also, lest a man should say: "I am a
> student of the law that was given to me and my ancestors, while
> you and your ancestors are not students of the law; your ancestors
> were strangers;" hence, it is written: An inheritance of the
> congregation of Jacob (Deut. 33:4). This tells us that the law was
> an inheritance for all who associate themselves with Jacob. Even
> outsiders who devote themselves to the law are equal to the High
> Priest, as it is said: Which if a man do, he shall live by them: I am
> the Lord (Lev. 18:5). It does not refer to priest or Levite or Israelite
> but merely to man. Thus, One law and one ordinance shall be
> both for you and for the stranger that sojourneth with you (Num.
> 15:16). [*Midrash Tanchuma, Vayakhel 8:2*][1]

Have you ever been in the Negev Desert? The landscape is truly awe-inspiring. The *midrash* tells us that we all have equal access to the desert; more than that, though, in the desert, we all are equal. We all have the same opportunity to accept the *mitzvot*. We all stood together at Sinai, whether we were born as children of Abraham and Sarah or came to seek adoption under the wings of the *Shekinah*. We are all equal in the eyes of God. What right does any of us have to think otherwise?

SIXTH ALIYAH: NUMBERS 15:17–26
FRIDAY, JUNE 19, 2020

Commandment Number One

In this reading, God warns the people through Moses regarding failure to observe "any one of the commandments" which is then equated to "anything that the Lord has enjoined upon you through Moses." Thus, the two phrases are treated as synonymous: God is warning the people regarding one specific sin that the people could commit which would be equivalent to all the others (combined). And what could that sin possibly be? Several sages (Rashi, Ramban, Rashbam) state unequivocally that this sin is idolatry. This sin—worship of other gods—was the first mentioned by God at Sinai. It probably was the only commandment that the people really heard before dispatching Moses to receive the commandments on their behalf because they were too frightened.

Why does this commandment receive top billing? Clearly, anyone who violates this is obviously violating all the others. If any other god (or thing, animate or inanimate) receives precedence over God, then obviously there is nothing obligating an individual to observe the *mitzvot*. The commandments only make sense in the context of a relationship with God. Therefore, the sages understand that this is the sin referred to in verses 22-23. Verse 26 tells us, *"The whole Israelite community and the stranger residing among them shall be forgiven, for it happened to the entire people through error"* [emphasis mine]. This follows yesterday's reading where we learned that there should be one law only for the native born and the resident stranger (convert). This verse seems to indicate that, in the event that the entire nation erred by committing idolatry, the strangers among them might be blamed. Just as the convert is subject to the same laws as everyone else, here everyone else is as guilty of wrongdoing as the convert.

Idolatry is serious business. It is one of only three sins for which *halacha* tells us we should allow ourselves to be killed rather than to be coerced into committing them. Even so, we see here that when it is committed inadvertently, God allows for forgiveness. That forgiveness is extended to all—native and foreign born—so long as they together bring one single sacrifice and acknowledge their communal guilt.

They Shall Be a Sign

My husband and I attended Lamaze classes when I was pregnant with each of my children. Many of you may have done the same as it was the big thing in childbirth in the '70s and '80s. Also known as "natural childbirth," it was designed as a method of giving birth without the use of any medication. Part of the training required that I learn "slow-chest breathing" as a method of relaxation while focusing on a specific object that I had designated, because it had significance to me.

Today's reading includes a very familiar passage [15:37-41]—the third paragraph of the *Shema*—that gives to the Jewish people something specific on which God tells us to focus our attention. God commands us to put fringes on the four corners of our garments (*tallit*); one of the fringes shall be blue; and looking at these fringes is to remind us of all the commandments of God. How does that happen? Here is a picture of the *tzitzit* on one corner of my *tallit* (that I received at ordination from JTS). Notice that there are five knots; these are to remind us of the five books of the Torah. You can see that there are eight strings (fringes); these are to remind us of the eight days between leaving Egypt and crossing the Red Sea. Notice also the *techelet*, the single blue strand; this is to remind us of the color of the sea, the sky, and God's Throne of Glory. The word *tzitzit*, in its most common spelling, has a *gematria* (numerical value) of six hundred. 600 + 5 [knots] + 8 [strings] = 613 [the number of commandments].

Thus, just as committing the one sin of idolatry is equivalent to violating all the commandments, observing the one *mitzvah* of *tzitzit* is equivalent to observing all the commandments.

Finally, as beautiful, and important as this passage is, we may ask why it is placed at the end of *parashat* Shelach Lecha. What does this have to do with the story of the spies who took up most of this week's reading? The answer lies in verse 39: the words "do not follow [your heart and your eyes]" in Hebrew are *v'lo-taturu.* The verb *taturu*☒ is the same verb used over and over earlier in the *parashah*, translated as "to spy." You may recall that I suggested a better translation was "to look for [something]." The spies went out looking for something and got themselves into trouble. Rashi says, "The heart and the eyes are the 'spies' of the body and act as its agents for sinning: the eye sees, the heart covets, and the body commits the sin."[2] The message God gives to us is this: keep your eyes focused on the *tzitzit*, remember the *mitzvot,* and don't go looking for something else.

I have often taught this lesson to teenagers, particularly those who question their Jewishness. Before you look for meaning in anything else, particularly any other religion, I suggest that you first learn exactly what it is that you are contemplating abandoning. If you honestly do that, I think that you may find that there is so much beauty to be experienced in our tradition that you really don't need to go anywhere else. And I believe that beauty is reflected in the *mitzvah* of *tzitzit.*

Parashat Korach

Feeling Canceled

In this *parashah*, we read the story of a group of men who banded together to stage a rebellion against Moses and Aaron. This group consisted of three smaller groups who banded together. Each group had their own separate grievance, but they were no doubt fired up by each other in a mob mentality. The first group, led by Korach, was from the tribe of Levi. Even more specifically, they were from the clan of the Kohathites. You may recall that this clan was responsible for carrying the ark and all the holy objects from inside the tabernacle. Even though they had been given this honor, elevated to the status of the second most important group in the camp, it still wasn't good enough for them and they envied Aaron and his sons for being chosen for the priesthood.

The second group, led by Dathan, Abiram, and On, were all members of the tribe of Reuben. Looking again at the map of the Israelite camp (see page 101), we can see that the Reubenites and Kohathites were located adjacent to each other, so these men were probably fired up by the rebellious Levites. Additionally, the Reubenites were resentful of the fact that, though Reuben was the firstborn son of Jacob, the blessing of the firstborn was passed to Judah, Jacob's fourth son. This was clearly an old gripe, but probably easily fomented on the strength of outside agitation.

It became a group of two hundred fifty leaders of the community representing all the tribes. Some sages (Ramban) say that these men were all firstborns who were resentful of the fact that they had been supplanted by the Levites in the service of the *mishkan*.[1] In truth, the Torah does not tell us exactly what their complaint(s) were. It may well have been multiple things.

As we have seen in our country in the last few months and weeks, when there is a feeling of general unrest in society, many groups will band together to give strength to their voices. That is exactly what happened here; "they combined against Moses and Aaron" [16:3]. Each group was resentful of some loss of status. Together, they focused their resentment on the two brothers, accusing them of taking too much upon themselves. In addition, they were able to capitalize on the general unrest in a nation of people who were resentful of their plight of being destined to wander in the desert for forty years as their fighting men gradually died off, all the while complaining about lack of food and water.

According to the Talmud, the specific challenge that Korach put to Moses had to do with *tzitzit*. Remember, this was the very last thing we read about in last week's *parashah*. We learned there that God directed that one of the *tzitzit* was supposed to be *techelet*, a specific shade of blue that is a sign of royalty, and reminds us of the sea, the sky, and the throne of God. Korach showed up wearing a garment made entirely of *techelet*. Since the blue dye was so expensive, this would have been a very ostentatious garment. It was, however, devoid of any fringes. Korach challenged Moses in front of the nation. Since the whole garment was *techelet*, did it need to have *tzitzit*?

Korach was not only challenging Moses' authority, he was also flaunting his wealth. He thought that perhaps he could buy his way into a position of leadership.

Moses' answer was yes, the garment still needed *tzitzit* since their purpose was to remind the wearer of God's *mitzvot*. Korach's garment was not able to do that.

Moses reminded Korach and his followers that, although they thought they were challenging Aaron because they envied his designation as High Priest, they were really challenging God, who had appointed Aaron to that position. Korach was blinded by his own wealth and his jealousy, losing sight of what was truly important. Though he had indeed received many blessings from God, they weren't enough for him.

It is often easy to get caught up in what others around us may have—be it wealth or position—and experience feelings of envy. As we shall see in the coming days, the story of Korach and his followers is a powerful reminder to use the gifts that have been given to us for good instead of feeling jealous of what others have.

Déjà Vu?

This reading picks up where the first one left off. Korach and company have challenged the leadership of Moses and Aaron; Moses has called out to Dathan and Abiram, two of the Reubenites, and asked them to come to him. Their response was to use his own words against him, saying that he has brought them *"from* a land flowing with milk and honey"* [16:13], applying the metaphor for the promised land to the land of Egypt instead. Moreover, they twice say to him *lo na'aleh*, translated here as "we will not come" [16:14]. But the Hebrew verb ע-ל-ה really means "to go *up*," either literally or metaphorically. In other words, they are stuck right where they are, with absolutely no intention of moving in a positive direction.

Most people look at Korach as a villain; certainly, that is the way he is painted by the rabbis. I do know at least one person, however, who thinks otherwise. There may or may not have been some validity to the challenges made by him and his followers. However, one who wishes to be an advocate for change is not only interested in complaining, agitating, and fomenting unrest in the community; one who really wants change is willing to sit down with the ones whose authority (s)he is challenging and talk about what can be done. This is "going up," so to speak—working for progress. This was where Korach and company went wrong as they refused to meet with Moses to discuss their concerns. All they wanted to do was accuse him.

As a result of their reticence, Moses tells them that tomorrow each of them is to bring his firepan and put incense in it and bring it before the Lord. Look at the similarity of language in the last two verses of our reading and these three verses from Leviticus:

> [16:18] Each of them took his fire pan, put fire in it, laid incense on it, . . . Now Aaron's sons Nadab and Abihu each took his fire pan, put fire in it, and laid incense on it; . . . [*Leviticus 10:1*]

> [16:19] Korah gathered the whole community against them at the entrance of the Tent of Meeting.
> Then the Presence of the LORD appeared to the whole community,

> . . . and assemble the whole community at the entrance of the Tent of Meeting. [*Leviticus 8:3*]

Mosesand Aaron then went inside the Tent of Meeting. When they came out, they blessed the people; and the Presence of the LORD appeared to all the people. [*Leviticus 9:23*]

The verses from Leviticus are from the story of the dedication of the *mishkan* and the installation of Aaron and his sons as priests. Korach was desirous of the priesthood, so he would be given the opportunity he desired.

However, he was so consumed with his envy that he couldn't see the major danger sign: these verses from Leviticus come out of the story of Aaron's ill-fated oldest sons, Nadav and Avihu.

We, the readers, should already be filled with foreboding. This can't end well.

THIRD ALIYAH: NUMBERS 16:20–17:8
TUESDAY, JUNE 23, 2020

Korach's Legacy?

The story of the confrontation between Korach and his followers, and Moses and Aaron continued. God is so angered by the rebels that God is ready to annihilate them all in an instant; only the intercession of Moses prevents that from happening [16:22]. God then instructs Moses to tell the people to remove themselves from "the abodes of Korah, Dathan, and Abiram." Interestingly, the phrase translated as "the abodes of Korah" is the *mishkan* of Korach. We know from our previous studies that the word *mishkan* usually refers to the Tent of Meeting, the Tabernacle, the holy abode of God among the people. Here (and again in verse 27) it refers to the living space, or dwelling place, of Korach, the leader of the rebellion. In other words, it could be translated as "the sanctuary of Korach."

Thus, if we follow that interpretation, we see that Korach truly did challenge the religious leadership of the nation. This word *mishkan* appears in various forms one hundred thirty-five times throughout the Bible, and in all but eighteen of those cases it refers to the Tabernacle, or later the Temple, that was at the center of the Israelite camp. Indeed, the two times that the term is used here in reference to the dwelling place of Korach are the first instances in the *Tanakh* that this word is used to apply to something other than the holy sanctuary. Thus, those who followed Korach sought an alternative sanctuary with him, either real or metaphorical. Korach sought to draw others away from God, Who now told the people to separate from it (the sanctuary) and him. Once that happened, the Earth opened and swallowed

Korach and all his people and their possessions [16:32]. They literally vanished from the face of the Earth [16:33]. And what of the men from the various tribes who had been instructed to bring their firepans with incense? Their fate was like the sons of Aaron: "And a fire went forth from the LORD and consumed the two hundred and fifty men offering the incense" [16:35]. Compare this to the following verse taken from the story of Nadab and Avihu: "And fire came forth from the LORD and consumed them; thus, they died at the instance of the LORD" [Leviticus 10:2].

The message to the people must be very clear by now: no one other than the descendants of Aaron should presume to bring the offering of incense before the Lord. God has given instructions regarding how we are to worship; it is not for us to try to change it.

Most people presume that when the Earth swallowed up "all Korah's people and all their possessions," and they literally vanished from the face of the Earth, that this included his entire family. We can find it understandable that God would want to make an example of them and erase their influence. Yet, a few chapters later in the book of Numbers, we read: "The sons of Korah, however, did not die" [26:11].

This tells us that Korach and his followers died, but that did not include his sons, who apparently did not follow in his footsteps. It appears that they lived on and fulfilled their duties as Levites. And how do we know this? Remember that the Levites were the ones responsible for the musical part of the worship in the Tabernacle, and, later, the Temple. Each of the Psalms begins with a dedication line. The overwhelming majority are attributed to King David. A few are attributed to Moses. Eleven of them are attributed to the descendants of Korach. So, though Korach was swallowed up by the Earth because of his rebellious actions, his descendants went on to participate in the worship in the *mishkan* and the Temple.

Each of us is given a choice to do good or not. Korach's sons could have followed in their father's footsteps, but they didn't. In a way, they, too, were rebellious against their father's rejection of God and Moses and Aaron. We make our own choices. Korach's sons followed their hearts to follow God despite the example that had been set for them by their father.

Korach's name is the one that appears on every one of those eleven Psalms. The legacy that lives on through his descendants is a positive, life-affirming one, though it still comes with a warning of what comes from a rebellious nature.

May we all follow the positive example set by the sons of Korach.

FOURTH ALIYAH: NUMBERS 17:9–15
WEDNESDAY, JUNE 24, 2020

Between the Living and the Dead

This short reading completes the story of Korach's rebellion. God turns on the people in anger and releases a plague. At Moses' instructions, Aaron takes his own firepan, with incense placed upon it, and runs among the people. The incense offers expiation for the people. Aaron literally stands as the dividing line between the living and the dead, and ultimately stays the plague, but not before 14,700 people lose their lives [17:14].

Not only did God need to squelch the rebellions of Korach and his followers, but God also needed to validate Aaron. The very same incense that had caused the deaths of Nadav and Avihu, and now two hundred fifty rebellious Israelites, was now the agent of healing but only because it was in the hands of the right person! Thus, God reinforced that Aaron alone was the chosen High Priest.

Putting this into a contemporary context: Aaron can be compared to the frontline medical staff, the doctors and nurses who have worked tirelessly to save lives and bring healing to the most critical COVID-19 patients. No doubt they feel at times as if they are standing between the living and the dead. Here in New York, the plague has been stayed (at least for now), even as it continues to climb dramatically in other places throughout the country. Many of these dedicated professionals have also been subjected to criticism and judgment when the crisis was at its peak. Now, they have been validated by the fact that our current rates of infection and death are so low. If we wish to continue in this positive direction, we need to acknowledge that healing belongs squarely in the hands of the professionals. Our responsibility is not to challenge their authority. Rather, it is to do everything in our power to support them.

FIFTH ALIYAH: NUMBERS 17:16–24
THURSDAY, JUNE 25, 2020

Validation

At the end of yesterday's reading, we saw that the people who witnessed the deaths of Korach and his followers, including the two hundred fifty men, now turned on Moses and Aaron, accusing them of being responsible for killing them all. Despite everything that had happened, the nation still challenged the authority of the two brothers. Therefore, God decided to set up a test that would prove to the people once and for all that God had indeed chosen Aaron and his sons to serve in the priesthood. Moses instructed the people that each tribe should bring a staff from one of its chieftains to him with the name of the chieftain (not the name of the tribe) inscribed on the staff. From the tribe of Levi, God specified that Aaron should be the one to submit his staff. In Hebrew, there is an interesting wordplay going on here: the word *matteh* has two meanings, "tribe" and "staff." By selecting one staff among the twelve, God will designate the tribe that has been chosen to lead the nation religiously. Choosing the tribe alone, however, would not have been enough (remember, Korach was a Levite, as were Moses and Aaron). God needed to show the people that Aaron alone was the choice for the High Priest, the *cohen gadol*. That is the reason that the chieftains had to put their names as well as their tribes on the staffs. In truth, the inscription probably read something like "Plony, from the tribe of Plonites." Aaron's therefore would have said, "Aaron, from the tribe of Levi."

In any event, Moses took the twelve staffs and placed them inside the holy of holies before the presence of the Lord. The next day, when Moses went to retrieve the staffs, eleven of them looked exactly as they had when he deposited them there the day before. The only exception was the staff of Aaron, which had produced sprouts, blossoms, and almonds.

The plural of *matteh* is *mattot*, regardless of the meaning. We see this word in verses 17 and 21. The Baal HaTurim points out, however, that the word is spelled defectively, missing the letter *vav* in verses 22 and 24.[2] These are the two instances where the word is used to refer to the eleven staffs from the other tribes, the ones that did not sprout. He says that this shows that these staffs were defective, dried out, when they were placed in the *mishkan,* and still dry when Moses retrieved them. There could be no doubt in anyone's mind that God had chosen Aaron as the spiritual leader of the nation.

Aside from validating the status of Aaron, I think that this story has a beautiful metaphor behind it. Many people come to prayer (either in the synagogue or individually) expecting to be moved spiritually. Often, they are disappointed when they come away feeling unchanged, unmoved. If we come before God feeling all dried up and looking for something to move us miraculously, we will most likely feel as dried up and defective as we did before we started. If, on the other hand, we come before God with sincerity and openness, then we come with the possibility of sprouting, producing fruit. It is at those times when we truly allow ourselves to open up and be vulnerable, to say to God, "choose me," that we have the opportunity to feel the Divine presence. And when we come away from an encounter like that, we can be a force for good in the world around us.

May we all be able to bring forth buds of potential, beautiful blossoms, and sweet fruit.

SIXTH ALIYAH: NUMBERS 17:25–18:20
FRIDAY, JUNE 26, 2020

Every Job has its Perks

Moses was now instructed by God to place Aaron's rod in the *mishkan*, inside the holy of holies as a perpetual sign to the nation. The hope was that this would end the complaining and accusations and challenges to Aaron's authority. Aaron had been endorsed by God once and for all.

Once again, God explained the responsibilities of both the *cohenim* (Aaron and his descendants) and the *Leviim* (the rest of the members of the tribe of Levi). The priests are to minister in the sanctuary; the Levites are to minister to the priests, but they may not enter the sanctuary under penalty of death. The priesthood comes with major responsibility. They must make sure that no one comes into the sanctuary, and at the same time make sure that there is no more anger or jealousy among the people over the priesthood.

Still in all, God tells Aaron that the priesthood is given to him and his sons as a gift [18:7], and that the Levites are given to the priests as a gift [18:6].

God then lists what parts of the sacrifices brought by the people belong to the priests. Since the occupation of the priests was to serve all the time in the sanctuary, they were not farmers; the sustenance for them and their families came from the crops and animals brought by the rest of the nation. This makes sense. Since they spent their days attending to the religious needs of the nation, it is only right that they should be supported by the nation.

Finally, God tells Aaron that he and his descendants will not own any land and that God alone is their inheritance.

Thinking about the lives and responsibilities of the *cohenim*, one might wonder exactly why the rest of the nation were so envious of them. Yes, they had the *kavod*—the honor and respect that came with their office—but they spent their days slaughtering animals and offering them as sacrifices. In between, they were responsible for making decisions about whether people and dwellings were pure or impure. And all the time that they spent in the sanctuary, they lived with the constant awareness of the danger of their jobs. If any unauthorized person entered the sanctuary, it would lead to death for both that person and the priests on that watch. And if any of them were to look at the presence of God above the ark, they would die. All of this while relying on others for sustenance because they owned no property. It doesn't exactly sound like a glamorous life, does it?

On the other hand, they got to spend their time in the service and presence of God. That part was a gift.

In a way, things are not much different today. The life of a rabbi is often scrutinized by congregants. Fortunately, we no longer have to offer sacrifices on behalf of congregants, but rabbis and their families often make sacrifices of their own in order to be able to serve the members of their congregations. Rabbis still depend on others for their sustenance and many rabbis do not own the homes they live in. And, depending on the size of a congregation, a rabbi can have several hundred "bosses" who place demands on his/her time.

But, despite the difficulties, just like the priests who served in the *mishkan*, we do get to spend more time in the service and presence of God. And that is still a gift.

SEVENTH ALIYAH: NUMBERS 18:21–32
WRITTEN FOR SATURDAY, SHABBAT, JUNE 27, 2020

Tzedakah: A Universal Obligation

Next, we turn our attention to the Levites who spent just as much time in the service of the sanctuary as the priests, as they were designated as the priestly supporters. One of their primary functions when the nation was not traveling was to make sure that no unauthorized people entered the sanctuary. When the nation was traveling, remember that the clan of the Kohathites were responsible for carrying the ark and the holiest objects from the *mishkan*, but they had to do so without looking at what they were transporting. Thus, the jobs of the Levites were very dangerous as either of the above situations could bring about death for the *Leviim*. At the same time, they no doubt did not receive the level of *kavod*, the honor and respect, that the priests did.

None of the members of the tribe of Levi owned land, for, just like the priests, they spent their days in the service of the sanctuary and had no time for planting and harvesting crops. Therefore, they, too, needed to be supported by the rest of the nation.

God instructed that the tithes (ten percent) of their crops that the members of the other tribes were required to donate were to be given to the Levites as their due [18:24]. However, even the Levites were required to tithe and were required to set aside ten percent of the tithe that they received [18:26-28]. This was to be given to the priests.

The final verse of this *parashah* instructs that the Levites "must not profane the sacred donations of the Israelites, lest you die." This meant that they were not to eat of the tithe that was given to them until they had first given their own tithe to the priests. Though God had commanded that the rest of the nation should provide for them, they were to take nothing for granted.

In a similar vein, the *Shulchan Aruch* deals with the subject of giving tzedakah:

> Every person must give charity according to his means. Even a poor person who is supported by charity, [must give charity . . .].
> . . . if he has a little money of his own that is not invested, he is permitted to receive charity, since he does not have enough capital to support himself from the profits of the capital. Nevertheless, since he does have from what to support himself, he is required to give charity from that which is given to him. Even if he can give only a small amount, he should not refrain from giving it, because his small contribution is as valued as the large contribution of the wealthy person . . . . However, anyone who has only enough for his own sustenance is not obligated to give charity because his own sustenance takes precedence over all others. [*Kitzur Shulchan Aruch* 34:2]

We are all obligated to give *tzedakah*. Even the poor person who is him/herself the recipient of *tzedakah* is obligated to give. The only exception is the person who has only enough for his own sustenance, with no extra.

Given the situation in our country today, with so many people relying on charity because jobs have been lost, taking this obligation of giving *tzedakah* seriously is more important than ever.

Parashat Chukkat

FIRST ALIYAH: NUMBERS 19:1–17
SUNDAY, JUNE 28, 2020

Remembering Yaakov

In this *aliyah*, we read about the strange ritual of the red heifer. God commanded Moses that a red cow, perfect, without blemish, never having been worked, was to be sacrificed and burned. The ashes were to be added to water to be used for purification by any person who had come into contact with a dead body [19:9-12]. Anyone who touched a corpse would become unclean for a period of seven days, after which (s)he could be made clean through these "waters of lustration."

Now, this whole thing may sound rather strange. Ralbag says that the purpose of this ritual cleansing was to prevent anyone from "lingering with their dead too long, consulting with mediums to seek information from the dead, and from treating the dead with disrespect . . ."[1] The goal was to accord every person who died the proper respect and dignity that they deserved, whether there were many family members left to mourn them, or even if there were none. In death, we are all equal.

As I write this, I think about the fact that tomorrow afternoon I will attend the funeral of a wonderful man, one of my former congregants from Congregation Agudas Israel in Newburgh, New York, where I served as interim rabbi during my final year of rabbinical school. His name was Yaakov Sullivan z"l. He was one of the sweetest, gentlest souls that I have had the privilege of knowing. Everyone who met him was touched by his sincerity and his love of his adopted Jewish faith (as you no doubt might have guessed from his name). His life was claimed by cancer, and he will be sorely missed.

One of the saddest things to me is that, as a convert who never had any children, Yaakov leaves behind no one who is halachically obligated to say *kaddish* for him. In Judaism, one of the highest honors one can pay someone is to remember them after they have died. And that is why, for the next year, whenever I have the opportunity to recite a mourner's *kaddish*, I will remember the name of *Yaakov ben Avraham v'Sarah z"l*. May his soul be remembered for good.

SECOND ALIYAH: NUMBERS 19:18–20:6
SUNDAY, JUNE 28, 2020

The Loss of Miriam

Now that the ritual of cleansing after contact with the dead through the ashes of the red heifer has been explained, we read about a very significant death for the nation. We are told that the people of Israel arrived in the wilderness of Zin "on the first new moon" [20:1], though we are not told the year. Based on other information that we find later in the reading, we will find that it was actually the fortieth year after leaving Egypt; we have read nothing since the second year. Therefore, virtually the entire time that the nation was wandering in the desert is unknown to us. What we do know is that, since this is the fortieth year, the whole generation of men who were destined to die after the incident with the spies are now gone, and the nation will soon be poised to enter the land. The three siblings who have been leading the nation all these years are still alive, though that is about to change. This same verse tells us that Miriam, older sister to both Moses and Aaron, died and was buried in the wilderness at Kadesh. The very next thing that the Torah tells us is that "the community was without water" [20:2]. From the juxtaposition of these two verses, the rabbis have derived the *midrash* that there was a well, "Miriam's well," that miraculously followed the nation around in the desert, providing the people with water [BT Taanit 9A:9]. Now that Miriam had died, the well dried up, leaving the people without water. Once again, they turned on Moses and Aaron, complaining of having no water, complaining of having been brought out of Egypt into the desert [20:3-5]. It is not enough that the brothers were dealing with the loss of their sister, they now had to deal with this rebellion.

Of all the things written by commentators about the death of Miriam, I think I most prefer Ralbag's commentary. He says, "I think Miriam, in her wisdom, must have drawn people to serve the Lord. It is as if the Torah were telling us that, had Miriam not died, the people would never have quarreled with Moses. Moreover, Moses and Aaron would have consulted with her when God told them to speak to the rock [see next reading], since she was a prophet and their elder; she would have kept them from doing anything stupid."[2]

We do know that Miriam (whose name literally means "sea of bitterness") was closely connected to water. The first time we met her in the Torah was when she stood on the shore of the Nile River, keeping an eye on the basket containing her baby brother (later named Moses, Egyptian for "drawn from the water") after Pharaoh had ordered the drowning in the river of all baby boys born to Israelite mothers. She watched as Pharaoh's daughter had her servant girls retrieved the basket then she stepped forward and offered to find a Hebrew wet nurse to nourish the baby for her [Exodus 2:5-9]. This turned out to be a cleverly devised plan to allow her mother, Yocheved, to be able to nurse her own child.

The next significant association of Miriam with water took place on the shores of the Red Sea. After Moses led the nation in the Song of the Sea, praising God for splitting the sea and saving the nation, Miriam took timbrels and tambourines and led the women of the nation in praising God for their salvation [Exodus 15:20-21].

Now, at her death, the nation found itself bereft not only of her presence, but, additionally, of the well that was the source of their water.

As Ralbag has pointed out, we will see that both of those losses will soon prove to be disastrous for the nation in general, and for Miriam's brothers, in particular.

THIRD ALIYAH: NUMBERS 20:7–13
MONDAY, JUNE 29, 2020

Asking the Difficult Questions

This is one of the most studied sections of the Torah. Moses and Aaron are instructed by God to take the staff of Aaron, assemble all the people of the entire nation before a particular rock, and to speak to the rock, ordering it to produce water for the nation [20:8]. Instead, Moses struck the rock twice with the rod to get it to produce water [20:11]. As a result of their disobedience, the two brothers are told that their punishment will be that they will not be able to go into the promised land with the people [20:12].

Does the punishment fit the "crime?" That seems to be the question that is hotly debated. What did Moses and Aaron do that was so terrible that it denied them entrance into the promised land?

One explanation is that they referred to the people as "you rebels" [20:10]. Despite the contentious nature of the people, they were still the nation that God had chosen. Therefore, it was inappropriate to refer to them this way.

Another explanation (Rabbenu Hananel) is that the brothers suggested that they, and not God, would be the source of the water that would come forth from the rock [20:10][3].

The most widely accepted explanation is that they simply did not follow directions. God told them to speak to the rock, and instead they struck the rock—not once, but twice—making it seem as though they, and not God, were the ones who produced the water. But even this is debated. After all, this is not the first time that they have faced a situation like this. We have the following from the book of Exodus:

(1) From the wilderness of Sin the whole Israelite community continued by stages as the LORD would command. They encamped at Rephidim, and there was no water for the people to drink. (2) The people quarreled with Moses. "Give us water to drink," they said; and Moses replied to them, "Why do you quarrel with me? Why do you try the LORD?" (3) But the people thirsted there for water; and the people grumbled against Moses and said, "Why did you bring us up from Egypt, to kill us and our children and livestock with thirst?" (4) Moses cried out to the LORD, saying, "What shall I do with this people? Before long, they will be stoning me!" (5) Then the LORD said to Moses, "Pass before the people, take with you some of the elders of Israel, and take along the rod with which you struck the Nile, and set out. (6) I will be standing there before you on the rock at Horeb. Strike the rock and water will issue from it, and the people will drink." And Moses did so in the sight of the elders of Israel. [Exodus 17:1-6]

In this instance, which had occurred at Sinai, Moses was specifically instructed by God to strike the rock with the rod to get it to produce water. In our story, we can't help but notice that God tells Moses to take the rod with him when approaching the rock (verse 8). Why? If he really was meant to only speak to the rock, then what need did he have of the rod? And if he had faced a similar situation before, and in that instance, he had to strike the rock, can he be blamed for "slipping up" and doing the same here? Another difference is that the incident in Exodus took place "in the sight of the elders of Israel" [Exodus 17:6], while in our current story, the "entire community" had been assembled (verse 8).

God told Moses and Aaron that they ". . . did not trust Me enough to affirm My sanctity in the sight of the Israelite people." The whole nation had been watching; this was an opportunity to affirm the power of God to provide for the people, not only the power but the care and concern for the people's needs. Instead, the critical moment was lost.

Many people feel that the penalty for the brothers was too severe. Or is it possible that they were held to a higher standard because of their positions of leadership? God expected more of them. There is no definitive answer; this is one of the mysteries of the Torah with which we struggle to find an explanation that we are comfortable with.

The bottom line, I think, is that if it hadn't been this, it would have been something else. I don't think that Moses and Aaron were ever destined to accompany the nation into the promised land. As great and revered as they may have been as leaders of the nation, they were, after all, only human. That much is clearly demonstrated in this story. They had done great things, for sure, but they were never meant to be revered as anything more than mortal.

Just like the rest of us, they made mistakes. Bekhor Shor explains that when they struck the rock the first time, the water did not flow from it because God was giving them an opportunity to think about what they were doing.[4] So, why did it come out after the second strike? According to Ralbag, it was so as not to embarrass them in front of the people.[4]

Even while telling them that they would receive the ultimate punishment, God still cared enough to protect their reputations among the people.

The story is complicated. I believe it is meant to be so. I believe that it is meant to give us pause, to make us ask the difficult questions. Why were they punished? And if Moses and Aaron could not live up to God's expectations of them, what hope was there for us?

I leave you to think about these things and decide for yourself.

FOURTH ALIYAH: NUMBERS 20:14–21
MONDAY, JUNE 29, 2020

Acknowledging Hospitality

This is a short passage with a short message. After the incident of the rock, the nation of Israel moved on from Kadesh. As they approached the territory of Edom (descendants of Esau, Jacob's older twin), Moses sent messengers to the king of Edom, asking permission to pass through their land. When Moses said, "we will not drink water from wells" [20:17], Rashi explains that he means to say that even though they have the manna provided by God, and the water provided by the miraculous well, they will not use them as a source of nourishment. As they pass through the land of Edom, they will buy food and water from them so that they, Edom, will benefit from the crossing of the Israelites. The lesson, Rashi says, is that a traveler should buy food from his host, giving him some benefit, even if he has brought his own food along.[5] One should never take advantage of the hospitality offered by another. If you benefit in some way from someone else, it behooves you to find some way to repay your host. This is true whether we speak of an individual, a family, a synagogue, a city or town, or a country.

When you read through the rest of this story, you will see that Edom did not offer the hospitality that was requested by Moses. How much more so must we acknowledge the one who grants our request and extends the hand of friendship to us?

FIFTH ALIYAH: NUMBERS 20:22–21:9
TUESDAY, JUNE 30, 2020

Sealed with a Kiss

In the second *aliyah* of *Chukat*, we read of the death of Miriam. Here in today's section, we read of the death of Aaron. God instructed Moses to take both Aaron and his son Eleazar up into the mountain. There, he was to remove the garments of the High Priest, the *cohen gadol*, from Aaron and place them immediately onto Eleazar [20:25]. You may remember from back in the book of Leviticus that there were four garments that every priest wore, and four additional garments for a total of eight garments that the High Priest wore.

The nation was not to be left bereft of a High Priest even for a moment. Later, when the Temple stood in Jerusalem, elaborate preparations were made in anticipation of the high holy days, and the one day each year that the High Priest was permitted to enter the holy of holies to make atonement for the people. In tractate Yoma, we learn that, starting a full month before Yom Kippur, the High Priest was placed into isolation for safe keeping, to be sure that nothing bad would happen to him in the interim. Not only that, but an additional priest was also chosen to be placed separately into isolation and would be called upon to step in immediately should anything happen to the High Priest. But wait, that's not all! A High Priest had to be married. So, additionally, a woman was chosen to succeed his wife at a moment's notice should his current wife suddenly die. Both women were also placed into isolation separately. All these elaborate orchestrations were designed to assure the nation that they would always have a *cohen gadol* [BT Yoma 2A].

That is the reason why Moses had to remove from Aaron the uniform of the High Priest and place it piece by piece on his son, who would succeed him. There is only one problem, though: Moses would have to remove all the garments from Aaron to be able to place them on Eleazer in the proper order. That would leave the nation, at least for some short period of time, without a High Priest. According to Ramban, there is a *midrash* that explains how this all happened miraculously: God clothed Aaron in garments of the Shekinah, the Divine Presence.[6] This did two things: it protected Aaron from embarrassment and it allowed Moses to remove the garments from Aaron in the order that he had put them on so that they could be placed upon his son in the proper order. Thus, we can imagine that with each garment that was transferred from father to son, the authority of the High Priest was also transferred little by little, until finally Eleazer stood clothed in the garments of the *cohen gadol* and his father was wrapped in the Shekinah. It was at that moment that Aaron died there on the mountain (verse 28).

The Baal haTurim has a beautiful commentary on this verse: he says that the phrase, "and Aaron died there" is equivalent in gematria (1,052) to the phrase, "this teaches that he died by a kiss."[7] What does this mean? Further on in the book of Numbers we read, "Aaron the priest ascended Mount Hor at the command of the LORD and died there . . ." [33:38].

The phrase that is translated here as "at the command of the Lord" really says, "by the mouth of the Lord." Just as in the Creation story in the book of Genesis, God breathed life into the first human being, here the reverse took place. Aaron literally died through a Divine kiss. This imagery, which we will later see applied to his brother Moses, as well, implies the most peaceful of deaths. After everything that Aaron had been through with this nation, he finally had a peaceful homecoming.

We also learn that the nation mourned for Aaron for thirty days [20:29]. It is from this text that we derive the idea of the *shloshim* period, the thirty-day period of mourning that is mandated for all relatives. It is always amazing to me to see the biblical origins of our traditions.

SIXTH ALIYAH: NUMBERS 21:10–20
TUESDAY, JUNE 30, 2020

Lessons from the Desert

Following the mourning period for Aaron, the nation travelled on. After circling around through several locations, they arrived back at the well where God had told Moses to gather the people together to give them water [21:16]. This is the well that we read about in the third *aliyah* where Moses made the mistake of hitting the rock instead of talking to it. After all the times that they have complained to Moses about lack of water, could it be that they have finally learned their lesson? This time, instead of arguing, their voices rise in song to praise the well. Rashi says that the "chieftains" who dug the well are Moses and Aaron, and that the staffs refer to the staff of Aaron that Moses used to hit the rock. *Midbar* is just that—the wilderness, where they received the well as a *mattanah* (gift) from God. Bechor Shor says that this spring was so miraculous that it flowed uphill.[8]

After forty long years of wandering in the desert, it seems perhaps that the nation is ready to take some responsibility and head into the promised land to claim their heritage. Acknowledging the gifts, the freedom, and the protection provided to them by God is a necessary prerequisite to entering the land. They have come by it the hard way.

Like the generation in the desert, we, too, have endured a great deal of suffering these last five months. We have endured isolation, just as they did. We have complained about the commodities we need but are in short supply of, just as they did. Many of us have endured sickness and suffered the loss of loved ones, just as they did.

Perhaps we all could/should take a page from their book. We can learn much from their experience.

SEVENTH ALIYAH: NUMBERS 21:21–22:1
WEDNESDAY, JULY 1, 2020

Goliath Had Nothing on This Guy

In this section, we read about several battles waged by the nation of Israel before they finally entered the land of Canaan. The people were now on the eastern side of the Jordan River. The territories they acquired through these battles were those belonging to Sihon, King of the Ammorites, and Og, King of Bashan. The area I refer to is on the northernmost part of the eastern shore of the Dead Sea, in an area which is today in the country of Jordan; this was the territory of Bashan. Directly south of it was the territory of Ammon. After these lands were conquered, they later became part of the land of Israel, and were given to the two and a half tribes of Gad, Reuven, and Menashe as their inheritance.

So, who was this Og, King of Bashan, and why did God have to tell Moses not to fear him? [21:34]

This is an interesting story and much of it is *midrash*.

The book of Genesis talks about Rephaim, giants who lived in the world before the time of Noah [Genesis 14:5, 15:20]. All of them were killed along with the rest of humankind at the time of the flood. That is, except for one: Og. The *midrash* says that Og survived the flood by hanging onto the ark as it floated through the boiling waters [BT, Zevachim 113B:12]. Furthermore, the *midrash* explains that Og cut a hole in the side of the ark through which Noah provided him with food every day.

The Book of Joshua does indeed mention Og as being one of the last of the giants who lived in Ashtarot and Edrei [Joshua 12:4]. And the Book of Deuteronomy talks about the size of his bed: ". . . His bedstead, an iron bedstead, . . . is nine cubits long and four cubits wide, by the standard cubit!" [Deuteronomy 3:11] Since a cubit is approximately 1.5 feet, these dimensions translate to approximately 13.5 feet by 6 feet! And how did Moses and the nation of Israel defeat him? The story from the Talmud is just too fantastical not to quote:

> . . . Og said: How large is the camp of Israel? It is three parasangs [a parasang is approximately 3.5 miles]. I will go and uproot a mountain three parasangs long and I will hurl it upon them and kill them. He went, uprooted a mountain three parasangs long, and brought it on his head. And The Holy One, Blessed be He, brought grasshoppers upon it and they pierced the peak of the mountain and it fell on his neck. Og wanted to remove it from his head; his teeth were extended to one side of his head and to the other and he was unable to remove it . . . . The story concludes: How tall was Moses? He was ten cubits [15 feet] tall. He took an axe ten cubits long, jumped up ten cubits [15 feet], and struck Og in the ankle and killed him. [*BT Brachot 54B:4*].

Wow! It sounds like all that Moses needs is a cape and a mask! The story, of course, is fantastical and totally unbelievable! But isn't that, after all, the point? Og has been made into a comic book figure.

Remember the story of the ten spies who brought back a bad report thirty-eight years earlier, making the people afraid to take the land? Remember what they were afraid of? The spies said that there were giants in the land! Now, after thirty-eight years, there really was a giant in the land, but God had reduced him to something comical, not to be feared. Now, the nation was able to take him and his land. Looking at it from a different perspective, the people were more capable of dealing rationally with the situation.

Sometimes it takes a situation so irrational, so unbelievable (like a pandemic?) to make us realize that, as much as we may like to think that we are in control, we aren't. But putting our trust in God allows us to deal with the overwhelming (i.e., giant) adversities that we are forced to endure. May we all be able to put our trust in God to see us through whatever still lies ahead in this fight against COVID-19.

Parashat Balak

Prophet or Charlatan?

Now that the Israelites had defeated both Og of Bashan and Sihon of Ammor, the Moabites, who were the next nation south of these kingdoms, became nervous about them. Balak, the king of the Moabites, decided to rely not just on the power of his army; instead, he sent messengers to Balaam, who was known to be a (non-Jewish) prophet, or soothsayer, to ask him to curse the people of Israel. Balaam's response was to ask them to stay the night while he inquired of God what to do. God appeared to him in a dream, telling him not to go with his visitors, and not to curse Israel because they are blessed.

The first thing that we should notice is that, at no point are Balaam's abilities to either curse or bless a people questioned. As a matter of fact, the leaders of the Moabites acknowledge that whomever Balaam blesses is blessed, and whomever he curses is cursed [22:6]. Apparently, he does seem to have some form of supernatural power. According to Jacob Milgrom, "Balaam is a diviner, one who predicts the future, not a sorcerer, one who can alter the future (through cursing and blessing)."[1] The Torah never says that there aren't people who have some kind of psychic powers, only that we are not to consult them because we should only rely on God to determine our futures.

So, Balaam is being asked to curse the Israelite people, something God has warned him not to do. The fact that he doesn't immediately say "no" to the messengers is telling. Instead, he tells them that he will see what God tells him to do. It seems that he is secretly hoping that God will speak to him that night in a dream and give him permission to go with the messengers.

If you were Balaam, what would you do? And what do you think is going to happen? We'll soon see.

SECOND ALIYAH: NUMBERS 22:13–20
THURSDAY, JULY 2, 2020

Whose God is God, Anyway?

The next morning, Balaam sent Balak's dignitaries back to him with the message that God would not let him carry out Balak's request to curse the nation of Israel [22:13]. Undaunted, Balak sent another delegation of more important dignitaries to entreat Balaam further to grant his request and they came with the promise of a great reward [22:15-17]. Clearly, Balak thought that Balaam could be bought.

Now, Balaam traditionally is not painted in a very favorable light, which we shall see as the story unfolds. However, in looking at this passage again, one tiny word jumped out at me in Balaam's response to them. He told them that not even for all the riches that Balak could give him could he say anything "contrary to the command of the Lord my God" [22:18]. Though Balaam was not a Jew, he claimed the sovereignty of God. He acknowledged that the God of Israel is more powerful than the pagan Baal worshipped by the people of Moab. Perhaps that was the reason that when God came to Balaam a second time that night, God gave him permission to go with these men with the caveat that he could only act at Divine command [22:20].

I have been asked many times—as I'm sure all rabbis are—how Jews feel about people who are faithful to other religions. My answer is that we Jews do not say, "you must be like me and believe exactly as I do to be "saved." We recognize the legitimacy of other monotheistic faiths which exhort their followers to lead an ethical, moral life. Our goal is not to make the whole world Jewish; our goal is to work peacefully together with others for the betterment of the world that God has given to us all.

Do You Believe in Miracles?

As if the story of Og wasn't fantastical enough, here we have a story of a talking donkey. God was angry with Balaam for departing with Balak's men [22:22]. How could that be? Didn't we just read at the end of the last section that God had given him permission to go? According to Ramban, Balaam's mistake was that he gave Balak's men the impression that he was indeed going with them to curse Israel. The verse goes on to say that an angel placed himself in Balaam's path as an adversary. Rashi points out that this angel was not an adversary "against him" but rather an adversary "for him." The angel was, he says, trying to prevent Balaam from sinning.[2] The problem was that Balaam didn't see the angel, but his donkey did! Three times she tried to get away, first wandering off the path into a field, then pressing up against a wall, squeezing Balaam's foot in the process, then finally laying down in the path. Each time, Balaam beat her. Both verse 22 and verse 27 use the same Hebrew phrase, "he was angry." The first states that God was angry with Balaam, the second states that Balaam was angry with his donkey. Thus, we infer that Balaam was as angry with his donkey as God was with him.

After the third time, when the donkey finally just laid down in the path rather than continue on, we are told that God opened the donkey's mouth, and she asked Balaam why he had beaten her three times [22:28]. Without batting an eye, he responded to her that she had made a fool of him and that if he had had a sword, he would have killed her [22:29]. (Ironically, unbeknownst to him, the angel did have a sword which was part of the reason for the donkey's fear.) The donkey spoke again, saying basically, "Look, I'm your donkey. You ride me all the time. Have I ever done this to you before?" (Who's making more sense here?) It is only at that point that Balaam finally saw the angel, who, coming to the donkey's defense, said that he should have killed him [22:33]. Balaam realized he had been wrong and said that he would go back if the angel disapproved of him going with the Moabite men [22:34]. The angel told him that he should continue on, but that he must say only what the angel would tell him to say [22:35].

Why did it take a talking donkey for Balaam to learn his lesson? Ramban says that it was to show that God was no less the source of Balaam's ability to speak than of the donkey's ability to do so, and to show that God could take away the ability to speak just as easily as God could give it.[3] Balaam was renowned as an orator and he needed to remember where that gift came from.

We have now seen a number of things in the Torah that defy the laws of nature. In Pirkei Avot, we are told that there were ten things that were created at twilight on the sixth day of Creation, in the last moments before Shabbat, as the time for creating drew to a close:

> Ten things were created on the eve of the Sabbath at twilight, and these are they: [1] the mouth of the Earth [that opened up and swallowed Korach], [2] the mouth of the well [Miriam's well, that miraculously followed the nation through the desert], [3] the mouth of the donkey, [4] the rainbow [after the flood], [5] the manna [that fed the people in the desert], [6] the staff [of Moses], [7] the shamir [a magical worm that was able to split the stones that were used to build the Temple], [8] the letters [of the tablets], [9] the writing [that appeared miraculously on the wall at the time of Daniel], [10] and the tablets [that contained the Ten Commandments]. And some say also the demons, the grave of Moses, and the ram of Abraham, our father [that he sacrificed in place of Isaac] ... [Pirkei Avot 5:6]

What is the significance of this *mishna*? It comes to teach us that everything that exists was created at the beginning of the world, that God does not create anything new. Therefore, we should not pray for or expect miracles that defy the laws of nature. Additionally, this comes to remind us that God is the source of all creation, not human beings.

FOURTH ALIYAH: NUMBERS 22:39–23:12
FRIDAY, JULY 3, 2020

Jews Don't Believe in an Afterlife—Right?

So, Balaam went with Balak to a place where he could see only a portion of the nation of Israel (keep in mind the way in which the camp was set up, with three tribes facing each of the four directions). He thought that if he could actually see the people of Israel, it would be easier for him to concentrate on them, and therefore to curse them. After instructing Balak to offer seven bulls and seven rams on seven altars, Balaam went off by himself to see if God would give him some instruction as "God manifested [Godself] to Balaam." Literally, this says that God called out to Balaam (you may remember the first section from the book of Leviticus, where God called out to Moses, but the word was *vayikra*, with a small *aleph*, representing someone with whom God wanted to have an intimate relationship, as opposed to *vayikar*, which we see here, representing someone with whom God simply wants to communicate). Here God literally put words in Balaam's mouth, telling him what to say [23:5]. Needless to say, he ended up blessing, instead of cursing, the people. He even went so far as to say, "May my fate be like theirs" [23:10]. According to the Bekhor Shor, this is evidence in the Torah that Jews believe in an afterlife. He says that, if we Jews did not receive a posthumous reward, then why would Balaam have made such a statement?[4] Why would he care what kind of death he had? Sforno says that Balaam was expressing a desire that his descendants would be like the descendants of the Jews.[4]

If a non-Jewish prophet can recognize that there is an afterlife, how much more so should we, the children of Israel, embrace this belief? While we do not talk about heaven and hell, we do talk about the soul living on after death. That is the reason we recite *Kaddish* in memory of lost loved ones—that their memories should be for a blessing. May those of you who mourning the loss of a loved one during this extremely difficult time, especially if you have lost any friends or family members to COVID-19, be comforted with the assurance that their souls live on.

FIFTH ALIYAH: NUMBERS 23:13–26
FRIDAY, JULY 3, 2020

You Can Lead a Horse to Water, but . . .

So, naturally, Balak was not a happy camper. He had brought Balaam to a place where he could see part of the nation, made sacrifices of fourteen animals, only to have Balaam bless the people of Israel instead of cursing them. To be fair, Balaam had told him multiple times that he could only say what God wanted him to say, and that he could not curse someone who was blessed by God. So, Balak brought Balaam to another location, which afforded him a view of a larger piece of the nation and asked him to try again. Once again, the requisite fourteen animals were sacrificed, and Balaam went off to see what the Lord would say to him. God not only manifested Godself to Balaam (*vayikar*), but also God put a "thing" in Balaam's mouth [23:16]. Rashi explains that Balaam, knowing he could not do what Balak wanted him to do, was tempted to not even return to Balak. Therefore, the "thing" that God put in Balaam's mouth was like a bit that one puts in the mouth of a horse or donkey to lead the animal to go where you want it to go. With this,

God visibly demonstrated that Balaam would have to go back to Balak.[5] The message that God wanted Balaam to deliver was that, unlike humans, God is not capricious, and God does not change God's mind. God has promised to bless the people of Israel and will not go back on that promise [23:19].

Balaam says, "No harm is in sight for Jacob." [23:21] Actually, a better translation of the Hebrew is, "God had beheld no iniquity in Jacob." Rashi says that this leads to the following beautiful midrashic interpretation: when the people of Israel transgress, God does not pay attention to it.[6] Rashbam says that God has not seen any iniquity in the people of Israel because God does not want to see it.[7] Like the parent who does not want to see any fault in their child, so, too, does God wish to ignore our imperfections. In any event, once again, Balaam failed to fulfill Balak's request to curse the people of Israel, leaving him completely frustrated. But we have not yet seen the end of this story.

SIXTH ALIYAH: NUMBERS 23:27–24:13
WRITTEN FOR SATURDAY, SHABBAT JULY 4, 2020

Our Dwelling Places and Our Sanctuaries are One and the Same

So, my husband likes to remind me that the definition of insanity is "doing the same thing over and over again and expecting a different result." In his frustration, Balak brought Balaam to a third location overlooking the nation of Israel, once again sacrificed seven bulls and seven rams on seven altars and waited for the results. This time, Balaam did not even look for guidance from God, since he realized that God wanted only for him to bless the nation. The words that begin his speech this time should be familiar to anyone who has regularly attended morning *minyan*: "How goodly are your dwelling places, O Jacob, Your sanctuaries, O Israel!" [24:5]. These words begin the morning *shacharit* service and are to be recited upon entering the synagogue. Rashi says that when Balaam looked down at the tents, the dwelling places of Israel, he saw that none of the entrances of their homes faced each other, allowing for privacy. At the same time, all their dwellings were open on all sides, demonstrating hospitality.[8] The Hebrew word that is translated as "your dwellings" is *mishkanotecha*, literally, "your *mishkanim*," your tabernacles. Each of our houses is a mini sanctuary, a place where God dwells.

Unfortunately, in these days of COVID-19, our houses cannot extend the hospitality that we would like, to invite others into our homes to share our shabbat table or anything else with us. We can, however, and even must continue to reach out and invite the *Shekinah*, the presence of God, to come and dwell in our houses with us. In the absence of human companionship, we need Divine company more than ever.

SEVENTH ALIYAH: NUMBERS 24:14–25:9
WRITTEN FOR SHABBAT, SATURDAY, JULY 4, 2020

We Couldn't Leave Well Enough Alone

In this last section of the Torah reading for this week, we see two things happen. First, unbidden by Balak, who finally was defeated, Balaam took it upon himself to make one more proclamation about the people of Israel. He talked about the future, about all the nations which will be subdued by Israel [24:17-24].

Now, it would be great if the *parashah* ended right here. Unfortunately, that is not the case. We have just seen that the nation is so holy to God that Balaam is unable to curse them. Instead, each attempt ends in blessings. Lest we get too carried away with ourselves, we see that no sooner did Balaam leave to return to his homeland than the men of Israel profaned themselves by having sexual relations with the women of Moab, the people of Balak! This led them to begin worshipping the Moabite god, Baal [25:1-2]. What Balak and Balaam were unable to accomplish, the men of Israel did to themselves! God instructed Moses that the ringleaders should all be impaled, and that the leaders of each tribe should kill the members of their tribe who were involved in this harlotry [25:4-5].

Amid all of this, one man brought the woman he was involved with right up to the door of the *mishkan,* right in the faces of Moses and all the community leaders. The priest Pinchas, son of the now *cohen gadol* Eleazer and grandson of Aaron, took matters into his own hands. Right there in the holy place, he took a spear and thrust it through the "bellies" (read "private parts") of the two of them. This action ended the scourge caused by the nation's harlotry and idolatry. In all, 24,000 people lost their lives [24:6-9].

This story catches us off guard after all the good that we have heard throughout the rest of the *parashah*. The rabbis, too, are uncomfortable with Pinchas. His action was decisive and finally stayed the plague. Yet, his action was violent and impulsive. He took matters into his own hands and there is no indication that he was acting at the command of the Lord (in contrast with Balaam, a non-Jewish prophet, who was).

Throughout history, we have had our share of zealots. Often, these stories do not end well. What are your thoughts about Pinchas? If you feel uncomfortable, that is to be expected. It's that same feeling we all get when the latest villain in the news happens to be Jewish (Madoff, Weinstein, Epstein, etc.).

We will hear more about the story of Pinchas in the coming week.

Parashat Pinchas

FIRST ALIYAH: NUMBERS 25:10–26:4
SUNDAY JULY 5, 2020

God's Making a List and Checking it Twice

This reading concludes the story of Pinchas which we read in the last *parashah*, Balak. Pinchas, son of the new *cohen gadol*, Eleazer and grandson of Aaron, took matters into his own hands when the men of Israel were enticed into sexual relationships with the Midianite women. When one man brought the woman he was involved with (whom we find out later in this reading was the daughter of their king), Pinchas stabbed them through with one spear at the door of the tabernacle. This stopped the plague. As a result, he was greatly rewarded by God for his actions [25:12-13]. This story is certainly controversial as it is one of those parts of the Torah that makes us feel uncomfortable, to be sure. It is not, however, what I would like to focus on. I would like to look at something a little more uplifting and less troubling.

Because so many people had died in the plague, and the nation now prepared to enter Canaan, God ordered Moses to take another census. God wanted to have an accounting of the number of people in the nation.

I want to look at the very last verse of this reading, "[these are] the descendants of the Israelites who came out of the land of Egypt" [26:4]. The listing of the names does not begin until the first verse of the next reading. The separation of the list from this verse thus leaves our reading on a pregnant pause: who were these descendants? Additionally, the word *ha-yotzim*, translated as "who came out" (of Egypt), is really a participle form of the verb, better translated as "who are coming out" (of Egypt) as if the action took place in the present tense.

167

What? You say that that doesn't make sense? I would like to think that it does. As a matter of fact, I think it presents a profound idea to contemplate. Think of the words of the *Haggadah:* each of us is to view ourselves as though we ourselves were there (in Egypt) and were the direct beneficiaries of God's redemption. In the response to the wicked child, we even say that "had he been there, he would not have been redeemed."

Taken metaphorically, then, we are called to examine our lives. We need to ask ourselves: what are the things or situations in our lives that enslave us, hold us captive, hold us back from moving forward?

When we can find the strength to move forward, then we are indeed "coming out of Egypt." It is an ongoing process which is why the verb is in a present tense form, indicating ongoing action.

Right now, many of us look forward to the time when we can all emerge from the grasp of the pandemic of COVID-19. We long for our lives to return to the Promised Land that we call "normal," whatever that means. The process is and will be long. We have all been changed by COVID. May we all emerge from this trying time having been strengthened by the experience.

God is taking a census. Is your name on the list of those who are (will be) coming out of Egypt?

SECOND ALIYAH: NUMBERS 26:5–51
MONDAY, JULY 6, 2020

Who's Your Daddy?

This is one of those readings that one might think is particularly difficult to write about. It is a very long reading consisting of the results of the census. The genealogy is listed by name, and then by clan. Remember that this is a list of those who left (are leaving) Egypt. There are several things I would like to point out about this reading.

The first is verse 11, which I cited previously. It tells us that "the sons of Korach . . . did not die." The Baal HaTurim cites a *midrash* that tells that when the ground opened up, there was actually a place set up for them high in Gehenna [Hell] where they sat and recited songs of praise of God [BT Sanhedrin 110a].[1] Eleven Psalms [45-49, 84-85, and 87-88] are attributed to the sons of Korach. One of these, Psalm 48, is the daily psalm for Monday. We don't know the names of the sons of Korach because scripture doesn't tell us. Thus, when these psalms contain the tagline "a psalm of the sons of Korach," it is as if they were redeeming their father's memory. They took no credit for the psalms themselves.

The second thing that struck me occurs in verse 46. Amid this long genealogy that (almost) exclusively consists of the names of men, we are told that Asher's daughter's name was Serah. Several *midrashim* are told about Serah. She is believed to have lived for a very long time. There are a total of three instances of her name being listed in a genealogy in the *Tanakh* (besides this one, the other two occur in Genesis chapter 46 and 1 Chronicles chapter 7). In each case, the names of her brothers are also listed. So, we are not sure exactly why she is the only woman whose name appears in these lists. Clearly, she must have been important.

The third thing I noticed—and this is the one I find to be the most beautiful of the three—is something that occurs repeatedly in this list. As each clan is named, the same pattern is followed. In English, the suffix "ite" is added on to the name of the clan's founder to get the name of the clan. It is far more interesting in the Hebrew; here are the first several examples:

Chanoch mishpachat hachanochi
[l']Falu mishpachat haFalui
[l']Chetzron mishpachat haChetzroni
[l']Nemuel mishpachat haNnemueli
[l']Yamin mishpachat haYamini

(The [l'] in each case on the left is not part of the name. It is simply a prefix meaning "of.")

So, we notice that the name of the clan consists of the name of the founder with the letter *heh* attached to the front and the letter *yud* attached to the end. These two letters form the shortened form of the four-letter name of God that we do not pronounce, but rather read as *Adonai*. In his commentary on verse 5, Rashi explains this in a beautiful *midrash*. The other nations mocked the people of Israel for being so precise with their genealogy. After all, if the Egyptians had held control over the Israelites in every way during the time that they enslaved them, it stands to reason that they had also had their way with the Israelite women. By adding God's own name to the head of every clan, God was showing that they all were legitimately children of their Israelite fathers.[2] At the same time, it becomes abundantly clear that God was claiming them as God's own.

I would also add to this the physical appearance of the name of the tribe in written form shows that God is literally surrounding each tribe with God's own protective, loving divine presence. In addition, we can see that the same identical process is repeated again and again in the list of clans. One after another, God claims every clan for Godself. Everyone is equally important to God.

We, too, are all equally important in the eyes of the Divine. Sometimes it's hard to feel that protective presence of God surrounding us. During the very difficult times that we have been dealing with these last five to six months, many of us may have felt alone and isolated. We long for human presence and human contact. We long to see our friends and family members in person instead of on a computer screen. We long for physical contact—how we wish we could hug our loved ones. Though we cannot experience the physical sensation of a human embrace, through prayer and study we can experience a Divine embrace. May we all find the strength that we need to endure, finding safe harbor under the wings of the *Shechina*.

THIRD ALIYAH: NUMBERS 26:52–27:5
TUESDAY, JULY 7, 2020

You Won't Know the Answer if You Don't Ask the Question

In this *aliyah*, we read that the land will be divided up between all the tribes of Israel. Since this was an agricultural society, land ownership was of primary importance. The land apportioned to each tribe was further divided between each of the clans of that tribe, and then further subdivided between all the members of a clan. Land was passed down from a father to his sons, with a double portion allotted for the firstborn. (Thus, if a man had three sons, for example, the property was divided into four equal portions, and two of those went to the firstborn son. If he had four sons, the property was divided into five equal portions, and two of those went to the firstborn son. If he had five sons, the property was divided into six equal portions, and two of those went to the firstborn son. And so on.)

Following this line of reasoning, what happened to a man's property if he had no sons? That is the question that is brought to Moses by the five daughters of a man named Zelophechad from the tribe of Menashe [27:1]. They explain to Moses that their father died leaving behind the five of them but no sons, and as a result his name will be lost among the tribe of Menashe as his property will just pass to the rest of the clan/tribe unless Moses allows for these five women to inherit their father's property. They point out that their father was not part of the band of people who followed Korach. Rather, they say that he died in the wilderness because of "his own sin" [27:3]. According to Rashi, this means that, though he did something wrong, he did not entice others to follow him.[3] The daughters do not mention what his actual sin was, only that he was not among the rebellious followers of Korach. So, the rabbis wonder, what exactly was the sin of which Zelophehad was guilty? Rabbi Akiva points to the following passage from earlier in the book of Numbers:

(32) Once, when the Israelites were in the wilderness, they came upon a man gathering wood on the sabbath day. (33) Those who found him as he was gathering wood brought him before Moses Aaron, and the whole community. (34) He was placed in custody, for it had not been specified what should be done to him.
(35) Then the LORD said to Moses "The man shall be put to death: the whole community shall pelt him with stones outside the camp." (36) So, the whole community took him outside the camp and stoned him to death, as the LORD had commanded Moses. [*Numbers 15:32-36*]

This unnamed man committed a major violation of the Shabbat. However, he acted entirely on his own. Rabbi Akiva holds that this man was Zelophehad, the father of these five women.[3] He committed a major violation by desecrating Shabbat, but he acted on his own.

Rabbi Shimon says that Zelophehad's sin was that he was among the people who decided to go out after God had sent a plague in the wake of the bad report from the 12 spies.[3] Moses told them not to go because God was not with them. They went anyway. The results, as we have seen, were disastrous. If this was Zelophehad's sin, then it was misguided, for sure, but he did not influence anyone else to follow him.

Regardless of what his specific sin was, his five daughters stood before Moses imploring him to give them their father's land as an inheritance. Moses' answer? He does not know, so he brings the matter "before the Lord" [27:5]. For this, the *midrash* says Moses is to be praised for setting an example for Jewish leaders for all time: never assume that you know everything; if something is too difficult for you to make a ruling on, consult God.[4]

As times change and the world presents new and more demanding situations than ever before (such as a pandemic! Combined with social unrest! And political unrest!) we rabbis find ourselves facing more and greater challenges than ever before. The pandemic has forced upon us many and various *halachic* issues that we never had to think about before. Whether dealing with these new questions or questions on any other topic, a rabbi who is not too proud to say, "I'm not sure, but I will seek an answer for you" sets an important example for us all. Saying, "I don't know, but I'll find out" means that one is open to whatever answer comes forth from God.

It means putting one's total trust in God. It means being willing to accept even an answer that we might not be comfortable with. Such is the ever-evolving nature of *halachah*.

Even for those who may not be rabbis, we all need to be open to asking the questions, and accepting the answers, even—or especially—when we find those answers difficult to agree with.

FOURTH ALIYAH: NUMBERS 27:6–23
WEDNESDAY, JULY 8, 2020

Who Will Fill Moses' Sandals?

Here we see the answer to Moses' inquiry of God regarding the daughters of Zelophehad. Yes, they should be allowed to inherit their father's land [27:7]. This passage can be (and is) used to support the idea of women's rights in the Torah. While not exactly being declared equal to male progeny (we shall see why in due time), they are permitted to have their father's land "transferred" to them.

Now, have you ever participated in a discussion where a rabbi (or someone else who is teaching) has just given an answer to a question that was posed? What happens? You know we Jews are never satisfied. Someone else will now ask, "Yeah, but what if . . . ?" That question is answered. Someone else says, "Yeah, but, what if . . . ?" And so on and so on. Every minute possibility is raised. This is not surprising. After all, this is the nature of most of the Talmudic disputes between rabbis. Every possible iteration of a situation must be raised and considered.

So, reading the answer that God gave to Moses here, it sounds as if God is already anticipating the "what if's." The entire order of inheritance is given: if a man has no male heirs, his daughters inherit his property. If he has no children at all, then his property goes to his brothers. If he has no brothers, then his father's brothers will receive his property. And if he has no uncles on his father's side, then the property passes to whomever is the next closest male relative [27:8-11]. Notice that, aside from the daughters, all the other inheritors are males. The goal is to keep the land within the tribe. In a very real way, this makes sense as each tribe was allotted a specific geographic area. If someone from another tribe owned a plot in the middle of one tribe's area, that could surely make for a difficult situation.

Additionally in this reading, God tells Moses that he, Moses, will eventually go up to the mountain to die, just as his brother Aaron had done [27:13].

The difference is that Aaron already knew before he died that his son Eleazer would succeed him but Moses does not know who his successor will be. He implores God to appoint an appropriate person to follow him who will care for the nation as he has. God instructs him to choose Joshua, and to designate him by the laying on of hands [27:18, 23].

How interesting it is that juxtaposed in the same reading we have the line of inheritance followed through male relatives (preferably sons), and then Moses, who must designate as his successor someone who is not related to him at all (Joshua), despite the fact that he has two sons. So, we are left to wonder: why do we not hear anything about Moses' sons? It appears that, though Moses was a great leader of the nation, he was not a great father. His sons, apparently, were not trained or prepared to assume the mantle of leadership. In fact, we hear virtually nothing more about them in the entire Tanakh. Instead, Joshua becomes the designated successor.

Would Joshua have been Moses' first choice? For that matter, would Moses have been comfortable with anyone being chosen to succeed him? There can be little doubt that he must have had some very mixed feelings as he laid his hands on Joshua, designating him as the next leader of the nation.

FIFTH ALIYAH: NUMBERS 28:1–15
THURSDAY, JULY 9, 2020

Singing About Sacrifices?

The Torah now switches gears. God tells Moses to instruct the people about the daily offerings and the cycle of the year. We have read about the special days designated throughout the year, and the agricultural reasons for each holiday. Now the specifics of the required sacrifices are delineated. God commands that we are to "be punctilious" in offering these sacrifices at the required times [28:2].

First and foremost, every day required the sacrifice of two lambs, one in the morning and one in the evening. These offerings are referred to as *olah tamid*, a regular (not perpetual) burnt offering [28:3]. During all the time that the *mishkan*, and later the *Temples*, stood, these two sacrifices were offered daily by the priests, as per God's command. Since the destruction of the Second Temple in the year 70 CE, we no longer have a place to offer animal sacrifices. Hence, these offerings have been replaced by daily prayer services: *shacharit* (morning) and *arvit* (evening). These sacrifices are, indeed, regular, as they are prayed daily even today, but not perpetual, as they no longer are offered in their original form. Could it be that God already knew what would ultimately become of the animal sacrifices?

Next, we learn about the sacrifices of the Sabbath [28:9–10]. In addition to the two lambs sacrificed every day, another two lambs are to be sacrificed immediately after the daily morning sacrifice. The name for this additional sacrifice that was added onto the *shacharit* service is *musaf*. This has become the concluding service added onto our Shabbat and holiday morning services, following the Torah service.

The passage continues, outlining the additional sacrifices that are required on the sabbath: two-year-old lambs without blemish, along with two-tenths of a measure of choice flour with oil mixed in, and the proper libation. The words of these two verses are part of the liturgy for the *amidah* of the Shabbat *musaf* service. Some people are uncomfortable including this in their *davening*. Recognizing this, some prayer books, including both the Lev Shalem and Sim Shalom *siddurim* published by the Rabbinical Assembly, in an effort to be sensitive to all worshippers, offer an alternate text on the following page, which does not talk about animal sacrifices.

What's your opinion? Do you/will you use the alternate text, or do you/will you stick to the traditional text? Or will you do one thing one week and something else the next?

The point is that it is important to realize what sentiments are expressed in our prayers, not just to sing along because they have a catchy tune. Sometimes that calls for wrestling with one's conscience a bit.

In this way, our prayer takes on greater personal significance. Even though we pray together using a prescribed set of prayers, it is important to make it your own and really own the prayer experience.

This may prove to be even more of a challenge in these days of Zoom and livestreaming. On the other hand, these are precisely the days when we need more than ever to internalize our prayers.

SIXTH ALIYAH: NUMBERS 28:16–29:11
FRIDAY, JULY 10, 2020

Celebrating by the Light of the Moon

This *aliyah* begins to lay out the calendar of special days of the year, days on which an additional sacrifice is required beyond the daily sacrifice. The year begins with *Pesach*, the first day of which is celebrated on the fifteenth day of the first month (Nissan) and celebrated for seven days

[28:17-25]. The central commandment for the people of Israel during this holiday, as we know, is to eat only unleavened bread. The sacrifices are to consist of two bulls, one ram, and seven lambs. Interestingly, we note that the animal sacrifices are accompanied, as usual, by a meal offering of flour mixed with water [28:20]! Though we may not eat chametz, it seems that God can! The first and seventh days are holy days on which no work is permitted.

Following this is the "day of the first fruits" [28:26] (i.e., *Shavuot*). This is a holy day on which no work is permitted. The sacrifices for this day are the same as for *Pesach*: two bulls, one ram, and seven lambs, along with a meal offering [28:27-28].

Then the first day of the seventh month (Tishrei) is a holy day when "the horn is blown" [29:1]. This is, of course, Rosh Hashanah and the sacrifices are one bull, one ram, and seven lambs [29:2], along with a meal offering. Interestingly, we note that both *Pesach* and *Shavuot* have one more bull than Rosh Hashanah. Why do you think that might be?

The passage goes on: on the tenth day of the seventh month (Tishrei) is a day when we afflict our souls, and we do not work [29:7]. This is obviously Yom Kippur. The sacrifices for this day also consist of one bull, one ram, and seven lambs [29:8], along with a meal offering. Keep in mind that the animal sacrifices have been replaced by prayer services since the destruction of the Temple.

I want to point out that the first day of *Pesach* falls on the fifteenth day of Nisan. We will see in the next reading that *Sukkot* begins on the fifteenth day of Tishrei. Other days on our calendar fall on the fifteenth of the month as well. *Tu B'Shvat*, the New Year for Trees, literally means "the fifteenth of Shevat." In the month of Av, six days after the solemn commemoration of *Tisha b'Av* (the ninth of Av), we have a somewhat unknown day of celebration, *Tu b'Av* (literally, the fifteenth of Av), which is a Jewish form of Valentine's Day. *Shushan Purim*, the day after *Purim*, marks the day on which the celebration continued in the outlying areas on the fifteenth of Adar.

Our calendar is based on a lunar cycle. Rosh Chodesh, the beginning of each new month, falls when there is no moon. The fifteenth of the month is when there is a full moon. On any of the holidays I listed above, if you look up in the night sky you will see that it is illuminated by a brilliant full moon. A full moon lights up the *sukkah* as we sit in it to observe Sukkot. A full moon lit the way as the nation of Israel left Egypt and traveled into the desert.

Just as the moon illuminates the night sky, so, too, do our holidays and holy days literally illuminate our lives.

Oh, Won't You Stay Just A Little Bit Longer?[5]

The cycle of holy days concludes with the harvest festival of Sukkot, which, as I mentioned in the previous reading, begins on the fifteenth of Tishrei and is celebrated for seven days. Unlike *Pesach*, where the number of animals sacrificed was the same every day, here the number of bulls was thirteen on the first day and decreased by one each day (twelve on day two, eleven on day three, ten on day four, nine on day five, eight on day six, seven on day seven). Additionally, two rams and fourteen lambs were sacrificed each day. Adding up the numbers of bulls gives us 13+12+11+10+9+8+7=70. One bull was sacrificed for each of the seventy nations of the world. During Sukkot, in the ceremony of *Ushpizin*, we symbolically invite a different distinguished guest to share in each day of our holiday celebration; the list includes the three patriarchs Abraham, Isaac, and Jacob; the leaders of the liberation, Moses and Aaron; Joseph; and King David.

Immediately following Sukkot, we have the one-day holiday of *Shemini Atzeret*, the eighth day of assembly. On this day, the sacrifices consisted of only one bull, one ram, and seven lambs. This extra day, as I have discussed before, was a day just for the nation of Israel which is the reason that there is only one bull. On this day, God wanted us to linger and spend one more day with God, for after this day there would be six months before the holiday of *Pesach* would occur once more, beginning the annual cycle yet again.

On every *Rosh Chodesh* and every holiday mentioned in this *aliyah* and the previous one, we add a musaf service to remember the additional offerings that God commanded us to bring on each of those days. May we take advantage of the opportunities presented to us by these additional services to linger a little longer in prayer and praise, dwelling in the presence of the Divine.

Parashat Mattot

FIRST ALIYAH: NUMBERS 30:2–17
SUNDAY, JULY 12, 2020

Promises, Promises

This section talks about vows, which we will see were taken very seriously in biblical times. Any man who makes a vow to God is obligated to fulfill that vow [30:3]. And what if a woman makes a vow? It takes fourteen verses to cover the answer to that:

- A father of an unmarried woman living in his house has the right to annul that vow. However, if he does not do so on the day that he learns of it, the vow stands [30:4-6].
- A husband who learns that his wife made a vow either prior to or after marrying him has the right to annul the vow but if he does not do so on the day that he learns of it, the vow stands [30:7-9, 11-13].
- A vow made by a widow or divorcee (a woman who is not under the authority of a man) stands [30:10].

So, a man had autonomy when it came to vows, but a woman did not. Additionally, an unfulfilled vow to God was considered a sin and required that a guilt offering be brought.

Interestingly, we have two stories of vows in the *Tanakh*, one tragic and one auspicious, one made by a man, and one made by a woman.

The first is the story of the judge Jephthah. Before going into battle with the Ammonites, he made a promise to God that, "whatever comes out of the door of my house to meet me on my safe return from the Ammonites shall be the LORD's and shall be offered by me as a burnt offering." When returning home after defeating the enemy, he was met by his daughter, his only child, coming out to meet him "with timbrel and dance!" Rending his clothes, he informed her of the irretractable vow that he had made. After allowing her time to mourn her fate, he did indeed follow through with his promise [Judges 1130-35].

Tragically, Jephthah made a careless vow, and ended up losing his daughter.

The second story of a vow is of a childless Hannah who made a promise that if God would bless her with a son she would give her son back to God to serve in the Temple. God indeed answered her prayer, and she named her son, "Samuel, meaning, 'I asked the LORD for him'" [1 Samuel 1:11-20].

Hannah fulfilled her vow, and later was blessed with five additional children as her reward.

Both Jephthah and Hannah vowed to give some unknown person to God as a sacrifice; Jephthah frivolously made a vow to sacrifice some human being as a burnt offering to God; Hannah vowed to give the child yet to be born to God as a holy sacrifice to serve in the Temple. Both fulfilled their respective vows. Jephthah's flippant proclamation led to a tragic loss of life; Hannah's led to a sanctification of her offspring for dedicated service to God. Jephthah paid a heavy price for his careless attitude; Hannah was rewarded for her selfless act of devotion. Jephthah's sacrifice was meaning*less*, Hannah's meaning*ful*.

The advice, then, borne out by these two examples, was not to take vows lightly. In the words of Ecclesiastes, "When you make a vow to God, do not delay to fulfill it. For He has no pleasure in fools; what you vow, fulfill. It is better not to vow at all than to vow and not fulfill" [5:3-4].

SECOND ALIYAH: NUMBERS 31:1–12
SUNDAY, JULY 12, 2020

To Sin or Not to Sin—That is the Question

God now tells Moses that he has one final task to complete before he, too, is to be "gathered to his kin." He is to instruct the people to avenge the death of the 24,000 who died as a consequence of the immorality with the Midianite women. Each tribe was to provide one thousand men for the battle, which was to be fought under the leadership of Pinchas [31:4-6]. The Israelites slew all the males among the Midianites, including their five kings [31:8]. Then the text tells us something interesting: they also killed Balaam.

Wait, what? The last time we heard from him, he blessed the nation of Israel when he had been asked to curse them by Balak no less than three times! Why did they need to take his life as part of God's revenge? Part of the answer can be found in the next reading, which tells us that the Midianite women had seduced the Israelite men, "at the bidding of Balaam." [31:16] How do we know this? Moses Chaim Luzzatto, the eighteenth century Italian commentator explains it this way:

> On his way back home, Balaam passed through Midian and heard how the Israelites had committed harlotry with the daughters of Moab and had thereby been led into idolatry. He then realized that this was the only sure method of undermining Israel. He therefore advised the Midianites to send their choicest maidens to seduce the Israelites into idolatry. In this way, they would forfeit the Almighty's protection.[1]

Okay, so Balaam was guilty of instigating. But, we might wonder, why does the Torah neglect to tell us of Balaam's complicity with the Midianites until after he has already been killed? Wouldn't his killing have made more sense to us if we had known this earlier?

This is the very question that is asked by Nehama Leibovitz, a well-known twentieth century Israeli commentator. Her answer is essentially this that "the moral responsibility ultimately rested on the Israelites themselves. They were guilty . . . . Every individual is responsible for his [or her] own acts. Provocation does not free the victim of responsibility."[2]

The message is clear: regardless of what kind of enticements to sin may be placed before us, each of us makes our own decision to sin or not. If you see someone's expensive Rolex watch out in full view and no one is around, you may be tempted to take it. On the other hand, you may decide not to take it, and thereby not to incur upon yourself the guilt of theft. Someone else, though, may give in to the temptation, and thereby become guilty of stealing. We each make our own choices.

I think, however, if we look again at the passage from Luzzatto, there is another message here. Balaam had finally found the Israelites' weak spot: immoral sexual behavior with foreign women. Therefore, he advised the Midianites to send their most enticing women (that is the reason that Zimri was caught by Pinchas with Cozbi, the daughter of a Midianite king). Balaam took advantage of their weakness, knowing that it would be easy to cause them to give in to their passion.

Balaam, therefore, was no different than someone who hands a drink to an alcoholic, a cigarette to someone trying to quit smoking, a calorie-laden candy bar or pastry to a dieter, or the signup sheet for a football pool to a compulsive gambler. Whether or not these activities are "sinful" is debatable. Nevertheless, putting something tempting like that right in the way of a person struggling to avoid their vice could very well be considered a sin. Rather, we need to offer support and encouragement when someone is struggling. Otherwise, we are no better than Balaam—and he was deemed by God to be worthy of death!

THIRD ALIYAH: NUMBERS 31:13–24
MONDAY, JULY 13, 2020

Cleansing the Camp?

Here we read what happened when those who had gone out to battle the Midianites returned to camp. This is one of those passages that some of us have difficulty grappling with. Normally in battle, only the men were slain, and that is what happened here. However, in this case, since the women, through their seduction of the men of Israel, had been the source of the immorality, Moses told the army of Israel that they must go back and also kill any woman among the Midianites who was not a virgin. The virgins could be spared since they were the only women who they could be certain had not taken part in the seduction and immorality. This was really a very wide-reaching standard, and, no doubt, many women who were not complicit in the seduction lost their lives.

Okay, so even if we can bring ourselves to accept the violent fate of the women, what are we to make of the fact that the same verse [31:17] begins with a commandment to "slay every male among the children" [of the Midianites]? The rationale, of course, is that these children could grow up to be fighters against the nation of Israel. The thing that struck me about this, however, is that it sounds an awful lot like what Pharaoh decreed against the people of Israel when we were enslaved in Egypt. He instructed the midwives to drown all the male babies born to Israelite women in the Nile for precisely the same reason.

It appears that there is a double standard at work here.

Reading further, we see that those who were involved in this killing needed to cleanse themselves and remain outside the camp for seven days. It seems that God also knew that what they were doing was problematic. Though God commanded them to do these things, they could not have done them without being affected psychologically and emotionally. No doubt the seven days of isolation outside the camp afforded them plenty of time to think about the things that they had done. Even though they had committed these heinous acts at the command of God, they still needed to be remorseful for having taken human lives and needed to cleanse their souls. And that, perhaps, is the lesson to be learned here.

Still, I can't help but wonder if God would also need to spend some time outside the camp. And if the answer to that question is yes then has God been spending time outside the camp these last four to five months?

FOURTH ALIYAH: NUMBERS 31:25–41
MONDAY, JULY 13, 2020

Not Liberty, but Justice, for All

Here we learn about the *terumah*, the contribution, which was required to be rendered to the sanctuary to the priests and the Levites. Through a complicated mathematical formula, the exact numbers of animals to be dedicated was calculated. Additionally, we notice that 32,000 human beings (i.e. (young) women who were virgins) had been taken captive. When young women were taken captive in war, they could be taken as wives, but not as slaves. A text in Deuteronomy outlines exactly what was to be done to a young woman who had been taken captive in war: if a man saw a beautiful woman whom he wanted to marry, she was to be brought into his house, have her hair cut and nails trimmed, and be given a month to mourn for the loss of her parents and her previous life. Only then could he take her as his wife. If at any time he changed his mind, he was to let her go free. He was not permitted to sell or enslave her [21:10-14]. She was not to be made to suffer for his actions. Thus, a warrior had to think very carefully before taking a female captive and could not act impulsively out of lust.

Again, to our modern sensitivities, the whole thing seems reprehensible. Yet, we know that even today there are, unfortunately, women who are taken captive as victims of war. There are women all over the world who are the victims of sex traffickers.

These women described in the *parashah*, who were basically captives of war, were totally vulnerable. They had no one who would defend them or fight for their rights. Surely women who found themselves in similar situations in the surrounding nations were voiceless and powerless. The Midianite women, however, who were captives in Israel, did have a Defender. God insisted that they not be treated as chattel, that their humanity be recognized.

I think that we would be hard pressed to find any other society or culture of that time that dictated that the woman's dignity must be considered in deciding her fate. We, like God, must strive to preserve the dignity of every human being, for we are all created in the Divine image.

FIFTH ALIYAH: NUMBERS 31:42–54
TUESDAY, JULY 14, 2020

Fighting for the Right Reasons

After returning from battle, a census was taken of the Israelites as well as of the items which they had taken as booty. Remember that only a total of 12,000 soldiers (one thousand per tribe) went out to battle the Midianites and were far outnumbered by their foes. Based on statistics alone, we would have expected that God would once again ask for a census to be taken of the warriors when they returned. Miraculously, they report that "Not one of us is missing" [31:49]. How can that be? The Talmud explains it this way: ". . . The intent of that verse is that not one man of us is missing due to transgression, i.e., none of them sinned" [BT Yevamot 61A:4].

The Baal HaTurim explains that not one of these men succumbed to the temptations of the women of Midian and therefore received God's protection when they went into battle.[3] In other words, their motivation was correct because they went to battle to defend the honor of God.

This is a far cry from the men who, thirty-eight years before, were afraid to go in and take the land that God had promised them. Then they were afraid of being outnumbered and overpowered. Now they are surely outnumbered, but not afraid of being overpowered.

Throughout our history, we Jews have been but a tiny minority in the world's population. We have always been severely outnumbered. Yet we have remained tied to our Torah and its teachings. And that has helped us to maintain our place in the world.

No Man (or Woman) is an Island

In today's reading, we see that two of the tribes, Gad and Reuven (and they were later joined by the half tribe of Menashe) approached Moses to ask if they could stay and settle in this land that they had conquered from the Midianites, even though it was not physically part of the land that God had promised to Israel and was on the other side of the Jordan River. Their rationale was that these lands had plenty of grazing room, and they, as it turns out, had lots of cattle. Moses' reaction was to become angry with them as he was afraid that the situation was déjà vu and that, even after thirty-eight years in the desert, the people had still not learned their lesson from the incident with the spies. They hastened to assure him that he was mistaken; they said that they would be "shock troops" [32:17] and be the first line of defense when the nation was under attack. Additionally, they assured him that they would not return home to their families until each member of the nation had received his portion of the land as a possession [32:18].

In Pirkei Avot chapter 2:5, we read "do not separate yourself from the community." These tribes may have been physically separated from the rest of the nation but spiritually they were joined as one, committed to defending the land and the other tribes if the need arose.

Though we Jews are scattered throughout the world today, nevertheless we are enjoined to remember this idea. A Jew cannot live in isolation; we need the companionship of others. These days, when we are living in physical isolation, this need for community is felt even more accurately. Thankfully, many of us are able to join together online through the wonders of Zoom. Many more people are taking advantage of online learning than ever before, and many synagogues find that more people participate in online services when they are offered than did by physically attending synagogue services in the past.

We long to be together, to see each other, to laugh together, to sing together, just to talk together. Zoom may not be perfect, but it is perhaps the next best thing. Until we can safely gather again in shul, I'll see you on the computer!

Honey, I'm Home!

This last section of *Parashat* Mattot continues the story of the request of the Reubenites and Gadites to remain and settle in the land east of the Jordan River that had been captured from the Midianites and Moabites. We have already seen that they promised Moses that, in the event of war, they would be the "shock troops," the first line of defense of the land of Canaan, thus remaining united with the rest of the nation. We read today that Moses gave them permission to stay and build in the land. But he told them that the land would only officially become theirs once they had proven themselves. When a battle arose, every man of fighting age (twenty to fifty) would be obligated to cross the Jordan and fight alongside the rest of the nation. This would prove their sincerity, and the land would then be theirs. If they did not go over and fight, they would suffer the consequences of their sin [32:20-24].

The particular verse that caught my attention is verse 26: the surety that they provided Moses was to tell him, "Our children, our wives, our flocks, and all of our other livestock will stay behind." Clearly, their intention was to return as they feel connected to this land. It is home.

I was struck by the contrast between this situation and that which occurred back in Egypt. Following the plague of hail, Pharaoh called Moses and Aaron to ask them whom they intended to take with them if he were to grant their request to go out into the desert to worship the Lord. Moses answered him, "We will all go, young and old: we will go with our sons and daughters, our flocks and herds; for we must observe the LORD's festival" [Exodus 10:9]. It's no wonder that Pharaoh said no at this point. Everyone was going—men, women, children, flocks. Clearly, it seemed, they had no intention of returning.

Two more plagues followed: locusts and darkness. Once again, Pharaoh called the brothers to him, saying, "Go, worship the LORD! Only your flocks and your herds shall be left behind; even your children may go with you" [Exodus 10:24]. Moses said that they were not leaving without the animals, since they needed them for sacrifices.

A final confrontation took place after the tenth and final plague, the death of the firstborn. Now, in exasperation, Pharaoh finally told them, "Up, depart from among my people, you and the Israelites with you! Go, worship the LORD as you said! Take also your flocks and your herds, as you said, and begone!" [Exodus 12:31-32].

Clearly, the nation had no ties to Egypt. They wanted out. That was reflected in Moses' insistence that they take everyone and everything with them, leaving nothing, not even one animal behind. Forty years later, we see that the tribes of Reuven and Gad have found the land where they are willing to leave their wives, children, and flocks—and to know that they will return to it.

As of this writing, I have been to Israel five times. It is the only country other than Canada to which I have traveled more than once. The last time I was there was for the first semester of my third year of Rabbinical School. I rented an apartment in Jerusalem and lived there for three months. Every time I leave Eretz Israel, I leave with the feeling that I'm going to be back, I just don't know when. But I do know that when I am there, as a Jew, I feel like I am home.

Parashat Masei

FIRST ALIYAH: NUMBERS 33:1–10
WEDNESDAY, JULY 15, 2020

We're Always Starting Over

This last *parashah* of the book of Numbers begins by recounting the journeys of the people of Israel from Egypt to Canaan, an eleven-day journey that had taken them forty years to complete. God told Moses to record all of the places that they stayed in for any amount of time along the way [33:2]; the journey was to be chronicled for all future generations to read. Notice that the places are called "starting points," not stopping points. That is because none of these places was designated as their final destination. So, while they may have stayed in each place for a certain amount of time, they ultimately departed from each on their way to what was designated to be their final destination, Canaan. Yes, they were on a physical journey, but no less so were they also on a spiritual journey, learning what it meant to be in a relationship with God, learning to trust God, and preparing themselves for life in the promised land.

We, too, are each on a spiritual journey in our relationship with God. As you look back, can you remember specific starting points along the way? Were there places or events that caused you to take a turn in a different direction?

These past five to six months have affected many of us spiritually. We have developed a new understanding of the fragility of life. With a lack of human companionship, many of us have leaned more on God to see us through. And in the future, when, God-willing, this pandemic will finally draw to a close (may it be soon) I pray that we each will be able to look back at this time as one of our starting points on our spiritual journey.

SECOND ALIYAH: NUMBERS 33:11–49
THURSDAY, JULY 16, 2020

Ya Gotta Have Heart[1]

This *aliyah* finishes what was begun in the last *aliyah*: a recounting of all the places the nation stopped on their journey from Egypt to Canaan. Keeping in mind the idea of starting points, we see the language in each case: they set out from X and camped at Y.

Reading the list of place names makes it sound as if they were constantly on the move. Forty verses tell us nothing more than the places they camped along the way. If we count the number of places, we will find that there were forty-two of them in all. But the journey can be split up into three parts:

- The first part, leading up to their initial arrival at the border of Canaan and the disastrous incident of the spies. This all took place in the first year, and there were fourteen encampments.
- The second part, wandering in the wilderness for thirty-eight years. There were twenty encampments.
- The third part, following the death of Aaron, and until they arrived once again at the border of Canaan. This all took place in the last year and there were eight encampments.

Notice that there was a lot of traveling in the first and last years. In between, twenty encampments over the course of thirty-eight years was not as hectic as we might have thought.

As we travel on our spiritual journeys, we make note of the significant places along the way, those moments and experiences that draw us closer to God. Sometimes the journey moves quickly, like fourteen times in a year; other times things move much more slowly, like twenty times in thirty-eight years. During these past several months, the isolation brought about by the pandemic has forced us all to slow down the pace of our lives. Many of us have experienced a level of spiritual growth that is inversely proportional to our level of involvement in the more mundane aspects of the material world. May we be blessed to have our hearts learn to cling to God as we each travel on our own journey to claim the covenant which is our inheritance.

Border Song[2]

Now that the nation stands ready to go in and conquer the land of Canaan, Moses issues a final set of instructions: all the inhabitants are to be dispossessed, and any altars or shrines of theirs are to be destroyed. The people of Israel are to go in and take possession of the land, settling it in designated tribal areas. If any inhabitants of the land are not dispossessed, they will become thorns in their sides. God will punish the people of Israel [33:52-56].

The balance of the reading [34:1-15], lays out very specifically where the borders of the land of Canaan will be. If you look at a map that shows the land distribution among the tribes, you will see that the designated area is much larger than the modern State of Israel; the entire area that was assigned to the tribes of Gad, Reuven and Menasseh on the eastern side of the Jordan River is today in the nation of Jordan.

Some people have very strong opinions about where the borders of Israel should be today. Many religious Jews are purists, believing that everything that was originally promised to us by God is part of our heritage for all time, and that therefore it should all be part of Israel today (this, of course, would not include the land on the eastern side of the Jordan since that had not been part of the land that God had promised. Rather, the two and a half tribes had requested it. Many liberal Jews, however, do not agree. Many would be willing to give up parts of the land if a guarantee of peace would be offered in exchange.

The borders of the modern State of Israel were established, not by God, but by human beings and they have also changed several times since the founding of the State of Israel in 1948. The history of the relationship between the Jews and Arabs of Israel, between Israel and the Palestinians, between Israel and the Arab nations that surround it is a complicated one. Often, the documentation of that history in the American media is less than accurate, to say the least. It can be difficult to read or listen to everything and decide what is truthful and accurate, and what is false and/or an exaggeration.

I won't suggest how you should feel about annexation. I only suggest that whatever opinion you have should be based on a well-informed understanding of the situation.

FOURTH ALIYAH: NUMBERS 34:16–29
FRIDAY, JULY 17, 2020

Apportioning the Land

We are approaching the end of the book of Numbers, and just like at the beginning of the book, we have a list of names—this time of the chieftains of the tribes. In the beginning of the book, these men were taking a census of the members of their respective tribes. Now, they are to oversee the apportioning of the land once the people have crossed the Jordan and conquered it [34:18]. We should note that the two tribes of Gad and Reuven are not represented on this list because they already received their portion when they requested to stay on the eastern side of the Jordan. We should also note, however, that, aside from the chieftains, there are two additional names on the list: Aaron's son Eleazar, who is now the *cohen gadol*, the High Priest; and Joshua, who has already been appointed to be Moses' successor [34:17]. At this point, Moses already knows that he will not be allowed to cross into the land with the people. Therefore, he himself will not be involved in the apportioning of the land.

I think it is significant that the chieftains will be accompanied in this task by both a military/political leader and a religious leader; and that those two men are the successors of Moses and Aaron, respectively, the brothers who were responsible for bringing them out of Egypt and to the brink of the promised land. In commenting on the fact that Eleazar is named before Joshua, Rabbeinu Bayha explains that Joshua was subject to the authority of the High Priest and was not able to initiate a war unless he first obtained his approval.[3]

As the people prepare to enter the promised land, they are reminded once again that their relationship with God takes precedence in their lives. We, too, must care for our spiritual well-being and connection with God, even as we live out our daily lives in the material world.

FIFTH ALIYAH: NUMBERS 35:1–8
FRIDAY, JULY 17, 2020

Are We There Yet?

Here we find out where the Levites are to live. Remember, the Levites did not own any land because they worked in the *mishkan* and they did not farm the land. But God also instructed that they should be provided for. Here we find that the nation was to set aside six cities, three on either side of the Jordan, which would be designated "cities of refuge" (more on these in the next reading). These six towns would be for the Levites to live in. In addition, the nation was to set aside forty-two more towns for the Levites, making a total of forty-eight towns. They were also to receive land surrounding each of their towns for pasturing their cattle.

The first verse of this section tells us that the nation is standing in the steppes of "Moab at the Jordan of Jericho." We read earlier in this *parashah* about the forty-two places that the nation of Israelites encamped in the forty years that they traveled in the desert. I compared their physical journey to the spiritual journey that we each find ourselves on. We will see that the book ends here on the brink of the promised land. The Torah never takes us into the land. If we want to read that part, we must continue reading on past the Torah to the next book of the *Tanakh*, the book of Joshua. But the Torah itself keeps us continually on a journey that we don't get to see to completion. It's a beautiful metaphor of the spiritual quest to draw closer to God that we all are pursuing. We're constantly on a journey, and we don't know what the end will be.

SIXTH ALIYAH: NUMBERS 35:9–34
WRITTEN FOR SATURDAY, SHABBAT JULY 18

Seeking Refuge

In these last two readings, Moses is taking care of the last-minute details of instructing the people about what they need to do once they get into the land. Here he gives the details concerning the cities of refuge that they are to set up; these offered protection to those found to be guilty of unintentional murder.

Among most societies in the Near East at the time, the idea of justified revenge killing of a murderer by the nearest male kin was prevalent. Therefore, it was a concept present in Israelite society, as well (again, to our modern sensitivities this sounds almost incomprehensible but we need to consider the time and place in which all of this was taking place). There was a difference, however, between the nation of Israel and the surrounding nations: each murderer was tried by the state to determine whether he was guilty of intentional or unintentional murder. The criteria used to determine what the murderer was guilty of were as follows: the kind of weapon that was used, whether the murderer and victim had prior enmity for each other or not, and the circumstances of the murder. If it was deemed that the murder was unintentional, then the *goel*, the redeemer, the blood relative who was responsible for avenging the murder, was not permitted to do so. Instead, the murderer was sentenced to live in one of these cities of refuge and as long as he stayed there, he could not be killed by the *goel*. He was to stay in the city of refuge until one of two things happened: either he himself died, or the *cohen gadol*, the High Priest, died [25: 25]. The death of a High Priest effected expiation for all those who had died on his watch.

And what was the reason for all of this? God had agreed to dwell among the people in the land and murder in the land made the land unclean. Therefore, God would not be able to abide the presence of murder in the land. God does not desire more bloodshed, yet God requires that expiation be made.

What message can this have for us today, when most of us, thankfully, are not guilty of murder? Only that we each need to examine our own lives. What are the things in our lives that God's presence cannot abide? If we wish to have a close relationship with God, we need to find them and root them out. Many of us have found that we dwell more in solitude today due to the isolation caused by social distancing. May we each take advantage of this time to draw closer to the Divine, seeking out the presence of the *Shechinah*. May God's presence be our city of refuge, keeping us safe in these difficult times.

SEVENTH ALIYAH: NUMBERS 36:1–13
WRITTEN FOR SHABBAT, SATURDAY, JULY 18, 2020

Two Steps Forward, One Step Back

Like many Conservative congregations throughout North America, the synagogue of which I am a member transitioned from a non-egalitarian to an egalitarian synagogue through a long and gradual process. And, even as the main sanctuary allowed more and more participation of women in the services, the morning *minyan* that met in the small chapel was the last service to do so. Women's requests for equal participation in that service were met with a great deal of resistance.

One Monday morning many years ago, our regular Torah reader was not present at the service, and there were no other men there who knew how to *leyn*. As I sat staring into my *siddur*, I was approached by the *minyan* leader, who said to me very matter-of-factly, "You know you're going to have to read Torah today, don't you?" After getting over my initial shock, I was excited to fulfill his request, and proudly did so. What an opportunity! However, on the following Thursday morning when our regular Torah reader returned, I was not asked to read again even though the reading was identical to the one that I had done on Monday morning. In fact, it would be several years before I again had the opportunity to read Torah at the morning service. I was good enough to *leyn* only in the absence of any qualified men. Otherwise, I wasn't good enough on my own merit.

Why do I tell you this story now? Because it reminds me of Zelophehad's daughters. We read about them several weeks back: five sisters whose father died in the wilderness, leaving behind no male heirs. They petitioned Moses to be able to inherit their father's estate. After Moses consulted with God, their request was granted. Many point to this story as a rare example of women's rights being recognized in the Torah.

This reading tells us, however, that that was not quite the case. Now that the nation was about to enter the land, and the land would be apportioned by tribe and clan, the members of the tribe of Menashe, Zelophehad's tribe, complained to Moses: what if any of these women were to marry outside their tribe? Then her portion would pass to her husband, and thereby to another tribe [36:1-4]. Again, Moses consulted God; the instructions came back that each of these five women, and indeed any unmarried woman who should find herself in a similar situation, was required to marry within her tribe so that the land would stay a part of the tribe's holdings [36:5-9]. These five women dutifully complied, marrying their first cousins [36:10-12]. Additionally, several commentators point out that this exception was only allowed for that specific generation that was going in to possess the land.

So, these women were, in a sense, placeholders. They were permitted to inherit their father's portion only because there were no male heirs, and thereafter it passed only to male relatives—to their sons, not their daughters.

To be fair, all of this took place in an extremely patriarchal society that pretty much reflected the way of the world at that time. In light of that reality, the daughters are to be commended for speaking up with their request, and it was rather momentous that it was granted, but it wasn't quite the achievement of equality that many people would like to believe that it was.

The more things change, the more they remain the same.

With this *aliyah*, we have concluded the study of the book of *Bamidbar*, Numbers.

חֲזַק חֲזַק וְנִתְחַזֵּק!

BOOK OF DEVARIM
Parashat Devarim

FIRST ALIYAH: DEUTERONOMY 1:1–10
SUNDAY, JULY 19, 2020

Time to Move On

This final book of the Torah consists of the three final speeches given by Moses to the nation. He begins his first speech by reprimanding the people. The six places named by Moses in the first verse are all places at which the nation had rebelled against God during the last forty years. He continues by reminding them that the journey from Horeb (Mt. Sinai) to Kadesh Barnea should have taken only eleven days. Yet it was, at the time of this speech, the fortieth year after leaving Egypt [1:3]. Moses is not being very subtle in intimating that it is due to the frequent disobedience of the nation that what should have been an eleven-day trip became instead a forty-year journey.

When the Israelites left Egypt, it took them two months to arrive at Mt. Sinai. Once there, they encamped and stayed for approximately two years, during which time Moses spent two periods of forty days and nights on the mountain receiving the two sets of tablets, respectively, that contained the Ten Commandments. The instructions for the construction of the *mishkan* and the installation of the priests were given by God and carried out by the people while camped at Sinai. Finally, though, Moses says that God told the people: *rav-lachem shevet bahar hazeh* (You have stayed long enough at this mountain). The phrase *rav lachem* really implies that something is too much. A better translation of this verse would be "you have stayed too long at this mountain." This phrase caught my attention, and I knew exactly where I had seen it before—twice in the story of Korach and his rebellion. The first was when Korach accused Moses and Aaron of taking "too much" upon themselves, saying to them, "You have gone too far! For all the community are holy, all of them . . . [Numbers 16:3]. In the second instance, Moses accused Korach of doing the exact same thing: "You have gone too far, sons of Levi!" [Numbers 16:7]. We see in both cases that these words are used as a form of rebuke. Additionally, we know that this situation did not work out well for Korach and his followers.

A search revealed that this phrase occurs exactly twice more in the Torah, and both are right in this week's *parashah*. Once again, we will see that God tells the people they have stayed too long at the mountain: "You have been skirting this hill country long enough [too long]; now turn north" [2:3].

Finally, in recounting Moses' instructions to the tribes of Gad and Reuven, who wanted to settle on the other side of the Jordan, he cited their justification for their request: ". . . I know that you have too much live-stock . . ." Here, with the use of this phrase, we can see that Moses really was rebuking them for their choice of a place to settle.

All of this brings me back to the use of the phrase in our verse: God is rebuking the people for overstaying their time at Mt. Sinai. I'm sure it must have felt comfortable and easy to stay where they felt safe, knowing that God was there with them. But God was impatient for them to get to the promised land. They needed to get on with their lives. That is why in the very next verse God said to them, "start out and make your way . . ."

Sometimes it's hard to move on in our lives, even though we know we need to. It's difficult to leave a place where we feel safe and protected, and to venture out into the unknown. For those of us who have been very cautious about going out during this COVID-19 pandemic, there can be no doubt that once a vaccine is available and we can emerge once more from our solitude and the safety of our homes, it will be overwhelming and a bit scary to do so. As much as we long to have our lives return to what they were (and I'm not sure that that is ever going to fully happen), it may still be difficult for some to make those first ventures out. Nevertheless, whether we are talking about the physical spaces that we have been inhabiting or the metaphorical spaces in the protective company of the Divine, I, for one, long for the day when we can feel the presence of God saying to us, "You have spent too long in this place. It is time to start out and make your way again."

Going Boldly Where No Man Has Gone Before

In this reading, Moses recounted the setting up of the judicial system, with judges set up over groups of thousands, hundreds, fifties, and tens; the people were not to be partial in their judgment in any way.

Then Moses reminded the people that they did, indeed, finally set out from Horeb (Mt. Sinai), and travel into the wilderness—that is described as "the great and terrible wilderness." What exactly is meant by "great and terrible?" Rashi says that it contained "snakes as big as a wooden beam and scorpions the size of a longbow."[1] Sforno says that it was "where no one had gone before; God wanted their journey to be as short as possible so they could enter the land immediately."[1]

I like Sforno's explanation: they entered uncharted territory and that is precisely what made it so frightening to them. But he also says that they entered *virgin* territory. (Sorry, but I can't help but hear Captain James T. Kirk in my head: "to boldly go where no man has gone before . . .").[2]

This phrase "great and terrible" was another that stuck in my head. A search revealed that it occurs only six more times in the entire *Tanakh*. I want to look more closely at five of these seven verses:

> We set out from Horeb and traveled the **great and terrible** wilderness that you saw, along the road to the hill country of the Amorites, as the LORD our God had commanded us. [our verse here] [1:19]
> . . . who led you through the **great and terrible** wilderness with its seraph serpents and scorpions, a parched land with no water in it, who brought forth water for you from the flinty rock; [8:15]
> I prayed to the LORD my God, making confession thus: "O Lord, **great and awesome** God, who stays faithful to His covenant with those who love Him and keep His commandments! [Daniel 9:4]
> I said, "O LORD, God of Heaven, **great and awesome** God, who stays faithful to His covenant with those who love Him and keep His commandments! [Nehemiah 1:5]
> . . . "Do not be afraid of them! Think of the **great and awesome** Lord, and fight for your brothers, your sons and daughters, your wives, and homes!" [Nehemiah 4:8]

Now let's see what is being described as great and awesome: the wilderness (the first two verses), and God (Daniel and the two Nehemiah verses).

(For the record, the other two verses are Joel 3:4 and Malachi 3:23. Both mention the future apocalyptic Day of the Lord, possibly referring to the coming of the messiah.)

So, what is the connection between the wilderness (desert) and God? If you have ever been to Israel and traveled to the Negev Desert, then you know the feeling of absolute and utter awe one experiences there. The silence, the vastness and beauty of the landscape are difficult to describe. Many people experience a feeling of closeness to God. Now just imagine living in that environment for forty years!

The people may have felt that they were leaving the presence of God when they left Mt. Sinai, but remember that, as they set out into the wilderness, they were led by the cloud of glory and that second ark containing the broken tablets. In a very real sense, as they journeyed toward the land of Canaan, they had two destinations: the physical destination of the promised land, and the more esoteric destination of the realization of their covenantal relationship with God. Both the wilderness and the presence of God were unknown, but great and awesome.

These last several months of the pandemic have certainly brought us through a time and experience that is like nothing that any of us has ever known. We have watched with awe and dread as the virus grips our nation and our world, claiming lives in numbers that we find difficult to comprehend. At the same time, many of us have felt the need to turn to God for the emotional and spiritual strengthening that we so desperately need to guide us through this unknown wilderness.

The promised land that we await here is a world free of COVID-19. May God grant us the strength to continue the journey until we arrive safely on the opposite shores of this metaphoric Jordan River.

THIRD ALIYAH: DEUTERONOMY 1:22–38
TUESDAY, JULY 21, 2020

Practicing Protection

In this reading, Moses recounts the incident with the spies, how the people were frightened by the report brought back by ten of the spies and refused to go in and take the land of Canaan. As a result, God decreed not only that none of the men of that generation save for Joshua and Caleb would live to see the land. Additionally, Moses would be denied the opportunity to see the promised land.

What caught my attention in this *aliyah* was the beautiful imagery used by Moses in explaining to the people why they should have trusted God: God carried them in the wilderness like a father carries a child [22:31]. What a beautiful image of God's love and care for the nation. And then there is verse 33. The first half recounts how God went before the nation in all their travels to "scout" (*latur*) the place where they should encamp. This no doubt refers to that second ark that contained the broken fragments of the first set of tablets of the Ten Commandments. This was the ark that went out ahead of the nation looking for a place for them to stop. In fact, you may remember from where this story was told in the book of Bamidbar that the word *latur*, usually translated as "to spy," really implies looking for something specific. This word appears eight times in the Torah. Six of them are in the story of the spies as it is told in the book of Bamidbar, and they all refer to the twelve men "spying" out the land of Canaan. The connotation is surely not positive.

The first occurrence of this word precedes the incident of the spies: "They marched from the mountain of the LORD a distance of three days. The Ark of the Covenant of the LORD traveled in front of them on that three days' journey to seek out a resting place for them . . ." [Numbers 10:33]. The last occurrence of this word in the Torah is in the verse we are presently considering: ". . . who goes before you on your journeys—to scout the place where you are to encamp—in fire by night and in cloud by day, in order to guide you on the route you are to follow" [1:33].

Both these verses use the word *latur* to refer to the presence of God (in the form of the ark) going before the nation to look for a resting place for them. Like bookends, they surround the six verses that refer to the spies looking for an excuse to not go into the land. Thus, their mistake was in not trusting God to do the spying, the looking, for them.

In the second half of verse 33, Moses calls to mind the pillar of fire and the cloud of glory that led the people by night and day, respectively. This is beautifully elaborated in the following *midrash*:

> . . . There were seven clouds—four on their four sides, one above, one below (to cushion their feet), and one before them, which lowered what was high and raised what was low, and killed the serpents and the scorpions, and swept and sprinkled before them. [*Sifrei Bamidbar 10:34*][3]

Taken together with the image from verse 11 of a father carrying his child, Moses presents a beautiful image of the tender love that God has for Israel. The wilderness may have been an unknown entity filled with scary creatures, but God carried them along, surrounding them protectively on all sides by seven clouds.

It is no wonder that God became angry when the people rejected God. How different the story would have been had they not done so. We, too, need to be appreciative of God's protective presence.

Now, more than ever, as we navigate these long, oftentimes lonely days of the COVID-19 pandemic, we, too, need to feel this comforting, protective presence of the *Shechinah*. At the same time, we shouldn't be presumptuous and rely solely on God's protection. Until a vaccine is found, we need to practice the protective measures we have available to us, such as wearing masks and social distancing. When we desire God's protection, we must also do everything in our power to protect ourselves and all those around us. The Torah obligates us to place primary importance on the lives and safety of all human beings.

FOURTH ALIYAH: DEUTERONOMY 1:39–2:1
WEDNESDAY, JULY22, 2020

Turn Around and Go a Different Way

Moses now recounts the disastrous results of the nation not trusting God when the twelve spies came back with their report after scouting out the land. He includes the story of the men who decided, after the fact, after they had already been chastised by Moses, that they would try to go in and take the land at that point. This was even though Moses had warned them not to go into the land because God was no longer with them. The Amorites, who were likened to a swarm of bees, came out and crushed them. Many more lives were lost. The nation was forced to turn back into the wilderness.

A phrase that caught my attention is "turn [around] and go" [1:40]. I knew this phrase sounded familiar, so I did a search. I found that we have already seen this phrase in this week's *parashah*, in the first *aliyah*, when God told the nation that they had stayed too long at Mt. Sinai and needed to move on: "Start out and make your way to the hill country of the Amorites and to all their neighbors in the Arabah, the hill country, the Shephelah, the Negeb, the seacoast, the land of the Canaanites, and the Lebanon, as far as the Great River, the river Euphrates" [1:7].

Here these words were used with such hope, instructing the people to start out on their journey to the promised land. In our verse above, however, they are used to tell the nation to resume their journey, this time away from the promised land. The ironic use of the same exact phrase really brings home to us how incredibly sad this moment was, and how much God was disappointed with the nation. Tigay describes it this way:

> "turn about and march into the wilderness. This command makes God's reversal of [God's] promise palpable: from the border of the promised land the people are sent away from the land, back where they have just come from; their journey 'through the great and terrible wilderness' was for naught. The wording of this command underscores the reversal with irony, for its first three words are identical to those with which the command to proceed to the land in verse 7." [4]

Going backwards in our relationship with God is never something we want to do. Fallible beings that we are, however, it is inevitable that it will happen at one time or another. Some of you may feel that you have walked backwards or gone in circles somewhat during these last five to six months. Times of isolation and depression can easily cause that.

Yet if we remember where this *parashah* began—on the banks of the Jordan River at the border with the land of Canaan—we know that the nation eventually did make their way there. They just needed to take a longer, slower—even circuitous—route to get there. The first time they had been there, they clearly hadn't been ready. In much the same way, if you find yourself going the wrong way, dwell on the idea that perhaps you're not ready to be there yet. You need to take a longer, slower route. You'll get there. Just make sure you continue the journey, for ceasing to try is the one thing that will surely guarantee failure.

FIFTH ALIYAH: DEUTERONOMY 2:2–30
THURSDAY, JULY 23, 2020

This Land is Your Land, This Land is My Land[5]

In this *aliyah*, we read about the beginnings of the journey of the nation through the wilderness. The first place that they will pass through is Seir, where the descendants of Esau live [2:4]. God warns them not to provoke these people because God will not allow them to conquer and/or take any part of this land. The reason, God says, is that God has given this land to the descendants of Esau as a possession [inheritance]. Furthermore, the people of Israel are told that, as they pass through the land, they are to pay for anything they need in the way of food or drink; they are to give the Edomites their due, and not take advantage of them in any way.

At first glance, this seems rather strange to us. The language used sounds very much like the language used to describe the land of Canaan for the people of Israel. God gave them the land and we are not entitled to it. Ramban said, ". . . it would not be right to steal this land from them; the Holy One would be as angry at Israel for stealing it as He would [be] at a nation who stole Israel's land . . ."[6] (The land we are talking about here is the land called Edom, which lay at the southernmost end of the Dead Sea.) Reading further, we find that the nation next came to the area of Moab, just north and east of the land of Edom. God told them not to engage in battle with the Moabites because God would not give them any of their land, either, as God had given it to the sons of Lot [the Moabites] as a possession [inheritance] [2:9]. Once again, the language is very similar to that used to describe the land of Canaan as the inheritance of the Israelites.

Continuing, we read that, after being in the desert for thirty-eight years and having all the fighting men of the generation of the spies die off, we finally approached the area of the Ammonites, again north and east of the land of the Moabites. (These lands, of the Moabites and of the Ammonites, were in part of what is today the country of Jordan.) Once again, God told the Israelites not to harass the people of Ammon since God would not give them the land of the Ammonites because "God has given it to the sons of Ammon as a possession [inheritance]" [2:19]. A third time, the language is very similar to that used regarding the land of Canaan for the people of Israel.

So, what's going on here? Many find this surprising. Weren't we the only ones who had been given a land as an inheritance by God? What is the significance of these three nations? The answer is that these people are all *mishpacha* to us! The Edomites are the descendants of Esau "your brother" [2:4]; Esau, as Jacob's twin brother, was also descended from Isaac, and therefore from Abraham. Though he gave up his birthright to his younger brother, nevertheless he was still a blood relative.

And what about the Moabites and the Ammonites? They are both descended from Lot, albeit through incest but that was because, after the destruction of Sodom and Gemorrah, Lot and his daughters thought that they were the only people left on Earth. Therefore, the two daughters took turns getting their father drunk and then seducing him so that he would impregnate them.

And who was Lot? Abraham's nephew, who had left his country behind to follow his uncle Abraham to an unknown place. His loyalty to his uncle was counted to him as if he were Abraham's own offspring.

Therefore, these three nations, the Edomites, the Moabites, and the Ammonites, are considered descendants of Abraham no less than we, the people of Israel, are. That is the reason that we are not permitted to take any of the land belonging to any of them.

Additionally, Rashi says that, when God was about to give the Torah to the people of Israel, God first offered it to both Esau and Ishmael (Abraham's son by his concubine Hagar). "Even though [God] knew perfectly well they would not accept it, nonetheless [God] extended an offer of peace to them."[7]

So, why mention all of this now? These three nations were already living in the land that God had given to them as an inheritance. The nation of Israel was not yet living in their promised land, all through their own disobedience and faithlessness. Now they were ready to assume their destiny and their strength could be bolstered by the evidence of God's providence of their relatives' lands. If God could provide for these other nations to be able to live in the land that God had given them, how much more so would God be able to bring the nation of Israel safely into the land of promise. They could proceed forward to take the land, confident in the knowledge that God does, indeed, keep promises.

SIXTH ALIYAH: DEUTERONOMY 2:31–3:14
FRIDAY, JULY 24, 2020

Giants and Their Iron Beds

This *aliyah* tells us of the beginning of the conquest of the land. First, we conquered the land of Sihon; all the people were killed and only the animals were taken as booty [2:31-35]. Then we moved on to the territory of Og, King of Bashan, and conquered all his territory, as well [3:1-7]. This is King Og that I wrote about several weeks back. We are told here that he was the last of the Rephaim, an ancient race of giants. We are also told here that his bed was made of iron and measured 9 cubits long by 4 cubits wide [3:11]. (Since a cubit was approximately 1.5 feet, that means that the bed was approximately 13.5 feet by 6 feet.) He was so big that the bed had to be made from iron as wood was not strong enough to hold him. That would have made Og himself approximately 6 or 7 cubits tall (between 9 and 10.5 feet). As if that wasn't fantastical enough, Rashbam says that it wasn't even his bed—it was his cradle from when he was a child—that was described here.[8] Even though he was defeated by the Israelites, we are told that this bed/cradle was kept as an artifact. We read that God told Moses not to fear him because God would deliver him into their hands.

This was a real test. When they originally were frightened away from entering the land from the bad report of the spies, it was because they had been told that there were giants in the land. Now, God presented them with the same challenge, telling them at the same time not to be afraid.

Sometimes we are presented with things or situations that seem like giants to us, things that may be too big to handle. Certainly, many people have been feeling this way during these last several months. As the daily number of people infected with COVID and the number of deaths continue to climb in our country and the world with no end in sight, coupled with the continuing social unrest in our country, it can be easy to feel overwhelmed with despair. The situation of our lives can seem like that big, heavy, imposing iron bed. When we feel this way, we need to remember that God tells us not to be afraid. I know that sounds simplistic, and easier said than done. It is right now, more than any other time, that we need to help each other to not be afraid. We need to be the strength that others need.

God-willing we will make it through this and get to a point where we can live freely in our land again. May it be soon.

SEVENTH ALIYAH: DEUTERONOMY 3:15–22
WRITTEN FOR SHABBAT, SATURDAY, JULY 25, 2020

The Original Pioneers

Here Moses recounts how these lands on the eastern side of the Jordan River were apportioned to the tribes of Gad and Reuven and the half-tribe of Menashe. Then he reminds them that the remaining nine and a half tribes do not yet have possession of the land where they will settle. Though these tribes are settled and comfortable in their lands, the greater part of the nation are not. Moses reminds them that, until all the tribes are settled in the land of Canaan, they are obligated (by their own oath, you may recall) to go and fight with the rest of the nation. Indeed, they are to be the "shock troops" the troops that went in front of the rest of the army [3:15-18]. It is very appropriate, then, that the Hebrew word that is translated here as "shock troops" is *chalutzim*. In modern Hebrew, this word is translated as "pioneers" and was used for the earliest eastern European Jews who came to settle the land that would become the State of Israel. Like the Reubenites and Gadites in their day, the Chalutzim were the first people to settle in the land, preparing it for the next generations.

As we continue in the coming weeks through the book of Devarim, we will be moving ever closer to the promised land, but also to the loss of Moses. His successor, Joshua, has already been designated. Moses tells him to remember all that he has seen when he takes the nation into the land of Canaan. And Moses tells him not to be afraid.

Parashat Vaetchanan

FIRST ALIYAH: DEUTERONOMY 3:23–4:4
SUNDAY, JULY 26, 2020

We Are Still Here

In the beginning of this week's *parashah*, we see that the nation is finally poised to go in and take possession of the land of Canaan, and Moses pleads with God one last time to allow him to go into the land with the people [3:23-25]. Though Moses has been able to convince God to relent when it came to the nation, he is unable to do so for himself. God said to him, *rav-lach*, translated here as "enough!" [3:26]. (This is the singular form of the phrase that we looked at in the previous *parashah*, *rav lachem*, which is probably better translated as "too much." It is the only time in the entire *Tanakh* that this phrase appears in its singular form.) Even Moses, who has led the people now for over forty years and been a trusted confidante of the Divine, has worn out God's patience, much as a child wears out a parent's patience by asking for something again and again despite being told "no." God tells Moses to go to the top of the mountain and look out upon the land in all directions. Then he is to come down and give to Joshua all the instructions he will need as Moses' successor. As a parting blow, God says to Moses that Joshua will allot to the people the land that he, Moses, "may only see" [3:27-28]. Wow! Talk about rubbing it in!

Following this, Moses is about to begin to reiterate all the laws and rules, the *mitzvot*, that he has transmitted to the people over the course of these last forty years. He prefaces that, however, with a strict warning: "You shall not add anything to what I command you or take anything away from it but keep the commandments of the LORD your God that I enjoin upon you" [4:2]. In essence, we are not to change the words of the

Torah that have been given to us. What is meant by adding? Most commentators say it refers to doing more of what God has commanded, such as putting five sets of fringes on our garment instead of four, putting five species in the *lulav* instead of four, putting five biblical passages into the *tefillin* instead of four, etc. Chizkuni says that this is what the people were guilty of doing when they decided to send spies into the land. God told them to go and take possession of the land, and they said that they would do so on condition that they send in spies first.[1]

This does not refer to rabbinic stringencies that were put in place as what we call "a fence around the Torah," such as the expansion of the laws of *kashrut* and *Shabbat* observance. The idea behind these is actually to try to prevent someone from violating the commandments given in the Torah. This is a topic that could be discussed at length, but I will leave that for another time.

On the other hand, we may not detract from the commandments as they are given in the Torah. That is the reason that the evolution of *halachah* is sometimes difficult: we cannot disregard something that is contained in the Torah simply because we are uncomfortable with it. Instead, we must grapple with it (a perfect example of this is Leviticus 18:22, that forbids lying "with a man as with a woman"). Again, a lengthy discussion for another time.

Finally, the first *aliyah* concludes with a verse familiar to many of us from the Shabbat morning Torah service: "you, who held fast to the LORD your God, are all alive today" [4:4]. This verse is the last part of the introduction read by the *gabbai rishon* just before calling up the *cohen* for the first *aliyah*. When Moses said it, he was referring to all the people who stood in front of him, who had survived all the plagues and the difficult years in the desert to get to where they were. When we say it today, we refer to all the people gathered in the synagogue who have the privilege of being able to convene to worship together and listen to the words of the Torah. These words have never felt more poignant to me than the last three weeks, when a small number of us have returned to the sanctuary on *shabbat* morning for a service that was being livestreamed to the rest of the congregation. After being kept away from the sanctuary for four months by a pandemic, it has been very emotional to realize how much we had missed being there.

Heart and Soul

This passage is one long exhortation to the nation to observe all the *mitzvot* that Moses transmitted to them. He tells them that their observance of the *mitzvot* will be evidence to the other nations around of how wise and discerning they are [4:6]. No other nation has such perfect laws or a god who is so close at hand [4:7-8]. They must not forget the *mitzvot* and they must transmit them to their children [4:9]. They heard the voice of God at Mt. Sinai when the Ten Commandments were given [4:10-13]. Since they only heard God's voice but did not see God, they should not be tempted to make any kind of physical image to represent God [4:14-19, 23-24]. God decreed that Moses would not go into the land with the nation [4:21-22]. If they are disobedient, they will be exiled from the land [4:23-28]. If they seek God, God will remember the covenant with them [4:29-31]. No other nation has had a god like ours [4:32-38]. Observing the commandments will assure that things will go well for them in the land [4:40].

One phrase which caught my attention is that we are told to seek God, "with all your heart and with all your soul" [4:29]. This phrase is, of course, familiar to us. In total, it occurs seven times in the Torah, all of them in the book of Devarim, two of them in our *parashah* alone:

> But if you search there for the LORD your God, you will find Him, if
> only you seek Him **with all your heart and soul**—[4:29] [our verse]
> You shall love the LORD your God with all your heart and **with**
> **all your soul and with all your might.** [6:5] [from the sixth *Aliyah*,
> the first paragraph of the Shema]
> And now, O Israel, what does the LORD your God demand of you?
> Only this: to revere the LORD your God, to walk only in His paths,
> to love Him, and to serve the LORD your God **with all your heart**
> **and soul . . .** [10:12]
> The LORD your God commands you this day to observe these laws and
> rules; observe them faithfully **with all your heart and soul.** [26:16]
> . . . and you return to the LORD your God, and you and your
> children heed His command **with all your heart and soul,** just as I
> enjoin upon you this day, [30:2]
> Then the LORD your God will open up your heart and the hearts
> of your offspring to love the LORD your God **with all your heart**
> **and soul,** in order that you may live. [30:6]

...since you will be heeding the LORD your God and keeping
His commandments and laws that are recorded in this book of the
Teaching—once you return to the LORD your God **with all your
heart and soul.** [30:10]

These seven verses express a common theme. The phrase "with all your
heart and all your soul" is applied to the observance of the *mitzvot* in each of
them. So, in that context, what does it mean? What is the difference between
"heart" and "soul?"

"Heart" refers to thoughts and intentions, while "soul" refers to emotions and desires. There are those who have an intellectual relationship with
God, trying to make sense of all the commandments and everything that
they read in the Torah, Talmud, or any of our other holy sources. This person
lacks that emotional part of the relationship with God.

On the other hand, there are those who are so involved emotionally with
God that they question nothing, living in a kind of bubble. They don't put
enough thought into making sense of what God asks of them.

The point is that either one of them without the other is not enough.
Combining the two implies serving God with the totality of one's being, both
intellectual and emotional (i.e., undivided dedication). That balance is not
easy to achieve. But that, after all, is the point. Those of us who vacillate
between the two parts of our relationship with God are being honest with
ourselves and with God. An honest and open communion with God is ever-
changing and something we need to work on for our entire life. It may be
difficult, but it is well worth the effort.

THIRD ALIYAH: DEUTERONOMY 4:41–49
TUESDAY, JULY 28, 2020

This is the Torah

Moses begins here by taking a brief sidetrack to mention once again the
three cities of refuge that were set up on the east side of the Jordan. Remember that these were cities where those guilty of committing unintentional
murder could live and remain safe from the revenge of his/her victim's relatives. Here the cities are named [4:41-43].

Following this, Moses returns to reminding the people that he is about
to reiterate to them all the *mitzvot* that he had previously taught them.
Among these are "the decrees, the laws, and the rules" [41:45]. So, what's

the difference between these three terms? According to Rashi, the decrees are warnings regarding things not to do. The laws are those commandments that have no apparent rationale for them and the rules are the *mitzvot* that have obvious rationales.[2] The point is that all of them originate with God, and, therefore, are equally binding.

This is brought out clearly in verse 44, which is very familiar to all of us: "This is the Teaching [Torah] that Moses set before the Israelites." These are the words that we sing when witnessing *hagbah,* the lifting of the *sefer* Torah whenever it has been read. By singing these words, we acknowledge that this scroll does indeed contain the Torah that was given to us by Moses, at the command of God. And it is the same Torah from which the same *parashah* is read and can be heard in any synagogue in the world on any given week. And it is the same Torah that continues to unite us as a people just as it has for over three thousand years.

FOURTH ALIYAH: DEUTERONOMY 5:1–18
WEDNESDAY, JULY 29, 2020

We Were Slaves

Beginning with verse 6, we have Moses reciting the Ten Commandments for a second time. These are viewed as the foundation for all other commandments. The commandments are essentially broken down into two groups of five each: the first five govern our relationship with God, and most have an explanation of their rationale. The second five govern our relationship with other human beings, and generally do not require any explanation.

The ten are: prohibition of worshipping other gods [5:6-7]; prohibition of making idols [5:8-10]; prohibition of swearing false oaths [5:11]; keeping, observing the sabbath [5:12-15]; honor, fear mother and father [5:16]; prohibition of murder, prohibition of adultery, prohibition of stealing, prohibition of giving false witness [5:17]; prohibition of coveting [5:18]. Though the two lists are essentially the same, there are some differences between the commandments as they are given here and as they appear in the text from the book of Exodus.

So, there are three places where there is extra wording in the Deuteronomy text that is not in the Exodus text: Deuteronomy reminds us that the obligation of Shabbat observance is, "as the LORD your God has commanded you" [5:12]; no such qualifier exists in the Exodus text. The same phenomenon occurs in the commandment to honor father and mother [5:16].

Both texts include the stranger or the servant (slave) in the obligation to refrain from work on the sabbath. Only the Deuteronomy text explains, "so that your male and female slave may rest as you do" [5:14].

In addition, there are three places where the wording is different in the two texts: Exodus tells us to remember the sabbath [20:8], Deuteronomy tells us to observe it [5:12]. Continuing with *Shabbat*, Exodus tells us to remember it in in relation to the six days of creation [20:11], while Deuteronomy relates it to the Exodus from Egypt [5:15]. Finally, regarding the last commandment, Exodus tells us not to covet our neighbor's house or wife (or anything else that belongs to him) [20:14], while Deuteronomy tells us not to covet his wife, or crave anything else that belongs to him [5:18].

The biggest of these differences seems to be in the rationale for *Shabbat* observance. In Exodus, we are told that it is a remembrance of creation and the fact that God rested on the seventh day. Therefore, we emulate God's behavior on that day. In Deuteronomy, we are told that it is to remember that we were slaves in Egypt and God redeemed us from there. This is coupled with the addition in the previous verse about not working on *Shabbat* "so that your male and female slave may rest as you do." Putting aside the question of slavery being morally acceptable in biblical times (I have discussed this before, and biblical slavery was a different situation in many ways than slavery in America), we notice here that Deuteronomy is an advancement, so to speak, over the Exodus text. Observing *shabbat* means that we remember that in Egypt there was no such thing as a day off for us—ever—and, therefore, when we rest on the seventh day, we are to make sure that our slaves have the day to rest, as well. In other words, the Deuteronomy text starts to give us a sensitivity and a conscience. This is a theme we shall see several times going forward in the study of this last book of the Torah.

As we have witnessed, unfortunately, in our own country, suddenly outlawing slavery and stating that it was morally offensive didn't affect a change in the attitudes of many, thereby laying the groundwork for the problems of racism that we still see today. What the Deuteronomy text seems to attempt is to develop a sensitivity to those slaves and their very human needs and feelings. And if that can take place on a societal level, that would be a much more effective path to abolition of the institution of slavery.

But that, of course, is the difference between a democratic society and a religious one.

FIFTH ALIYAH: DEUTERONOMY 5:19–6:3
THURSDAY, JULY 30, 2020

Listening to the Divine

In this *aliyah*, Moses recounts to the nation how frightened they were when they heard the voice of God at Sinai. They only heard the beginning of the Ten Commandments and then were afraid to hear any more for fear that they would die. Instead, they pleaded with Moses to go and receive the Instruction [Torah] from God on their behalf then come back and impart it to them. That is indeed what happened. After meeting with God, Moses came back and began to share with them what he had been told by God, exhorting them to faithfully obey all of God's instructions, imparting them to their children. Faithful observance, he said, would be good for them and their future generations, resulting in long lives in the land of Canaan [5:26].

As I read through these fifteen verses, I was struck by how many times the verb *shema* (to hear, or better, to listen, and sometimes, to obey), is used here: nine times!

- Moses says to the people, "when **you heard**" (the voice of God) [5:20]
- The people say to Moses, "when **we heard**" (the voice of God) [5:21]
- The people say to Moses, "if **we** continue **to hear**" (the voice of God) [5:22]
- The people say to Moses, "what **human being** ever **heard**" (the voice of God) [5:23]
- The people say to Moses, "**you** go and **hear**" (what God says) and the people say to Moses, "**we will do [obey]**" (everything that God says) [5:24]
- Moses says that "**the Lord heard**" (the plea of the people) and God says to Moses, "**I have heard**" (the voice of the people) [5:25]
- Moses exhorts the people to "**obey**" (all of God's instructions) [6:3]

In writing or retelling a story, most authors will try to avoid using the same word too frequently. The fact that this verb comes up so often in this passage cannot be a coincidence. I think that the Torah wishes to show us that real communication is going on here: between Moses and the people, between Moses and God, and between God and the people. They are all speaking to each other. And, more importantly, they are all listening to each other.

Having a relationship, a connection, with God requires open communication with the Divine, listening to hear God's voice and instruction (in whatever form that may take) and communicating our thoughts and feelings to God in return. When we can do that, then it is good for us. God still speaks to us today through the written words of the Torah, and through the words of sages who interpret those words for us.

It is our job to keep the lines of communication open.

All of this, of course, is a natural lead-in to tomorrow's reading, as we shall soon see!

SIXTH ALIYAH: DEUTERONOMY 6:4–25
FRIDAY, JULY 31, 2020

L'Dor VaDor

This *aliyah* contains several sections that are very familiar. Let's start with the first six verses: this is the first paragraph of the Shema; one could arguably say that this is the most well-known passage from the Torah. The Shema has come to be for many the prayer that represents our belief in God, the prayer that symbolizes that we are Jews. This is the prayer that we are to recite twice daily, once in the morning and once in the evening, based on the instructions in the prayer itself. This is the first prayer that most children learn to recite each night at bedtime. Throughout our history, this has also been the prayer that is recited at the moment of death. In short, this is the prayer that symbolizes our faith.

What are the commandments that are contained in these six verses?

- Love the Lord your God with all your heart, soul and might. [6:5]
- Teach them [these words] to your children and recite them twice daily, when you lie down at night, and when you rise up in the morning. [6:7]
- Bind them [these words] on your hand and your forehead. [6:8] This, of course, refers to the *tefilin*.
- Inscribe them [these words] on your doorposts and your gates. [6:9] This, of course, refers to the *mezuzah*.

We must bear in mind that in biblical times, Jewish worship was centralized and communal. In the desert, everyone was required to come to the *mishkan* to offer their sacrifices. Later, when the Temple(s) stood in Jerusalem, this was the place at which all were commanded to appear three times a year to bring their sacrifices. The Second Temple was destroyed in the year 70 CE. Since then, we have been disbursed throughout the globe with no central place to worship. So, what is it that has kept us faithful to God and our heritage for nearly two thousand years with no central place of worship?

The answer, I think, can be found right here in the Shema. The commandments contained in it have forced us to personalize and internalize our observance, bringing it into our psyches and our homes. The commanded recitation of the Shema itself has caused many of us to memorize the words of these verses. The commandment of the *tefilin* causes us to place straps on our arm and forehead containing the words of God; we literally wear the words of God on our bodies. The commandment of the *mezuzah* makes each of our houses into a mini Temple, a place where the *mitzvot* and the traditions are observed.

And what is the reason for all of this? To teach our children. When we sit in a *sukkah* on a chilly fall evening or wave together the four species of the *lulav* or turn our houses upside-down searching for *chametz* before the arrival of *Pesach* or behave like fools on Purim to drown out the name of Haman or do any other of the many things that may seem strange to others, we are told that our children will ask what we are doing [6:20]. This verse is familiar to us from the *Haggadah* and is the question asked by the wise child. The answer is also familiar to us: *avadim hayinu l'pharaoh b'mitzrayim* (we were slaves to Pharaoh in Egypt) [6:21].

The point is that we do all these things to teach our children. When they ask us why we do the things we do, that is our opportunity to explain that God, who redeemed us from slavery in Egypt, asks this of us. We display our love of and faith in God by observing the *mitzvot*. The message we convey to them is that they, too, should become the next generation of Jews who are faithful and loyal to God. And we hope that they, in turn, will do the same for their children. This is how we Jews have survived for thousands of years and will continue to survive long into the future.

SEVENTH ALIYAH: DEUTERONOMY 7:1–11
WRITTEN FOR SATURDAY, SHABBAT, AUGUST 1, 2020

To Know God is to Love God

In this last section of the *parashah*, Moses issues some final warnings to the people: when they enter the land, they are not to intermarry with the people there whom they will dispossess and they are to destroy all their altars and idols. The concern is for the negative influence that they could potentially have on the people of Israel.

Moses goes on to explain the reason for God having chosen them to be God's special treasure among the nations: it was not because they were a large and mighty nation. On the contrary, they were the smallest of nations [7:7]. No, Moses says, plain and simple, God chose Israel because God loved them [7:8]. Therefore, one last time, Moses reminds them (and us) to observe all the Instruction [Torah], laws and rules that he transmitted to them. These are, after all, the things that we know God wants us to do. Even in a human relationship, when you love someone, your desire is to please them by doing things that they want you to do. How much more so should we desire to please our God?

This relationship of mutual love between us and God is described most beautifully in the two verses that I recite, just like everyone else, each morning as I wind the strap of my hand *tefilin* around my fingers: "And I will betroth you forever: I will betroth you with righteousness and justice, And with goodness and mercy, And I will betroth you with faithfulness; Then you shall know the LORD" [Hosea 2:20-21].

If you are (or ever were) married, think back to the excitement of the time you and your spouse first became engaged. It was most likely a happy and exciting time, filled with anticipation. That is the kind of feeling that is expressed about God each morning when donning *tefilin*. In Hebrew, when we use the word *yodea* (to know) when referencing a person, it does not mean "know" in the sense of "being acquainted with." Rather, it refers to a relationship of intimacy. When the last part of this passage from Hosea says that you will know God, therefore, it is describing an intimate relationship with the Divine.

May we all be privileged to experience this special covenantal bond of love that God has with the people whom God has chosen.

Parashat Ekev

FIRST ALIYAH: DEUTERONOMY 7:12–8:10
SUNDAY, AUGUST 2, 2020

Showing Gratitude

In this first *aliyah* of *parashat* Ekev, Moses continues to exhort the nation to observe all the commandments while listing all the blessings that God will bestow on them for being faithful to the covenant. Among these will be fertility for both them and their flocks, abundance of yield from their crops and vineyards, lack of sickness and disease (oh, if only we could have that today!), and deliverance from all their enemies. Again, he reminds them that all the idols and altars of the people that they will displace are to be destroyed.

Moses continues by reminding the people of all the ways that God has cared for them during their forty-year trek through the wilderness: providing sustenance in the form of manna, miraculously preventing their clothing from wearing out (some even say that the children's clothes inexplicably grew along with them!), and preventing their feet from swelling.

There are two specific verses that caught my attention in this reading. The first explains the justification for the manna. [8:3] Moses says that "man does not live by bread alone, but by everything that goes out from the mouth of the Lord." (Many people think that Jesus was the originator of this statement, but this clearly shows that he was merely quoting the Torah when he said it.) So, what was Moses trying to say? God provided the people with manna so that they would not be consumed by worry about where their food would come from. Instead, they were to put their efforts into learning and understanding the Instruction [Torah] that they had received from God and committing themselves to observing it. This, in turn, was also intended to foster an appreciation for everything that God had done/was doing for them, and to instill in them a sense of gratitude (which, we saw, had often been lacking during their desert wanderings, when there were multiple incidents of ingratitude and complaining). The last verse of the reading [3:10] instructs them (and us), "when you have eaten and are satisfied, give thanks [bless] to the Lord your God for the good land which [God] has given you." It is from this verse that we derive the commandment to recite *birkat hamazon,* the grace after meals. Whenever we have eaten, we are obligated to express our gratitude to the One who is the source of all sustenance. At the same time, we are also commanded by the verse to offer thanks to God for the land. According to Ramban, "You must thank God at all times, both for having eaten your fill and for the land that [God] gave you as an eternal possession."[1] He goes on to say that we are obligated to do this no matter where we might be, whether we are living in the land of Israel or in the Diaspora. Even if we are not living in the land, it is nevertheless the eternal inheritance of all Jews.

Many of us have developed during these last six months or so a deeper appreciation for the blessings that we have; for food on the table, for our homes and our families, and hopefully, our health. If you are fortunate enough to not have been directly affected by COVID-19, then that fact, especially, is worthy of your gratitude.

On the other hand, for some of us it is difficult to feel grateful when we are going through such trying times. We can't experience the freedom we had last year; we are unable to move about and go anywhere we want or do whatever we want; we should be wearing masks and we must self-distance. Many of us long for human physical contact. Just a simple hug would mean so much. Many are dealing with financial hardship such as loss of a job and worrying about potential loss of housing.

And that is why it is so important for us all to reach out and support each other, now more than ever.

SECOND ALIYAH: DEUTERONOMY 8:11–9:3
MONDAY, AUGUST 3, 2020

The Path Less Taken

In the previous reading, we read about all the blessings which God had promised to give to the people of Israel if they would be faithful to the covenant and the observance of the *mitzvot* once they had crossed over into the land of Canaan: wealth, prosperity, progeny, health, victory over their enemies. In today's reading, Moses cautions them that human nature being what it is, they might be tempted in the future to think that they had achieved all of this on their own, to forget about God and all that God had done for them in Egypt and in the wilderness. Moses goes on to warn the people that if in the future they will forget God and be tempted to worship the pagan gods of the other nations around them, there will be consequences and they, too, will perish [8:19-20].

This is a lesson that, I think, many of us have come to realize in the last six months or so. Many of us led comfortable lives, some more so than others. Good jobs, nice homes, happy families. Many of us may have neglected the spiritual part of our lives, wrapped up in the hustle and bustle of our hectic lives of work and family responsibilities.

And then COVID-19 arrived. The great equalizer. It does not distinguish between the wealthy and the poor, those who live in big fancy houses and those who are homeless, those who have good family lives and those who don't. We are all equally vulnerable. The lives of all of us have been affected by it.

We can react to this situation in one of two ways: either by turning towards God for support, acknowledging our hurt and our need, or turning away from God, putting the blame for our plight and the plight of the world on God, using it as justification for rejecting God.

The problem with the second option is that it is a very lonely choice. Freedom means that we can reject God. We should not, however, be surprised if God, in turn, rejects us.

The first option is difficult for some of us. When things become difficult, we may feel so defeated that we are unable to trust God and we find ourselves unable to allow ourselves to be vulnerable. It's scary and it hurts. But, in the end, it is so much better than a life lived without a connection to the Divine. Having a spiritual connection to God requires effort on our parts that will be equally met from the other side.

The choice is yours. Which way have you responded to the hardships of the pandemic? And which way will you respond going forward?

THIRD ALIYAH DEUTERONOMY 9:4–29
TUESDAY, AUGUST 4, 2020

Saving the Broken Shards

In this *aliyah*, Moses retells the story of the giving of the (first set) of the tablets containing the Ten Commandments. After the people said that they were afraid to hear God's voice anymore, Moses went up to the top of Mt. Sinai to meet with God. He remained up there communing with God for forty days and nights, eating and drinking nothing. At the end of that time, God gave him the tablets containing the words of the Ten Commandments; Moses describes them as having been "inscribed by the finger of God" [9:10]. What a precious gift to receive! These tablets represented the covenant that God had forged with the nation of Israel. Rashi notes that, in the Hebrew, the word for tablets, *luchot*, is here spelled without a letter *vav* that is indicative of a feminine plural noun. Therefore, he says, the word is not obviously plural. According to Rashi, that is to indicate that both tablets were equally important.[2] Now, remember that the first five contained commandments regarding our relationship to God, and the second five contained commandments regarding our relationship to our fellow human beings. Thus, we cannot have one of those relationships without the other as each of them influences and infuses the other.

Of course, we know that, while Moses was on the mountain, the people grew impatient waiting for his return and ended up convincing Aaron to build them a golden calf to represent God, a clear violation of the commandments that God had just given. We learn from today's text that they were doing this at the exact time that Moses was receiving those precious tablets. At God's urging, Moses descended the mountain to see what the people were doing. Upon seeing them worshipping the calf, Moses became so enraged that he destroyed those precious tablets. The word *va-ashlichem* (I threw them) is also misspelled [9:17]; there is a missing letter *yud*, which has a numerical value of ten in gematria. The Baal HaTurim says that the absence of this letter here is to indicate that the letters of the Ten Commandments flew away off the tablets when they broke.[3] This is supported by the Talmud, which says, ". . . The tablets were broken, and the letters are flying and returning to their point of origin" [BT Pesachim 87B:22].

The letters flew back up to heaven to the One who had inscribed them on the stone in the first place, leaving nothing but shards of shattered stone. The people had shown themselves to be unfaithful to God, with Whom they had just entered a covenant relationship. They had broken their end of the relationship and Moses brought that home to them in a very real way by smashing the tablets before their eyes.

Moses prostrated himself before God, fasting for another forty days and nights, interceding for the people, pleading with God not to break off the relationship entirely. He implored God to honor the covenant, not because the people deserved it, but to honor the promises that God had made to their ancestors, Abraham, Isaac, and Jacob [9:26-27].

And what became of those broken shards of stone that for a few brief moments had held so much promise, so much beauty, so much holiness? Though they longer had any letters on them, they still retained some holiness due to their original designation as holy. Every single little piece had to be gathered up and collected. These, we learn, were placed in the ark and carried along with the nation as they traveled through the desert. You may remember from the book of Leviticus that there was a second ark that went out ahead of the people when they were traveling and sought out a place to stop. This ark, it is believed, contained those broken shards.

In this way, the nation was always reminded of the grave error that they had made in worshipping the golden calf; presumably, this would prevent them from repeating a similar mistake.

More than that, I think those shards were a reminder that, though they had committed this tremendous sin, God had in the end forgiven them and renewed the covenant.

So, what message can this have for us today? I would ask you: what broken shards do you have in your life? Do you carry them with you? And what have you learned from them?

FOURTH ALIYAH: DEUTERONOMY 10:1–11
WEDNESDAY, AUGUST 5, 2020

One Ark or Two?

In this *aliyah*, Moses recounts the story of the second set of tablets. After Moses had interceded for the nation with God for a second forty-day and forty-night period, we see that God relented in God's plan to destroy the nation. God was ready to reconcile with the people and give them a second chance in the form of a second set of tablets. There were a couple of differences this time, though. The first time around, God presented the tablets to Moses as a completed project. This time, God told Moses that he, Moses, was to carve the set of tablets, and carry them up to the mountain with him [10:1] where God would then inscribe them with the words of the Ten Commandments, just like the first set.

Additionally, before Moses set out on his ascent up the mountain, he was instructed by God to build an ark of wood where the new tablets would be deposited when he returned [10:3]. This ark had to have been constructed before the building of the *mishkan*, which had not yet been built before this point in the story. Therefore, it was different from the ark that had the gold cover and the two cherubim perched on the top. It is from here that we derive the tradition of the two arks. This ark was a plain wooden ark. When Moses returned with the second set of tablets, they were placed in this ark, along with the broken fragments of the first set. Both sets remained there together until the construction of the *mishkan* was completed, along with that gold ark. Once that ark was completed, this second set of tablets was placed in it, and it remained inside the tabernacle in the holy of holies. That was the ark that was carried by the Levites when the Israelite camp was in motion. The broken fragments of the first set of tablets, however, remained inside this simple wooden ark. This was the ark that went before the nation when they traveled, searching for a new resting place.

The first set of tablets was given to us as a completed object, a gift from God. This second set came about as a collaborative effort between man and God: Moses carved the tablets and carried them up the mountain, and God inscribed them. No doubt, both Moses and the people had much more that they personally invested in these tablets. They played a part in the creation of the nation.

This is much more representative of an ideal relationship with God. We should present to God the blank tablets of our heart, allowing God to inscribe on them the *mitzvot,* the Instruction—the Torah—which defines the parameters of that relationship. We should open the lines of communication with God and allow God to teach us what God desires from us. At the same time, we need to uphold—as Moses literally did—our part of the agreement. And we also need to find a safe place inside our hearts to protect that relationship.

And all of this while keeping a watchful eye on those broken fragments of the first set of tablets, reminding ourselves of what can happen if we let the tablets drop.

FIFTH ALIYAH: DEUTERONOMY 10:12–11:9
THURSDAY, AUGUST 6, 2020

What Does God Ask of Us?

This *aliyah* begins with a question. Moses asks the people, "What does the Lord your God require of you?" Then he immediately goes on to answer his own question: "only" this—revere God, walk in God's ways, love God, and serve God with all your heart and soul, and keep God's commandments [10:12-13]. But here is the most important part of this statement: all of this is for your [own] good. How many of us can remember those words being spoken to us by a parent at some point? In a moment of semi-omnipotence, a mother or father told us that they knew better than we did what actions would be beneficial and which would be harmful. In much the same way, the

Ramban points out in reference to this verse that God is not demanding something of us that God needs, indeed God doesn't really need anything from us. Rather, he says, God demands these things from us because we need to do them.[4] Being in a positive, open relationship with God is good for us—psychologically, emotionally, spiritually. Moses points out the blessings we will receive/have received from God because of this unique partnership with the Divine. This relationship needs to be initiated and cultivated by us, and Moses promises that God will respond in kind.

Moses continues by reminding the people of all that God has done for them, all the miracles that they personally witnessed with their own eyes: the exponential growth of the seventy people who initially went into Egypt to a nation of over 600,000 fighting men (approximately 2,000,000 people altogether), the plagues brought about in Egypt, the parting of the Red Sea, the manna, and the water in the wilderness. An appreciation of these things alone should inspire them to observe the *mitzvot*.

One more phrase that struck me is *v'shamarta mi'shmarto* (*keep* [God's] charge) [11:1]. A better translation of this phrase, again according to Ramban, is "protect what [God] protects."[5] God protects the poor, the widow, the orphan, the stranger. We, in turn, must do the same. Being committed to God means being committed to those things that are important to God. It means becoming an advocate for those who are unable to protect themselves.

For us as Jews today, in these times of great social upheaval, this is a responsibility that we dare not shirk.

What is important to God must also be important to us.

SIXTH ALIYAH: DEUTERONOMY 11:10–21
FRIDAY, AUGUST 7, 2020

Hear, O Israel . . .

Most of this reading comprises the second paragraph of the Shema [11:13-21]. You may recall that the sixth reading of last week's *parashah*, Vaetchanan, contained the first paragraph. Last week, I wrote about that section at length. It allowed for the observance of Judaism to move from the communal to the personal level.

Let's compare these two passages. Clearly, they have a lot in common:

• In the first paragraph, we are told to love God with all of our
heart, soul, and might [6:5]. In the second, we are told to

serve God with our heart and soul [11:13]. The first paragraph is written to *you*, second person singular, the second to *you*, second person plural.

- Both paragraphs tell us to teach our children, and to recite these words at home and away, when we lie down and when we get up. [6:7, 11:19]
- Both paragraphs tell us to bind the words as a sign on the hand and a symbol on the forehead. [6:8, 11:18]
- In both paragraphs, we are told to inscribe God's words on the doorposts of our houses and on our gates. [6:9, 11:19]

The difference is that the second paragraph is longer, with an additional section in the middle, and another one at the end. The middle section promises what God will do if the people are obedient: God will provide rain that will in turn provide for sustenance for the people and their cattle. Conversely, if they forget God, all these things will be denied to them. The end section explains that their obedience to God and the obedience of future generations will assure that they will be able to live and remain in the land of Canaan.

The first paragraph gives us a series of commandments designed to keep us ever mindful of the presence of God in our lives. The second paragraph reiterates all of that and tells us both what the reward for obedience will be and what the penalty for disobedience will be.

I am reminded of this famous verse from the book of Exodus: "Then he took the record of the covenant and read it aloud to the people. And they said, 'All that the LORD has spoken we will [hear and we will] do!'" [24:7]. It seems counterintuitive to us, but observing the commandments comes before understanding and understanding comes with doing.

Additionally, we have the idea that the commandments are written to the individual in the first paragraph and to the nation in the second paragraph. We must first each accept the yoke of the *mitzvot* individually, but then we must also acknowledge the fact that we are obligated to the *mitzvot* because we are a part of the nation of Israel. And we are obligated to recite these words twice daily, to always remember who we are and what God asks of us.

What Would God Do?

In this short final reading, Moses reiterates once again all the blessings that God will bestow on the nation if they will faithfully observe the Instruction [Torah] that God has commanded. This is defined as loving God and walking in all [God's] ways [11:22]. Rashi explains that this means emulating God, doing as God does: "As [God] is compassionate, so must you be compassionate; as [God] does acts of kindness, so must you do acts of kindness."[6]

In the book of Genesis, we are told that human beings are created "in the image of God." That means that we have the capacity to do good as God's emissaries in the world. So, when faced with an opportunity to effect some positive change, ask yourself, "What would God do?"

Parashat Re'eh

It's Your Choice

The first word of this *parashah*, *re'eh*, is a verb in the imperative form: see. An interesting choice of words. Moses doesn't say to the people, "look," which would make more sense. Instead, he says, "see." In other words, the people are being told to really take notice of what he is about to tell them: they will be blessed if they obey God's commandments, cursed if they do not. Additionally, as is pointed out by Ibn Ezra, this verb is in the second person singular imperative form; thus, it is directed at each one of us individually.[1] Each of us is to see the choice that lies before us, between obedience and disobedience, between blessing and curse. Each of us makes our own choice. This first verse contains one more important word: today. The choice to obey or not is a choice that we make anew every day as we face new situations and challenges.

Continuing in the reading, Moses cautions the people not to worship the gods of the people with whom they come into contact, instructing them to tear down their altars and wipe out any physical reminders of them, "obliterating their name from that place" [12:3]. Immediately following this, Moses says, "Do not worship the Lord your God in like manner" [12:4]. Putting these two verses together, Rashi says that the implication is that we are not to obliterate God's name in the way that we eliminate the names of the idols.[2] So, it is from here that we derive the idea that we are not to erase God's name. Therefore, to avoid erasing it, we do not write God's name in the first place. We also do not throw away any pages or books on which God's name is written, we bury them. Many people have the custom of taking this to an extreme, writing "G-d" instead of "God." Technically speaking, the name that is referred to here is *yud-hey-vav-hey*, the Hebrew name of the deity, which we do not pronounce. This is the name which we do avoid writing, printing it instead as 'ה.

Putting these two ideas together, we make a choice each day: choosing to obey the *mitzvot* means choosing to not erase God from our lives, to not obliterate the bond that we have with the Divine.

SECOND ALIYAH: DEUTERONOMY 12:11–28
MONDAY, AUGUST 10, 2020

Right Makes Might

In this *aliyah,* Moses begins by reminding the people that their sacrifices can only be made in one place, the central place of worship: the tabernacle (*mishkan*) in the wilderness, and later the Temple(s) in Jerusalem. The sacrifices could only be made by the priests, the *cohenim*. For many people, these were opportunities to have large family feasts; slaughtering an animal, after all, produced a large quantity of meat, all of which needed to be consumed in a short amount of time. This meant that for many these were also the only opportunities to eat meat [12:11-14, 17-18, 27].

Moses goes on, however, to remind the people that, should they desire to eat meat, they may do so [12:15-16, 20-25]. It is imperative, however, that the animal be properly slaughtered, and, above all, that the blood be poured out on the ground and never consumed. In this way, we should always remain cognizant of the fact that life is not in our hands but, rather, God is the ultimate source of all life. The blood represents the life, the *nefesh,* the soul. Indeed, we are told that the blood is the life [the soul] [12:23]. We have no claim on that.

Finally, Moses exhorts the people: "Be careful to heed [keep and obey] all these commandments that I enjoin upon you; thus, it will go well with you and with your descendants after you forever, for you will be doing what is good and right in the sight of the LORD your God" [12:28].

In this verse. the word *shamor* (guard or keep) represents, according to Rashi, retaining the commandments through careful study of them; internalizing them so as not to forget them.[3] This will make it much more likely that you will not, indeed, disobey them.

This, for me, emphasizes the great importance of personal study. For as long as I have been a Jew (and even before), study has been a high priority for me. Understanding our sacred texts and teachings bolsters my faith like nothing else can.

And that is also why I love teaching so much. It is the reason I began this Torah study series back in March. It is my hope and prayer that those of you who have been studying with me have been inspired to ask questions and to study further on your own. There is so much to learn.

THIRD ALIYAH: DEUTERONOMY 12:29–13:19
TUESDAY, AUGUST 11, 2020

Searching for Answers

This is another section in which the verb *shema* (hear, listen, or obey) is a dominant theme, appearing in one form or another six times in twenty-two verses. In general, the passage deals with three different scenarios in which one might be enticed to investigate, follow, or worship other gods:

- When a false prophet arises, who seems to be validated by some sign, and attempts to entice you to worship another god. [13:2-6]
  - Here we are told not to listen to this false prophet, but rather to listen to God alone.

- When a family member or friend proposes worshipping another god. [13:7-12]
  - We are told not to listen to him; and when all Israel hears about his punishment (stoning), they will know not to be drawn away by such people.

- When someone has convinced an entire town among you to follow another god. [13:13-18]
  - If you hear of it, you are to doom the town to destruction.

Worshipping other gods is clearly something not to be taken lightly. It is the very first thing that we were warned about in the Ten Commandments. Finally, Moses gives the antidote to all three situations described above: "You shall heed [listen to, obey] the Lord your God, obeying all of [God's] commandments that I command you today, doing what is right in the sight of the Lord your God" [13:19].

This ties in closely with yesterday's section. The antidote to being enticed to follow other gods is to be educated about what our God desires of us.

Over the years, I have been challenged many times by doubters or questioners (particularly young people) about why we should follow the beliefs and practices of Judaism as opposed to any other religion. I invariably challenge them in return: before you reject Judaism, know what you are rejecting. There is so much beauty to be found in our tradition. If you haven't found it, you haven't looked hard enough yet. We all have questions and sometimes doubts; the solution to this situation, however, isn't to just walk away. Rather, it is to look for answers, to wrestle with the traditions, to study the texts.

I believe that if someone embarks on such a quest with a truly open mind, (s)he will not find it so easy to abandon his/her faith. Doing what is right in the sight of the Lord isn't always easy but, in the end, it is spiritually satisfying and worth the effort.

FOURTH ALIYAH: DEUTERONOMY 14:1–21
WEDNESDAY, AUGUST 12, 2020

About that Chicken Parmesan . . .

After a short reminder that we are not to make any gashes on ourselves when mourning a death [14:1], the balance of this reading is devoted to the laws of *kashrut*. Here, in a much more concise form than we had in Leviticus, is a description and listing of all the animals which we are or are not permitted to eat:

- animals that have split hooves and chew their cud may be eaten, including ox, sheep, goat, deer, gazelle, roebuck, wild goat, ibex, antelope, mountain sheep. [14:4-6]
- animals that have split hooves but don't chew their cud (pig) or animals that chew their cud but don't have split hooves (camel, hare, daman) may not be eaten. [14:7-8]
- animals in the water must have both fins and scales for us to be able to eat them. [14:9-10]
- all "clean" birds can be eaten. [14:11] (This term is not defined. Presumably, a clean bird is one that does not appear on the next list.)
- the following birds are forbidden for consumption: eagle, vulture, black vulture, kite, falcon, buzzard, raven, ostrich, night

hawk, seagull, hawk, great owl, little owl, white owl, pelican, bustard, cormorant, stork, heron, hoopoe, and bat. [14:12–18]
- among insects, anything that is winged and swarming is forbidden. [14:19]
- clean winged creatures (again, this term is not specifically defined) may be eaten. [14:20]
- anything that has died a natural death is forbidden [14:21]. This is because an animal must be properly slaughtered and have its blood drained before it can be consumed.

All of this was covered, although in a little more detail, in the text in Leviticus. The list of birds is essentially the same but there are a couple of slight differences.

There is one major difference between this text and the one in Leviticus, and it comes literally at the very end of the section: "You shall not boil a kid in its mother's milk" [14:21]. It is from this verse that the rabbis derived the mandate of separation of meat and milk products. This commandment does not appear in the text in Leviticus. It does, however, appear twice in the book of Exodus [23:19, 24:36].

These two verses in Exodus appear in the context of the laws regarding the festival holidays (*Pesach*, Shavuot, Sukkot). Therefore, some scholars believe that this was something that actually was practiced by some of the other nations as part of pagan fertility rites. The rationale for this prohibition is humanitarian: milking a new mother and using that milk as a liquid in which to boil her own kid shows grave insensitivity to animal life. And that is, of course, just a step away from insensitivity to human life.

Probably no statement in the Torah has been more discussed and debated by scholars and lay people than this one. Some sages say that the commandment is very specific, applying only to exactly what it says: forbidding a kid (i.e., a goat) to be boiled in its own mother's milk. Some even say that only the animal itself is forbidden to us, not the milk.

Then, of course, there is the question about birds. Since they do not produce milk, many people ask why this restriction even applies to them. Why can't we eat chicken parmesan? Indeed, even in the Talmud, there is evidence that some communities did not apply this to birds:

In the locale of Rabbi Yosei HaGelili, they would eat poultry meat in milk, as Rabbi Yosei HaGelili held that the prohibition of meat in milk does not include poultry. The Gemara relates: Levi happened to come to the house of Yosef the hunter. They served him the head of a peacock [*tavsa*] in milk and he did not eat. When Levi came before Rabbi Yehuda HaNasi, the latter said to him: Why did you not excommunicate these people who eat poultry in milk, contrary to the decree of the Sages? Levi said to him: It was in the locale of Rabbi Yehuda ben Beteira, and I said: Perhaps he taught them that the *halakha* is in accordance with the opinion of Rabbi Yosei HaGelili, who permits the eating of poultry meat in milk. Given the possibility that their rabbi rules that it is permitted, I cannot come and prohibit it, and I certainly cannot excommunicate them for it. [*BT Shabbat 130A:9–10*]

What I find amazing about this story is the respect shown by Rabbi Levi. While he himself refrained from eating the poultry in the milk, he did not reprove the people of that town for doing so. Not only that, but he also recognized that another sage, Rabbi Yosei HaGelili, held that this practice was acceptable and therefore did not publicly disagree with him or criticize his followers.

I don't know of any *kashruth*-observant Jews today who eat poultry with milk. However, there are arguments in the kosher world all the time. Which *hecksher* is acceptable? Who is the rabbi who supervises a product or a restaurant? Does one observe *chalav Israel* or not? Is it *glatt* kosher or not? And so on. In today's Jewish world, there is probably no other issue (except possibly *Shabbat* observance) that has proven to be more divisive for the Jewish people. Perhaps we all could learn a lesson from Rabbi Levi.

FIFTH ALIYAH: DEUTERONOMY 14:22–29
THURSDAY, AUGUST 13, 2020

Nine for Me, One for You

Moses now turns his attention to the tithes. We previously read about these in Leviticus: ten percent of one's crops belonged to God. Verse 22 contains the phrase "every year" but the phrase literally says, "year [by] year." In other words, each year the tithe must be taken from that year's produce and could not come from anything left over from a previous year. The reason for this is that the tithe was designed to cause us to appreciate God and to recognize that God alone is the ultimate source of all our sustenance.

So, what was one supposed to do with this amount that was tithed? It was brought to the place that God would choose to place his name (Jerusalem) and consumed there, along with the firstborn from the flock, which were to be sacrificed there. Everyone had a big feast! This was designed to cause us to "revere the Lord your God forever" [14:23].

And what if God's blessing of your crops had been so great that the ten percent was an amount too large and unwieldy to carry all the way to Jerusalem? We learn that the produce could be sold and the currency received for it was to be carried to Jerusalem. There it was to be converted back into sustenance—anything your heart desired to add to the feast, including "wine or other intoxicant" [14:25-26]. This was truly meant to be a festive occasion, causing us to rejoice with God. However, it only took place in years one, two, four, and five of every seven-year cycle.

In the third and sixth years, one was still obligated to gather his tithe. However, instead of bringing it to Jerusalem, it was to be made available in the area where one lived for the Levites, who had no inheritance but were supported by the rest of the nation, and for the poor in the community (the stranger, the orphan, and the widow) [14:27-29].

In this way, the tithe was both an opportunity to enjoy the bounty with which one was blessed by God, and an opportunity to share one's bounty with others who had not been as fortunate as oneself—and both were mandated by God. The lesson is still important for us to learn today— especially today.

SIXTH ALIYAH: DEUTERONOMY 15:1–18
FRIDAY, AUGUST 14, 2020

Reparations

The first major idea addressed in this passage is the topic of the needy in our midst [15:4-11]. Moses begins this section by saying that there will be no poor among the nation because God will greatly bless the nation. But this will be the case only if the people are careful to listen to God's voice and observe all the commandments. Recognizing human nature for what it is, Moses goes on to instruct the people what they are to do if they do encounter a poor person in their midst: you shall open your hand wide to him and lend him what he needs. This reminds me of a *drash* that I gave many years ago at the annual Interfaith service that takes place on Thanksgiving Eve in my community. The theme of the evening was: "enough." The Hebrew word for "enough" is *dai*. If we reverse the two letters of this word, we get the word *yad* (hand). So, when we feel that we have "enough" that God has blessed us then that is the time that we turn our hand over and open it up wide to offer to our less fortunate neighbors whatever they need. This is not to be done grudgingly; rather, if we do it without hesitation, Moses tells us that God will bless us. Though this section began with the idea that God desires that there be no poor among us, it finishes with this statement: "The poor will never cease out of the land" [15:11]. This is then followed by what is now stated as a commandment: "you shall [surely] open your hand wide to your brother, your poor and to your needy in your land." Ideally, God wishes that we would be motivated to do this on our own. However, if there is not enough intrinsic motivation, God has turned it into an obligation. The overriding concern is that the needs of the poor be met.

The second major idea addressed in this section is the freeing of slaves [15:12-18]. You may remember that back in the book of Leviticus we read about how a Jew who fell upon hard times could become a slave to a fellow Israelite. At the same time, we learned about the *schmitah* year, the last year in every seven-year cycle when all debts were canceled and all slaves were set free. Two very important verses here are 13 and 14: "when you set him free, do not let him go empty handed. Furnish him out of the flock, threshing floor and vat, with which the Lord has blessed you." Furthermore, the last verse says that we should not view this as a hardship because for six years he has given you double the value of a hired man (since you didn't have to pay him).

For six years, you have been the beneficiary of his labors. Therefore, you may not just grant him his freedom and tell him to go. You must provide him with the wherewithal to be able to live on his own and support his family with dignity. In other words, you are to provide him with reparations. You owe him that.

How different our country would be today if our American forefathers had followed this Torah law when slavery was abolished. Many people today still believe that it is not too late, that we owe reparations to the members of the black community who are descended from slaves.

Whether you feel this is an appropriate action or not, we all need to be concerned about the racial unrest in our country today. It is important that we all ask what we can do to be part of the solution instead of the problem. If we all can honestly answer that question, and then act on it, then perhaps there is some hope for the future of America.

You *Will* Be Happy

Endings and beginnings—which do we celebrate? Many of us gather on December 31 to celebrate the secular New Year. We mark the end of the year that is passing and look with hope to the clean slate of the year that is dawning, having no idea what the coming twelve months will bring. Where were you this past New Year's Eve? Many of us looked forward to the coming year with excitement, making a big deal out of its redundant number, and listening to memes of Barbara Walters reciting her iconic line, "I'm Barbara Walters, and *this* is 2020!" Now having lived through the first eight and a half months, we wonder what we were thinking. Between a pandemic, an economic crisis, social unrest, a tropical storm, a confrontational election—this year can't end soon enough!

This *parashah* finishes with Moses giving a shortened, abbreviated discussion of the cycle of holidays of the year. He naturally begins with *Pesach*, which takes place in the month of Aviv, the first month of the year [16:1-8]. He reviews the laws of the Passover sacrifice and the prohibition of eating leavened bread. Next, he goes on to talk about the Feast of Weeks (Shavuot) [16:9-12] that takes place exactly seven weeks after the beginning of *Pesach*. He mentions the obligation to bring a freewill offering to God. Finally, he mentions the Feast of Booths (Succot) [16:13-15]. He talks about keeping a feast to the Lord for seven days. Finally, Moses finishes up with a general statement about these three festival holidays (*chagim*) [16:16-17]. These are the three times each year when every male is required to appear before God in Jerusalem, and they are not permitted to arrive empty handed and must bring an offering of thanks for all that God has given.

Regarding both Shavuot and Succot, we are commanded to rejoice before the Lord. So, the first question that we might ask is, "why only on these two? Why are we not commanded to rejoice on *Pesach*?" I have some theories, but I'll let you contemplate and see what you think. Another question we might ask is, "how can we be commanded to rejoice? Can an emotion be mandated?" The answer to this question is that we are to celebrate the holidays with gratitude for God's gifts to us and in recognition of what has already happened, not in anticipation of the unknown that lies ahead.

Verse 15, which is the end of the description of Succot, contains this unusual phrase: *v'hayita ach sameach"* often translated as "you shall surely rejoice." In our text above, the translation is "you shall have nothing but joy." The literal translation of the phrase is, "you will be [very] happy."

As Rashi points out, this is not really a commandment but is more a statement, a promise.[4]

Succot marks the end of the cycle of festival holidays, but it occurs only about halfway through the calendar year. So, the end of one annual cycle of holidays is completely separated from the beginning of the next, making each cycle an entity unto itself. The text here tells us that when we reach the end of the cycle, we will be happy because we will have an appreciation of all the blessings that we have received from God.

This year, our celebration of the fall holidays will, no doubt, be much more subdued than we are used to. Nevertheless, we all should take the time to look back over the cycle of holidays that we have marked during 2020 beginning with our small, Zoomed Passover seders celebrated in a strange new reality brought about by a pandemic. Instead of seeing our friends and family members face to face, we saw them on our computer screens, which had a prominent place at the seder table. Succot being essentially an outdoor holiday may bring a different type of celebration. If your *succah* is big enough for social distancing, perhaps you will be able to celebrate with a small group of people face to face.

More importantly, instead of dwelling on all the inconveniences and sadness and loneliness of these past months, ask yourself what blessings you have received from God this year that you never could have received in any other "normal" year? Did you have time to slow down? Did you do things that you don't normally have time for? See and talk to people that you don't communicate with often enough, even if it was by Zoom or Skype or Facetime? If you haven't yet been able to do so, try to develop an appreciation for any good things that may have come your way. If you can do that, then *v'hayita ach sameach*, you will be happy. And, heaven knows, we all could use some happiness this year.

Parashat Shoftim

FIRST ALIYAH: DEUTERONOMY 16:18–17:13
SUNDAY, AUGUST 16, 2020

Justice, Justice Shall You Pursue

Parashat Shoftim begins with Moses talking about setting up a judicial system; the first two words are here translated as "magistrates and officials." In other texts, they are often translated as "judges and officers." In either case, the former were the people responsible for rendering judgements, and the latter were responsible for making sure that the decisions were carried out. Moses instructs that these officials should be set up everywhere. Moreover, justice must be pure and correct and the judges must not show any impartiality or take any bribes [16:18-19].

The first sin to be rooted out in the land is idolatry. Any person found and proven guilty of this sin is to be brought out to the gates of the city and stoned by the rest of the people [16:21, 22, 17:2-5].

Next, we read about a very important judicial rule in Israel: for a crime whose penalty is death, a person can only be found guilty if there are two or three corroborating witnesses, not on the word of one witness alone [17:6]. This certainly makes a lot of sense as it prevents anyone who holds a grudge against another person from falsely accusing them. Additionally, a tremendous responsibility was put upon those who would testify against their fellow. They had to be totally united, in agreement on their testimony. So, how do we know that one couldn't try to exert undue influence on the other to support his testimony? We read that the witnesses together had to be the first ones to stone the convicted individual [17:7]! Bearing testimony carried with it the responsibility of being an executioner. This would, no doubt, cause anyone to think twice before falsely accusing another person.

One of the things I noticed about this entire passage (except for the very last verse, 13) is that all the verbs of Moses' instructions here are in the second person singular. Though these judicial instructions were a charge to the entire nation, every individual needed to internalize them and realize that each one is responsible for assuring that we live in a just society, as defined by the covenant and commandments that God has given us.

A very famous phrase comes from this Torah reading: "Justice [only] justice shall you pursue" [16:20]. (Some translations include the word only, some do not.) Looking at the Hebrew, we can clearly see that the first two words of this phrase are identical. This has led to much discussion over the course of many centuries: since no word in the Torah is viewed as superfluous, what is the meaning of this repeated word? Several answers have been suggested:

- Ibn Ezra said that it means that justice should be pursued whether it brings profit or loss; or that justice should be pursued time after time.[1]
- Ramban said that it means that each individual should pursue justice, and also go where the judges are superior.[1]
- Jeffrey Tigay says that it means "justice alone, justice and only justice."[2]
- Resh Lakish said that it means we should be deliberate and careful in judgment, not rushing into a decision.[3]
- Rambam said that it means that we should consult with others and receive as many opinions as possible before rendering a decision.[4]
- Some say that it shows that justice is the responsibility of each of us, not just the judges.
- Some say that it indicates the need for compromise when two claims are in direct contradiction to each other.
- Some say that it comes to tell us that justice extends to non-Jews as well as Jews.

All these ideas have merit. I suggest that it is connected to those two or three witnesses who, though they are individuals, must be united in their rendering of judgment.

I also think that people spend so much time worrying about explaining the repetition of the word "justice" that they don't pay attention to the third word in this phrase, "you shall pursue." We are instructed to literally chase after justice, to ensure that we live in a just and non-biased society. This becomes even more incumbent upon us when we see justice being denied to others. We don't have the right to just sit back and be complacent, or to say, "Why bother? Nothing's going to change. I'm just one person." Remember that everything in this section is written in the singular and thus directed at the individual.

God speaks to each of us as a member of the Jewish people and of society as a whole: Justice, justice shall you pursue.

SECOND ALIYAH: DEUTERONOMY 17:14–20
MONDAY, AUGUST 17, 2020

Choosing the Leader of the Nation

In this very short (but timely) section, we learn something about choosing a political leader. Moses tells the people that when they enter the land and live there, they will have a desire to have a king, just like all the other nations around. The stories of the kings of Israel are recorded in the next part of the Tanakh, the Prophets (*Neviim*). The history recorded here shows that God was not happy about the people's desire to have a king; God alone was supposed to rule over them. We see in our reading for today that God made a concession to the people: they could have a king, but God would lay out the ground rules:

- God would choose the candidate, who would come from the nation of Israel; he could not be a stranger. [17:15]

- He was not to acquire a large number of horses. He could have only what he would need for military purposes, but none for his own personal wealth. He was not to go back to Egypt to acquire these horses (Egypt was apparently a large exporter of horses). He was not to be dependent on Egypt for anything. [17:16]

- He was not to have many wives as this would be distracting both from his duties as a monarch as well as from God's teachings. Nor was he to amass large amounts of silver and gold but only what was needed to support the army and his personal needs but not personal excesses. This would keep him from imposing heavy taxes on the nation. [17:17]

- He was to have his own personal copy of the Torah written for him, and this was to be always with him. He was to study it,

learn the commandments of God, and observe them. [17:18]
This was perhaps the most important requirement.

• He was not to become haughty, feeling that he was better than
  his fellow Israelites, whom he was to treat as brothers and
  equals. He was to recognize that he had been chosen to be their
  leader, but not their master. [17:20]

Thus, we see that the king was to be humble before God, recognizing Who is the true Sovereign of Israel, and by whose authority he sat on the throne. He was not to be a power grabber of any kind, ruling rather for the benefit of all the people. He was obligated to observe the same laws put forth by God for the nation and he was not above the law. Indeed, he always had to be conscious of this. The most precious thing he had at all times was his own personal scroll of the Torah, which was meant to keep him grounded.

All of this, of course, sounds so very different and distant from what we witness in our country today. This week is the Democratic Convention, next week will be the Republican. No matter which party you belong to, there is no denying that the political mudslinging that we are subjected to every day is a far cry from the Torah's ideal for a national leader.

Nevertheless, we do have to make a choice. The very fabric of our nation depends on it. So, ask yourself which candidate represents for you that moral high ground, the candidate who feels like he is a member of the nation, not its master. Which candidate will lead the nation with the needs of us all foremost in his mind? Which candidate will not be carried away with his power, but will rather use his power for the good of the nation?

Unlike the people of ancient Israel, we do have a say in who our president will be. And it is the responsibility of each of us to cast our vote on Election Day.

THIRD ALIYAH: DEUTERONOMY 18:1–5
TUESDAY, AUGUST 18, 2020

Supporting Those Who Support Us

This short *aliyah* talks about the members of the tribe of Levi, the priests and Levites who are responsible for the religious life of the nation. After the king, this is the next most important leadership group. They are, as Ibn Ezra points out, the ones who will teach the Torah to the king (as well as the rest of the people).[5]

We are reminded that the Levites have no territorial inheritance. They would, after all, have no time for farming as their job was to be involved in the sacrifices and worship in the *mishkan*, and later the Temple. Since they serve the entire nation, the responsibility for their maintenance falls on all the remaining tribes. We are to provide for all their basic needs: food (the choicest parts of every sacrificed animal; grain, wine, and oil) and clothing (wool from the sheep). We (and they) are told that their portion is the Lord [18:4]. Therefore, when we provide for their needs, it is as if we are giving these things as an offering to God.

Today, of course, the titles of *Cohen* and *Levi* are largely ceremonial since the Temple is no longer standing. How, then, can we observe this *mitzvah* today, fulfilling our responsibility of supporting the Levites? Today, we support our local synagogues as they are the modern replacements for the Temple.

Unfortunately, the synagogue is a very different entity today than it was back in January before the pandemic shut down our world. Who knows if it will ever be the same as it was before the arrival of COVID-19? In many ways, the American synagogue has been changed forever. New ways are being explored all the time to meet all our religious needs. This is truly a challenging time for our clergy and our lay leaders; they need our support as much as we need theirs.

The synagogue needs our financial support now more than it ever has, but it also needs our contributions in other ways. About five months ago, Rabbi Aaron Benson, my own congregational rabbi, asked me if I had any ideas what I would like to do to contribute to the spiritual life of the congregation during the time of lockdown; I suggested doing a daily Torah study. That is how this writing endeavor was born. It has been a challenge for me, and a lot of work has been required to maintain this, but a number of people have told me how much they are enjoying it as well as how much they are learning. Additionally, my own personal learning has expanded dramatically through this endeavor.

The synagogue emails have also become much longer lately, packed full of offerings and activities for just about every interest. Many members of the synagogue community are stepping up to the plate.

Our congregations provide for our spiritual needs, making sure that, just like the Levites in the Temple, we each can say "the Lord is my portion." They need and deserve our support now more than ever.

FOURTH ALIYAH: DEUTERONOMY 18:6–13
WEDNESDAY, AUGUST 19, 2020

A Lesson from Marty McFly

This short section cautions us about the things practiced by other nations that God finds abhorrent. All forms of worship that involve child sacrifice, all forms of divination, magic, necromancy (consulting the dead), astrology, casting spells, and all ways of trying to know/predict the future are forbidden.

The Torah does not say that the reason we should not consult with these types of people is that they are all charlatans and deceivers (many are, apparently, legitimately doing the things that they claim to be doing). Rather, though most of us wish we could know the future, we need to accept that these answers lie in the hands of heaven. God created the world and set everything in motion according to the natural order. When we try to ascertain knowledge of the future, we try to exercise power over God's creation, to say that we are more powerful than God. And what would we do if we knew what was going to happen in the future? Attempt to change it? Much as we might think so, that's not our decision to make. Even Marty McFly found that, when he inadvertently went back to the future and changed it, the consequences for his parents and subsequently for his own future were disastrous.[6]

God desires for us to rely just on God to make our way in this world. Sometimes we are given information about the future through the words of prophets (although not so much today anymore). Most often, it comes down to accepting our fate by having faith in the divine order of the world.

All of this is summed up in the last verse: "You must be wholehearted with the Lord your God" [8:13]. Rashi says that this means that, instead of trying to ascertain the future, we should wholeheartedly accept whatever comes our way.[7] Rashbam says we are to address our inquiries to God, not to the dead.[7] Ramban says that we are to worship God with unblemished integrity.[7] Ibn Ezra says that if we wish to know about the future, we should address our inquiries only to God.[7]

The Baal HaTurim says that the word *tamim* (pure, wholehearted) in this last verse is customarily written in the *sefer* Torah with the first letter, the *tav*, enlarged.[8] He explains that this indicates that anyone who can be wholehearted with God will be considered to have fulfilled the entire Torah from from*aleph* to *tav*, from beginning to end. This doesn't come easily and is something to be worked on every day.

May we all strive to be wholehearted with our God.

HINDSIGHT IS 2020

Prophets True and False

The first part of this reading [18:14-22] addresses the role of a prophet. Like the king, the prophet will come from "your brothers," the people of Israel. Moses begins by reminding the people of what they said at Horeb (Mt. Sinai): after hearing the beginning of the Ten Commandments, the people became frightened and told Moses to go in their place. They were afraid to hear the voice of God anymore, lest they die. God's response to this, as transmitted to Moses, was that they had spoken well. To that end, God would send a prophet to take the place of Moses, who was soon going to die. God would speak to the people through this prophet whom God would appoint. God would put God's own words into this prophet whom God had appointed, and instructed that everyone was to heed the words of such a prophet. God promised to hold accountable anyone who did not heed the words of one of God's prophets.

Tigay points out that this last statement places the prophet as the highest human authority, higher even than the king, about whom no such promise is made.[9]

All of this is followed by a discussion of how to tell a true prophet from a false prophet (basically, if he speaks in the name of God, and what he prophesies comes to pass, then he is a true prophet), and what should be done to one who is revealed to be a false prophet. If he presumes to speak falsely in the name of God, he will suffer the penalty of death for trying to mislead the people of Israel.

So, what does all this mean for us today, when we generally do not have prophets in our midst? The "prophets" whom we encounter today are, more often than not, of the false variety. I know this from personal experience. Those who try to pervert the words of the Torah, those who try to mix the words of the Torah with the words of Jesus—many of them would use their charisma to entice us to follow them. Trust me, the results of choosing to do so can only be disastrous.

Today, we need to put our trust and faith in the words of our sages and Torah scholars who have preceded us. Should we just accept something blindly even though we have some difficulty agreeing with it? Not at all! Being Jewish sometimes means wrestling and struggling with ideas with which we are uncomfortable. It means asking those difficult questions. Sometimes it is very difficult to deal with these kinds of issues. But we should not reject the teachings of our heritage, nor abandon the Jewish people. Any person or movement that would try to convince us otherwise is not to be given any credence.

We must remain steadfast to our Jewish heritage. "If the prophet speaks in the name of the LORD and the oracle does not come true, that oracle was not spoken by the Lord; the prophet has uttered it presumptuously: do not stand in dread of him."

SIXTH ALIYAH: DEUTERONOMY 19:14–20:9
FRIDAY, AUGUST 21, 2020

Do Not Be Afraid

In this reading, we learn some of the rules of warfare by which the nation is told they must abide. The magistrates (the *shotrim* from the first verse of the *parashah*) address several types of men who are exempt from going into battle [20:5-9]:

- One who has just built a new house but not yet had a chance to dedicate it (with a huge celebratory feast as was customary).
- One who has planted a vineyard but not yet been able to harvest it. This would not be until the vines are four years old, as harvesting fruit and grapes was prohibited for the first three years.
- One who has betrothed a bride but not yet been able to marry her.

In each case, the individual has important unfinished business on his mind. He would be worried that he would be killed in battle and therefore would not be able to complete his task (dedicate his house, harvest his vineyard, marry his wife) and that someone else would [be required to] complete the task for him, benefiting from his untimely demise. Abarbanel comments that each of these individuals will be prevented from fulfilling a *mitzvah*: the first from building a parapet on his roof (we will read about this in next week's *parashah*, Ki Teitzei), the second from being able to bring his first fruits as an offering to God, and the third from procreating (the first commandment given to men, be fruitful and multiply).[10]

In any event, the belief was that any of these three types of individuals would be so distracted by worrying about his predicament that he would be a danger to himself and other fighting men in the battle. So, these rules about exempting some fighting men from battle had both a practical and a humanitarian rationale.

But the magistrates continue: anyone who is afraid or disheartened should also return home so that his lack of courage should not influence others to be afraid, as well. Again, this makes perfect sense as a fearful soldier is a liability, not an asset. This law, too, is given two rationales: R. Yose the Galilean says that this refers to a person who knows he has committed some sin and is therefore afraid that he will fall in battle as punishment for his sins.[10] Rashi elaborates on this, saying that, because the previous three categories of exemptions have already been stated, anyone who saw a man returning from the battle would assume that he fell into one of those three categories. They would not presume that he was a sinner and thus, even the sinner is spared the embarrassment of having to disclose his state.[10] But carrying that guilt internally could prove to be unbearable on his conscience. On the other hand, Rabbi Akiva says that perhaps this person is genuinely afraid of warfare and such a person does not belong on the battlefield.[10] But Ramban explains that such a person is also, indeed, a sinner![10] You might ask how this can be. For that, I would direct you back to the beginning of the speech of the magistrates [20:1-4].

Here, the magistrates tell the people that they should not be afraid of an enemy that they face in battle because God marches with them. So, therefore, one who is afraid to go into battle is one who would deny the power of God to walk with them into battle.

And yet, the one who is afraid is allowed to go home.

What message does this have for us today? Let's look at verse 3: How does the magistrate gain the attention of the people? With the words "Hear, O Israel!" The very same words that we have previously been commanded to recite twice daily, the words that have come to embody our faith, these are the words with which we are addressed before going into battle. And we are reminded that it is the Lord your God who walks with you to do battle with you against your enemies, to bring you victory.

What are the enemies we face today? That would cause us to be afraid? The enemy of an uncertain future, dominated by the specter of COVID-19? The uncertainty of the future of our country? The uncertainty of employment or safe housing? There is much that would cause us to be afraid today.

There are those who would challenge our allegiance to our God and to the Jewish people. But this passage comes to remind us that the daily recitation of the *Shema*, the prayer that calls us to unite in our allegiance to our God, keeps us grounded. It reminds us that God is there to walk with us, and to strengthen us. And, as difficult as it might be, it reminds us that we should not be afraid. Rather, we should turn to God, twice daily in the recitation of the *Shema*, and not be afraid.

Easier said than done, you say. I know, I say, I know.

Let us venture to move forward, put our faith and trust in God who walks with us, and to not be afraid.

SEVENTH ALIYAH: DEUTERONOMY 20:10–21:9
WRITTEN FOR SHABBAT, SATURDAY, AUGUST 22, 2020

Respect for Society's Castoffs

At the end of today's reading, we read the unusual ritual of the unidentified corpse that is found lying in the open, somewhere in between major cities [21:1-9]. Representatives of the three closest towns come out to measure the distance between the corpse and the cities to see which one is actually the closest. The elders of that town are then to take a heifer and break its neck. The priests come forward and wash their hands over the heifer (symbolic of washing themselves of the guilt of this crime) and declare, "our hands did not shed this blood, nor did our eyes see it done." They go on to ask God to absolve them of the guilt of this crime (the murder of this individual).

What is up with this? What is going on?

According to Bekhor Shor, "the entire complicated procedure is meant to demonstrate what a fuss the Holy One makes about a single life."[11] This case, if it occurred today, would probably end up in the cold case files: unsolved, unknown, unimportant. This corpse is deprived of both its life and its dignity.

But God has made it clear that the land of Israel cannot tolerate the shedding of innocent blood. This is a theme going back to the first murder recorded in the Torah when Cain murdered his brother Abel, and God said to Cain, "What have you done? The voice of your brother's blood cries out to me from the ground" [Genesis 4:9]. When the land of Israel is forced to absorb the blood of innocents, it is a defilement of the land. If this defilement is allowed to build up, it will force the exile of the people from the land. If the murderer of this individual were known, then his family members would have the right to seek revenge, and this would provide expiation for the shedding of innocent blood. Here, the murderer is unknown, but the assumption is that (s)he comes from the nearest town. By performing this strange ritual, the priests of that town are providing the needed expiation of innocent blood. It is as if they are saying, "If we had done a better job of educating these people about observing the *mitzvot*, then this never would have happened. And if we had done a better job of investigating this murder, then we would be freed of the responsibility of performing this expiation." We as humans may neglect our responsibilities towards the homeless, seemingly important people in our world.

This story shows us that we have a greater responsibility toward them than those whose murderers we can identify. We need to see those whom society rejects and take ownership for being a part of a society that allows injustices like this to happen. And, more importantly, we need to work toward preventing such a situation in the first place—not just the murder, but the plight of the homeless.

Though the message is several thousand years old, it is perhaps more timely today than it has ever been.

Parashat Ki Tetzei

FIRST ALIYAH: DEUTERONOMY 21:10–21
SUNDAY, AUGUST 23, 2020

Mourning for a Lost Life

Parashat Ki Teitzei begins with a discussion of the captive woman who could be taken as a wife. If the nation were to go out to war and emerge victorious, they were permitted to take captives from the survivors. If a man saw a woman among the captives who he found attractive and wanted to marry, he could do so, provided that he followed the prescribed protocol: she was to come and live in his house, trim her hair, cut her nails, and take off the clothing of a captive. He was not permitted to take her outright as his wife. All these physical changes were designed to make her less attractive. This was not supposed to be an impulsive act on his part; if he really wanted to marry her, he would have to wait and give her time. It is very important to note the following: during this initial time in his house, she would undergo a conversion process and without such, he would not be able to marry her. This is an unusual conversion procedure since it was, in a way, coerced, not voluntary. She had to be given time to contemplate her situation and her future. Additionally, the text tells us that she had to be allowed to take a full month to mourn the loss of her father and mother [21:13], whom we naturally assume had died. This is quite possible since the woman arrived in his house as a captive of war. It was, however, possible that they might still be alive and if that were the case, she would then mourn the fact that she would be losing contact with them forever. Therefore, the text tells us that she must be given a full month—the traditional period of mourning—to lament the loss not only of her parents but also of her previous life.

As a Jew by Choice, I took notice of this part of the process. Traditional *halachah* says that a person who converts to Judaism is like a newborn, and that (s)he is to have no contact with their birth relatives. Included in this is the idea that a convert is not supposed to say *kaddish* for non-Jewish birth relatives.

And yet I can tell you how harsh this idea can be. I lost my father very unexpectedly six months after my conversion to Judaism. I knew that I had to be with my mother and siblings for the wake and funeral, but I also knew that these observances, as meaningful as they were to the rest of my family, held no solace or comfort for me. And so it was that I reached out to my rabbi at the time, Rabbi Moshe Edelman, for advice. Recognizing my need to observe the loss of my father with traditional Jewish practice, he pinned the black ribbon of a mourner on me and, doing the requisite tear, told me that after the funeral I should return home and sit *shiva*, saying *kaddish* for the year, and observing the *yahrzeit* in future years. It meant so much to me to be able to mark my father's passing according to appropriate Jewish practice. Twenty-eight years later, when my mother passed away, I did the same thing. The members of the congregation came out at that time to comfort me in my *shiva* period, and I felt tremendously supported by my Jewish community.

Not all Jews by Choice make the decision to mourn their relatives in a traditional Jewish manner, but I know many others besides myself who have. We need to continue to support our converts in this and other ways, recognizing that many have given up quite a bit in terms of their relationships with their birth family. Even when the relationships remain strong, it is next to impossible to not be affected by the differences in mourning practice. Many have the experience of feeling like a fish out of water at a time that is already disorienting by its very nature.

This directive in today's *parashah* underlines this need. This young woman, who has been totally uprooted from family, country, and anything she might have known in her previous life, must be given the month's time to mourn that loss. We can do no less for those who choose to cast their lot with the Jewish people.

One Thing Leads to Another

Abarbanel explains that *parashat* Ki Tetzei is organized in such a way as to show that one *mitzvah* leads to the opportunity to observe another, and, similarly, one sin leads to another.[1] This concept, known as *mitzvah goreret mitzvah, averah goreret averah,* is elaborated on in Pirkei Avot: "Ben Azzai said: Be quick in performing a minor commandment as in the case of a major one, and flee from transgression; For one commandment leads to another commandment, and transgression leads to another transgression; For the reward for performing a commandment is another commandment and the reward for committing a transgression is a transgression" [Pirkei Avot 4:2].

This teaching describes a way of training the heart and the conscience. The more we observe the commandments, the more we will be inclined to do so and the converse is, of course, also true.

This concept is vividly shown in this short *aliyah*, which includes an explanation of several *mitzvot* in rapid order:

- The body of someone who has been impaled for committing a capital offense must be buried the same day [21:22-23]. Though the person was guilty of a grave offense, we still are commanded to show respect for the dead.

- If you find an animal, a garment, or anything else that belongs to your neighbor, you must do everything possible (short of incurring personal loss) to return it to him or her [22:1-4]. If you have ever lost something valuable and then felt the relief when someone returned it, you know how important this is. We are especially commanded to observe this even—especially—when the item belongs to our enemy.

- Women should not wear men's clothing, nor should men wear women's clothing [22:5]. This is another verse which tends to be controversial if taken out of context and brings up many questions, and is often misunderstood. On a lighter note, we may wonder about drag queens such as RuPaul. A large segment of the entertainment industry revolves around men dressing up as women. Many of them look very beautiful yet we, the audience, all know that they are men underneath all the makeup and clothes. Are they violating this commandment? On a more serious and a contemporary note, today we are much more aware that there are many levels of gender nonconformity. As members of the LGBTQ+ community choose to dress in a manner that is authentically reflective of their true identity, we may wonder if this commandment condemns them for doing so. And what about an actor playing a character of the gender opposite their own? Or someone who dresses up for Purim as a character of a different gender from their own? Or those who criticize me and many other female rabbis and observant women for wearing a *kippah*, a *tallit*, or *tefilin*, telling us that these are a man's garments? According to Rashi, none of the people are violating this commandment. He says that this commandment refers to a woman who dresses like a man specifically so that she will be able to spend time in their company, and, ultimately commit adultery with one or more of them. It also refers to a man who dresses like a woman so that he will be able to spend time with women unnoticed, which could also lead to immorality.[2] In other words, these are people who are crossdressing because they are looking to engage in illicit behavior. Summing up these two cases, Rashi says that "the Torah forbids only the wearing of a garb that leads to abomination (unchastity)."[2] Now, Rashi's comments are also reflective of different societal norms and perspectives, to be sure, but I think the bottom line is this: it is the intention behind the act that we need to be concerned about. If someone dons the garments of a different gender with the intention of deceiving someone for the ultimate purpose of doing them harm in some way, then that is what this verse forbids.

• If you come upon a nest where the mother bird is sitting on either eggs or baby birds, you may not take them all; you may let the mother go and take only the young [22:6-7]. The rationale for this is both practical and humane. Presumably, the only reason you are taking anything from the nest is for food. If you were to take the mother, there is a good chance that the young will not survive, but if you let the mother go, she can have more babies in the future, which is the practical side. Additionally, and perhaps more important, we chase the mother away before taking the eggs or the babies to spare her from seeing her young taken away, which is the humanitarian side.

The first three of these *mitzvot* train an individual to be more sensitive to the needs and feelings of other human beings—perhaps even those whom we normally might not care about so much. The fourth trains us to be sensitive to the needs and feelings of animals.

Mitzvah goreret mitzvah, one *mitzvah* leads to another. As we have entered the month of Elul that leads us up to the celebration of Rosh Hashanah, may we draw close to God by training our hearts to observe more of the commandments, and become more thoughtful about our fellow human beings as well as the animals in our world.

THIRD ALIYAH: DEUTERONOMY 22:8–23:7
TUESDAY, AUGUST 25, 2020

Protecting Ourselves and Others

This *aliyah* continues the idea of *mitzvah goreret mitzvah* (one *mitzvah* leads to another). These are some of the commandments that are defined here:

- You may not mix different kinds of seeds (crops), work animals, clothing fibers. [22:9-11]
- You must put fringes (*tzitzit*) on the four corners of your garment. [22:12]
- A man who falsely accuses his wife of not being a virgin shall be flogged and required to pay a fine to his father-in-law; he is not permitted to divorce her. [22:13-19]
- A woman whose husband accuses her of not being a virgin, and the charges are proven to be true shall be stoned. [22:20-21]
- A man who has sexual relations with another man's wife shall be killed, along with the woman. [22:22]
- A man who has sexual relations with a woman who is betrothed to another man in town shall be stoned along with the woman; if the rape occurs in the field, only the man shall be stoned; if the woman is not betrothed, the man must pay her father the bride price and marry her—and he will never be permitted to divorce her. [22:23-29]
- A man may not marry his father's former wife. [23:1]
- A eunuch, a *mamzer*, an Ammonite or a Moabite may not be a part of Israel. [23:2-5]

Much can be said regarding any one of these. The one that caught my attention (possibly because it seemed like the least controversial) was the one preceding all of these: "When you build a new house, you shall make a parapet for your roof, so that you do not bring bloodguilt on your house if anyone should fall from it" [22:8].

Houses in biblical times had flat roofs that were used for several purposes, including sleeping, drying produce, and socializing. All of this, however, could prove to be very dangerous, and even fatal, as it was obviously very easy to fall off. Therefore, all homeowners were commanded to construct a barrier or low wall called a parapet all along the edges. In this way, the homeowner could not be held liable should someone fall from the roof and be injured or killed. Thus, the parapet served to protect both the homeowner and anyone else who spent time on the roof of his house.

Several of the commentators expand on this idea, saying that a home-owner should remove all such things which could potentially cause harm or death to others: an unstable ladder should be removed, as should a dog which is known to be vicious or to have bitten people before; a pit should be filled in or roped off.

Some have taken this further, saying that we should worry about anything that poses a potential danger to ourselves as much as others. This means that we should refrain from activities such as abusing alcohol or drugs or smoking. Many people might say about such activities, "I'm only hurting myself, it's my business." Of course, we know that that is not true as much has been said about the dangers of second-hand smoke, as well as the emotional and psychological toll on families and friends of those addicted to alcohol or drugs. How often do we read about tragic accidents caused by impaired drivers?

Today, of course, we have a huge controversy raging in this country over the proper etiquette in this time of COVID-19. Wearing masks and social distancing have become flashpoints of disagreement. And yet, as Jews, if we place it in the context of the *mitzvah* of not doing anything that could be potentially harmful to another person, then there should be no question. The mask that you wear is there to protect others from *your* germs, the mask that they wear protects *you* from their germs. Keeping six feet or more apart protects you *both*.

It's all about protecting both ourselves and others from potential danger. This, it would seem, is our present-day parapet—and God commands us to construct it.

My Enemy May Not be My Friend, but I May Not Hate Him

This *aliyah* also continues a list of commandments—*mitzvah goreret mitzvah:*

- When going off to war, the camp must remain holy [23:10-15]: Anyone rendered unclean by a nocturnal emission must leave the camp until evening, when he must immerse himself before returning. There must be a designated place outside the camp for relieving oneself. And all excrement must be covered over with dirt or sand.
- A (non-Jewish) slave who seeks refuge in Israel shall not be returned to his master. [23:16-17]
- There are to be no cult prostitutes in Israel, male or female. [23:8]
- No Israelite is to borrow from his fellow Israelite at interest. [23:20]
- Any vows made to God must be fulfilled [23:22-24].

Again, the very first commandment of the *aliyah* caught my eye: "You shall not abhor an Edomite, for he is your kinsman. You shall not abhor an Egyptian, for you were a stranger in his land" [23:8].

In this verse, there are two nations whom we are instructed not to abhor, but for very different reasons (that is why, I think, there is a letter *samech* separating the two clauses of this verse, which begin with the exact same wording). The Edomites are the descendants of Esau, Jacob's older twin brother, from whom he took the birthright of the firstborn through deception. Esau vowed to kill Jacob, but never followed through on that. Esau had every right to be angry with Jacob yet, many years later when they reunited in the desert as Jacob returned to Canaan with his family and his flocks, they parted peacefully. So, the Edomites are our relatives, descendants of Abraham through Isaac, no less than we are. That is why we are told not to abhor them.

But what about the Egyptians? We know all too well that they were the people who enslaved us for several hundred years; we spend a good deal of time at our *seders* talking about the horrible treatment we suffered at their hands. And the single most repeated commandment in the Torah is to love the stranger because we ourselves were strangers in the land of Egypt. And yet here that is the exact reason given for us to not abhor the Egyptians—because we were strangers in their land. How can that be? We need to remember how we came to be in Egypt in the first place. Our ancestor

Joseph had been made second in command to Pharaoh and was charged with overseeing the gathering and distribution of food during the time of famine. It was because of his merit that Jacob was invited to move to Goshen in Egypt with his entire family to be able to escape the famine. In other words, their actions saved us initially. In addition, many of the Egyptians were very generous to us when we left, bestowing on us gifts of gold and silver. We therefore owe them a debt of gratitude, and therefore we may not abhor them.

This tells us a lot about how we treat our enemies and adversaries. It is human nature to carry grudges, to remember all the horrible things that someone did or said to or about us. This passage teaches us to look beyond all of that to find the positives in the relationship, even if they may be very overshadowed by the negatives, as was certainly the case with the Egyptians.

In our country today, we are strongly divided along political lines and social lines. The question is this: can we look across the aisle to see what we have in common, and then be able to work together for good? Can we support those who are protesting for racial equality while supporting our police officers at the same time? Easier said than done, I know. But this, I believe, is the message of this verse. God calls us to recognize our brothers, and to recognize the humanity in our adversaries.

FIFTH ALIYAH: DEUTERONOMY 23:25–24:4
THURSDAY, AUGUST 27, 2020

Take Only What You Need

The first two verses [23:25-26] of this very short *aliyah* specify what one may take when entering another person's vineyard or field: in the first case, enough grapes to fill oneself up, or, in the second case, as many ears as can be plucked with one's hand. In both cases, there is a strong warning against gluttony: you must not put any grapes into your bag or use a sickle to harvest grain.

All of the commentators agree that these two verses refer to someone who has been hired to work in a vineyard or field at the time of harvest. If everyone were told that they could freely go into their neighbor's vineyard or field and eat their fill or harvest what they could, this would be grossly unfair to the farmer who had planted and tended the crop all summer long.

The situation of the hired workers, on the other hand, is a different story. If they are working in the vineyards and fields and harvesting the crop, it would be difficult and unnatural for them to not taste some of the fruits of their labor. Additionally, the farmer is obligated to provide the hired workers with a meal for the day. They are entitled to take what they need but, again, allowing them to fill up bags and carts to take home more than what they themselves require is not only gluttony, it is tantamount to stealing from the farmer.

So, what lesson can we take from this? I think we can view the world around us as the vineyard/field of God, Who created it all and has placed it into our hands for maintenance and safekeeping. We are the hired laborers working in the vineyard; we are entitled to take what we need. We are not entitled to hoard more than that. Taking our responsibility to tend this vineyard seriously means ensuring that there is enough of the harvest left to sustain all the other workers, as well.

Responsible stewardship of God's vineyard means recognizing that it does not belong to us individually, but rather to us collectively.

SIXTH ALIYAH: DEUTERONOMY 24:5–13
FRIDAY, AUGUST 28, 2020

Preserving Dignity

This is another short *aliyah* that delineates several *mitzvot*. The part that I would like to focus on this time comes from the end of the reading: "When you make a loan of any sort to your countryman, you must not enter his house to seize his pledge. You must remain outside, while the man to whom you made the loan brings the pledge out to you. If he is a needy man, you shall not go to sleep in his pledge; you must [surely] return the pledge to him at sundown, that he may sleep in his cloth and bless you; and it will be to your merit before the LORD your God" [24:10-13].

The situation that is described here involves a poor man who has borrowed something from you but is unable to repay it. You are permitted to take and hold an item of his as collateral until the loan is repaid. But this man is so poor that he has only one item to give as collateral: a garment. The assumption is that it is most likely a garment or blanket that he uses for warmth at night. Since he has an absolute need for this item, you may not keep it at night when he needs it. Therefore, you are required to return it to him every evening before nightfall, and then he will return it to you again in the morning. Many commentators say that the words "you must surely return" indicate that you must continue to collect it and return it to him again and again every day, even if it means that you do this a hundred times or more. Of course, if the item is a daytime garment, then you collect it from him each evening and return it to him every morning.

After doing this multiple times, you might say to yourself, "This is ridiculous. Why should I go out of my way to do this day after day? It's more aggravation than it's worth." Additionally, as pointed out by some of the commentators, if the item is a nighttime garment, and you are gathering it each morning so that it is in your possession during the daytime, you might also say to yourself, "Why am I doing this? What use do I have for this nighttime garment during the daytime?" Conversely, if it is a daytime garment, and you collect it again in the evening so that it is in your possession during the overnight hours, you might ask of what use this garment is to you during the nighttime. The answer, as it says in the last verse, is that he will bless you, and thereby you will gain merit in the eyes of God.

The goal of all of this, it would seem, is to allow the debtor to maintain his dignity. If you were to say to him, "I have no need of your garment. You keep it." Then he becomes a charity case, a ward of the state. On the other hand, by taking his pledge daily, even if it is inconvenient to you, you say to him, "I know that you will pay me someday. You may not have the ability to do so right now, but I know that your intention is to pay me back." This, it seems to me, is a value that many of us have forgotten these days while in the throes of the contentious society in which we find ourselves. Every member of society, no matter how wealthy or poor, deserves to be treated with dignity and respect. Keep in mind that if the winds of change had blown in the opposite direction, then perhaps the situations might have reversed, leaving you as the person who would need to reclaim your garment each day.

SEVENTH ALIYAH: DEUTERONOMY 24:14–25:19
WRITTEN FOR SHABBAT, SATURDAY, AUGUST 29, 2020

Do Not Forget to Remember What Amalek Did (Does) to You

This last *aliyah* of *parashat Ki Teitzei* is also filled with many *mitzvot* dealing with interpersonal relationships. The three verses I would like to concentrate on are the last three: "Remember what Amalek did to you on your journey, after you left Egypt— how, undeterred by fear of God, he surprised you on the march, when you were famished and weary, and cut down all the stragglers in your rear. Therefore, when the LORD your God grants you safety from all your enemies around you, in the land that the LORD your God is giving you as a hereditary portion, you shall blot out the memory of Amalek from under heaven. Do not forget!" [25:17-19].

In contrast to what we were told about the Edomites and Egyptians—that we are not to abhor them—here we are told never to forget what the Amalekites did to us in the wilderness but also to totally blot out the name and memory of Amalek. And what was it that they did? They came upon us by surprise, attacking us from the rear, and attacking the most weak and vulnerable among us, the stragglers in the rear. This is the most cowardly kind of action that an enemy could take in confronting a people.

These three verses are read every year as the maftir reading on *Shabbat Zachor,* which takes its name from the first word, an imperative verb form instructing us to "remember!" This is the shabbat that occurs immediately preceding the holiday of Purim.

Later in the *Tanakh,* in chapter 15 of the book of 1 Samuel, we read the story of Saul, from the tribe of Benjamin, Israel's first king, who defeated the Amalekites in battle. He did not, however, wipe them all out, as he should have done, according to the instructions in these verses from our *parashah;* instead, he kept the Amalekite King Agag alive. Though Agag was killed by Samuel, the *midrash* tells us that one of his sons somehow managed to escape. Generations later, this conflict between Israel and Amalek was played out again with very different results in Shushan, where another member of the tribe of Benjamin, Mordecai, and his cousin Esther, were victorious over Haman the *Agagite,* who had plotted to wipe out all the Jews. This, of course, is the story of Purim. And it is from the verse in our *parashah* that tells us to blot out the name of Amalek forever that we get the custom of making a lot of noise and waving graggers every time that his descendant Haman's name is mentioned as we read the *megillah.*

These three verses will always carry a special significance for me. They are the verses upon which I based by senior sermon during my final year of rabbinical school at the Jewish Theological Seminary.[3] I spoke of how today we all metaphorically became Amalek, both to ourselves and others, causing us to doubt both ourselves and God. Like Amalek, doubt attacks as where we are most vulnerable, sometimes crippling us emotionally and preventing us from moving forward. Just as we drown out the name of Haman from the *megillah* reading, we must also drown out the voices that tear us down whether they come from other people or are just in our own heads. Sometimes easier said than done.

Parashat Ki Tavo

Bringing Our First Fruits to God

Parashat Ki Tavo begins with a description of the first fruits ceremony. Now that the people are preparing to enter the land, they will be required to bring some of the first fruits of every crop to the Temple as an offering to God. The offering is to be brought in a basket that is placed in front of the priest, who puts it down in front of the altar. The prescribed speech that the Israelite recites in this instance should be familiar to you from the Passover seder and it marks the beginning of the *maggid* section of the *Haggadah*, the retelling of the story, starting with our very humble beginning: My father was a wandering Aramean . . . [26:5]. Most commentators say that this refers to Jacob, who ran away from his home in Canaan when his brother Esau wanted to kill him for taking his firstborn blessing by deceit. He headed to the land and home of his uncle Laban, arriving there with basically nothing to his name. He ended up staying there twenty years. During this time, he acquired two wives and twelve children, along with many flocks of sheep and goats. He left Aram greatly enlarged. Though he did return to Canaan, he ultimately had to move his family to Egypt during the famine. He went down to Egypt with meager numbers (seventy people in all), [but] there he became a great and populous nation (approximately 2,000,000 people). The Egyptians dealt harshly with us and oppressed us [26:6]—by throwing the baby boys into the Nile River and making us build the cities of Pithom and Rameses. They imposed heavy labor upon us. The Lord freed us from Egypt by a mighty hand, an outstretched arm and awesome power, and by signs and portents . . . [26:8]. This refers to the ten plagues that God brought upon the Egyptians. He brought us to this place and gave us this land, a land flowing with milk and honey [26:9]. This, of course, refers to Eretz Israel.

Many of us know the adage that one should never forget where (s)he came from. We remember not only our humble beginnings, but also how we got to where we are, and, more importantly, Who it was that was responsible for that happening. This first fruits ceremony was designed to remind the individual that God is the true owner of the land and source of its fertility; we are merely the benefactors.

Every year on *Pesach*, we re-enact this story as we read the *Haggadah*. But we are also reminded daily in our prayers, and in every Shabbat and holiday kiddush, of the fact that God delivered us from Egypt with a mighty hand and an outstretched arm.

Perhaps this lesson is even more important for us to remember in these difficult times. Though things are going well, and our numbers are still low in New York, our lives are still anything but normal. Many of us are dealing with some level of depression stemming from dealing with this pandemic for seven months or more, without a definite end in sight. As difficult as things may be sometimes, we do need to appreciate our freedom and ability to practice our faith. And we need to look to God, the true source of all our blessings, with gratitude for what we have, including (and especially) our health.

SECOND ALIYAH: DEUTERONOMY 26:12–15
MONDAY, AUGUST 31, 2020

Bringing the Poor Tithe

This very short *aliyah* describes the ritual of the poor-tithe. Every three years when an individual had designated the ten percent of his crop as his tithe for the year, instead of bringing it to the Temple and giving it to the priests, he distributed it to all those in his community who had no means of self-support: the Levites, widows, orphans, and strangers. Since the tithe was used for this holy purpose, it was just as important as—or perhaps even more important than—the tithe that was brought to the Temple. The bringing of this tithe was accompanied by this specific declaration, stating that the complete tithe was gathered, that it was not handled incorrectly, and that it was distributed to the poor in the community in fulfillment of God's commandments [26:13-14]. Following the declaration, the individual concluded with a short prayer [26:15] asking for God to bless all the people of Israel and the land, as well. Though the declaration was individual, the prayer is communal, asking for God's blessings for the entire nation. Our prayers are almost always universal in nature: we never ask for blessings for ourselves alone. Rather, we pray on behalf of Jews everywhere, indeed sometimes on behalf of all people, Jew, and non-Jew alike. Most importantly, in this particular case, this would, of course, include asking God's blessings for the very people to whom the tithe had just been distributed. We recognize that in the blink of an eye the situation could be reversed, and we could ourselves become poor and in need of receiving the tithe; and we recognize that we must play our part in helping to bring blessings to their lives.

THIRD ALIYAH: DEUTERONOMY 26:16–19
TUESDAY, SEPTEMBER 1, 2020

We Are God's Treasure

Here we have another very short section. The listing of commandments has concluded; with these four verses, Moses reiterates the nature of the covenantal relationship between the people of Israel and God.

The very first word is *hayom* (today). Moses tells the people that God commands them today, really meaning every day, to observe all the commandments. Rashi says that the message is that "they should always seem as new to you as on the day you were first commanded to observe them."[1] Every day we renew our covenant relationship with God by recommitting ourselves to the observance of the *mitzvot*.

Next, the two sides of the relationship and commitment are unequivocally stated. First, Israel affirms that Adonai is our God, and that therefore they will walk in God's ways, keeping all the *mitzvot* [26:17]. Then, Adonai affirms that the people of Israel have become God's "treasured people" [26:18].

Being in a covenantal relationship with God brings with it all the blessings that God chooses to bestow on us, and all the responsibility of being role models to the rest of the world. Being faithful to the commandments is good for us personally, and good for the world at large.

Blessed are the Peacemakers

In this section, Moses begins to describe an unusual and profound ritual which is to take place when the people cross over the Jordan and enter the land of Canaan. They are to set up large stone pillars on Mt. Ebal. These stones are to be coated with plaster, and then they are to "inscribe [on them] every word of this Teaching most distinctly" [27:8]. Most of the commentators say that the Teaching refers to the Torah: the entire text, from Genesis through Deuteronomy, is to be carved into these stones. "Most directly" means that the text was to be written in all seventy languages of the Earth [at that time]. Ramban says that the text even included the *"tagin,"* the decorative crowns that are placed on some of the letters in the Torah.[2]

The significance of this ceremony is explained in verse 9. It is so important that the people are told, *"Shema Israel"* (Listen up, Israel!). But this time the familiar injunction is preceded by another imperative spoken by Moses and the elders: Quiet! [i.e., Silence!]. What was taking place was so important that no one was to miss a single moment of it. And what was happening? "Today, you have become the people of the Lord your God."

Wait a minute! Didn't that already happen at Sinai thirty-eight years ago? Yes, the process was begun then when the Ten Commandments were given. But thirty-eight years of wandering in the desert have ensued. Thirty-eight years of arguing with God and learning how to trust God. Thirty-eight years of forging a relationship with God. And that process is only completed now that all the final *mitzvot* have been given. Being in a covenant relationship with God means that we are obligated to observe all the *mitzvot*.

Along with these stone pillars, the people are also commanded to construct an altar of stones [27:5-6] on which sacrifices of well-being will be offered. God commands that the stones of this altar are to be unhewn (uncut) and that no iron tool is to be used on them. Why? Mishnah Middot 3:4 explains it this way: "Since iron was created to shorten man's days and the altar was created to prolong man's days, and it is not right therefore that that which shortens should be lifted against that which prolongs."[3]

Iron, since it is used to make weapons, shortens man's days. The altar, since it is used for sacrifice to draw close to God, lengthens man's days. That is the reason that iron tools may not be used to cut the stones.

In *Midrash* Tanchuma, Rabbi Yochanan ben Zakkai explains that the altar is designed to bring peace between the people of Israel and God. This, he says, is the reason that iron, which is used to make weapons of war, may not be used on the stones of the altar. He goes on to say that if these inanimate stones, which neither see nor hear, can affect peace between man and God, how much more so should someone who promotes peace between a man and his wife, or between a man and his fellow man, merit having his days and years prolonged.[4]

The message is clear: God calls us to be peacemakers. With all the turmoil and strife in our country today, between political rivalry, and those protesting for Black Lives Matter and those protesting in support of the police, not to mention mask wearers versus non-mask wearers, there is plenty of strife and division surrounding us. Our goal should be to get people from opposing sides to honestly listen to each other just as the people of Israel were told to listen up to God's instructions. We may not get anyone to change their minds, but if we can get two people with opposing views to respect one another and their views, then that is at least a beginning.

And the best place to start, of course, is with yourself. With whom will you make your peace?

FIFTH ALIYAH: DEUTERONOMY 27:11–28:6
THURSDAY, SEPTEMBER 3, 2020

Blessings and Curses

The description of this strange and dramatic ritual continues. Six of the tribes will stand on Mt. Gerizim when the blessings are pronounced on the nation and the remaining six will stand on Mt. Ebal when the curses are pronounced on the nation. The Levites (those who ministered in the *mishkan,* the men between ages twenty and sixty) stood in the valley between them to pronounce the blessings and the curses. They turned towards Mt. Gerizim when pronouncing the blessings, and towards Mt. Ebal when pronouncing the curses. In this section, twelve curses are pronounced, corresponding to the twelve tribes; after each curse is pronounced, all the people are to say "amen." Each of the first eleven curses addresses a sin that is committed in secret, say the commentators. The twelfth curse is on "he who will not uphold the terms of this Teaching and observe them" [27:26]. Ramban explains that this refers to someone who invalidates one of the commandments, not one who disobeys one of the commandments.[5] In other words, the one who denies the legitimacy of one of the commandments is the person described here. As evidence, he points to the fact that the verse does not say "one who does not do the terms of this Teaching," rather it says, "one who does not uphold the terms of this Teaching." This makes sense. Think about it: if any of us were to be cursed for disobeying any of the commandments, what hope would there possibly be for us? We are all guilty of violating commandments—sometimes daily. If that were the meaning, there would be no hope for any of us. Clearly, disavowing the validity of the commandments is fundamentally a much more serious offense.

We are accustomed to the practice of saying, "amen" [let it be so; I agree with you] every time we hear someone else recite a *brachah*. Indeed, we are supposed to do this. But here we see that we are also to give the same acknowledgment to a curse when we hear it pronounced (on behalf of God).

The reading concludes with four lines of blessings: the people of Israel are told that they will be blessed in the city and the country through their children, and the offspring of their cattle, and their produce, in their basket and their kneading bowl, in their comings and their goings. These blessings are conditional upon obedience to God and to all the Commandments, at least in principle. So, let us all say, "amen."

SIXTH ALIYAH: DEUTERONOMY 28:7–69
FRIDAY, SEPTEMBER 4, 2020

Verses and Verses of Curses Upon Curses

This very long *aliyah* begins with eight verses of blessings. These continue the blessings begun at the very end of the last *aliyah*. This section culminates with the promise that "The LORD will make you the head, not the tail; you will always be at the top and never at the bottom" [28:13]. There is, however, a caveat: Israel will be the recipient of all these blessings only if they maintain observance of all of the commandments, without deviation [28:14].

At this point, a transition takes place. Verse 15 says what will happen if the people are not stringent in their observance of the *mitzvot*: all these curses [that follow] will be brought upon them. The curses take up almost the entire balance of the *aliyah* [28:16-68] in a section referred to as the *tochechah* (warning). (We previously encountered a smaller *tochechah* section in Leviticus 26.) Practically every vile punishment that one can think of is included in these verses. So severe is the *tochechah* that it is traditionally read in an undertone by the Torah reader, and many people are reluctant to assign or to receive this *aliyah*. Here is a listing of some of the horrendous things included in these curses:

- Verses 16-19 completely undo the blessings of verses 3-6 of the last *aliyah*: your offspring, your cattle, your produce shall all be cursed.
- Disease: pestilence (meaning "a virulent epidemic"), consumption (tuberculosis); blight and mildew affecting the crops
- Drought, military disaster, pox, scab, itching, hemorrhoids
- Madness and blindness, loss of sanity, severe inflammation
- Exile, destruction of crops (locusts), children taken into captivity
- Resident aliens will become their creditors
- Another nation will overtake them; that nation will consume their produce and the newborn of their cattle
- They will become cannibalistic, eating their own children
- Plagues and sickness
- They will be reduced in numbers (instead of increased)
- They will be scattered throughout the nations and become despondent

All these horrific things (and more) are described in great detail. These will be the results of disobedience. Clearly, all of this is designed to frighten the people (and us) and deter them (and us) from disobeying the command-ments. As we read through the list, we become traumatized and sickened by the litany of punishments. Eventually, after fifty-three verses of curses (if it weren't so terrifying, it would sound like something out of Dr. Seuss!) we can become numb to the threats and promises. It is almost too much to take in. Could the God who loves us so much and has chosen our nation alone among all the peoples of the Earth as a unique treasure, and forged a cov-enant relationship with us really inflict that amount of punishment on us?

Just when we think we might not be able to take any more, along comes verse 69 to finish out the *aliyah*:

"These are the terms of the covenant which the LORD commanded Moses to conclude with the Israelites in the land of Moab, in addition to the covenant which He had made with them at Horeb."

In this last verse, God reiterates the idea that these are the words of the covenant, the *brit*, that God forged with us. The covenant was begun at Sinai and finished here, forty years later, as the people prepared to enter the land. Could it be that this verse comes to remind not only us, but also Godself about the covenant? For, no matter how bad things may seem, we are still bound to God in an eternal covenantal relationship.

What we see here is a classic example of a phenomenon in the divisions of Torah reading. Indeed, you may be wondering why we had several short (some *very* short) Torah readings in this *parashah*, and here we have one which is sixty-three verses long. The answer is that the custom is to never end a Torah reading on a negative note; we should always be left with a positive thought. Therefore, once the litany of curses began in this chapter, we entered a very negative section. We do not reach a verse that is positive in nature until we get to verse 69.

The message of this is important for us today as we navigate the world of a pandemic, wondering when (if?) we will ever see an end to this. We see from this Torah reading that, indeed, there will be an end, a time to renew our bonds to God. Just like this Torah reading, it may seem like the difficult times are *very* long, and, at times, unbearable. But, just like this Torah reading, there will be an end, a renewal of the covenant. May it be soon.

SEVENTH ALIYAH: DEUTERONOMY 29:1–8
WRITTEN FOR SHABBAT, SATURDAY, SEPTEMBER 5, 2020

Recognizing God's Providence

Once again, we have a very short *aliyah*. Now that all the blessings and curses have been pronounced, Moses gives a *very* abridged version of what happened during the last forty years. He switches back and forth between speaking in the first person and speaking in the third person (on behalf of God).

He reminds the nation of all the wondrous things they saw in Egypt (the plagues), and on the way out of Egypt (the Red Sea, Mt. Sinai) [29:1–2]. But then he continues by saying that they did not have enough understanding or perception to understand the significance of it all. We see that this is so from all their rebellious acts while traveling in the wilderness. Still, God cared for them for these forty years, providing them with food and drink and clothing, and protection from all the nations who tried attacking them. All this so that they would come to know and understand God's love for them.

It is only now, after these forty years, and the vision of hindsight, that they can truly see how God has cared for them. Verses 3 and 4 are explained in the Talmud this way:

> Yet even Moses our teacher, who said this to the Jewish people, did
> not allude to the Jewish people until after forty years that they
> should have stated this request, as it is stated: "And I have led
> you forty years in the wilderness" (Deuteronomy 29:4), which
> shows that Moses was speaking forty years after the revelation at
> Sinai. And at that point it is written: "But the Lord has not given

you a heart to know, and eyes to see, and ears to hear, until this day" [Deuteronomy 29:3]. Rabba said: Conclude from here that a person does not understand the opinion of his teacher until after forty years, as Mosessaid this to the Jewish people only after forty years of learning Torah. [*BT, Avodah Zarah 5B:2*]

During the long period of isolation in the wilderness, the people often complained about their lot; though God provided for all their needs, they couldn't see God's providence or the blessings that were bestowed on them. Now that they were standing finally on the brink of the promised land, at last ready to claim their heritage, only now did they have a mind to understand, eyes to see and ears to hear.

Similarly, we, who are living through a prolonged period of difficulty—for some of us, punctuated by loneliness and isolation like being in a desert—may feel like doing nothing but complaining. Indeed, many of us do *kvetch* a lot. We're becoming really tired of this and can't see an end. It's hard to see God's hand in all of this. "Where is God?" many of us ask.

Unlike the Talmud's statement, I do not think that it will be forty years before we see an end to this (please, God!). Nor do I think it will even be forty months; Forty weeks, probably. But whenever it is, may we all reap the benefit of a new understanding of and appreciation for God's love and care. May we emerge with a new realization of the many blessings we have, and may we move forward in our lives with a deepened faith in both God and each other.

Parashat Nitzavim

NITZAVIM FIRST ALIYAH: DEUTERONOMY 29:9–11
SUNDAY, SEPTEMBER 7, 2020

Hayom, Hayom, Hayom

This very short *aliyah* has some very important lessons to teach us. The word that is the name of the *parashah*, *Nitzavim*, is translated as "you [pl.] stand." It is not the standard word used for standing, however (that word is *omed*). This word is more formal, as in the sense of standing together for presentation. This is an important moment: all the people are presenting themselves to enter the covenant with God. Though the word "all" certainly seems universally inclusive, Moses continues by listing who is included in this group: the leaders, the men, the women, the children, the strangers, the menial workers. Though the people of the nation stand together, the message to each and every one is that acceptance of the covenant is an individual affair; no one can do that for you (i.e., the men must do it for themselves, not through the agency of their leaders; the women must do it for themselves, not through the agency of their husbands; the children must do it for themselves, not through the agency of their parents). Indeed, this message is subtly conveyed in the language of Moses. Though he speaks to the entire assembled nation, he switches from addressing them in the second person plural [29:9] to the second person singular [29:11].

Additionally, the verb used for entering the covenant is *l'avrecha*, from the root *avar* (to cross over). The implication is that committing oneself to this covenantal relationship with God is transformational, moving from one state of being to another.

Finally, we see both at the beginning and the end of this reading the word *hayom* (this day, or today). This means that one should enter the covenant today and recommit oneself to it again every day anew.

This message is as viable today as it was when Moses gathered the nation before him on the banks of the Jordan River. Each of us should begin every day by recommitting ourselves to the covenant with God that connects us together as one people.

SECOND ALIYAH: DEUTERONOMY 29:12–14
SUNDAY, SEPTEMBER 7, 2020

Did I See You at Sinai?

Here we have another very short reading. Continuing to talk to the assembled nation, Moses says on behalf of God that the covenant is being made not with them alone, "but both with those who are standing here with us this day before the LORD our God and with those who are not with us here this day" [29:1]. The question asked by many commentators is this: since we already know that the entire nation was gathered before him, who could he possibly mean when he speaks of "those who are not with us here this day"?

There are two different answers that are frequently given. The first is that it refers to all past and future generations of Jews, as we read in these two sources:

> All the generations which have arisen from the days of old until now stand with thee to-day before the Lord your God, and all the generations which are to arise after us stand also here with us to-day. [*Targum Jerusalem*][1]

> . . . but all the generations which have arisen from the days of old stand with us today before the Lord our God, and all the generations which are to arise unto the end of the world, all of them stand with us here this day. [*Targum Jonathan*][2]

This same idea is expressed in this very beautiful *midrash*:

> You should know that every soul, from Adam to the end of the world, was formed during the six days of creation, and that all of

them were present in the Garden of Eden and at the time of the giving of the Torah, as it is said: With him that standeth here with us this day, and also with him that is not here with us this day. [*Midrash Tanhum Pikudei 3:4*][3]

The other explanation, according to the Bekhor Shor and others, is that these words refer to the souls of all those who would come to join the Jewish people through conversion from that time forward into the future.[4] This interpretation reinforces the idea that Jews by Choice are equal to born Jews in the eyes of God.

The most important point of all of this, according to Jeffrey Tigay is that "the mutual commitments made here by God and Israel are binding for all future generations."[5]

The same covenant that God forged with the generation gathered before Moses is still binding in our generation today.

THIRD ALIYAH: DEUTERONOMY 29:15–28
MONDAY, SEPTEMBER 8, 2020

Seeing Spots

This is the longest *aliyah* of the two *parshiyot* that we are studying this week. A large part of the text consists of a warning: Moses reminds the people of all the idolatry that they have seen in Egypt, and in the surrounding nations since they have left Egypt. Moses warns the people that if any of them thinks in secret that they can go against God and worship the gods of the other nations, that person will be subject to all the curses that were laid out in the book (this is referring to the curses we read about last week in the *tochecha* section of Ki Tavo). And in future generations, everyone who sees this will ask what happened; everyone will know that it was because they rejected God and worshipped idols. They will become an example for many generations into the future.

The verse in this section which is most discussed and commented on is the last one: "Concealed acts concern the LORD our God; but with overt acts, it is for us and our children ever to apply [do] all the provisions of this Teaching" [29:28].

According to most commentators, the "concealed acts" of the first phrase refers to the reasons for the commandments. These, according to the verse, are the concern of God. God alone knows the rationale for each of the commandments. As we have seen over the last few months, there are many *mitzvot* for which we can know the rationale; but there are many others (such as the laws of *Kashrut*) for which we have not yet discerned the meaning. On the other hand, the overt acts of the second phrase of this verse refer to the actual performance of the *mitzvot*. This is our territory, not God's. It is a great partnership that we have: God understands why the *mitzvot* are important and should be observed; but God cannot observe the *mitzvot*.God needs us for that.

The other reason that this verse is discussed and commented on so much is the way that it appears in the Torah: there are dots over the words translated as "for us and our children [for]ever." There are eleven dots in all: three on the first word, seven on the second, and one on the last. There are other places in the Torah where we find these *nekudot,* but this is the only place that has so many of them so close together. There are several theories about their significance. One theory posits that there is some question about the text, that perhaps a mistake was made in copying the words at some point, and then that error became tradition and was continued. Another theory states that the markings indicate that an important ethical lesson is being conveyed by the text. No one knows with certainty the significance of the dots, but it certainly is impossible to ignore them.

As the verse itself tells us, the meaning is part of the things that are concealed from us at the present time by God; nevertheless, we continue the tradition. Indeed, a Torah scroll is considered invalid if these dots are not included. So, we continue to ponder their meaning. Isn't that, after all, what Torah study is all about?

FOURTH ALIYAH: DEUTERONOMY 30:1–6
MONDAY, SEPTEMBER 8, 2020

Mending a Broken Spirit

This *aliyah* talks about people who did in fact abandon their belief in God and were subsequently exiled from the land. During that time, however, they experienced a change of heart and returned to a belief in God. Verse 3 expresses a beautiful statement: "then the LORD your God will restore your fortunes and take you back in love. He will bring you together again from all the peoples where the LORD your God has scattered you."

God will restore your fortunes and take you back in love, no matter where in the world you may have been scattered to. A *midrash* explains that, when Israel goes into exile, the *Shechinah* goes with them. Even though the exile may be the result of sin, God accompanies us into exile, endures our suffering with us, and only returns to the land when we do. The next three verses continue to describe this glorious return: we will return to the land and be more numerous and prosperous than our ancestors. Verse 6 promises that God will open our hearts and the hearts of our children, removing any impediments, allowing us to love God with the devotion of a whole heart. When we have the desire to return to God, God gives us the help we need to be able to do so. Because, just as we desire to be reunited with God, so, too, does God desire to be reunited with us.

Parashat Netzavim is read every year on the Shabbat immediately preceding Rosh Hashanah. The process of return that I have just described is indeed the process of *teshuvah* (repentance) that we are called to observe during these solemn ten days that are coming. Indeed, the five words that I highlighted above are all based on the Hebrew root *shuv* (return), the same one from which we derive the word *teshuvah*.

Additionally, as pointed out by the Baal HaTurim, the first letters of the four-word phrase "your heart and the hearts [of your children]," spell out the word *Elul*, the month that we are in now, leading up to and culminating at Rosh Hashanah, the season of repentance.[6]

When we restore our relationship with God through *teshuvah,* then, according to Gersonides, when this last verse tells us that "the Lord your God will open up your heart," it means that we will finally be able to understand the "hidden things" that are referred to in verse 28, the last verse of the first part of the third *aliyah* (see above).[7]

This year, the High Holidays come with new significance for many of us who feel that our relationships with God have been strained with the events of the past eight months. I know I do. Now, more than ever, we pray to be able to return from the spiritual exile that has been imposed on us by COVID-19. Now, more than ever, we need *teshuvah*, and we also need God's help to repair our broken trust.

FIFTH ALIYAH: DEUTERONOMY 30:7–10
TUESDAY, SEPTEMBER 9, 2020

God is Waiting for You

Once again, in this short reading, Moses reiterates to the nation what will result when they repent of their wrongdoing and return to God: prosperity, fertility, abundant crops, a renewed relationship with God.

We also notice that, of the four verses in this reading, three of them contain a word with the root *shuv* (return). Again, this is the root upon which we base the word *teshuvah* (repentance). In this last week before Rosh Hashanah, the message is clear: God is waiting for us all to repair our broken relationships with the Divine, to seek out that closeness to God. When we do, God promises to take delight in our repentance.

So, you need to ask yourself if you want to return to a close, covenantal relationship with God. If so, what must you do to make it happen? Or are you having difficulty reconnecting with God? Do you feel very far removed from God because of everything you have experienced for the last six to seven months? Again, what must you do to make it happen?

Our reading promises that God is there waiting to accept us back; God wants to reunite with us, and to bestow God's blessings upon us. So, the ball is in your court. What will you do?

SIXTH ALIYAH: DEUTERONOMY 30:11–14
TUESDAY, SEPTEMBER 9, 2020

The Answer is Within Reach

In this short reading, Moses assures the people that the Torah of God is not beyond their reach, it is not beyond their comprehension [30:11], it is not in the heavens [30:12] or beyond the sea [30:13].

This is still true for us today. No matter what level we are at in terms of Torah study, the Torah speaks to us at that level. The Torah is the instruction from God, designed to draw us closer to God. How could it possibly make sense for it to be too difficult for us to comprehend? I believe that Torah study is also fluid. What it says to us today is not what it said to us last year, nor is it what it will say to us a year from now.

The last verse tells us, "No, the thing is very close to you, in your mouth and in your heart, to observe it" [30:14]. Very close to you. Have you ever found yourself looking for something that you misplaced, looking high and low, only to find that it was right under your nose the whole time? The study of Torah is like that. Sometimes you can search high and low to find the answers you need but until you open your eyes and your heart, you won't see the answers that are waiting within it for you, right under your nose.

In your mouth. Torah study often requires recitation for memorization. The Hebrew phrase that says "in your heart" is equivalent to the English phrase "by heart." In your heart. Your heart is what motivates you to keep the commandments of God out of love for God.

All these elements of Torah study come together to effect *teshuvah*. According to the Bekhor Shor, "something that is in the mouth but not the heart is meaningless, and something that is in the heart but does not prompt speech or action is not worth that much."[8]

Torah study can and must lead to action if we wish to bring about a change in our lives.

SEVENTH ALIYAH: DEUTERONOMY 30:15–20
WEDNESDAY, SEPTEMBER 9, 2020

The Choice is Yours

In this final *aliyah* of parashat Nitzavim, Moses sums up everything he has been speaking about to the nation by telling them that they have been given a choice: life and prosperity versus death and adversity [30:15]. The choice of life, with its resulting prosperity, comes from choosing to walk with God and obey God's commandments [30:16]. The choice of death [evil], with its resulting adversity, comes from choosing to worship other gods [30:17].

As Ramban points out, though clearly Moses and God favor one path over the other, we really are free to choose which way to go; neither God nor any human being will prevent us from making either choice.[8]

There is a very important word regarding this choice in the first verse, *hayom* (today, this day). For truly we are given the opportunity to choose anew every day.

I have also written before about the idea that God requires not one, but two, witnesses to any transaction (we have two witnesses sign a ketubah, a get, a conversion). According to verse 19, the witnesses called by God to witness our choice are none other than heaven and Earth! Our choice is witnessed in both our realm and God's realm; all of creation is called to "sign the document." Why? Because both will be involved in enacting the reward or the punishment, depending on our choice.

Verse 19 is the primary verse in this reading, summing up the choice: "I call heaven and Earth to witness against you this day: I have put before you life and death, blessing and curse. Choose life—if you and your offspring would live—"

If you have ever been to the National Holocaust Museum in Washington, D.C., you most likely have seen this verse. The exhibition actually begins on the third floor of the museum, and as you work your way through it, you gradually work your way down to the first floor, where your journey brings you out into the Hall of Remembrance, a large room designed to induce contemplation of all that you have just seen (witnessed) yourself. Engraved above the benches on the right side of the room as you enter is this exact verse. In the context of the Holocaust, the verse takes on an entirely new meaning. This, too, is a message as important today as it ever was.

Choose Life!

Parashat Veyelech

FIRST ALIYAH: DEUTERONOMY 31:1–3
WEDNESDAY, SEPTEMBER 9, 2020

Moses Takes His Leave of the Nation

Moses had now finished his final address to the nation. The people, who were all gathered together to hear his message, had returned to their tribes and their homes. Moses knew that he was about to die, but he cared so much for the people that he "went [walked] and spoke these things to Israel" [31:1]. The commentators say that he literally went and walked among all the tribes and all the people to tell them that he was about to die, and that Joshua would succeed him. He wanted to take his personal leave of them.

The nation numbered about 2,000,000 people—that's a lot of walking! Yet he tells them, "I can no longer be active," literally, "I can no longer go out and come in" [31:2]. Since he prefaced this by saying that he was one hundred twenty years old, we might say that this makes sense. However, that doesn't jive with all of that walking that he did! Indeed, we shall see in *parashat* V'zot haBrachah that he had not lost his strength at all. In fact, God had maintained it, since he surely had needed it to lead the people for forty years in the desert. Instead of saying that he was physically incapable of leading the nation, Rashi says that Moses was telling the people that he was no longer permitted to do anything for them.[1] The time had come to pass the mantle of leadership on to Joshua, who would lead the people across the Jordan and into Canaan.

Ramban says that what Moses was doing here can be compared to someone who wants to take his leave of a friend and goes to the friend to get his/her permission to leave.[2] This makes the moment much more poignant. Despite all the difficulties of leading these people for forty years, the

279

challenges to his authority, the complaining and disobedience, and having to intercede on their behalf with God on multiple occasions—even still, Moses was saddened to leave them. He wanted to go out and meet with them one last time, to speak with them, and to listen to them. He truly cared for them and wanted them to succeed. This is a sign of a true leader.

VAYELECH SECOND ALIYAH: DEUTERONOMY 31:4–6
THURSDAY SEPTEMBER 10

You'll Never Walk Alone[3]

In this short *aliyah*, Moses assures the nation that they will be victorious over the idolatrous nations that they will need to displace once they enter the land. He begins by reminding them of what happened to Sihon and Og, kings of the Amorites, who attacked the Israelites as they approached the promised land. With God's help, the Israelites were not only able to be victorious over them, but also to route them and acquire their land. Moses assures the people that they will be victorious over these nations, as well.

To reassure the nation and bolster their resolve, Moses tells them not to fear because "the Lord your God Himself marches with you." Not behind you, not in front of you, *with* you.

According to Tigay, this kind of promise, that God will be with someone, is often given in the Bible to someone whom God is sending on a mission, especially a military one, as we see here.[4] It is meant as an assurance of God's help and protection. Moses knows this promise well because he first heard it over forty years before when he stood at the burning bush, listening to God charge him with his mission to go to Pharaoh and procure the freedom of the Israelites from Egyptian slavery. Moses asked God, "Who am I, that I should go to Pharaoh, and that I should bring forth the people of Israel out of Egypt?" (Exodus 3:11). God's answer was ". . . I will be with you; that shall be your sign that it was I who sent you. And when you have freed the people from Egypt, you shall worship God at this mountain" [*Exodus 3:12*].

At this point, certainly Moses knows that God has kept that promise to him for well over forty years. Now that he is preparing to take his leave of the people, he tries to give them the same reassurance that God gave to him. We shall see later in the next *aliyah* that Moses makes this same promise to Joshua, his successor: God will be with Joshua no less than God has been with Moses for all these years.

As we continue to navigate the uncertain world around us in this time of pandemic, many of us are in dire need of God's reassurance. We face a formidable enemy, whose strength is truly unknown to us.

"Fear not," God says. "I will be with you." May we all be fortified by the strength of God's presence, helping us to navigate through these long and difficult days.

THIRD ALIYAH: DEUTERONOMY 33:7–9
THURSDAY SEPTEMBER 10

The Torah is a Living Document

Continuing from where we left off, this short *aliyah* begins with Moses' reassurance to Joshua that God will be with him as he assumes the leadership of the nation.

With that, the Teaching (the book of Deuteronomy) was complete. We read that Moses wrote it down and gave it to the priests and Levites, who carried the holy ark [33:3]. This written record was to be placed in the ark alongside the tablets containing the Ten Commandments.

Now, if we stop and think about that for a moment, it means that the entire written Torah was not given at Sinai. Only part of it was. Moses wrote that part down and continued writing over the course of the next forty years as new segments were revealed to him.

Based on the contents of the book, Abarbanel says that before departing from Sinai, Moses wrote down the books of Genesis, Exodus, and Leviticus. From then until now, as new parts of the story occurred and new teaching was revealed, Moses wrote them down.[5] In other words, the rest was written down as it was communicated and revealed to him. That means that whatever we know as written Torah originated as Oral Torah.

Thus, we see that, from the beginning, Torah was a living, changing document, revealed by God not all at once, but rather in installments.

This is no less true today. While the written text of the Torah itself remains unchanged, there is no end to the commentary that has been and is being written all the time. What I am doing with these daily writings—teachings—add to the body of Torah.

May you search and study and find your own sacred Torah to add to that which has existed since Sinai.

FOURTH ALIYAH: DEUTERONOMY 31:10–13
FRIDAY, SEPTEMBER 11, 2020

The Torah Belongs to Us All

Now that the Torah, including this final book of Deuteronomy, has been written down, Moses gives instructions for how the contents are to be shared with all the people. There are two things that need to be remembered here: the vast majority of the population could not read and there were very few copies of the scroll. Therefore, the Torah needed to be transmitted to the people through public readings. That, of course, meant that this was not going to be a frequent occurrence. Thus, when these public readings took place, they were that much more precious to their audience.

To that end, the proper time and place needed to be selected. Moses instructed that in the seventh, or sabbatical, years, at the time of the Feast of Booths (Sukkot) [31:10], everyone—men, women, children, and strangers—was to be gathered at the Temple in Jerusalem [31:12] to hear the public reading, so that they would develop a love for its teachings and the observance of the *mitzvot*.

This was the perfect time: since it was the sabbatical year, they had a lot of leisure time on their hands. Sukkot was the time of the fall harvest, the end of the agricultural year. As such, it was the time that the highest number of people would be in Jerusalem.

There are several important messages here: the words of the Torah belong to everyone; all people—men, women, children, and strangers are obligated to study Torah and learn its teachings; the Torah must be made accessible to everyone; and it should be studied again and again throughout one's lifetime.

Today there is no end to the books of Torah commentary that have been written by scholars for centuries in virtually every part of the world. With the advent of the internet, it has become even easier for just about anyone to access any number of sources for study.

Now, the Torah is studied every Monday, Thursday, and Shabbat morning, as well as every minor and major holiday and every Rosh Chodesh. *That* is formal, public Torah study. A specific time for personal, private Torah study is not mandated; each of us is responsible for making time for ourselves to study. In our normal busy lives, often we find it difficult to find the time. In recent months, with more time on our hands, it has been much easier for many of us to find time for study. For many, like me, Torah study has given strength and solace during the long, isolated days. May we all create the opportunity for meaningful study both now, and in the future, when, God-willing, we will be able to return to a more "normal" lifestyle.

A Peaceful Transfer of Power

Now that Moses is about to die, the mantle of leadership will soon be passed on to Joshua. The people must know that he is God's choice, so both men are summoned by God to the Tent of Meeting, the *mishkan;* this is the place where God has always met with Moses to communicate with him. Now the cloud descends once again upon the tent. This is a clear sign to the people that God has chosen Joshua. More importantly, perhaps, it is a sign to *Joshua* that God has chosen him.

It can be difficult to assume a leadership role at any time. If you have ever served in any such role—as president of an organization, or as someone with authority over others in the workplace—it can seem rather daunting at first, no matter how well prepared you think you are. This feeling can be exacerbated if your predecessor was particularly skilled. Imagine how Joshua must have felt, taking over the reins of leadership from Moses, the person who led the nation out of Egypt, through the Red Sea, through forty years in the desert—the only leader the nation has ever known.

God goes so far as to tell Moses that the people would rebel yet again after his death, turning to idolatry because they will think that God is no longer among them. This will make things even more challenging for Joshua.

God tells Moses that there is one last poem that he is to recite for the nation before he dies. More importantly, he is to write it down and "put it in their mouths" (i.e., have them memorize it). The poem itself will serve as a witness against the people (we will read this poem in the next *parashah*); they will complain that God abandoned them, but the poem will show that they were forewarned of the consequences of their behavior. The fact that the poem is written down, and committed to their memory, will present incontrovertible evidence.

All of this is to bolster Joshua's confidence. Moses will be gone, but, together with God, he will have left something behind to ease the transition.

SIXTH ALIYAH: DEUTERONOMY 31:20–24
WRITTEN FOR SHABBAT, SATURDAY, SEPTEMBER 12, 2020

What a Difference a Letter Can Make

The job of a *gabbai* is to follow the Torah reading and correct a reader if (s) he makes a mistake; it requires careful attention to detail. Mistakes in the trope (the musical note) do not need to be corrected but mistakes in the Hebrew pronunciation must be corrected, no matter how minor they may seem. A mispronounced Hebrew word can completely change the meaning of the text. In this *parashah*, we have a wonderful example of this. In this *aliyah*, Moses speaks to Joshua on behalf of God, when he tells him, "Be strong and resolute: for you shall bring [תָּבִיא] the Israelites into the land that I promised them on oath" [31:23].

Back in the third *aliyah*, we had this verse: "Then Moses called Joshua and said to him in the sight of all Israel: 'Be strong and resolute, for it is you who shall go [תָּבוֹא] with this people into the land that the

LORD swore to their fathers to give them, and it is you who shall apportion it to them'" [31:7].

The phrasing of the verses is very similar, but look at the Hebrew verbs. In verse 7, the verb is *tavo* (you will go) [with this people]. In our verse 23, the verb is *tavi* (you will bring) (the Israelites = the people). In Hebrew, the verbs differ by only one letter, and therefore one sound. (Both come from the same root, *bo;* one is a *paal* form, and one is a *hiphil* form, for those of you who understand Hebrew grammar.) Why is the difference so significant in our text?

Joshua is first told that he is to go with the people; only later is he told to bring the people. Joshua first needs to remember that he is one of the people, before he can become the one who leads them. A true leader must understand and identify with the people that (s)he leads. A leader must have empathy with the people (s)he leads.

In this case, Joshua needs to remember that when they left Egypt, he was just like everyone else. He is now about to assume the mantle of leadership of the nation because God has chosen him for the job; God has seen qualities in him that God desires in a leader. God is elevating him to that role, but he has come from among the people.

And, therefore, if the Torah reader interchanges these words, the *gabbai* needs to correct them. Going with the people must precede bringing them along.

Forewarned is Forearmed

Moses was finally finished explaining the Torah and the *mitzvot* to the people. It was all written down and the scroll(s) placed in the ark, along with the tablets containing the Ten Commandments. The tablets had been given to them forty years prior at Mt. Sinai and, as we previously read this week, the rest was written down on scrolls gradually as it was revealed to Moses. The tablets and the scrolls are bookends representing the beginning and end of their desert trials and tests. In time to come, they will serve as two witnesses against the nation when it becomes rebellious. The people will not be able to say that they did not know what the consequences of their actions would be. Later, Jewish history bore out the truth of God's words as the nation was exiled from the land, first under the Assyrians, later the Babylonians, and finally under the Romans. It is only the last one hundred fifty or so years that have seen the return of a significant Jewish presence in the land.

All that remains for Moses to do is to recite the last poem to the nation whch we will read in the next *parashah*, Ha'azinu.

Parashat Ha'azinu

FIRST ALIYAH: DEUTERONOMY 32:1–6
MONDAY, SEPTEMBER 14, 2020

Providing Nourishment for Our Souls

Parashat Ha'azinu, the penultimate *parashah* in the Torah, consists entirely of the last song, the last message that Moses wanted to transmit to the nation before he died. He begins by calling witnesses to what he is about to say; the witnesses that he calls are the heavens and the Earth [32:1]. As pointed out by Ramban, these witnesses have existed literally since the beginning of creation.[1] In the beginning, God created the heavens and the Earth [Genesis 1:1].

Ibn Ezra says that "the point of invoking heaven and Earth as witnesses is that they last forever."[1]

Moses thus calls upon witnesses that have existed since the beginning of time and will continue throughout time and these very same witnesses exist today. It makes sense: if you are asking someone to witness something, you would want witnesses that are going to exist forever so your words will never be forgotten. The words that Moses was about to impart to the nation of Israel were meant not only for the generation of people standing before him in the moment but for all future generations of Jews, including our own.

There is some very beautiful imagery in these first few verses. Moses calls upon both the heavens and the Earth to hear (listen to) what he is about to say [32:1]. The word used when addressing the Earth is *vatishma*, which comes from the verb *shema,* that is so familiar to us. More interesting to me is the word used to address the heavens, the first word of the *parashah, ha'azinu.* We can see in this word the root of the word *ozen* (ear). It is a *hiphil,* or causative, verb form. It is almost as if Moses is saying to the heavens, "make yourselves into ears [for me]." In other words, Moses is calling upon the heavens to become his ears after he is gone. Most of us will behave differently if we know (or suspect) that someone is listening. The same heavens and Earth that have been watching and listening since the time of Moses are still watching and listening to us today.

Moses compares his words to rain [32:2]—showers, droplets; the image is of a gentle, nourishing rain. Rashi says, "just as rainy winds strengthen the grasses and help them grow, so words of Torah strengthen those who study them, and help them grow."[2] What a beautiful image! Just as food provides the nourishment for our physical bodies, so does Torah provide the nourishment for our spiritual sides, our souls, our *neshamah*.

Now, let's think about this a little. Our biblical ancestors were very dependent on the rain falling in its season for, if it didn't happen, the nation would fast and pray until God sent the rain. Today, we have recourse. How many of us have sprinklers to maintain lush, green lawns? We have the opportunity and ability to provide water to nourish our grass and our gardens even if it doesn't rain.

In the same way, we have the opportunity and ability to provide the nourishment that our souls need through Torah study. Not only do we have physical books available, but all the sources we might need can be found online through the wonders of the internet. If you are reading this right now, you are engaging in Torah study.

And that, my dear readers, is the reason I do this. For myself as well as all of you, I pray that these daily Torah studies provide spiritual nourishment for your souls. I know that my soul is nourished through the study that I engage in when preparing to write each day.

May we continue to provide the nutrition that our souls need to thrive as we enter a new year on the Hebrew Calendar.

SECOND ALIYAH: DEUTERONOMY 32:7–12
TUESDAY, SEPTEMBER 15, 2020

On the Wings of Eagles

Moses continues his final song/poem, adding more beautiful imagery. He begins by telling the people to "remember the days of old" [32:7]. Ramban says that this phrase refers specifically to the six days of Creation in Bereshit; he says that already as the world was being formed, the Kadosh Baruch Hu already had Israel in mind.[3] Elaborating on this point, the Bekhor

Shor says, "God had prepared a specific land on Earth for the Jewish people already long before they had come into existence."[4] This means that from the very beginning of Creation, God already had us in mind. Moses tells the people that "the LORD's portion is His people" [32:9]. In all of God's creation, we are the nation that God has chosen as God's own.

The metaphor is continued in verse 10, where we are told that God "Guarded him [Israel] as the pupil of His eye." Rabbeinu Bachya explains that "the pupil of the eye is known in classical Hebrew as *ishon*. The reason is that it contains within it something which resembles a human being, *ish*. The word, or rather the ending -*on*, suggests something small . . ."[5]

This means that we are always directly in God's line of sight.

The Bekhor Shor says that the word *ishon*, means "eyelid" and actually is related to the word *sheinah* (sleep).[6] When we sleep, our eyelids close over our eyes and cover them protectively. That, he says, resembles the way that God watches over and protects Israel.

Finally, we are told that "Like an eagle who rouses his nestlings, gliding down to his young, so did [God] spread [God's] wings and take him [Israel], Bear him along on His pinions" [32:11].

Rashi explains that an eagle is tender with its young, not entering the nest suddenly:

> When it comes to remove . . . (the young) from one place to another, it does not take them with its claws, as other birds do: because other birds are afraid of the eagle that soars so high and flies above them, therefore they carry . . . (the young) by . . . (the mother's) claws for fear of the eagle. But the eagle is afraid only of an arrow, therefore it carries . . . (the young) on its wings, saying, "It is better that the arrow pierce me than that it should pierce my young". So, too, the Holy One, blessed be He, says, (Exodus 19:4) "I bare you as on eagles' wings"[7]

Ibn Ezra says that the eagle takes each of the chicks one at a time onto his wings, since they are not strong enough to fly on their own.[8]

As we enter this most unusual of High Holiday seasons, still facing so many unknowns in the coming months, many of us find ourselves in great need of the reassurance of God's love and providence that comes from the beautiful imageries of these verses. May you feel God's comforting protection like the eyelid that protects the eye, and when you need strength may you feel supported and carried as the eagle tenderly carries its young.

Celebrating God's Feminine Side

In this next *aliyah* of *parashat* Ha'azinu, Moses continues his last song/poem, his last message to the nation before he dies. The first three verses still continue the recounting of the history of all the good things that God did for Israel; they describe the nourishment that God provided for the nation. Though God is referred to here with masculine pronouns, God is described using a verb that is distinctly feminine in nature: "He set him atop the highlands, To feast on the yield of the earth; He fed him honey from the crag, And oil from the flinty rock . . ." [32:13]. The word *vayenikehu* is translated here as "he fed [him]" but several commentators point out that this word really means "he suckled [him]." This metaphor portrays God as a nursing mother and conveys the idea that God provided all of Israel's nourishment from God's own creation. Israel was totally dependent upon God for their sustenance. This metaphor conveys the idea of God as a tender, loving parent.

The word that follows this word is *dvash*, usually translated as "honey," as it is here. However, a few commentators point out that what is referred to is not what we usually think of as honey. This honey is not produced by bees but comes from dates which are, of course, very prolific in *Eretz* Israel. If you have never tasted this, I strongly recommend it. Additionally, most commentators agree that the "foaming grape-blood" of verse 14 refers to wine; Ibn Ezra says that "there will be so much wine that you can drink it whenever you want."[9] Wine not only provides sustenance; in our tradition, it symbolizes joy. That is the reason that each Shabbat and Yom Tov begins with *kiddush*, sanctification of the day by reciting a blessing over a cup of wine.

Beginning with verse 15, the poem/song takes an ominous turn. Moses begins to talk about the nation's rejection of God, straying after idols. To really convey the seriousness of this, Moses continues to use amazing imagery to define the relationship with God that they will be turning their backs on. In the final verse of the *aliyah*, we read, "You neglected the Rock that begot you, Forgot the God who brought you forth" [32:18]. The word *yaladcha* is translated here as "[he] begot [you]." More precisely, it means, "[he] gave birth to [you]," again applying that feminine imagery. The final word of this section, *m'chol'lecha*, is translated here as "brought [you] forth." Tigay says that this word really applies to labor pains.[10] Hizkuni says that this word really means, "to dance," implying that God had "danced" the nation out of Egypt accompanied by song[11], which is reminiscent of the people singing and dancing at the Red Sea after they had safely made it through to the other side.

In the next few days, we will be starting the celebration of the High Holidays. One of the most beautiful, soaring prayers that we sing over these days is the *Avinu Malkeynu* (Our Father, our King) prayer. Many of us love the imagery; some of us are troubled by the masculinity of it. *Parashat* Ha'azinu makes up for that.

God has both masculine and feminine aspects. God is a loving parent to us—sometimes father, sometimes mother. We need both.

As we prepare to celebrate this unusual High Holiday season, may you experience the love and tenderness of the *Shekinah*, God's feminine side, as well as the protective love of *Avinu Malkenu*.

FOURTH ALIYAH: DEUTERONOMY 32:19–28
MONDAY, SEPTEMBER 21, 2020

In Exile, We Find Our Way Home

As the final song/poem of Moses continues, the mood changes in this *aliyah*. Though Moses speaks in his own voice up until this point, a change occurs in verse 20 and he speaks as the voice of God, warning the people of what can/will happen in future time when/if they turn away from God and indulge in idol worship. Famine, plague, pestilence, dangerous beasts, the sword of their enemies will all be unleashed against them. It's a very dire warning.

But then we have this interesting phrasing: "I might have reduced them to naught, Made their memory cease among men . . ." [32:26]. We know that this refers to the future exile(s) of the nation from the land, the ultimate punishment. God says that it would have been possible to wipe out the nation completely, so that even the very memory of them would cease. During the final exile from the land, the Roman Exile in the first century CE, the Jews were literally scattered throughout the known world. Abarbanel says that this was really a blessing in disguise. He says that this scattering was a great act of charity by the Kadosh Baruch Hu.[12] Think of the nations and civilizations that no longer exist, the Trojans, for example. Since their remnant was all concentrated in one tiny spot in the world, it was relatively easy for the Greeks to obliterate them.

Think of all the nations that expelled us at various times throughout history: England, France, Spain, and more. Think of all the nations that persecuted us and violently tried to destroy us: the Spanish Inquisition, the pogroms of Russia, and, of course, the Nazi Holocaust. Without question, each of these incidents resulted in the loss of thousands, if not millions, of lives. At the same time, though, each of these incidents inspired those who survived to travel to more and further spots on the globe. Thus, though we may be small in number on the worldwide stage, we are still here. As Abarbanel explains it, "it is only being scattered throughout the world that has kept us alive."

I would take this one step further. Two passages in the Talmud explain the rationale for the exile this way:

> And Rabbi Elazar said: The Holy One, Blessed be He, exiled Israel among the nations only so that converts would join them, as it is stated: "And I will sow her to Me in the land" [Hosea 2:25]. Does a person sow a *se'a* of grain for any reason other than to bring in several *kor* of grain during the harvest? So too, the exile is to enable converts from the nations to join the Jewish people. [*BT Pesachim 87b:14*]
> And there are *meforshim* [who say] that because of converts Israel is in exile, as it says: Why are Israel scattered in many lands? They are scattered through the nations in order for them to add to them converts . . . [*Tosafot on Kiddushin 70B:15*][13]

Not only was the nation scattered in order to preserve the remnant of those who escaped from and survived persecution but also to attract and bring new members into the fold! For those of us who are Jews by Choice— or if you know or are related to someone who has chosen to join the Jewish people (and, let's face it, these days, who doesn't?)—this is an awesome thought. Not only did God not wipe out the nation, but its future has also been assured by adding new members.

And that is why it is possible to find Jews whose last names are Sullivan, Velazquez, and even Cella! May we be blessed to continue to welcome into our fold those who choose to come under the wings of the *Shekinah*.

FIFTH ALIYAH: DEUTERONOMY 32:29–39
TUESDAY, SEPTEMBER 22, 2020

God Does Teshuvah, Too

In this part of the poem/song, God's anger is turned toward the enemies of Israel and they are to be punished for all the things that they did to Israel. Though they were the agents through whom God wreaked punishment on

Israel for their sins, they, too, needed to learn a lesson. They were not to become carried away with themselves or attribute their success over Israel to their own strength.

In the middle of the reading, we have the following verse: "For the LORD will vindicate His people And take revenge for His servants, When He sees that their might is gone, And neither bond nor free is left" [32:36]. The word *yitnecham* is translated here as "take revenge for." Rashi points out that the real meaning of this verb is "to change one's mind, converting an intention to do evil into one to do good or vice versa."[14] The Old JPS Translation of this phrase is, "For the Lord will judge His people, and repent Himself for His servants . . ." When God sees the suffering of Israel at the hands of their enemies, God regrets what God has done and changesGod's mind.

The thought continues in the final verse of the *aliyah*: "See, then, that I, I am He; There is no god beside Me. I deal death and give life; I wounded and I will heal: None can deliver from My hand" [32:39].

God is still speaking here, and the word "I," is repeated. No, God is not stuttering. God elaborates: "I deal death and [I] give life. I wounded and I will heal." It is as if God is acknowledging wrongdoing and vowing to make up for it. In other words, God repents for the way that God has treated Israel.

What a timely message, as we prepare to mark Yom Kippur. God does not ask of us what God is not willing to do Godself. Girded with this knowledge, we can approach the Day of Atonement with the expectation that a repentant God stands ready to accept us, the repentant human beings. A repentant God is an empathetic God, an approachable God.

May we all be sealed together in God's book. I wish you a *gmar chatima tovah*.

SIXTH ALIYAH: DEUTERONOMY 32:40–43
WEDNESDAY, SEPTEMBER 22, 2020

What Kind of Role Model Will You Be?

These four verses are the conclusion of Moses' final song/poem to the people of Israel. Verses 40-42 are spoken in the voice of God, and they complete the description of the revenge that God will exact on the enemies of Israel, those who attacked them and took advantage of their disadvantaged state brought about by their disobedience to God.

The final verse switches back to Moses as the speaker: "O nations, acclaim His people! For He'll avenge the blood of His servants, Wreak vengeance on His foes, And cleanse the land of His people" [32:43]. According to

Rashbam, the phrase *harninu goyim amo* is better translated as: "O nations, acclaim [God] along with His people!"[15]

Thus, Moses brings the poem/song to its conclusion by exhorting the nations of the world to celebrate God's deliverance of Israel from the hands of their oppressors. In other words, if the other nations of the world come to believe in God and desire to serve God as we do, that will naturally lead them to praise God. This, in turn, will result in them receiving the same blessings and protection that Israel receives.

This finally gets to the heart of the matter. Israel's designation as God's "Chosen People" is a concept that makes some of us uncomfortable. We need to understand, however, that this is not a designation of privilege; rather, it is one of responsibility. God had tried twice to forge a covenantal relationship with all of humankind: once with Adam and Eve, and then later with Noah. Both efforts were thwarted by the free will with which God has endowed all of us. Finally, God decided to designate one people, one nation, the descendants of Abraham to be an example to the rest of the nations of what it is to live in communion with God. When we can live such an exemplary life, and receive God's blessings for doing so, we serve as a *dugma*, a role model, to those around us.

Looked at in this light, we can see why God becomes so angry with the people of Israel when they are disobedient. In this case, the example being set is the completely wrong one.

During this introspective period of the year, let us each examine our deeds and ask ourselves, "Would my behavior inspire or discourage others to/from extolling God's praises?" Since none of us is perfect, there will be times when the latter choice is the honest answer. So, then the question becomes, "What can I do to fix this?"

May we all be the example that God calls us to be in this new year 5,781. Our nation and our world need it now more than ever.

SEVENTH ALIYAH: DEUTERONOMY 32:44–52
THURSDAY, SEPTEMBER 24, 2020

It Is Your Very Life

Once Moses had finished his last song/poem that comprised the entirety of this *parashah* up to this point, he enjoined them one last time to take the words of the Torah to heart, teaching them to their children [32:46]. Next, he describes the words of Torah, the teaching of God: "For this is not a trifling thing for you: it is your very life; through it you shall long endure on the land that you are to possess upon crossing the Jordan" [32:47]. The Hebrew word translated here as "trifling" is *reyk*, which literally means, "empty." Additionally, the word translated here as "for you" is *mikem*, which literally means, "from you." That would mean that a more literal translation is: "For this is not an empty thing from you, it is your very life."

This is explained this way in the Jerusalem Talmud:

> [*Peah 1:1 15B*]: there is nothing empty in the Torah; if it seems that way to you (either unclear or meaningless)—then that is coming from you. It is because you have failed to study it thoroughly.

Moses has done and said all that he can to the people. He has recited to them the words of the Torah and given them the tablets and the scrolls with the written words. Now the rest will be up to them, and to us.

Immediately following this last exhortation from Moses, God tells him that he is to go up into Mt. Nebo, from where he will be able to look down and see the land of Canaan. He will not, however, be allowed to enter the land. Like his brother Aaron did on Mt. Hor several weeks earlier, he is going up into the mountain to die.

Parashat V'zot HaBrachah

Claiming Our Inheritance

And so, we have come to the last *parashah* of the Torah, V'Zot HaBrachah. This *parashah* has the distinction of being the only *parashah* that is never read on a Shabbat morning outside the land of Israel. The only time this *parashah* is ever read in the synagogue is on Simchat Torah, the holiday on which we celebrate the completion of the annual Torah reading cycle.

The previous *parashah*, Ha'azinu, contained the final song/poem with which Moses addressed the nation, but it contained some grim predictions and threats for the future. After leading the people for forty years, Moses did not wish to leave them on a note of negativity. To that end, the first verse tells us, "This is the blessing with which Moses the man of God, bade the Israelites farewell before he died." The first six *aliyot* of this *parashah* are comprised of Moses's final blessing of the nation.

This first *aliyah* contains one of the most well-known verses in the Torah: *Torah tziva-lanu Moses morasha kehilat Yaakov* (When Moses charged us with the Teaching [Torah] as the heritage of the congregation of Jacob) [33:4]. This verse should be familiar to you as it is very often sung by the congregation as the Torah is dressed at the end of the public reading in the synagogue. With just seven words, we state our fundamental belief that the Torah was transmitted to us by Moses, that it belongs to us all, and that it is our heritage. The Baal HaTurim explains that it is our heritage, but not our inheritance.[1] What's the difference, you might ask? He says that "every Israelite bequeaths [it] to his children; but Torah knowledge does not come as an inheritance—it can be acquired only through diligent study." In other words, each of us needs to claim his/her heritage.

Since the synagogue that I attend began having live-streamed Shabbat services in the middle of July, I have been one of the people privileged with being present in the sanctuary because I serve as a *gabbai* and a Torah reader. We do a carefully calculated dance at the reading table: the honoree reads the blessing and moves away, then the Torah reader reads from the scroll and moves away, and then the honoree approaches to recite the final blessing. The *gabbaiim* are seated on either side of the *Shulchan* in the first pew rather than standing next to it. Each person who reads from the Torah uses an anti-bacterial wipe to wipe down the handles of the scroll after they have finished. It was less than a year ago that we were carrying the scroll around the sanctuary before and after the Torah reading, allowing anyone who wanted to touch it to do so with their *tzitzit*, their *siddur*, or even their fingers. Now, sadly, for safety reasons, it has become off limits to most of us. And that fact, to me, is very sad. And yet . . .

The Torah itself is not off limits to any of us. The words contained in the scroll belong to us all. And they are accessible to us all through printed texts, through online texts, through Zoom classes and, indeed, through these writings that I have been doing since March. That, my friends, is the very reason that I do this, to bring the words of Torah to you. Torah study has always been something about which I am passionate. It is what brought me to Judaism in the first place, what strengthened my commitment to Judaism, and what allowed me to be able to take on the challenge of Rabbinical School.

Now, I don't mean to imply that you need to study to the level that I have. Rather, I would encourage you to study at whatever level you are right now, and to continue to study. Find personal meaning in the words and struggle with the parts that make you uncomfortable.

You may be physically separated from the scroll but you are not separated from the Torah. Claim your heritage.

SECOND ALIYAH: DEUTERONOMY 33:8–12
WEDNESDAY, SEPTEMBER 30, 2020

Left or Right—Both are Equally Correct

Moses began his last blessing with words addressed to the entire nation. He then progressed to addressing words to the individual tribes. In the first *aliyah*, he spoke to the tribes of Reuven and Judah. Here he speaks to Levi and Benjamin. Of the latter, he says this: "Beloved of the LORD, He rests securely beside Him; Ever does He protect him, As he rests between His shoulders" [33:12]. I was intrigued by this image that "he rests between his shoulders." It can be interpreted in two ways, as it is not totally clear if Benjamin is the subject or the object in this phrase.

If Benjamin is the subject, then God is the object; Benjamin rests between God's shoulders. The image conjured here is that of a parent carrying a child on his/her shoulders. Just about all of us who are parents can relate to this image, thinking back to a time when we did this with our own children. How happy our kids were sitting up there, riding on Mom or Dad's shoulders instead of having to walk, literally having a birds-eye view of their surroundings. Happy memories are generated for both parents and child alike. In this analogy, the tribe of Benjamin feels safe in the protective presence of God.

But what if Benjamin is the object in this phrase, and God is the subject, meaning that God rests between Benjamin's shoulders? This, too, conjures up images of safe protection. Some say that this alludes to the fact that the Temple, when it was constructed, stood in Jerusalem at the center of the territory of Benjamin.

The name Benjamin literally means, "son of my right hand." Ironically, we learn from later stories in the *Tanakh* that the members of the tribe of Benjamin were known for being left-handed, or, at the very least, ambidextrous. But God rests right in the middle between the two sides, not showing any preference for either side, a protective presence guarding Benjamin from behind. In more instances than I can count, our tradition shows a preference for the right hand/side, as a symbol of strength, at the same time relegating the left to represent weakness and darkness. As a left-handed person myself, this never sits well with me. That's why I love this imagery of God perched protectively between Benjamin's shoulders, balancing equally between the left and the right.

THIRD ALIYAH: DEUTERONOMY 33:13–17
THURSDAY, OCTOBER 1, 2020

And the Bush Was Not Consumed

Moses continues with his blessings of the individual tribes. Here he turns his attention to Joseph, whom he describes as "the elect of his brothers" [33:16]. This, of course, refers to the fact that he was loved and favored by his father Jacob more than his ten older brothers. Moses wishes many wonderful things for Joseph's descendants: blessings on the land, dew, abundant fruits, fertility in their herds, and all the bounties that the land and the mountains have to offer. But the most beautiful wish by far is for the favor of the Presence in the Bush [33:16]. With this wonderfully expressive phrase, Moses hearkens back to his first encounter with God at Horeb (Mt. Sinai). While he tended the sheep of his father-in-law Jethro, God called to him from the bush that appeared to be burning, and yet "was not consumed" [Exodus 3:2]. This was when Moses received his commission to go to Egypt to tell Pharaoh to let the people of Israel go and this was the beginning of the special relationship between Moses and God. Moses was reluctant to agree to do what God asked of him, arguing that he didn't/couldn't speak well. In the end, we know that he finally did agree to go with the assurance from God that Aaron would go with him as a spokesperson.

Here we are, forty years later, and Moses shared a closeness with the Divine that no one else has ever done before or since. They met a second (and third) time on Mt. Sinai when Moses received the first, and then the second, set of tablets from God. After that, they met in the *mishkan*, the tabernacle. Clearly, Moses has gotten over his fear of public speaking and almost the entire book of Devarim (Deuteronomy) has been comprised of him speaking to the people. And here, in his final blessings, he wishes for Joseph, "the favor of the Presence in the bush." In other words, Moses wishes for Joseph the favor of God. He wishes for them the same kind of relationship with God that he himself had all these years.

Throughout these last four books of the Torah, we have seen Moses talk to God, plead with God, become angry with God, praise God, implore God, and pour his heart out to God. Sometimes he was able to convince God to change God's mind and sometimes he was unable to. We have seen him plead with God several times to be able to enter the land of Canaan with the nation, only to be told, "No. You must go up into the mountain to die. You may look down and see the land, but you may not enter the land."

Through it all, their relationship was based on open communication. Though we may not be called to the greatness of Moses, we can pour out our hearts to God just as Moses did. We may not (and most likely will not) hear God speak to us in return. Nevertheless, through prayer and study we can keep the lines of communication open.

My wish for us all is that we, too, may be blessed with "the favor of the Presence in the bush."

Searching for Hidden Treasure

Moses continues his final blessing of the tribes of Israel, here speaking first to Zevulun and then to Gad. Zevulun's territory bordered on the [Mediterranean] Sea. According to Rashi, the members of this tribe complained to God about this.[2] Why were they not given fields and vineyards like some of the others? God said that their reward was different: "they draw from the riches of the sea And the hidden hoards of the sand" [33:19]. Hizkuni explained that the Zebulonites would go out each day after the tide had gone out and retrieve hidden treasures that had been buried in the sand. These treasures were more than just seashells—sometimes they were valuable items that had come from boats that had been shipwrecked.[3] The medieval French commentator Gersonides metaphorically compared these perfect hidden treasures to the wisdom hidden in the Torah, waiting to be discovered and dug out.[3]

Living here on Long Island, we are surrounded by beaches. Think what it's like walking on the beach at low tide. You look carefully down at your feet to see what you can find peeking out at you from the sand. Sometimes it's just sitting there, waiting for you to pick it up. Often, only part of it is visible, peeking out of the sand. You need to stop and brush some sand out of the way to reveal the item in its entirety. And sometimes you might spot something that someone else misses. This is what Gersonides refers to: sometimes Torah study readily provides its gems to us but much of the time only a small part of the treasure is there to catch our attention. If we aren't looking closely, it would be easy to miss these hidden treasures. If we put in the effort to find these things that are glinting at us, and then work to extract them intact from the sand, we will be well rewarded for our efforts.

There are so many gems of wisdom hidden in the Torah, just waiting there for you to uncover them. But you must be looking for them, and you need to stop and take the time to extract them. And when you do, you will be richly rewarded for your efforts.

Sons and Daughters

Moses continues his final blessings of the tribes of Israel. After speaking to Dan and Naphtali, he moves on to address the tribe of Asher: "Most blessed of sons be Asher; May he be the favorite of his brothers . . ." [33: 24]. In commenting on this verse, Rashi quotes Sifrei Devarim 355:19, which states, "You will find none of the tribes who was so blessed with [sons] as Asher"; yet he goes on to say, ". . . I do not know how this was so."[4] Ramban also comments that no tribe was blessed with sons as much as Asher.[5]

Interestingly, however, when the genealogy of the children and grandchildren of Jacob is recounted in chapter 46 of Genesis, we read the following: "Asher's sons: Imnah, Ishvah, Ishvi, and Beriah, and their sister, Serah. Beriah's sons: Heber and Malchiel" [Genesis 46:17].

And later, when the genealogy is again delineated in the book of Numbers, the listing of the descendants of Asher includes this verse: "The name of Asher's daughter was Serah" [Numbers 26:46].

Both citations catch our attention, since women are rarely mentioned in a biblical genealogy. Indeed, the entire listing in both instances includes the names of fifty-three grandsons of Jacob, and only one granddaughter, Serah, the daughter of Asher. From this, the commentators derive that she must have been very important (I have mentioned her previously, in *Parashat* Pinchas). Consequently, several *midrashim* have been derived about her. One of these says that she was the first person to tell Jacob that Joseph was still alive in Egypt.

The Talmud tells another well-known *midrash* about her:

> . . . And from where did Moses . . . know where Joseph was buried? . . . Serah, the daughter of Asher, remained from that generation that initially descended to Egypt with Jacob. Moses went . . . and said to her: Do you know anything about where Joseph is buried? She said to him: The Egyptians fashioned a metal casket for him and set it in the Nile . . . River . . . so that its water would be blessed. Moses went and stood on the bank of the Nile. He said to Joseph: Joseph, Joseph, the time has arrived about which the Holy One, Blessed be He, took an oath saying that I, . . . God, will redeem you. And the time for fulfillment of the oath that you administered to the Jewish people that they will bury you in Eretz Yisrael has arrived. If you show yourself, it is good, but if

not, we are clear from your oath. Immediately, the casket of Joseph floated to the top of the water. [*BT Sotah 13A:14*]

It should be noted that, since Serah is listed in the names of the family who first went down into Egypt, this would have made her well over two hundred years old at the time the nation of Israel left Egypt.

According to a different *midrash*, Serah had an additional distinction:

> There were nine . . . who entered the Garden of Eden alive, . . . :
> Enoch the son of Yered, Elijah, the Messiah, Eliezer the servant of
> Abraham, Hiram, king of Tyre, . . . Ebed-melech the Cushite, Jabez
> the son of R. Judah the Prince, Bithiah the daughter of Pharaoh,
> and Serah the daughter of Asher. Some say: Also R. Joshua b. Levi.
> [*Derekh Eretz 1:18*][6]

According to the legend, these nine people were taken up into Olam HaBah, the afterlife, here referred to as the Garden of Eden, without dying. Note that only two of the nine are women: Serah, and Pharaoh's daughter, Bithiah (who rescued Moses from the Nile, named him, and raised him as her own son).

Oh, and what of Asher's sons Imnah, Ishvah, Ishvi, and Beriah, who are also listed in the genealogy? There are no such legends about them. In fact, there is nothing to tell us anything distinguishing about them. Which brings me back to Rashi's comment on this verse: none of the tribes were blessed with as many sons as Asher, but "I do not know how this was so."

Asher's daughter, on the other hand, is another story. For those of us who search for the hidden women of the Torah, Serah is a shining example. May we draw inspiration from her story.

SIXTH ALIYAH: DEUTERONOMY 33:27–29
WEDNESDAY, OCTOBER 7, 2020

Who is Like You?

With these three verses, Moses finishes up his last words to the nation. After giving his final blessings to the individual tribes, he now returns to addressing the entire nation with words of support and praise. In verse 29, we find these very familiar Hebrew words: Who is like you? We recognize these words from the morning service, where we recite them shortly before the *amidah:* "Who is like You, Adonai, among the mighty! Who is like you, adorned in holiness, revered in praise, working wonders!" [Exodus 15:11].

This verse comes from *Shirat haYam,* the Song of the Sea that the people of Israel sang after their deliverance at the Red Sea when the waters miraculously parted for them, allowing them to escape the pursuing Egyptians. Here these words are used to praise God. No other god can possibly compare.

The phrase "who is like You?" appears four additional times in the *Tanakh:*

All my bones shall say, "LORD, who is like You? You save the poor
from one stronger than he, the poor and needy from his despoiler."
[*Psalm 35:10*]
Your beneficence, high as the heavens, O God, You who have done
great things; O God, who is Your peer! [*Psalm 71:19*]
O LORD, God of hosts, who is mighty like You, O LORD? Your
faithfulness surrounds You; [*Psalm 89:9*]
O happy *Israel!* Who is like you, A people delivered by the LORD,
Your protecting Shield, your Sword triumphant! Your enemies
shall come cringing before you, And you shall tread on their backs.
[*Deuteronomy 33:29*]

Like the words from *Shirat haYam,* the three verses from the Psalms all extol the greatness of God, praising God for God's providence, beneficence, and faithfulness. Quite understandably, the words, "who is like You" are usually used in reference to God. As a question, it is, of course, rhetorical, since truly no one, no person, no god, can compare to God. We say these words in awe of our God.

But the last verse in this chart is our verse from this reading at the end of Deuteronomy; and we see that in this verse the phrase "who is like you" is not of God, but of Israel—of us. Here Moses stands in awe of the blessings that we have received from God, of the unique relationship that we have with God. It is as if he is saying, "how fortunate are we"—again, a rhetorical question, since truly no other nation is as fortunate as we are.

We must be very careful, though. This thought must humble us, not make us haughty. Being the recipients of God's beneficence obligates us to care for others, providing for their needs as God provides for ours. Being the benefactors of God's goodness obligates us to make the world a better place.

This is the last thought with which Moses leaves the nation.

SEVENTH ALIYAH: DEUTERONOMY 34:1–12
FRIDAY, OCTOBER 9, 2020

Sealed with a Kiss

So, here we have arrived at the last *aliyah* of the Torah. Moses has finished his final blessing of the nation and God tells him once again to ascend the mountain so that he will be able to see the entire land of Canaan from there. God reminds him yet again that he, Moses, may not cross over into the land with the nation. He is going up to the mountain to die. No one is accompanying him. God will meet him there on the mountain, as God has done before.

And then we read: "So Moses the servant of the LORD died there, in the land of Moab, at the command [the mouth of], the LORD" [34:5]. You may recall that Aaron's death was described the same way: he died "at the mouth of" God [Numbers 33:38]. What exactly does this mean? The Talmud elaborates:

> It was also taught in a *baraita*: Nine hundred and three types of death were created in the world, . . . The Gemara explains that the most difficult of all these types of death is croup . . . while the easiest is the kiss of death . . . . The kiss of death is like drawing a hair from milk. One should pray that he does not die a painful death. [*BT Brachot 8a:13*]

To die at the mouth of God is described as dying by the kiss of God. All the way back in Genesis (which we will read next), we are told that God breathed life into the first human being (Adam). Now, at the end of the Torah, we read how God takes life away the same way—by a kiss. The imagery is beautiful. The Talmud describes it as "drawing a hair from milk," silent, simple, almost imperceptible. Peaceful. The very lips that, in arguing with God at the burning bush, Moses had described as "uncircumcised," the lips that stuttered, the lips that had difficulty speaking, but in the end developed so well that they have been speaking to men and God for literally the last four books of the Torah. Those very same lips finally yield back to God the soul which God had infused into them.

There is no more beautiful way to describe a death. As much as Moses wanted to go into the land with the nation, he also was tired—and ready—to hand the reigns over to Joshua.

We also know that no one accompanied Moses up to the mountain. We are told in verse 6: "He [God] buried him in the valley in the land of Moab, near Beth-peor; and no one knows his burial place to this day." God was Moses' grave digger. You all have, no doubt, experienced a Jewish burial at some point, when everyone present participated in the ritual of shoveling dirt into the grave. For Moshe Rabbeinu, God undertook this ritual alone. Theirs was truly a relationship of love.

So, my friends, we have arrived at the end of the book of Deuteronomy, the end of the Torah. Very shortly, we will celebrate Simchat Torah. We end the annual cycle of Torah reading, only to immediately begin it again. Next, we begin the study of Bereshit.

In the meantime,

חֲזַק חֲזַק וְנִתְחַזֵּק!

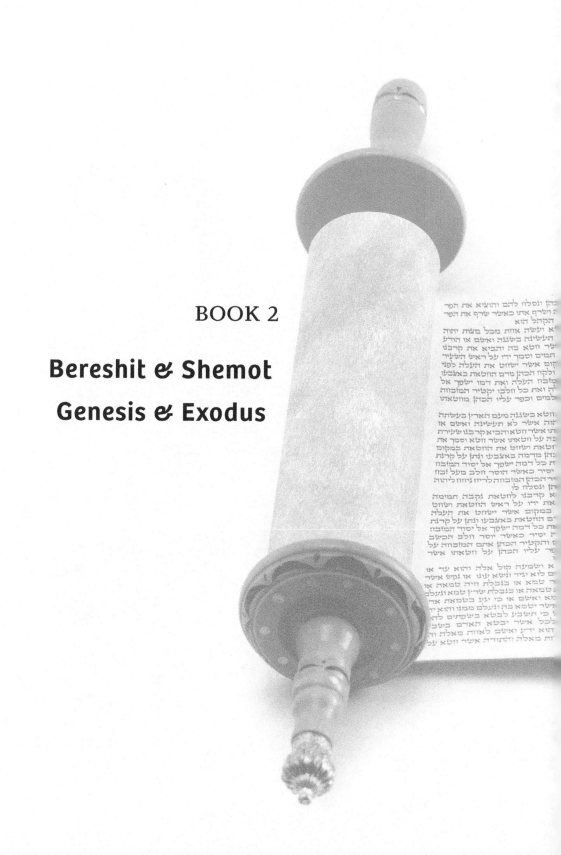

BOOK 2

Bereshit & Shemot
Genesis & Exodus

ואת כל החלב אשר על הקרב ואת שתי הכלית
ואת החלב אשר עליהן על הכסלים ואת
היתרת על הכבד על הכלית יסירנה והקטירם
הכהן המזבחה לחם אשה לריח ניחח כל חלב
ליהוה חקת עולם לדרתיכם בכל מושבתיכם
כל חלב וכל דם לא תאכלו
וידבר יהוה אל משה לאמר דבר אל בני ישראל
לאמר נפש כי תחטא בשגגה מכל מצות יהוה
אשר לא תעשינה ועשה מאחת מהנה אם הכהן
המשיח יחטא לאשמת העם והקריב על חטאתו
אשר חטא פר בן בקר תמים ליהוה לחטאת
והביא את הפר אל פתח אהל מועד לפני יהוה
וסמך את ידו על ראש הפר ושחט את הפר לפני
יהוה ולקח הכהן המשיח מדם הפר והביא אתו
אל אהל מועד וטבל הכהן את אצבעו בדם והזה
מן הדם שבע פעמים לפני יהוה את פני פרכת
הקדש ונתן הכהן מן הדם על קרנות מזבח קטרת
הסמים לפני יהוה אשר באהל מועד ואת כל דם
הפר ישפך אל יסוד מזבח העלה אשר פתח אהל
מועד ואת כל חלב פר החטאת ירים ממנו את
החלב המכסה על הקרב ואת כל החלב אשר על
הקרב ואת שתי הכלית ואת החלב אשר עליהן
אשר על הכסלים ואת היתרת על הכבד על
הכלית יסירנה כאשר יורם משור זבח השלמים
והקטיר הכהן על מזבח העלה ואת עור הפר ואת
כל בשרו על ראשו ועל כרעיו וקרבו ופרשו
והוציא את כל הפר אל מחוץ למחנה אל מקום
טהור אל שפך הדשן ושרף אתו על עצים באש
על שפך הדשן ישרף

BOOK OF BERESHIT
Parashat Bereshit

Creating Order Out of Chaos

This first *aliyah* outlines the systematic order of creation, from the light and darkness created on the first day, leading all the way up to the pinnacle of God's creation, human beings, on the sixth day. What catches my attention, particularly now at this moment in time, is the two-word Hebrew phrase *tohu va'vohu* [1:2]. It is used to describe the primordial chaos that existed when God began the process of creation. This phrase is most often translated as, "unformed and void." The elements that God needed to create the world were all there but were just all jumbled up together in one unformed, chaotic mess. Beginning on day one, God methodically went through these elements and sorted them out, step by step putting order into the world. With each step, the Earth moved closer to the ideal world that God wished to place under the authority of mankind. Human beings were not equipped to handle a creation of chaos. At the same time, neither were they capable of sorting everything out and placing it in its proper place. Not only did God do this, but as each successive day saw more of the world sorted out, it was completed with God's declaration that "it was good" [1:4,10,12,18,21,25].

Right now, for many of us, our world seems like it is in total chaos while we deal with social unrest, political unrest, and a global pandemic. Additionally, many people in our world are dealing with financial crisis, as well, having lost jobs or suffering reduced income. Our children are sometimes confused by having to navigate both in-person and virtual learning. Parents never know from one day to the next if their kids will be able to go to school, or if they will have to arrange childcare because someone in their kids' school tested positive for COVID and the school must be closed for a day or two.

Very little in our world seems as it should be. We desperately need God to make some sense of the chaos for us. Following the example of Genesis, we need to see that the answers will not come all at once but need to come in an orderly fashion, one logical step after another. The social unrest cannot possibly be solved unless and until the political unrest has been settled. The financial and educational woes cannot possibly be solved unless and until a vaccine is found to fight the pandemic.

The difference is this: in the creation story of Bereshit, human beings did not come into existence until after the ordering of the rest of Creation had already taken place. This time, we are here to witness the ordering of our chaos. But we also learned in Bereshit that we, human beings, were created to be partners with God in maintaining Creation. That means that this time, as God begins to order the chaos of our world, we must play our part as well. We must exercise our right to vote. We must be willing to take a vaccine once one has proven to be safe (and, in the meantime, we must show our concern for the welfare of ourselves and others by wearing a mask). We must do what we can to help those who are struggling financially. We must commit ourselves to a world of true racial and gender equality.

Order will come out of this chaos only if and when we commit ourselves to working together with each other and the Divine to make it happen.

And when we do, then once again God will say that it is "very good" [1:31].

SECOND ALIYAH: GENESIS 2:4–19
MONDAY, OCTOBER 12, 2020

A Divine Breath of Life

Though the complete order of creation was described in the first *aliyah*, here the text goes back over some details. Strangely enough, we notice not only a change in the order, but a seemingly very different description of the creation of human beings. Many scholars feel that there actually are two different creation stories, one in chapter 1 and one in chapter 2.

In any event, here we have the creation of the plants and vegetation [2:5-6], followed by the creation of a human being [2:7], then the trees [2:9], and finally the animals [2:19].

I want to look at the one single verse that talks about the creation of the human being: "the LORD God formed man from the dust of the earth . . ." [2:7].

The raw material used by God to create the human [ha-adam] is "the dust of the ground [ha-adamah]." The name for the physical body is closely related to the earth from which it came. The spiritual body, the soul, is different: ". . . [God] blew into his nostrils the breath of life, and man became a living being" [2:7].

Just last week, we read about the death of Moses, described as a kiss from God, gently reclaiming his soul. Here we read the opposite: the soul, the *neshama*, was breathed into the body of the first human through his nostrils by God. What a beautiful description! Mankind is the only one of God's creations to receive the soul directly from the breath of the Divine. In the same way, God infuses each of us with a unique soul as we take our first breath at birth. The Talmud expands on this teaching:

> And this serves to tell of the greatness of the Holy One, Blessed
> be He, as when a person stamps several coins with one seal, they
> are all similar to each other. But the supreme King of kings, the
> Holy One, Blessed be He, stamped all people with the seal of
> Adam the first man, as all of them are his offspring, and not one of
> them is similar to another. Therefore, since all humanity descends
> from one person, each and every person is obligated to say: The
> world was created for me, as one person can be the source of
> all humanity and recognize the significance of his actions. [*BT
> Sanhedrin 37A:15*]

Each of us is unique, yet we are all descended from one common ancestor. Each of us is equally important in the eyes of our Creator. This is exactly why we Jews place such high value on human life.

[Note: some of you may wonder whether I believe that these early stories in the Torah, or any of the later stories for that matter, truly occurred according to the biblical account. My answer is that I think spending time arguing over the veracity of the biblical accounts misses the point. The more important question to ask and answer, in my opinion, is *why* is this story in the Torah, and *what* am I (we) supposed to learn from it? Our Torah has survived (relatively) intact for over three thousand years. It is our sacred document, and the same text is read in every synagogue in the world by Jews of every denomination and nationality. The same text that spoke to our ancestors before us speaks to us today and will speak to our descendants in the future, but only if we are listening.]

THIRD ALIYAH: GENESIS 2:20–3:21
TUESDAY, OCTOBER 13, 2020

Male and Female He Created Them

This *aliyah* continues the second creation story. After the man named all the animals, none was found to be a fitting helper. Therefore, God decided to create woman. This is the story we are all so familiar with: God put the man to sleep, removed one of his ribs, and from it fashioned a female version of the man, who then named her Woman, since the raw material from which she was created came directly from his own body.

This is also the story that many women have difficulty accepting. Here, Woman was created second, after the man, and from his body, for the expressed purpose of being a helper to him. This story has bolstered the long-held belief of many Jews and Christians alike that women are inferior to men, and that this is by the design of God.

But let's look at the first creation story from chapter 1. You might have missed it, but let's look at how differently this is described there: "*And God said,* "Let us make man in our image, after our likeness . . . . And God created man in His image, in the image of God He created him; male and female He created them" [1:26-27].

You may be familiar with these verses, but did you ever really look at them? The first question one might ask is: to whom is God speaking when God says, "Let us make man? Generally, the interpretation is that all the angels, and, indeed, all of God's creation form the audience.

The next question might be: what does it mean to be created "in the image of God?" The answer is related to what I discussed in yesterday's *aliyah*: [hu]man [beings] alone among God's creations are endowed with a God-given soul. [Hu]man [beings] alone are created with free will, and autonomy over their own lives. [Hu]man [beings] alone are created to be God's partners in maintaining the world that God created.

In this context, it must be noted, the word, *adam*, translated as "man" refers to humankind, not to a specifically male human being.

Most importantly, in this story, when God created man in God's image, we are also told, "male and female created He them." Rashi explains, and Ibn Ezra and others concur, that the meaning of this is that God's original creation was one single human being with two faces, one male and one female.[1] In this telling, both genders are equally important. Neither is subservient to the other, as they were created in partnership, sharing one physical body.

In an attempt to reconcile these two creation stories, Rashi further explains that the word translated as "rib" in the second creation story really implies not just a single bone, but rather, an entire side of him.[2] In other words, the second story really describes how God took the one unified human being that God had originally created and separated it into two, a male and a female. This was, of course, necessitated by the fact that God had commanded man to "be fruitful and multiply" [1:28], and the one single being was incapable of doing that on its own.

For some, this idea may seem strange and difficult to grasp. What is important to me is the implication that from the very beginning God's intention was to create males and females as equals and as equally matched partners. If we look at it that way, then working to perfect God's creation means working to put men and women back on equal footing.

The rest of this *aliyah* is spent on the also very familiar story of the man and the woman and the snake—eating the fruit that God had forbidden them to eat, with the result that they were banished from the Garden of Eden. I encourage you to read through that on your own. It has much to tell us about good and evil, obedience and disobedience, and free will.

FOURTH ALIYAH: GENESIS 3:22–4:18
WEDNESDAY, OCTOBER 14, 2020

Yes, I Am My Brother's Keeper

This *aliyah* recounts the stories of the first and second human births, and the first human death. This is made all the more tragic by the fact that it is not a natural death, but a murder. The first instance of one human being taking the life (the very precious life, as we read about in the last *aliyah*) of another—and not just any other—indeed, the first human death—the first human murder—was a case of fratricide.

This made it even more urgent that the first two human beings—the male and the female—fulfill the first commandment that had been given to them by God: *p'ru ur'vu,* (be fruitful and multiply) [1:28]. Adam "knew" his wife (biblical expression for having sexual relations) twice. Their first son was named Cain and their second was named Abel [4:1-3].

Cain, the farmer, brought to God an offering from his harvest, and Abel, his younger brother, the shepherd, brought to God an offering from his flock [4:3-5]. God favored Abel and his sacrifice [4:4-6], and rejected Cain and his, thus causing Cain to be envious of his younger brother. Despite a warning from God, Cain gave in to his anger and killed his sibling [4:8], and then, when questioned by God, tried to feign ignorance with the very famous question, "Am I my brother's keeper?" [4:9].

God's answer is very poignant: "your brother's blood cries out to Me from the ground!" [4:10].

God let Cain know that he could not escape his fate. His brother's very blood (which is, of course, the life-giving part of the body) had developed a voice, crying out to God—from *ha-adamah,* the ground; that which had provided the raw material for the creation of the physical body had now received it back. Additionally, the word that is translated here as "blood," *d'mei,* literally means, "bloods"—the word is plural! Why is that? Rashi and Ibn Ezra (quoting Onkelos) explain that it is both Abel's blood, and the blood of all the unborn generations that could have descended from him, but now will never exist, that are crying out to God for justice.[3] From this, we derive the idea that one who takes a life has taken the life of the whole world.

In a world plagued with so much social unrest, when we are witnessing the brutal murders of so many black men at the hands of white men, we have also witnessed these past several months the record numbers of people in this country who are stepping up and saying, "I am my brother's keeper." The only way to overturn the centuries-old tide of racism in this country is for us all to recognize our responsibilities to each other. The voice of our brothers' blood cries out to us from the ground.

FIFTH ALIYAH: GENESIS 4:19–26
THURSDAY, OCTOBER 15, 2020

Turning to God in Prayer

As part of his punishment for killing his brother, Cain was sent out of the land, away from his parents, now essentially leaving them bereft of children. The Torah then traces the genealogy of the descendants of Cain (no, it does not explain where his wife came from). Adam, on the other hand, was now essentially childless. So, we are told that Adam once again "knew" (had sexual relations with) his wife, Eve [4:25]. Eve once again gave birth to a son, this time naming him Seth, because, she said, "God has provided me with another offspring in place of Abel" [4:25]. It seems that it was not only God who had rejected Cain but his parents had, as well. Their only hopes for having descendants were now pinned on this third son, brought into the world to replace the brother(s) he would never know. Seth, finally, provides them with a grandson (again, we do not know where his wife came from) whom he named Enosh. In Bereshit Rabbah 20:29, it is explained regarding Seth, "with him the world was created anew." His son's name, Enosh, means "man," just as his father's name also bears the same meaning.

A very important development occurred here in terms of the relationship between human beings and God: the development of prayer. It was with the generation of Enosh that, "men began to invoke the Lord by name" [4:26]. The lines of communication with God were opened up. Human beings began to acknowledge that their very existence depended on God. The text tells us, essentially, that both Seth and his son Enosh were, indeed, monotheists.

We, like Seth, need to recognize and acknowledge the fragility of our daily existence and open and maintain the lines of communication with God.

SIXTH ALIYAH: GENESIS 5:1–24
FRIDAY, OCTOBER 16, 2020

Partners in Creation

This *aliyah* recounts the genealogy of the descendants of the first man, called Adam. We are reminded that Adam had been created in the image of God [5:1]. Then we read the following: "When Adam had lived one hundred thirty years, he begot a son in his likeness after his image, and he named him Seth" [5:3].

We see that Adam was able to beget a son "in his likeness after his image." In other words, Adam was able to mimic his own creation. Just as he had been created in the Divine image, he was now able to pass that Divine image down to his own son.

We also notice something interesting about the genealogy. It makes no mention of Adam's first two sons, Cain and Abel. We know that Abel died. We also know that, though Cain was banished, he did have offspring. We read his genealogy in the last *aliyah* of this *parashah*. These offspring, however, were not counted among the offspring of Adam. Indeed, we will see going forward that the line of Cain all died in the flood at the time of Noah (whom we will see was a direct descendant of Seth).

The commentators all explain that for one hundred thirty years Adam had not been intimate with Eve. He realized that he had messed things up with his first two offspring. This was probably a direct result of the incident with the snake in the Garden of Eden. Adam had become sinful and had passed that on to his first two sons; the results, as we read, were disastrous, resulting in the ultimate loss of both. Therefore, Adam separated from his wife for a time to work on repairing his relationship with God.

Only when he felt reunited with God, when he himself could acknowledge the godliness in his own being, was he able to come together with Eve again, knowing that his new offspring would inherit the image of God just as he himself had done. The fate of the world would now rest on that son, Seth. This idea is expanded on in the Talmud:

> § The Sages taught: There are three partners in the creation of a person: The Holy One, Blessed be He, and his father, and his mother. His father emits the white seed, from which the following body parts are formed: The bones, the sinews, the nails, the brain that is in its head, and the white of the eye. His mother emits red seed, from which are formed the skin, the flesh, the hair, and the black of the eye. And the Holy One, Blessed be He, inserts into him a spirit, a soul, his countenance . . . eyesight, hearing of the ear, the capability of speech of the mouth, the capability of walking with the legs, understanding, and wisdom. [BT Niddah 31A:9]

Of course, we understand the biological process so much better today than the Talmudic sages did. We know that the father contributes a sperm (instead of a "white seed") and the mother contributes an egg (instead of a "red seed"); and we know that the physical characteristics can be determined by either parent, or, more likely, a combination of the two. We, like the rabbis, still understand that both parents contribute to the creation of the physical body of a child. Yet, even with our much more sophisticated understanding of biology, we are still mystified when it comes to understanding how the body becomes a living being. The soul is placed in the body by the *Kadosh Baruch Hu*. The creation of a new life really does require the contributions of three partners, two human and one Divine.

Becoming and being a parent is an awesome responsibility. *L'dor vador.*

SEVENTH ALIYAH: GENESIS 5:25–6:8
WRITTEN FOR SHABBAT, SATURDAY, OCTOBER 17, 2020

Ad Meah v'Esrim

Here we see the continuation of the genealogy of Adam, continuing for ten generations until the birth of Noah [5:29]. Following this, we read the strange idea of some divine beings (angels?) being intimate with earthly women to the displeasure of God [6:2,4]. There is also mention of the Nephilim appearing on Earth, possibly as the result of these unholy unions; these were mythical creatures who were giants. The most well-known of these is the giant Og, whom we have met before, in *Parashat* Chukkat.

In any event, all of this is very displeasing to God. There are two things that result from these strange couplings. First, God decides to limit the life span of human beings. The number is not insignificant. God says that God will limit a human being's lifespan to one hundred twenty years (even though we will see many people who live far beyond this age). This number sounds familiar as it was only last week that we read about the death of Moses at one hundred twenty years old! So, once again, we see the end of the Torah cycling back to the beginning.

More importantly, we are told about God's reaction to the lawlessness of human beings: "And the LORD regretted that He had made man on Earth . . ." [6:6].

God regretted having created human beings. Wow! That didn't take long, did it? Only ten generations, and God was so disgusted with us that God decided to wipe out human beings from the face of the Earth. We had disappointed God and had not become God's full partners in maintaining God's creation.

At the same time, we remember that when God had the same feeling in the book of Exodus and again in Deuteronomy about the nation of Israel, it was Moses who interceded and convinced God to relent and not destroy the people. Here in Genesis, there is no Moses to say to God, "hold on, don't do this. What will the people of the world think?"

We do read that "Noah found favor with the Lord" [6:8]. As we will see, Noah was chosen to be the one through whom humanity would continue. Noah was the best person that God could find to fill that role. But Noah was no Moses. He followed God's orders to save himself and his family and the animals, but there is no evidence that he tried to intercede on behalf of the rest of humanity.

God asks us to be more like Moses than Noah. That means taking up the causes of others and being willing to fight for them, even with God. With the current state of affairs in our world, with all the social turmoil, this is perhaps more important now than it ever has been.

Parashat Noach

FIRST ALIYAH: GENESIS 6:9–22
SUNDAY, OCTOBER 18, 2020

It's All Relative

We met Noah at the end of last week's *parashah*, *Bereshit*. He appears in the genealogy exactly ten generations after Adam. We read that by that time the people of the Earth had become corrupt and lawless, and, as a result, God came to regret the creation of human beings. Noah is described here at the beginning of this week's *parashah*: "This is the line of Noah. Noah was a righteous man; he was blameless in his age; Noah walked with God" [6:9].

Noah was both a righteous man (*ish tzadik*) and blameless (*tamim*). There is some debate about exactly what this means. What kind of a person was Noah, exactly? The conduct of a righteous person is considered to be beyond reproach. The word *tamim* is usually translated as "pure," especially when it is used to describe the animals that are acceptable for sacrifice. It really means "without blame." But this characteristic is qualified in the verse: he was righteous and pure in his time (generation). In other words, Noah was righteous and pure when compared to the rest of the people of his time. We already know, because the Torah has told us, that all the people of the world were corrupt and immoral. The Talmud explains this as follows:

> With regard to the verse: "These are the generations of
> Noah; Noah was a righteous man, and wholehearted in his
> generation." Rabbi Yohanan says: Relative to the other people
> of his generation he was righteous and wholehearted, but not
> relative to those of other generations. And Reish Lakish says:

In his generation he was righteous and wholehearted despite
being surrounded by bad influences; all the more so would
he have been considered righteous and wholehearted in other
generations. [BT Sanhedrin 108A:17]

There are two differing opinions here. Rabbi Yohanan says that Noah was
only righteous when compared to his contemporaries. Because they were so
reprehensible, it was easy for him to look good. Had he lived at another time,
however, such as ten generations hence in the generation of Abraham, his
goodness would have paled in comparison to the patriarch. As a matter of
fact, there is no evidence in the text that Noah did anything to try to warn
or save any of his fellow human beings. We will see in the coming weeks that
Abraham did do exactly that when faced with a similar situation.

Reish Lakish says exactly the opposite. He says that Noah was righteous
despite the fact that he was surrounded by lawless people. Since he could
be righteous when surrounded by so much sinfulness, it would have been
much easier for him to be righteous if he were in the company of other like-
minded people. I will leave it to you to decide which you think it is.

Finally, the verse tells us that "Noah walked with God." I have discussed
this word holech (walk) before when it is used to describe one's relationship with God. The verb form used here (the hitpael, for those of you who
know Hebrew grammar) really means "to walk about" or "stroll." Most of
the commentators say that the relationship means that Noah walked side
by side with God, relying on God for support and guidance. What I envision
is a partnership, a friendship.

In the rest of this reading, God instructs Noah how to build the ark
including what its dimensions should be and what raw materials he should
use. God says that God will bring a flood to destroy the earth, and that Noah,
his wife, his three sons, and his three daughters-in-law will be the only
people to survive. God will establish a covenant with Noah. Noah is to gather
a male and female couple of every animal into the ark, as well as food for all
of them.

This reading finishes by telling us that Noah did exactly what God had
commanded him to do [6:22]. This was the natural result of the partnership
that they shared.

I think we can learn from what Noah did as well as from what he did not
do. His loyalty to God is admirable, to be sure, and something to which we
can all aspire. However, unlike Abraham and Moses, he didn't care enough
about other human beings, be they sinful or not, to contend with God, to
question God's decisions, to intercede for others. Obedience is admirable;
blind obedience, questionable.

SECOND ALIYAH: GENESIS 7:1–16
MONDAY, OCTOBER 19, 2020

Let it Rain

In this second *aliyah*, we see Noah and his family entering the ark at God's invitation, as well as bringing along the animals in pairs. Then we read about the beginning of the flood.

There are some interesting differences in the story from what we read in the first *aliyah*. First, when God is speaking to Noah, God tells him that he alone has been found to be righteous in his generation [7:1]. But in the last chapter, Noah was described as righteous and pure in his generation. Rashi says that full praise of a person should only be offered when they are not present. In their presence, only partial praise should be given.[1] Presumably, the reason would be that the object of your praise should not get too much of a swelled head. As wonderful as that person may be, humility is also a desirable virtue to have.

Another difference we can't help but notice between this reading and the previous one is the numbers of the animals to be brought into the ark. In the last chapter, the commandment was very straightforward: two of each species, a male and female pair. Here, Noah is told by God to bring one pair of the unclean animals only; of the clean animals, and the birds, he is to bring seven male-female pairs [7:2-3]. The first question we might ask is what is meant by clean versus unclean animals? From the book of Leviticus, we know that these terms refer to two things: animals that are acceptable for sacrifice and animals that are acceptable for eating. One may wonder how Noah knew which were clean and which unclean. Since God did not really explain that to him, we don't know. But we do know that Noah had been instructed to bring food for his family onto the ark, and we will also see later that the first thing that Noah did when he came out of the ark was to offer sacrifices to God. So, that is the reason for the additional animals.

Like last chapter, we once again read that Noah did exactly as God commanded him [7:5].

Let's look more closely at verse 1: "Then the LORD said to Noah, 'Go into the ark, with all your household . . .'" The translation here says that God said to Noah, "go into the ark," but the Hebrew word *bo* really means, "come." So, God is really saying to Noah, "Come into the ark." It is as if God says to Noah, "I am in the ark. Come in here and join me. I will be with you, and I will keep you safe." How beautifully reassuring this seems in light of what can only be thought of as an extremely daunting and overwhelming situation for Noah. Indeed, the chapter finishes by telling us that once Noah and his family entered the ark, "the Lord shut them in" [7:16]. Even as God prepares to destroy the rest of creation, God looks lovingly after those whom God has chosen to keep alive.

Finally, I want to make note of the significance of numbers in this chapter (I'm a former math teacher and you know I can't resist!). The number that appears most often is seven, which is used twice in reference to the numbers of pairs of animals [7:2,3] and twice in reference to the number of days until it began to rain [7:4,10]. Additionally, there are seven different instances where some form of the verb bo (come) appears [7:1,7,9,13,15, and twice in verse 16]. Seven is the number of completeness or perfection. The animals here are "perfect" and the time needed for the final preparations for the flood will be complete. That will happen when all the animals and people who are going to be saved have entered the ark.

Additionally, we are told twice [7:4,12] that it rained for forty days and forty nights. Forty in the *Tanakh* is often used just to represent a long period of time, but it can also represent, according to Sarna, purification and the purging of sin.[2] That, of course, is very fitting to describe God's purpose for the flood: purifying the Earth and cleansing creation of sin. (The other most famous event in the Torah that required forty days and nights for completion was the giving of the Torah on Mt. Sinai—both sets of tablets.)

Finally, we are told the date on which the flood began: "in the second month, on the seventeenth day of the month" [7:11]. This makes sense. The second month is Marcheshvan, the month that just began today. This is the start of the rainy season in Israel. This year, the seventeenth of Marcheshvan begins on Tuesday evening, November 3 (I kid you not!).* I think I'll just leave that here.

THIRD ALIYAH: GENESIS 7:17–8:14
TUESDAY, OCTOBER 20, 2020

We Are Not in Control

This is the story of the flood itself. Here we have the ultimate case of sheltering in place. God closed the door on the ark. The directions for constructing the ark had not included a rudder of any kind so there was no way for Noah to steer the ark in any way. It merely floated on top of the water [7:17,18].

---

*November 3, 2020 was Election Day

The eight people in the ark, along with all the animals, were totally dependent on God for their very existence.

Once again, there is an abundance of numbers and dates in this *aliyah*. It rained for forty days and nights [7:17], the waters rose to a height of 15 cubits (approximately 22.5 feet) above the highest mountaintop [7:20], and the waters stayed on the earth for one hundred fifty days (five months) before receding [7:24, 8:3]. Noah waited forty days before opening the window and sending out the raven [8:6], seven days before sending out the dove [8:10], and seven days before sending out the dove again [7:12]. We have already talked about the significance of the numbers forty and seven.

Let's look at some of the dates in this passage: "in the seventh month, on the seventeenth day of the month, the ark came to rest on the mountains of Ararat" [8:4]. The seventh month is Nisan, and the seventeenth day of that month is the first day of *chol hamoed* (the intermediate days of) *Pesach*. Passover celebrates deliverance from Egyptian slavery and here Noah begins to see his deliverance from the flood. "The waters went on diminishing until the tenth month; in the tenth month, on the first of the month, the tops of the mountains became visible" [8:5]. This would be the first day of Tammuz, sometime in the early summer. "In the six hundred and first year, in the first month, on the first of the month, the waters began to dry from the Earth" [8:13]. This would be the first day of Tishrei—Rosh Hashanah. How appropriate that this would be the beginning of the "new Earth," so to speak. Finally, "in the second month, on the twenty-seventh day of the month, the Earth was dry" [8:14]. This would be the twenty-seventh day of Marcheshvan, thus making the time that Noah spent in the ark exactly one year and ten days.

Especially this year, 2020, this story carries a special significance. Our world was turned upside down in March of this year, and experts say that it probably will not be until spring or summer of 2021 that a vaccine will become widely available, thereby making our time in isolation or semi-isolation slightly over a year.

The comparison is even more poignant when we read what was happening outside the haven of the ark: "All in whose nostrils was the merest breath of life . . . died" [8:22]. How achingly tragic! Think back to the creation of human beings that we read about just last week, when God breathed the soul into the first humans, giving them life. Here, God reclaimed all those precious souls. Though things may be relatively quiet here in New York right now, we still watch each day as the tallies of people who fall victim to the coronavirus continue to rise to unbelievable numbers. In the coming weeks, we will pass more than a quarter of a million deaths in the United States. It is a number that we have difficulty wrapping our head around.

Both the story of Noah in biblical times and the true saga of COVID-19 in our times come to teach us the fragility of life. We learn that no matter how much we may try, we are ultimately not in control of our own lives. Let us all, like Noah, who was righteous and pure in his generation, rely on our relationship with God to guard and preserve us through this crisis.

FOURTH ALIYAH: GENESIS 8:15–9:7
WEDNESDAY, OCTOBER 21, 2020

A Whole New World

In today's *aliyah*, we read about what happened after Noah and his family came out of the ark. Just imagine how Noah (and the others) must have felt at this point. He had been locked up inside the ark for over a year. During that time, he, no doubt, had a lot of time to think. It would have been impossible to ignore the fact that, while these eight people were tucked safely inside, under the watchful care of God, outside, the rest of humanity was dying. Did Noah feel some twinges of guilt now for not having argued with God about what God planned to do, or for not trying to warn any of the others of their impending doom?

Perhaps there was more than a little trepidation at the thought of leaving the protective cocoon of the ark. What would the Earth look like now after the flood? How would he live in a world where there were no other people around? We see here that, just as God had invited Noah to enter the ark, now Noah had to be invited to exit the ark. You may recall from the second reading that God didn't really tell Noah to go into the ark. Rather, God used the word *bo*, saying instead "come into the ark." Similarly, here we see that God said, "come [*tzeh*] out of the ark" [8:16]. But the word *tzeh* really means "leave" or "go out." Thus, God is really saying to Noah, "leave the ark." So, we see that God has, indeed, been with him for the entire journey inside the ark, and now must encourage Noah to leave the safety of the ark and go out into the unknown.

Once Noah came out onto dry land with his family and the animals, we are told that he "built an altar to the LORD and, taking of every clean animal and of every clean bird, he offered burnt offerings on the altar" [8:20]. So, this was indeed the purpose for the seven pairs of all the clean animals and the birds. Most commentators have assumed that this was a sacrifice of thanksgiving for God's deliverance. However, some have suggested that perhaps Noah was bringing a sin offering, asking God's forgiveness for not having done more to mitigate the horrific consequences of the world's sinfulness.

Next, we see that Noah and his sons have a major responsibility: God twice commands them to "be fruitful and multiply" [9:1,7]. This was the same commandment that God had given to Adam and Eve in the Garden of Eden. Here, the world had been created anew, so to speak, with these eight people; if the Earth were to be repopulated, it would happen through them. That has got to seem very daunting!

Finally, we see that here, for the first time, God gives human beings permission to eat meat: "Every creature that lives shall be yours to eat" [9:3]. This is a major concession that God makes. However, God is also aware that allowing human beings to be carnivorous has the potential to desensitize us to taking the life of a living creature. We already saw what happened with Cain and Abel, the first murder of a human being. Therefore, God issues a very stern warning, "Whoever sheds the blood of man, By man shall his blood be shed; For in His image Did God make man" [9:6]. One who commits murder destroys the image of God not only in his victim, but also in himself, making himself guilty of committing this most cardinal of sins. God breathed a soul into each human being, and only God should be privileged to reclaim it at the appointed time. None of us has the right to eclipse that.

FIFTH ALIYAH: GENESIS 9:8–17
THURSDAY, OCTOBER 22, 2020

A Weapon Becomes a Thing of Beauty

In this passage, we see that perhaps Noah was not the only one experiencing some guilt and regret. Perhaps God also felt some regret over causing such major destruction and loss of life. This concept of God feeling regret may seem strange to us. Yet wasn't that exactly what we were told was the impetus for all of this in the first place? When God saw the wickedness of human beings, God regretted having created them [6:6].

Now, God makes a covenant with Noah and all his descendants (i.e., all of humankind), vowing "never again shall all flesh be cut off by the waters of a flood, and never again shall there be a flood to destroy the Earth" [9:11]. When a covenant is made, it is usually accompanied by a physical sign of some sort. We are all familiar with the sign provided by God as a reminder of this promise: "I have set My bow in the clouds, and it shall serve as a sign of the covenant between Me and the Earth" [9:13].

We all call this a rainbow because it appears in the sky only after a rainfall, but notice that God only calls it a "bow." Indeed, the word *keshet* used here, is only used in the Bible to refer to a bow, the most common weapon of warfare in ancient times. Ramban points out that the bow that is God's sign is pointing down, with its legs on the ground, instead of up. He says that human beings do the same thing, turning their bows 180-degrees when they wish to make an overture of peace to their antagonists.[3] With this bow pointing in the direction that it is facing, it could not possibly be used to aim any arrows at the Earth. Additionally, it has no string. It is God's overture of peace to humankind. Most of us are in the habit of looking for a rainbow after a rainfall, particularly a very heavy one. We marvel over their beauty and take pictures when we see them, but not all of us know that there is also a blessing one is supposed to say upon seeing a rainbow:

> Blessed are You, Lord our God, Ruler of the universe, who
> remembers the covenant,
> and is faithful to His covenant, and keeps His promise.

May we all be blessed with many more rainbows, and when we see them may we always remember God's overture of peace.

SIXTH ALIYAH: GENESIS 9:18–10:32
FRIDAY, OCTOBER 23, 2020

A Biblical Origin Story

In this *aliyah*, we read about a potentially embarrassing incident for Noah, and its ramifications for his descendants. The way that it is described in the Torah text almost makes it sound as if it happened practically right away after Noah offered his sacrifices to God, soon after exiting the ark. If we think about it, we realize that several years had to have elapsed before this incident occurred. We are told that Noah was the first person to plant a vineyard [9:20]. Clearly, this would take several years before the vines would produce enough grapes to ferment into wine, and the wine could be produced. Skipping over all of that, we are told in the very next verse that Noah drank the wine and became drunk [9:21]. Reading this today with our modern sensitivities, many of us immediately form a negative opinion of Noah. What happened to the man whom God thought of as righteous and pure, the man who walked with God?

Some of the commentators are not so harsh on Noah. Abarbanel says that "he had good reason never to want to see water again, let alone to drink it."[4] Sarna says that "no blame attaches to Noah since he was oblivious to the intoxicating effects of his discovery."[5]

In 2020, we, too, should have more sympathy for Noah. God had commanded him and his sons to be fruitful and multiply; yet the genealogies in the rest of this *parashah* show that Noah himself was unable to do this and only his original three sons are listed [10:1]. The three of them all had children, but Noah himself did not. Whatever issues Noah had (and no doubt there were many) he had no contemporaries to talk to; his life had to have been lonely and solitary. Not only that, but the next few verses also show that he had problems with his children. We learn that because of his drunkenness, he "uncovered himself in his tent." [10:21] A better translation is "he was uncovered within his tent." This wording implies that possibly someone else was responsible for this, for embarrassing Noah in his state of incapacity. Some of the commentators go so far as to suggest that a castration or a rape had occurred.

In any event, he was discovered by his youngest son, Ham, whose response was to go and tell his two brothers about it, perhaps mocking their father. Shem and Japheth took a cloth and walked into their father's tent backwards, turning their faces away so as not to see his nakedness, covered him with the cloth and then exited. This was an ultimate show of respect.

What follows is essentially an origin story (since those are so popular today). When Noah discovered what happened, he cursed not Ham, but his son Canaan (does that name sound familiar?) and his descendants going forward. He said that they would be slaves to the descendants of Shem. He went on to bless Shem, referring to God as "the God of Shem." We will see later in the genealogy that Shem's famous descendant is Abraham. Having already read the end of the Torah, where the nation of Israel stood poised to enter and claim the land of Canaan, we have already seen how all this this played out in the future.

SEVENTH ALIYAH: GENESIS 11:1–32
WRITTEN FOR SHABBAT, SATURDAY, OCTOBER 24, 2020

Blah, Blah, Blah, Blah, Blah, Blah . . .

After reading of the death of Noah and the listing of the names of the subsequent generations, we see that the population of the Earth began to swell.

However, having all descended from one man, they all spoke the same language [11:1], and they were all living in close proximity to one another. They devised a plan to build a city and a tower with its top in the sky, to build a name for themselves [11:4]. Their motivations were vain and selfish and their intention was to challenge the authority of God. Ironically, their desire was to reach heaven because that was where they thought God was. God, instead, came down to earth to inspect their project. God's fear was that there would be nothing that they would not attempt if they continued to be united in speaking one language. Additionally, Rashbam says that a greater sin that they were guilty of was not following God's commandment to "be fruitful and multiply and fill the Earth."[6] Instead, they lived together in one place, and their motivation for building their city and their tower was, "lest we be scattered all over the world" [11:4].

This generation had learned nothing from the generation of the flood. God was once again very disappointed with human beings, but had vowed never again to destroy all of humankind. Instead, God's solution was to "confound their speech, so that they will not understand one another" [11:7]. That is why the tower was called Babel, because that is exactly what everything suddenly sounded like [11:9]!

Today, working together with someone who speaks a different language than you do creates a situation where one needs to work much harder to make it happen. Unity is still a desired outcome.

On the other hand, as I sat and wrote this, I watched the final presidential debate between Donald Trump and Joe Biden prior to the election. In so many ways, it was a microcosm of where we are as a country: most of us speak the same language, and yet it sounds like so much babble. Even with a common tongue, it seems we are so far removed from being able to work together for the common good.

Those who attempted to construct the Tower of Babel wished to be in control of their world and their destiny. If there is anything that we have learned this past year, it is that, ultimately, we do not have complete control over our world. We have all read about the Bubonic Plague, the Spanish Flu, and any number of other pandemics that wreaked havoc with the Earth's population. None of us were prepared to deal with one in our own generation. We have been jolted out of our complacency in a harrowing way. May we learn the hard lessons that our biblical ancestors did not, and may we find a way to work through this crisis—united, not divided.

Finally, the story of the Tower of Babel is followed by another genealogy. In the last seven verses, we are introduced to Shem's most famous descendant, Abram, and his wife Sarai. We will read much more about them in the coming weeks.

Parashat Lech Lecha

FIRST ALIYAH: GENESIS 12:1–13
SUNDAY, OCTOBER 25, 2020

Leaving it all Behind

We first met Abram at the end of last week's *parashah*; he was a tenth-generation descendant of Noah through his son Shem. His story officially begins here, with God's call to him to leave his land and set out on his own. The English translation of verse 1 does not accurately convey the fact that there were in fact three things that God told Abram to leave and go out from: your land (country), and your birthplace (i.e., extended family), and your father's house (i.e., immediate family).

Much has been made of the order in which these three things are listed. At first glance, it seems that the order is the reverse of what it should be: if Abram left his country, then wouldn't he de facto also automatically have left both his birthplace and his father's house? On the other hand, isn't it indeed possible that he could leave his father's house, but still be in his birthplace? Or that he could leave his birthplace, but still be in his land? The three places are listed in reverse order, from the most general and largest area to the most specific and smallest area. The rabbis, however, explain that the order is indeed correct: the places are listed according to the level of difficulty that Abram would have in separating himself from them. It would be difficult for him to leave his country, even harder to leave his birthplace, and harder still to leave his father's house.

Next, we see the promises of things that God will do to bring blessings to Abram as a reward for his willingness to do what God asks [12:2-3]. Interestingly, we notice that there are also three things that God promises, and that they are listed in the reverse order of the three places that he left behind: I will bless you (and make your name great); and I will bless those who bless you (and curse those who curse you); and all the families of the Earth will bless themselves through you.

The blessings go from the very specific (Abram himself) to those with whom he interacts, and finally to the most general, to all of humankind.

We see here an inverse relationship: the harder it is to give something up, the greater the rewards received for doing so.

We, too, are sometimes called to make sacrifices, to give things up because of our lives as Jews. We must give up certain foods that perhaps we really like to eat, or certain activities that we like to do. The rewards, however, for living a life of *mitzvot*, are great; they extend not only to us, but to our families, and to those with whom we come into contact. Like paying it forward, if those with whom we come into contact also live a life of *mitzvot* then the circle of blessings widens even further. Like ripples left in the water by a rock thrown into it, we may never know how far our sphere of positive influence can extend.

Our world needs a lot of blessings right now. I challenge us all to commit ourselves to walking more closely with God, just as Abram did. Let's all do our part. And remember not to concentrate on the negatives or what you may have to leave behind. Count instead on the blessings that will follow.

SECOND ALIYAH: GENESIS 12:14–13:4
MONDAY, OCTOBER 26, 2020

Take My Wife—Please[1]

We have just learned about Abram setting out from his home with his wife Sarai and his nephew Lot and all he owns and heading for a land that God would show him. No sooner had he arrived than the Torah tells us he ran into a problem: a severe famine in the land. So, we read at the end of the last reading that he went down to Egypt to wait out the famine; presumably, there was food in Egypt. We also read that Abram made a strange request of his wife as they were about to enter the land: ". . . he said to his wife Sarai, 'I know what a beautiful woman you are. If the Egyptians see you, and think, 'She is his wife,' they will kill me and let you live. Please say that you are my sister, that it may go well with me because of you, and that I may remain alive thanks to you'" [12:11-13].

Apparently, this was a somewhat accepted practice in the ancient world, that a foreign woman entering the land could be "claimed" by the leader of that land for himself. Abram, knowing how beautiful his wife was, appeared to have resigned himself to the idea that she would be taken. However, if the Egyptians knew that she was married, they would have to kill her husband before claiming her. To avoid that possibility, he asked her to lie, saying instead that she was his sister, not his wife! Suddenly our new hero seems tainted. To our modern sensitivities, especially considering the #MeToo movement, this request is unconscionable. Not only was Sarai taken into Pharaoh's palace, helpless to do anything, but her husband would profit by the situation: "And because of her, it went well with Abram; he acquired sheep, oxen, asses, male and female slaves, she-asses, and camels" [12:16].

Though Abram was reluctant to speak up in defense of his wife, God came to her rescue by bringing plagues on Egypt [12:17]. Pharaoh angrily summoned Abram to him and chastised him for his dishonesty, and then told him to leave the land, sending him out with everything he owned, including all the new wealth he had just acquired—dishonestly—in Egypt.

From Sarai's point of view, this is a horrible story. In essence, her husband pimped her out for his own safety and personal gain. She remained silent throughout; the Torah does not give her a voice. Even Pharaoh's words to Abram are very telling: "Why did you say, 'She is my sister,' so that I took her as my wife?" [12:18]. This would indicate that, despite asking Sarai to lie to Pharaoh, Abram himself told Pharaoh that she was his sister. Some people question whether Pharaoh really went so far as to consummate a relationship with Sarai, claiming that God's intervention through the unnamed plagues surely must have prevented that from happening. But notice in Pharaoh's statement above that he clearly said that he took her as his wife; in the ancient world, there is only one thing that could possibly mean. (Amazingly, we will see this same exact scenario played out again later in the Book of Genesis with Abram and Sarai, and again after that, with Isaac and Rebekah.)

There are also some who point out that this situation is a metaphor for what we will see later in the book of Exodus: Sarai represents the nation of Israel, who are taken into Egypt by their divine spouse (in this case, God) because of a famine in Canaan, only to become abused by Pharaoh, helpless to improve their situation until God intervenes with plagues.

In researching this passage, I found that there are several commentators who are also uncomfortable with Abram's conduct here. In the following *midrash*, the story is retold with a little more detail, and Sarai is given not only a voice, but empowerment:

> And when the princes of Pharaoh saw Sarai, they were greatly
> surprised at her beauty, and all the princes assembled and
> hastened unto Pharaoh and informed him concerning what [had]

happened, and they praised Sarai's beauty [to] the king. And the king ordered his servants to bring Sarai [to him]. And Pharaoh saw Sarai, and he was greatly pleased with her, and the king was greatly astonished at her beauty . . . And the woman was taken [immediately] into the house of Pharaoh. And Abram was greatly grieved about his wife, and he prayed fervently [to] the Lord to deliver Sarai from the hands of Pharaoh. And Sarai likewise prayed [to] the Lord, saying: . . . oh Lord, behold we have done as [You have] commanded . . . us, and we have left our country and our family, and we went forth [to] a foreign land among people whom we have not known, neither yesterday nor day before yesterday. And now after we have come into this country to save our household from famine this unfortunate event [has] befallen me. And therefore, oh Lord my God, save and deliver me from the hands of this oppressor, and show kindness [to] me for the sake of [Your mercy]. And the Lord [listened to] the voice of Sarai and the Lord sent an angel to deliver her from the hands of Pharaoh. And Pharaoh came and seated himself in the presence of Sarai, and the angel of the Lord stood by her side, visible only unto her, and the angel said unto Sarai: Fear not, for the Lord [has] heard [your] prayer. And the king approached Sarai and said [to] her: Who is the man that brought [you here]? And she said: He is my brother. And the king continued: It is my desire to make him great and exalted, and to do [to] him all kindness which [you may] ask concerning him. And the king [sent] at the same time [to] Abram silver and gold and pearls and precious stones in great abundance, and sheep and cattle and [male] servants and [female] servants. And the king gave orders and they brought Abram to dwell in the court of the royal palace, and the king made Abram very great even in that night. And the king came near to Sarai, and he stretched out his hand to touch her, when the angel of the Lord dealt him a severe blow, and the king was scared and he abstained from trying to touch her once more. But the king came near Sarai once more when the angel [knocked] him to the ground, and the angel continued [this way] through the whole night and the king was greatly terrified. And the servants of the king likewise, as also all the people of his household were stricken by the angel with a grievous plague on account of Sarai, and there was a great crying and weeping in the household of Pharaoh that night. And Pharaoh seeing the great evil which [had] befallen him said: [Truly] for the sake of this woman all this is done [to] us; and Pharaoh kept away at a distance from her, and he spoke [to] her very kind words. And the king said: Do give me the true information concerning the man [you came] with? And Sarai replied: Know then that this man I came with is my husband, yet I said he is my brother for fear [that you] might kill him in your wickedness. And the king decided to release Sarai, and the plagues at once ceased, [by which] the angel of the Lord had smitten him and his people, and Pharaoh was convinced that on account of Sarai he [had] suffered all that great evil, and the king wondered greatly. [*Sefer HaYashar, Book of Genesis, Lech Lecha* 5][2]

In this account, we are told that both Abram and Sarai prayed to God, yet only the words of Sarai's prayer are recorded, and she prayed on behalf of both herself and her husband. God heard her prayer and sent an angel to protect her; the angel prevented Pharaoh from even touching her.

None of this, of course, is in the biblical text. This is a classic example of a *midrash* that is told to not only fill in the gaps, but also to correct several perceived wrongs that we may see in the original text. For women trying to reclaim our place in the Torah, this is a much better version of the story.

THIRD ALIYAH: GENESIS 13:5–18
TUESDAY, OCTOBER 27, 2020

Things Are Looking Up

After the incident in Egypt, Abram returned to Canaan. There he found that there was not enough room for both him and his flocks, and Lot and his flocks, and thus quarrelling resulted between their shepherds. Realizing that they had to separate, Abram offered the choice to Lot: one would go north and the other would go south. We are told that, "Lot raised his eyes and saw" how well-watered the plain of the Jordan was [13:10] and the lush green land appeared ideal for grazing his sheep. Rather than graciously offering that side to Abram, he chose it for himself, and moved out. After they were separated, God commanded Abram, "raise your eyes and look . . . to the north and south, to the east and west" in all four directions [13:14]. God promised Abram that God would give to Abram's descendants all the land that he could see. Lot may have thought that he was getting the better deal, but he had limited his vision. God told Abram not to limit his vision, but rather to look everywhere.

Generations later, God gave the same command to Moses: "Go up to the summit of Pisgah and gaze about, to the west, the north, the south, and the east. Look at it well, for you shall not go across yonder Jordan" [Deuteronomy 3:27].

Now God told Moses to look out over the same land, again in all four directions. Though he would not enter the land, the nation of Abram's descendants stood ready to enter the land and take possession of it, finally fulfilling God's promise to Abram. Like bookends, the commandment appears at the beginning and end of the Torah, first with unrealized potential, and later with the anticipation of fulfillment. Clearly, the message is that God keeps God's promises.

There are three additional instances in Abraham's life when he "raised his eyes and saw" something that was life-changing:

> Looking up, he saw three men standing near him. As soon as he
> saw them, he ran from the entrance of the tent to greet them and,
> bowing to the ground, [18:2]
> On the third day, Abraham looked up and saw the place from afar. [22:4]
> When Abraham looked up, his eye fell upon a ram, caught in the
> thicket by its horns. So, Abraham went and took the ram and
> offered it up as a burnt offering in place of his son. [22:13)]

In the first instance, Abram saw three "men" approaching his tent; they turned out to be three angels, one of them bringing a message from God that Sarah would have a child.

In the second, he saw the place on which God would ask him to sacrifice that child.

In the third, he saw a ram caught in a thicket that an angel told him to sacrifice in place of that child.

In each instance, unlike Lot, he looked up, raising his eyes all the way to take in his surroundings. He saw what God wanted him to see and, as a result, was the beneficiary of God's blessings.

We, too, need to look up—to raise our eyes and see—the things that God would reveal to us. If we don't, then, like Lot, we don't see the whole picture; we limit our vision, and consequently, also limit our opportunity to see God's blessings. That's not always so easy to do, I know, but just think about what you might be missing. Why limit yourself?

Abram Steps Up His Game

Here we have a very strange and unusual passage in the Torah, which almost doesn't seem to fit in with the rest of the text. Basically, we are reading the first biblical account of warfare. A group of four eastern kings waged war against a group of five kings from the west, including the kings of Sodom and Gomorrah (this was the area where Lot had settled when Abram gave him the choice of where to go). As a result of all of this, Lot and his family were taken captive, and all their possessions were taken as well [14:12]. Upon hearing the news, Abram put together an army of three hundred eighteen of his servants and went off to fight against Lot's captors. Speedily defeating them, he brought back Lot, his wife, and the rest of his family, and all his possessions.

One of the functions of this story is to serve as vindication for Abram; Lot had selfishly chosen what looked like the better tract of land, but that decision was what led to him being taken captive. Abram appears here as the hero. It is the only story in the Torah that presents him in a militaristic mode.

Another function is to present Abram in a more positive, assertive character mode, in contrast to his behavior in Egypt, where he appeared to be very cowardly and non-assertive.

Finally, Abram is to be lauded here for observing the *mitzvah* of *pidyon shevuyim,* ransoming the captives. Abram could rightfully have borne resentment against his nephew for selfishly choosing the better plot of land to settle on. Instead, his feelings of familial loyalty took over (notice that he did not get involved in the conflict between the warring groups of kings until he was told that Lot and his family had been taken). Throughout Jewish history, this *mitzvah* of *pidyon shevuyim,* ransoming the captives, has been one of extraordinary importance. The Talmud explains it:

> . . . the Gemara relates that Ifera Hurmiz, the mother of King
> Shapur, king of Persia, sent a purse . . . full of dinars to Rav Yosef.
> She said to him: Let the money be used for a great *mitzva.* Rav
> Yosef sat and considered the question: What did Ifera Hurmiz
> mean when she attached a condition to the gift, saying that
> it should be used for a great *mitzva?* Abaye said to him: From
> what Rav Shmuel bar Yehuda taught, that one does not impose
> a charity obligation on orphans even for the sake of redeeming
> captives, learn from this . . .
> . . . that redeeming captives is a great *mitzva.* [*BT Bava Batra 8A:18–8B:1*]

This *mitzvah* is considered more important than feeding and clothing the poor. Communal funds were to be allocated for ransoming captives. According to Maimonides, if one delays fulfilling this *mitzvah*, it is as serious as if he had committed murder.[3]

In modern times, this *mitzvah* has taken precedence in Israel, when IDF soldiers have been taken captive in a wartime setting. A captive should never be ransomed for an unrealistically exorbitant sum of money. Yet the State of Israel has sometimes exchanged large numbers of Arab prisoners for one Israeli soldier. Look up the story of Gilad Shalit.[4]

In any event, at the end of today's reading, we see that Abram received blessings from King Melchizedek for his actions.

After the failure of the first generation of human beings, as well as the failure of the generation of Noah, God needed to be sure that Abram and his descendants would not fail. In this instance, it seems, Abram has passed one more test.

FIFTH ALIYAH: GENESIS 14:21–15:6
THURSDAY, OCTOBER 29, 2020

Not Seeing is Believing

In this *aliyah* we have the first recorded conversation between Abram and God. God begins the dialogue by telling Abram that, going forward, God will be a *magen* (shield) to him [15:1] and Abram will not have to engage in warfare anymore. God had bigger plans for him, therefore, God would be his protector. It is from here that we derive the term *Magen Avraham*, Shield of Abraham, to refer to God. (This should sound familiar to you from the second opening blessing of every *Amidah*.) In the second half of the verse, God continued, telling Abram that he would receive a great reward. Abram's first recorded words to God are, "O Lord GOD, what can You give me, seeing that I shall die childless?" [15:2]. In other words, Abram assumed that God referred to a material reward of some kind. As he was already advanced in years and had no progeny, all his wealth would pass on to his servant. There would be no remnant and Abram's line would die off with him. So, he seemed to be asking God, "what good will anything that You give me do for me?"

In response, God assured him that, despite his advanced age, "none but your very own issue shall be your heir" [15:4]. Then, as if that weren't enough, God brought Abram outside and said to him, "Look toward heaven and count the stars, if you are able to count them . . . So shall your off-spring be" [15:5]. Most of us are familiar with this promise that God made to Abram.

If you've ever been in the desert, or the mountains, or out on the water—any place far away from the light pollution of our cities and suburbs—and looked up at the night sky, you know that feeling of seeing more stars in the night sky than you ever have before. You know you can't possibly count them and, if you know anything at all about modern astronomy, you know that there are so many more that are out there in the universe that none of us can see.

That is what I have always thought of when I read about God saying to Abram, "count the stars, if you are able to count them." However, this year I realized something I never did before: based on what happens next in the biblical text, we know that this conversation took place during the daytime! So, when God instructed Abram to count the stars "if he can," that was because he could not even see them! God was asking Abram to believe in something that he was not even able to see! Intuitively, Abram could envision what the night sky looked like—he knew the stars were up there—but in that moment, he truly was not even capable of seeing them.

So many people spend a great deal of time looking for scientific evidence to prove or disprove the validity of biblical events. How does the big bang theory jive with the story of creation? Are there scientific explanations of the plagues in Egypt? Can we determine which mountain was Mt. Sinai? Are there remnants of Noah's Ark on Mt. Ararat? On and on it goes. Such questions have been explored practically since the Torah was written down. In the end, people who explore questions like these spend so much time looking for "proof" that they miss the messages that the Torah comes to teach us.

We will see in the coming chapters of Genesis that, when Abram is able to believe in God's promise even though he cannot see the evidence of it, then he will merit receiving all the blessings that God is promising to bestow on him, beginning with an heir. In the same way, when we can study the Torah, recognizing its intrinsic holiness, even though we cannot prove or disprove its historic accuracy, then, we too, like Abram, will merit receiving the blessings that come with a relationship with the Divine.

So, I challenge you: count the stars, if you can!

Playing God

In the first part of this long reading, we have this strange story of the second recorded conversation between Abram and God. In this dialogue, two significant things happen: first, God foretells the Egyptian enslavement by telling Abram that his offspring will be strangers in a foreign land for four hundred years, and that God will free them from there [15:13-14]; and second, God promises Abram that the land in which he is standing (Canaan) will be given to his descendants.

The balance of this reading deals with the story of the birth of Abram's first child. This is another story that does not shine a positive light on either Abram or Sarai.

We have known since the first time that Sarai was introduced to us at the end of last week's *parashah* that she was barren. Now that God had promised Abram that he would have a son of his own, her barrenness could clearly be a deterrent to that happening. Therefore, she concocted a scheme that involved her servant, Hagar (who, by the way, is Egyptian. No doubt that she was part of the gifts that Pharaoh gave to Abram after the incident with Sarai). Sarai wanted Abram to impregnate Hagar, and Sarai would claim the child as her own [17:2]. Once Hagar conceived, however, she looked down on Sarai [17:4] since she had been able to do what Sarai could not. Clearly, Abram was not the infertile party here.

This, in turn, led to strife between husband and wife: she complained to him that Hagar now despised her, and he told her to deal with it on her own [17:5-6]. Sarai then treated her handmaid harshly, and, as a result, Hagar ran away into the wilderness. There she was met by an angel of God, who ultimately told her to return to Sarai's home, promising her that she would give birth to a son, and that she would have too many descendants to be counted [17:10-11]. The angel instructed her to name her son Ishmael, meaning "God has heard."

Hagar followed the angel's instructions and this part of the story finishes with the birth of Ishmael when Abram is eight-six years old [17:15-16].

At the end of this section, the Torah jumps ahead to Abram's ninety-ninth year. We have no idea what happened in those thirteen intervening years and can only assume that Abram learned to trust God more during that time. Now, God once again promised him that he would be a father to many nations [17:4,6], and God changed his name by adding an extra letter *heh*, making his name Avraham (Abraham). In the Torah, a name change is usually indicative of a major life change. We will see in the next reading what God has in mind for our patriarch.

Hagar, whose name could translate to "the one who lives [with you]" is the unwitting victim in this story. She is not seen by either her mistress or her master as anything more than a means to an end; neither one of them ever calls her by her name. She is first addressed by her name by the angel who meets her in the desert [17:8]; indeed, she is the first person in the Torah to be visited by an angel. Though the human beings do not really see her as a person, God sees her. She is the only woman in the Torah to receive a promise of many descendants (the very same promise that God had made to Abram). She is the first woman in the Bible to be told by God (through the angel) that she will have a child and, as we will see in the next chapter, she is the first person in the Torah to cry.

And she is the first woman to give Abram a son (though Ishmael is not, we shall see, the son to whom God referred to when God promised Abram an heir of his own). This son, as you may be aware, later goes on to be the progenitor of the Arabic peoples and is regarded as a prophet by Muslims.

We have in the story of Hagar and Ishmael an origin story. And both are innocent victims here.

Hagar is the most admirable human character in this story. Abram and Sarai, in addition to grossly mistreating Hagar, are guilty of "playing God." Since God had told Abram that he would have a child of his own, they took things into their own hands, and tried to force it to happen, only to be met with drastic consequences, and two human victims of their inability to trust God to fulfill God's promise.

Sometimes, it's hard to trust God. We become impatient waiting for God to bestow blessings upon us.

Right now, many of us are impatient to see a vaccine and a potential end to this pandemic that is raging again elsewhere in our country, and the world. But if a vaccine is pushed through too quickly because we do not trust either God or the doctors who have been entrusted by God with the medical abilities to develop that vaccine, the consequences could be disastrous, and there could be many human victims. Let us not, like Abram and Sarai, complicate what is already a very difficult situation.

And let us not look at others without using their names, without recognizing their humanity. May we recognize that we are all partners in God's creation, and in this fight to conquer COVID-19.

SEVENTH ALIYAH: GENESIS 17:7–27
WRITTEN FOR SHABBAT, SATURDAY, OCTOBER 31, 2020

It's All in a Name

In this last section, God instructs Abraham that the sign of the covenant between God and Israel will be that all males will be circumcised on the eighth day of life [17:10-12]. This, of course, is where the *brit milah* (covenant of circumcision) comes from.

Next, God changes Sarai's name: replacing the *yud* with a *heh*, her name now becomes Sarah. Now she, too, is ready for a major life change and is going to bear a son whom they are to name *Yitzchak,* Isaac. Sarah is ten years younger than Abraham and will be ninety years old when she gives birth to her first and only son. Isaac will be the son through whom God will make Abraham numerous, as well.

I want to show you something I noticed about the name changes for our first patriarch and matriarch: they maintain the covenant. God promises also to bless Ishmael and make him his descendant.

Abraham had a *heh* added to his name. Sarah had a *yud* removed from her name and replaced with a *heh*. The numerical value of *yud* is ten, the numerical value of *heh* is five. So, we see that the ten that was removed from Sarai's name was split equally between herself and her husband—they each received exactly half of it, five.

To me, this is symbolic of the idea that they are more united now, working in unison with each other.

As I mentioned once before, the Talmud teaches that there are three partners in the creation of each child: mother, father, and God [Kiddushin 30B:21, Niddah 31A:1,9]. With this dual name change, Abraham and Sarah are finally ready to become partners in becoming parents to the child that they have desired for so long, and with whom God is now ready to bless them.

Parashat Vayera

FIRST ALIYAH: GENESIS 18:1–14
SUNDAY, NOVEMBER 1, 2020

She's Laughing, but It's No Joke

Here we have the story of the celestial visitors to the tent of Abraham and Sarah. Though they are acknowledged as being non-humans masquerading in human form, there is some disagreement about who, or what, they are. Some say that they are three angels, some say that they are two angels accompanying God. In any event, Abraham sees them approaching at what was possibly the hottest part of the day and insists that they turn aside into his tent to rest a bit from their journey. Much has been written about Abraham in this passage. His visitors are there to observe the *mitzvah* of visiting the sick (he had just been circumcised at the end of the previous *parashah* at the age of ninety-nine). And he is the consummate example of someone who extends hospitality to the wayfarer.

Yet, throughout this passage, Abraham is referred to more often through masculine third person singular pronouns (he, him) rather than by name. His name does not appear until verse 6. Sarah, on the other hand, is only referred to by her name, never by an impersonal pronoun. The implication would be, therefore, that she takes precedence over him in this reading. Indeed, it seems, the primary purpose of their visit is to announce to Sarah the news that she will have a son the following year. Some say that the original intent was to inform her directly of her impending motherhood, since God had already told Abraham. What's more, the visitors asked Abraham where Sarah was before addressing their host: "They said to him, 'Where is your wife Sarah?'" [18:9]. Notice that the word *elav* (to him) is written with three dots over it, to call our attention to it. Gersonides says that the dots come to tell us that the messengers' original intention had been to give their news to Sarah alone (since Abraham already knew), but she disappeared behind the door of the tent out of respect for them, forcing them to ask Abraham where she was.[1] Once that information was ascertained, the pronouncement was made to Abraham since he was the only person physically in front of them, yet it was said loudly enough that she could hear.

Think about it: in the previous *parashah*, Hagar received a personal announcement from an angel about her impending motherhood. Though Ishmael is Abraham's son, he is not the one through whom the covenant will be sealed. How much more so should Sarah, Abraham's wife, who will become the mother of the promised heir, be the beneficiary of the annunciation? Additionally, this birth will be truly miraculous: Sarah will be ninety years old and her husband one hundred years old when this baby is born. There can be no question that there is a Divine hand in this birth.

We will see that God did indeed have something to discuss with Abraham, but that occurred later, on the road, as the three visitors departed. Clearly, God did not need to come into the tent to talk with Abraham. They have had several conversations out in the open air. God did, however, need to come into the tent to talk to Sarah, for that was where she spent most of her time.

Viewing this conversation in this light puts Abraham and Sarah on equal footing. They both have wanted this child, and they will parent this child together. It is no surprise that each of them, separately, laughed—probably from both incredulity and happiness—when they heard the news.

SECOND ALIYAH: GENESIS 18:15–33
MONDAY, NOVEMBER 2, 2020

Arguing with God

Here we have the famous story of Abraham "arguing" with God over the fate of the people of Sodom and Gemorrah. As Abraham accompanies his three guests when they depart from his tent, the one who is God (or representing God) tells him that God is about to destroy the cities because the outcry from them is so great, and their sin is so grievous [18:20]. Knowing that his nephew Lot and his family live in Sodom, Abraham tries to bargain with God [18:23-33] saying that it would be unjust for God to destroy the innocent along with the guilty. What if there are fifty righteous people in the cities? God says that the cities will not be destroyed in that case. Abraham asks, what about forty-five? No, the cities will not be destroyed. Forty? No. Thirty? No. Twenty? No. Finally, ten? No, the cities still will not be destroyed. And the bargaining stops there.

This story shows Abraham to be more righteous than Noah since he intercedes with God on behalf of others. In addition, since he goes no lower than ten with his count, this is one of the texts from which the rabbis derive the number of ten as the minimum number of Jews required for a prayer quorum, a *minyan*. Ten is the minimum number of Jews that make up a community.

A bigger question that has been contemplated by many is this: what exactly was the great sin that warranted the destruction of Sodom and Gemorrah? The text does not tell us. Because of what follows in the next section of the *parashah*, many sages say the people were guilty of sexual immorality.

Others are not happy with this explanation. Pointing to the word *za-akat*, which literally means "her outcry," they say that the word "her" does not really refer to the city, as is usually thought, but rather refers to a single individual, a woman named Peletit. According to the *midrash*, she was one of Lot's daughters, and was married to an aristocrat. Her "crime" was having compassion for the poor of the city and trying to help them:

> Rabbi Jehudah said: They made a proclamation in Sodom (saying):
> Everyone who strengthens the hand of the poor or the needy with
> a loaf of bread shall be [burned] by fire. Peleṭith, daughter of Lot,
> was wedded to one of the magnates of Sodom. She saw a certain
> very poor man in the street of the city, and her soul was grieved
> on his account . . . What did she do? Every day when she went
> out to draw water she put in her bucket all sorts of provisions
> from her home, and she fed that poor man. The men of Sodom
> said: How does this poor man live? When they ascertained the
> facts, they brought her forth to be [burned] with fire. She said:
> Sovereign of all worlds! Maintain my right and my cause (at the
> hands of) the men of Sodom. And her cry ascended before the
> Throne of Glory. In that hour the Holy One, blessed be He, said:
> "I will now descend, and I will see" whether the men of Sodom
> have done according to the cry of this young woman . . . as it
> is said, "I will now descend, and I will see whether they have
> done altogether according to her cry, which [has] come unto me"
> "According to their cry" is not written here (in the text), only
> "According to her cry." [Pirkei de Rabbi Eliezer 25:8][2]

The same story is told slightly differently in the Talmud. Her "crime" is the same, as is her fate, though it was actualized slightly differently:

There was a young woman who would take bread out to the
poor people in a pitcher so the people of Sodom would not see it.
The matter was revealed, and they smeared her with honey and
positioned her on the wall of the city, and the hornets came and
consumed her. And that is the meaning of that which is written:
"And the Lord said: Because the cry of Sodom and Gomorrah is
great [*rabba*]" . . . And Rav Yehuda says that Rav says: *Rabba* is an
allusion to the matter of the young woman [*riva*] who was killed
for her act of kindness. It is due to that sin that the fate of the
people of Sodom was sealed. [*Sanhedrin 109B:9*]

A society that would not only not care for its poor, but, worse yet, would
take the life of someone who does reach out to help them is a society in
which all the values of justice and compassion are turned upside down. This
kind of depravity constitutes a society totally devoid of Torah values. This is
the kind of sin that would capture the attention of God and bring about the
destruction of such a city.

So, once again, just like the generation of the flood, we see people behaving with such depravity that they are judged and condemned to death. Noah
walked with God, and followed God's instructions, to save himself and his
family, but did nothing to try to save anyone else. Abraham walked before God
and tried (unsuccessfully) to convince God to save the cities from destruction.

Still, neither man spoke to any of the doomed people to try to convince
them to give up their sinful ways!

In our world today, we see many of our values trampled daily, by leaders
and ordinary citizens, as well. We dare not stand by and watch it happen. We
must speak out when we view rampant injustice. We must do what we can
to care for those who are unable to provide for themselves. For if we do not,
then we ourselves are complicit.

THIRD ALIYAH: GENESIS 19:1–20
TUESDAY, NOVEMBER 3, 2020

Breaking Up is Hard to Do[3]

As God (or the angel representing God) remained behind to talk with Abraham, the other two angels continued to Sodom, to check out first-hand what
was going on in the city. What follows is one of the more disturbing sections
of the Torah. As the angels enter town, they encounter Lot, who prevails

upon them to spend the night at his residence [19:1-3]. Since we are told that he prepared for them cakes of unleavened bread, some commentators tell us that this incident took place during *Pesach*. Before long, we are told, all the men of Sodom surround Lot's house, demanding that he send out his visitors so that they may "be intimate with them" [19:4-5]. At this point, we do not know whether Lot realizes that his guests are in reality angelic emissaries. What we do know is that he wishes to protect them from the angry mob outside. Sounds noble, right? That is until we realize what he offers to the townsmen instead to appease them: his own two unmarried daughters [19:8]! Ramban says that this indicates that Lot was essentially an evil person—one to whom sexual abuse of women meant little.[4] Indeed, especially when we view this incident in light of the #MeToo Movement, we wonder how depraved one must be to offer his own daughters to an angry mob for sexual favors? This leads us to wonder further: why does Lot even warrant this divine intervention to save his life?

Indeed, the angels intervene, pulling him into the house to save him from the rioting crowd, and then blinding them with a bright light [19:10-11]. After an unsuccessful attempt to convince his sons-in-law to come with him, he still needs to be pushed to leave. Still, he delays and must be physically removed from the town by the angels [19:16]. They tell him, "Flee for your life! Do not look behind you, nor stop anywhere in the Plain; flee to the hills, lest you be swept away" [19:17]. Even now, once more, Lot asks if he can't go to a town that is closer instead [19:20]. This is where the story leaves us.

This whole scenario leaves us very uncomfortable, and with many questions. In answer to the question posed above regarding why Lot warranted divine intervention to save his life, I think it is only the merit of Abraham that sent the two angels to visit Lot in the first place. Lot has shown himself to be devoid of moral character. He was drawn to Sodom by the lush green pastureland for his flocks. Even after he was kidnapped from Sodom in the battle of the kings, he still returned to live in a society that had become morally corrupt. Rather than rise above it, he allowed two of his daughters to marry into the society and was willing to offer up his remaining two daughters as a sacrifice to the corrupt townspeople. When given the chance to leave, he hesitated time and time again.

Returning to Abraham, we may wonder why he did not do more to save his nephew; after all, he was the one who had previously mustered up an army of men and gone to free Lot when he was taken captive. Even as Abraham bargained with God over the number of people who might be saved from Sodom, he never mentioned Lot by name.

We may also wonder why, when the angels told Lot to leave Sodom, he was not given the option to return to Canaan and live with Abraham. After all, they were the last remaining family members that each had from the "old country."

Putting all of this together, I think that all of this happened because Abraham needed to separate from Lot once and for all. His presence had become toxic.

Abraham and Sarah had both just had their names changed by God and been assured that they were about to have their much longed-for child, and that God would establish his covenant with their descendants. The last thing they needed to worry about was Lot and his poor decisions.

Sometimes ending relationships, particularly with family members, is necessary for one's own well-being. That doesn't make it any easier to do so.

FOURTH ALIYAH: GENESIS 19:21–21:4
WEDNESDAY, NOVEMBER 4, 2020

One Death, Three Births, One Bris

This *aliyah* has a lot going on in it. First, we have the completion of the story of the destruction of Sodom and Gomorrah [19:21-29] when God rains down fire from heaven on the cities, but you may recall that the angel had told Lot and his family not to look back as they left the city. Here we have the familiar account of his wife looking back and being turned into a pillar of salt. If you have been in Israel and traveled to the shores of the Dead Sea, with its high salt concentration, you can almost envision this happening. We may wonder why Lot's wife suffers this strange demise, particularly at this time. To be sure, the story that follows most likely could not/would not have occurred as it is described had she still been alive. The depravity of Lot's family, it seems, knows no end. Finally, we are, indeed, told that the reason that Lot was spared was for Abraham's sake, not for any merit of his own.

Following this, we have a very disturbing story of what became of Lot and his two unmarried daughters [19:30-38]. The three of them find themselves living in a cave. The older of the two daughters says to her sister, "there is not a man on earth to consort with us in the way of all the world." Many commentators interpret this to mean that the daughters truly thought that the rest of the world had been destroyed, and that they were the last three people left alive. This is, quite possibly, the only way that we can even rationalize these events. This is, however, not realistic. Surely, they must have realized that Abraham and his family had not been destroyed. Kimhi suggests that no man would be interested in Lot's daughters because they had come from

Sodom, which had a reputation as an immoral place.[5] In any event, the Torah recounts that the two daughters took turns getting their father Lot drunk, and then seducing him while he was in his drunken state. As a result, each of them found herself pregnant. As time went on, Lot should have realized that he was the father of both of his newest potential grandchildren. He had earlier said that his daughters had not "known" any man and that he was the only man around. In any event, what we have here is another origin story—the daughters become the maternal ancestors of the Moabites, and the Ammonites, respectfully—these nations later became eternal enemies of Israel.

Next, we have a repeat of the story of Abraham leaving the land and trying to pass Sarah off as his sister [20:1-18]. This time, however, there are several differences in the story. First, we are not told why he left the land. Second, Abraham himself tells the people of Gerar that Sarah is his sister instead of asking her to lie for him. Third, God protects Sarah by coming to Abimelech in a dream by night to tell him that he will die for taking Sarah since she is a married woman (apparently Abimelech had not yet been intimate with her). I found Abimelech's response very interesting: "O Lord, will You slay people even though innocent?" It reminded me of Abraham's bargaining with God over the people of Sodom and Gemorrah, asking if God would slay the innocent with the wicked [21:4]. Once again, the king accuses Abraham of bringing great distress on himself and his kingdom, tells him to take his wife and go, and gives Abraham great riches before sending him on his way.

Finally, we are told that when he was leaving the land, Abraham had to pray for the people of Gerar, "for the LORD had closed fast every womb of the household of Abimelech because of Sarah, the wife of Abraham." What are we to make of this? How would making all the women of Abimelech's house barren have helped protect Sarah? Some commentators explain that what was really going on here is that none of the women was able to conceive, because Abimelech was unable to perform sexually! That would certainly have protected Sarah! And why does this even need to be explained to us?

A big difference exists between this story and the first time that Abraham tried to pass off his wife as his sister. Then, we knew that Sarah was barren, so she would not have conceived in any event. Here, however, Sarah has just been told by God that she is finally going to have the child she has desired for so long. This is the promised child, Abraham's heir, the one through whom the covenant will be established. If Abimelech had indeed been intimate with her then that would have raised a question about the parentage of Isaac. After everything that they have been through to bring them to this point, God could not allow that to happen now.

Indeed, the final verses of this *aliyah* [21:1-4] tell us that God did finally bless Sarah and cause her to conceive, that she gave birth at long last to a son who was named Isaac, and that he was circumcised at the age of eight days in fulfillment of God's commandment.

So, in this *aliyah*, we have three births: two born of unholy alliances and one born of a holy alliance. For many generations into the future, there will be enmity between their descendants.

FIFTH ALIYAH: GENESIS 21:5–21
THURSDAY, NOVEMBER 5, 2020

See Me

In this *aliyah*, which is also the Torah reading for the first day of Rosh Hashanah, Abraham gains a new son, but also loses another son. The birth of Isaac brings great joy to his parents. Three years pass and it is time for Isaac to be weaned, so Abraham hosts a large feast [21:8]. During the celebration, Sarah notices that Ishmael, who is sixteen years old already, is playing with (i.e., making fun of) Isaac [21:9]. We can only imagine how he must have felt about this new younger brother, fourteen years his junior, who was going to supplant him as the heir. Some of the commentators even suggest that Ishmael, who was known to be an archer, was shooting arrows at his younger sibling. Notice that Ishmael does not even have a name here, and neither does his mother Hagar. He is referred to by Sarah as, "the son whom Hagar the Egyptian had borne to Abraham" and his mother is called "that slave woman" [21:9-10]. Angrily, Sarah demands that Abraham send them out of the house. We are told that Abraham was greatly distressed over the matter, because it "concerned a son of his" [21:11]. This is the reaction one would expect him to have, yet we will see quite a contrast in the story told later in the seventh *aliyah* of this *parashah*. In any event, God tells Abraham to heed the voice of his wife Sarah, and then gives him the following assurance: "it is through Isaac that offspring shall be continued for you. As for the son of the slave-woman, I will make a nation of him, too, for he is your seed" [21:12-13]. Interestingly, even God does not refer to either of them by name. God does reiterate two things, though: Isaac is the son through whom Abraham's inheritance will be continued, but God will make a nation out of Ishmael, as well. God is telling Abraham to give Hagar and her son their freedom. So, early next morning, Abraham sends Hagar and Ishmael out into the wilderness with a loaf of bread and a skin of water.

This is another story that is jarring to our sensibilities. Abraham and Sarah have passed so many of God's tests. They are supposed to be the exemplary couple. Yet neither of them looks very good here. Rather, they both appear to be uncaring and cruel. It seems that both parties are complicit in this heartless act.

When we read on further, however, we see that once again Hagar is encountered by an angel in the desert, just as Ishmael seems at the point of death. The angel reveals a well of water and assures Hagar that God will make a great nation of her son [21:18].

Truthfully, for Hagar and Ishmael, leaving the home of Abraham and Sarah was probably the best thing that could have happened. We know from before Ishmael's birth that Sarah already was mistreating Hagar. Unfortunately, the rivalry between him and his new little brother has only made that situation much worse. Now, at least, they both have their freedom. Apparently, Ishmael grows and thrives, and his mother finds a wife for him.

Hagar and Ishmael are really the innocent victims here. As a slave, Hagar has no autonomy. And Ishmael's birth was brought about through the machinations of Sarah and Abraham, coming up with their own scheme to have a child instead of waiting for God to fulfill the promise of an heir. Now that Isaac has arrived, they have no more use for Hagar as a slave, and Sarah wants her son to be Abraham's sole heir.

Sometimes we lose sight of who might be the unwitting victims of our actions. Sometimes we may not realize how much we hurt someone emotionally or psychologically. It's much easier to look past the others around us if we don't see them for who they are—if they don't have a name to us. Today in our country, it's easy to look past someone simply because his/her political views or views about COVID-19 don't align with ours. But instead of tossing them out of the house, so to speak, we would do better to open our eyes, to really see them, and to learn to live together. We and our children will benefit from that in the long run.

SIXTH ALIYAH: GENESIS 21:22–34
FRIDAY, NOVEMBER 6, 2020

Be Our Guest[6]

This short, somewhat strange *aliyah* almost seems kind of out of place here, plunked right down in the middle of the narrative about Abraham, Sarah, and Isaac. Whereas the other stories in this *parashah* are much more elaborate in their detail, this one seems to have a paucity of details.

Suddenly, we are talking about Abimelech again (this was the king who most recently had taken Sarah into his harem after Abraham had tried to pass her off as his sister). Here, Abimelech asks Abraham to make a pact with him and extend it to their descendants, to treat each other fairly and honestly. Abraham agrees to do so and this is significantly the first oath taken by anyone in the Torah.

In addition, Abraham purchases a well. This is notable because it is the first purchase of land that he has made and is yet one more piece of the puzzle: in addition to descendants, God has promised him land. The place is named for what took place there: "that place was called Beer-sheba [well of oath], for there the two of them swore an oath" [21:31].

Finally, we are told that Abraham planted a tamarisk tree, *eschel*, at Beer-sheba [21:33]. The *midrash* explains the significance of this:

> . . . even righteousness itself was sleeping until Abraham awakened it. How did Abraham do this? He made an inn and opened doors in every direction in order to receive all those passing by, as it says, "He planted a tamarisk (eshel) at Beer-sheba . . ." R' Azaria said: what is this eshel . . . ? It is an acronym for eating (. . . *achilah*), drinking (. . . *shtiyah*) and escorting one's guests (. . . *leviyah*). This is "righteousness met wherever he set his foot . . ." [*Midrash Tehillim 110:1*][7]

Abraham became known for his hospitality, according to this *midrash*. The welcome that he had extended to his three angelic visitors earlier in the *parashah* was apparently the norm for him. That's why he was sitting by the door of his tent that day when they came by—he made it a practice to look for travelers and invite them in. Notice that the *midrash* says that there were doors opened on all sides. Perhaps you have heard this explained by a rabbi officiating at a wedding: the *chuppah* is representative of the tent of Abraham, open on all sides. Every couple embarking on a married life is encouraged to emulate Abraham in extending hospitality in the new home that they will be establishing together.

Unfortunately, these days, this is a *mitzvah* that has become difficult for us to observe, especially now that we head towards winter and the weather grows cooler, making it less practical to eat outdoors.

We all long for the day when we can invite people into our homes again to socialize. We especially long to be able to celebrate our holidays with family and friends. May we safely see that day soon.

Did He, or Didn't He?

This *aliyah* tells one of the most well-known stories in the life of Abraham: the *Akedah*. This is Abraham's final test, and we are told from the very first verse that God was testing Abraham here. The nature of the test is that God instructs him to take Isaac to a mountain far off and offer him up as a sacrifice, specifically a burnt offering [22:2]. Abraham sets out the next morning with Isaac and two servants to fulfill his mission. Eventually, he tells the two servants to wait behind while he and Isaac will go on ahead. On the mountain, Abraham places his son on top of the altar and raises his knife to slay him. At that moment, he is stopped by an angel who tells him that he has passed the test. Since God saw that he was ready to do what God asked, his descendants will be many, and they will be blessed. Additionally, all the other nations of the Earth will be blessed through his descendants [22:16-18]. Abraham spots a ram caught in the bush by its horn [think shofar] and sacrifices it in place of his son.

This chapter of the Torah has been studied by more scholars—Jewish, Christian, and Muslim alike—practically since it was first written down on a scroll. As a matter of fact, during my senior year of Rabbinical School, I took a full semester course which covered just these two stories—Hagar and Ishmael and their expulsion from the home, and Abraham's attempted sacrifice of Isaac. You may also know that these two stories constitute the Torah readings for the two days of Rosh Hashanah. So, clearly, this is one of the most important passages in the Torah.

"God tests Abraham, and Abraham passes the test," could be a succinct title for this chapter. But a close reading of the text leaves us with many questions.

To begin with, Abraham says nothing to God when God tells him what he is to do—not one word! To anyone who is a parent, this is almost inconceivable. The omission seems even greater when we recall that, in the last chapter, when God told him to send Ishmael away, we were told that Abraham was very distressed about it because it concerned his son. Why not speak up now, when it concerns his other son? Clearly, the rabbis were disturbed by this, as well. There is a famous *midrash* told by Rashi that says that the following conversation, which is an expansion of verse 2, is what really transpired between God and Abraham:

"Take your son—"But I have two sons."

"—your [only] one—" "But each is the only son of his mother."
"—Isaac, whom you love . . ."

Another question we might ask is whether Abraham really believed that God would ever actually let him slay his own son. Logic would say that the request doesn't even make sense: this is the son of promise, the long-awaited heir through whom God has promised to maintain the covenant. None of that can happen if Abraham takes his life, and surely, Abraham and Sarah are far too old to have another child now. So, could it be that Abraham, realizing all of this, was confident all along that God would stop him before he completed the deed? I think that that could well be the case. We note that when Isaac points out that they have everything they need to make a sacrifice, except the animal, Abraham answers him this way: "God will see to the sheep for His burnt offering, my son" [22:8].

Additionally, we note what Abraham says to the servants when he tells them to wait behind: "You stay here with the ass. The boy and I will go up there; we will worship, and we will return to you." It could be argued, of course, that he is just saying this to throw Isaac off. I don't really think so, though.

A big question is what was going through Isaac's mind through all of this? Again, the text doesn't tell us. While he is referred to as "the boy" several times in the text, he was at least a teenager, and may have been as old as thirty-seven according to some calculations. He could easily have overpowered his father, who was one hundred years older than he! But again, the Torah is silent on this question. Other than the already mentioned question to his father regarding the missing sacrifice, there are no other words uttered by Isaac anywhere in this passage.

There is, however, something very telling in the story. Twice we are told that on the way to Mt. Moriah, Abraham and Isaac walked together [22:6,8]. But after the encounter with the angel/God and the sacrifice of the lamb, we read "Abraham then returned to his servants, and they departed together for Beer-sheba; and Abraham stayed in Beer-sheba." Where was Isaac? I believe that this incident, no doubt, caused some strife between father and son. Think about it. Would you want to be with your father if he had just attempted to kill you? I think that Isaac did not return with his father; I believe they became estranged for some period of time. Where did Isaac go? Hold that thought—I'll answer that in the next *parashah*.

There is even a *midrash* that says that Isaac really died that day and was brought back to life!

R. Judah says: When the sword touched Isaac's throat, his soul

HINDSIGHT IS 2020

flew clean out of him. And when [God] let His voice be heard from between the cherubim, "Lay not [your] hand upon the lad." The lad's soul was returned to his body. Then his father unbound him, and Isaac rose, knowing that in this way the dead would come back to life in the future; whereupon he began to recite, "Blessed are You, LORD, who resurrects the dead." [*Pirkei de Rabbi Elieazer 31:10*][8]

For those of you who ask whether we Jews believe in an afterlife, clearly some scholars do! This blessing that is placed in the mouth of Isaac is today part of our *Amidah*.

There are many other things that can be said about this passage. The bottom line, I think, is this: I believe that, in a very real way, Abraham has now sacrificed not one, but two sons. The first, Ishmael, he drove out of his home. The second, Isaac, it seems, he also drove away.

And yet, Abraham has been assured by God that he and his descendants will be blessed because of his unwavering faith and obedience.

I encourage you to study the story of the *Akedah*. Ask questions. Wrestle with the text. Allow it to speak to you. Read between the lines. This text is sacred to us, because it has so much to say to us.

Parashat Chaye Sarah

FIRST ALIYAH: GENESIS 23:1–16
SUNDAY, NOVEMBER 8, 2020

A Grief Too Great to Bear

This week's *parashah* is the only one in the entire Torah that is named for a woman. Surprisingly, though the name means "the lives of Sarah," it begins by telling us about Sarah's death at the age of one hundred twenty-seven. Several things are interesting here. First, we are told that Abraham came to mourn for his wife [23:2]. The strange wording implies that he was not physically with her at the time that she died. Where was he? Well, think back to the last story that we read about Abraham in the previous *parashah*: the *Akedah*, the attempted sacrifice of Isaac. Several commentators suggest that Abraham was not with Sarah when she died because he was on Mt. Moriah, where he had almost taken their son's life at God's command. Surely, he had not told her before leaving home with Isaac and the two servants what he was planning to do as, no doubt, she would have tried to stop him. Here, though, some commentators suggest that someone (perhaps Satan?) came and told Sarah about what had transpired on Mt. Moriah. Upon hearing the news, she had a heart attack and died. That would seem to imply, though, that she didn't get the full story of what happened and that the attempt had been aborted by the angel. Her reaction would not have been quite as drastic if she thought that Isaac was still alive. It was her great grief at the thought that her son had died that caused her to lose her own life. Then there is this *midrash*:

> . . . Another way of looking at the words [*vayehiyu chayeh* Sarah]
> is that they refer to the hereafter. This would reflect the fact that
> the Torah reported her death immediately after she had heard that

Yitzchak's soul had "flown" to heaven as a result of his having been offered to [God] as a sacrifice. The form [*vayehiyu*] would hint that both her soul and that of Yitzchak departed from Earth at the same time to take up permanent residence in the celestial regions. [*Rabbeinu Bahya, Bereshit 23:1:7-11*][1]

According to this, both mother and son lost their lives at the same moment.

Most commentators agree that the main purpose of this story in the Torah is to show that Abraham purchased the Cave of Machpelah as a burial place, thus finally establishing some ownership of property. This cave ultimately became the burial place for the three patriarchs and three of the matriarchs. Abraham and Sarah, Isaac and Rebekah, Jacob and Leah were all buried there; only Rachel, who died on the side of the road after giving birth to Benjamin as the family traveled back to Canaan was not buried there. But legend has it that there actually are four couples buried in the cave. Who is the fourth couple? Adam and Eve.

Finally, even as we read of Sarah's death, we have already seen a hint of who will take her place as the next matriarch in Israel. It appeared at the very end of last week's *parashah*, where we read a short genealogy of the family of Abraham's brother back in the old country, Nahor: "Some time later, Abraham was told, "Milcah too has borne children to your brother Nahor: Uz the firstborn, and Buz his brother, and Kemuel the father of Aram; and Chesed, Hazo, Pildash, Jidlaph, and Bethuel." Bethuel being the father of Rebekah. These eight Milcah bore to Nahor, Abraham's brother" [22:20-23].

As I have mentioned before, women are generally not mentioned in genealogies. Therefore, when they are, we notice it as there must be a reason that they are mentioned by name. It seems as if this whole family tree is listed here for the express purpose of introducing us to the woman who will ultimately come to comfort Isaac for the loss of his mother.

SECOND ALIYAH: GENESIS 23:17–24:9
MONDAY, NOVEMBER 9, 2020

My Seder Plate has an Orange on It

This passage holds special meaning to me as it is the first about which I wrote an in-depth *d'var Torah*; the occasion was my adult *bat mitzvah* in November 1984. The *parashah* was Chaye Sarah, but I concentrated specifically on five short words in the Hebrew text.

The subject of this passage is Abraham's concern for finding the right wife for Isaac. Sarah died and Abraham, now one hundred thirty-seven years old, must be concerned that he may not be far behind. For the covenant to continue between God and his family, Isaac must marry and have an heir. Since that covenant relationship is so special, Abraham was concerned that the right kind of woman be found for his son. He enlists the aid of his servant Eliezer, giving him specific instructions: Isaac must not marry a Canaanite woman. Therefore, the servant is instructed to go back to the land that Abraham left behind, to Abraham's family, to find the right candidate. Under no circumstances is Eliezer to bring Isaac back there with him. Since Abraham was told at the end of the previous *parashah* about the children (and one grandchild) that had been born to his brother Nahor, it could well be that he specifically had Rebekah in mind, though he did not mention her by name to Eliezer.

The object of my *d'var Torah* was the second half of verse 24:1: "and the LORD had blessed Abraham in all things [*bakol*]." You will see from the following sources (seven that I have listed here but there are many more) that the question argued by the sages is basically this: How could the Torah tell us that God had blessed Abraham with all things, since, according to the Torah text, God had not given him a daughter? The rabbis have differing opinions on this:

> ...Rabbi Meir says: The blessing was that he did not have a daughter. Rabbi Yehuda says: The blessing was that he had a daughter, and her name was Bakkol. Evidently, Rabbi Yehuda understands the birth of a daughter to be a blessing. The Gemara explains the difficulty: Say that you heard Rabbi Yehuda explain that the blessing was that the Merciful One did not even deprive Abraham of a daughter, in addition to his sons. Did you hear him say that a daughter is preferable to a son? [*BT Bava Batra 141A:6*] and similarly [*BT Bava Batra 16B:10*] and [*Ein Yaakov, Bava Batra 1:41*][2]

> ...Rabbi Meir learns he didn't have a daughter and this was a blessing for him for he wouldn't have been able to marry her to anyone but the cursed children of Canaan. And if he would send her to his homeland [to marry one of his relatives] she too would worship idols like them, for a wife is under the jurisdiction of her husband. Avra[ha]m wouldn't want his worthy offspring from his wife Sarah to go outside the land (Israel) and all the more so worship idols! And Rabbi Yehuda learns that Avra[ha]m did have a daughter, meaning that [God] didn't cause him to lack even a

daughter. And this was the blessing of "With everything," that he had everything that people desire in life; he lacked nothing. Then the "Others" came and mentioned the name of the daughter . . . in this matter that the Torah is saying that [God] blessed him with one daughter whose name was [Bakol]! [*Ramban on Genesis 24:1:1*][3]

. . . Rabbi Yehudah simply felt that one cannot describe someone as enjoying "all of G'd's blessings," unless such a person had also been blessed with having a daughter. [*Rabbeinu Bahya, Bereshit 24:1:3-5*][4]

. . . The numerical value of the word *bakol* is equal to that of *ben* (a son)—suggesting that God had blessed Abraham with a son and since he had a son he had to find him a wife. [*Rashi on Genesis 24:1:1*][5]

So, the answers to our question are: (1) He did not have a daughter, and that was a blessing. (R. Meir) since he would not be able to marry her to any of the Canaanites, but he would have to send her away to her husband's family's home where there were likely to be idolaters, and he would not want that to happen; (2) He did have a daughter, and that was a blessing. (R. Yehudah); (3) The name of his daughter was Bakol—the word that is translated as "with all things" (R. Yehudah or others); (4) The numerical value of the word *Bakol* (thirty) is equal to that of *ben* (a son); (5) Therefore, being blessed with a son was equivalent to being blessed with everything (implication: so, who needs a daughter?)

When I wrote my *d'var Torah* back in 1984, it was a very different world. The Conservative Movement was not yet ordaining women as rabbis. I was bothered by the condescending attitude towards women. After a lengthy examination of all these sources, I finally arrived at the following conclusion:

My Hebrew name is *Margalit Moriel bat Abraham v'Sarah* [now, in addition, it is preceded by the title *Harav*]. Today, I can say that Abraham has indeed been blessed with a daughter. I am proud to be a daughter of Abraham and I am also proud to be one of a large and growing number of Conservative women who bear the title *Rabbi.*

Thinking on this more, I think that this discussion is particularly relevant in our nation this week as we have seen the first woman elected to national office, our new Vice President Elect, Kamala Harris.

In biblical times, in a patriarchal society, there were few roles that women could fill besides wife and mother. We have come far in our fight for equality. May all the women who have been ordained continue to bring blessings to our movement and may our new Vice President bring blessings to our country.

A Prayer is Answered

In this *aliyah*, Abraham's servant Eliezer sets out on his mission to find a wife for Isaac, taking along ten camels and many gifts for the prospective bride and her family. Arriving in town at evening, he heads straight to the well to water his camels. The well was typically the place in town to which a stranger went first because it was the place to find out anything you needed to know about the town. It was also the place to go to find out about possible hospitality for the night.

He offered a prayer to God, asking for success for his mission: "O LORD, God of my master Abraham, grant me good fortune this day, and deal graciously with my master Abraham: Here I stand by the spring as the daughters of the townsmen come out to draw water; let the maiden to whom I say, 'Please, lower your jar that I may drink,' and who replies, 'Drink, and I will also water your camels'—let her be the one whom You have decreed for Your servant Isaac. Thereby shall I know that You have dealt graciously with my master" [24:12-14].

What is notable is that this is the first such instance in the Torah of someone addressing God in prayer. His words are simple and straightforward, not following a prescribed order of prayer; they are spontaneous, and they are his own.

Many of us can take a lesson from the words of Eliezer. We Jews are so used to the established orders of the *Shacharit, Minchah,* and *Maariv* Services; we're very good at opening a *siddur* and following along. But extemporaneous prayer is another thing altogether. Many Jews are awkward and uncomfortable praying in their own words, associating it more with Christian style of worship. Many people whom I have visited in the hospital have told me that they feel a need to pray, but have said to me, "Rabbi, I don't know how." The answer is simple: just say what's in your heart. The words don't need to be elegant; they need to be honest.

It is also interesting to note what Eliezer is looking for in a wife for Isaac: someone who would help a stranger and his animals. He does not ask for beauty or riches and instead asks for good character.

It is also interesting to note that, despite Abraham's explicit instructions, Eliezer does not specify that God send him someone from Abraham's family. Yet, that is exactly whom he encounters, the very Rebekah that Abraham had recently heard about. Twice in this section, we are given not only her name, but her complete family identification. We, the readers, know immediately that God has answered his simple, heartfelt prayer: "He had scarcely finished speaking when Rebekah, who was born to Bethuel, the son of Milcah the wife of Abraham's brother Nahor, came out with her jar on her shoulder" [24:15].

Rebekah not only gives him water, she even draws water for those ten camels, as well. No small task!

By this, Eliezer knows her generous character. It is only at this point, after she has watered all ten camels, that he asks her identity. She responds: ". . . I am the daughter of Bethuel the son of Milcah, whom she bore to Nahor" [24:24].

With her answer, Eliezer, like us, knows that God has not only answered his prayer, God has sent him someone from the family of Abraham. He receives further affirmation when she offers him lodging in her father's home for the night. So far, his mission looks like it is going to be successful. Now, he just needs to get the approval of her family.

FOURTH ALIYAH: GENESIS 24:27–52
WEDNESDAY, NOVEMBER 11, 2020

Faithfulness is Rewarded

This *aliyah* begins with the servant's second prayer to God. This time, it is a prayer of thanks for having been led to the family of Abraham. Once again, the prayer is heartfelt and sincere. Upon hearing his prayer, Rebekah runs home to tell her family what has happened. Now, suddenly, we learn that she has a brother, Laban [24:29]. This is curious because when the genealogy of Nahor's descendants was given at the end of the last *parashah*, we noted that it was unusual that Rebekah, a woman, was mentioned. Additionally, there was no mention of Laban at that time. This is even more unusual that she should be included, and he excluded. We are already being led to think highly of her, and not very highly of him.

We see that Laban runs out to meet Eliezer, and, according to the text, once he sees the earrings and bracelets that he had given to his sister, and he sees all (ten of the) camels, he invites him to come into the house [24:31].

What's going on here? Many of the commentators say that from the very beginning we are seeing Laban's true colors (no pun intended for those who understand Hebrew—*Lavan* means "white"). He is drawn by the sight of the valuable gifts that Eliezer brings and is greedy and materialistic.

In this *aliyah*, the hero, the character we are to emulate, in contrast to Laban, is Eliezer, Abraham's servant. And the contrast is very stark.

After being welcomed into the home of Nahor, Laban, and Rebekah, a meal is placed in front of Eliezer. No doubt he is hungry after the journey with the camels, but he declines to eat until he has spoken [24:33], telling them the whole story of his mission, beginning with Abraham's charge to him. The retelling of the story goes on for thirteen verses. Many have wondered why this is. So often in the Torah, stories are told devoid of details, skipping over large chunks of time. And yet, here we have the same story retold in very specific detail. The reason for this, according to many commentators, is to emphasize the faithfulness of Abraham's servant. He was committed to his mission and trusted in God to make it successful. His dedication is rewarded in verses 50-51. As he finishes retelling the story, he asks her family to give him an answer regarding her betrothal right away. Here is the response of both her father and her brother: ". . . The matter was decreed by the LORD; we cannot speak to you bad or good. Here is Rebekah before you; take her and go and let her be a wife to your master's son, as the LORD has spoken" [24:50-51].

He receives an affirmative response and then worships God for his success [24:52]. There may have been a clear omission of Laban's name in the genealogy, but Eliezer's devotion is rewarded.

The message is clear: keep the lines of communication with God open, devote yourself to fulfilling your vows, be grateful, and extol the greatness of God to others.

I think there is also a secondary message at play here: the sincere, heartfelt prayers of a non-Jew are recognized, acknowledged—and answered—by God. We Jews do not have exclusive access to the attention or favor of God.

FIFTH ALIYAH: GENESIS 24:53–67
THURSDAY, NOVEMBER 12, 2020

Love at First Sight

There are several interesting things going on in this reading. Now that Rebekah's family has agreed to the marriage, the servant gives them gifts, then eats and drinks with them, and then stays the night. In the morning, he is anxious to get underway on his return journey. After being questioned by her family [24:58], Rebekah agrees to go immediately with Eliezer. They send her off with the following blessing: "O sister! May you grow into thousands of myriads; may your offspring seize the gates of their foes" [24:60]. The first part obviously expresses a wish that she should have many children, a typical blessing for a bride in that society. The second part sounds a little odd for blessing a bride; additionally, it should be noted that we have heard these words before: "I will bestow My blessing upon you and make your descendants as numerous as the stars of heaven and the sands on the seashore; and your descendants shall seize the gates of their foes" [Genesis 22:17].

This verse is from the previous *parashah*; they were spoken to Abraham by the angel after the *Akedah*, after he had almost sacrificed Isaac as a burnt offering. Now they are being spoken to Rebekah, the young woman who is about to become Isaac's wife, the one through whom the promise to Abraham will be continued. Only Isaac himself does not receive a blessing with these words. He is, however, clearly the heir of Abraham, so the promise would naturally pass to him from his father. The coincidence of the words indicate that Isaac and Rebekah together will continue God's covenant to the next generation.

The servant sets out on his return journey, bringing with him Rebekah and her nursemaid, who, once assigned to Rebekah at birth, became her servant for life. And where do we read that Isaac is? We are told that he had settled in the Negev, and that he was just returning from Beer-lahai-roi. We heard of this place once before: "Therefore, the well was called Beer-lahai-roi; it is between Kadesh and Bered" [16:14].

This verse is from the story of the first time that Hagar was in the wilderness, when she ran away from Sarah. This is the well where the angel encountered her and foretold the birth of Ishmael. Our present verse implies that this was a place that Isaac visited frequently. Could it be that after the *Akedah*, instead of going back home with Abraham, Isaac went in search of his half-brother? Did he possibly wish to reestablish ties with him? It's an interesting thought to ponder.

The other thing that we are told about Abraham's designated heir is the following: "...Isaac went out walking in the field toward evening..." [24:63].

There is much speculation about what exactly is the meaning of the verb, *lasuach*, that we see used here. Rashbam translates it as "to shrub," meaning that he went out to plant trees; Ibn Ezra translates it as "bushwacking" or walking among the bushes; Ramban translates it as "to talk."[6] Interestingly, Hizkuni says that the phrase "he went out" means that he went out from Egypt, where he had been for the last three years since the *Akedah*.[6]

The more popular translation follows Rashi, who interprets it as "meditate," and Abarbanel, who says that he was "praying."[6] Indeed, this idea is mentioned in the Talmud:

Isaac instituted the afternoon prayer, as it is stated: "And Isaac went out to converse [*lasuah*] in the field toward evening" [Genesis 24:63], and conversation means nothing other than prayer, as it is stated: "A prayer of the afflicted when he is faint and pours out his complaint [*siho*] before the Lord" [Psalms 102:1]. Obviously, Isaac was the first to pray as evening approached, at the time of the afternoon prayer. [*BT Brachot 26B:6*]

According to this interpretation, since Isaac was praying towards evening, it was still late afternoon; therefore, he is credited with instituting the *minchah* service. (This same passage attributes the *shacharit* service to Abraham, and the *maariv* service to Jacob.)

Next, we have the magical moment when Isaac and Rebekah literally lay eyes on each other for the first time. We read about Isaac, ". . . he raised his eyes [looked up] and saw . . ." [24:63] We read about Rebekah, ". . . she raised her eyes [looked up] and saw . . ." [24:64] The fact that the same exact phrase is used to refer to both (except that the first is, naturally, masculine and the second feminine) could almost have come straight out of a romance novel. They both saw each other at the same moment.

Finally, the *aliyah* finishes with this: "Isaac then brought her into the tent of his mother Sarah, and he took Rebekah as his wife. Isaac loved her, and thus found comfort after his mother's death" [24:67].

This is the first time in the Torah that we are told that there was love between two spouses. Despite the lengthy relationship that Abraham and Sarah had, we were never told that they loved each other. Isaac and Rebekah, it seems, are not only destined to fulfill the covenant, they will do so because they love each other. Love is now established as an important element of the marital relationship.

SIXTH ALIYAH: GENESIS 25:1–11
FRIDAY, NOVEMBER 13, 2020

Together in Eternity

Now that Isaac has been settled with Rebekah, Abraham feels free to find another spouse for himself. We read: ". . . Abraham took another wife, whose name was Keturah" [25:11].

While there is disagreement over the identity of this woman, there are several commentators who believe that Keturah and Hagar are one and the same. Rashi says that Hagar had not married or been with any other man since having been sent out of Abraham's house.[7] We do remember how upset Abraham was about sending her and Ishmael out into the wilderness. Let me remind you of the following verse from the previous *aliyah*: "Isaac had just come back from the vicinity of Beer-lahai-roi, for he was settled in the region of the Negeb" [24:62].

Rashi says that the reason that Isaac had gone to Beer-lahai-roi was to bring back Hagar, so that Abraham could marry her.[7] While no other commentator has the same thought, it still has a nice implication. If it were true, it would mean that both father and son were simultaneously looking to find a wife for each other! Each wanted to provide comfort for the other after suffering the loss of Sarah.

After this, we are given a genealogy of all the descendants Abraham had with Keturah [25:2-4]. Since Ishmael is not included in this list, that would bolster the case of those who say that she was not Hagar. Abraham gives gifts to these six sons, but wills that everything he has go to Isaac [25:5-6]. Then, it seems that we have come full circle: ". . . This was the total span of Abraham's life: one hundred and seventy-five years." [25:7]. Notice the similarity of language to the very first verse of this *parashah,* which told us of the death and life span of Sarah. Additionally, we are told that, "His sons Isaac and Ishmael buried him in the cave of Machpelah . . ." [25:9].

We see then from the Torah text that Abraham's two oldest sons had indeed reconciled and come together to bury their father. Abraham was buried in the Cave of Machpelah, along with his beloved Sarah. We find the following poignant *midrash* in the Talmud:

> . . . Rabbi Bena'a was marking burial caves for the purpose of helping to prevent the contracting of ritual impurity. When he arrived at the cave of Abraham, i.e., the Cave of Machpelah, he encountered Eliezer, the servant of Abraham, who was standing before the entrance. Rabbi Bena'a said to him: What is Abraham doing at this moment? Eliezer said to him: He is lying in the arms of Sarah, and she is examining his head. [BT Bava Batra 58A:3]

Thus, Abraham and Sarah were spending eternity locked in a loving embrace, and their gravesite was being watched over by Abraham's trusted servant Eliezer.

Finally, to finish the *aliyah*, we read that, ". . . Isaac settled near Beer-lahai-roi" [25:11].

So, it seems possible that Isaac and Ishmael had reunited for more than just their father's death. Their three parents had never been able to work out their problems so that they would be able to live together. Indeed, the next generation was able to accomplish what their parents could not. Would that the descendants of Isaac and the descendants of Ishmael would be able to coexist peacefully today.

SEVENTH ALIYAH: GENESIS 25:12–18
WRITTEN FOR SHABBAT, SATURDAY, NOVEMBER 14, 2020

The Twelve Tribes of—Ishmael(?)

This very short *aliyah* which concludes our *parashah* comes to show us that the promise that God had made to both Hagar and Abraham regarding Ishmael was fulfilled. He did indeed become the father of many nations. We are given the names of his twelve sons, who are described "twelve chieftains of as many tribes" [25:15-16]. Indeed, there were twelve tribes that descended from Ishmael. In addition, a later verse from Genesis tells us that Esau married: ". . . also Basemath daughter of Ishmael and sister of Nebaioth. [36:3] That would mean that Ishmael had twelve sons and one daughter, exactly the same as Isaac's son Jacob.

Finally, Ishmael's life, too, comes to an end. We see that the verse describing Ishmael's death is practically identical to the verse describing Abraham's death from the last *aliyah*: "These were the years of the life of Ishmael: one hundred and thirty-seven years; then he breathed his last and died and was gathered to his kin. This was the total span of Abraham's life: one hundred and seventy-five years. And Abraham breathed his last, dying . . . and he was gathered to his kin." [25:7-8]

Rashi says that the phrase, "he breathed his last" is used only when speaking of the death of someone who was righteous.[8] Ramban says that it refers to a quick and painless death, but when used together with the phrase "was gathered to his kin," it definitely implies that the person was righteous.[8]

The implication, therefore, is that Ishmael, the son who was spurned, lived a life that emulated his father.

Starting next week, we shall see what happened to Isaac, the son of promise.

Parashat Toldot

FIRST ALIYAH: GENESIS 25:19–26:5
SUNDAY, NOVEMBER 15, 2020

God Speaks to Us All

This *parashah* tells the story of Isaac, through whom, according to God's promise to Abraham, the covenant would be fulfilled. The previous *parashah* ended with Isaac marrying Rebekah and taking her into his mother's tent. Here we are told that Isaac was forty years old when they married [25:20]. We do not know exactly how old Rebekah was, but she was believed to be considerably younger than her husband (many of the commentators believe that she was just three years old (!); one says fourteen). In any event, we are told that Rebekah, like Sarah before her, was also barren. Isaac knew that he needed to produce offspring for his father's legacy to continue. He also did not wish to resort to attaining fatherhood through a concubine as his father had done as he had witnessed firsthand the disastrous effects that this had had on his family's dynamic. Besides, he genuinely loved Rebekah, so he didn't want to have children with any other woman besides her. And so, "Isaac pleaded with the LORD on behalf of his wife" [25:21]. The word "pleaded" implies a fervent, heartfelt prayer, intense petitioning. Additionally, Rashi says the following about this verse:

> FACING HIS WIFE—He stood in one corner and prayed whilst she stood in the other corner and prayed [Genesis Rabbah 63:5].[1]

Here we have the idea that not only Isaac, but also Rebekah, offered entreaties to God, and they did so simultaneously. Though they were in opposite corners, they prayed together. Rebekah did not depend on her husband's intercession alone; she herself reached out to God. The *midrash* elaborates further:

> ...What is "opposite his wife"? Rather this teaches that Isaac was prostrated on one side and Rebecca was on the other side, and he said, "Master of the World, all the children which you are going to give to me, may they be from this righteous woman." [*Ruth Rabbah 7:14*][2]

These are, indeed, poignant, heartfelt words. In any event, the verse tells us that God heeded Isaac's prayer and Rebecca conceived. Unfortunately, it turned out to be a very difficult pregnancy, and Rebekah was particularly uncomfortable. This time, she went directly to God herself to inquire about her situation:

> "she went in order to enquire from God." ...Ramban understands the words [*vatalach lidrosh et Hashem*], to mean that Rivkah appealed directly to God in prayer seeing that she felt so much anguish. [*Tur HaAroch, Genesis 25:22:3*][3]

Rebekah is the first woman in the Torah who felt empowered enough to reach out to God herself without necessarily depending on her husband as an intermediary. God told her that she was carrying twins, that there would be strife between the offspring as they grew older, and that the older would serve the younger [25:23]. How ironic! Isaac had wanted to avoid this very situation by having children only with his wife. Now she was being told by God that it would happen anyway.

Next, we read about the birth of the babies, Esau, the older, and Jacob, the younger. We are told that Isaac was sixty years old when they were born [25:26] so a full twenty years had elapsed since he and Rebekah had married. God had promised Abraham that his descendants would be greater in number than anyone would be able to count, and Isaac, no doubt, knew about that promise. Interestingly, these twins would be the only children that Isaac (and Rebekah) would have.

Additionally, it seems that Isaac did not learn anything from his own fractured family dynamics about the deleterious effects of parental favoritism: "Isaac favored [loved] Esau . . .; but Rebekah favored [loved] Jacob." We will soon see the devastating results of these conflicting parental preferences.

As the *aliyah* goes on, we read the story of Esau selling his birthright to his brother Jacob in a moment of desperation. This is a story that many find troubling. We know by the way the sons are described that Jacob is the one who is intended by God to carry out the covenant of Abraham. Why, then, was he not born first? Why did he have to obtain the birthright deceitfully? And is this something that was even possible to be transferred from one son to another? It becomes clear from the story as it unfolds that their father Isaac was not informed of this transaction; Rebekah, however, does seem to be aware of it later with the likely assumption being that Jacob told her. Here's a big question to ponder: to what extent was this influenced by the conflicting parental preferences of the two brothers?

A new famine in the land caused Isaac to seek out Abimelech because God had told him not to go to Egypt, entreating him to stay where he was, and reiterating the promise that God had made to Abraham: his descendants would be as numerous as the stars, and all the nations of the Earth would bless themselves through them [26:1-5]. We will see again how Isaac failed to learn from his father's poor example.

SECOND ALIYAH: GENESIS 26:6–12
MONDAY, NOVEMBER 16, 2020

Sometimes We Bring Out the Worst in Each Other

This *aliyah* picks up the story of the famine. Following God's request, Isaac did not go down to Egypt during the famine. This is significant because Egypt was the place that Abraham traveled to the first time that he encountered a famine (and, not coincidentally, the first time that he tried to pass off his wife Sarah as his sister). However, we need to take note of where Isaac was living at the time of this story: in Gerar [26:6]! This is the same location to which Abraham had traveled, the second time that he encountered a famine (and, not coincidentally, also the second time that he had tried to pass Sarah off as his sister). You may recall that this second time Sarah was taken into the harem of the King Abimelech and was only saved from being defiled by an angel who came to speak to the king.

Here we see that Isaac was already in Gerar, and the king's name is once again Abimelech (probably a son or grandson of the one from the Abraham story). In this story, Rebekah was not taken into the palace of the king; however, the men of Gerar took notice of her beauty. Fearing for his life just as his father before him had done, Isaac reacted in precisely the same cowardly manner and told the people of Gerar that Rebekah was his sister [26:7]! Here, however, there was no angel stepping in to reveal the truth. Instead, Isaac's own actions gave him away. Looking out the window,

Abimelech saw Isaac and Rebekah together. Our translation says that he was "fondling" his wife but the Hebrew word is *metzachek*, which connotes more than fondling. The implication is that they were at that moment involved in sexual relations.

This word is interesting for two reasons. First, it is a play on his own name, Itzchak. Secondly, and perhaps more disturbing, there is only one other place in the Torah (indeed, in the entire Tanakh) where this word appears, and we encountered it two weeks ago in Parashat Vayera: "Sarah saw the son whom Hagar the Egyptian had borne to Abraham playing [*metzachek*]" [26:9].

This was the incident that had led Sarah to demand that Abraham banish Hagar and Ishmael from the home. In this instance, we see the word is translated as "playing," but based on its usage in our current passage, we know now that it really has a much darker meaning. The implication of this is something very disturbing, something we don't even wish to contemplate. Something that would cause us to say that, if that is indeed what was happening, then, yes, now we understand why Ishmael was sent away.

Indeed, there are some who say that there really was incest taking place in the incident of Ishmael's mistreatment of Isaac. Is that what you're thinking right now?

On the other hand, did you see how far we were able to go based on just one word? Before, we felt pity for Ishmael, exiled with his mother, abandoned by his father to die in the desert, but the biblical account needs for us to have a negative opinion of him. We need to justify the idea that his descendants will later become enemies of Isaac's descendants. So, it's easy to get carried away when we consider the potential meaning of one little word.

We often are very quick to jump to conclusions, forming negative opinions of someone based on very little information. In our world today, so dominated by social media and people still arguing over differing political views, this happens all the time. I challenge you to honestly examine yourself and ask whether you've ever found yourself being too judgmental, too quick to form an opinion before examining all the facts.

Unless and until we can all learn to change this behavior, we will not be able to bring the healing that our country and our world need so badly right now.

Living Waters

Isaac continued living in the land of Gerar where he prospered and grew wealthy [26:13], causing the native people to become jealous of his flocks [26:14]. As a result, they stopped up all the wells that Abraham had dug [26:15] and Abimelech asked him to leave [26:16]. So, Isaac moved to the wadi Gerar and re-dug wells that Abraham had previously dug there and the Philistines had since stopped up [26:17-18]. While doing this, his servants dug a well that we are told contained *maim chaim* (living water) [26:19]. In this case, this phrase refers to fresh spring water. Radak explains in his commentary:

> [they found there a well of living water], after they kept digging, they found this additional well beneath the old well. This is why the Torah did not write that they found . . . simply water, but [a well] that they found a new source of water. [*Radak on Genesis 26:19:2*][4]

The rabbis of the Talmud also commented on this verse:

> . . . Rabbi Ḥanina said: One who sees a well in a dream sees peace, as it is said: "And Isaac's servants dug in the valley and found there a well of living water" . . . and ultimately there was peace. Rabbi Natan says: One who sees a well in his dream it is a symbol that he has found Torah, as the well symbolizes Torah. As it is stated with regard to the Torah: "For whoever finds me finds life" [Proverbs 8:35], and it is written here: "A well of living water," and we see that a well is linked to Torah as both are associated with life. [*BT Brachot 56B:7*]

Now we understand the significance of this phrase, "living water." We know how important water is as it is literally life-giving. Therefore, the water comes to symbolize the Torah, which, for us, is also life-giving. Just as water provides sustenance for the physical body, Torah provides sustenance for the soul, for the spiritual self.

This verse is the first of eight times that the phrase "living water" is used in the *Tanakh*.

In the book of Jeremiah, at a time when the nation had been particularly rebellious, God spoke to them: "For My people have done a twofold wrong:

They have forsaken Me, the Fount of living waters, And hewed them out cisterns, broken cisterns, Which cannot even hold water" [Jeremiah 2:13].

Here, God is described as the source of these living waters; God says that the wells that the people have dug for themselves are broken and unable to hold water. So is the rebellious heart—unable to hold words of living Torah. May we all be sustained by the living waters of the Torah, and may God, the source of Torah be our strength, especially during these difficult times.

FOURTH ALIYAH: GENESIS 26:23–29
WEDNESDAY, NOVEMBER 18, 2020

Abraham, Isaac, Jacob, Moses, and—Caleb?

After the incident with the wells, Isaac returns to the area of Beersheva [26:23] where he has a nighttime encounter with God who self-identifies as "the God of Abraham" and tells him not to be afraid [26:24]. God promises to bless and increase Isaac "for the sake of My servant Abraham."

As recently as last week, we have seen the image of a faithful servant in Eliezer, who lovingly swore to his master Abraham that he would carry out his wishes (to find a wife for his son), and then went to great lengths to do so. According to Sarna, there are only five individuals in the Torah who are referred to as God's servants: Abraham, Isaac, Jacob, Moses, and Caleb.[5] It is easy to understand how this term, which is ascribed to righteous individuals, could be applied to the first four people on this list, who were all known as important leaders in Israel. Caleb, along with Joshua, was one of the two spies who did not bring back a bad report about Canaan, who wanted to go in and take possession of the land. Joshua's importance is indisputable as he was designated as Moses' successor. Yet, Joshua does not earn the title "servant of God," Caleb does. We understand the significance of this title from the following verse in which God describes Caleb: "But My servant Caleb, because he was imbued with a different spirit and remained loyal to Me—him will I bring into the land that he entered, and his offspring shall hold it as a possession" [Numbers 14:24].

Despite being severely outnumbered by the other ten spies and their evil report about the land, Caleb and Joshua remained faithful to God and displayed great courage in facing an angry nation that was ready to stone them, all the while entreating the people to listen to them and not be afraid to go in and take possession of the land.

The connection between Caleb and Moses is obvious; they were contemporaries (Caleb was also Moses' brother-in-law, husband of Miriam). But what is the connection between Caleb and the three patriarchs?

There is a *midrash* that tells how Caleb, alone among the twelve spies once they had entered the land of Canaan, went off on his own to visit the Cave of Machpelah to seek the guidance of those who were buried there and pray for strength from God to successfully complete his mission:

It is also stated with regard to the spies: "And they went up into the south, and he came to Hebron" [Numbers 13:22]. Why is the phrase "and he came" written in the singular form? The verse should have said: And they came. Rava says: This teaches that Caleb separated himself from the counsel of the other spies and went and prostrated himself on the graves of the forefathers in Hebron. He said to them: My forefathers, pray for mercy for me so that I will be saved from the counsel of the spies. [*BT Sotah 34B:7*]

It is often difficult to be able to remain faithful to the values of our faith. Sometimes it takes courage to speak up and do the right thing, especially when far outnumbered by those who would say otherwise. May we all have the strength and courage to follow in Caleb's example, to remain loyal and faithful to the teachings of God in a world that often eschews religious values.

FIFTH ALIYAH: GENESIS 26:30–27:27
THURSDAY, NOVEMBER 19, 2020

Who Are You, My Child?

This *aliyah* and the next tell the story of Jacob deceiving his father Isaac into giving him the blessing that was intended for his brother Esau. The stage is set when we are told that Isaac was old, and his eyesight was "dimmed" [27:1]. Apparently, Isaac seemed to think that he was near death (in reality, according to the biblical account, he lived for a long time after this). In any event, he wanted to give Esau a special blessing before he died. To that end, he instructed Esau to go out hunting for venison and prepare a special meal for him to eat prior to giving him the blessing [27:3-4]. After Esau left to fulfill his father's request, Rebekah, who apparently was eavesdropping during this conversation, called Jacob to her, instructing him to bring her two goats from the flock that she could prepare for him to bring to Isaac; then he would receive the blessing instead of Esau [27:8-10]. Jacob was concerned that Isaac would touch him and realize that he was trying to deceive him and Rebekah's solution was to dress Jacob in Esau's clothing and place the skins of the animals on his arms and his neck [27:11-16]. When Jacob brought the food to Isaac, his father was not quite sure that he believed that the person standing before him was indeed Esau. No less than three times he asked for verification that he was speaking with Esau, and Jacob claimed that he was. After the final time, Isaac called Jacob to him, smelling him, and finally declared that the man standing before him smelled like the fields and therefore must be Esau.

The *aliyah* ends right here, bringing us to the brink and then interrupting the narrative. If we didn't know the story, what would we think at the end of this *aliyah*? Does the deception work or not? Does Jacob receive the blessing that was intended for Esau or not?

The Torah, by splitting the *aliyah* this way, causes us to concentrate on Jacob's behavior (we certainly could ponder Rebekah's culpability here, as well, but the emphasis is decidedly on Jacob). What do we think about Jacob here? We know that even before the twins were born, God told Rebekah that the older would serve the younger (this, of course, explains the stake that she holds in it). Clearly, it seems that Rebekah was willing to go to great lengths to make the prophecy come true. It does not appear that she ever told Esau about this prophecy. It does seem, though, that Jacob is well aware of it.

In any event, as I read through this story, it occurred to me how many times the word "son" appears in various forms: my son (*beni*), eleven times; his son (*beno*), third times; her son (*benah*), four times.

All of this in just seventeen verses (that does not include the number of occurrences in the continuation of the story in the next *aliyah*). Time and time again, both Esau and Jacob are addressed by their parents as "my son," a fitting title in any case. But we the readers are aware of the familial relationships of the four characters in this story. Why do we need to be reminded of them so frequently? In my opinion, it adds to the confusion and, in a way, it seems as if they are all participating in the deception.

The climax of this section, I think, comes in verse 18, when Isaac asks Jacob, "Who are you, my son?" This is the most direct question posed to Jacob by his father. This is the moment where he decides if he will be truthful or not. His answer is very telling: "I am Esau, your firstborn." Well, that statement is partially true. It is interesting that the word *bechorcha* (your firstborn), appears only this one time in the whole section. We know that Esau sold his birthright to Jacob; thus, Jacob considers himself the rightful recipient of the blessings of the firstborn. But Esau and Jacob are referred to as his/her older son and his/her younger son, respectively, when mentioning them in terms of their relationship to Isaac or Rebekah.

I think that Isaac's question to Jacob is a challenge not only to be honest with his father, but to be honest with himself. It is as if Isaac is asking him,

"Why are you doing this? Do you know? Are you aware of who and what you have become, my son?"

Self-awareness is so difficult sometimes. It's hard to be honest with ourselves about our motivations, particularly when our actions, like Jacob's, might be less than admirable. It is precisely at moments like this that it is so important to be able to face ourselves honestly. Yes, the ultimate goal for which we are aiming may be an admirable goal but are we following the right path to get there? And who might we be hurting along the way?

One positive thing about this year, I think, is that we have been given a lot of time and opportunity for introspection. May we all use that time for good, working to make ourselves better people. When we come out of our COVID-induced cocoons next year, may we emerge as better people, ready to work together to form a better world.

SIXTH ALIYAH: GENESIS 27:28–28:4
FRIDAY, NOVEMBER 20, 2020

Who Are You Really, My Child?

Here we have the second part of the story of the "purloined blessing." We see that Isaac does, indeed, give his special blessing to Jacob, who is masquerading as his brother Esau [27;28-29]. He begins with a blessing for enjoying the bounties of the Earth: dew from heaven, the fatness of the Earth, grain, and wine. Then he goes on to say that nations will bow down to him, his brothers will bow down to him (why the plural? He only has one!), anyone who curses him will be cursed, and anyone who blesses him will be blessed. This is the part of the blessing that is specifically designated for the first born.

We hardly have time to contemplate the meaning of any of this as Jacob no sooner leaves Isaac's presence than Esau comes home with game that he had caught [27:30-31], ready to present his father with a meal. We, the readers, are filled with a sense of foreboding.

When Esau brings his game to his father, we once again see that Isaac asks this question: "Who are you?" but this time he does so without naming the person to whom the question is addressed. Sarna says that this is because Isaac has difficulty accepting the idea that his own progeny would have deceived him.[6]

As a matter of fact, in this part there are not nearly as many words that mean "son" as in the previous *aliyah*: my son (*beni*), twice; his son (*beno*), once; your son (*bincha*), once; her son (*benah*), twice.

The answer that is given to Isaac's question is essentially the same he had received just as little while before: "I am your son, Esau, your first-born!" (Jacob had answered, "I am Esau, your firstborn.") Both Jacob and Esau claimed to be the firstborn; yet only one of them—Jacob—noted that he was Isaac's son.

Isaac realizes that he has been deceived, but also realizes that the blessing, once given, cannot be rescinded. Esau's reaction is truly heart-breaking; three times he begs his father to give him a blessing as well [27:34,36,38]. The last is accompanied with bitter wailing, "Have you but one blessing, Father? Bless me, too, Father!" When we read this, we cannot help but be moved; we can feel Esau's anguish.

Isaac responds by giving him a blessing, the beginning of which is almost identical to the one that he had given to Jacob: Esau will also enjoy the fatness of the Earth and the dew of heaven [27:39]. Notice, however, that the order of these is reversed from Jacob's blessing. Isaac continues, however, by telling Esau that he will live by the sword, and that he will serve his brother.

As a result of all of this, Esau vows to kill Jacob as soon as Isaac dies. To protect Jacob (and herself), Rebekah tells Isaac that she is distressed by the Hittite women whom Esau has married. She suggests to Isaac that they send Jacob away to her brother's house to find a wife.

So, which of the four parties in this story is innocent? Certainly not Jacob, who carried out a deception on his father. And not Rebekah, who assisted her son in the deception.

What about Esau? Yes, we feel sorry for him. But at the same time, he, too, was guilty of deceiving his father. When Isaac first called him to tell him to go hunting for a meal so that he could give him his special blessing—Esau knew at that moment that he long ago had sold his birthright to Jacob. Esau knew that Jacob was the one who should be receiving the blessing, but he did not tell his father. He fully intended to receive that blessing himself, in which case he would have been the one to have deceived his brother, depriving him of the blessing that he had told him years before he was giving to him.

And what of Isaac? He would seem to be the least culpable here. He was the victim of deception from all three members of his immediate family. At the same time, it is quite clear from the story that he was never quite sure who was standing before him when he gave that first blessing. He didn't know if it was Jacob or Esau but he did know that the person was his son, and that is perhaps why that word shows up so frequently in the first part of the story, but not the second.

In the end, God's intention for the twins has been borne out, but only because, once again, the humans involved have taken things into their own hands to bring it to fruition. And the results are disastrous.

A question to ask here is, "Do the ends justify the means?" When we try to play God, the results can never be good. God's intention was for Jacob to rule over his brother. Certainly, the Creator of the world could make that happen.

All four players in this story are culpable to a certain extent. And all four end up suffering in the end.

Engaging in deception, even if one's motives might be construed as possible, is fraught with the possibility of bringing about unexpected, unfortunate, and unwanted consequences. This story should be a warning to us all.

SEVENTH ALIYAH: GENESIS 28:5–9
WRITTEN FOR SHABBAT, SATURDAY, NOVEMBER 21, 2020

We Are All Flawed

This very short *aliyah* closes out this episode of sibling rivalry and birthrights. Jacob has been sent off to Laban, Rebekah's brother, to find a wife. Esau, realizing that his parents are distressed over the two women whom he has married, takes a third wife—this one the daughter of his uncle Ishmael. Since Jacob has been instructed to marry a daughter of his mother's brother, Esau reasons that his parents will be appeased if he marries the daughter of his father's brother. The text does not tell us what their reaction to this union was.

In the end, the last part of Isaac's life has turned out to be not much better than his father Avraham's final years. Like Abraham, Isaac has two sons, and he is apparently estranged from them both, just as his father had been estranged from himself and Ishmael. Abraham lost his wife when she heard that he had tried to kill their son. Isaac has not lost his wife, but, no doubt, their relationship is strained by having to send away the son whom Rebekah loved.

Finally, we must remember that Abraham had sent his servant to Paddan-Aram to find a wife for Isaac, and to bring her back to Canaan with him. He had been very explicit about one thing with Eliezer: "Do not take my son back there," he told him in no uncertain terms. Now, that same son, Isaac, needs to find a wife for his designated heir, Jacob. The wife must also come from Paddan-Aram, from the same family, Bethuel and Laban (Rebekah's father and brother). But Isaac, unlike his father, sends his son back there, deeming it a safer place for him to be, given his brother's anger.

After this, we hear nothing more about Isaac until his death at the age of one hundred eighty. It seems that the family with whom God has chosen to have a covenant relationship has a long way to go and many lessons to learn before their destiny can be realized.

But isn't that, in the end, really the point? Had they been perfect, we would have been presented with an unattainable reality, a bar too high to strive for. Instead, we are presented with human beings with flaws, just like us. We can look at the mistakes they made and, hopefully, learn from them instead of repeating them.

Parashat Vayetzei

FIRST ALIYAH: GENESIS 28:10–22
SUNDAY, NOVEMBER 22, 2020

A Stairway to Heaven[1]

With this *parashah*, we begin the story of Jacob, the third of the patriarchs. At the end of the previous *parashah*, he had been sent away from Beersheva by his parents because his brother Esau was so angry with him that he had vowed to kill him. His father Isaac instructed him to go to the home of Laban, Rebekah's brother, to find a wife. Here we find him at a place along the road where he stops for the night. Laying down, he takes a stone and places it under his head as a pillow [28:11]. He soon falls into a deep sleep, during which he has a vision. In his dream he sees a ladder (or a staircase) reaching from the ground beside him up to heaven (anyone hearing Led Zeppelin right now?). There are angels going up and down the ladder and God is standing beside him. God promises to give him the land where he currently is and reiterates to him the same promise that had been made to both his grandfather and his father before him that his descendants would be as numerous as the stars in the sky, and all the other nations of the Earth would bless themselves through them. Finally, God promises to bring Jacob back to this place [28:13- 15].

Reading through this passage, I am reminded of the sanctuary of my home synagogue, North Shore Jewish Center in Port Jefferson Station, on Long Island in New York. Our very beautiful, distinctive ark depicts this scene of Jacob's dream. At the bottom of the ark, we can see Jacob reclining with the stone under his head. The ladder twists above him all the way up to the top of the ark, which is very tall. All along the ladder, there are little appendages that resemble the letter "*yud*" that are supposed to represent the angels. The names of the twelve tribes, the sons of Jacob, are attached to the ladder, as well.

When Jacob awakens from his dream, he says, "Surely the LORD is present in this place, and I did not know it!" [28:16]. Realizing that the place is holy, Jacob goes on to utter the following phrase: "This is none other than the abode of God, and that is the gateway to heaven" [28:17]. This phrase appears on the walls of our sanctuary, in Hebrew and English, on either side of the bimah, surrounding the ark.

Jacob's vision of the ladder has been discussed by many commentators with various interpretations of its symbolism. The Baal HaTurim interprets it using gematria: the numerical value of the word *"sulam"* (ladder) is sixty. Another word that has the same numerical value is *kol* (voice). He says, "the prayers of the righteous serve as a ladder upon which the angels may ascend . . . whoever focuses his intent upon his prayers causes the ladder to be complete with all its rungs, and they (i.e., the angels) are able to ascend."[2]

Most commentators say that this place, which Jacob called Bethel (*Beit El, house of God*) was really Mt. Moriah, the exact place at which his grandfather Abraham had attempted to sacrifice his son and Jacob's father Isaac. It was also, then, the place where both Temples later stood in Jerusalem. The heavenly sanctuary is said to be at the top of Jacob's ladder, directly above the spot of the earthly sanctuary. Once again, when I envision our synagogue ark, all the way on the very top (therefore, top of the ladder) there is a depiction of the heavenly Jerusalem of gold.

Though we cannot all physically gather in the sanctuary right now, we can livestream the service, viewing it on our computers at home. Through the camera's eye, we can see the *bimah* and our beautiful ark, and the inscription on the walls reminding us of this passage. Whether we are in the sanctuary or in our living rooms, may the sound of our prayers ascend together to heaven, providing a portal for God's angels to ascend with our prayers of praise and supplication, and to descend, bringing healing and comfort to our very needy world.

SECOND ALIYAH: GENESIS 29:1–17
MONDAY, NOVEMBER 23, 2020

We Can't See the Forest for the Trees

In this *aliyah*, Jacob meets his future wife at the well where she has come with her father's sheep. The scene is reminiscent of Eliezer's encounter with Rebekah at the well when he came in search of a wife for Isaac. Unlike Eliezer, however, who first observed Rebekah watering the camels before inquiring who she was, Jacob knows already who Rachel is before he even speaks to her, having first spoken to some shepherds he met at the well. Additionally, unlike Eliezer, who came with ten camels and laden with gifts, Jacob is alone and has nothing to give to his prospective bride. Therefore, he will have to work for his uncle Laban. Still in all, if we were to freeze the action right here, after verse 15, it seems that everything is going according to plan. Jacob has come in search of his uncle Laban, from whose family he has been instructed to find a wife. Not only has he met Laban, but he has also met his daughter and he is apparently already smitten with her.

Suddenly, however, the text takes a moment to interject a piece of information that we didn't have before: Rachel has an older sister, Leah. Not only that, but we are also offered a comparison of the two sisters: "Leah had weak eyes; Rachel was shapely and beautiful" [29:17]. One is praised for her beauty and the only thing we know about the other is that she had "weak" eyes.

There is much discussion among the commentators regarding what exactly is meant by "weak eyes." The word *rakot*, here translated as "weak," appears nowhere else in the *Tanakh*. Most commentators agree that it does not mean that she was cross-eyed or that she was visually impaired, as so many assume it does. Many translate it as "soft." Some say that Leah was aware that Rebekah had two sons and had heard horrible stories about Esau. However, she assumed that since she was the older of the two sisters, she would have to marry the older of the two brothers. We read in the previous *parashah* that Esau took the daughter of Ishmael as his third wife so, if Leah were to marry him, she would become wife number four. She was so unhappy at the prospect that she had spent a lot of time crying, and that is what made her eyes appear to be soft. Other than that, she was said to be as physically attractive as her younger sister.

In any event, the *aliyah* ends right here. We, the readers, know of course what is going to happen when we read on in the next *aliyah*.

I was struck by the recurring theme of the following three verses from the book of Genesis: "When Isaac was old and his eyes were too dim to see, he called his older son Esau and said to him, 'My son.' He answered, 'Here I am.'" [27:1]; "Leah had weak **eyes**; Rachel was shapely and beautiful." [29:17]; and "Now Israel's eyes were dim with age; he could not see. So [Joseph] brought them close to him, and he kissed them and embraced them" [48:10].

The first verse here is from the previous *parashah* and begins the story of Jacob deceiving his father Isaac to receive his brother Esau's blessing.

The second is our verse here about Leah's eyes. We already know that Jacob will marry both Leah and Rachel, but Rachel will be the object of his affection.

The third is from the end of the book of Genesis when Joseph brings his two sons to his father Israel (Jacob) for him to bless them. Since Jacob's own eyesight is then failing him, he reverses his hands, placing his right hand on the head of the younger son, Ephraim, instead of his older brother, Menashe.

There is one common theme to all three of these stories from the life of Jacob: all three involve the younger of two siblings usurping the place of the older. And in all three stories, there is something faulty about the eyes of one of the characters. And in all three stories, the outcome was exactly the way that God intended it to be.

Sometimes, we get so distracted by what we can see with our eyes that we cannot see what is really happening. Often, in the moment, we are uncomprehending of why something is happening to us. "Why me?" we may ask. Or "why now?" or "why did it have to happen this way?" It is not until later, when we can look back on the situation, that we can see the logic.

Right now, many of us find it difficult to deal with the rising incidence of COVID-19, and the very real need to be more cautious and conservative again like we were back in the springtime. At the same time, no less than three pharmaceutical companies have announced that they have developed vaccines that are highly effective, and they will soon seek approval for their distribution. There is some light ahead, but we need to be patient if we want to get there. May the year 2021 offer us the opportunity to look back on this time and know that, though it may be difficult to refrain from doing many of the things we want to do right now, it will have been the right decision in the end.

May we all remain safe and healthy so that we will be able to see that day.

THIRD ALIYAH: GENESIS 29:18–30:13
TUESDAY, NOVEMBER 24, 2020

Eight is Enough (Or is It?)[3]

In this *aliyah*, Jacob becomes the victim, rather than the perpetrator, of deceit. He makes an agreement with Laban that he will work for him for seven years in exchange for being able to marry his younger daughter Rachel [29:18-19]. When the seven years are up, he asks Laban to give him Rachel as his wife [29:20-21]. After throwing a big wedding celebration, Laban gives him Leah instead of Rachel [29:22-23]. When Jacob realizes in the morning what has happened, he confronts Laban, who tells him that their custom is not to marry off a younger daughter before the older [29:25-26] then promises to give him Rachel as well in exchange for seven more years of work [29:27-28]. Each of the daughters also comes with a maidservant: Leah has Zilpah, Rachel has Bilhah. According to Chizkuni, each of these was also Laban's daughter, born of one of his concubines.[4] That would mean, therefore, that Jacob's four wives were all sisters or half-sisters.

The Torah then goes on to tell us the following about the two sisters: "The LORD saw that Leah was unloved and he opened her womb; but Rachel was barren" [29:31]. We may wonder why Leah was unloved (some translations even say "hated" but most commentators shy away from such strong language). In any event, from the start, Rachel had been the object of Jacob's affections. Additionally, Jacob, himself a great deceiver, viewed Leah as being complicit with her father's deception. After all, she spent the entire bridal night with him and never divulged her true identity. Though we can possibly understand her motivation (she may well have viewed this as her only chance to be married), we can also hold her accountable for her part of the deception. Jacob, it would seem, has received his just desserts, poetic justice at its best. Here, however, we see the usual sibling switch-eroo following a path opposite the familiar one of the younger usurping the older. Here, the older has usurped the place of the younger and taken her place as his wife.

The verse tells us outright that Rachel was barren (this seems to be a recurring theme with the wives of the patriarchs) but the fact that we are told that "the Lord . . . opened her womb" implies that, at the outset, Leah was barren, as well. Abarbanel says that God's original plan was to play a providential role in the births of all the children of Jacob.[5] In any event, because of Jacob's feelings regarding his two wives, God grants fertility to the less favored wife while retaining the barrenness of the favored wife. Now we see that Jacob's progeny appears with great frequency. In rapid succession, Leah gives birth to four sons, Reuben, Simeon, Levi, and Judah then she ceases from bearing children. Rachel, meanwhile, remains childless. Finally, in desperation, and after confronting her husband to ask him why he wasn't praying for her as his father Isaac had prayed for his mother Rebekah, she resorts to the same method of attaining motherhood as Sarah had done with Hagar and offers her maidservant Bilhah to Jacob. Bilhah bears two sons, Dan and Naphtali. Seeing that she has ceased from childbearing, Leah resorts to the same method and offers her maidservant Zilpah to Jacob. Zilpah also bears sons, Gad and Asher. Jacob already has four times as many sons as either his father or his grandfather. And we will see in the next *aliyah* that he is not done yet.

Cheaper by the Dozen?

This *aliyah* continues the story of the births of Jacob's children. It begins by telling us that Leah's son, Reuben, who the commentators estimate is about seven years old at this point, discovers some mandrakes in the field and brings them to his mother [30:14]. So, what were these mandrakes? They came from some kind of plant that was either thought to assure fertility or was perceived to be an aphrodisiac (not necessarily the same thing!). In any event, Rachel, who remains childless, asks Leah to give her some of the mandrakes. Leah's answer is very telling: it wasn't enough that you took my husband away, now you want these mandrakes, too? [30:15]. From this, the commentators deduce that Jacob had ceased to be intimate with Leah (how else to explain the abrupt cessation of her pregnancies when she had been so fertile in the first four years?). Additionally, the reason that Leah has stopped conceiving is that Jacob is spending all his time with Rachel, whom he loves most, and who as yet has been unable to conceive. So, the sisters bargain with each other for the opportunity to have conjugal relations with their mutual husband. Rachel "allows" Leah one night with Jacob in exchange for some of the mandrakes. Wanting to guarantee that Leah would have to follow through on this agreement, Leah meets Jacob as he comes in from the fields and tells him he must sleep with her that night [30:16]. From this encounter, God grants Leah not only a fifth son (Issachar), but apparently also her husband's renewed interest, as she goes on to have a sixth son (Zebulon) [30:18-20]. There is a passing mention of the fact that she also bore a seventh child for Jacob, their daughter, Dinah [30:21].

So, just to refresh your memory, at this point, Jacob has ten sons (six with Leah, two with Rachel's handmaiden Bilhah, and two with Leah's handmaiden Zilpah), and one daughter (with Leah). Then, finally, at long last, God remembers Rachel and opens her womb, healing her barrenness (just as had happened with the two previous matriarchs, Sarah and Rebekah). She gives birth to a son, naming him Joseph (in Hebrew, *Yosef*, meaning "he will add"), expressing the hope that she will have one more son after this [30:22-24]. At this point, the narration of the birth of Jacob's children ceases.

There is, however, a very interesting take on the relationship between the two sisters. Even though Leah was not as loved by Jacob as Rachel was, she felt compassion for Rachel's childless plight. The Talmud tells the following story:

... "And afterwards she bore a daughter, and called her name Dinah" ... The Gemara asks: What is meant by the addition of the word: Afterwards? What does the verse seek to convey by emphasizing that after the birth of Zebulun she gave birth to Dinah? Rav said: After Leah passed judgment on herself and said: Twelve tribes are destined to descend from Jacob, six came from me and four from the maidservants, that is ten, and if this fetus is male, my sister Rachel will not even be the equivalent of one the maidservants; immediately, the fetus was transformed into a daughter, as it is stated: And she called her name Dinah, meaning she named her after her judgment [din] [*BT Brachot 60A:12*]

According to this *midrash*, when Leah conceived for a seventh time, the child was originally supposed to be Joseph. However, she knew prophetically that Jacob was ordained by God to have twelve sons. She already had six, Bilhah had two, and Zilpah had two. If Leah were to have another boy, then Rachel would only be able to have one, making her less important than either of the two maidservants. Therefore, Leah prayed, asking God to make her fetus female—and the gender of the fetus was changed. This child became Dinah, and Joseph was later born to Rachel.

This story in the Talmud is part of a longer discussion about whether one may pray, asking God that their fetus may be a specific gender. If the child has already been conceived, couldn't this be a prayer in vain? The ultimate decision is that one may make such a prayer up until forty days after conception and after that will be too late. (Actually, modern studies have shown that genitals begin forming in a fetus at about seven weeks, so this isn't too far off.)

What struck me about this *midrash* is that the fetus was transformed into a daughter. The *midrash* is saying that the fetus, which was originally male, changed to female. Could this be a way in which the rabbis tried to explain individuals who identified as transgender? It's not something that they talk about much, but it would be foolish to think that there were no individuals who identified as such back then. It surely does give us pause.

In any event, though the story of Jacob's children seems to come to an end here, we know from the count that there will be one more child. And if Leah is right, he will be Rachel's second son.

How Long, Oh Lord?

Here we have a very strange story. Apparently, the fourteen years that Jacob has promised to work for Laban in exchange for his two wives have come to an end. He now decides that it is time to go back to Canaan to his family. He has essentially been an indentured servant to Laban. So, when he expresses a wish to leave, Laban asks him what he desires as wages for the time that he has worked for him. Jacob sets up an elaborate scheme with his uncle/father-in-law regarding the flocks: he will take in the future all the cattle that are speckled and spotted, the sheep that are brown, and the speckled and spotted goats. (Genetically, all of these are uncommon in the Middle East.) We then read about various things he does over the course of the next seven years to induce the sheep, cattle, and goats to produce these genetically recessive traits. Eventually, he is very successful and becomes very wealthy. By that point, the feelings of his wife's family towards him deteriorate and he calls Rachel and Leah to discuss the idea of leaving.

So, rather than dwelling on this genetic manipulation, I want to think about the following: Jacob wanted to go home again. He wanted to go back and see his parents (yes, his father Isaac was still alive!), even though, as far as he knew, his brother still wanted to do him harm and/or kill him. However, in the fourteen years since he left home, his own family had expanded greatly: two wives, two handmaiden/wives, twelve children. He could not leave unless he could provide for them.

Today is Thanksgiving. Most of us celebrated either alone or with the family members with whom we live/associate. Most of us longed to have our traditional Thanksgiving celebrations together with our extended family and friends. As I write this, the numbers of COVID cases in the New York area are skyrocketing to levels that we haven't seen since the springtime. In my synagogue, we received the word today that there will no longer be any congregants attending Shabbat services, only the clergy. What happened?

Like Jacob, we long to "go home." We want to go back to what our lives were before. We want everything to return to "normal." And we would go back in a heartbeat, if we could, even though there is still this horrible virus lurking, waiting to do us harm and perhaps even kill us. But the statistics of the last week or so show us that we simply are not ready. Yes, we have heard encouraging news that there may be as many as three vaccines on the horizon and they may be approved soon. But it will be several months at best before they will be available to most of us.

We need to find our speckled and spotted sheep. We need to find what will sustain us over the next few months and beyond. We thought we were ready, then we became lax.

When we do emerge from this virus, God-willing sometime next year, it will be to a new world. We need to use the time that has been granted to us now to help us prepare for our new reality.

Jacob had to be patient for seven more years. May God grant us the patience to hold on for several more months.

SIXTH ALIYAH: GENESIS 31:17–42
FRIDAY, NOVEMBER 27, 2020

As the Fonz Would Say: Sit On It, Rachel![6]

Finally deciding to make a break with Laban, Jacob packed up his wives, children, servants, and animals, and headed back towards Canaan. To avoid a confrontation with his father-in-law, he chose to leave when Laban had gone off to shear his sheep, apparently about a three days' journey in the opposite direction from the way in which they would be traveling. In her father's absence, we are told that, "Rachel stole her father's household idols" [31:19].

We know that Laban was an idol-worshipper who also practiced divination. But we wonder, what reason could Rachel possibly have had for stealing the idols? The commentators put forth several theories, none of them wishing to consider the possibility that she wanted them for herself. The most popular thought is that she did not want Laban to use them to discover through divination which way they had gone and where they had stopped. There are two problems that I see with that theory: it actually imbues these idols with magical powers, and he clearly somehow managed to find out anyway since he was able to chase after them and overtake them on the journey. Rashi says that Rachel desired to free her father from idol worship.[7] Rabbeinu Chananel elaborates on this idea:

> . . . she stole them in order that he would reconsider his actions,
> saying to himself that any deity which allows itself to be stolen
> surely cannot be much good to anyone. [*Rabbeinu Chananel*][8]

She wished to show him that the idols were, in fact, powerless. This is a similar idea to the famous *midrash* about Avraham as a boy smashing all his father's idols except for one, in whose hands he placed the hammer he had used, later telling his father that the idol had done the damage. When his father doubted the credulity of that story, Abraham pointed out to him the futility of idol worship.

In any event, to be sure to deny her father access to his idols, Rachel took them with her instead of just burying them somewhere. All of this was done without Jacob's knowledge. We know this because, when Laban caught up with him and asked him why he had stolen the gods, we are told that Jacob said: "anyone with whom you find your gods shall not remain alive! In the presence of our kinsmen, point out what I have of yours and take it." Jacob, of course, did not know that Rachel had stolen them [31:32].

Jacob would hardly have made such a vow had he known in whose possession the idols in fact were. In any event, because of this vow, the situation became more dire as Laban launched a full-scale search of all the tents. Taking advantage of the fact that he began with Jacob's and Leah's tents, we are told that Rachel took the idols from her tent and stored them in the camel cushion on which she sat. When her father approached her, she said to him: "Let not my lord take it amiss that I cannot rise before you, for the period of women is upon me" [31:35].

This reminded me of the following Talmudic passage:

> . . . A person should always converse euphemistically, as one finds in the following verses. The first: "And whichever saddle that the *zav* [impure man] rides upon shall be ritually impure" [Leviticus 15:9] which discusses the impurity imparted by a *zav* to an object on which he sits, calls this action riding. And the verse: "And anyone who touches anything on which she sat" [Leviticus 15:22], which discusses the parallel ritual impurity of a woman, a *zava*, calls the action sitting. Since riding is slightly demeaning for a woman, as it involves an immodest splaying of the legs, the verse avoids the term riding and opts to convey the more modest image of sitting . . . . one should be clever when speaking and avoid inappropriate phrases. [*Pesachim 3A:12*][9]

We know that women were encouraged to ride side-saddle out of a sense of modesty. However, it simply is not possible to do that on a camel! Additionally, Rachel didn't speak euphemistically at all, but came right out and told her father exactly what her "condition" was. (In reality, we do not even know if she was telling him this truthfully, or just making it up.) This was enough to cause Laban to back away and leave her alone. Eventually, he gave up the search.

Now, finally, Jacob felt emboldened enough to speak up to his father-in-law, recounting how he had taken advantage of his son-in-law for twenty years, despite Jacob's great and honest servitude. The *aliyah* ends with Jacob attributing his success to the protection and providence of God in contrast to Laban, who now literally found himself godless.

Jacob now appears to be ready to rightfully take his place as the grandson of Abraham and son of Isaac as the heir to the covenant with God.

SEVENTH ALIYAH: GENESIS 31:43–32:3
WRITTEN FOR SHABBAT, SATURDAY, NOVEMBER 28, 2020

Longing to be Together

Realizing that Jacob is leaving with his daughters and his grandsons, Laban offers to make a pact with Jacob [31:44]. Jacob erects a pillar and has his servants set up a mound which will mark the demarcation point between the two men [31:45-46]. Laban declared the place to be a witness of the agreement being solemnified between the two men: "and [it was called] Mizpah, because he [Laban] said, "May the LORD watch between you and me, when we are out of sight of each other" [31:49].

This verse is well recognized by many people. Perhaps you have seen something called a *mizpah* coin, particularly in gift shops in Israel. It is made up of two separate pieces that fit together like puzzle pieces, and usually contains the words I just quoted. It is designed to be separated between two people who share a special relationship but who may not be geographically close to one another. Each will wear one piece of the coin, knowing that its mate is being worn by the other. In addition to representing the idea that their relationship is incomplete unless they are together, it expresses a fervent wish for God to watch over their beloved friend/relative while they are apart, and to bring them together again at some future time.

I think that this is a fitting sentiment for us all to keep in mind during this time that we are physically separated once again due to the rising incidence of COVID cases, unable to come together in the synagogue to worship. It is made perhaps even more difficult for us this second time than it was back in the early days of the pandemic. After having had the opportunity to come together, albeit in limited numbers, for four and a half months since July. In our hearts, we all carry a piece of the *Mizpah* that connects us as the family of Israel. May the Lord watch over us all, keeping us safe, so that we will once again be able to join together in prayer and praise of God. *Ken yehi ratzon,* may it come speedily in our day.

Parashat Vayishlach

FIRST ALIYAH: GENESIS 32:4–13
SUNDAY, NOVEMBER 29, 2020

Setting the Bar Too High

Having made his pact with his father-in-law Laban, Jacob set his sights on reuniting with his brother Esau. Remember that the last time they saw each other was twenty years ago, after the incident of the stolen blessing, and Esau was so angry with his brother then that he said he wanted to kill him. Jacob sends messengers ahead to tell Esau what has happened in his life during these twenty years and expresses a desire to gain his favor [32:4-6]. The messengers return, apparently without having spoken with Esau, but with the news that he is coming to meet Jacob together with four hundred men. This, we are told, causes Jacob to be "greatly frightened," causing him, in turn, to divide up his family, servants, and flocks into two camps, hoping that Esau will not realize it, and that at least if he attacks one camp, the other will escape his wrath. Jacob then prays to God for deliverance [32:7-13].

The Baal HaTurim has an interesting observation on verse 5.[1] Jacob's message to Esau contains the information "I dwelled with Laban." The word *garti*, translated here as "I dwelled" or "I lived" is made up of four letters, *gimmel, resh, tav, yud*. These letters can be rearranged to spell *taryag*, a kind of made-up word whose significance is its *gematria*, or numerical value, of six hundred thirteen. In other words, *taryag* represents the six hundred thirteen *mitzvot*. According to the *midrash*, Jacob was trying to say to his brother that, even though he had lived with his idol-worshipping father-in-law for the past twenty years, he continued to observe all the *mitzvot* during that time. This is an interesting comment. Most of the rabbis like to believe that all the patriarchs observed all the commandments even though the entirety of them were not given until the time of Moses. The thought is that they were so righteous that they just intuitively knew them all.

This is particularly interesting in light of a discussion regarding verse 8. The question that is posed is: "What did Jacob have to be afraid of?" Rashi says that he was afraid of being killed, or, worse yet, that he might have to shed blood.[2] Clearly, as we can see from verse 12 that he was afraid for the lives of his wives and children. At the same time, he reminds God in his prayer that God had promised to be with him and protect him, and to make his descendants as many as the grains of sand in the sea (actually, God only said that to Abraham and Isaac, not to Jacob). Therefore, if Jacob had faith that God would keep those promises, his fear should have been unfounded. So perhaps there's another explanation:

"Yaakov was greatly afraid;" seeing that Yaakov had had many assurances from God, why would he be afraid of the encounter with his brother Esau? He realized—belatedly—that he had erred in staying with Lavan after having completed his fourteen years of service in order to marry. During the years when he had worked to amass material wealth, his brother Esau had performed the commandment of honoring father and mother. He was afraid that he did not have sufficient merits to overcome Esau's lead in that department [B'reshit Rabbah 76,2]. According to the *Midrash*, G-d's promise to protect him was limited to while he was outside the borders of the Holy Land. [*Daat Zkenim*][3]

According to this theory, Jacob was afraid that Esau had been more observant of one very important *mitzvah* than he himself had been during the last six years that he had lived with Laban: the *mitzvah* of honoring parents.

Thus, we have two conflicting visions of our patriarch: either he was totally observant of all the *mitzvot* or he was distressed because there was at least one *mitzvah* that he had been negligent about. I think I prefer the second alternative. One who is totally diligent in his observance presents an impossibly perfect role model, a standard that the rest of us cannot achieve. One who is not perfect yet is disappointed with him or herself when (s)he finds that (s)he is falling short of the mark is someone I can identify with. Like everyone else, I sometimes fall short in my observance; but when I realize my shortcomings and am uncomfortable with them, I can work on improving them. That, I believe, is an accurate description of how we are called to live our lives as Jews, and that goal is attainable for all of us.

Where's Dinah?

In preparation for his encounter with Esau, Jacob sent ahead massive numbers of animals as gifts, instructing each servant to let Esau know that the gifts were from his brother Jacob, who was following behind [32:14-22]. Then, despite having separated his group into two camps, he now brought his entire family, all his flocks and his servants and possessions across the river Jabbok, remaining on the other side alone. During the night, he had a strange wrestling encounter with a "man" (most likely, really an angel). Realizing that he was not prevailing over Jacob, the man/angel took his leave just before dawn, but not before changing Jacob's name to Israel [32:23-30]. This, of course, is a well-known story from the Torah.

I, however, noticed something earlier on in the reading that I had never noticed before: when Jacob is sending his family over to the other side of the river for safety, we are told that he took "his two wives, his two maidservants and his eleven children" [32:23]—and, indeed, the Hebrew word used is his children, not his sons. Did someone lose count? Last we saw, there were twelve children in all, eleven sons and one daughter. So, who is not included in this count, and why? Naturally, the first assumption is that the one not accounted for is Jacob's lone daughter, Dinah. But if she were not among the eleven children mentioned, the question then becomes: where was she? The commentators also were bothered by this:

> . . . But where was Dinah? He placed her in a chest and locked her in so that Esau should not set his fancy upon her (desire to marry her). On this account, Jacob was punished because he had kept her away from his brother for she might have led him back to the right path [Genesis Rabbah 76:9]. [Rashi][4]

Jacob did not want his brother Esau to marry his daughter (at last count, Esau already had three wives, all of whom his parents disapproved of), so he hid her. Well, okay (maybe?), but wouldn't she still have been moved to the other side of the river, even if it was inside of a box?

> Dinah was included in the words "and his two wives," as she was always close to Leah, her mother . . . . Jacob had put her into a box that he had locked. His concern had been that if Esau would see her, he would take her by force. [Radak][5]

Radak cites the same source but says that Dinah did not have to be mentioned or counted separately because she was so close to her mother Leah. He also says that Jacob was afraid that Esau would take his daughter by force (i.e., rape). Make sure you remember all of this—it will come back to haunt Jacob—and us—bigtime!

Sifrei Chachamim also raises the possibility that the missing child from our verse may have been one of the sons instead of Dinah. Citing a blessing that Joseph gave to Benjamin late in life [43:29], he explains that Benjamin needed to be blessed since he had not yet been born at the time of our current story and thus was not included in Jacob's statement to Esau that these were, "the children whom [God] has graciously granted your servant" [33:5]. But, if that were the case, he asks, why would Joseph not have also included another brother in his blessing, if he, too, had been missing at the time of our story? Since he didn't, Sifrei Chachamim concludes, the uncounted child must have been Dinah.[6]

So, there we have it. Poor Dinah is hidden away in a box because of her gender, in much the same way that her grandmother Rebekah and great-grandmother Sarah were passed off as their respective husbands' sisters. With all the testosterone floating around in her family, one wonders if anyone really paid much attention to her. It is almost no wonder that she went out on her own looking for love. We will see the disastrous results of all of this later in the parashah.

THIRD ALIYAH: GENESIS 32:31–33:5
TUESDAY, DECEMBER 1, 2020

Renewing Family Ties

As the sun rose, when Jacob left the place where he had encountered the man/angel, naming it Peniel (face of God), he was limping from where the angel had wounded his thigh. Almost as a side note, the Torah tells us that we do not eat the part of the meat containing the sciatica to this day [32: 33]. This is where we get the prohibition of eating filet mignon (kosher filet mignon does exist, but it is very expensive, as the nerve must be removed through a very tedious process).

No sooner had Jacob left the encounter with Peniel than he raised his eyes to see Esau and his four hundred men descending upon him. He had each of the children join their respective mothers and then arranged them by Bilhah and Zilpah first, followed by Leah, and finally Rachel. Jacob bowed before Esau seven times and Esau embraced him and kissed him; they both wept [33:1–4].

The Hebrew text contains something unusual in verse 4. The word *vay-ishakehu* (he kissed him) looks strange. Our eyes are drawn to those little dots over the word—six in all, one on each letter (it looks like seven, but one is the dot for the *shin*). These even appear in the Torah scroll (which, of course, has no vowels). Whenever this phenomenon appears, the rabbis assume that there must be some significance to those dots. Therefore, they attempt to find a rationale:

> . . . originally Esau had intended to bite Yaakov's neck feigning an embrace. God made his teeth as soft as wax and Yaakov's neck as hard as ivory. [They wept] one on account of his neck, the other on account of his teeth. [Radak][7]

> . . . Rabbi Simeon ben Elazar said . . . it teaches that [Esau] felt compassion in that moment and kissed [Jacob] with all his heart. Rabbi Yannai said to him: If so, why is ['kissed'] dotted? On the contrary, it teaches that [Esau] came not to kiss [Jacob] but to bite him, but our ancestor Jacob's neck became like marble and that wicked man's teeth were blunted. Hence, 'and they wept' teaches that [Jacob] wept because of his neck and [Esau] wept because of his teeth. [Bereshit Rabbah 78:9][8]

> . . . a difference of opinion is expressed . . . as to what these dots are intended to suggest: some explain the dotting as meaning that he did not kiss him with his whole heart, whereas R Simeon the son of Johai said: Is it not well-known that Esau hated Jacob? But at that moment his pity was really aroused and he kissed him with his whole heart. [Sifrei Bamidbar 69.2][9]

These are just three examples of the variations of opinions among the commentators. On the one hand, we have those who view Esau as a completely unchanged man whose hatred caused him to attempt to bite his long-lost brother on his neck. In this case, Jacob's neck fantastically was transformed into either marble or ivory, damaging Esau's teeth. On the other hand, we have those who view Esau as a man who put his hatred for his brother aside, sincerely embracing him out of fraternal love.

Both extremes demonstrate an unnatural, unexpected occurrence that some might dub a "miracle." Which is easier to believe? The second, of course. Which do we prefer to believe? Again, the second.

For two brothers who have been separated by circumstance for twenty years, we choose to accept an outcome that allows them to reunite and put their differences aside. Both have prospered, both have been blessed with many children, and both still love their parents, who are still alive. Perhaps those of us who have familial relationships that have been strained during these difficult days of COVID, or due to some other reason, will be able to heal those tensions and come together soon in a sincere embrace, just as Jacob and Esau did. *Ken yehi ratzon.*

FOURTH ALIYAH: GENESIS 33:6–20
WEDNESDAY, DECEMBER 2, 2020

Passing the Birthright

When Jacob and Esau finally encountered each other face to face, Esau asked about all the animals that Jacob had sent on ahead, and Jacob said that (they were gifts) offered to win Esau's favor [33:8]. Esau, like Jacob, had prospered in the last twenty years, as evidenced by the fact that he was meeting his brother with four hundred men. As Sarna points out, the proper etiquette of the Middle East dictates that one should make a show of refusing a gift when it is offered, so that the one who offers the gift should be insistent, and the recipient ultimately accepts it reluctantly.[10] It is a charade that they are required to carry out. Therefore, we see that Esau told his brother, "I have enough, my brother; let what you have remain yours" [33:9]. When Esau said that he had enough (and therefore he didn't need Jacob's gifts), he appeared to be following the script. It is the second part that catches the attention of the commentators, Esau went on to say that what Jacob had should remain his. This was not part of the script and was an unnecessary addendum. So, what was Esau trying to say here? Most of the rabbis say that Esau was stating that he was finally signing off on the birthright and the blessing, acknowledging that they belonged to Jacob. He had done well without them. In addition, to carry forth the grudge that he had had for the past twenty years would only be counterproductive. By accepting this idea, and stating out loud that he could do so, he freed both himself and his brother to carry on with their lives and fulfill their destinies. Jacob no longer needed to be afraid of his brother, and Esau no longer needed to allow himself to be consumed by hatred. Esau's actions are commendable here.

Ultimately, the brothers parted ways peacefully after Jacob refused Esau's offer of men to help guide and protect him and his family on their way.

Jacob, we are told, settled near the city of Sukkot with his family. This city was, at least, in the land of Canaan. Most of the commentators think that he took up residence there for about eighteen months to allow himself time to replenish his flocks after the gift that he had given to Esau.

I cannot help but think of all of this in light of the current political situation in our country. Our election was held a full month ago, and a clear winner was chosen. Yet, we have a president and his followers who are unable to accept that. The turmoil that has been created by this failure to acknowledge that the voters have chosen the other candidate is taking its toll on us all in so many ways.

I think that the present administration would do well to take a cue from Esau: accept and acknowledge that the birthright and the blessing has passed to someone else and allow us all to get on with our lives.

FIFTH ALIYAH: GENESIS 34:1–35:1
THURSDAY, DECEMBER 3, 2020

The Victimization of Dinah

The story contained in this *aliya* is disturbing on several levels. We are told that Dinah, Jacob's only daughter, "went out to see the daughters of the land" [34:1]. This seems reasonable. With all those brothers, she undoubtedly longed for female companionship. Additionally, we have seen that little attention was paid to her by her family. Her motivation was not wrong but, unfortunately, her actions might have been careless. She apparently caught the attention of Shechem, the son of Hamor, the leader of the city near which they had settled. However, rather than try to woo her properly, he raped her. Afterwards, he asked his father to arrange for him to be able to marry Dinah [34:2–4]. (Sounds backwards, no?)

Hamor approached Jacob and his sons (who were naturally very angry when they heard about this) to try to secure not only Dinah as a bride for his son, but a general agreement between their two peoples to live together, trade together, and marry each other's women. Shechem himself spoke up, basically saying that he would do whatever they asked [34:5–12]. Dinah's brothers laid out their terms: Hamor's men must all agree to be circumcised. Hamor and Shechem not only agreed to their terms, but they also went back to speak with all the other men of their city to convince them, and all the men of the city were then circumcised on the same day [34:13–24]. Three days later, Simeon and Levi (who were two of the sons of Leah, and therefore full brothers to Dinah) entered the city and killed all the men of the city while they were incapacitated. They rescued Dinah and brought her back home. Then the remainder of their brothers plundered all the animals and possessions of the people of Shechem while taking their women and children captive [34:25-29]. Jacob was angry with his sons and berated them for what they had done. Their motivation had been essentially to defend Dinah's honor. Jacob, however, was more concerned that they had now put themselves in danger from the other surrounding peoples [34:30-31]. We, as readers, seem to be more outraged and embarrassed by the extreme behavior of the sons than their father Jacob. Sadly, Dinah is not heard from again in the biblical narrative. She, the innocent victim, fades into obscurity.

As I said, there is so much about this story that seems problematic, beginning with Shechem feeling free to take Dinah by force then seemingly thinking that it was okay because he wanted to marry her. His father, too, does not seem troubled by his son's violent deed. Dinah's own father's reaction is subdued and passive, hardly what one would expect from a father whose daughter has just been raped. He does not deal with Hamor and Shechem himself, but rather leaves it for his sons and then is upset afterwards that they made him look bad in the eyes of his neighbors.

Then, of course, there are the brothers. Their indignation at their sister's fate is admirable. Certainly, the cultural rules of the time called for them to exact justice on her behalf—against her attacker. What justification was there for deceiving and then killing all the men of the city? (Some commentators say that they needed to take sweeping, decisive revenge in order to avoid an endless cycle of killing. If they had just killed Shechem, then his family would have taken revenge on them, etc.) There is also the method of killing to be considered: using the sign of the covenant between God and Israel as a ruse to incapacitate them. Sarna says that this is classic irony: "the part of the body used by Shechem in his violent passion will itself become the source of his own punishment."[11]

Perhaps most troubling is the treatment of Dinah by all the men in the story. Abarbanel actually says that "the whole story is written here to demonstrate how difficult it is to have a daughter. Dinah brought Jacob more trouble than all twelve of his sons put together."[12] This is a classic case of blaming the victim. And just like that, poor neglected Dinah, whom we heard almost nothing about, whose only "mistake" was seeking friendship from other women, disappears from the Torah. It is as if this one story is the justification for her existence.

I would not even begin to try to explain or justify all these things. As I said, it is one of the parts of the Torah that we struggle with. One thing I would say is that we need not be complicit. We should be outraged. At the same time, that outrage must trigger some results in us. Thankfully, we live in a time and place when the treatment for most women is far better than what we see in this story. But not all. What can and should we be doing today to change societal attitudes, and in what ways can we exact justice on the perpetrators of sexual crimes? And what can we do to help support the victims? These are the kinds of things that this story should cause us to think about.

SIXTH ALIYAH: GENESIS 35:12–36:19
FRIDAY, DECEMBER 4, 2020

Jacob Gains a Son, but Loses a Wife

Finally, after a number of years, Jacob is headed back to the home of his parents. He is already in the land of Canaan. Along the way, we are told that Rachel is, at long last, pregnant again. However, her labor is difficult. Informed by the midwife that her child is another boy, she names him Ben-Oni, meaning "son of my sorrow." After Rachel dies, Jacob changes his name to Benyamin—Benjamin—usually translated as "son of my right hand" [35:16-20]. All of Jacob's eleven older sons were named by their mothers (or Leah or Rachel in the case of the sons of the handmaidens). Jacob had nothing to do with naming any of his children—until now. There is not total agreement about the meaning of the name, or why Jacob chose to change it. If we take the names at face value, it would surely be understandable that he would not want to saddle his son with a name that would remind him, Jacob, of Rachel's death every time he looked at him. In addition, the right hand was considered to be the source of strength (another stereotype that I have difficulty with), so Jacob wanted to put a positive spin on it. (Ironically, the tribe of Benjamin was later known for being left-handed, or at least ambidextrous.)

I like Chizkuni's explanation better: interchanging a final *mem* for a final *nun* (a legitimate grammatical occurrence in biblical Hebrew) would make the name Benyamim—meaning son of (many) days—implying that Benjamin was born in Jacob's old age and would be his support as he continued to grow older.[13]

Since they are traveling on the road, and much too far from the Cave of Machpelah, Rachel is buried on the side of the road. Later, Jacob will be buried together with Leah in the Cave. Though Leah was slighted by Jacob in this world, it was she who got to spend eternity with him.

Now that Jacob has twelve sons, his family is complete, so we are given a summary of the names of the sons and their mothers. There is no mention of Dinah. Jacob finally makes his way to his father's home. Though we were never told about it in the text, his beloved mother Rebekah, with whom he was so close, has by this time passed away.

Ironically, Isaac, who was considered to be old and frail already at the time of the incident that precipitated Jacob's departure from home, that of the stolen blessing, is still alive at one hundred eighty years old. We are told that Isaac was "gathered to his kin" just as Abraham had been before him. And, just as Abraham's two sons came together to bury him when he died, so, too, do Isaac's two sons come together to bury him [35:28-29]. It is interesting to note, however, the order of the names: it is said that Isaac was buried by "his sons Esau and Jacob." Though Jacob had received the birthright and the blessing, and Esau had accepted that fact, here Esau is recognized as the oldest son. How fitting is this as Isaac had always favored him over his brother. Most importantly, the two brothers are able to come together again to honor their father, whom they both loved, by participating together in his burial.

With this, we will now be given the genealogy of the descendants of Esau, and the story of Esau will draw to a close. The brothers are able to part ways, each to fulfill his own destiny.

SEVENTH ALIYAH: GENESIS 36:20–43
WRITTEN FOR SHABBAT, SATURDAY, DECEMBER 5, 2020

Don't Mess with God's Creation

This is an *aliyah* that is a little challenging to find something to write about. At the end of the last *aliyah*, we were given the genealogy of the descendants of Esau. When he separated from Jacob, Esau settled in the land of Seir. What we have here is a listing of the clans and kings of the Horites, the people living in the land before Esau conquered it.

We do have one interesting *midrash* about one of the individuals mentioned here. In verse 24, we are told about Anah, who "discovered the hot springs in the wilderness while pasturing the asses of his father Zibeon." Here the word *ha-yeymim* is translated as "hot springs." However, most of the commentators say that the real meaning of the word is "the mules." The verse does tell us that this occurred while he was tending his father's donkeys in the wilderness. As the story goes, according to Rashi, Anah, himself the product of an incestuous relationship, discovered that he could breed a male donkey with a female horse, thus producing a mule.[14] The key word

HINDSIGHT IS 2020

here is "breed." Apparently, prior to this, the animals had sometimes been doing this on their own. Chizkuni explains it this way:

> . . . these were animals that resulted from crossbreeding, and
> the Torah names him in order to chastise him for having
> successfully violated the principle of not crossbreeding . . . we
> have to understand this verse as follows: Anah was the first
> person who deliberately mated donkeys with horses. Prior to
> this, mules existed but they resulted from the mother animal
> having mated with a horse of its own account . . . . he developed
> a system of breeding such animals successfully . . . Seeing that
> G-d is very displeased with such procedures being undertaken
> by man, he is blamed for such practices having been introduced.
> Another interpretation: the Torah wishes the reader to know that
> the animals resulting from crossbreeding are not included in the
> blessing given by the Creator to all the creatures He had created.
> Proof of this is the fact that such creatures cannot sire or give
> birth to another generation of their breed.[336]

The blessing mentioned here, which is said to not apply to mules, is the commandment to "be fruitful and multiply," which God gave to all the animals in the Garden of Eden [1:22]. However, since these animals had not been created by God, they were not subject to this commandment. That, therefore, is the explanation for the infertility of mules!

The real message, if there is one, is this: don't mess with God's creation! For to do so is to imply that God's creation is imperfect, and that we humans can improve on it. God will not bless such meddling.

But if we are not supposed to interfere with God's creation by introducing new species, perhaps a more interesting and relevant question for us to consider is this: is it permissible to interfere with God's creation by allowing existing species to become extinct, and not doing everything we can to prevent that from happening? What is our responsibility in preserving the lives of animals that are on the endangered species list, and in what way should that responsibility be shaped by our Jewish values?

Something to think about over Shabbat, as we celebrate creation.

Parashat Vayeshev

FIRST ALIYAH: GENESIS 37:1–11
SUNDAY, DECEMBER 6, 2020

Parental Favoritism is Still Not a Good Idea

With this week's *parashah*, we begin the story of the next generation, the story of Joseph, beginning when he was seventeen years old. Right from the start, we see that, even though he had ten older brothers, the narrative is going to be centered on him. This should be our first clue that there continued to be problems with the family dynamic. We are told that he was tending Jacob's sheep along with his half-brothers who were the sons of the two maidservants Bilhah and Zilpah [37:2]. Here is our second clue: Joseph was hanging out with the four sons of the two concubines, not with the six sons of Leah. Clue number three is that Joseph was a tattletale and brought back bad reports of his brothers to their father. Surely, this would not be the best way to endear himself to them.

Then verse 3 says it all: "Now Israel loved Joseph best of all his sons, for he was the child of his old age; and he had made him an ornamented tunic."

What?! Like his father and grandfather before him, Jacob was guilty of favoritism! Did he learn nothing from his own experience with his brother Esau? Wasn't it just in the last *parashah* that we were reading about how frightened he had been about reuniting with him?

We are told outright that Jacob loved Joseph more than any of his other sons and the reason that is given is that Joseph was the "child of his old age." However, some of the brothers were fairly close to him in age. Not only that, but Benjamin also clearly fits that description as he truly is the baby of the family. In reality, it is more likely the fact that Joseph is the firstborn son of the favorite wife Rachel, who waited so long to conceive, and he no doubt bears a physical resemblance to her, that makes him the object of his father's affection.

As if that weren't irritating enough to his brothers, Jacob greatly exacerbated the situation by giving Joseph an ornamented tunic. Exactly what this means is not quite clear. Rashi says that it means that the tunic had bands of fine wool around the cuff. Rashbam says it was a fancy cloak. Ibn Ezra says it was an embroidered coat. Bekhor Shor says that it had a nice appearance.

Kimhi says it was a striped tunic, each stripe a different color.[1] This is probably the closest to what most of us envision it looked like. Then, of course, the modern commentator Andrew Lloyd Weber dubbed it an "Amazing Technicolor Dreamcoat."[2]

Whatever it looked like, it was clearly a garment that designated Joseph as his father's favorite, and the result was that his brothers hated him so much that they could not even speak civilly to him [37: 4].

To make matters even worse, we see that Joseph's brothers found his behavior toward them very irritating. He told them of two dreams that he had. In the first dream, they were all binding sheaves of wheat in the field; his sheaf stood upright, and theirs all bowed to it [37:7]. The implication is that they would all come to bow down to Joseph at some point. (As Ramban points out, we will see that a quest for wheat during the famine will be the exact cause for them to bow down to him in the future.)[3]

In the second dream, the sun, the moon, and eleven stars bowed down to him [37:9]. This one was told to Jacob as well as his brothers. While the eleven stars represent the brothers, the sun and moon are interpreted to mean his father and mother. (We know that his mother, Rachel, was no longer alive at this point. Some say that Leah is meant here. Others, such as Rashi and Ibn Ezra, say that the interpretation refers to Rachel's maidservant Bilhah, who raised Joseph as if he were her own.)[3]

In any event, the die is cast (no pun intended). This short first *aliyah* should leave us with a sense of foreboding. In each of the two previous generations, there were only two sons and they were rivals of each other. Now there are ten sons aggrieved by the special treatment that their younger brother receives (Benjamin, who was Joseph's full brother, was very young at this point, so was not really involved in this sibling rivalry).

Being a parent is never easy, whether our children are young or adults themselves. Anyone who is a parent knows how easy it is for one child, like Tom Smothers to his brother Dick, to say, "Mom [or Dad] always liked you best."[4] We walk a fine line when we try to balance our affections for our offspring. On the other hand, some parents try so hard to not show any favoritism that they end up not recognizing each of their children for their individual talents and traits. We need to love them all equally for the things that makes each of them special.

I know—sometimes easier said than done.

SECOND ALIYAH: GENESIS 37:12–22
MONDAY, DECEMBER 7, 2020

Up Close and Personal

To set the stage for this *aliyah*, we are told [37:12] that Joseph's ten older brothers had gone off to pasture Jacob's flocks in—where? Shechem? This place should sound familiar as it is the city where Simeon and Levi killed all the men as revenge for the rape of their sister Dinah. Supposedly, there was great pastureland there and Jacob had even bought a plot of land there prior to the attack on his daughter [23:19]. Still, this probably was not the best choice of a place to go. Naturally, Jacob might have been concerned about their welfare. His solution, however, demonstrates poor judgement. He sends his seventeen-year-old son, whom he is aware that these brothers all despise, to go and check on them and bring back word [37:13-14]. Joseph's tale-bearing was one of the sources of their anger with him, yet that is exactly what Jacob asks him to do here. Joseph, it appears, is more than happy to fulfill his father's request.

When he arrives in Shechem, however, he is unable to locate his brothers. We are told that "a man came upon him wandering in the fields" [37:15]. Many commentators have pondered this verse. Who was this man? Where did he come from? How did he know who Joseph's brothers were and where they had gone? Often in the Torah an unnamed character who comes along at an opportune time is thought to be an angel. One clue here is the word *to-eh* (wandering) used to describe Joseph's actions. This word appears only one other time in the Torah: "When you encounter your enemy's ox or ass wandering, you must take it back to him" [Exodus 23:4]. In this case, the animal in question is lost from its owner and it is a *mitzvah* to return it to him/her. The Baal HaTurim reasons that, since it is an obligation to return a lost animal, setting it on its way, how much more so are we obligated to help a person who has lost his/her way, and return him to himself, to the road on which he is supposed to go?[5] Could it be that Joseph was having second thoughts about fulfilling his father's request? This unnamed man was placed here to find him and set him back on his mission. Many commentators say that the man was really the angel Gabriel. In any case, he tells Joseph that he heard his brothers talking amongst themselves and that they decided to go further on to Dothan. Now, Joseph could have said to himself, "Dad only said to go to Shechem. I could go home and tell him they were gone when I got here." Instead, he decides to continue to Dothan to find them [37:17].

As he approaches, his brothers see him coming from far away [37:18]. (I'm sure it was fairly easy to spot him wearing that special coat that their father had given him.) The text tells us that they saw him from far away and decided to kill him. This indicates the kind of relationship they had with their younger brother—they didn't really see him close up (i.e., they didn't really know him). They hated him for his dreams, and they hated him because their father loved him more than he did them. They were unable to look past these things and didn't allow themselves to really get to know him. He, in turn, did not try to get close to them either and wearing that coat all the time just rubbed their noses in the situation. We see here the dire consequences of a dysfunctional family relationship.

To a man, the brothers all decide to kill Joseph and throw him (his body) into a pit, and then tell Jacob that a wild beast killed him [37:20]. Leaving someone to die without a proper burial would be considered a great dishonor, but this is what they planned for their brother. One brother, Reuben, breaks rank with them and suggests that they not kill him, but rather just throw him into one of the pits [37:21-22]. Reuben's intent was to come back later and remove Joseph from the pit. One wonders why he didn't try to convince them not to harm Joseph at all. Perhaps he was concerned for his own safety if he made such a suggestion. So, instead, he plans to deceive them, just as they are planning to deceive their father, and just as their father deceived their grandfather, only to be deceived in turn by his father-in-law.

We can already sense that the situation that is about to unfold is not a good one, and most likely will not end well. Once again, we are witnessing the tragic results of sibling rivalry and parental favoritism.

We would do well to learn to look at each other up close, not just from afar.

THIRD ALIYAH: GENESIS 37:23–36
TUESDAY, DECEMBER 8, 2020

Deception Has Consequences

Following Reuben's suggestion, the brothers took Joseph, stripped him of his special tunic and threw him into a pit; we are told that the pit was empty [37:23-24]. The pit may have been empty of water (telling us therefore that this probably took place in the fall, before the beginning of the rainy season), but, according to Rashi, it did have snakes and scorpions in it.[6] We can only imagine the fright that Joseph must have felt. It is interesting to note, however, that, as we read through the story, we are told nothing about his reaction to this situation. The Torah leaves him mute.

It was not long, however, before the brothers changed their minds yet again. Reuben had apparently left the area, intending to come back later and retrieve Joseph from the pit. When the remaining nine brothers spotted a caravan of Ishmaelite merchants, Judah proposed a different fate for Joseph: they should sell him as a slave. At least this way, they would get some profit from the situation, and they would not be directly responsible for killing him [37:25-27]. In the end, they sold their brother for twenty pieces of silver. There does seem to be some confusion about whom he was sold to, though. Rashi resolves the conflict by explaining that he was sold to the Ishmaelites, who in turn sold him to the Midianites, who in turn sold him to the Egyptians [37:28].[7] Reuben, meanwhile, returned to the pit, and, not finding Joseph there, assumed that he was dead. He tore his clothes in mourning, but it seems he mourned his own fate more than his brother's, assuming that, as the oldest, he would take the blame for the loss of Joseph [37:29-30]. The other brothers apparently did not tell him the truth about what they had done; at least, there is no evidence in the text that they did so.

Finally, following up on their original thought, the brothers cruelly led their father to believe that Joseph was dead by killing a goat, dipping Joseph's tunic in it, and then sending it to Jacob, asking if he recognized it [37:31-33]. Sarna points out the extreme irony here: when Jacob was younger, he had used the skins of a goat and the garments of his brother to deceive his father Isaac into giving him his brother's blessing.[8] Now, his ten oldest sons used the blood of a goat and their brother's garment to deceive him.

Additionally, the whole firstborn issue seems to be repeating itself yet again in the next generation. By rights, Reuben, as the oldest of Jacob's sons, was the firstborn. However, in a verse that I did not discuss from last week's *parashah*, Reuben had committed a grave sin against his father: ". . . Reuben went and lay with Bilhah, his father's concubine, and Israel found out" [35:22].

Bilhah, you may recall, was Rachel's maidservant, and the woman who raised Benjamin as her own after Rachel died. No doubt, she became a second mother to Joseph, as well. Most importantly, as far as Jacob was concerned, she was one of Jacob's wives. Therefore, this was the greatest insult that Reuben could have committed against his father. That is why, some commentators suggest, Reuben had persuaded his brothers not to kill Joseph as he hoped to come back to the pit to rescue Joseph, not because he cared so much about him, but because he hoped to redeem himself with his father. That is also the reason he was so upset when he returned to the pit only to find Joseph missing. To compound matters, we find the following verse in the book of 1 Chronicles: "The sons of Reuben the firstborn of Israel. (He was the firstborn, but when he defiled his father's bed, his birthright was given to the sons of Joseph son of Israel, so he is not reckoned as firstborn in the genealogy . . ." [1 Chronicles 5:1].

In truth, this is the only place in the *Tanakh* where this idea of Joseph receiving the birthright is mentioned. We will see at the end of the book of Genesis, when Jacob gives his sons his final blessing before dying, that he does indeed remove prominence from Reuben, stating as his reason the fact that he "went up to his father's bed" [49:4]. He does, however, appear to give prominence to Judah at that time.

Our reading today ends on one final twist of irony: we read that Jacob says essentially that he will spend the rest of his life mourning Joseph [37:35]. Then the scene changes abruptly: "The Midianites, meanwhile, sold him in Egypt to Potiphar, a courtier of Pharaoh and his chief steward" [37:36]. The Hebrew wording is unusual here because the word "meanwhile" implies that this action is concurrent with the action of the previous verse. In other words, at the exact moment that Jacob began mourning for his son, the Midianites were selling him in Egypt.

There is clearly a great deal of irony here in addition to the layers and layers of deception. The message is a warning that deception leads to more deception and it always has victims, some of them innocent, and it can never be good. We are left wondering two things: What was Joseph feeling through all of this? And did the brothers have any feelings of guilt, not only for their treatment of Joseph, but for the great sorrow that they caused their father?

FOURTH ALIYAH: GENESIS 38:1–30
WEDNESDAY, DECEMBER 9, 2020

OMG, I'm Becoming My Mother (or Father)!

This *aliyah* consists of an entire chapter of Genesis that seems at first glance to be interjected here in the middle of the story of Joseph. This is the story of Judah and his daughter-in-law Tamar. Here is some perspective before we look at the story: Judah was the fourth son of Jacob (and Leah). When we last left the story of Joseph, Judah was the brother who suggested not leaving Joseph in the pit to die, but rather selling him to the passing band of Ishmaelites. Judah, as I previously mentioned, was the brother who rose to prominence in Jacob's deathbed blessings of his sons. The firstborn, Reuben, had slept with his father's concubine/wife Bilhah; and the second and third sons, Shimon, and Levi, had been responsible for slaying all the men of Shechem as punishment for the rape of Dinah.

So, what's going on in this chapter? Judah left his brothers and married an unnamed Canaanite woman [38:1-2]; you may recall that both Abraham and Isaac were adamant that their sons should *not* marry Canaanite women). In what seems like rapid succession, she bears three sons for him: Er, Onan, and Shelah [38:3-5]. Judah, fulfilling his paternal responsibility, finds a wife for his firstborn son, Er. Her name is Tamar [38:6]. Because Er is wicked in God's sight (an interesting wordplay here: Er is spelled *ayin-raysh*, and the word *rah* (wicked) is spelled *raysh-ayin*), God takes his life. Judah tells his second son, Onan, to fulfill his responsibility and provide his deceased brother with an heir by having sexual relations with Tamar [38:7-8]. However, Onan is reluctant to father a child who will not be considered his own, and consequently has an unnatural form of sex with Tamar that will not impregnate her, and as a result, God takes his life, as well [38:9-10]. Afraid of possibly losing his third son, Judah asks Tamar to hang out and wait then Judah's wife dies [38:11]. Realizing that her father-in-law appears to be withholding his third son from her, Tamar takes matters into her own hands and disguises herself as a prostitute, including veiling her face, and waits by the side of the road for Judah to pass by [38:13-15]. She catches his attention (he doesn't recognize her because of the veil). They negotiate a price and he says that he will send her a kid from his flock, and she asks for something as a pledge that he will keep his promise. As a pledge, she requests his signet, his bracelets, and his staff (all of which would have been readily recognizable). They have sex, she conceives, he leaves, she removes her disguise [38:16-19]. Judah attempts to send the kid as payment to the harlot, but no one can find her. Judah basically says, "Oh well, I tried" [38:20-23]. Three months later, Judah is told of Tamar's pregnancy as the result of harlotry. Declaring that she should be burned, he orders that she be brought to him. She comes bearing his very own signet, bracelets, and staff as identifiers of the man who has fathered her child, and Judah recognizes that she was right to do what she did since he had withheld his third son from her [38:24-26]. Tamar gives birth to twins. When one of them sticks his hand out first, the midwife puts an identifying scarlet bracelet on his wrist, which he then withdraws. This allows his brother to be born first (this is a very similar scenario to the birth of Jacob and Esau. Once again, one supplants the other at birth). The twins are named Perez and Zarah [38:27-30].

At first glance, we may ask what this story is doing here, right in the middle of the Joseph story. Aside from trying to develop the character of Judah more fully, we see once again several ironic coincidences that tie this chapter to the previous one:

- Both stories continue the theme of deception
- Once again, the deception involves clothing and a kid (goat)
- Both stories continue the theme of a younger brother displacing an older
- Most notable: the phrase, *haker-na* (please examine (this)) appears in both stories. In the last chapter, it was placed in the mouth of the brothers when they asked Jacob if he recognized Joseph's tunic. In this chapter, it is placed in the mouth of Tamar when she asks Judah if he recognizes his own personal possessions. This is not just coincidence: these are the only two instances in which this phrase appears in the entire Tanakh.

Which one of us has not had the experience of seeing our image in the mirror, or hearing words come out of our mouth, and saying to ourselves, "OMG, I have become my mother (or father)!" There is even a series of commercials on television now that call attention to this phenomenon. We may joke about it, but there definitely is a serious side to it. When we are young, we all think that we are going to be different, that we are going to rebel. Yet, as we grow older (and hopefully wiser), many of us come to a better understanding and appreciation of our parents, especially as we find ourselves to be the older generation in dealing with our children. Maybe Mom and Dad really did know what they were talking about after all? And if they didn't, at least maybe (and perhaps more importantly) we understand them better now. Their experiences have become ours. We must decide to either repeat their mistakes or to forge a way of change.

As Judah's personality is formed, he is called upon by God to see that he is not so different from his father Jacob, who wasn't so different from Isaac, who wasn't so different from Abraham.

So, the next time you look in the mirror or hear familiar words escaping from your lips, say to yourself, *haker-na* (examine this). Do you recognize it?

Good Looks are a Curse . . .

This short *aliyah* shifts the scene to Egypt, bringing us back to the story of Joseph. Right from the very first verse, we see God's providence in the situation. Of all the households that Joseph could have ended up in as a slave, he finds himself in the home of an important Egyptian official, named Potiphar. Just in case we might have any doubt about who is the mastermind of this situation, we are told twice in these six verses that "the Lord was with Joseph" [39:2,3]. Joseph was assigned to work in the house and everything in the house was put in his care, except for the food that Potiphar ate. This phrase is meant both literally and euphemistically. Egyptians did not eat with foreigners. And Potiphar's "bed" was also off limits. It is interesting that directly on the heels of this phrase we are told the following about Joseph: ". . . Now Joseph was well built and handsome" [39:6].

This is interesting for several reasons. First, he is the only man in the entire *Tanakh* who is described this way. Second, his mother was described similarly: ". . . Rachel was shapely and beautiful" [29:17]. From this we can deduce that Joseph must have resembled his mother. This, no doubt, contributed to Jacob's great love for him—he clearly must have reminded him of Rachel.

While we might think that this was one of God's many blessings that Joseph benefited from, we will soon see that it turned out to be a detriment to this young slave. Indeed, ending the *aliyah* on this note gives us a hint of what lies ahead.

It is also interesting to note that we have not heard a word out of Joseph's mouth since he asked the unknown stranger to tell him where his brothers had gone. All of this has happened to him—the horrible treatment of his brothers, the descent into Egypt after having been sold as a slave—and we do not know what went through his mind or what emotions he felt. We have heard so much about him, but almost nothing from him. That is, of course, about to change in a big way.

SIXTH ALIYAH: GENESIS 39:7–23
FRIDAY, DECEMBER 1, 2020

Did He or Didn't He?

This is the famous story of the temptation of Joseph by the wife of his master Potiphar. We were told at the very end of the last *aliyah* that Joseph was very handsome and that Potiphar had given Joseph command over his entire household, except for his bed (i.e., his wife). Here we read the consequences of that situation: Potiphar's wife is so taken with Joseph's youthful, physical appearance that she boldly and persistently tries to seduce him, pressuring him to have sex with her. To fully understand the situation that Joseph finds himself in here, we need to remember that Joseph is a slave in the home of a wealthy government official, whose wife is now pressuring him to have sex with her. The pressure to give in to her plays to his baser emotions, but the more he refuses her advances, it seems, the harder she tries. We are told simply that "he refused" [39:8] and his moral self withstood the challenge. But we wonder if it was really so simple. There is a clue in the Hebrew text. The word which means "he refused," *vayima-eyn*, has an unusual note above the *aleph* that looks like a lightning bolt. That's called a *shalshelet*; I have written about it previously (in *parashat Tzav*). For a Torah reader, it presents a challenge: three repetitions of three notes up followed by three notes down. The voice wavers. This note appears only four times in the entire Torah and each occurrence is a situation in which the protagonist can be perceived as wavering or hesitating, just like the note. So that would indicate that Joseph's refusal was not so outright and perhaps he really was tempted. Perhaps he hesitated, not quite so resolute in his refusal. At least, some of the sages of the Talmud think so, as we can see from the following strange and fantastic *midrash*:

> . . . At that moment, his father's image came and appeared to him in the window. The image said to him: Joseph, . . . Do you desire your name to be erased from among [your brothers], and to be called an associate of promiscuous women?
> Immediately: "And his bow abode firm" . . . This means that his bow (i.e., his penis) returned to its strength as he overcame his desire. The verse about Joseph continues: "And the arms of his hands were made supple" [Genesis 49:24], meaning that he dug his hands into the ground and his semen was emitted between his fingernails. [*BT Sotah 36B:13-14*]

We can certainly understand his being overcome with feelings of guilt if he thought about what his father would say at that moment. This story says that he literally saw the image of his father in the window and he heard his father warning him not to do this. Apparently, though, it was at the exact moment when he was about to complete the deed that he regained his senses and somehow was able to strengthen his arms, channeling his semen to exit his body through his fingertips. (In this way, he was not technically guilty of "spilling his seed," which would have been considered a grave sin as we saw in the last chapter.) Why do the sages go to such great lengths to come up with such a totally unbelievable story? Because they can't believe that Joseph, being human, would not have been tempted. Yet they cannot bring themselves to believe that he really would have followed through and acted on the temptation.

On a more serious note, let's look at his actual response from the Torah text. For the first time in a long time, we hear Joseph's voice: "Look, with me here, my master gives no thought to anything in this house, and all that he owns he has placed in my hands . . . . He wields no more authority in this house than I, and he has withheld nothing from me except yourself, since you are his wife. How then could I do this most wicked thing, and sin before God?" [39:12]. In very simple, logical terms he states his case: to do this would be an insult to Potiphar and a violation of the trust that he has placed in Joseph, and would also mean committing a sinful act, betraying the covenant relationship he has with God. With these words, he states his case. He does not reprove her for her actions, nor does he judge her. He merely states why he himself cannot morally fathom committing this act.

With this, Joseph sets an example for us all. We are called upon by God to live a life of righteousness and justice, and commitment to the mitzvot. We each make decisions for ourselves to do what is right and good, or not. We cannot make that decision for anyone else. We can and should stand in judgement of our own actions but we may not stand in self-righteous judgement of the actions of others.

We live in a world where more and more we are subject to the judgement of others. We in turn judge others for their political beliefs, for their ethics and morals, or for wearing or not wearing a mask. We would do well to follow Joseph's example, to be sure enough in ourselves to know what is the right behavior that God expects from us and to act on that without feeling the need to judge the behavior of others.

SEVENTH ALIYAH: GENESIS 40:1–23
WRITTEN FOR SHABBAT, SATURDAY, DECEMBER 12, 2020

Forget Me Not

As a result of the incident with Potiphar's wife, when she complained loudly to both the other servants of the household, and then to her husband, accusing Joseph of attempting to rape her, Joseph found himself in prison where he was not treated as just any ordinary prisoner. He was in the section reserved for royal prisoners, those wrongdoers who normally serve either Pharaoh or his courtiers (which Potiphar was). Just as God was with Joseph in Potiphar's house, advancing him to a place of prominence, so, too, did God assure that Joseph rose to a place of prominence in the prison and was placed in charge of the other prisoners. Here he met up with two men who served in Pharaoh's palace: his cupbearer and his baker. Both men had dreams in the same night that they were unable to interpret. Here, finally, we see Joseph's dream interpretation skills coming into play. Telling them that "God can interpret your dreams" [40:8], he asked each to tell him what they dreamed, and he explained to them the meanings. For the cupbearer, the news was good and he would be restored to his post in three days' time. For the baker, the news was not so good and in three days' time, Pharaoh would have him killed. Joseph asked the cupbearer to remember him when he would be freed from prison, mentioning his name to Pharaoh, and putting in a good word for him, so that he, too, could be released. The *aliyah* ends by telling us that both dreams were fulfilled just as Joseph said.

The last thing we are told is that "the cupbearer did not think of Joseph; he forgot him."

Because this is stated in two ways, there are various interpretations of what he did. Bekhor Shor says it means that his actions were not intentional, he was simply forgetful.[347] Abarbanel says that it means that he forgot to either do anything for Joseph himself to show his gratitude, or to mention him to Pharaoh as he had promised.[347] Rashi and Rashbam say that it is stated twice to show that he didn't remember Joseph when he was released, nor did he remember him with the passing of time.[9] Ibn Ezra says that the double meaning is that he didn't think about Joseph, nor did he speak about him.[9]

No matter how you interpret it, the cupbearer appears to be rather ungrateful.

I would bet, however, that we all are guilty of similar thoughts and actions from time to time. Sometimes we fail to thank those who have done something for us, or to do anything for them in return. It's not necessarily intentional or malicious—sometimes we just forget. With the passing of time, it becomes easier to put it out of our minds.

With everything that's going on in our world today—all the negativity—perhaps now would be a good time to sit down and consciously think about those who have done something positive for us, whether it was some small thing or they really went out of their way and, if possible, do something to express your gratitude. Don't wait until it's too late.

Parashat Miketz

Perchance to Dream[1]

Two years passed and Joseph was still in prison. The action now switches to the royal palace where we learn that Pharaoh has had not one, but two dreams. In the first, seven healthy cows come out of the Nile, followed by seven thin cows; the thin cows consume the healthy cows, and Pharaoh awakens from his dream [41:2-4]. Returning to sleep, he sees seven solid, healthy ears of corn growing on a stalk, and then seven thin, scorched ears of corn growing on the same stalk; the thin stalks consume the healthy ones, and once again Pharaoh awakens [41:5-7]. Clearly, the similarity of the dreams indicates that they both represent the same theme. As a matter of fact, the word *chalomo*, translated here as "his dreams," is really written in the singular in the Hebrew, "his dream." The fact that the dream essentially repeats itself indicates an urgency to the message. However, none of his magicians are able to interpret the dreams [41:8]. Finally, at that point, the cupbearer's memory is jogged, and he tells Pharaoh of his encounter with Joseph in prison [41:9-13].

Pharaoh now calls for Joseph to be brought to him *min habor*, translated here as "from the dungeon," but the actual translation is "from the pit." The Hebrew word is the same word used earlier in the story to refer to the pit that Joseph's brothers originally threw him into. Additionally, we read that once again, clothing comes into play: Joseph is cleaned up and made presentable to go before Pharaoh, with a fresh change of clothes and a haircut [41:14]. This concurrent change of clothes and action portend a change that is about to occur in Joseph's fortunes.

It is quite evident to us by now that dreams, both his own and others, play a major role in Joseph's story. We also have seen and are about to see again that Joseph had the ability to interpret dreams, which he credited to God. We have previously read in both the Book of Leviticus and the Book of Deuteronomy that God commands us not to engage in any kind of magic or sorcery. Dream interpretation does not fall into that category. On the contrary, dreams were always felt to be a primary means of God communicating messages to human beings. We have already seen a number of dreams besides Joseph's: Abimelech was warned in a dream not to touch Sarah; Jacob had his dream of the ladder, as well as a dream about the speckled and spotted sheep; Laban was warned by God in a dream not to confront Jacob when he had left with his family; Balaam was warned by God not to go with the servants of Balak. There will be several more instances of consequential dreams in the *Tanakh*. Indeed, God often communicated with the prophets through dreams.

Many still believe today that our dreams carry messages to us. When you find yourself remembering a vivid dream, think about what it could possibly mean. In the Talmud, there is a lengthy discussion of the subject of dreams. Here is one small part of it:

> . . . One who sees a dream from which his soul is distraught
> should go and have it interpreted . . . The Gemara is surprised by
> this: Interpreted? Didn't Rav Ḥisda say: A dream not interpreted
> is like a letter not read? [*BT Berachot 55B:7*]

I love that last sentence. If we want to put it into a modern context, we could replace the word "letter" with the word "text." Many of us receive multiple texts a day, from multiple people. It is our modern form of communication, and, of course, we respond to them. Think of some of the more meaningful texts that you have received from friends or relatives. Now just imagine if you had never read those texts. What messages might you have missed out on?

Remember this the next time you have a dream. And ask if it could have a hidden meaning. We all need to dream. I hope that yours are pleasant.

How Much is Enough?

Pharaoh says to Joseph, *chalom chalamti*, which literally translates as "I dreamed a dream" (anybody hearing Fantine in Les Mis right now?).[2] Again, he speaks of one dream. He tells Joseph that no one has been able to interpret the dream(s) for him, but he is basically counting on Joseph to be able to do it. Joseph says that not he but God will offer the interpretation [41:15-16]. Pharaoh recounts his two dreams [41:17-24]. Joseph interprets them as one dream with one meaning: the seven healthy cows and the seven healthy stalks represent seven good years of prosperity; the seven skinny cows and the seven thin stalks represent seven years of famine. God is sending Pharaoh a message about what God is about to do. The land is about to enjoy seven years of the greatest prosperity followed by seven years of the greatest adversity [41:25-31]. The fact that Pharaoh has had the same dream twice will essentially serve as a warning: God is telling Pharaoh that this is definitely going to happen, so Pharaoh should use this time to prepare. If Pharaoh is wise, he will appoint someone to oversee the project, directing the people of Egypt to gather up and store their surplus grain now so that they will have it during the seven lean years when they will really need it [41:32-37]. The *aliyah* ends with Pharaoh musing to his courtiers, asking whether they will find anyone more suitable for the position than Joseph [41:38].

The discussion in the Talmud about dream interpretation continues with the following:

> Rabbi Yoḥanan also said: Three dreams are fulfilled: A dream of
> the morning, a dream that one's fellow dreamed about him, and a
> dream that is interpreted within a dream. And some say that
> a dream that is repeated several times is also fulfilled, as it is
> stated: "And for that the dream was doubled unto Pharaoh twice,
> it is because the thing is established by God, and God will shortly
> bring it to pass" [Genesis 41:32]. [*BT Berachot 55B:20*]

Have you ever had a recurring dream? Something that repeated itself in the same night? Or subsequent nights? Perhaps you should look at it more closely.

On a different note, I want to look at this idea of the seven good years being canceled out by the seven lean years. It reminds me of a message I delivered many years ago at the annual Thanksgiving Interfaith Service in our local community. That year, the theme was "Enough." The Hebrew word for "enough" is *dai*. However, I pointed out, if we reverse the letters of this tiny word, we get the Hebrew word *yad* (hand).

In Pharaoh's dream, the seven bad years of famine canceled out the seven good years of prosperity, but God sent him a warning about this so that he could preemptively do something to change the ultimate outcome. We will soon see exactly how that happened and how Joseph was involved.

The message I gave on that Thanksgiving Eve was this: when you are fortunate enough to feel that you have enough, then you should open your hand to share your prosperity with those who may not be as fortunate. You have the ability to do something to alleviate the misfortune of others.

And how much is "enough?" Each of us must answer that for ourselves. Just so, each of us has the ability to affect change in some way.

This was, as I said, a message I delivered quite a few years ago (at least ten, if not more). Yet it is just as relevant, if not more so, today, when the many months of the pandemic have resulted in high rates of unemployment and people in need of assistance. Perhaps as you read this you find yourself in this position—there should be no shame in this. As we read further in the story, we will see that Jacob's own family found themselves having to go to Egypt to beg for food. Joseph saw fit to provide for their needs. May our modern twenty-first century Jewish community rise to the occasion by opening hearts and hands to bring equity to our world.

And, by the way, the words, *dai* (enough) and *yad* (hand) each have the same *gematria* (numerical value): fourteen, which is also the same as the sum of seven (good years) plus seven (bad years).

The power to change the world is literally in the hands of each and every one of us. May we use the opportunity that has been presented to us for good.

THIRD ALIYAH: GENESIS 41:39–52
TUESDAY, DECEMBER 15, 2020

Who Are You?

Once again, we see Joseph's life completely transformed. Pharaoh is so impressed with him that he makes him vizier in Egypt, second in command only to Pharaoh himself. Joseph will be charged with overseeing the effort to gather up and store grain during the years of plenty in anticipation of the years of famine. As such, his appearance requires an overhaul: he will wear Pharaoh's signet ring and a gold chain around his neck and be dressed in robes of fine linen [41:42]. According to Ralbag, these robes were very expensive, and Hizkuni says that only kings and noblemen were even permitted to wear them.[3] In other words, Joseph has become Egyptianized, at least in his outward appearance. No doubt, this was necessary for the Egyptian people to be able to pay him the respect of his office, as well as to be able to trust him to carry out his mission. Sarna points out that Joseph's Egyptian appearance was also an important detail in the story.[4] We shall see how it prevented his brothers from recognizing him when they came to Egypt.

Joseph's transformation, however, did not end with his appearance: Pharaoh gave him an Egyptian name, Zaphnath-Paaneah [41:45], which most commentators say means "revealer of hidden things," a nod to his skills at dream interpretation. In the same verse, we are also told that Pharaoh gave Joseph a wife, Asenat, the daughter of Potiphera, priest of On (there seems to be some disagreement over whether this is the same Potiphar who was Joseph's former master). However, the commentators have difficulty with the idea of Joseph marrying an Egyptian, so many of them cite the following *Midrash*:

> Dinah went forth to see those girls who were making merry and he [Shechem] seized her, and he slept with her, and she conceived and bare Asenath. The sons of Israel said that she should be killed, for they said that now people would say in all the land that there was an immoral daughter in the tents of Jacob. What did (Jacob) do? He wrote the Holy Name upon a golden plate and suspended it about her neck and sent her away. She went her way. Everything is revealed before the Holy One, blessed be He, and Michael the angel descended and took her, and brought her down to Egypt to the house of Potiphera because Asenath was destined to become the wife of Joseph. Now the wife of Potiphera was barren, and (Asenath) grew up with her as a daughter. When Joseph came down to Egypt, he married her, as it is said, "And he gave him to wife Asenath the daughter of Potiphera priest of On" [*Pirkei de Rabbi Eliezer 38*][5]

Not only does this story provide Joseph with a Jewish wife, but it also puts a final positive spin on the story of Dinah: sending her daughter off to Egypt to be adopted by Potiphar and his wife. It was only natural that the Hebrew daughter would become the wife of the Hebrew slave who rose to vizier of Egypt.

Together, Joseph and Asenat have two sons who are given Hebrew names: Manasseh and Ephraim [41:50-52].

So, now Joseph has been transformed. He looks like an Egyptian, dresses like an Egyptian, no doubt has learned to talk like an Egyptian, and, of course, like the song says, walks like an Egyptian.[6]

But for all his outward physical changes, was he truly an Egyptian? Or did he remain faithful to his Hebrew heritage?

The changes effected in Joseph were physical, outward changes. Despite everything, the commentators all agree that, inwardly, he never lost sight of who and what he was. He could see that his youthful dreams were starting to come to fruition, and he was in a position of rulership. He was biding his time waiting for their full completion with a reunion with his family. Despite what others may have seen when they looked at him, the truth of the matter is that Joseph himself knew and always remembered that he was *Yosef ben Yaakov*.

Often in our daily lives, it is easy to lose sight of the Jewish part of our identity, getting swept up in the secular activities of our lives. Yet we need to remember that we can't (or shouldn't) ever separate ourselves from our Jewish identity. Indeed, the values of our faith, the values of justice and compassion for others should infuse the decisions we make not only in the synagogue, but also in the home, the workplace, the school, the grocery store—and in these days especially—the hospitals.

FOURTH ALIYAH: GENESIS 41:53–42:18
WEDNESDAY, DECEMBER 16, 2020

Do You Recognize This?

Just as Joseph had predicted, the seven years of plenty came to an end, and the years of famine began. The famine was severe in the land of Egypt. When the people cried out to Pharaoh for bread, he directed them to go to Joseph, who had previously organized the gathering up and storing of surplus grain during the seven years of abundance. But the famine was very extensive, reaching far beyond the borders of Egypt, so much so that people from other nations came to Egypt to buy grain [41:53-57].

The famine had reached as far as Canaan, prompting Jacob to send his ten oldest sons to Egypt to buy food for the extended family. Only Benjamin, Jacob's youngest son and, to his knowledge, the only remaining son of his beloved Rachel, was not permitted by Jacob to go [42:1-4]. So, exactly who went down to Egypt? It is interesting to look at how they are described. We are told that Jacob spoke to "his sons," telling them to go down to Egypt. Only two verses later, we are told that "ten of Joseph's brothers" went to Egypt. The description changed. Why? We are receiving a hint that Joseph's dream is about to be fulfilled. The action from this point on is dependent on the brothers' relationship with Joseph. Yet verse 4 tells us that Jacob did not send "Joseph's brother Benjamin" with "his brothers." The word "his" is ambiguous here. Does it refer to Joseph or to Benjamin? It is unclear. However, either way, it puts Joseph and Benjamin in a subgroup of their own, the sons of Jacob's beloved Rachel. Finally, in verse 5, as they arrive in Egypt, they are described as "the sons of Israel," foretelling the fact that this encounter will eventually lead to the entire nation of Israel coming down to Egypt.

Arriving in Egypt, the brothers, like everyone else, must stand before Joseph to ask for food. Though he recognizes them, they do not recognize him [42:6-8]. We have seen this verb, *haker*, before. The word "he recognized" is the same word that showed up in 38:26 when Judah recognized his cloak that he had left with Tamar as a pledge. It is also the same verb that was used when Tamar asked Judah if he recognized his cloak, and again when the ten brothers asked Jacob if he recognized Joseph's coat. In both cases, the object that was recognized was something precious that had been forgotten, something that might have been assumed to be lost forever but a second chance was given to reclaim the coat—and the brothers. Yet Joseph "acted like a stranger" (literally, "made himself unrecognizable") to his brothers. He did not tell them who he was. He spoke only Egyptian, pretending not to be able to speak or understand Hebrew. In addition, Joseph realized that his dream was being fulfilled, while his brothers did not. Deciding to test them, he accused them of being spies, and told them they would have to bring their youngest brother (Benjamin) to Egypt to prove themselves [42:9-18].

Sometimes we don't recognize when God sends us a message. Sometimes we don't recognize the blessings in our lives. Sometimes something stirs us, saying, "Do you recognize this?" We all need to occasionally take some time to stop and reevaluate our lives. Are there precious things that were perhaps forgotten and need to be reclaimed? Relationships that need to be rekindled or repaired? If so, will you reveal yourself, or make yourself unrecognizable?

Working to repair broken relationships is never easy. It wasn't easy for Joseph and his brothers either, as we will see. It takes work and making oneself vulnerable, and tears, and fear. But it can bring so many blessings in the end.

Brothers—the Ties that Bind

Joseph sends his brothers on their way, giving them each enough food for their family. However, he instructs them that they are to bring Benjamin back with them. As surety, he keeps Simeon as a prisoner in Egypt. Among themselves, the brothers begin to speculate that this is their punishment for their treatment of Joseph. They still do not realize that he is standing right in front of them and understands every word they say [42:19-24]!

Unbeknownst to the brothers, when Joseph orders that the brothers' sacks be filled with food, he also instructs that their money should be placed back into their sacks. When they later discover it on their way home, they are filled with dread. After all, they had assured the Egyptian vizier that they were honest men [42:25-28]! Arriving back home, the brothers tell Jacob everything that has happened, including the fact that they may not return to Egypt unless Benjamin accompanies them. Jacob, however, says that he will not allow that to happen [42:29-38].

Unfortunately for Jacob, the time comes when he has no choice. The famine persists. As their food supply dwindles once again, he tells his nine older sons to return to Egypt. Judah reminds him of the vizier's demand and tells his father that they will go to Egypt if and only if Benjamin is with them. When Jacob realizes that he has no choice, he sends them off, telling them to take not only their youngest brother, but twice the amount of money they had the first time so that they can pay for the original grain and for new supplies, as well [43:1-15].

In these thirty-five verses, there are no less than seventeen instances where the word "brother(s)" is used: nine of them refer to Benjamin, two refer to Joseph, and six refer to Simeon, or the collective brothers. There can be little doubt what message is conveyed here. The brothers are being reminded of their fraternal ties to Joseph, whom they sold into slavery because they hated him and could not speak a pleasant word to him; to Benjamin, upon whom their father apparently showers the same favoritism that he did to Joseph; to Simeon, whom they have left behind in Egypt; and to each other, all sons of the same man and members of the same family. The question is: will they remain mired in their distrust and resentment of each other, or will they rise above the pattern of sibling rivalry that has plagued their family for several generations, to be able to fulfill their destiny? They certainly face some difficult times during the famine, and we know that they face much more difficult times in the coming generations as they become enslaved in

Egypt. They will need to be united if they are to survive that. If not, what will become of the hopes and dreams of a nation of Israel living in the land promised to Abraham, in a covenant relationship with the God of Avraham, Isaac, and Jacob?

The future of the nation depends on the brothers—all twelve of them the sons of Jacob—being able to resolve their differences.

Sometimes these difficult days of the pandemic put strains on relationships: family relationships, friends, and even work colleagues. If we allow those relationships to be damaged now, it will be difficult to overcome that when things return to "normal." So, we, too, need to ask ourselves: will I allow myself to be mired down by resentments and hurts or will I be able to rise above them?

SIXTH ALIYAH: GENESIS 43:16–29
FRIDAY, DECEMBER 18, 2020

"We Came Indeed Down"

Think back to the previous readings—Jacob had become a wealthy man by the time he parted from his uncle/father-in-law Laban, having obtained many flocks, cattle, and servants. But famine is non-discriminatory and strikes everyone. The fortunes of the brothers, it seems, have been reversed, and they now find themselves in the position of having to ask someone else for the food that they themselves are unable to provide for their families. We can only imagine what they must have been feeling—not only fear, but shame, humility, and embarrassment, especially since they find themselves in the position of pleading their case to a servant.

This rings so true to what we are seeing in our world today. Day after day, we see reports on television or in the newspapers about the unprecedented numbers of people who find themselves at food banks, many of them in this situation for the first time in their lives. The pandemic has wreaked havoc with our economy, putting unemployment numbers at levels we have never seen. Most likely, you know one or more people or families who are in this position or perhaps you yourself have been affected. Like Joseph's brothers, people do whatever is necessary to provide for their families, but it is hard not to feel shame in doing so.

If we look back at the text, the way in which the steward treats the brothers is notable. First, he gently reassures them: "All is well with you; do not be afraid. Your God, the God of your father, must have put treasure in your bags for you. I got your payment" [43:23]. He puts them at ease and tells them essentially not to worry about the money. He does not express any kind of disbelief of their story, even though it is rather incredible. Then he brings them in, allows them to relax and wash their feet while having their animals fed [43:24]. He treats them with dignity even though Hebrews were really looked down upon in Egypt.

In this sense, the steward models the way in which we should treat people who may look to us for help. If you find yourself in a position to be able to help others, particularly now at the time of the holidays, and when it is so cold outside, then you should do so. Remember that those who need your help do not find themselves in that position voluntarily. Be generous with your kindness as well as your charity. People are suffering more than enough. They do not need to suffer insults or indignity as well.

SEVENTH ALIYAH: GENESIS 43:30–44:17
WRITTEN FOR SHABBAT, SATURDAY, DECEMBER 19, 2020

Yes, I Am My Brother's Keeper

In this last *aliyah,* we see that Joseph continues to test his brothers. When the meal is served, the brothers are seated separately from Joseph and his servants because, we are told, it was abhorrent to the Egyptians to eat with the Hebrews. However, the Egyptians do not eat with Joseph because he is the grand vizier. How reflective is this of Joseph's identity crisis; he eats neither with the Hebrews nor with the Egyptians. He is not comfortable with either one. Yet he is really both, seemingly unable to reconcile the two parts of his identity.

In any event, the brothers are confused because they are seated in age order, which is not necessarily intuitive since several of them were born in fairly close chronological proximity. Additionally, Benjamin, their youngest brother, is served a portion several times larger than that of the others. Was this intentional? Did Joseph really want to shower so much more on his full brother or was he testing the loyalty of their ten older brothers to see if they would become jealous of him [43:30-34]?

The next morning, Joseph sets up another situation that is designed to frame them. He instructs his house steward (the same one in whom they confided in the previous *aliyah*) once again to put all their money back in their sacks, and to place Joseph's very own silver goblet in the sack which belongs to the youngest [44:1-2]. The scene that ensues is reminiscent of Laban pursuing Jacob in search of his household gods. The difference is that here the evidence was planted by Joseph. The brothers, like their father Jacob, are ignorant of the actual "theft." Therefore, like Jacob, they make a foolish oath: the one who has the goblet will die and all the others will become slaves [44:1-9].

When the goblet is discovered in Benjamin's sack, the brothers tear their clothes, a common sign of mourning. You may recall that this is what Jacob did when they showed him Joseph's cloak dipped in the goat's blood. Now they themselves are emotionally brought to the same level to which they had brought their father; they feel the same level of sorrow that he felt. Knowing that they have no choice, the brothers pack up their animals to return to the city, resigned to face their fate. However, once again, we must note how they are defined: "when Judah and his brothers returned to the city . . ." [44:14]. This clearly indicates to us that Judah is going to take a prominent role here.

Judah was the brother who:

- suggested selling Joseph instead of leaving him in the pit to die.
- Fathered twins by his daughter-in-law Tamar after she deceived him by dressing as a prostitute.
- Promised their father Jacob that he himself would serve as surety for the safety of Benjamin when the brothers took him down to Egypt with them.
- Would emerge as the leader of his brothers after Reuben, the firstborn, angered his father by having sex with his concubine/ wife Bilhah.

Judah now tells the vizier (Joseph, though the brothers are still unaware of that) that they will all serve him as slaves, not just the one with whom the goblet was found [44:16].

Joseph set up the perfect situation for the brothers to be angry with and separate from Benjamin. Yet there is no evidence in the Torah text that they reproach him in any way, even though they clearly saw the goblet in his sack. It would have been easy for them to assume under the circumstances that he was the one who put the money back in their sacks. Instead, the brothers present a united front, standing with Benjamin.

Additionally, Judah does not blame Joseph for putting the goblet in Benjamin's sack or for putting the money back in their sacks. Instead, he tells Joseph that God has uncovered their crime. In other words, God has brought about this whole situation to enable them to come to terms with their guilt for having mistreated their brother Joseph and to test them, seeing if they will repeat their mistakes with Benjamin.

The *aliyah* ends with Joseph saying that he will not hold them all guilty for the "crime" of the one. Could it be that he spoke metaphorically, saying that he will no longer hold them guilty for the crimes that they long ago committed against him? Joseph, too, must come to terms with his own role in the situation; after all, he was also guilty of antagonizing them, taunting them with his dreams and his coat. We begin to see hope of reconciliation among the twelve sons of Jacob, reconciliation that can only happen when all of them are able to recognize their own individual guilt before both their brothers and God.

I wish you a peaceful Shabbat.

Parashat Vayigash

FIRST ALIYAH: GENESIS 44:18–30
SUNDAY, DECEMBER 20, 2020

Speaking in the Voice of Another

The brothers have all been brought back before Joseph, who has said that he will keep Benjamin as a slave for having "stolen his goblet" while allowing the others to go. Now Judah, the one who convinced Jacob to allow Benjamin to come to Egypt, offers himself as surety and steps forward to speak directly to Joseph. In what is the longest speech in the entire book of Genesis, he pleads his case.

Judah begins by reminding Joseph that, when he had asked them on their first trip to Egypt whether they had a father or a brother, they told him about Benjamin: "We have an old father, and there is a child of his old age, the youngest; his full brother is dead, so that he alone is left of his mother, and his father dotes on him" [44:20]. How difficult it must have been for Judah to make this statement. In truth, he is justifying his father's favoritism towards his youngest brother. This is what Joseph has been waiting to hear. If Judah can make such a statement honestly and without malice then Joseph knows that the brothers do not display the same jealousy towards Benjamin that they did toward him. It is interesting to note that Judah says that Benjamin's full brother (i.e., Joseph) is dead (he previously had said that he was no longer with them). Essentially, this part of his statement is a lie. As far as Judah and the other brothers know, Joseph is still alive. They led their father to believe that he was dead, though they themselves know otherwise. Benjamin also, no doubt, believes that Joseph is dead. We can only imagine what Joseph must have felt to hear that said about himself.

Judah continues to recount the story: Joseph told them to bring Benjamin down to Egypt so that he himself could see him. Their answer had been to tell Joseph, "The boy cannot leave his father for if he were to leave him, [he] would die" [44:22]. (Note that the translation above says, "his father would die." However, the word "father" does not appear in the Hebrew.) The verse is, therefore, ambiguous. Many obviously assume that the pronoun "he" refers to Jacob, who was inconsolable at the loss of Joseph and wouldn't be able to bear the loss of Benjamin. There are several commentators, however, who say that the word really refers to Benjamin, who was apparently as attached to his father as his father was to him; he would despair of never seeing Jacob again. In addition, Benjamin had no doubt been told the story of his birth, how his mother had died while on a journey, and he was afraid that he would suffer the same fate. The Baal haTurim says that the ambiguity is intentional as it applies to both father and son because "neither could live without the other."[1]

Judah then goes on to recount the conversation that he and his brothers had with Jacob, explaining that the vizier had told them not to return unless Benjamin was with them. He quotes Jacob's words: "As you know, my wife bore me two sons. But one is gone from me, and I said: Alas, he was torn by a beast! And I have not seen him since. If you take this one from me, too, and he meets with disaster, you will send my white head down to Sheol in sorrow" [44:27-29]. Again, Judah describes Jacob's favoritism for his two youngest sons (and even for their mother). Rather than recounting this with malice, he explains why he cannot return without Benjamin. Instead of criticizing his father or being angry with him, Judah appears to genuinely understand his father. He attempts to evoke Joseph's sympathy for him. The *aliyah* ends midsentence; the last thought expressed here by Judah is: "his own life is so bound up with his." With this, Judah demonstrates a genuine empathy for his father and his brother, and an understanding and appreciation of the bond that they share.

Giving voice to the feelings of someone else demonstrates a true understanding of their thoughts and motivations. Today, there are still so many issues that divide us as a nation—politics, response to the pandemic, response to social unrest, and the racial divide. Whatever our feelings, we all have strong emotionsabout all these things. But the reason that we have such divisions is because we find ourselves unable to give voice to those with opposing views, unable to even begin to try to understand them.

Perhaps we can all take a lesson from Judah.

At Last, Joseph Wept

The first *aliyah* left off in the middle of Judah's entreaty to Joseph—literally midsentence. The second *aliyah* begins with the completion of that speech. Judah goes on to explain to the vizier of Egypt (Joseph) that he offered himself as surety to Jacob for the safety of his brother Benjamin to allow him to come to Egypt with his brothers. Judah offers himself as a slave in Benjamin's place, saying that his father would die of grief if Benjamin did not come home. Indeed, in the last verse of his speech [44:34], Judah says that he would not be able to go home again if Benjamin were not with him because he would not be able to bear to see his father's reaction. Indeed, if the brothers were to return to their father and Benjamin were not among them, Jacob would assume that his youngest son was dead, just as he had done with Joseph.

Between the two *aliyot*, Judah's speech is seventeen verses long. In those seventeen verses, he uses some version of the word "father" no less than thirteen times: *av* (father), once; *aviv* (his (Benjamin's) father), three times; *avi* (my father), seven times; *avinu* (our father), twice. The whole speech is designed to evoke sympathy for Jacob in the heart of the Egyptian who is "the equal of Pharaoh." Every time that Judah uses the word "my father," it surely must eat away at Joseph, reminding him of the close relationship that he himself had had with Jacob. Every time that he used the word "our father," Joseph must have felt the irony—yes, "our father" indeed. And every time that he used the word "his father," Joseph no doubt felt the pang of realizing that Benjamin shared the relationship with Jacob that he himself had once enjoyed. The pressure on Joseph must have been palpable. There were already two other times in the story where Joseph had almost broken down but had to turn away to hide his tears. Here, finally, he can take it no more. Ordering everyone except his brothers to leave the room, Joseph releases the emotion that had been pent up for thirteen years and he breaks down and cries and wails. So heartrending is his cry that it is heard all the way in Pharaoh's palace. Finally, the word "my father" is spoken one more time as Joseph reveals himself to his brothers: "I am Joseph. Is my father still well [alive]?" [45:3]. Of course, Joseph knew that his father was indeed alive based on everything that Judah had just said to him. It is almost as if he is saying, "is my father really still alive?" Overcome with the emotion of the moment, he finds it almost impossible to believe.

The brothers are naturally confused by this turn of events. Not only are they confused, but we are told that they were "frightened by his presence" (OJPS translation). Why would they be frightened? In an instant, they realize how powerful their brother has become, and they think that he might want to take revenge on them for having sold him into slavery. He quickly assures them that they need not worry, for it was all part of God's plan: God had sent him on ahead to Egypt so that he would be able to save lives, including those of his brothers.

This story of Joseph interacting over these many months with his brothers and not being able to reveal himself is in many ways reminiscent of the relationships that many of us have had with family members and friends during these last nine months of the pandemic. In some cases, we can see each other only through a computer screen. When we can see each other in person, it is only behind the protection of a mask. Touching is strictly off limits. Now, just imagine how you will feel that first time you are able to fully reunite again—the first time you are able to touch, to hug, to kiss. Imagine how you will feel. No doubt, all the pent-up emotions that have been brought by COVID-induced separation will come pouring out when we can truly renew precious relationships again, just as Joseph does now with his brothers, and anticipates being able to do soon with his beloved father.

May we have the patience that Joseph had to be able to wait until the time is right, to be able to say to one another at that time that this was part of God's plan to save lives. May it come speedily in our day.

THIRD ALIYAH: GENESIS 45:8–18
TUESDAY, DECEMBER 22, 2020

Absence Makes the Heart Grow Fonder

Now that the dam of emotions has burst, Joseph can hardly contain himself. His speech is not nearly as long as Judah's was. Nevertheless, it began with the last four verses of the previous *aliyah* and continues through the first six verses of this *aliyah*. He uses the word *avi* (my father) no less than four times. How long he must have yearned to be able to utter that word!

He instructs them to go back to Jacob, telling him that they come with a message from "your son Joseph" [45:9]. *Bincha* (your son), no doubt, this was another word that he had longed to be able to say. More importantly, he puts it in the mouths of his brothers, who once were not able to speak to him civilly. He says to them, "you can see for yourselves" then says that his brother Benjamin "can see for himself" that it is indeed Joseph who is speaking to him [45:12]. Some wonder about this. It almost seems that he is singling Benjamin out again. Rather, he is saying to them, "Look, you know I do not hold a grudge against Benjamin because he was not involved in the incidents that took place in the desert. Just as I hold no ill feelings towards him, so, too, do I harbor no ill feelings toward the rest of you." With that, he kisses Benjamin and then kisses all his brothers [45:14-15]. As Rashi points out, the verb form that is used here implies not one single kiss, but rather multiple kisses.[2] Joseph showers his brothers with kisses, making up for the many years that he had not been able to do so, going all the way back to the days of his youth when they harbored hatred for him.

Joseph instructs his brothers to tell Jacob to pack up everything—his family and his animals—and come down to Egypt where Joseph will settle them in Goshen. In this way, Joseph will have his father close to him and Joseph will be able to care for his whole family. Joseph says that Jacob should make the journey with great haste—without delay. Of course, we realize that this would entail Jacob leaving the promised land of Canaan to go into exile. However, Joseph was not free to leave Egypt due to his position; nor was it possible for him to keep sending food back to Jacob without arousing the suspicions of the Egyptians. In addition, they were only two years into the years of famine with still five more to go! Had Jacob remained where he was, he would have become destitute, and, as the Baal HaTurim points out, this would have caused Jacob to be distracted from being able to study.[3] He could grow resentful, causing his relationship with God to suffer. Therefore, under the circumstances, packing up and moving to Goshen made more sense.

Finally, I would like to return to the Talmud's discussion of dreams that we touched on last week:

> From the same source, Rabbi Levi said: One should always anticipate fulfillment of a good dream up to twenty-two years after the dream. From where do we derive this? From Joseph, as it is written in the story of Joseph's dream: "These are the generations of Jacob. Joseph, being seventeen years old, was feeding the flock with his brethren" [Genesis 37:2]; and it is written: "And Joseph was thirty years old when he stood before Pharaoh King of Egypt" [Genesis 41:46]. From seventeen to thirty, how many years are they? Thirteen; and add seven years of plenty and two of famine; the total is twenty-two and only then was the dream fulfilled when his brothers came and bowed down to him. [BT Berachot 55B:2]

Joseph waited twenty-two years for his dreams to be fulfilled! Think of all that happened to him in those twenty-two years. No doubt there were many times when it seemed highly unlikely that he would ever see the realization of his dreams. Yet here he was, standing before his brothers.

Thinking of this should give us some hope and consolation. If Joseph could wait twenty-two years to see his dreams fulfilled, enduring separation from his family that included slavery and imprisonment, then surely, we can hold out another six to nine months, if need be, to realize the dream of being able to reunite with loved ones, kissing and embracing them as Joseph does with his long-estranged brothers. Throughout those long twenty-two years, Joseph played his part, doing everything that was expected of him, biding his time. So, too, do we need to do our parts, doing everything that is expected of us, biding our time as we wait for our time of separation to end.

FOURTH ALIYAH: GENESIS 45:19–27
WEDNESDAY, DECEMBER 23, 2020

Breaking the News Gently

At the command of Pharaoh, Joseph dispatched his brothers with wagons to use for transporting the members of their extended family back to Egypt. He also sent them with provisions for the journey, as well as a clean garment for each; Benjamin, however, received five new garments and three hundred pieces of silver. Twenty donkeys, ten male and ten female, were sent to Jacob, laden down with "all of the good things of Egypt" [45:18-23].

When the brothers arrived home, they told their father that Joseph was not only still alive, but he was also now the vizier of Egypt. Jacob could not believe them at first until he saw all the things that Joseph had sent to him and then his spirit revived [45:25-27].

Why did Joseph have to tell his brothers not to "be quarrelsome on the way" [45:24]? There are several theories put forth by the sages: they would argue over an issue of *halachah* (Rashi, really?); they would worry that they might be waylaid by robbers (Rashbam, Ramban, Bechor Shor); they would argue over whose fault all of this was—who had caused Joseph to be sent to Egypt in the first place (Rashi, Ibn Ezra).[4] I think there is another likely possibility.

Just try to imagine for a moment how they might have worried about telling Jacob the news of Joseph. After all, telling him that Joseph was alive and in Egypt would require admitting what they had initially done to their brother all those years ago. It would require admitting that they had allowed their father to suffer in his grief, believing that his son was dead, instead of telling him the truth. Now, they no doubt might have argued over how Jacob should be told, and who should tell him. As a possible answer, there is a beautiful *midrash* about Serah, the daughter of Asher, whom I wrote about twice before (in *parashat* Pinchas, and *parashat* V'zot Brachah). She is the only female (other than Dinah) to ever be listed in a genealogy of Jacob's family. She is mentioned three times specifically in the *Tanakh*, and they occur very far apart timewise. The implication is that she lived for a very long time—some even say forever! And what was so special about her that she merited this long life? The *midrash* tells us:

> And when they [the brothers] came to the boundaries of the land, they said to one another: What shall we do in bringing this matter before our father? For if we impart it to him suddenly, and tell him all about it, he will be greatly astounded at our words and he will refuse to listen to us. And when they went on until they approached their houses, they met Serach coming towards them, and the damsel was exceedingly beautiful and wise, and a skilled player on the harp; and they called her and she came unto them and she kissed them. And they took her and gave her a harp saying unto her: Go, we pray thee, before our father and sit down before him and strike this harp and speak unto him according to these words. And they instructed her concerning what she had to say, and she hastened unto Jacob and she sat down before him. And she sang and she played beautifully upon the harp, and she sang in the sweetness of her voice: Joseph, my uncle, is alive and he reign[s] over all the land of Egypt; he is not dead. And she often repeated these words. And Jacob heard her words and it pleased him greatly, and when he heard her sing it twice and three times, the heart of Jacob was possessed by joy, through the sweetness of her voice, and the spirit of God came over him, and he knew that all her words were true. And Jacob blessed Serach for singing these words before him, and he said: My daughter, may death never prevail against thee forever, for thou hast revi[v]ed my spirit, only repeat . . . this song once more before me, for [you have] caused me gladness with [your] words. And she sang once more the same words and Jacob listened, and he was pleased and he rejoiced, and the spirit of God came over him. And while he was yet speaking with her, his sons came before him with horses and chariots and royal garments and servants running

before them. And Jacob arose and went to meet them, and he saw his sons dressed in royal garments and all the good things that Joseph sent [to] them. And they said [to] him: [know] that our brother Joseph live[s], and that he rule[s] over the whole land of Egypt, and it is he who ha[s] spoken [to] us all we have told [you]. And Jacob heard all the words of his sons and his heart fainted, for he believed them not, until he saw all that Joseph had given [to] them and all that Joseph had sent along with them, and all the signs he had spoken of unto them. And they unpacked all the things before him, and they displayed all that Joseph had sent, and they gave to every one of them what Joseph had sent him. And Jacob knew that they ha[d] spoken the truth, and Jacob . . . greatly rejoiced [because] of his son. [*Sefer haYashar (midrash), Book of Genesis, Vayigash 9*].[5]

Because Serah broke the news that Joseph was still alive—words that he never believed that he would hear—to her grandfather gently, allowing him to gradually comprehend it in joy before the brothers appeared before him with the evidence of the veracity of what she was saying, the situation was diffused. Jacob rejoiced in the news of his son Joseph before he ever heard it from the others. It is because of this that Jacob blessed his granddaughter Serah and rewarded her with the promise of a long life.

FIFTH ALIYAH: GENESIS 45:28–46:27
THURSDAY, DECEMBER 24, 2020

"I Myself Will Go With You"

Without hesitation, Jacob immediately packed up everything he had and set out for Egypt. Stopping in Beersheba to offer a sacrifice, he was visited by God in a vision by night. God told him not to be afraid and promised Jacob that he would be made into a nation in Egypt. God promised to go down to Egypt with Jacob, and to bring him out again. No doubt this means after death, as the last promise is that Joseph will close his eyes when he dies.

What follows in the rest of the *aliyah* is a complete listing of the descendants of Jacob who went down to Egypt with him, sons, and daughters (though Dinah is the only daughter we know of), grandsons and granddaughters (again, Serah is the only one listed by name). A tabulation is given after the listing of the offspring of each of Jacob's wives: Leah, thirty-three;

Zilpah, sixteen; Rachel, fourteen; and Bilhah, seven. Then we are told that the total who came to Egypt with Jacob was sixty-six [46:26]. In addition, Joseph's two sons were born in Egypt. Then we are told that the total is seventy. How can that be? 66+2+1 (Jacob himself) = 69. Where does the other 1 come from? We already saw the answer: "I Myself will go down with you to Egypt" [46:4].

The seventieth soul that went down to Egypt was the *Shechinah*, the presence of God. Though Jacob was leaving the land to go into exile, he needed to be reassured and reminded that God does not dwell only in the promised land of Canaan. Indeed, God had previously promised to be with Jacob when he had run away from home to his uncle Laban to escape the wrath of his brother Esau. There Jacob had expanded his family to include four wives and thirteen children and had also acquired many flocks and cattle. God had blessed him there and he had prospered.

Now Jacob knew he was heading into the final chapter of his life, but he knew he would be accompanied by the presence of his God and the presence of all twelve of his sons.

There is no more beautiful promise that God could make to anyone than "do not be afraid of what lies ahead, because I Myself will go (down) with you." We have all endured some difficult days this past year. In another week, we will (thankfully) put the year 2020 behind us. There is hope that comes with the beginning of a new secular year and the arrival of a vaccine. And yet at every turn we are told that things will get worse before they get better and that the worst is still ahead of us. If we wish to have the strength to make it through whatever lies ahead, we all need to listen to the promise God makes to us just as it was given to Jacob: Do not worry. I Myself will go with you.

SIXTH ALIYAH: GENESIS 46:28–47:10
FRIDAY, DECEMBER 25, 2020

You Were Strangers in the Land of Egypt

Joseph's family arrives in Goshen, with Judah leading the way. Anxious to be reunited with his father, Joseph saddles up his own chariot and goes out to meet him. We read, "he presented himself to him and, embracing him around the neck, he wept on his neck a good while" [46:29]. The wording is ambiguous: who is doing the weeping here, Joseph or Jacob? The natural assumption is that it refers to Joseph. After all, the first half of the verse talks about him and we have already seen copious tears from him when he reunited with his brothers. And yet it also makes sense that it could be Jacob as he had wept for his son since the day he was presented with his torn and bloodied coat. Ramban says, "Who would weep more, the elderly father who finds his son alive after years of loss and mourning, or the young son who is the ruler of Egypt?"[6] Indeed, the next person to speak is Jacob, telling Joseph that he feels that he could die now since he has seen his son's face [46:30]. So, it could be either one. I'll leave it for you to decide.

Joseph now prepares his brothers for meeting with Pharaoh, telling them that when they are asked what their occupation is, they should respond that they are shepherds, after which they would be granted permission to settle in Goshen [46:31-34]. Joseph chooses five of his brothers to go with him before Pharaoh, and they respond as he has instructed them. They elaborate a little on what Joseph has instructed them to say: "We have come . . . to sojourn in this land, for there is no pasture for your servants' flocks, the famine being severe in the land of Canaan" [47:4]. From the very beginning, they are aware of their status as outsiders; Joseph told them that shepherds were abominations to the Egyptians and that this would be justification for them to live in Goshen, a separate area of the land. It is because of this awareness that the single most mentioned *mitzvah* in the Torah is love for the stranger. This sensitivity to the feelings of the other is mentioned no less than four times in the Torah as the reason for loving the stranger:

> You shall not wrong a stranger or oppress him, for you were
> strangers in the land of Egypt. [Exodus 22:20]
> You shall not oppress a stranger, for you know the feelings of the
> stranger, having yourselves been strangers in the land of Egypt.
> [Exodus 23:9]
> The stranger who resides with you shall be to you as one of your
> citizens; you shall love him as yourself, for you were strangers in
> the land of Egypt: I the LORD am your God.
> [Leviticus 19:34]
> You too must befriend the stranger, for you were strangers in the
> land of Egypt. [Deuteronomy10:19]

Human nature is so often not to trust, but rather to be suspicious of, or look down upon, someone different, someone that some would say is tres-passing on our land, taking advantage of everything that our country has to offer. Because of this, God reminds us that this was precisely the situation our ancestors found themselves in when they first came to Egypt. The need for this sensitivity is as important today as it ever has been, perhaps more so. We live today in a divided country, one in which the differences between us are often emphasized, and not in a positive way. We, as Jews, still find ourselves amongst the groups who are marginalized; we know what it feels like to be strangers in a strange land. We, as Jews, need to fight for social justice, speaking up for those in our society who have been labelled "other." The values of our Torah require nothing less from us.

SEVENTH ALIYAH: GENESIS 47:11–27
WRITTEN FOR SHABBAT, SATURDAY, DECEMBER 26, 2020

Promises, Promises

So here we learn that Joseph settled his family in the land of Goshen, providing food to sustain them all. The famine was severe in both Egypt and Canaan. As the years continued, the famine didn't let up, and each year, the people of Egypt came to Joseph pleading for his help. Every year, the people had to resort to more drastic measures to ensure their survival. First, they had to give all of their money to Joseph in exchange for food. The next year, they had to bring all of their animals—horses, flocks, cattle, donkeys. The following year, they were forced to sign over their land to him. Then, they themselves became serfs. Finally, Joseph decreed that twenty percent of all the crops they grew belonged to Pharaoh. Everything that Joseph collected went into the treasury of Pharaoh and he kept nothing for himself. Joseph never got carried away. He was always conscious of his position and used his gifts to save others, primarily Egyptians.

The last verse is a foreshadowing of the future. After settling in Goshen in the land of Egypt, the people of Israel, the descendants of Jacob, "were fertile and increased greatly" [47:27]. God's promise to Abraham, to Isaac, and to Jacob was finally coming to fruition. Israel was finally becoming a nation.

Two weeks from now, when we begin the book of Shemot, the great fertility of Jacob's descendants will lead to the descent into slavery and the fulfillment of a promise God had made to Abraham.

Parashat Vayechi

FIRST ALIYAH: GENESIS 47:28–49:9
SUNDAY, DECEMBER 27, 2020

I'm Alive!

In the previous *parashah*, when Pharaoh asked Jacob his age, the answer was one hundred thirty. This last *parashah* of the book of Genesis begins by telling us, "Jacob lived seventeen years in the land of Egypt" [47:28]. The verse then concludes by telling us that Jacob's total life span was one hundred forty-seven years. So, we wonder: since we can easily see that 147-130=17, why does the Torah need to tell us specifically that Jacob lived seventeen years in Egypt? The number seventeen has additional significance. It is the age of Joseph when he was sold into slavery in Egypt (i.e., the age when he was removed from his father's life). This can hardly be a coincidence. The commentators have a lot to say about this:

> . . . all the years of Yaakov until he settled in Egypt could not truly be described as "life," seeing that they were all clouded by different kinds of anguish. It was only during his last seventeen years in Egypt that his mind was at rest and not beset by serious worries of one kind or another . . . Joseph . . . was the cause of Yaakov's last seventeen years being happy years. During those seventeen years, he repaid his father who had sustained him for the first seventeen years of his life by providing for him during the last seventeen years of his life. He had been seventeen years old when he had been sold. [*Chizkuni*][1]
>
> . . . The Torah underlines that these were the only years which Jacob could really be described as having enjoyed by writing,

"these years were full of life." These seventeen years were truly, "Jacob's years." [*Or HaChaim*][2]

. . . just as Joseph was under the protection of his father for the first seventeen years of his life, so his father was under Joseph's protection for the last seventeen years of his life. [*Radak*][3]

. . . [Joseph spent the first seventeen years of his life under the care of his father, whereas his father spent the last seventeen years of his life under the care of Joseph. [*Tur HaAroch*][4] Corresponding to the seventeen years during which Jacob raised Joseph, Joseph provided for Jacob for seventeen years. [*Baal HaTurim*][5]

Just as Joseph lived in Jacob's care for seventeen years, so Jacob lived in Joseph's care for seventeen years. [*Kimchi*][6]

All these comments and more give us the feeling that Jacob finally found some peace in his life once he was reunited with his beloved son, Joseph.

I think there is more to it, though, that the commentators do not touch on. I think that Jacob's peace came not just from his renewed relationship with Joseph; I think it came from the renewed relationship shared by all his sons. Perhaps he, too, had finally been able to reconcile himself with his own role in contributing to the jealousy and animosity that Joseph's ten older brothers had harbored against him.

Some wonder whether Jacob ever asked his sons what had transpired in the desert, and how they could have been so cruel as to let him believe that Joseph was dead. We don't really know because the Torah doesn't comment on it one way or the other. Perhaps Jacob intentionally did not ask them. His sons are all grown men with children of their own now. Seeing that they were united now, and that Joseph himself has insisted that this was God's plan to send him on ahead to provide for them all perhaps was enough for Jacob to finally feel at peace. No doubt, that, too, was also part of God's plan all along.

SECOND ALIYAH: GENESIS 48:10–16
MONDAY, DECEMBER 28, 2020

The Younger Supersedes the Older, Yet Again

Before he dies, Jacob wants to bless Joseph's two sons and adopt them as his own. The scene is clearly reminiscent of Jacob receiving from his father the blessing intended for his brother Esau. Just as Isaac's eyes were dimmed so that he could not see which of his sons stood before him, here we are told that Jacob's eyes, too, have become dim with age [48:10]. Ironically, Jacob now tells his son, "I never expected to see you again, and here God has let me see your children as well." Apparently, he was not totally blind, but he could only see someone if they were very close to him. In any event, Joseph brings both boys to his father at the same time, and once again, the birth order is switched, with the primary blessing going to the younger child, not the firstborn. The difference is that this time it appears to be intentional on Jacob's part.

Joseph approaches his father with his two sons, Menashe, his firstborn, and Ephraim, his younger son.

The right hand, since it is associated with the strong arm of God, is usually interpreted as representing strength. In the Talmud, instructions are given for the manner in which three people should align themselves when walking together:

> . . . it was taught in a *baraita*: Three people who were walking on the road should not walk in single file but should walk with the teacher in the middle, the greater of the students on his right, and the lesser of them to his left. [*BT Yoma 37A:10*]

Following this dictum would mean that Menashe should have been on Joseph's right and Ephraim on his left as they approached Jacob. However, it was apparently equally important that the right hand, the hand representing strength, should be placed on the head of the firstborn when the blessing was given; it certainly seems to have mattered to Joseph, even as he himself was essentially displacing Reuven as the designated firstborn among his brothers (this is evidenced by the fact that Jacob adopted the two boys as his own, essentially giving a double portion of the inheritance to Joseph). In any event, knowing that Jacob's eyesight is failing him, Joseph reverses the position of the boys, placing the firstborn Menashe on his left and the younger Ephraim on his right. This way, when they are facing Jacob, they will be positioned correctly for the blessing, Menashe at Jacob's right hand and Ephraim at his left (if this sounds confusing to you, think what happens when you look in the mirror—your right hand touches your reflection's left hand, and vice versa). Joseph is therefore surprised at what happens next: "But Israel stretched out his right hand and laid it on Ephraim's head, though he was the younger, and his left hand on Manasseh's head—thus crossing his hands—although Manasseh was the firstborn" [48: 14]. And with that, Jacob begins by blessing Joseph, and then moving on to the boys.

Once again, we see that the younger displaces the older, a theme that has played out in every generation of this family so far. The difference here is that Jacob does not appear to be doing this out of favoritism. Furthermore, there is no deception taking place; Jacob appears to know exactly what he is doing.

The rest of this scene, including a blessing familiar to anyone who is the parent of a son, continues in the next *aliyah*.

THIRD ALIYAH: GENESIS 48:17–22
TUESDAY, DECEMBER 29, 2020

May All of Our Children be Blessed

Jacob's blessing of his grandsons continues. Joseph, seeing that his father has switched his hands, thinks that he is simply making a mistake, assuming that Joseph would naturally have placed Menashe, as his firstborn, on his right, and Ephraim on his left. So, Joseph himself reaches out to switch his father's hands back again, indicating that the boy on Jacob's right is indeed the firstborn. He apparently forgot, however, that Jacob seemed to be capable of seeing up close. In any event, Jacob does not allow Joseph to reverse his hands, saying "I know." Repeating these words a second time, he assures his son that he absolutely is aware of what he is doing. He is not showing favoritism. He is basing his action on a foreknowledge that both boys will be blessed, but Ephraim, the younger, will be greater than Menashe, the older [48:17-19].

Jacob then continues with the blessing, declaring that all Israel will invoke blessings [on their sons] saying: "[May] God make you like Ephraim and Manasseh." With that, Jacob has spoken the formula by which Jews would (will) forever bless their sons. All over the world, Jewish parents invoke this blessing on male children every Shabbat evening, and on every major life cycle event, such as *bris* or *bar mitzvah*.

So, you may wonder: what was it about these two boys that merited being the ones in whom the males of Israel all receive a blessing? I suggest that the answer is twofold.

First, though the birth order was once again upended, this was the first instance in which there was no animosity displayed between the brothers. They accepted their grandfather's blessing without complaint or objection.

Second, one of the reasons that Jacob felt he needed to adopt these boys as his own was because they were his only offspring to be born outside the land of Canaan—in exile, in the diaspora. They had spent their entire lives in Egypt, surrounded by a foreign culture in which they were decidedly a minority, yet they had remained faithful to their heritage, to the covenant established by God with the nation of Israel. No matter where on earth we live, or in what generation, we can wish no less for our sons.

But what about our daughters? Nowhere in the Torah are we given a formula for blessing our female offspring. Yet anyone who is a parent of a daughter is familiar with the accepted formula: May God make you like Sarah, Rebecca, Rachel, and Leah.

We wish for our daughters that they should be like the four matriarchs of Israel. Each of these women was a strong woman trying to forge her way in a distinctly patrilineal society. Though they could not divorce themselves from the role assigned by their society, nevertheless they each endured some kind of hardship, and each fulfilled her destiny as a mother in Israel.

Like Ephraim and Menashe, the matriarchs, as well as all women in Israel, were outsiders in a way; but, like the sons of Joseph, they nevertheless remained faithful to their heritage, to the covenant established by God with the nation of Israel. And, like the sons of Joseph, we choose today to bring them in and make them equal partners with their male constituents. No matter where on Earth we live or in what generation, we can wish no less for our daughters.

FOURTH ALIYAH: GENESIS 49:1–18
WEDNESDAY, DECEMBER 30, 2020

Blessing the "Kinder"

Jacob is at the point of death, so he calls all his sons to him, so that he can "bless" them, or tell them what awaits them in the future. Neither Abraham nor Isaac, who each had only two sons, was able to do this before their deaths. For each of them, a reunion of their offspring only occurred after their death, when their sons came together to bury them.

Though Reuben is listed first among Jacob's sons, he has lost the designation of firstborn due to having been intimate with Bilhah, one of the two concubine/wives. Mounting his father's bed was the worst insult that Reuben could possibly have inflicted upon him. Reuben was both the oldest of Jacob's sons, and also the firstborn of his wife Leah. With the adoption of Ephraim and Menashe, the designation of firstborn has been passed to Joseph, the firstborn of Jacob's wife Rachel [49:3-4]. Jacob's second and third sons, Shimon and Levi are linked together in their father's declaration. He describes them as lawless men who slay other men in their anger [49:5-6]. This, Rashi points out, is based on two incidents: first, the brutal slaying of all the men of Shechem in retaliation for the rape of Dinah; and second, they were the brothers who, when seeing Joseph approaching in the desert, said to each other, "Here comes that dreamer. Come now, let us kill him" [37:19-20].[7] Of them, Jacob says, "I will divide them in Jacob, Scatter them in Israel." Indeed, as we saw in the books of Leviticus, Numbers, and Deuteronomy, the tribe of Levi, since they were designated to work in the *mishkan*, were not given any tribal territory. Instead, they had cities in the territory of each of the other tribes, literally scattering them in Israel.

For his fourth son, Judah, Jacob gives praise rather than reproof. He tells him that his brothers will praise him, and his father's sons will bow low to him [49: 8]. Note that the second terminology includes both Judah's brothers and his half-brothers—all of Jacob's sons. He compares him to a young lion [49:9]. It is from here that we derive the symbol of the lion of Judah. Here we find the following well-known phrase that alludes to the eventual reign of King David and his descendants in the Southern Kingdom of Israel, which included the holy city of Jerusalem: "The scepter shall not depart from Judah, Nor the ruler's staff from between his feet" [49:10]. This verse also inspires the belief that the messiah will eventually come from the descendants of Judah. His territory will also have abundant wine and milk [49:12]. Judah's descendants will prosper and be leaders and all of this can be construed as his reward for having stepped forward and taken a leading role in the reconciliation of the brothers, and the reuniting of the family.

Next, Jacob moves on to Zevulun and Issachar, the two youngest sons of Leah. Once again, the birth order is reversed. Though Issachar is the older of the two, Zevulun is mentioned first. Jacob foretells that his descendants will dwell by the seashore, and they will be involved in trade and commerce [49:13]. Issachar is described as a "strong-boned ass, crouching among the sheepfolds" [49:14]. Rashi interprets this to mean that his descendants will be involved in Torah study, supported by the descendants of Zevulun.[8] Rashbam interprets it to mean that they will work the land instead of being involved in commerce.[9] Jacob says, "He bent his shoulder to the burden, and became a toiling serf" [49:15]. This is interpreted to mean that they did both: work the land to benefit all their brothers, since they did not wish to go to war, and take on the burden of Torah study, passing on their knowledge to their brothers.

Jacob now moves on to the four sons of Bilhah and Zilpah. Beginning with the oldest, Dan, Bilhah's firstborn, Jacob pronounces that this tribe will govern, or judge, in Israel. They are compared to a serpent who lies in wait by the side of the road until the right moment to come out and attack its foes [49:16-17].

Jacob's predictions for his sons and their descendants are briefly inter-rupted at this point by verse 18: "I wait for Your deliverance, O LORD!" Jacob calls upon God to give him strength to complete his "blessings," his predic-tions for all his sons before he dies.

FIFTH ALIYAH: GENESIS 49:19–26
THURSDAY, DECEMBER 31, 2020

Blessings for Jacob's Favorite Son

Jacob now moves on to Gad, the firstborn of Zilpah, who is described as a tribe of warriors [49:19]. Next comes Asher, Zilpah's second born. Asher's "bread shall be rich" [49:20] because his territory will be fertile and abun-dant in olive trees and the tribe will prosper. Finally, Jacob addresses the last of the four sons of the concubines, Naphtali, Bilhah's second born. Once again using animal imagery, this tribe is likened to a hind, a graceful, beau-tiful animal also known for its speed [49:21]. Their territory will produce abundant fruit, and they will be known as swift-footed messengers.

Finally, we come to Jacob's favorite son, Joseph, whose blessing, like Judah's, is lengthier than the others. Though Jacob speaks to Joseph, we need to remember that these words are really for Ephraim and Menashe, who will now become two "half-tribes," replacing their father in terms of inheritance. Joseph is described as a "wild ass" [49:22], although several commentators translate this as a "fruitful vine." Yes, he did have two sons but most of his brothers had more than that. The "wild colts on a hillside" are interpreted to be the many Egyptian girls who would line up on the wall to get a glimpse of him because he was known for his great beauty (which had attracted Poti-phar's wife earlier). We read that wild archers assailed him and shot at him [49:23], which is, of course, figurative. It could refer to the treatment Joseph received at the hands of his brothers, or, more likely, to the treatment he received from Potiphar and his wife. Continuing this theme, we are told that "his bow remained taut" [49:24]. This is a thinly veiled phallic reference, hinting that Joseph had been aroused in his confrontation with Potiphar's wife. The verse continues by saying, "his arms remained strong." This is strangely interpreted to mean that his semen passed through his arms and exited his body through his fingers and into the ground, thus enabling him to resist her advances.[10]

Here, in Jacob's words to Joseph, is the first time that the word "bless/blessing" appears in this entire speech and it appears no less than six times in these last two verses! It is also the first time that the name of God is invoked. It seems that Jacob shows favoritism to Joseph right up until the end. Jacob asks that God bless Joseph with abundant rain, fruitfulness, fertility, and all the blessings which Jacob himself has enjoyed as part of the covenantal relationship with God. The blessing finishes by designating Joseph as the "elect of his brothers" [49: 26].

The remarkable and wondrous thing here is that Jacob can give this blessing without worrying about jealousy and strife arising between Joseph and his brothers.

So, Jacob is almost done. There is one son left.

SIXTH ALIYAH: GENESIS 49:27–50:20
FRIDAY, JANUARY 1, 2021

Jacob Died—or Did He?

Benjamin is compared to a "ravenous wolf" [49: 27] as the tribe of Benjamin was known to be comprised of fierce warriors. The first king of Israel, Saul, came from the tribe of Benjamin.

With this, Jacob has completed his blessings/predictions for his sons. Acknowledging that he is about to die, he instructs all his sons (he had previously asked Joseph to swear to him) to make sure that he is buried in the Cave of Machpelah along with his grandparents Avraham and Sarah, his parents Isaac and Rebekah, and his first wife, Leah [49:29-32].

Following this, Jacob takes his leave of Earth [49: 33]. Let's compare the verses that describe the deaths of our three patriarchs:

> And Abraham breathed his last, dying at a good ripe age, old and contented; and he was gathered to his kin. [25:8]
> when he [Isaac] breathed his last and died. He was gathered to his kin in ripe old age; and he was buried by his sons Esau and Jacob. [35:29]
> When Jacob finished his instructions to his sons, he drew his feet into the bed and, breathing his last, he was gathered to his people. [49:33]

Comparing the three, there is one glaring omission; all three breathe their last and all three are gathered to their people. However, only in the case of Avraham and Isaac does the Torah say that they died. The word *vayamot* (he died) does not appear in the verse describing the death of Jacob. This leads some of the sages to question whether Jacob really expired. Indeed, we have the following Talmudic reference:

> After they had eaten, Rabbi Yitzhak said to Rav Naḥman that
> Rabbi Yoḥanan said as follows: Our patriarch Jacob did not die.
> [BT Taanit 5B:9]

Clearly, from the rest of our reading in Genesis, we see that Jacob is embalmed (a forty-day process), and mourned (another thirty days), buried in the Cave of Machpelah, and mourned by his sons for another seven days [50:1-14]. So, how can anyone say that Jacob did not die?

I think the answer lies in the fact that Jacob was given a second name, Israel, when he wrestled with the angel the night before he reunited with his brother Esau. This was the name that sealed the covenant between him and his descendants and the Divine. This was the name with which he would fulfill his destiny of becoming a great nation. Indeed, in this reading we find the first occurrence in the Torah of the phrase "tribes of Israel" in reference to the descendants of Jacob [49:28]. We, all of us today, are the present-day descendants of Jacob, the descendants of Israel. Our very existence is testimony to the fact that the covenant between God and Israel is still binding and we are the heirs. So long as we remain faithful to that covenant, then indeed it can be said that Jacob did not die.

SEVENTH ALIYAH: GENESIS 50:21–26
WRITTEN FOR SHABBAT, SATURDAY, JANUARY 2, 2021

The End of the Beginning

After Jacob's burial in Canaan in the Cave of Machpelah, his sons return to Egypt. With Joseph in the powerful role of vizier and their father gone, the brothers again become anxious that Joseph will exact revenge for their having sold him into slavery so many years before. He reassures them that they need not worry [50:21].

Time passes. Joseph lives until the age of one hundred ten, seeing descendants to the third and fourth generation [50:22-23]. Realizing that his death is at hand, he has his brothers swear that when they eventually leave Egypt, they will bring his bones with them to bury him in the land of Canaan. As the Bekhor Shor points out, Joseph will no doubt receive a highly honored burial in

Egypt due to his high rank and position. Nevertheless, what ultimately matters more to him is to be buried among his own people in his own land.[11]

What is noticeable here is what he says to his brothers: "God will surely take notice of you" [50:24]. The verb form used here is what is known as an infinitive absolute, an expression of emphasis. Noticeably, with the repetition of the verb, we also see the repetition of the letter *peh*, which has a numerical value of eighty. Since Joseph ascended to power at the age of thirty and died at one hundred ten, he ruled over Egypt for eighty years.

Rashi points out the relationship of this verse to the following verse from next week's Torah reading in the book of Shemot: "Go and assemble the elders of Israel and say to them: the LORD, the God of your fathers, the God of Abraham, Isaac, and Jacob, has appeared to me and said, 'I have taken note of you and of what is being done to you in Egypt" [Exodus 3:16][12]

These words, using the same verb and the same verb form, also show the repetition of the letter *peh*. They were spoken to Moses at the burning bush when God first called to him regarding sending him to Egypt to redeem the nation from slavery. Moses was eighty years old when that happened!

So, even as one book ends and the nation of Israel has descended into Egypt where they will eventually be enslaved, the Torah already provides a hint, a glimpse, into the ultimate redemption that God will provide.

With this, we have completed the study of the Book of Bereshit. We have reached the end of the beginning (*Bereshit* means "in the beginning"). The descendants of Abraham, Isaac, and Jacob have become a nation. Now they will need to become a sovereign nation, dwelling once again in the land promised to them by God. That story begins in the book of Shemot.

חֲזַק חֲזַק וְנִתְחַזֵּק!

BOOK OF SHEMOT
Parashat Shemot

FIRST ALIYAH: EXODUS 1:1–17
SUNDAY, JANUARY 3, 2021

What's in a Name?

We have begun a new book of the Torah: Shemot, which means "names."
There is, however, a definite connection to the book of Genesis, indicating a
continuation of the story from one to the other in the first word *v'eleh*, ([and]
these are). Though the English translation usually does not include the word
"and," it is clearly indicated by the letter *vav* at the beginning of the first
word. The last verse of Genesis told us that Joseph died, and we go directly
from there to "[And] These are the names of the sons of Israel who came to
Egypt" [1:1]. The Baal HaTurim points out that the use of the phrase "the
names of the sons of Israel" indicates that the Jews in Egypt did not change
their Hebrew names (along with not changing their language, and not being
involved in gossip, this was one of the three things for which they merited
being redeemed from Egypt).[1] By connecting this first verse to the last verse
of Genesis through that *vav*, we are told that Joseph had told the Jews not to
change their names in Egypt. "They changed my name to Zaphenath-panea,"
he told them, "But you should not change your names." This name, you may
recall, was given to Joseph when he became the vizier of Egypt. Because of
his position as second in command to Pharaoh, it was necessary that he
assume an Egyptian identity. However, he did not want the members of his
extended family to assume an Egyptian identity.

Generations passed and the people of Israel were fertile and prolific,
multiplying greatly. Then we read that "A new king arose over Egypt who
did not know Joseph" [1: 8]. Fearing their numbers, he prevailed upon the
Egyptian people to oppress the Israelites severely, ultimately leading to

their enslavement. Since we are talking about names here, it is very ironic that this new Egyptian king is unnamed. Consequently, there is only speculation, no real certainty, about which Pharaoh is specifically referred to here. More importantly, much has been said about the second part of the verse, where we are told that this new king, "did not know Joseph." No matter how many generations had elapsed, we must wonder how he could possibly not have known Joseph. Surely, given the important position that Joseph had held in the Egyptian court, and the fact that he had literally saved the nation (as well as other surrounding nations) by collecting and then rationing food through the years of famine, his name surely would have been recorded in any accounting of Egyptian history. However, he would have been recorded there as Zaphenath-paneah, not as Joseph. As Sforno points out, it never occurred to this new Pharaoh that the vizier of Egypt could have been a Hebrew.[2] Hence, that is why we are told that he did not know Joseph.

Joseph was dressed in royal robes and rode in a royal chariot; his appearance, by necessity, was totally that of an Egyptian. Yet he knew himself that he was not Zaphenath-paneah, he was Yosef ben Yaakov. Despite his appearance and how he had to live his life, Joseph remained loyal to the faith of his ancestors, giving his sons Hebrew names, speaking to them in Hebrew, and raising them as Jews. We saw in the last *parashah* how, because they remained faithful to God, his sons Ephraim and Menashe merited to be the ones by whom all Jewish boys are blessed for all time.

Each of us has a Hebrew name. Though my driver's license identifies me as Margaret M. Cella, my conversion papers identify me as Margalit Moriel bat Avraham v'Sarah, and my ordination certificate added the title "HaRav" to the front of that. I wear a necklace that has my Hebrew name on it and very rarely take it off. For me, this is my true, more important identity, regardless of whatever else I may be involved in during my daily life. Even in a world that affords us freedom to exercise our faith, it is important that our identities be infused with our Torah values, and that we model the behavior that God demands of us. We must remain strong and confident in who and what we are and not allow our spirits to be subjugated to others.

So, ask yourself: by what name are you known to others?

God Sees the Goodness in Us All

At the end of the first *aliyah*, we read how Pharaoh had charged the mid-wives who attended to the Israelite women (who may or may not have been Israelites themselves, depending on how one reads the verse) to drown all the baby boys born to Jewish women. The two women, however, Shifrah and Puah, were unable to do so. At the beginning of this *aliyah*, Pharaoh confronts them about this and they answer that the Israelite women complete their labor too quickly, delivering (and presumably hiding) their babies before the midwives even arrive [1:18-19]. In response, Pharaoh now extends his instruction to the entire Egyptian population. All Jewish male babies are to be drowned in the Nile; only the females are to be permitted to live [1: 22].

All of this serves as background information for what comes next. We are told at the beginning of chapter two that a man from the tribe of Levi married a woman from the same tribe [2:1]. Though they are not named here, we know from subsequent events that these are Amram and Yocheved, the parents of Moses. Now, we also know from elsewhere in the Torah that Moses had two older siblings, Aaron and Miriam. That being the case, one of two scenarios must have occurred between verses 1 and 2 of this second chapter: these first two children were born, but their births were not recorded or (and this is the explanation that is favored by Rashi and Ramban, among others) the parents had actually divorced after the births of their first two children because of the harshness of Pharaoh's decree, but now were remarried.

In either case, verse 2 tells of Moses' birth: "The woman conceived and bore a son; and when she saw how beautiful he was, she hid him for three months." There is a wealth of commentary about this verse. The first question we may ask is: why did she have to hide him? The obvious answer is to protect him from any Egyptian who would seek to drown him in the Nile in compliance with Pharaoh's decree. But Rashi says there is more to it and notes that the Hebrew says, "she saw that he was good." This verse calls to mind the first chapter of Genesis and the creation story: "God saw that the light was good . . ." [1:4].

Indeed, in the Genesis story, the phrase, ". . . was good" is used no less than seven times to describe various parts of God's creation. Now the very same phrase is used to describe this child in his mother's eyes. According to Sarna, this "suggests that the birth of Moses is intended to be understood as the dawn of a new creative era."[3] Moreover, the Talmud states that since this phrase is used in reference to light in Genesis and Moses in Exodus, this tells us that the whole house was filled with light when he was born [*BT Sotah 12a:17*]. It was for this reason that his mother knew that she had to hide him because she was afraid that the Egyptians would see the light, enabling them to find the baby. Additionally, the great light would indicate to them that this child was destined to become the redeemer who would lead the nation of Israel out of Egyptian slavery. And finally, she knew that the great light of creation had been hidden away by God until a future time. So, too, she thought that she had to hide him away until the right time would arrive for him to redeem the nation.

Rashbam concentrates on the last part of the verse, which tells us that she hid the baby for three months. He points out that Moses' mother "saw" him, just as God "saw" the light of creation. In other words, she examined him carefully before announcing that he was good. Why? Because, Rashbam says, Moses was born three months prematurely, but his mother was able to ascertain that he was healthy and perfectly formed.[4] This, however, also explains why she was able to hide him away for three months. No one was expecting her to give birth for another three months, so no one came looking for her baby.

When the three months were up, she knew she could hide him no longer. Planning to tell anyone who came looking for her baby that she had had a stillbirth, she devised a drastic but clever plan. She placed him in a basket and set it floating in the Nile [2:3-4]. Once more, we find an interesting word play here. The word *teva*, used here to refer to the basket, occurs in only one other place in the *Tanakh*. It is the word used to refer to the ark that preserved the lives of Noah and his family during the great flood. Both items were life-preserving vessels that floated freely on the surface of the water, keeping their respective occupants alive through Divine providence.

As the well-known story of Moses continues, Miriam stands nearby to observe her baby brother's fate; Pharaoh's daughter discovers the basket when she comes to the Nile to bathe. Realizing that this is most likely an Israelite infant, she nevertheless decides to keep him and raise him herself. Miriam steps forward, offering to find a wetnurse for her among the Israelite women. She of course finds her own mother, Jocheved, who thereby is able to continue to nurse her own son. When he is weaned, she returns him to the palace, where Bitya (Pharaoh's daughter) adopts him as her own, naming him Moses (Moshe), meaning "I drew him from the water."

Moses, like Joseph, will be raised as an Egyptian in the royal palace. However, unlike Joseph, who was well aware of, and carefully guarded, his Jewish identity, Moses is only aware of his Egyptian identity and does not know that he has another name:

. . . Rabbi Meir says: "Tov" is his, Moses', real name, as it was given to him by his parents when he was born. Rabbi Yehuda says: His name was Toviya. Rabbi Neḥemya says: They said he was good because they saw that he was fit for prophecy. [*BT Sotah 12A:17*]

Unlike Joseph, Moses will have to discover his Hebrew identity. Moses will have to discover how good he is in the eyes of God. For now, his goodness will have to remain hidden.

Each of us, just like Moses, was created *b'tzelem Elohim,* in the image of God. Therefore, each of us has the potential for goodness. How does your Jewish identity shine through in your daily life?

THIRD ALIYAH: EXODUS 2:11–25
TUESDAY, JANUARY 5, 2021

Who Are You?

In this *aliyah,* Moses first begins to experience an identity crisis. The *aliyah* begins by telling us that Moses went out to his brothers to see their burdens [2:11]. Though we do not know for sure, the use of the term "his brothers" implies that Moses was somehow aware of the fact that the people of Israel were his kinsmen. My guess would be that this was a somewhat recent occurrence, and that that revelation had been the impetus for him to go out among his brothers. In any event, while he was checking out the status of his kinsmen, he spotted an Egyptian beating one of the Israelites. The Torah does not tell us the motivation for this beating; Rashi tells a *midrash* that the Egyptian had called the Hebrew out to work in the middle of the night so that he himself could go in and take advantage of the man's wife, who thought, due to her inability to see in the darkness, that she was having sex with her husband. The Hebrew returned home and realized what had happened. Consequently, the Egyptian, in trying to prevent the man from taking revenge on him, worked him very hard all day long and when he didn't work hard or fast enough, the Egyptian beat him. This, according to Rashi, was the scene that Moses came upon in his walk that day.[5]

We are told what Moses' reaction was to this scene: he "turned this way and that and, seeing no one about, he struck down the Egyptian and hid him in the sand" [2:12]. Upon first reading this verse, one might be inclined to think that Moses was looking around to see if anyone would see what he was about to do. A better interpretation is that Moses looked about, and, seeing no one else around to step into the situation, took it upon himself to intercede.

In any event, he killed the Egyptian and buried the body in the sand.

The next day when he went out among his kinsmen, he noticed two Jews struggling with each other. This time, when he went to intercede, he was rebuked by one of them, who asked, "Who made you ruler over us? Do you intend to kill me like you killed the Egyptian?" [2:14].

Moses realized that others were indeed aware of what he had done, including all the way into the palace, where Pharaoh already intended to kill him [2:15]. As a result, Moses ran away, leaving Egypt.

Arriving in the land of Midian, he went to the usual gathering place, the well. There he encountered seven shepherdesses, sisters who were the daughters of Jethro, the (High) Priest of Midian, and who were apparently being bullied by the other shepherds. Moses once again interceded, watering the women's flocks for them as his great-grandmother Rebekah had done so many years before for the camels of Eliezer, the servant of Abraham.

In telling their father about the encounter, Jethro's daughters said to him, "an Egyptian rescued us from the shepherds." Moses' clothing was still that of Egypt and, no doubt, the way in which he conducted himself also labelled him as an Egyptian (not to mention that Egyptian name). Moses knew he was a Jew, had even interceded on behalf of a fellow Jew. Other than that, however, he still carried himself as an Egyptian.

Yitro (also known here as Reuel) gave Moses his oldest daughter Tzippora as a wife [2:21]. Very soon, they had their first child, a son whom Moses named Gershom, which literally means, "[I have been] a stranger there." Once again, names are significant. What place was Moses referring to with the word "there?" He was referring back to Egypt where he himself had found that he was a stranger in a strange land—a Hebrew among Egyptians, an Egyptian among Hebrews. And now he was an Egyptian/Hebrew living with the priest of Midian and his family. Moses was by this time eighty years old. Having run away when he was still young, he had been struggling with his identity for a very long time.

Suddenly, the narrative switches back to Egypt, where the Pharaoh had died, only to be replaced by a new, crueler Pharaoh, who made the lives of the Israelites even more harsh than his predecessor. In their pain, the people of Israel cried out to God, who heard their call. God heard their cry and was determined to address the situation.

Whether Moses realized it or not, and indeed whether he was ready for it or not, his identity crisis was about to be resolved in a very vivid, decisive, and profound way.

We, too, sometimes face an identity crisis. Have you ever been asked whether you consider yourself to be a Jewish American or an American Jew? The question asks you to consider which of those two parts of your identity—American and Jew—is the dominant one, and which modifies the other. This is not always an easy question to answer. The way you answer it today may not be the way you answer it tomorrow, but it is important to contemplate.

FOURTH ALIYAH: EXODUS 3:1–15
WEDNESDAY, JANUARY 6, 2021

The Most Important Name of All

This *aliyah* contains what is likely the most important name in the entire Torah.

This is, of course, the well-known story of the burning bush. Moses, out tending the sheep of his father-in-law, encounters this bush that appears to be in flames, and yet, "the bush was not consumed" [3:2]. This verse has been adopted by the Jewish Theological Seminary as its motto, symbolic of the idea that the living fire of Torah study continues today, igniting the souls of all who study there without consuming them.

God speaks to Moses from the bush, telling him that God has heard the cry of the people from Egypt, and that God wants to send Moses to liberate them from bondage. With this, a lengthy discussion/disagreement ensues between Moses and God, in which Moses attempts to convince God that he is not the right man for the job. The first thing that he says is very telling: "who am I to go to Pharaoh?" [3:11]. I think that this is reflective of an internal identity crisis, as I mentioned in yesterday's reading; is he Egyptian or Hebrew, royalty or common man? The question could also indicate that he does not know what name to apply to himself. It is interesting that, unlike Joseph, whom we always refer to by his Hebrew name, Moses is forever known by the name that was bestowed upon him by the princess of Egypt, not the name that was given to him by his Hebrew parents. This *midrash* explains why that happened:

> And she called his name "Moses." From here, you can learn about
> the merit of those that perform acts of kindness. Even though
> Moses had many names, the only name that was set throughout
> the Torah was the name that Bathyah, daughter of Pharaoh, called
> him. Even the Holy One Blessed is He did not call him by another
> name. [*Shemot Rabbah 1:26*][6]

Continuing the discussion, God assures Moses that God will be with him, guaranteeing fulfillment of his mission and ultimately bringing him back to this same mountain together with the freed nation of Israel to worship God there [3:12]. Moses next asks what he is to tell the nation when he says that the God of Israel has sent him to them, and they ask: "what is His name?" [3:13]. The answer is *"ehiyeh asher ehiyeh."* This phrase has been studied and commented on for thousands of years. Several translations have been suggested: "I am that I am" (OJPS); "I will be as I will be" (Rashi)[7]; "I will be forever" (Rashbam)[7]; "I always am" (Ibn Ezra)[7]; "I will be with whom I will be" (Ramban)[8]; "I shall be as I shall be."

The first and third words of this phrase, which are identical in the Hebrew, are a verb: the third person masculine singular future form of the verb "to be." Based on this, some have coined the phrase, "God is a verb." What should be clear from all of this is the fluid nature of the Divine. God is both constant and ever-changing.

God is a constant source of strength and support in difficult times. Yet what exactly we need is not always the same, nor is it the same for every individual in similar circumstances.

As I write this, the Congress of the United States has reconvened after the disturbing events of this afternoon when angry mobs of protesters stormed the Capitol building.

We as a nation are hurting right now. We are shocked to the core by what we have witnessed today, something totally unlike anything we have ever seen in our lifetimes or even imagined that we would see.

May we, as a Jewish community, turn to our faith and turn to each other, and look to our God as a source of comfort in our time of need.

The final verse of this reading reiterates this for all time: This shall be My name forever, This My appellation for all eternity [3:15].

FIFTH ALIYAH: EXODUS 3:16–4:17
THURSDAY, JANUARY 7, 2021

Who Am I?

The discussion/disagreement continues between God and Moses, though God seems to be doing most of the talking. After promising once again to be with Moses in leading the people out of Egypt to a land flowing with milk and honey, God instructs Moses to go to the king of Egypt and tell him that the Israelites need to go a three days' journey into the wilderness to worship. God indicates to Moses, however, that the Pharaoh will not let them go until God exerts some force, and that when they eventually leave, the Egyptian people will give them gifts of gold and silver [3:18-22].

Moses speaks up again, protesting that the people of Israel will not believe him. In response, God gives him three signs that he can use: his rod will turn into a serpent, his hand will turn leprous when he puts it into his cloak and brings it out again, and he will be able to turn water from the Nile into blood [4:1-9].

Still unconvinced, Moses has a further objection: "I am slow of speech and slow of tongue" [4:10]. Some commentators suggest that this simply means that Moses' objection was that it had been so many years since he had spoken Egyptian that he wasn't very good at it anymore, having forgotten a lot. But most feel that Moses is saying that he had some form of speech impediment. A *midrash* tells this story of what happened when Moses was a baby:

> . . . And it was that Pharaoh would kiss him (Moses) and hug him, and he would remove Pharaoh's crown and place it on his own head . . . And some of the observers sitting among them were the magicians of Egypt that said, "We are wary of this, that he is taking your crown and placing it on his head, that he not be the one we . . . [prophesy] that will take the kingship from you." Some said to kill him and some said to burn him. And Jethro was sitting among them and said to them, "This child has no intent [to take the throne]. Rather, test him by bringing in a bowl [a piece of] gold and a coal. If he outstretches his hand towards the gold, [surely] he has intent [to take the throne], and you should kill him. And if he outstretches his hand towards the coal, he [surely] does not have intent [to take the throne], and he does not deserve the death penalty." They immediately brought the bowl before him (Moses), and he outstretched his hand to take the gold, and [the angel] Gabriel came and pushed his (Moses) hand, and he grabbed the coal. He then brought his hand along with the coal into his mouth and burned his tongue, and from this he was made "slow of speech and slow of tongue." [*Shemot Rabbah 1:26*][9]

And what exactly was this speech impediment? Most commentators say that Moses stuttered. This would explain his objection that he was "slow of speech and slow of tongue." In response, God asks Moses, "Who gives man speech?" [4:11]. Once again, God promises to be with Moses and to instruct him what to say. Surely, since the implication is that God gives the power of speech, it must also be true that God could heal Moses' speech impediment. Clearly, that was not part of God's plan. Bekhor Shor says that God meant to say, "I could heal you, but I will look more impressive if I can make a stutterer perform my mission."[10] In other words, how much greater would it be if, instead of taking Moses' stutter away, God would give him the confidence to speak to the people and the Pharaoh with his stutter.

Moses interrupts God one more time (he seems to be speaking okay here!) to try one last time, begging God to send someone else. Finally, God becomes angry, promising to send his brother Aaron with Moses to the people and Pharaoh. Aaron will be his spokesman [4:13-17].

Ironically, we have already seen in the final three books of the Torah (and we will see in this book as well) that Moses did most of the talking. Moses spoke a lot and Aaron spoke very little. He was apparently able to overcome his stutter and become an effective leader in Israel.

I think that this is no coincidence that we are reading this story this week as the Congress has finally certified the results of the Electoral College, affirming that Joseph Biden will be our next president. It is well known that President Elect Biden had a stuttering problem in his younger years and has worked hard to overcome it. It is still noticeable at times when he speaks today, when he sometimes needs to slow down to get a word out. He has had a long career in public service and politics, and, in addition to his speech difficulties, has had to deal with great personal adversity in the tragic loss of his first wife and daughter, and in recent years his son.

God promised to be with Moses so long as he undertook the leadership of the nation of Israel—even with a stutter—and to give him the strength and support that he would need to guide the people through difficult times. So, too, should we all be praying that God will be with our incoming president as he undertakes the leadership of the United States—even with a stutter—and give him the strength and support that he will need to guide our nation through very turbulent times. The well-being of each of us, and, indeed, of the entire country, depends on it.

Dereliction of Duty

And so, finally convinced, Moses asks Jethro if he can take his leave of him [4:18]. God assures Moses that all those who had wanted to kill him (i.e., the Pharaoh) have died (a new Pharaoh sits on the throne [4:19]). Moses sets out with his wife Tzipora and their two sons (yes, there is a second, Eliezer, though we haven't heard anything about him yet) [4:20]. God assures Moses that, even though he will perform all the signs that God had given to him, God will harden Pharaoh's heart so that he will not let the people of Israel go. Moses is to tell Pharaoh that Israel is God's firstborn, and that, in return for not letting them go, God will kill his firstborn [4:21-23].

What follows next is indeed a very strange incident [4:24-26]. We are told that along the way, God sought to kill "him." It is not entirely clear whom this refers to. Moses? His firstborn son, Gershom? Or possibly, though not likely, Moses' second son, Eliezer? In any event, somehow Tziporah is able to discern the reason for this sudden attack and learns that Moses' son(s) is/are not circumcised. Now, if Moses was unsure of his identity (Egyptian or Israelite? And living as a Midianite?) that could possibly explain why he had never circumcised his son(s). However, he is headed back to be the one who will lead the people of Israel out of Egyptian slavery. We already know that he will have difficulty getting the people to accept him. If he has not fulfilled the primary *mitzvah* representing the covenant between God and Israel, what kind of role model will he be? Tzipora takes matters into her own hands, literally. Picking up a piece of flint (these desert stones are extremely sharp), she performs the circumcision herself, throwing the foreskin at her husband and calling him a "bridegroom of blood."

As a point of fact, we do not hear about Tzipora again until much later on, in the book of Deuteronomy, as the nation prepares to enter the land. It seems that Moses sent her and the boys back to Midian so they would not distract him from fulfilling his mission of redeeming the nation from Egyptian slavery. In effect, from this point on, Tzipora and Moses become estranged.

The obligation to circumcise one's son belongs to the father. Was Moses ashamed that his wife had had to do this since he himself had not? Or were they already experiencing marital difficulties by this point, and Tziporah's harsh reaction to having to do what Moses neglected to do was merely a reflection of that? It's difficult to say.

One thing is for sure: those who are called to fulfill important roles for God as Moses often had find that their family relationships suffer and spouses and children become estranged due to lack of attention. Having such a close relationship with the Divine doesn't offer time or space for close relationships with human beings. That is the tragic part of being a leader.

What about those of us who are not great leaders like Moses? Those of us who are just "regular people?" Are there things that come between us and those we love? Work? Other interests? Or maybe sometimes just lack of awareness? And these days maybe COVID? All of these can put strains on relationships. If there is anything that this last year has taught us, it must be that we need to examine our lives and our priorities. We have all read far too many stories of people who unexpectedly and tragically lost loved ones this year, sometimes without having an opportunity to say goodbye. If any of this rings true for you, then perhaps it is time to reexamine your priorities. Don't allow a spouse to become a "bridegroom of blood."

SEVENTH ALIYAH: EXODUS 5:1–6:1
WRITTEN FOR SHABBAT, SATURDAY, JANUARY 9, 2021

Do You Know God?

Finally, Moses and Aaron go to visit Pharaoh and deliver the message that they received from God: "Let my people go that they may serve me in the wilderness." What was Pharaoh's response? "I don't know the Lord, and I will not let you go" [5:2].

In *Midrash Mishlei*, the story is told that when Pharaoh ascended the throne, he received congratulatory letters from kingdoms all around him (in much the same way that President Elect Biden has received congratulatory messages and phone calls from world leaders around the globe). But Pharaoh did not recall having received a message from "the Lord," so he had his royal servants bring to him all the communications he had received. Sure enough, there was nothing in there that said it was from God. Therefore, Pharaoh said that he did not know God.[11] Pharaoh made it all about himself and his perspective. If he didn't/couldn't know God, then how important could this God have been? After all, didn't the Egyptians consider Pharaoh himself to be a god? Of course, we know how this ends: Pharaoh will come to know the God of Israel the hard way through being on the receiving end of the ten plagues!

Moses and Aaron, on the other hand, have a very profound answer. They tell Pharaoh, "The God of the Hebrews has manifested Himself to us . . ." [5:3]. We might ask, what exactly does that mean? Some translations say that God "has met with us" but I think that the meaning goes deeper than

HINDSIGHT IS 2020

that. The Hebrew verb *nikrah* used here comes from the root *koreh*, which usually has to do with being "named." For example, in the Torah we often see the phrase, "and he called his name . . ." in reference to giving a child a name. But the verb form used in our phrase is a reflexive form called *nifal*, meaning "to be called" or "to meet (unexpectedly)" or "to (chance to) be present." This meeting implies an intimate encounter, coming to know someone by name.

We have seen that God was revealed to Moses by name at the burning bush when Moses asked what name he should use to describe the One who dispatched him to save the people from slavery. God was introduced to Moses in a state of intimacy, and then Moses in turn introduced God to the rest of the nation in the same spirit.

Pharaoh doesn't know God because he is looking for a god who will meet him on his terms, praising him as the ruler of Egypt. Moses, and by extension the nation of Israel, know God in an open, intimate relationship.

And so, we have come full circle in this first *parashah* of the book of Shemot (names). It began with the names of all those who went down to Egypt. We learned that Joseph, a Hebrew who served as the vizier of Egypt, was apparently unknown to the Egyptians by his Hebrew name. We learned that Moses, the designated redeemer of Israel, was known only by his Egyptian name. And we learned that Moses asked God to reveal to him what name to use to refer to the Divine. And here we learn that this is the name by which God becomes manifest to us, the name by which God is present with us.

God is present with us today no less than God was with the fledgling nation looking for freedom. We, too, long for freedom today: freedom from oppression for the members of our society, freedom from want for ourselves and others, freedom from the feelings of anxiety and insecurity that come from experiencing events like those that occurred in our nation's capital this week, and most of all, we long for freedom from COVID-19. May we be blessed to reclaim the intimate relationship with God that allows us to say, "God has made himself known to us . . ."

Parashat Vaera

FIRST ALIYAH: EXODUS 6:2–13
SUNDAY, JANUARY 10, 2021

We All Must Play a Part

God tells Moses that God revealed God's self to the three patriarchs, Abraham, Isaac, and Jacob [6:2]. In one of those early conversations with Abraham, God foretold the Egyptian slavery: ". . . Know well that your offspring shall be strangers in a land not theirs, and they shall be enslaved and oppressed four hundred years . . ." [Genesis 15:13].

God told Abraham that the period of slavery would be four hundred years but in actuality, it was "only" two hundred ten years. There are various explanations of this given by the commentators. Among these is an interesting *midrash* cited by the Baal HaTurim.[1] The three patriarchs stood before God and interceded on behalf of their descendants for the duration of the time they were enslaved, asking God to release them from their Egyptian bondage. God challenged all three of them: were any of them willing to give up letters from their name? If so, God would reduce the number of years of slavery by the numerical value of the letters they gave up. Both Abraham and Jacob insisted that they needed all of the letters in their names [remember that they had both had their names changed by God]. Isaac, however, insisted that his name should not be spelled *Yitzchak* (יצחק) [with a *tzadee*]. Instead, it should be spelled as it is in this verse from Psalms: ". . . that He made with Abraham, swore to Isaac," *Yischak,* (ישחק) [with a *sin*] [Psalm 105:9].

Notice that there is a difference of one letter and the usual *tzadee* (ninety) is replaced by a *sin* (three hundred). Since 300- 90=210, Isaac, the one patriarch who had never had his name changed by God, suggested that the years of slavery should be reduced to two hundred ten.

The story doesn't necessarily have any great profound meaning. Nevertheless, due to my love of all things having to do with numbers, I find it fascinating.

In any event, there is another, probably more well-known, and certainly more relevant, numerical citation that comes from this *aliyah*. God directs Moses to tell the people all the things that God is going to do for them to end their enslavement [6:6-7]. There are four verbs that are used by God that indicate promises being made: I will free you, [I will] deliver you, [I will] redeem you, and I will take you.

According to both the Palestinian Talmud and *Midrash* Bereshit Rabbah, these four citations are the reason for the four cups of wine at our seders. Wine at the seder is a symbol of joy; each of these promises, made and fulfilled by God, is a cause for rejoicing. Some scholars, however, note that there is really a fifth verb: "and I will be your God" [6-7]. The first four actions all occurred in the biblical account but this fifth action began in the Torah and is an ongoing verb in each generation, time, and place: I will be. Each of us today can experience this intimate relationship with the Divine no less than the generation of the Exodus. And so, some people consider Elijah's cup to be a fifth cup, representing this fifth verb and the promise of future redemption. Each family has its own traditions at the seder. At my seder, Elijah's cup sits on the table empty until we get to that point in the Haggadah. We then pass the cup around the table and each person pours a little bit of wine from his/her own cup into Elijah's, symbolizing the idea that each of us needs to play our part in ushering in this future redemption of the world. Each of us needs to be involved in perfecting the world that has been entrusted to us by God. Not only that, but we also need to pool our efforts together to make that happen. Redemption can happen only when we can all work together. That is the symbolism of Elijah's Cup.

I will be that I will be.

SECOND ALIYAH: EXODUS 6:14–28
MONDAY, JANUARY 11, 2021

Rivalry No More

At this point in the story, there is a break for genealogy. Unlike the one given at the beginning of the book of Exodus, however, this does not include the descendants of all the sons of Jacob. Instead, it is limited in scope, calling attention to one tribe in particular.

It begins normally enough by listing the descendants of Reuben then Simeon (Jacob's first two sons) [6:14-15]. Next is Levi. The names of his sons are given, along with his age [6:16] and already we notice a difference. Next, we learn the names of the sons of all of Levi's sons [6:17-19]. Clearly, we see some favoritism shown here to the tribe of Levi. Why? The answer becomes clear when we read the next verse. We read that a man and a woman from the tribe of Levi, Amram and Yocheved, married, and she gave birth to two sons, Aaron and Moses [6:20]. This is the reason for the genealogy—to give us the lineage of the two brothers who are about to become the main players in this story, who will be the leaders of the nation of Israel, shepherding them from slavery to freedom. It is very strange, though, that in a genealogy that does include the names of some women, among them Moses' and Aaron's mother, and Aaron's wife, there does seem to be one glaring omission. Left out of the list is their sister Miriam, who will also play a part in the leadership of the nation. (There do exist, however, other versions of the text that include the words, "and their sister Miriam.")

After delineating the sons of two of Levi's grandsons [6:21-22], we are told the name and lineage of Aaron's wife, Elisheva, as well as the names of the four sons she bore to Aaron, and then the name of one of Aaron's grandsons [6:25].

Finally, it is reiterated to us (just in case we didn't know or couldn't figure it out by now) that these are the same Aaron and Moses who went to speak to Pharaoh [6:26-27]. Since they are about to embark on their important leadership roles, we are given their *yichus*, their credentials. Just as Moses needed to know what name to use when telling the nation Who sent him, the people also needed to know whothese men were who were about to begin a mission to lead them out of slavery to freedom.

One significant trend that they seem to upend is the rivalry between brothers which we have seen as an ongoing theme, with the younger invariably upstaging the firstborn. Moses is younger, and clearly has the stronger leadership role. Nevertheless, we know that Aaron is destined to become the first *Cohen Gadol,* the first High Priest, and the ancestor of the priesthood.

To bring this home, in verse 26, the brothers are listed as Aaron and Moses; in verse 27, they are listed as Moses and Aaron. Together, they form a partnership. For their mission to be successful, that is a necessity.

Pride Comes Before the Fall

Now that we have seen the pedigree of Aaron and Moses, God tells them again what is going to happen: the two of them will go to speak to Pharaoh, repeating to him everything that God has told them to say. As such, they will operate as God's messengers [6:29-7:3]. However, God tells them in advance that Pharaoh will not listen to them, but instead God will harden his heart. Much has been made of this by the commentators. If God hardened Pharaoh's heart, what does that say about free will? Did Pharaoh have no chance to repent, to change his mind? The answer given is that, for the first five plagues, the text tells us that Pharaoh himself hardened his own heart. It will not be until the sixth plague that we are told that God hardened his heart. Pharaoh did indeed have the opportunity to repent. Not only did he not do that, but, with each time that he hardened his heart it became more and more difficult for him to do so. After five plagues, Pharaoh's continued obstinance increasingly became a danger to himself and his people, who no doubt followed his lead in denying God and God's powers. This all began because Pharaoh had said, "Who is [God] that I should heed his voice . . . ? I do not know [God]." Apparently, his arrogant attitude had spread to the rest of the Egyptians because here we read that the reason God would harden Pharaoh's heart is so that God would be able to demonstrate God's power, multiplying the number and intensity of the plagues, in order that "the Egyptians shall know that I am the LORD" [7:5]. Pharaoh and his people did not recognize the power or the authority of the Lord. Yet, in the end, they were not able to escape that power or authority. Unable to admit that he was wrong, Pharaoh was stubbornly entrenched in his denial of the inevitable—that the people of Israel would indeed be freed from Egypt. At the same time, he remained unwilling/unable to see the damaging effects of his behavior.

I have never been able to understand how Pharaoh (or any other person, for that matter) could continue to harden his heart, despite all the proof of God's power shown to him, until he reached a point where he was incapable of conceding, unable to admit that he was powerless to change the situation.

I still don't understand it. But, sadly, like the rest of our nation, I have seen with my own eyes that it can, indeed, happen.

I'll Believe It When I See It

Here, at last, the confrontation between Moses and Aaron and the Pharaoh of Egypt begins. Following God's instructions, the brothers produced the first sign. Aaron cast down his rod and it turned into a serpent (or some type of large reptile. The text is not quite clear). Nonplussed, Pharaoh called his magicians, who were able to replicate this with their own rods. However, God's power was demonstrated when the snake that had been Aaron's rod swallowed up the snakes that had been the rods of the Egyptian magicians [7:8-12]. As God had foretold to Moses, "Pharaoh's heart was stiffened," and he refused to let the people of Israel go [7:13]. This thought is reiterated in verse 14: *kaved lev Paroh*, translated here as "Pharaoh is stubborn," but it really means "Pharaoh's heart is hardened."

Pharaoh still needed to be convinced of God's power and authority over creation and it was time for the plagues to begin. God instructed Moses and Aaron to meet Pharaoh at the Nile, where he regularly went every morning. After announcing what they were about to do, Aaron was to strike the waters of the river with his rod. The waters would turn to blood and, as a result, all the fish would die, causing a great stink to arise in the land, and the people of Egypt would have no desire to drink the water [7:15-21]. The Egyptian sorcerers were able to locate some water that had not turned to blood, and they were able to replicate the miracle. Nevertheless, Pharaoh's heart would continue to be hardened [7:22-23]. The waters of the Nile would remain as blood for seven full days, leaving the Egyptians with nothing to drink [7:25].

This was followed by the plague of frogs. Once again, the waters of the Nile played a role. Aaron stretched out his hand over the water, and the frogs came up out of the river and inundated the land. They were literally everywhere: in the bedrooms, on the people, in the ovens. Once again, the magicians were also able to replicate this miracle. However, they were unable to make the frogs go away as only God and his servants could do that [7:26-8:7].

That these first two plagues struck the Nile was significant because the river was a god to the Egyptians. Clearly, God was demonstrating that He has mastery over the gods of Egypt. Moreover, water is essential for life. Yet we also know that God has told us repeatedly that the life of humans and animals is in the blood and that is why, since the time of Noah, we are forbidden to eat any blood.

Additionally, the first plague clearly shines a light on the callousness of the Egyptian people who all had participated in the drowning of the Israelite male babies, thus who all had blood on their hands (there was blood throughout the land of Egypt) [7:21]. Now that blood could clearly be seen by all. Because the fish died and the water stank, they were loath to drink from the water [7:18]. One has to wonder if they had been okay with drinking the water when it was filled with the blood of Israelite babies.

When the river brought forth the frogs of the second plague, it was as if the river was punishing the Egyptian people for making it complicit in the murders of the Israelite children.

At the same time, God was sending a message to the people of Israel: the sin of the Egyptians is known and has been brought to light and God is punishing them. God had said that the purpose of the plagues was to cause both Pharaoh and his people to know that God is the Lord. In addition, the people of Israel also needed to be convinced of God's power. They had been so beaten down and oppressed for such a long time that it was difficult for them to perceive God's immanence.

We, too, may find it difficult to see God's providence in our world today. The social, political, and physical problems we have lived with for almost a year are wearing us down. The turmoil our country has experienced, including today's contentious second impeachment of President Trump in one year's time, and the fear of more and increased violence in the next week leading up to the inauguration, are wearing on the nerves of us all. Many suffer from high levels of anxiety. Yet, in the midst of all this, many of us are receiving or will soon receive our vaccinations for COVID-19. And in a week's time, we will have a new president. There is hope that we will be released from much that has plagued us this past year. Let us hold fast to that hope and move forward together to heal our country and our world.

FIFTH ALIYAH: EXODUS 8:7–18
THURSDAY, JANUARY 14, 2021

Frogs, Lice, and Insects—Oh My!

Moses entreated God to stop the plague of the frogs and the frogs died and piled up all over the land, causing it to stink yet again. Still, Pharaoh hardened his heart [8:7–11].

The next plague came without warning to Pharaoh. Aaron used his rod to strike the dust and it became lice throughout the land of Egypt, once again making everyone miserable. Those of you who have children can no doubt remember at least one time when that fateful note came home from school, informing you that a student in your child's class was found to have head lice. I remember well the first time this happened when my kids were young. By the time they came home with the notice, we found that all four of us already had lice! Everything in the house had to be stripped and washed and we all had to use delousing shampoo. It was horrible! I'm sure many of you can relate. We can only imagine what it must have been like in Egypt.

This time, the Egyptian magicians were unable to replicate the miracle. In acknowledging that this is beyond the scope of their capabilities, they said to Pharaoh, "this is the finger of God." This is an interesting phrase and appears only two other times in the Torah: "When He [God] finished speaking with him [Moses] on Mount Sinai, He gave Moses the two tablets of the Pact, stone tablets inscribed with the finger of God [31:18]. And ". . . the LORD gave me the two tablets of stone inscribed by the finger of God with the exact words that the LORD had addressed to you on the mountain out of the fire . . . [Deuteronomy 9:10].

Each of these other verses refer to the tablets of stone on which the Ten Commandments were written with "the finger of God." How strange that the same phrase should be used to describe the tablets and the lice. Sarna says that it refers to "a supernatural phenomenon beyond human control."[2] So, it seems that Pharaoh's servants are now coming to the point of recognizing and knowing the presence and handiwork of God, whereas their ruler, on the other hand, continues to harden his heart [8:15].

Time for another plague. So, God told Moses and Aaron to go back to Pharaoh in the morning and inform him that the land would be filled with swarms of insects that would be everywhere—on their persons, in their houses, on the ground [8:15-17]. No doubt, with all those dead fish and frogs laying around, the insects found plenty to feast on. Some scholars say that these were not really swarms of insects, but rather swarms of wolves or foxes or some mixture of other species that would have made them deadly, not just annoying.

There is one thing that is different about this plague. For the first time, God announced that there would be a separation between Egypt proper and Goshen so that the people of Israel would not be affected by this plague [8:18]. This, of course, could also leave no doubt in their minds Who was the source of this plague, for the animals (especially if they were insects) could not possibly be that discerning.

Once again, the message was meant not only for Pharaoh and his people, but also for the people of Israel: God has the power to control nature, for, after all, everything in nature has been created by God. Now, in addition, they could see that the plagues were aimed solely at the Egyptians with the aim of convincing them to allow the people of Israel go free. Unfortunately, Pharaoh wasn't getting the message yet, and, therefore, sadly, neither were his people.

SIXTH ALIYAH: EXODUS 8:19–9:16
FRIDAY, JANUARY 15, 2021

Past the Point of No Return?

This *aliyah* picks up where the last one left off, with God telling Pharaoh (through Moses) that with this plague, there will be a distinction between the Egyptians and the Israelites. True to God's word, that is exactly what happened [8:19-20]. Pharaoh begins to suspect that God was angry because the Israelites had not been able to offer sacrifices, which were a common form of worship for most near-Eastern cultures in the ancient world. To that end, Pharaoh told Moses and Aaron to go and sacrifice in the land of Egypt. This, of course, was not what they had asked for; they had asked to be given permission to go into the desert to sacrifice. Moses explained to Pharaoh that he thought that the sight of them sacrificing animals to God would appear as an abomination to the Egyptians, who apparently did not eat meat. Moses said that they would go instead on a three days' journey into the wilderness. Pharaoh agreed, admonishing them not to go too far (how far did he think 2,000,000 people would get in three days?). Moses asked God to remove the swarms and warned Pharaoh not to go back on his word again. God removed the insects completely. Pharaoh apparently had a very short memory, and so his heart was hardened yet again, refusing to let the people go [8:21-28].

Time for the next plague. This time, it would be more than annoying: it would be a deadly pestilence affecting the cattle and livestock of the Egyptians. Before, Pharaoh's magicians had recognized the work of the "finger of God." Now, Moses declared that the "hand of God" would be on the animals of Egypt. The hand of God is representative of God's power and strength. God again declared that there would be a distinction between the Egyptian animals and those of the Israelites so that only Egyptian animals would die. In this case, the separation between Egyptians and Israelites would be even more obvious, as all the animals grazed in the same area, both near and among each other. Pharaoh sent for news, only to have it affirmed to him that not one of the Israelites' animals perished. And yet even with this evidence of the specificity of God's power, Pharaoh's heart remains hardened [9:1-7].

Time for another plague. This one would physically affect human beings as well as animals, not killing them but making them extremely uncomfortable. Moses and Aaron threw handfuls of dust from the furnace into the air and it dissipated, becoming boils and sores on people and animals throughout Egypt [9:8-9]. We haven't heard about the magicians since the plague of the lice, which they were not able to duplicate. It would be reasonable, however, to assume that Pharaoh called them to him with each new plague to see if they had the power to reproduce it. Here, because the magicians themselves were afflicted with boils, they were unable to even appear before Pharaoh and Moses as they were utterly defeated and embarrassed. Thus, God was showing definitively that the gods of Egypt were no match for God. Now, finally, we are told that the Lord hardened Pharaoh's heart [9:10-12]. Ramban suggests that, prior to this, whenever we were told that Pharaoh's heart was hardened, it was due to the influence of his magicians. Now, without them there to egg him on, he did it himself.[3]

The more evidence of God's power and authority is presented to Pharaoh, the more he digs in his heels, refusing to acknowledge the reality of what is being shown to him, all the while dragging his people down with him. Sound familiar?

Now Moses told Pharaoh once again that he must let the Israelites go in order that they could serve God. If not, God warned that, "I will send all My plagues upon your person . . ." [9:14]. However, the Hebrew really says, "upon your heart." In other words, it was now no holds barred. Pharaoh's stubbornness meant that God would now hurl upon him, and his people, plagues even more severe, calling upon every element of God's creation. Ultimately, the tenth plague will break Pharaoh's heart. Because he has refused to allow God's firstborn, the nation of Israel, to go free, he himself will lose his own firstborn son.

SEVENTH ALIYAH: EXODUS 9:17–35
WRITTEN FOR SHABBAT, SATURDAY, JANUARY 16, 2021

It Didn't Have to Be This Way

Moses, speaking for God, accused Pharaoh of continuing to "thwart" the nation of Israel [9:17]. Several commentators (Rashi, Rashbam) say that this really means "suppress."[4] Because the Egyptians continued to treat the Israelites harshly with cruel punishment and enslavement, God was meting out this harsh punishment on them in return. Ibn Ezra says that it means "you continue to extol yourself."[4] In other words, you continue to praise yourself, saying how great you are, and thinking that God cannot force you to do anything that you don't want to do. Pride and arrogance prevent Pharaoh from feeling either remorse or compassion.

Moses announced that the next plague, beginning the next day, would be hail so severe that any person or animal caught outside would die. He warned the Egyptians not only to stay inside themselves, but also to bring in their slaves and their animals [9:18-19]. Some say that this warning demonstrated God's compassion, allowing the people of Egypt an opportunity to save themselves, that God did not want to kill them, only punish them. Truthfully, we know from two verses that seem to be almost out of place here [9:31-32] what crops were ruined by the hail—flax and barley—crops upon which the Egyptian economy was heavily dependent. Thus, this is believed to be the real rationale for the plague: economic destruction.

Those who paid no heed to, or disregarded, the word of the Lord, did not bring in their slaves and animals from outside [9:21]. The Hebrew phrase, however, is literally, "did not set his heart towards" the word of the Lord. These are people who clearly followed Pharaoh's lead, hardening their own hearts, and failing to acknowledge the power of God. Egypt is a land that rarely sees rain—much less hail—so they failed to believe that what Moses told them would indeed occur.

And so, Moses stretched out his hand towards heaven and brought forth the hail and thunder so severe that it behaved in unnatural ways: fire rained down (instead of up) and hail (which is made from frozen water) mixed with fire. Two opposing substances worked together at the will of their Creator. Again, this is further evidence of God's sovereignty over nature (and therefore all the gods of Egypt). Once again, the land of Goshen was spared, and the hail and fire stopped at the border [9:21-26].

Pharaoh called Moses and Aaron to him. Expressing contrition, he asked Moses to pray to God, asking that the fire and hail cease. If they do so, he says that he will keep them in Egypt no longer [9:27-29]. Yet, once again, after God heeds Moses' prayer and the hail and thunder cease, Pharaoh continues to harden his heart, changes his mind, and does not allow the people of Israel to leave [9:33-35].

We are witnessing a battle of wills between a human ruler and a Divine ruler. God had made the lives of the Egyptians miserable with water turned to blood, frogs, lice, insects, cattle disease, boils, and hail; their animals had died, their crops had been destroyed, and they had suffered physically themselves. Yet so many of them had blindly followed Pharaoh's lead, all the while denying God's power and ultimately prolonging the inevitable. Pharaoh was so blinded by his own rage that he cared little how much his own people suffered.

But not all the Egyptians felt this way. We will see that, just as God predicted, many Egyptians showered Israelites with jewelry and gifts when they finally left Egypt and many even decided to go with them.

We can only wonder how different things might have been if Pharaoh had not been so stubborn.

Parashat Bo

FIRST ALIYAH: EXODUS 10:1–11
SUNDAY, JANUARY 17, 2021

It's All About the *Kinder*

The story continues. God wants Moses to return to Pharaoh's presence yet again to announce the next plague. God calls to Moses and says *"bo el Paroh,"* translated here as *"go to Pharaoh."* However, the Hebrew word *"bo"* from which the *parashah* gets its name, really means "come." How can that be? That would seem to be a major error in translation. The commentators were uncomfortable with the idea of God saying "come to Pharaoh" for that would imply that God was with Pharaoh, an idea that they were unable to reconcile. The Bechor Shor translates this way: "come with me, and I will go with you."[1] This is a very different way of looking at the situation. God is promising to be with Moses from the outset when he goes to Pharaoh. God is not sending Moses on a mission alone because God is by his side as they approach the Egyptian monarch together.

Why does God make this promise for this plague? Because by this time, Pharaoh's heart is beyond repentance: "I have hardened his heart and the heart of his courtiers" [10:1]. Their hearts are beyond repenting; Egypt cannot be spared the further punishments God will mete out on them for enslaving the people of Israel. But remember that God has a second purpose here. Not only the Egyptians, but also the Israelites, need to be convinced of God's power, "that you may recount in the hearing of your sons and of your sons' sons how I made a mockery of the Egyptians" [10:2]. And this is exactly what we have done at our seders right on down through the present day. We tell our children and grandchildren about the great wonders that God performed for us to redeem us from slavery.

This idea is reflected again later in the reading after Moses has declared to Pharaoh that the next plague visited upon his people will be locusts. Pharaoh's courtiers urge him to let the men of Israel go to worship their God [10:7]. Pharaoh calls Aaron and Moses back to him to ask who will go to participate in this worship. Moses answers: "We will all go, young and old: we will go with our sons and daughters" [10:9]. Moses is adamant that the entire nation is included. Pharaoh's courtiers had said *shalach et ha'anashim* (let the men go) [10:7]. The Baal haTurim points out that the gematria of this phrase is equivalent to that of the phrase *gedolim im katanim* (adults and children).[2] Moses is not leaving without the children. They are the ones who will have the opportunity to enter the promised land. They are the future!

And so it has been for us as Jews ever since. Every year on *Pesach,* we sit down to the seder to reenact the story of the Exodus from Egypt. The children ask the questions and we adults provide the answers. So important is this *mitzvah* that last year the members of the CJLS (Committee on Jewish Law and Standards, the governing body on *halachah* for the Rabbinical Assembly of the Conservative Movement) enabled us to use technology to host a seder by Zoom. The question, "How is this night different from all other nights?" suddenly took on a new meaning.

This year, *Pesach* comes early, at the end of March. Though vaccine distribution has begun, it still seems likely that for many of us the seders will take place over the internet once again. And God-willing, before the year is out, we will be redeemed from the imprisonment that has been imposed on us by COVID-19.

May we see the day, in the not-so-distant future, when we will be able to regather in the synagogue to worship. All of us, young and old, will go, with our sons and our daughters.

SECOND ALIYAH: EXODUS 10:12–23
MONDAY, JANUARY 18, 2021

Reach Out in the Darkness[3]

This reading begins with the eighth plague. Locusts descended upon the land of Egypt in unprecedented numbers, covering every possible space, devouring all the greenery of the land. Pharaoh called Moses to him yet again, asking him to entreat God to remove the locusts. As he left Pharaoh's presence, Moses did so. God caused a strong west wind to come up and drive all the locusts into the sea. Once again, however, as soon as the immediate threat was removed, Pharaoh's heart was hardened and he changed his mind, refusing to allow the people of Israel to leave [10:12-20].

Time for plague number nine: darkness. Like plagues three and six, this one came upon the Egyptians unannounced. Moses raised his hands towards the sky and a thick, tangible darkness descended upon Egypt, so thick that people could feel it, so thick that people were immobilized, unable to move from their place for three days' time [10: 21-23]. Darkness can be very frightening because it contains the unknown. Every horror movie ever made has seminal scenes that occur when scary things come out of the dark. The audience waits with bated breath on the edge of their seats, knowing that something waits in the darkness to terrorize them, and they have no control over.

A friend who owned a sailboat once told me about traveling from Florida to New York. She described the darkness out on the ocean at night where nothing can be seen but the stars overhead. I can only imagine what that must be like.

This was the darkness that Pharaoh and his people felt. Not only could they literally not see their hands in front of their face, but they could also feel the darkness like a physical entity. And it enveloped them.

I think this darkness is symbolic of where Pharaoh and his followers were spiritually. He had hardened his heart to the point where he was incapable of recognizing the power or goodness of God or believing in God at all. And his courtiers had blindly (no pun intended) followed his example. He also could not or would not see how his actions had affected those around him. He was truly in a very dark place, from which he seemed to have been incapable of extricating himself.

Additionally, we are told in the last verse that "people could not see one another" [10:23]. While this may have been a literal darkness that caused the lack of visibility, I think that in our country today we have a metaphorical darkness. We, as a society, are so strongly divided on so many issues—political, social, environmental, religious—all exacerbated by the shadow of a pandemic, that many of us cannot/will not see our neighbors who are standing right in front of us. The strong opposing opinion prevents us from seeing the person who holds that opinion. Friendships and family relationships are strained to the brink.

In contrast to the darkness, however, the same verse tells us: "the Israelites enjoyed light in all of their dwellings." The people of Israel basked in the light of God's providence, hopeful that the time of their redemption from slavery would soon be at hand. We, too, look forward to a modern-day redemption from the darkness that sometimes feels like it is engulfing us.

The Power of Ten

Pharaoh called Moses back to him. As evidence of just how deeply enveloped in the darkness he was, we see that he did not even ask Moses to pray to God about removing the darkness, as he had with other plagues. Instead, he told Moses to go with his people and worship the Lord. He said that they could even take their children. There was just one major problem: he told them to leave their flocks behind! Why would he say this? Because he needed to hold on to something of value as collateral, otherwise there would be no reason for them to come back. However, the animals (at least some of them) would be needed for the sacrificial component of their worship. Once more, the Torah tells us that "the Lord stiffened Pharaoh's heart," and he refused to allow the Israelites to leave [10:24-27].

God confided to Moses that there would be one more plague. This one would be so devastating to Egypt that Pharaoh would not only let the people go, but he would also drive them out "one and all" [11:1]. No one would be left behind—not the women, nor the children, nor the older people, nor the animals. This would finally be the freedom that they had been waiting for. In preparation for that, God instructed Moses to tell all the people of Israel to ask the Egyptians to give them gold and silver valuables.

So, even though it hadn't officially been announced, we, the readers, share with Moses the knowledge that it would take ten plagues to convince Pharaoh to release the nation of Israel. At the culmination of this redemption, we have the dramatic scene that takes place at Mt. Sinai, in which the covenant between God and Israel is formalized through the Ten Commandments.

Like bookends, these two tens define the Exodus from Egypt. The number ten occurs often in our tradition and symbolizes completeness, perfection. With ten plagues, God completed and secured our freedom from slavery, and with Ten Commandments, God perfected and secured our commitment to a life of service. The last of the ten plagues finally convinced Pharaoh of the supremacy of the God of Israel, and the first of the Ten Commandments declared to Israel the supremacy of our God.

And, to this day, we Jews require that ten of us be united and present together to declare the greatness of God. May the day come soon that we will once again be able to gather together to worship our God, freed from the worry and constrictions brought about by this wretched pandemic.

Signs, Signs, Everywhere a Sign[4]

Moses announces the final devastating plague. Around midnight, all the firstborn in the land of Egypt will be struck dead. This plague will reach all the way from Pharaoh's palace to the poorest Egyptian servant girl; the animals of Egypt will be stricken, as well. After this, the Egyptian people will tell Moses to get out of their land, and to take all his people with him. After making this pronouncement to Pharaoh, Moses leaves in anger. One final time, we are told that "the Lord stiffened Pharaoh's heart" and he would not let the people go" [11:4-10].

Before the plague is enacted, God issues instructions for Moses and Aaron to transmit to their people: this month (Nisan) is to mark the beginning of the year and on the tenth day of the month, every household is to designate a lamb that will be used for the *Pesach* sacrifice. The actual sacrifice is to be made on the fourteenth day of the month, on which day the meat is to be eaten together with unleavened bread and bitter herbs, and the blood is to be smeared on the doorposts of the houses [12:1-12]. Verse 13 elaborates on this commandment regarding the blood: "And the blood on the houses where you are staying shall be a sign for you: when I see the blood, I will pass over you, so that no plague will destroy you when I strike the land of Egypt."

We all know about the blood on the doorposts and that it was intended as a sign. Yet a careful reading of this verse does not indicate that it is a sign for God; rather, the sign is for you (i.e., the people of Israel). Think about it—every plague leading up to this point showed a demarcation between the Egyptians and the Israelites because God knew exactly where each lived and wished to afflict the Egyptians while sparing the Israelites. There would be no reason to think that suddenly God no longer knew where the people of Israel lived and needed a physical sign from them.

Rashi goes so far as to say that the blood didn't even go on the outside of the doorpost. Rather, he says, it went on the inside of the door where it could be seen by the home's inhabitants as a physical reminder of the sacrifice that God had commanded them to make, for them to be able to differentiate themselves from the people of Egypt.[5]

Do we have other signs in our lives that remind us of our relationship with God? Of course. And, like the blood on the doorposts, many of them appear inside our homes. Every time we make a distinction between a meat dish and a dairy dish, that is a sign. Every time we light shabbat or *yom tov* candles, that is a sign. Many of us put *mezuzot* on our interior and exterior doorposts, and that is a sign. Every time we celebrate *shabbat* or a holiday, designating sacred time, that is a sign.

If we were to neglect to observe any one of these signs, either intentionally or unintentionally, who would know? Only God and we ourselves. No one else. The signs exist within our homes. They are for our benefit. They are outward manifestations of the covenant relationship we have with God.

These past ten months or so, we have spent most of our time confined to our houses, some of us more than others. No doubt, we have all had the opportunity for a good deal of introspection. Are there signs that you have clung to with even greater tenacity, signs that grounded you, signs that reminded you of the presence of God in your life? What signs have sustained you through this time of pandemic? How has your observance of those signs changed? And what will you do with those signs when you once again have the freedom to move out of your house unencumbered?

The remainder of this reading goes on to describe the proscribed observance of *Pesach* for all generations. Beginning with the fourteenth day of the first month (Nisan), unleavened bread is to be eaten for seven days, the first and seventh days are holy days on which no work is to be done, leavened bread is not even to be found in the home [12:14-20]. Perhaps more than any other holiday in our yearly cycle, the observance of *Pesach* takes place in the home, and the entire eight days are a sign of the miracles that God performed for us so long ago.

May your life be enriched by the signs that point to the presence of God in your home, and in your heart.

FIFTH ALIYAH: EXODUS 12:21–28
THURSDAY, JANUARY 21, 2021

The Power of Eight

Moses continued his instructions to the people. Each family was to choose its own lamb to sacrifice and a bunch of hyssop was to be used to spread the blood of the sacrifice on the doorposts and the lintel. When the Lord passed through the land, the Lord would see this blood and pass over the house, sparing the firstborn. Even if the blood was on the inside, God would still see it. It would be a sign to the people inside, as I explained in the last *aliyah*. Additionally, it would be a sign to God that the people inside the house were doing what God had asked of them.

Think about what the doorposts must have looked like with the three sides painted with blood. The shape resembles the letter *chet*. This letter resembles a gateway through which one enters and exits.[6] As the people of Israel observed the first *Pesach*, recognizing God's protective presence while awaiting their redemption from slavery, they entered a deeper relationship with the Divine, aware of the major change that was about to take place. The letter *chet* has a numerical value of eight. This is the number of continuities, the number that points to the future. Think of the eights in our lives as Jews: a baby boy's *bris* on the eighth day of life; the eight days that the oil of Chanukah lasted, thus giving us eight branches on our menorahs; the eight strings of *tzitzit* on one corner of a *tallit*, reminding us of all of the *mitzvot*; *Shemini Atzeret*, the Eighth Day of Assembly, extending the holiday of Sukkot by one more day; and perhaps most relevant to this discussion, the eight days that we celebrate *Pesach* in the Diaspora.

To this day, *Pesach*, more than any other holiday, is the quintessential holiday that is celebrated primarily inside the house, just as the nation of Israel did on that first *Pesach* so long ago. Today, we don't slaughter a lamb or put blood on the doorpost, but we do have a celebratory meal in which we reenact the first Passover. And we encourage our children to ask questions: "And when your children ask you, 'What do you mean by this rite?' you shall say, 'It is the Passover sacrifice to Adonai, who passed over the houses of the Israelites in Egypt when smiting the Egyptians but saved our houses'" [12:26-27].

So, this *Pesach*, when you pass through your doorway, imagine what it would look like with the blood painted on it and imagine the letter *chet* superimposed on the entryway/exit. Think about how the experiences of the past year have allowed you to enter a deeper, stronger relationship with God. And when the time comes that we can fully exit from our houses back out into the world, take those lessons with you.

SIXTH ALIYAH: EXODUS 12:29–51
FRIDAY, JANUARY 22, 2021

A Night of Vigil

Here we read of the tenth and final plague: the death of the firstborn. It occurred, as promised, at midnight. No one in Egypt was sleeping that midnight. We are told that there was not a single household in Egypt that did not suffer the loss of a firstborn. Therefore, a great cry arose in the land, emanating literally from every family in Egypt. Pharaoh himself suffered the loss of his son. This, coupled with the mournful cry of his people ringing in his ears, prompted him to call Moses and Aaron to him while it was yet night, telling them to take their people and their animals and be gone from the land [12:29-33].

Having to prepare to leave in the middle of the night, the people of Israel packed up to leave with their dough, which had not yet leavened. Pressing the Egyptians to give them items of gold and silver, they were successful, and left Egypt greatly enriched. The figure of 600,000 who left only represented the men between the ages of twenty and sixty. By the time the children, the older men, and the women were also counted, the estimate is that the nation of Israel numbered some 2,000,000 people.

God then gave further instructions regarding the *Pesach* offering (which we represent with the shank bone on our seder plates). A stranger, a foreigner, and a hired servant may not eat it but a servant who had been circumcised may. It must all be consumed in one house. All Israelites are to keep it. A stranger who wishes to partake in it must be circumcised first, and once he is, his status is the same as that of any man born a Jew [12:43-49].

In between the description of the plague and the delineating of the ordinances of the *Pesach* sacrifice, we read: "That was for the LORD a night of vigil to bring them out of the land of Egypt; that same night is the LORD's, one of vigil for all the children of Israel throughout the ages" [12:42]. The word *shimurim*, translated here as "vigil," appears twice in this verse, and nowhere else in the entire *Tanakh*. The first use of the word "vigil" in this verse refers to God and the second refers to the people of Israel.

Why was God keeping vigil the night of the first *Pesach*? According to Rashi, Rashbam, and Ramban, God had first made the promise of the future deliverance of the people from slavery to Abraham, and God had been waiting since that night—for over four hundred years—for this night to come in order to fulfill that promise.[7] Now that the time had finally arrived, God watched over their houses to protect them from the angel of death. God's vigil came with a requirement of the people about to be freed: "the night of vigil kept for them must be kept by them" [Ramban][8]. God has enjoined upon us the obligation for all time to keep vigil on that night in remembrance of what God did for us. Hence, the Passover seder. We retell the story and the more details and questions, the better. Many of our seders go long into the night, rivalling the five rabbis that we read about in the *Haggadah* who argued all night until their students came and told them it was time for the morning *shema*. This gives literal meaning to the word "vigil."

Another interpretation is given by Kli Yakar:

> . . . This can be likened to two companions who said to one another, "You hold my lamp and I will hold yours." The two "lamps" are that of the mitzvah . . . and that of the human soul . . . Thus [God] told B'nei Yisrael that if they would guard the "lamp" of the *Pesach* sacrifice, He would guard their souls by not allowing the destroyer to enter their homes. And about this guarding, it stated, "a night of watching for [God] to bring them out of the Land of Egypt." And corresponding to Israel's guarding the *mitzvot*, it stated, "watching for all of the Children of Israel throughout their generations."[9]

By faithfully observing all the *mitzvot* of *Pesach*, we keep vigil over the souls that God has entrusted to us—our own and those of our children and grandchildren.

SEVENTH ALIYAH: EXODUS 13:1–16
WRITTEN FOR SHABBAT, SATURDAY, JANUARY 23, 2021

And Even More Signs

Earlier in this *parashah*, I wrote about the sign of the blood on the doorpost. In this last *aliyah*, we learn of several additional signs.

First, there are the signs specifically tied to the observance of the holiday. For seven days, the people of Israel are enjoined not only to eat unleavened bread, but also to make sure that there is no leavened bread in the house. They are not to even see it. For days or weeks ahead of *Pesach*, we clean and scrub every single nook and cranny of our homes, purging the *chametz* from the house. And when that's done, we search the house with a candle and a feather in a quest for several pieces of *chametz* that we planted there. We rid the house of the *chametz* to fulfill the commandment. We do the search largely for the benefit of children, to involve them in the process, and so that they will be inspired to ask why we are doing such *narrishkeit*. We read: "And you shall explain to your son on that day, 'It is because of what the LORD did for me when I went free from Egypt'" [13:8]. This should sound familiar to you as it is the answer given in the *Hagaddah* to the wicked child. It continues: "For me, and not for you. Had you been there, you would not have been redeemed."

Additionally, ". . . when, in time to come, your son asks you, saying, 'What does this mean?' you shall say to him, 'It was with a mighty hand that the LORD brought us out from Egypt, the house of bondage" [13:14]. This is the answer that we give to the child who does not even know how to ask a question. The seder is filled with signs that define the parameters of the vigil we have been commanded to keep throughout all time.

But what about all the other days of the year? What sign do we have that reminds us of the Exodus on those days? Twice in this passage we have the answer: ". . . this shall serve you as a sign on your hand and as a reminder on your forehead—in order that the Teaching of the LORD may be in your mouth—that with a mighty hand the LORD freed you from Egypt" and ". . . so it shall be as a sign upon your hand and as a symbol on your forehead that with a mighty hand the LORD freed us from Egypt" [13:9,16].

A sign on your hand and a sign on your heart refer, of course, to the *tefilin* worn every weekday morning. The single compartment inside the box of the arm *tefilin,* along with the four compartments inside the box of the head *tefilin,* contain parchments upon which are written these and two additional verses from the Torah that allude to the *tefilin*. The arm *tefilin*, worn on the individual's non-dominant arm, is to remind us of the strong arm of God that strengthens us and by which we were delivered out of slavery in Egypt. The head *tefilin* is placed on the forehead, symbolic of absorbing the words they contain into our consciousness. The *tefilin* are worn so that we are reminded of the Exodus from Egypt not just once a year on *Pesach,* but rather every day of the year.

Some people view *tefilin* as a bizarre, antiquated ritual. I view it as one of the most important *mitzvot* in my daily life. To me, they are a beautiful reminder of the relationship I have with God, a commitment which I reenact every morning. I start my day by clothing myself in the uniform of *mitzvot*. Some people—policemen, firefighters, doctors, nurses, judges, delivery people, and more—wear uniforms that identify their occupation. So, too, we Jews are required by God to wear our uniforms of *tallit* and *tefilin*, signs to remind us of who we are and Who is our God, and what our God did for us in Egypt and continues to do for us today and every day.

Parashat Beshallach

FIRST ALIYAH: EXODUS 13:17–14:8
SUNDAY, JANUARY 24, 2021

Take Me with You

At long last, the people of Israel have left the land of Egypt and the slavery that its people had afflicted upon them. We can only imagine how they must have felt, especially after several hundred years of servitude. No doubt, they were overjoyed. But they were also in a precarious frame of mind, as none of this generation had ever experienced anything but slavery. They were not at all prepared for a life of freedom. It was for this reason that we are told that God did not lead them through the way of the Philistines even though it might have been a shorter route [13:17]. God was concerned that seeing the warriors there would frighten them enough that they would consider returning to Egypt. Instead, God led the nation through the wilderness of the Red Sea [13:18].

Moses had one final mission to carry out as they left Egypt: "And Moses took with him the bones of Joseph, who had exacted an oath from the children of Israel, saying, 'God will be sure to take notice of you, then you shall carry up my bones from here with you'" [13:19].

Back at the very end of the book of Genesis, just before Joseph died, he exacted this promise from his brothers. Not long before that, he himself had fulfilled this same promise that he had made to his father Jacob, taking his bones out of Egypt and burying them in the Cave of Machpelah. However, Joseph, being considered Egyptian royalty, had to be buried in Egypt at the time of his death. According to *midrash*, his coffin, made of metal, was sunk in the Nile by the Egyptians. Now Moses needed to find it if he was going to carry out the promise made by Joseph's brothers so long ago, that now bound their descendants as they were about to enjoy thefreedom that Joseph had spoken of. How, after all this time, was Moses to locate Joseph's coffin? The *midrash* tells us that, once again, Serach, the daughter of Asher, who miraculously was still alive, stepped forward to help:

> ...But how did Moses know where Joseph was buried? It was said that Serach, the daughter of Asher, was of the previous generation and to her Moses went and asked whether she knew where Joseph was buried, and she said: "An iron casket was made by the Egyptians wherein he was placed and sunk in the River Nile, so that the water of the Nile should be blessed through him." Thereupon, Moses went and stationed himself on the brink of the Nile and said, "Joseph, the time which the Holy One, praised be He, gave an oath to redeem Israel has expired; the oath with which thou hast adjured Israel is now to be fulfilled. If thou wilt reveal thyself, well, but if not, then we shall be free from the obligation of thy oath." Immediately did the casket of Joseph float the water. [*Ein Yaakov Sotah* 1:9][1]

And so, once again, it was this mysterious woman in Israel, mentioned briefly in the genealogies, who merited being the bearer of the knowledge needed by Moses to carry out his mission, fulfilling the vow that had been made so long ago to Joseph.

Additionally, we have this beautiful *midrash* which speaks of the merits of showing honor to the dead by participating in their burial:

> ...Joseph merited to bury his father, resulting in a display of great honor to his father, and there was none among his brothers greater than he in importance, for he was viceroy of Egypt, as it is stated: "And Joseph went up to bury his father; and with him went up all the servants of Pharaoh, the Elders of his house, and all the Elders of the land of Egypt, and all the house of Joseph, and his brethren, and his father's house; ...[Genesis 50:7-9] .... Moses merited to be the only person involved in the transportation of Joseph's bones to be buried in Eretz Yisrael, and there was none among the Jewish people greater than he, as it is stated: "And Moses took the bones of Joseph with him" [Exodus 13:19]. Who had a greater burial than Moses, as no one involved himself in his burial other than the Omnipresent Himself, as it is stated: "And He buried him in the valley in the land of Moab over against Beth Peor; and no man knows of his sepulcher unto

this day" [Deuteronomy 34:6] . . . . Not only with regard to Moses did the Sages say that God takes part in his burial, but also with regard to all the righteous individuals. [*Mishnah Sotah 1:9*][2]

Before he died, Jacob exacted a promise from Joseph to bury him in the Cave of Machpelah; Joseph was the greatest in stature of his brothers, so it was he who merited the honor of interring his father. In turn, when Joseph himself died, he merited to be buried by the greatest man of the generation that would carry out his request. Therefore, Joseph merited to be buried by no one less than Moses, the redeemer and liberator of the nation who had been sent by God. Thereafter, Moses merited to be buried by the greatest of the generation that he had led to the brink of the promised land. However, he himself was the greatest person of his generation. Even Joshua, his successor, did not rise to his level of greatness. Therefore, as you may recall from the end of the Book of Deuteronomy, Moses was buried not by any human being, but by God alone. The Mishnah goes on to say that this honor is accorded not only to Moses, but to all righteous individuals.

When we attend a funeral and participate in the solemn ritual of shoveling dirt into the grave, covering the coffin, we show the greatest honor to the deceased that we possibly can. This is a situation where the person who benefits from our deeds cannot possibly repay us. Instead, we pay it forward, showing *kavod* to the one who can no longer perform any *mitzvot*. In return, we merit receiving the same *kavod* from those we leave behind, and from God, Who will also accompany us on our journey home, and welcome us in *olam habah*.

SECOND ALIYAH: EXODUS 14:9–14
MONDAY, JANUARY 25, 2021

Be Still and Wait for the Lord

As the people of Israel escaped into the desert, the Egyptians gave chase. After realizing what he had done in allowing them to go free, Pharaoh had once again changed his mind, gathered up all his forces, and headed out after them. From the previous reading, we learned that Pharaoh came out with six hundred chariots [14:7]. The Israelite men of fighting age (between the ages of twenty and sixty) numbered 600,000. That comparison alone is one Egyptian for every thousand men of Israel (and that does not even include the older men, the women, or the children).

And yet, even with these overwhelming odds, the Israelites were "greatly frightened" [14:10]. Unused to being free people who left behind the land of their captivity, they became paralyzed with fear at the sight of their former captors. Though they were large in number, they didn't have the slightest idea how to fight or defend themselves and they were menaced by the mightiest men of Pharaoh's army.

In their fear, they lashed out at Moses: What have you done to us? Weren't there enough graves in Egypt you had to bring us out here to the desert to die? Didn't we tell you to leave us alone and let us serve the Egyptians? That would have been better than dying out here [14:11-12]. Actually, there is no evidence in the Torah that they ever made that last statement.

It seems that they were panicking and were saying things that made no sense and taking it out on the one person who had done more for them than anyone else. If any of you has been a parent, a teacher, a police officer, a tour guide—anyone who has ever had the responsibility of leading groups of people—then you can probably remember or imagine a situation in which one or two people (over)reacted quickly and loudly to something that occurred so that in a matter of minutes you were dealing with a cacophony of voices, everyone speaking excitedly at once. You wished you could just shake them and say, "Snap out of it!" but you knew it would be futile. You needed to be the calming influence. It was the same for Moses.

Moses could have fired back at them, and many would say he would have been justified in doing so, being the victim of their ingratitude. Certainly, we know from having already studied the subsequent books of the Torah that there were numerous times when the people complained, and Moses lashed out at them. But not here. Here it seems that Moses ignored the personal insult. Instead, demonstrating empathy and understanding, he tried to calm them by telling them not to fear, that God would deliver them from the hand of the Egyptians, whom they would not see again [14:13].

Finally, Moses simply says to them, "The LORD will battle for you; you hold your peace!" [14:14]. With these words, Moses attempted to diffuse the situation. His message was essentially this: Take a deep breath and try to stay calm. God will take care of the situation. You just need to be still and wait for it.

Sometimes we may feel like we are facing a daunting situation, an overwhelming enemy, human or otherwise. A natural human reaction might be to give in to our fear and assume the worst. And sometimes, there is not another person around to tell us to snap out of it. It is especially at those times that we need to learn to be still, to silence our pounding hearts, and wait for the deliverance of God, even when it appears there is no way out.

Take the First Step into the Sea

God turns to Moses and tells him that this is not the time for him to be engaging in lengthy prayers. Instead, he is to instruct the people to continue moving forward, even though they may not see a pathway out at this point. Moses is then instructed to lift his rod and hold it over the sea; the waters will split and the people will walk through on dry land [14:15-16]. The scene, which many of us envision taking place during the daytime, actually occurred at night. The pillar of cloud normally went in front of the people during the daytime, leading the way, and then disappeared when night fell and the pillar of fire took its place. Instead, here it went around behind the people as night fell, thus, together with the pillar of fire, protectively surrounding the people and separating them from the encroaching army of Pharaoh. We read that, "one could not come near [each] other all through the night" [14:20]. The night was dark. They were in the desert, after all, yet the pillar of fire gave off so much light that they could clearly see each other but could not come close to each other. The Hebrew words translated here as "each other," *zey-el-zeh*, appear only one other time in the entire *Tanakh:* "And one would call to the other, "Holy, holy, holy! The LORD of Hosts! His presence fills all the Earth!" [Isaiah 6:3].

This verse, which describes the angels in the heavenly court singing praises to God, should sound familiar to you as we sing it as part of the *kedushah* in every one of our services. We ourselves imitate the angels as we rise in prayer. There is a well-known *midrash* that links these two verses that contain this phrase. The Baal HaTurim explains that the angels also wished to sing praises to God when the waters of the Red Sea split.[3] God, however, stopped them, saying "My handiwork [the Egyptians] are drowning in the sea, and you want to sing songs?"

Thinking about all of this, I am reminded of our current situation, still living through the long dark night of the pandemic. We cannot yet see clearly to the other side of the sea, where safety awaits us on its shores. The night is dark yet the pillar of fire that we call the internet shines a bright light into our darkness. Through Zoom, Facetime, Skype, and Google Classroom, we can clearly see each other though we cannot come near each other. And as the death toll continues to rise in our nation and in the world, surely God tells the angels that now is not the time for songs of praise because so many are dying.

Yet as we continue reading today's *aliyah*, we see that deliverance for the people began to arrive "at the morning watch" [14:24]. In biblical times, the twenty-four-hour day was split into four-hour watches. According to Ibn Ezra, the time period that is referred to here is the third and final watch of the night, which covered the hours from 2 to 6 a.m. God's deliverance began to arrive while it was yet night, just before the dawn.

Our deliverance is still over the horizon, but the beginnings of it are beginning to appear. We have begun the process of vaccination. Many have received their shots, but many more are still waiting. Some are still afraid to do so. As the waters begin to part, providing a way forward, may we all have the courage to step boldly in, trusting that safety awaits us on the other side.

And then may they close behind us, drowning the coronavirus in the sea, and removing the threat to our lives. May it come soon and in our day.

FOURTH ALIYAH: EXODUS 14:26–15:26
WEDNESDAY, JANUARY 27, 2021

We All Need a Gentle Touch

As the last of the nation of Israel passed through the Red Sea, with the separated waters appearing as two walls on either side of them, God instructed Moses once again to raise his right hand, together with the rod, over the waters. This time, the waters closed back in on top of each other, drowning all of the Egyptians who had boldly followed them into the sea. Finally, at long last, the Torah tells us that the people of Israel believed in both God and Moses [14:26-31].

What follows next is one of the most beautiful parts of the Torah: one of the most well-known songs of praise in the entire *Tanakh*, *Shirat haYam*, the Song of the Sea. It is an expression of spontaneous praise for the One God who intervened directly in nature to deliver the people of Israel to freedom from slavery and oppression. The first thing that is notable about the song in the Torah scroll itself is the distinctive way in which it is written. The lines must be written in such a way that each has a blank space underneath it and that blank space must in turn have writing below it. (You should be able to see this clearly if you look at a copy of the Hebrew text).

Traditional explanations for this distinctive format of scribal calligraphy hold that it is meant to represent a wall put together by a bricklayer. A different analogy that I find preferable is that it resembles the walls of water being pulled apart on the left and the right, with the people passing through on the dry ground in the middle. In other words, it's a visual depiction of the very miracle that was wrought by God to facilitate the deliverance of the nation.

HINDSIGHT IS 2020

What about the actual language of the song? To be sure, there are large parts of it that we struggle with when viewed through the lens of our modern sensitivities, such as the verses 15:1,4-6,10,19 that commend God for tossing the Egyptians into the sea and drowning them. We struggle (rightfully so) with the idea of celebrating our freedom at the expense of the lives of others. Yet none of us knows the feeling of having been enslaved for our entire lives. It is difficult to judge the actions and words of our biblical ancestors without being able to place ourselves into their experience.

At the same time, the song also contains some beautiful imagery, much of which is very familiar to us because it has made its way into our liturgy: *mi kamocha ba-elim Adonai, mi kamocha nedar ba-kodesh, norah tehilot oseh feleh* (Who is like You, O LORD, among the celestials; Who is like You, majestic in holiness, Awesome in splendor, working wonders!) [15:11]. The question is, of course, rhetorical. There is no one among either Earthly or heavenly beings who compares to our God—no being as awesome or powerful, no being who loves us as much, that would go to the lengths that our God did to bring us to freedom! This verse is recited as part of the verses leading up to the recitation of the *Amidah*, the part of the worship service when we ourselves sing songs of praise to God. As we repeat these words, we not only validate their meaning, but we also simultaneously validate our connection today to those who came before, to our ancestors who crossed the sea on dry land. We acknowledge that even today we are privy to the same providential care from God.

A little further on in the reading we have this verse: *Adonai yimloch l'olam va-ed* (The LORD will reign for ever and ever!) [15:18]. This verse, too, is part of the section leading up to the recitation of the *amidah*. Repeating it affirms our faith in the providence and continuity of our God.

There are several other beautiful verses in here. I encourage you to study them on your own, to see which ones speak to you. I would like to touch on just one more all the way at the end of today's reading: "I the LORD am your healer" [15:26]. Ramban points out that the word *rofecha* (healer) is in reality not a noun, it is a verb: [I am] the One who heals you."[4] The Baal HaTurim points out that the second letter of this word is a soft letter *fay* instead of *pay*. He explains that this is indicative of the soft, gentle nature of healing that comes from God.[5]

Most, if not all, of us, need that gentle healing right now—physically, emotionally, spiritually. May we all be able to entrust ourselves to the Divine, to feel that soft, gentle touch of healing of both body and spirit that will give us the strength needed to endure this pandemic, to make it safely through, and to join our voices to sing songs of praise when we find ourselves delivered safely onto the shores on the other side.

FIFTH ALIYAH: EXODUS 15:27–16:10
THURSDAY, JANUARY 28, 2021

Am I My Brother's Keeper?

The nation of Israel travels in the desert, now in relative safety. The Egyptian threat has been removed and they can relax and enjoy their freedom. It doesn't take long, however, before they begin to grumble and complain. Towards the end of the last *aliyah* was the first time that they complained about the lack of water. Moses turned to God Who instructed him to throw a stick into water that was bitter. The waters turned sweet, and the people had plenty to drink [15:22-25].

In today's reading, they begin to agitate about lack of food to eat. We are told that the entire nation complained to Moses and Aharon, accusing them of bringing them out into the wilderness to die. They say that it would have been better to die in Egypt as at least there they had plenty to eat [16:2-3].

Many commentators find fault with the Israelites. After all that God has done for them—bringing the plagues on Egypt, parting the sea for them, giving them their freedom—how could they be so ungrateful? At the same time, they have never had to work for their own food. Though it might have been meager, whatever they had was provided by their Egyptian taskmasters because if a slave is undernourished, (s)he can hardly work. Not only do they not know how to obtain their own food, God has brought them out into the desert where food is scarce. Using modern terminology, we could say that the people of Israel are suffering from "food insecurity." This term, relatively new in our vocabulary, is variously defined as: a lack of consistent access to enough food for an active, healthy lifestyle; a household's inability to provide enough food for every person to live an active, healthy life; a condition in which a household lacks access to adequate food because of limited money or other resources.[6,7,8] We hear this term a great deal in the news these days because it has become rampant in our country, indeed, in our world, due to the pandemic. The potential ramifications are far reaching. When I was a teacher, I remember that we always had to be aware of the students in our classrooms who were receiving free or subsidized breakfast and lunch because a child who was chronically hungry was a child unable to fully concentrate on his/her studies. Therefore, food insecurity is detrimental to a child's education. The parent who is unable to provide for his/her child's nutrition is also vulnerable, feeling shame and inadequacy.

Through Moses, God tells the people that food will be provided for them, that it will rain down from the sky six days a week (not on Shabbat). We will learn more about this *manna* in the next *aliyah*. God says that the people are being tested to see whether they can obey God's Torah, which they are being prepared to receive in the next *parashah*. First, they may not be greedy; they are not to gather any more than they need for any given day. Rashbam says that even if they tried to gather more, they would find when they got it home that it was only equivalent to that day's portion.[9] On the other hand, on Friday mornings they would be required to gather a double portion so that they would have enough for Shabbat. If they failed to do so, they would be hungry on Shabbat, for none would fall on that day.

Bringing these two themes together, the Baal haTurim says that, "the Torah was given primarily to those who eat the manna."[10] As part of his further explanation, he asks, "is it possible for one to sit and expound on the Torah when he does not know from where his food and drink will come?" In other words, if they had to worry about where they would receive their sustenance, they would thus be distracted and unable to properly prepare themselves mentally, emotionally, or spiritually to receive the Torah. Therefore, God lovingly provided their sustenance but with caveats.

Today, we have so many people in our country who are food insufficient. If they worry about how they will provide for themselves and/or their children, there is little chance that they will be able to concentrate on their spiritual lives. That, in turn, will only exacerbate their feelings of inadequacy and abandonment, removing them further from the God whose comforting presence they so desperately need.

Therefore, it is incumbent upon those of us who are able to do so to help provide for their physical sustenance through donations of cash, goods, our time, or whatever we can.

When God asked Cain what had happened to his brother Abel, he feigned innocence, asking, "Am I my brother's keeper?" [Genesis 4:9]. The answer, my friends, today more than ever, is a resounding yes.

SIXTH ALIYAH: EXODUS 16:11–36
FRIDAY, JANUARY 29, 2021

Everything You Want and Need

This *aliyah* expands on the laws regarding this substance that God would provide every weekday morning, six days a week, for forty years until they reached the land of Canaan [16:35]. It appeared on the ground each morning as the dew melted away. The people named it *manna*, "for they did not know what it was." The fixed measure they were to gather was an *omer* per person [16:15-16]. Nothing was to be left over until morning. If it was, it turned to maggots [16:19-20]. However, when they gathered the double portion for Shabbat on Friday mornings, it did not spoil. Some people did go out on Shabbat morning to gather it but found nothing [16:22-30].

So, what did the *manna* taste like? One would hope that it was good since it sustained them for forty years. So, it had to be something that they would not tire of. The text says that ". . . it was like coriander seed, white, and it tasted like wafers in honey" [16:31]. The number of *midrashim* that have been written about the *manna* and its taste are numerous. Here is a sampling:

> With regard to the manna, it is written "bread" [Exodus 16:4], and it is written "oil"[Numbers 11:8], and . . . "honey" [Exodus 16:31]. How can we reconcile these verses? Rabbi Yosei, son of Rabbi Ḥanina, said: For the youth it was like bread, for the elderly it was like oil, and for the children it was like honey. Each received what was appropriate. [BT Yoma 75B:5]
> . . . The manna became whatever they wanted inside their mouths. [Bamidbar Rabbah 15:24][11]
> . . . One had only to desire a certain dish, and no sooner had he thought of it, than manna had the flavor of the dish desired. The same food had a different taste to everyone who partook of it, according to his age; to the little children it tasted like milk, to the strong youths like bread, to the old men like honey, to the sick like barley steeped in oil and honey. [Legends of the Jews 3:1:91][12]

Each of these conveys the idea that the *manna* had a different taste for different people and each person's taste fulfilled exactly what it was that they needed at that moment in time. Thus, the *manna* was custom made for the individual and for that specific day and it might change from one day to the next. It acquired the taste of not only what they needed but what they desired!

Tying this concept together with that of the last *aliyah*, we have this beautiful *midrash*:

> . . . R. Jose bar Hanina said: It was according to the capacity of each and every person that the Divine Word spoke with him, and do not be surprised at this fact. Since we find in the case of the manna that, when it came down to Israel, each one of them savored it according to his capacity . . . how much the more would the principle apply with the Divine Word! [Midrash Tanchuma Buber, Yitro 17:1][13]

The idea that each person savored the taste of the *manna* according to his/her own capacity or ability (or literally strength) was a foretaste of what awaited them at Mt. Sinai. Each person would receive the Torah of God individually, according to what (s)he needed and was capable of handling at that moment. The taste of Torah is different for each of us, but for all of us it is something sweet. It can sustain us for forty years (or more) and changes with time. Each day each of us receives exactly what we need, so long as we are willing to receive it on the terms that God wishes to offer it. But if we leave it overnight until the next day, it spoils, and we have squandered it.

May we each maintain open eyes and open hearts to receive the Torah that God will share with us each and every day. And may we appreciate its sweetness as we allow it to penetrate our hearts and draw us closer to the Divine.

SEVENTH ALIYAH: EXODUS 17:1–16
WRITTEN FOR SHABBAT, SATURDAY, JANUARY 30, 2021

Giving Support to Those Who Support Us

As the nation continued their journey through the wilderness, they again found themselves without water, and complained to Moses, accusing him yet one more time that bringing them out of Egypt to kill them. Moses turned to God yet again for guidance; God told him to go on ahead and when he arrived at Horeb (Sinai) he was to strike a rock with his rod, and water would come out [17:1-7]. So, the same rod that had been used to turn the waters of the Nile into blood, as well as to signal the parting of the waters of the Red Sea, was now used to bring precious water to the Israelites to drink. In a beautiful sense of irony, the rod that began by depriving the Egyptians of water to drink now provided water for the Israelites to drink.

Following this, we have the story of the battle against the people of Amalek, who, without provocation, came and attacked the people of Israel. Moses instructed Joshua to choose men to go to battle with him while he himself would stand on top of the mountain holding the rod in his hand. Before long, an unusual phenomenon emerged: "whenever Moses held up his hand, Israel prevailed; but whenever he let down his hand, Amalek prevailed" [17:11]. As the commentators explain, this is not to imply that Moses had some magical powers in his hands. Rather, since he was standing on the mountain and raising his hands, the people needed to raise up their eyes when they looked at him, thus looking towards heaven, and God, from

Whom their deliverance would come. However, Moses was, after all, only human. As he held his hands in the air, he grew tired; thus, Aaron and Hur propped him up on a rock and held his hands aloft all day until the sun went down, enabling an Israelite victory [17:8-13].

This story demonstrates vividly that our leaders (both politically and religiously) sometimes grow tired from the large, sometimes overbearing responsibilities of their office. These difficult days of the pandemic are especially difficult for our rabbis and lay leaders alike. For close to a year now, they have been trying to navigate the strange, new, unknown world of COVID-19 that has uprooted us entirely. They try to lift and hold us all up, but sometimes the collective weight of us can be too much to bear. It is at those times that we all need to hold up their hands, to literally lift them up, to release some of their burden, to work together with them to win the spiritual battles that plague us as a Jewish Community, and to assure victory over our unseen but powerful foes. May we all come together to support our clergy and lay leaders. Let us acknowledge that they hold their hands up as a signal of strength and that, we, in turn, must give them our support when their strength flags.

Parashat Yitro

FIRST ALIYAH: EXODUS 18:1–12
SUNDAY, JANUARY 31, 2021

Claim Your Torah

This *parashah* is considered by many to be the most important *parashah* in the entire Torah because it contains within it the account of the encounter of the nation with God at Mt. Sinai, where the two tablets containing the Ten Commandments were given. How strange it is, then, that it is named for someone who was not only not Jewish, but was a priest of Midian. We have met him before when Moses first fled Egypt to go into the wilderness. It was then that he encountered the seven daughters of Jethro at the well, and this encounter then led to him settling and staying with Yitro, whose daughter Tzipporah became his wife. At that time, Moses could feel honored to have such a prestigious father-in-law. Now, it seems, Yitro takes pride in his son-in-law, who has become the leader of a large nation of people for whom God has done wondrous things [18:1].

We are told here that Jethro came out to meet Moses, bringing with him Tzipporah and their two sons, Gershom and Eliezer [18:2-6]. Though the details were apparently omitted from the Torah, it seems that at some point, perhaps as he assumed the leadership of the people of Israel, Moses had sent his family back to live with Yitro in the wilderness. We do not know exactly why. Some speculate that he had actually divorced Tzipporah while others think that either Moses or God (or perhaps both) thought that the presence of his wife and sons would be either a distraction or a hindrance as he undertook his mission. Even here, we see that the rest of the reading reflects a conversation between the two men and there is no further mention of Moses' family at all.

The arrival of Yitro and his entourage is described this way: "Jethro, Moses' father-in-law, brought Moses' sons and wife to him in the wilderness . . ." [18:5] Commenting on the seemingly superfluous phrase "in[to] the wilderness" in this verse, Rashi says the following:

> . . . Indeed, we know that they were in the wilderness, and it
> appears unnecessary to state that Jethro came to Moses there. But
> by stressing this Scripture is speaking in praise of Jethro: that he
> was living amidst all the splendor that the world could provide,
> and nevertheless his heart prompted him to go forth into the
> desert, a waste place to hearken to the words of the Torah.[1]

Jethro was an individual of importance. In addition to being the priest of Midian, he was the senior statesman here. Yet, he chose to leave the comfort of his home to travel out into the desert to meet with Moses and hear the details of all that God had done for them. We are told that he rejoiced at Moses' words, he blessed God, and brought sacrifices.

There are many commentators who speculate that Yitro went so far as to convert to Judaism and there are probably equally as many who say that he did not. Those who say that he did point to this as one of their proof texts: (Yitro says), "now I know that the Lord is greater than all gods . . ." [18:11]. Those who say that he did not, point to the fact that at the end of this story Yitro returns home, even though he is invited to stay with the people of Israel.

A case can be made either way. Regardless of what you may think about that, Rashi's point is that Yitro is to be praised for leaving his home and going into the wilderness to learn Torah. Taken metaphorically, we can say that he was willing to leave behind what he knew, to move out of his comfort zone, into the unknown to learn about all the wonders that God had done for the people of Israel. And the result was an acknowledgment of the greatness of God.

If Yitro, who was not Jewish, can not only be willing to open himself to learn words of Torah, but also go out of his way to do so, how much more so should we, members of the nation of Israel who share a covenant relationship with God, be willing to open ourselves up to what our God has to teach us. Sometimes it means leaving our comfort zones and heading towards the unknown. Opening ourselves to what God has to teach us can be transformative. We owe it to ourselves to seek out words of Torah wherever we can—from books, from classes on Zoom (or in person when we are able to do that again), from podcasts, from doing our own research, from talking with others. The rewards await us.

It Is Not Good for One to be Alone

This reading tells the well-known story of Yitro, who offers some insight in response to observing Moses sitting for the entire day, answering questions, and rendering judgment for the individuals who approached him [18:13-16]. This was truly an impossible, daunting task for any human being, especially given the size of the nation. Jethro's suggestion is that Moses set up a hierarchal system of judges, appointing trustworthy men as chiefs over thousands, hundreds, fifties, and tens. They will judge the minor cases, leaving only the major rulings for Moses, which will relieve most of the burden from Moses's shoulders. It is believed that this system inspired our founding fathers to establish the judicial system of the United States.

In advising Moses, Yitro said to him, "[what] you are doing is not good . . . you cannot do it alone." This phrase appears only one other time in the entire Torah: "The LORD God said, 'It is not good for man to be alone; I will make a fitting helper for him'" [Genesis 2:18].

This verse, which precedes God's creation of the first woman in the Garden of Eden, expresses a similar sentiment. God determined that it is not good for Adam to have a solitary existence and Eve was created as a fitting helper for him. Adam had been charged by God with being a caretaker for the rest of God's creation. Again, this is too much for him to do all by himself, therefore God provided assistance for him. In our reading, God also provides needed assistance to Moses, this time in the words of advice that come from his father-in-law, who has just recently come to recognize the supremacy of God.

These days, many of us are spending more time in isolation or near isolation. These can be very trying times, especially for those who live on their own. It is not good to be alone, nor is it good to take too much upon oneself, trying to do it all alone. We all need the support we receive from interacting with others, be they friends or family. It is so important to maintain contact, if not in person, then by phone, Zoom, or email.

This, of course, works two ways: if you need some support, reach out to others, and ask for it, and if you know someone who needs support, reach out to him/her, and offer it.

Being a Jew means being part of the nation of Israel. It also means being a part of the human family. Remember, "[what] you are doing is not good . . . you cannot do it alone."

Choose Capable Men

In this very short section, we read that Moses followed his father-in-law's advice to set up a judicial system. The text says that he did just what Yitro had told him to do [18:24]. Well, not exactly. Yitro had suggested that Moses appoint "capable men who fear God, trustworthy men who spurn ill-gotten gain" [18:21]. Here we are told that he indeed appointed capable men [18:25]. As pointed out by Ibn Ezra and Chizkuni, only God really knows the hearts of men, so Moses was not able to choose men who feared God.[2,3] By the same token, according to Rashi, one who is trustworthy is one whose word is reliable, and one who would spurn ill-gotten gain would despise his own wealth if taken to court.[4] These qualities would also be impossible to ascertain completely. The only trait that Moses was able to judge accurately was whether a man was capable or not and if he possessed the knowledge necessary to decide judicial matters, or not.

Why might Moses have been reluctant to make decisions regarding the trustworthiness of others or whether they feared God? According to most commentators, this chapter is out of place; it is thought that the incidents described here actually occurred later, after the giving of the Ten Commandments on Mt. Sinai. That would place it after the story of the Golden Calf, when, unbeknownst to Moses, while he was on Mt. Sinai receiving the tablets from God, the people were below worshipping the calf that they had asked Aaron to make for them to worship. (We will read this story in *Parashat Ki Tissa.*) The people whom Moses had thought were ready to enter into a covenant relationship with God had betrayed them both. In anger, Moses smashed the precious tablets. He realized that the trust he had placed in these people was misplaced. When we look at our current story in light of this one, we can better understand why Moses would feel that he was able to appoint judges based only on their capabilities, on the qualities that he could see and assess.

Similarly, the same could be said about any of us. When we take on a position, either in our workplace or as a volunteer in the synagogue or some other setting, we hope that others will put their trust in us, but ultimately, we do need to prove ourselves worthy of that trust. Only God knows what is truly in our hearts, whether we are God-fearing or not, whether we are trustworthy or not. For that matter, only God knows what lies in the hearts of the others around us, as well. It is not within our power to judge.

On Eagles Wings Surrounded by Clouds

And now we come to the story of the giving of the Torah at Mt. Sinai. The date is given: the third new moon after they left Egypt, the month of Sivan. We are told that it was, "on that very day" they entered the wilderness [19:1]. Rashi explains that this phrase tells us that "the words of Torah should always be as new to you as on the day they were given."[5] Every day, we should not only study, but experience words of Torah, and we should approach our study with the same anticipation that we can only imagine that the people of Israel must have felt as they arrived at Mt. Sinai. As Ramban points out, this place was their intended destination.[5] Here they would enter a covenant relationship with God.

Arriving at their destination, the people made camp, and Moses hurried up the mountain to meet God and receive further instructions. God had a message for Moses to deliver, "to the house of Jacob and . . . the children of Israel" [19:3]. Rashi says that the first term refers to the women, the second refers to the men. Ibn Ezra says that the first group are the ones present at that moment, the second group are those who would be born later (including all of us). There are other explanations offered, but I personally like these the best. In the first case, I appreciate the idea that the women are included and are also listed before the men. The Torah was given to all of us, regardless of gender. The Torah is egalitarian. I also appreciate the second explanation, that each one of us should feel as if we ourselves were at Sinai and that the Torah was given directly to us no less than it was to the generation of the Exodus.

In the message that Moses was to deliver to the nation, God first reminded them of all that God had done for them so far: "I bore you on eagles' wings and brought you to Me" [19:4]. Several commentators have addressed the beautiful imagery of this verse. Rashi points out that, whereas other birds carry their young in their claws underneath them, the eagle instead carries its young on its wings. Coupling this with the idea that the eagle is said to fly higher than most other birds, we see that this shields the young protectively from danger below. Both Rashi and Ibn Ezra point out that others may fear the eagle, but the eagle fears nothing. Several described the eagle's great speed. Perhaps the comment that I like the best comes from Sforno: the swiftness of the eagle allows it "to go where no man had gone before."[6] I couldn't help but conjure up images of Captain Kirk and the Starship Enterprise when I read this!

A subtlety that is missed by many is that the phrase is really "on eagles' wings," meaning more than one eagle. Rabbeinu Bahya explains that the eagles are an allusion to the two pillars that accompanied the nation of Israel in the desert: the pillar of cloud by day and the pillar of fire at night, both guiding and protecting the nation as they traveled through the desert.[7] We read in the previous *parashah* how they surrounded the Israelites to fend off the charging Egyptians and their arrows.

The Ohr HaChaim describes additional clouds:

> The "wings of eagles" are a reference to . . . the clouds of [God's] glory, which were spread beneath the feet of the people so that they did not have to step on obstacles. Moses reminded the people of that in Deut. 8,4: "your feet never swelled during these forty years."[8]

Some take this even further, saying that there were a total of seven clouds that accompanied the nation on their journey: one on the left, one on the right, one in front of them, one behind them, one above them, and one below, all forming a kind of protective bubble, and one additional one in the front, leading the way.[9]

All this imagery is designed to show us the great love that God showed to the people of Israel, doing everything to draw them closer to the place where they would enter into a covenanted relationship. Like a groom anxiously awaiting his bride, God's desire was to bring them there with great speed. What awaited them at the mountain was something that no nation had ever experienced before. So, as you try to conjure up this image in your head, allow it also to stir in your heart the same anticipation of an encounter with the Divine that was no doubt experienced by our ancestors in the desert. May your Torah study inspire in you the same love for God that they must have felt. After all, each of us is to feel as if we were there at that time, standing at Sinai, preparing to meet our God.

FIFTH ALIYAH: EXODUS 19:7–19
THURSDAY, FEBRUARY 4, 2021

Tekiah!

This *aliyah* contains the final preparations that needed to be made before the giving of the Torah, all of which were transmitted to the people from Moses after his encounter with God on the mountain. The people were to wash their clothes and be ready for the third day when the revelation would take place. They were not to go up on or even touch the mountain. They were to abstain from sexual intimacy (that is the meaning of the commandment "do not come near a woman") for the duration of this three-day period [19:7-15]. Therefore, they were to appear before God as a bride: chaste, adorned in new clothes, and not entering the sacred area until the relationship had been consecrated.

All this drama was accompanied by awesome sights and sounds. The mountain, which was enshrouded in a thick cloud, was smoking and trembling, there was awesome thunder and lightning, and the sound of a shofar growing very loud. We can only imagine what it must have been like to be standing at Mt. Sinai that day. To us it sounds exciting but also somewhat intimidating, awe-inspiring but at the same time frightening [19:18-19].

The last verse of this section tells us that a manifestation of the Divine was imminent when the sound of the shofar grew louder and louder. According to the *midrash*, this wasn't any ordinary shofar:

> Rabbi Zechariah said: That ram, which was created at the twilight, ran and came to be offered up instead of Isaac . . . And it was caught by its two horns in the trees, as it is said, 'And Avraham lifted up his eyes, and looked, and behold, behind him a ram caught in the thicket by its horns' [Genesis 22:13] . . . He offered it up instead of Isaac his son, as it is said, 'And Avraham went and took the ram, and offered it up for a burnt offering in the stead of his son . . . From that ram, which was created at the twilight, nothing came forth which was useless . . . . The horn of the ram of the left side (was the one) wherein He blew upon Mt. Sinai, as it is said, 'And it shall come to pass, that when the ram's horn sound[s] long' . . . (The horn) of the right side, which is larger than that of the left, is destined in the future to be sounded in the world that is to come, as it is said, 'And it shall come to pass in that day, that a great trumpet shall be blown'" [Isa. 27:13] [*Pirke de Rabbi Eliezer* 31:11,13][10]

This *midrash* speaks of the ram that Abraham found caught in the thicket on Mt. Moriah and sacrificed in place of Isaac when God stopped him at the very moment that he was poised to take his son's life. Because this ram fulfilled such a holy purpose, it attained a special place in our tradition. Its (left) horn became the shofar through which God summoned the people to meet their holy Groom at the mountain. Later, this same horn was sounded at Jericho, causing the walls to fall for Joshua; it was the shofar whose blast announced the presence of God. The (right) horn has also been reserved for a future time, to announce the coming of the Mashiach. This shofar is mentioned three times in this reading. (The translations I give here may be a little bit different from what you see in your text, depending on the version you are using, but are, I believe, a more accurate representation of the Hebrew):

> verse 13: *bimshoch hayovel* (When the ram's horn sounds a long blast)
> verse 16: *v'kol shofar chazak* (the sound of the shofar grew stronger)
> verse 19: *vayehi kol hashofar holech v'chazak me'od* (and the sound of the shofar grew continuously stronger)

Just as the sound of this shofar called our ancestors to Sinai to the initial giving of the Torah, so, too, does it call us today to receive the words of the Torah, through study and a quest for deeper understanding. For our ancestors, the initial call was followed by a stronger blast, and then by a blast that grew continuously stronger. We, too, should make it our goal to dedicate ourselves to grow continuously stronger in our study and understanding of the Torah as we grow closer to God.

SIXTH ALIYAH: EXODUS 19:20–20:14
FRIDAY, FEBRUARY 5, 2021

Revelation

This *aliyah* contains the text of the Ten Commandments. Most of us are familiar with the commandments themselves, and I also did a comparison of this text with the text in Deuteronomy when we studied that *aliyah* several months ago. So, here I would like to share with you a *d'var Torah* that I wrote during my Pentateuch (i.e., Torah) class in my first semester of Rabbinical School at the Jewish Theological Seminary in Manhattan, based on an article written by my teacher, Professor Benjamin D. Sommer.[11] We see here that verses 20-25 of chapter 19 set the final stage for the Revelation: the people have gathered at the foot of the mountain, where Moses has told them not to go up. There they wait. There does seem to be some confusion about exactly where Moses was during this time. He seems to be putting in a lot of legwork going up and down the mountain, delivering messages from God to the people. The actual text of the Ten Commandments is contained in verses 1-14 of chapter 20. We have previously read about the sights and sounds that accompanied the giving of the Ten Commandments: the cloud on the mountain, the shofar blasts, the thunder, and the lightning. It was not only awe-inspiring, but it was also frightening to many of the people. We will see in the beginning of the next *aliyah* that at some point the people became so frightened that they asked Moses to go and talk to God for them, and then report back to them. The question then becomes: at what point did they make this request of Moses? Possible answers to this question are: 1) They asked Moses to go and speak with God on their behalf before the giving of the Ten Commandments, in which case they heard none of them; or 2) They asked him at some point during the giving of the Ten Commandments, in which case they heard some part of them; or 3) (least likely) they asked him after the Ten Commandments were given, in which case they heard all of them. We can quickly rule out the last possibility because if the people were so frightened by what they were seeing and hearing, it is highly unlikely that they would have listened to the whole recitation of the Decalogue and then said to Moses, "you go talk to God for us." So, now we need to answer the question, exactly how much did the people hear: nothing, or some part, of the Decalogue? It also does not seem likely that they made this request without hearing anything from God, which leaves us with the middle option. So, now we need to determine how much of the commandments they heard before deciding they had heard enough. Basing a conclusion on the fact that the first two commandments are given as though God is speaking to them directly, but the rest sound as if someone (Moses) is speaking on behalf of God (most likely due to the idea that the people were afraid and didn't want to hear any more), some scholars think that the people heard only the first two commandments. The late eighteenth-early nineteenth century Eastern European scholar R. Naftali Tzvi Horowitz (d. 1827) quotes Menachem Mendel of Rymaov (d. 1827) in suggesting this very minimalist theory: the only thing that the people heard was the *aleph*, the first letter of the first word *anochi* (which, in this case, is the more formal form of the first-person singular pronoun, "I"). Yet those who know Hebrew might say: How can this be? The *aleph* is a letter of silence. Without an accompanying vowel, it makes no sound at all. That would imply that, what the people really heard (quoting that great Jewish philosopher Paul Simon) was "the sound of silence." They each experienced the Revelation of the Torah at some profound, personal level as evidenced by the fact that each commandment is addressed in Hebrew to the individual (*atah* (you, second person singular)), not the plural (*atem* (you, second person plural)). Each one is written in the singular form. Thus, God spoke to the nation as a whole people, but each person experienced the Revelation as an individual, as if God were speaking to him/her personally. The following interesting theory was explained by Horowitz:

We can form an *aleph* by tilting a letter *vav* slightly to the left and attaching to it two *yuds*, one rightside-up and one upside-down: א

Furthermore, if we calculate the gematria of *vav* plus *yud* plus *yud*, the result is twenty-six. We receive the same result when we calculate the gematria of *yud-hey-vav-hey*, the unspeakable name of God. Both the *aleph* and God's ineffable name have a total value of twenty-six. Therefore, by implication, when we stood at Sinai and experienced the *aleph* of *anochi*, we were in direct communication with the Divine Presence. So, you might ask, what did we really hear since an *aleph* by itself is silent? Well, as it turns out, the *aleph* in the word *anochi* does have a vowel under it:

This *aleph* with a *kamatz* under it was like a quick rush of air: "aww." This was indeed how young yeshiva boys used to begin their formal education in *cheder* in eastern Europe: *Kamatz-Aleph*: aww. "The rest comes from God because God is the teacher" [Sommer].

This minimalist theory of Revelation implies that actually we heard little at Sinai, so it requires us to decipher and interpret the rest to find its meaning for our lives as individuals and as a nation. The *kol demamah*, the still small voice of Revelation, has not stopped. It does not stop. It continues to speak to us today. We just need to listen.

SEVENTH ALIYAH: EXODUS 20:14–22
WRITTEN FOR SHABBAT, SATURDAY, FEBRUARY 6, 2021

I'll Be There

This *aliyah* begins with the people telling Moses to go and speak to God on their behalf since they were both awestruck and frightened by the entire experience. Their senses were so overwhelmed by all the things that they were experiencing that the Torah text literally says that they saw the thunder and the lightning [20:15]. Usually only the latter of those can be experienced visually!

When Moses returns to the people, he brings the message that God has spelled out regarding the first two commandments specifically: we are commanded not to make any physical representations of God, not even of silver or gold. Rather, God commands that worship shall consist of making an altar on which sacrifices can be made [20:20-21]. As we have seen, sacrifices were an important component of biblical worship. (This form of worship ended with the destruction of the Second Temple in the year 70 CE. Since that time, sacrifice has been replaced with prayer.)

If the people do promise to abide by this request/commandment, God makes a beautiful promise: "... in every place where I cause My name to be mentioned I will come to you and bless you" [20:21].

When we offer our prayers to God, God promises to be with us. The Baal HaTurim points out that the word "I will come" has the gematria of ten.[12] Therefore, he interprets this to indicate that whenever a *minyan* of ten people gathers together in the synagogue, the Divine presence will come and dwell among them. This is also mentioned in the following Mishnah:

> Rabbi Halafta of Kefar Hanania said: when ten sit together and
> occupy themselves with Torah, the Shechinah abides among them,
> as it is said: "God stands in the congregation of God" [Psalm
> 82:1] [*Pirkei Avot 3:6*][13]

Some feel that God's promise to come to us when we worship applies even when fewer than ten gather together. The Mishnah continues:

> How do we know that the same is true even of five? As it is said: "This
> band of His He has established on Earth" [Amos 9:6]. How do we know
> that the same is true even of three? As it is said: "In the midst of the
> judges He judges" [Psalm 82:1]. How do we know that the same is true
> even of two? As it is said: "Then they that fear the Lord spoke one
> with another, and the Lord hearkened, and heard" [Malachi 3:16].[13]

During this past year, when social distancing has resulted in many times when we are not able to come together in a *minyan*, this idea has become especially relevant. Now more than ever we need to feel the comforting presence of the *Shekhinah* when we worship, often virtually, from our homes instead of the synagogue sanctuary.

And what of those who find themselves in a solitary worship experience? The *mishnah* continues . . .

> How do we know that the same is true even of one? As it is said:
> "In every place where I cause my name to be mentioned I will
> come unto you and bless you." [Exodus 20:21][13]

For most of the last year, except for a few short weeks in the fall, and Sunday mornings in the summertime, I have davened *shacharit* at home, alone. To make my experience more meaningful, I adopted the practice of davening outside on my back deck, which happens to face east. About the only thing that has kept me inside is either rain or snow in the morning. Even in chillier temperatures, I have gone outside. I have watched the seasons change as I am joined each morning by the songs of the birds in the yard augmenting my prayer experience. And I have also felt the presence of God as we greet each new day together.

Parashat Mishpatim

FIRST ALIYAH: EXODUS 21:1–19
SUNDAY, FEBRUARY 7, 2021

Don't Rely on Miracles

Parashat Mishpatim is chock full of interesting things. As the natural continuation of the Revelation of the Ten Commandments, it contains many of the subsequent *mitzvot* that Moses conveyed to the people (remember ten was just a start; there are six hundred three more!). Some find it interesting that the first issue to be addressed is that of slaves [21:1-11]. However, we need to remember that the audience who first received these verses had indeed just come out of several hundred years of slavery themselves. They were to remember what it felt like to be enslaved, and not inflict the same kind of suffering on anyone who came to be their slaves. (I have addressed this issue of slavery before, when it came up in the book of Leviticus in *parashat* Behar. Slavery was often not something inflicted on another against his/her will as it was here in the United States, but rather, it occurred when an individual who had become destitute entered such a commitment as a way of supporting himself and/or his family.

In any event, the following conditions were imposed upon a slavery situation: it could last six years at most, and slaves were freed in the Sabbatical (seventh) year. A wife and children who came with him at the beginning of his servitude would leave with him at the end, but a wife given to him by his master, and any children born of that union, stayed behind with the master. Additionally, a man could choose to stay permanently with the master but if a master changed his mind about a female slave whom he had taken, he could not send her away because he was still responsible for clothing and feeding her.

This is followed by a section on those who take the life of another, intentionally or otherwise [21:12-14]. One who takes a life shall lose his own. If it was not premeditated, he shall be allowed to escape to one of the cities of refuge (I have also discussed these previously, in *parashat* Masei and *parashat* Shoftim).

Then, in rapid succession, we have the following three categories of people who are to be put to death: one who strikes a parent, one who captures another and sells him, one who curses a parent [21:15-17].

Finally, in the last two verses of this *aliyah*, we have the situation of two men quarreling and one inflicts a (non-life-threatening) injury on the other [21:18-19]. The one who injured the other is responsible for paying for the other's loss of (productive working) time, and—this is the part I want to address—for bringing about the other's healing (in modern terms, we would say paying for his medical bills). Indeed, Onkelos says that he is required to pay the doctor's fee.[1] Ramban expands on this, explaining that he must pay the doctor(s) directly and they have to cure the victim, who may not collect the settlement money himself and then use it for something else.[1]

A number of scholars explain that the Hebrew phrase being discussed here, *v'rapo yerapeh*, ((he shall) cause him to be thoroughly healed), really serves as an authorization for physicians to practice medicine. This explanation of this phrase appears in the Talmud no less than twenty-two times. Here are just two of them:

> . . . When the verse states: "And shall cause him to be thoroughly healed [*verappo yerappe*]" . . . it is derived from here that permission is granted to a doctor to heal, and it is not considered to be an intervention counter to the will of God. [*BT Bava Kama 85A:15*]

> . . . Rav Aḥa is saying that people should not practice medicine as they lack the ability to heal; rather, healing should be left to God. Abaye responded and said: One should not say this, as it was taught in the school of Rabbi Yishmael that from the verse, "And shall cause him to be thoroughly healed" [Exodus 21:19], from here we derive that permission is granted to a doctor to heal. The practice of medicine is in accordance with the will of God. [*BT Brachot 60A:28-29*]

We notice in this second quote that there was a dispute here between two rabbis regarding whether or not people should rely on physicians and their medical skills. One, Rav Aha, said no, healing comes from God. Abbaye disagrees, saying that medical healing is indeed in accordance with the will of God.

This is an idea that has come very much to the forefront in our times. There are many (observant) Jews who are resistant to do what is necessary to fight COVID: wear a mask, socially distance, and get a vaccine. They feel that other *mitzvot* are equally as important (studying Torah, celebrating a wedding, escorting a deceased person to his/her grave). And they say that "God will protect me."

However, the *halachah* is clear here in the *Shulchan Aruch:*

> **The Torah permits a doctor to heal the sick,** as it is said, "And he shall [pay] to have him healed properly. "Therefore, **a sick person should not rely on a miracle, but is obliged to follow the accepted procedure and call a physician to heal him.** Many of the world's pious men have been cured by physicians. A person who refrains from calling in a physician (for himself) commits two wrongs: For one, **it is forbidden to rely on a miracle in a life-threatening situation.** This behavior causes one's sins to be remembered at a time of illness. Secondly, **it is arrogant and presumptuous to rely on your righteousness that you will be healed in some miraculous manner.** You should call the most competent physician but with all that, your heart should be turned to Heaven, and pray for mercy from the Faithful Healer, blessed is His Name trusting in Him alone. [*Kitzur Shulchan Aruch 192:3*][2] [emphasis mine]

The doctors and nurses who have been in the front lines of dealing with this coronavirus have given and continue to give countless hours of personal sacrifice, often putting themselves in harm's way to care for those afflicted with the disease. Our obligation as Jews, to God, to the healthcare workers, to others around us—and to ourselves—is to do everything in our power to keep ourselves healthy.

This is true no matter what our health issue is, not just COVID. Caring for our health is a primary responsibility. We dare not be presumptuous and rely on miracles.

SECOND ALIYAH: EXODUS 21:20–22:3
MONDAY, FEBRUARY 8, 2021

A Loss Without Recompense

This *aliyah* contains multiple laws having to do with restitution in various situations:

1. A man who strikes his servant is punished only if the servant dies. [21:20-21]
2. When two men quarrel and one inflicts damage on the other, the perpetrator shall receive the same injury that he inflicted (eye for eye, tooth for tooth, etc.). [21:23-25]
3. A man who strikes his servant and destroys either his eye or his tooth must let the servant go free. [21:26-27]
4. If an ox gores a person who then dies, the ox is stoned, but the owner is acquitted, unless the ox was in the habit of doing this and the owner had been warned. In that case, the ox is stoned, and the owner is put to death [21:28-29]. The same is true if the ox gores the fellow's child; if the ox gores a servant, its owner must make a payment of thirty shekels of silver. [21:31-32]
5. If a man digs an open pit and an ox or a donkey falls in and dies, he must pay damages to the owner of the animal, but he receives the carcass. [21:33-34]
6. If one man's ox kills another man's ox, the live ox is to be sold and the money received, as well as the carcass of the dead ox, are to be divided between the two men, unless the ox was in the habit of behaving this way. In this case, the live ox is given to the man whose ox was killed, and the owner of the errant ox receives the carcass of the dead ox. [21:35-36]
7. If a man steals an ox or a sheep, and subsequently either kills or sells it, he must make restitution: five oxen for an ox, four sheep for a sheep. [21:37]
8. If a thief breaks into a house at night, and the homeowner strikes him in self-defense and kills him, the homeowner is not liable. [22:1]

There is one law in here that I want to discuss in a little greater detail: "When men fight, and one of them pushes a pregnant woman and a miscarriage results, but no other damage ensues, the one responsible shall be fined according as the woman's husband may exact from him, the payment to be based on reckoning" [21:22].

Reading further into the next verse, we see that the one who caused the injury is required to compensate the injured woman's husband in equal measure: [the value of] an eye if she lost an eye, [the value of] a hand if she lost a hand, [the value of] a foot if she lost a foot, etc. Everything is calculated monetarily, comparing the value of the person (in this case the woman) if (s)he were to be sold as a slave before this injury occurred to her value after suffering the injury. Based on this logic, then, following the same reasoning, the verse indicates that the man who caused the woman to miscarry is required to compensate the husband for the difference of the woman's value were she to be sold in the slave market if she had still been pregnant as compared to when she is not. That seems to be the only reason that this injury is singled out from the other injuries. We can say "an eye for an eye, a hand for a hand" and so on but we can't exactly say "a fetus for a fetus," especially since the one who injured her was a man!

This all seems very crude and cold to our modern sensibilities, viewing everything monetarily; we have difficulty relating to it, especially those of us who are women.

The important thing to take away from this is the following: it is clear from this text that the loss of the fetus is viewed as an injury to the woman and is not considered a loss of life. This is one of the verses that is used to support Judaism's view that life begins at birth, not at conception.

We sometimes wrestle with this concept, especially those of us who have experienced the awesome feeling of a potential new life moving inside of us. We also must be mindful of the fact that, until modern times, with major advances in prenatal and pediatric care (among other things), the infant mortality rate was much higher than it is today. Certainly, in biblical and Talmudic times, it was a much more common occurrence for a woman to lose multiple children over the course of her lifetime, either during pregnancy or during their childhoods. We also need to remember that the biblical text reflects a patriarchal society, and all our early rabbis and commentators were men, as well. Perhaps this was their way of dealing with this phenomenon while trying to spare the mother heartbreak.

In any event, it is one of those instances where ancient viewpoints clash with our modern-day feelings. We struggle with it, we wrestle with it, we try to make some sense of it. Many rabbis today, recognizing the very real emotional pain that a mother (and a father, as well) experiences at the loss of a pregnancy, regardless of the cause, help the parents to find appropriate ways of expressing their grief. Appropriate religious rituals have been devised to honor the loss of a potential life, and to provide the needed support of a rabbi and the Jewish tradition at what is a most vulnerable time in the life of a parent.

I extend my sympathies to any of you who have experienced such a loss. May you experience the comforting presence of the *Shekhinah* to accompany you through your mourning.

THIRD ALIYAH: EXODUS 22:4–26
TUESDAY, FEBRUARY 9, 2021

Our Actions Surely Have Consequences

The list of *mitzvot* continues. In this *aliyah*, we have several command-ments regarding animals or other property that cause damage, or are lost, or stolen [22:2-14]. Next, we read about a man who seduces a girl/woman who is a virgin and not betrothed (committed to, designated for) someone else. He is obligated to pay her dowry to her father and marry her. Even if her father does not give permission for him to marry her, he must still pay the dowry. It is important that we note that the word used here is seduction, which does not involve force. Rape is addressed elsewhere in the Torah.

Following this, we have three seemingly disparate prohibitions: sorcery, bestiality, and offering sacrifices to other gods [22:17-19].

The last seven verses of the reading contain what could arguably be considered the most relevant, timeless (or timely?) commandments in this section, discussing the treatment of the most vulnerable people in society: the widow, the orphan, and the stranger [22:20-23].

First the stranger (i.e., the convert): you are not to wrong or oppress him/her for the simple reason that you yourselves were strangers in Egypt. In other words, you know what it feels like to be a stranger and it's not good, so don't do it to someone else.

Next, the widow and the orphan: do not afflict them. That's it. No ratio-nale. Just don't do it. In a patriarchal society, where all means of financial support devolved through the men, these were people with little to no means of providing for their own needs. But, if you do afflict them, and they cry out to God, God will hear them. Reading this verse should remind us of what God said to Moses from the burning bush: "I have now heard the moaning of the Israelites because the Egyptians are holding them in bondage, and I have remembered My covenant" [Exodus 6:5]. Just as God heard our cries when we were suffering in slavery in Egypt, so, too, will God hear the cries of the innocent victims whom we oppress.

These are followed by three verses cautioning us against charging interest from the poor if we lend them money [22:24-26]. If the only pledge a man has to offer is his garment, we are to give it back to him each day, for he will need it for sleeping (I have previously discussed this idea in *parashat Ki Tetzei*.

It is interesting to notice several things about the Hebrew grammar in this section. First, most of the verbs are written in the singular imperative form though sometimes they fluctuate to the plural imperative form. We are enjoined to recognize that these things are our individual obligations; each of us is directly commanded to be sensitive to the needs of the poor and oppressed in our midst. Yet, as individuals, our capacity to right these wrongs is limited. Our actual efforts to help them can be/are much more effective when we realize our obligations as a society, and we work together to address the needs of the disadvantaged.

Additionally, in verse 22, an uncommon verb form, the infinitive construct, occurs three times in one verse: *aneh taaneh, tza-ok yitzak, shamoa eshmah.* This form usually intensifies the meaning (If you will surely afflict them, they will surely cry out to me, I will surely hear them). The Baal HaTurim explains their presence here a little differently: "the double verb form implies that God will respond to every action that inflicts pain upon a widow or an orphan with a similar action against the perpetrator."[3] Every action has an equal and opposite reaction. In other words, our actions (or inactions) have consequences. If we cannot fulfill our obligations, if we ourselves cannot respond to the cries of the others, we can little expect God to respond to our cries when we find ourselves in a time of need.

FOURTH ALIYAH: EXODUS 22:27–23:5
WEDNESDAY, FEBRUARY 10, 2021

Actions Have Consequences

This short *aliyah* contains several *mitzvot* concerning our relationship with God.

We are not to revile God or an earthly ruler. Nor are we to withhold our first fruits or our firstborn from God, or the firstborn of our animals, nor are we to eat animals that die of natural causes [22:27-30],

This is followed by three verses relating to judgements. We are not to give a false testimony or throw our testimony in with the wicked; we are not to pervert justice; we are not to show favoritism to a poor man in a dispute [23:1-3]. The idea of not showing partiality in judgment, either to the rich and powerful, or to the poor and destitute, is strongly emphasized. Surely, we can understand being cautioned against favoring the rich and powerful because these are the people who have the means to offer a bribe or to exert undue influence on the rendering of a judgement. But the poor? We just finished discussing in the last *aliyah* how we need to be especially sensitive to the needs of the poor. But the truth is that this is precisely the reason for the present precaution. As Sarna points out, the mere fact that the Torah so frequently reminds us to have compassion for the poor might possibly cause us to have undue sympathies for them.[4] This, in turn, could easily cloud our judgement, influencing us to rule in their favor as a means of helping them out. Or HaChaim takes this even further by explaining it this way:

> . . . The extra word [*b'ribo*] contains a moral/ethical message . . . that the poor is liable to engage in a confrontation with God asking [God] why [God] supplies everyone else with their needs whereas he is hungry and naked. Everyone who gives even a copper coin to a poor [person] and thereby stills his hunger prevents the poor from complaining to God and accusing [God] that God is not gracious to the poor. On the other hand, at times when no one on Earth is gracious to the poor, his argument is very powerful. The Torah therefore commands us not to contribute to strengthening the voice of the poor who accuse God of insensitivity to their fate.[5]

According to this explanation, the poor person might naturally tend to accuse God of favoring others while neglecting them. This sentiment is only strengthened when others neglect his/her needs, and refrain from doing anything to help them. On the other hand, when others give him/her *tzedakah*, those actions serve to either prevent or delay him/her from cursing or accusing God.

Our concern for the poor should not only be for their physical needs, but for their emotional and spiritual needs, as well. Our actions should inspire praise for God, not curses, love for God, not disdain. Our actions must be representative of adherence to the *mitzvot*. Our own motivations will inspire like motivations in others. Actions inspired by a love for God can, in turn, inspire a love for God in those whose lives are affected by what we do. Conversely, actions inspired by an indifference to the needs of others can in turn inspire an indifference to God (or worse).

Once again, we see that our actions have consequences, sometimes far-reaching.

FIFTH ALIYAH: EXODUS 23:6–19
THURSDAY, FEBRUARY 11, 2021

Prayers in Motion

This *aliyah* begins with reiterations of several *mitzvot* that we have already seen. You are not to pervert justice or take bribes or show favoritism in judgement. You are not to oppress the stranger because you yourselves were strangers in Egypt and know how it feels to be an outsider. You are to work the land for six years and allow it to rest as a (sabbatical) year once every seven years. Similarly, once every seven days, you are to observe Shabbat as a day of rest for you, your servants, and your animals. You are not to even mention the names of any other gods [23:6-13].

This is followed by a section related to the calendar The first and last of these verses practically look like bookends: "Three times a year you shall hold a festival for Me." and "Three times a year all your males shall appear before the Sovereign, the LORD" [23:14-17].

In between these verses, we read of *Pesach, Shavuot,* and *Sukkot,* the three holidays which are specifically referred to as *chag, chagim.* These are what are sometimes referred to as the Three Pilgrimage Festivals: each required every Jewish male to travel to Jerusalem and appear at the Temple. (It is not a coincidence that the Hebrew word *chag* sounds very similar to the Arabic word *haj,* which is a word still used today to refer to Muslim pilgrimages to Mecca.)

Interestingly, the two verses cited above, both begin with the same two words in the English: "three times." The Hebrew, however, is not the same. The phrase *shalosh pe-amim* does literally mean "three times" [23:17] and the phrase *shalosh regalim* literally means "three feet" [23:14] but is considered a synonym of the first phrase. Observance of these three holidays takes place by using our feet.

Thinking about this reminded me of a famous saying, "praying with my feet." Many people attribute this saying to Rabbi Abraham Joshua Heschel, who, after marching side by side with Dr. Martin Luther King, Jr. in Selma, Alabama in 1965, was quoted as saying the following:

"For many of us, the march from Selma to Montgomery was about
protest and prayer. Legs are not lips and walking is not kneeling.
And yet our legs uttered songs. Even without words, our march
was worship. I felt my legs were praying."[6]

He was not, however, the originator of the concept. It can more accurately be traced to the famous abolitionist Stephen Douglass, who is quoted
as saying, "Praying for freedom never did me any good till I started praying
with my feet."[7]

No matter which way you phrase it, the message is the same: praying is
often meditative but unless it is also expressed by actions, it is ineffective.
Praying on our own or even in the synagogue must also inspire us to march
out into the world and work for social justice. This can take many forms:
fighting for racial equality, working on behalf of the poor in our midst, working to improve the environment, etc. In other words, our spiritual prayers
should inspire us to work for *tikkun olam*, repairing the world that we live
in. For if they do not, then our prayers benefit no one, not the world, not God,
not even ourselves.

SIXTH ALIYAH: EXODUS 23:20–25
FRIDAY, FEBRUARY 12, 2021

Come Together

This short *aliyah* concludes the extensive listing of *mitzvot* that have comprised the first five *aliyot* of this *parashah*. Here God speaks to the nation
of Israel telling them that an angel will be sent to guard them on their way
to the land of Canaan. The people are forewarned that they are not to provoke this angel, rather they are commanded to obey him. Moreover, they are
warned again that, once they get to the land, they are not to worship the gods
of the people who live there, but rather they are to destroy their idols to prevent themselves from even being tempted to do so [23:20-24].

The reading concludes with the following verse: "You shall serve the
LORD your God, and He will bless your bread and your water. And I will
remove sickness from your midst" [23:25].

What we can only see in the Hebrew, not the English, is that the first
part of the verse is written in the second person plural (you, your), and the
rest is written in the second person singular (you, your). The Baal HaTurim
explains that the commandment "you shall serve" is written in the plural

because it is referring to communal prayer, which is always (quarantine notwithstanding) preferable for us as Jews.[8] Praying as an individual is always acceptable, but our tradition tells us that God pays special attention when we come together to pray, especially when there are ten or more of us. There are multiple parts of the service, including the *kaddishes*, the *Amidah*, and the *barchu*, that can only be recited in the presence of a *minyan*. When we join our prayers together, we are uplifted by the prayers of others, and the shared experience of worshipping God together.

The Baal HaTurim goes on to explain that the second part of the verse, which tells us that God will bless "your bread" and "your water" and remove sickness from "your midst" is written in the singular because God blesses each of us according to our own personal needs.[8]

God's need is for us to join together in prayer and praise, and when we do that, we are blessed as a community. In addition, we each receive the individualized blessings that we need, as well.

These days, it is usually not possible to come together for an experience of communal prayer, and many of us miss it. We long to be able to join our prayers with others, to be able to say *kaddish* for our loved ones whom we have lost, or to answer the *barchu* call to prayer. Even though many rabbis have allowed for the possibility of convening a virtual *minyan* over Zoom, the experience is still not quite the same. At the same time, since we are so isolated spiritually, we need more than ever to receive God's blessings, to feel the comforting presence of the *Shekhinah*.

In two weeks' time, we will celebrate the joyous holiday of Purim—virtually. Many of us remember that this was the last holiday that we all celebrated together last March. That means that we are completing a full year's cycle of holidays celebrated in isolation. Who would ever have imagined that this pandemic would last so long?

Some of us are beginning to receive our vaccinations (I got my second dose yesterday!). As we begin a second cycle of holidays by planning for a second year of Zoom seders, we can begin to see some glimmers of hope. May God sustain you both spiritually and physically until we can join together physically in one location once again in communal prayer. And when that day comes, how joyous will our worship be!

Do You Hear What I Hear?

This last *aliyah* of *parashat Mishpatim* begins with several promises that God makes to the nation for the future time when they would be settled in the land [23:26-33], which, after all, is the ultimate destination for which they are headed. God tells them that none of the women will be barren, and none will miscarry, and that their enemies will gradually be driven out of the land before them. The boundaries of the land are delineated, and the people are commanded to have no agreements with the people of the land. Once again, they are reminded not to worship their gods.

The laws that will govern their relationship to God and the land are contained in the Torah that has begun to be revealed to them. God invites Moses and Aaron, along with Aaron's two oldest sons Nadav and Avihu (remember what later happened to them at the dedication of the *mishkan*?) and seventy elders to come up to the mountain to worship. There they will have a mystical experience, including a vision of God sitting on God's heavenly throne. Moses is invited to go up into the cloud, where he will remain for forty days and nights and receive the tablets upon which the Ten Commandments will be inscribed.

Before ascending, Moses recounts to the people all the words that he has heard from God. Their response to Moses is: *naaseh v'nishma*, literally, "All that the Lord has spoken we will do and we will hear [listen]." This phrase has been debated and discussed by many commentators. The order of the words seems as if they are backwards and should be reversed. How can doing precede hearing? Does this imply blind obedience?

Remember that prior to this the people were frightened to hear the "voice" of God. They heard only the very beginning of the Decalogue, and then implored Moses to go and speak with God on their behalf. When they say, "we will do," they commit themselves to the covenant as it has already been revealed through Moses. When they say, "we will hear," they commit to listening for/to God's instructions from this point forward. They commit themselves to obey (hear) a covenant formulated by ongoing revelation from God.

This should be our approach to our relationship with God, as well. The actual words, the text of Revelation that are recorded in our Torah remain unchanged. The Revelation of interpretation, however, is an ever-evolving phenomenon. In Pirkei Avot, we read:

> Rabbi Joshua ben Levi said: every day a *bat kol* (a heavenly voice)
> goes forth from Mount Horeb [Sinai] [Pirkei Avot 6:2][9]

To be a Jew is to live a life of commitment to the Torah that is already revealed and is being revealed anew every day. That can only be done by one whose ears are open to hear the still, small voice of God when it speaks to us.

I think it is hardly a coincidence that the seminal prayer of the Jewish people is the Shema—a prayer that begins by enjoining us to listen, to hear. Throughout Jewish history, God has called us to enter God's own presence, to commit ourselves to the eternal *brit* established at Sinai and to continue to listen to its ongoing instruction in our lives.

As we enter Shabbat, may your heart be opened to hear the words of your Creator.

Parashat Terumah

FIRST ALIYAH: EXODUS 25:1–16
SUNDAY, FEBRUARY 14, 2021

Take Me, Please

What is *Terumah*? It is a gift, an offering, which is brought willingly. The offering referred to here in this reading consists of the items needed for the construction of the *mishkan,* the Tabernacle, and all its accoutrements, which will accompany the nation of Israel as they travel through the desert.

Most Torah scholars feel that actually this *parashah* is out of chronological order, that the events described in it really took place after the incident with the Golden Calf, which is described in *parashat Ki Tissa*, that we will read two weeks from now.

The *parashah* begins with God instructing Moses to tell the people to bring gifts, *terumah,* to be used in the construction of the portable sanctuary. These free-will offerings are to be accepted from every person whose heart moves him/her to bring them [25:2]. At the end of the verse, the word appears again: *terumati.* With the possessive ending here, it means "my offering." Since the *mishkan* was to be a place for God to meet the people, we can interpret this to mean that God also contributed to the offering along with the people.

God goes on to list thirteen materials needed and requested for the construction of the Tabernacle, listed in order of importance [25:3-7]. We cannot help but notice what the first item on the list is: gold. We will see that a huge amount of this precious metal is required, both for the tent itself, and especially the ark that will house the tablets of the Ten Commandments. It seems as if this construction is meant to atone for the Golden Calf. There, in that incident, Aaron told the men to take the gold from the earrings their wives wore. Here, it was offered freely but there it was used to construct an idol, a physical representation of a god that they could see and worship. Here, it was used to construct a sanctuary to house the *Shekhinah*, the indwelling presence of God who can be experienced but not seen. The construction of the calf was a scene of chaos brought about by the panic and fear of the nation at the fact that they didn't know when their leader would return, whereas the construction of the Tabernacle was an orderly scene that took place in an orderly fashion according to the instructions given by God through the mouth of their leader, who was standing right in front of them. God leaves no doubt about what these materials are to be used for: "And let them make Me a sanctuary and I will dwell among them" [25:8]. When they build this sanctuary, they will have no need for physical representations of God because God promises to take up residence among the nation. The word *betocham* can better be translated as "within them." God promises that the *Shekhinah* will dwell inside the hearts of each individual and this is no less true today than it was then.

Moses relays the specific instructions, beginning with those for the ark, which is to be constructed before the Tabernacle itself [25:10-16]. It is to have very precise dimensions: "two and a half cubits long, a cubit and a half wide, and a cubit and a half high." Not one of the three dimensions is a whole number—2½ cubits by 1½ cubits by 1½ cubits. This comes to remind us that none of us is perfect, nor is our knowledge of Torah ever complete.

Pulling this all together, let us return to the second verse where God tells Moses to tell the people to bring their gifts, their *terumah*. God says, "let them take [for] me" [25:2]. A better translation leaves out the word "for:"

> The Holy One, blessed be He, said to Israel: The law is Mine, and if you accept it, you must accept Me with it [*Midrash Tanchuma, Terumah 3:3*][1]

The Baal haTurim paraphrases this beautifully: "The Holy One, Blessed is He, said to Israel, 'The Torah is Mine and you have taken it . . . take Me with it.'"[2] In a moving expression of love that resembles a marriage proposal, God asks us to accept not just the words of Torah, but also the indwelling presence of the *Shekhinah* that imparts meaning to those words.

SECOND ALIYAH: EXODUS 25:17–40
MONDAY, FEBRUARY 15, 2021

I Will Meet You There

This *aliyah* gives the details of the construction of all the furnishings of the *mishkan*, beginning with the covering, or *kapporet*, over the ark. It was to be a slab of pure gold, exactly the same size as the ark itself. A pair of of *keruvim*, angelic-faced beings, were placed, one on each end of the *kapporet*, facing each other with their faces turned slightly downward and their wings pointing upwards [25:17-21]. God tells Moses: "There I will meet with you, and I will impart to you—from above the cover, from between the two cherubim that are on top of the Ark of the Pact—all that I will command you concerning the Israelite people" [25:22]. In this small space between the wings of the *keruvim* and above the *kapporet*, is where God promises to talk with Moses. Some of us have trouble wrapping our heads around this idea. After all, God is infinite. How could it be that the *Shekhinah* could be contained in this tiny space? The rabbis, too, have struggled to understand this idea:

> That great glory, of which it is written, "Do I not fill heaven and Earth?"
> See how His love of Israel wrought upon this glory! The Lord, as it
> were, contracted Himself to speak from above the *kapporet* between the
> two cherubs! [*Sifra, Vayikra Dibbura d'Nedavah, Chapter 2 12*][3]

The God Who fills the universe contracted the Divine presence to fill this small, sacred space when speaking with Moses. And why would God do this? Out of love, as is explained in this *midrash:*

> There was a certain man who was saying about his marriage as he
> walked: When our love was strong, we could have slept on a bed
> that was the width of a sword. Now that our love is not strong, a
> bed of sixty cubits is not sufficient for us. Rav Huna said: Verses
> are written that convey these sentiments. Initially, it was written:
> "I will meet with you there and I will speak with you from above
> the Ark Cover" [Exodus 25:22], and it is taught in a *baraita:*
> . . . when God had great affection for Israel, the Divine Presence was
> revealed within the confines of this limited space . . . . And at the end, when
> Israel sinned, the whole of the space of the Temple was not expansive
> enough for the Divine Presence to rest within it [*BT Sanhedrin 7A:14-15*]

The image of God in the *mishkan* is compared to a newlywed groom, so in love with his bride that they commune together in intimacy in this tiny space above the ark. Sadly, the second half of this *midrash* conveys the image of a marriage relationship that has soured, where intimacy no longer exists, and the couple cannot find enough room to get away from each other. This was what happened centuries later when the nation became sinful.

As was discussed in the lesson of the first *aliyah*, today in the absence of the *mishkan* or the Temple, the *Shekhinah* can come and dwell within each of us if we open ourselves up to it. We also need to remember that, just like a marriage, we need to work on this relationship with the Divine. That requires making sure that our hearts are open to accepting the Divine Presence, as well as communicating with God in that very small space. That takes work on our part, work to learn the words of Torah, work to observe the *mitzvot*, work to put those values into practice for *tikkun olam*—doing our part to repair our broken world. And, like a marriage, sometimes we'll slip up and we may feel that God is angry with us. That just means we need to work harder to make things right again.

Then there are those moments of Divine intimacy when God's presence feels almost palpable. They come unexpectedly, perhaps when you are studying and are inspired by something new discovered in a text, or perhaps when you find new meaning in the words of a prayer, or when you witness a beautiful or strange phenomenon in nature. The feeling is difficult to describe, but if you've ever had moments like this you know exactly what I am talking about. They come infrequently, making them even more precious. And these are the moments that sustain us.

As we are marking more than a full year of living in the shadow of COVID-19, we need those kinds of moments more than ever.

THIRD ALIYAH: EXODUS 26:1–14
TUESDAY, FEBRUARY 16, 2021

A Unicorn in the Torah?

This *aliyah* gives the instructions for the coverings of the *mishkan*. There are four levels of coverings. The first consists of ten sheets of linen in shades of blue, purple, and scarlet, with one hundred loops and fifty clasps to join them together [26:1-6]. The second level consists of eleven curtains of goats' hair, again with one hundred loops and fifty clasps for joining them together [26:7-13]. The third level consists of rams' skins dyed red [26:14].

It's that fourth level that catches our attention. This layer consists of *orot techashim*, translated as "dolphin skins." What? Dolphin skins? In the middle of the desert? How could that be?

The rabbis, too, wondered about these. What exactly was a *tachash*? Since the word appears nowhere else besides the instructions for the *mishkan*, it is impossible to say for sure. There is a *midrash* that says that this was something entirely different:

... The *tahash* that existed in the days of Moses was a creature unto itself ... And it had a single horn on its forehead, and this *tahash* happened to come to Moses for the moment while the Tabernacle was being built, and he made the covering for the Tabernacle from it. And from then on, the *tahash* was suppressed and is no longer found. [*BT Shabbat 28B:6*]

According to this *midrash*, this unicorn appeared at the exact moment that Moses needed it to build the Tabernacle, and disappeared once the construction was done, never to be seen again. Furthermore, this *tachash* was said to be very colorful: It was a large pure animal, with a single horn in its forehead and a skin of six different colors that roamed the desert ... They captured one of them and from its skin made a covering for the ark. R. Nehemiah contended that it was a miraculous creature that [God] created for that precise moment, and that it disappeared immediately thereafter from Earth. Why is it called *orot tahashim*? Because the verse states: "The length of each curtain shall be thirty cubits." What known animal could supply enough skin for a curtain of thirty cubits? It must, indeed, have been a miraculous creation, which disappeared immediately after it was created [*Midrash Tanchuma, Terumah 6*].[4]

It is said that this *tachash*, this unicorn, this animal that had a single horn protruding from the middle of its head, rejoiced in its six colors, and was happy to fulfill the mission for which it had been created. This made me think about the item which God has commanded that we human beings place in the middle of our own foreheads.

Most people are familiar with the Hebrew word for six, *shesh*. The two *shins* that form this word remind me of the *tefilin shel rosh*, the head *tefilin*, which has two *shins* on it. The *shin* which is on the right side of the *bayit* (box) when the *tefilin* is placed on the head is a normal three-pronged *shin*, while the one on the left side is unusual: it has four prongs, something not seen anywhere else. Therefore, by combining the two letters, we get a

total of seven prongs. I like to think of the three prongs as representing our three patriarchs, and the four as representing our matriarchs. As we stand in prayer each morning, we are surrounded by the history of all those who came before us. More importantly, seven is the number that represents perfection, completeness, wholeness. Had that *shin* on the left been a normal letter, we would have had only six prongs. Instead, we have seven.

If the *tachash*, the unicorn, can rejoice in its six colors that were given to it, and praise God that it was given a purpose, becoming part of the structure of the *mishkan*—the place where Moses came to encounter God—how much more so should we rejoice in our "horn" with seven prongs, that helps us to focus our minds and hearts on our daily encounter with God. Whether that encounter takes place together with others in a *minyan*, or as individuals praying in our home sanctuaries, we still are surrounded by the *yichus* of the patriarchs and the matriarchs, who intercede for us as our prayers ascend to the Divine throne.

FOURTH ALIYAH: EXODUS 26:15–30
WEDNESDAY, FEBRUARY 17, 2021

Torah is Like Mother's Milk

This *aliyah* outlines the instructions for the wooden structure of the *mishkan*, comprised of planks and sockets which would be used to join all the pieces together. There were to be forty planks each for the northern and southern sides of the tent, eight for the western side and the eastern side was apparently to be left open. These components will complete the outside of the structure itself.

The *aliyah* concludes with God telling Moses to set up the Tabernacle according to the way it was shown to him on the mountain [26:30]. From this, the rabbis infer that the *mishkan* was not set up piece by piece as the various parts were constructed. Rather, it was only erected after all the pieces had been made and gathered so that it could be erected all at once. It is also believed that Moses himself erected the tent when it went up the very first time because he had been shown the blueprints when he was on the mountain receiving the tablets.

This portable sanctuary would serve the religious needs of the people for the entire time they traveled in the wilderness. Later, once the nation settled in the land and the monarchy had been established, it was King David who longed to set up a permanent place of worship in a central location in

Jerusalem, but, though his motivation was pure, his hands were stained with the bloodshed of war. Instead, God told him that his son, Solomon, would be the one to build the Temple. Indeed, Solomon constructed a large, grandiose structure. Upon its completion, it was dedicated with much singing, dancing, and rejoicing.

And yet, even then, as the nation joyously celebrated together the completion of the Temple, a *midrash* tells us that Solomon had a vision of its future destruction:

> ...In the hour that Shlomo built the Holy Temple, the whole world was filled with the fragrance of spices. In the end, he saw that it would be destroyed, and he wept, saying "this fragrance was all for naught!" The Holy One said to him "do not be distressed, I will build it as an eternal construction." [*Pesikta Rabbati 20:1*][5]

We know, of course, that Solomon's Temple was indeed destroyed by the Babylonians in the year 586 BCE. Later, the Second Temple was constructed on the same site. It, too, was destroyed, by the Romans, in the year 70 CE. Since then, we remember what God said to Moses at the beginning of these instructions: I will dwell inside them. This is the eternal construction that God spoke to Solomon about. It is compared to a young lover lying between the breasts of his beloved, where her heart lies [Shir Ha Shirim 1:13]. The image, both erotic and intimate, is also alluded to in the following Talmudic passage:

> The Gemara interprets another verse: "I am a wall and my breasts are like towers" [Song of Songs 8:10] . . . . Rava said: "I am a wall;" this is the Congregation of Israel. "And my breasts are like towers;" these are the synagogues and study halls in which the Congregation of Israel is nurtured by the Torah, from which it draws its spiritual strength. [*BT Pesachim 87A:8*]

God is portrayed in this text as a nursing mother to the nation of Israel, providing nourishment for our souls through the words of Torah. The Temple may no longer be standing, but God, appearing here as our loving mother (in contrast to the male imagery that is usually used to define God) perpetually provides the spiritual sustenance that we need. May we continue to draw on its strength and comfort.

The Best Kind of Hangup

The inside of the Tabernacle was separated into two sections, the innermost being the Holy of Holies (this is where the ark was to be placed), and the outer being the holy place. Here we read about the inner curtain, the *parochet*, that separated these two holy spaces. Today, the same word is used to refer to the curtain inside or in front of the ark in the sanctuary of a synagogue. In the *mishkan*, there was also an outer curtain, the *masach*, that separated the outer area from the area outside the tent. Each of these curtains, just like the first layer of coverings on the Tabernacle, was to be made from blue, purple, and crimson yarns, as well as *shesh moshzar*, fine twisted linen. Here the word *shesh* means "linen." However, since the other, more common meaning of this word is the number "six," Rashi interprets this to mean that each yarn used in the Tabernacle was woven of six strands.[6]

Additionally, each of the curtains was to be hung from hooks that were attached to four posts from which they were suspended. The word used to refer to these hooks is *vaveihem*, literally "(their) vavs." *Vav*, being the sixth letter of the alphabet, has a numerical value of six. However, that is not the only interesting connection to be made here. In the ancient form of writing the Hebrew letters, the *vav* was shaped like a capital letter Y and has been described as a two-pronged fork. This was said to be the shape of the hooks upon which the curtains of the *mishkan* were suspended.

Thinking of this reminded me of a Torah scroll. Many Torah readers can tell you that the best kind of Torah to read from is what is called a "Vav Scroll," so called because, apart from only four columns in the entire scroll, every column is written by the *sofer(et)*, the scribe, in such a way that it begins with the letter *vav*. These scrolls most closely resemble the alignment of the Hebrew text in the *tikkun*, the book used by those who read Torah to study and prepare a Torah text for public reading in the synagogue. Many synagogues have one or more of these scrolls in their *aron kodesh*.

Dr. David Z. Moster describes an interesting correlation between the *mishkan* and a *sefer* Torah.[7] He points out that the word *amudim* is used here to refer to the posts, or columns, upon which the hooks (*vavim*) from which the curtains are suspended are attached. The same word, *amudiim*, is used today to refer to the columns in a Torah scroll.

Additionally, the word *yeriot* is used elsewhere in *Parashat Terumah* to refer to the coverings of the Tabernacle, and today it is also used to refer to the individual pieces of parchment that are sewn together to make a *sefer* Torah. Thus, as explained by Moster, the *vavs* appear at the tops of the columns that are inscribed on the pieces of parchment, in much the same way that the hooks that held up the curtains were found at the top of the columns in the *mishkan*. In this way, the Torah scroll itself is a miniature representation of the Tabernacle.

Remembering that the Tabernacle was the place where Moses encountered God, we can see that for us today the place to encounter God is in the sacred words inscribed on the scroll of the Torah. The service in the *mishkan* was open only to the *cohenim* and *leviim*, the priests and the Levites, while the Torah is open to us all. It is an unsurpassed commodity. Torah knowledge can never be taken or stolen from you.

And, unlike anything else, when we share our Torah knowledge with others, our knowledge is increased rather than diminished. When two people come together to study Torah, each bringing his/her own learning and understanding, they each come away with twice as much knowledge as they had before.

Torah study is an ongoing process throughout our lives. When we receive an *aliyah* to the Torah, the blessing we recite is *"Baruch ata Adonai, noten haTorah"*—not the One who gave the Torah, rather the One who gives Torah. Now and forever.

SIXTH ALIYAH: EXODUS 27:1–8
FRIDAY, FEBRUARY 19, 2021

Perfection

This section moves to the courtyard directly outside of the *mishkan*. As with the inside, the first part which is described is the most important part: the altar and all its accoutrements. This altar is where the sacrificial offerings were made. After an animal was slaughtered, the priest on duty would dash or sprinkle the blood around the altar and the animal would then be burned on top of the altar. Through this, expiation could be attained for the one who had brought the sacrifice. This idea is expanded on in the following *midrash*:

> "you are to construct the altar, etc.;" the word [*mizbeach*] here
> may be understood as an acrostic of the words, [*mechilah, zechut,*
> *brachah, chaim*], "forgiveness, merit, blessing, life." [*Daat Zekenim*
> on Exodus 27:1][8]

Through bringing a sacrifice to be offered on the altar, an individual received each of these four things. Again, we need to remember that we cannot look at these practices through our twenty-first century eyes; animal sacrifice was a typical form of worship in the ancient Near East. The difference for the Jewish people is that the practice was regulated by the parameters set out by God. Not all people were permitted to offer the sacrifices. Instead, they had to be brought to the central location of the *mishkan* and carried out by the *cohenim*, the priests. An individual needed to be made aware of the fact that the animal lost its life on his/her behalf and that was not to be taken lightly. That is why the priest had to pour out the blood on the altar as God had stipulated that the life was in the blood. Therefore, the life that was taken needed to be given back to God.

God told Moses that the altar was to be constructed out of acacia wood and delineates the specific dimension that it was to have: "five cubits long and five cubits wide—the altar is to be square" [27:1]. Keeping in mind that a cubit was approximately 1.5 feet., that would make these dimensions 7.5 feet long, 7.5 feet wide, and 4.5 feet high. There is a great deal of symbolism contained in these dimensions:

> . . . The measurements of five-by-five cubits for the length and
> width of the altar corresponded to the two Tablets of the covenant
> on each of which five of God's directives had been engraved. The
> height described by the Torah (i.e., three cubits) is an allusion
> to the three redeemers of the Jewish people, Moses, Aaron, and
> Miriam. [*Rabbeinu Bahya*][9]

There is also a lengthy debate in the Talmud regarding the height of the altar, with a number of rabbis claiming that the altar was really 10 cubits (15 feet) high, which would make it extraordinarily large. That, of course, is the point that they wish to make with this assertion, adding an extra dimension (no pun intended) to the awe-inspiring sacrificial service. There is, however, no clear resolution of this idea.

There is also no disagreement about the length and width both being 5 cubits. Even this, however, generates commentary. Noting that nothing in the Torah is considered to be superfluous, the question is raised: if we have already been told that the length and width are both the same number, why do we need to be told that "the altar is to be square?" Ibn Ezra answers this by saying that the word *ravuah,* translated as "square," really just means a quadrilateral—something four-sided. Therefore, we need the dimensions to know that it is, indeed, square.[10] The square shape again implies perfection, all four sides being equal in length, and all four angles (the "horns" of the altar) also equal in measure. Once again, I was reminded of the *tefilin*. The *batim*, the two boxes, one for the head *tefilin*, and one for the arm *tefilin*, are also perfectly square. This is another natural connection, as our prayers today have taken the place of the sacrifices of biblical times. And what do the *batim* contain within them? Words of Torah. Once again, we see the connection between the *mishkan*, the Torah, and our prayers. When we offer our prayers in heartfelt sincerity, they are as perfect and desirable to God as the sacrifices offered by our biblical ancestors on the altar of the Tabernacle.

SEVENTH ALIYAH: EXODUS 27:9–19
WRITTEN FOR SHABBAT, SATURDAY, FEBRUARY 20, 2021

Connecting with the Divine

This last *aliyah* talks about the enclosure, the area which is demarcated to cordon off the *mishkan* and its outer courtyard. On the north and south sides, it was set apart by 100 cubits of hangings, and on the west side by 50 cubits of hangings, thus making it an enclosure that was exactly twice as long as it was wide. On the east side, there were 15 cubits of hangings on either side of a 20 cubit screen, or entrance to the outer courtyard. The area inside this enclosure was separated into two equal areas, the first of which was the outer courtyard, and the second of which contained the Tabernacle. This *parashah* contains a great deal of intricate details about construction: raw materials, measurements, placement, which are the nuts and bolts of creating sacred space. This is the kind of reading that, at first glance, may seem difficult to draw much spiritual meaning from. And yet throughout we have seen that God is in the details. These technicalities have evoked connections to our prayer experience, to Torah study, and to the *tefilin* that God has commanded us to place on our bodies for the purpose of enhancing our worship experience.

We saw at the beginning of this *parashah* in the first *aliyah* God's promise that if the people built a sanctuary, then God would dwell among (within) them. And that did, indeed, occur in the Tabernacle in the desert, and later in the Temple(s) in Jerusalem. But most of the people were not able to communicate directly with God; only Moses had direct access to the presence of the *Shekhinah* in the desert. In the *mishkan*, Moses enjoyed regular direct access to the Divine presence through entering the Holy of Holies. Today, however, we all can experience the same access to our Creator—the Torah is open to us all.

Parashat Tetzaveh

FIRST ALIYAH: EXODUS 27:20–28:12
SUNDAY, FEBRUARY 21, 2021

Come On, Baby, Light My Fire[1]

Later this week, we will be reading *Megillat* Esther as part of our Purim celebration. One of the unusual facts about this book is that nowhere in the book is the name of God mentioned. It is one of only two books in the entire *Tanakh* about which we can make this statement. The other is *Shir haShirim*, Song of Songs, which we read on the shabbat of *Pesach*. In this *parashah*, we have the human equivalent; from the beginning of the book of Shemot right through the end of the Torah, Moses is clearly the most important character. Yet, in *parashat Titzaveh*, even though it is obvious to us that God is continuing to speak to Moses, we find that it is the only *parashah* in the last four books of the Torah that is lacking his name.

Most likely the reason for this is that for much of this *parashah*, God is giving to Moses the instructions for those who will serve as *cohenim* in the *mishkan*: Moses' brother Aaron and his sons. In this one area, Moses must retreat to the background and allow his brother and nephews to enter the spotlight.

The first verses of this *Aliyah* [27:20-21] almost seem as if they could have been part of *parashat Terumah*, as they pertain to the lights that the priests are to light inside the Tabernacle. God's instructions are that the people are to bring a supply of oil for the priests: *l'ha-a lot ner tamid* (to kindle lamps regularly) or, according to the old JPS translation, "to cause a lamp to burn continuously." Once lit, the *menorah*, the light of which is representative of the presence of the *Shekhinah*, was never meant to go out. The Baal haTurim explains how this was accomplished: of the seven lamps on the *menorah*, the middle one, or western lamp, was the most prominent, facing the Holy of Holies, while the other six lamps, three on either side, faced inwards toward it, and it was supposed to be kept burning perpetually.[2] Each evening, the *cohen* on duty would enter the *mishkan* and extinguish the other six lamps (if they hadn't already gone out on their own). He would then take the (still-burning) wick of the western lamp, put it aside while all the lamps were cleaned out and new oil and wicks were placed in them, then rekindle all seven lamps from the saved wick. What if the wick of the western lamp had gone out? It first had to be rekindled from one of the other lamps that had not gone out, and then the priest would proceed as before. In this way, the lamp would burn continuously. The other important idea to keep in mind is that the purpose of the light of the *menorah* was not illumination. As I said before, it was a reminder of the presence of the *Shekhinah*, and, once that presence entered the *mishkan*, it was to be there continually.

Now remember that in our modern world, the *Shekhinah* no longer has a physical structure within which to take up residence. Instead, the presence of God dwells within our hearts. Applying this metaphor of lighting the menorah to our lives today implies that it is up to each of us to make sure that the indwelling presence of the Divine never departs from our hearts. Daily we must rekindle the lights of that presence.

"How do we do that?" you might ask. Well, prayer for one thing. Davening the daily prayers, either in a *minyan* if possible or one's own if that's not possible, is a crucial element in the daily rekindling of the flame. Torah study is another way to keep the light of the Divine presence burning within us. We can study on our own, or join a Zoom session, since there are so many of them that are readily available now.

As we are about to enter the second year of COVID-19 existence—in whatever form that will take—we are keenly aware that our world has been changed. Indeed, it is unlikely that it will ever again be exactly the same as it was pre-pandemic. Regardless of what unknowns the future may hold, however, the one constant that continues in our lives is the indwelling presence of the Divine, but only if we each individually rekindle the lights of God's presence every day.

Sibling Revelry

This *aliyah* deals specifically with the "breastplate of decision" worn by the *cohen gadol*, the High Priest, whenever he entered the *mishkan*. This was by far the most distinctive of the eight pieces of his required attire. On it were placed twelve precious stones in four rows of three stones each. These twelve stones were engraved with and represented the names of the twelve tribes of Israel [28:21]; the Baal haTurim explains that the four rows represent the four matriarchs and the three stones per row represented the three patriarchs.[3] Thus, as Aaron stood before God, he was keenly aware that he represented all the tribes of Israel, and that it was on the merits of the patriarchs and the matriarchs who came before him that he was able to do so. Finally, when Aaron wore this breastplate, he carried the names of the tribes, the twelve sons of Israel (Jacob) on his heart [28:29].

There is a beautiful story told about this in *Midrash Tanchuma* on Song of Songs 8:1 which says, "If only [you] could be like a brother to me." The *midrash* explains that the people of Israel expressed this desire to God.[4] The question that follows, however, is "which brother?" Is there a particular brotherly relationship that Israel would like to emulate in its relationship with God?

Examining the possibilities, the *midrash* rejects each of the following, since they are all clearly problematic on some level:

- Cain hated Abel so much that he killed him.
- Ishmael hated Isaac and he was banned from the household of Abraham when Sarah observed him "playing" with Isaac. Some say that the meaning is really that he was shooting arrows at Isaac because he wanted to kill him.
- Esau hated Jacob; he was so angry with his twin for taking his blessing that he vowed to kill him after Isaac died.
- Joseph's ten older brothers conspired against him, first wanting to kill him, then selling him instead into Egyptian servitude because they hated him.

Therefore, God questions Israel: Which brother [do you wish Me to be like?] After all, it seems that from the beginning of the creation of the world until now brothers have hated each other! Israel asks further: Do You mean like Moses and Aaron, since they loved and cherished each other? Referring to this incident, they point out that, even as Moses, who had led the nation out of Egyptian slavery, was now charged with consecrating his brother Aaron to be the High Priest, they were not jealous of each other. "In fact," the *midrash* says, "they rejoiced in each other's exalted role."

We saw in *parashat* Shemot how, at the burning bush, Moses pleaded with God to send someone else in his place. He knew that Aaron had been a leader in his own right back in Egypt during all the years that he, Moses, had been in the desert. Therefore, he did not want to intrude on Aaron's domain. God assured him that, rather than being upset, Aaron would be happy. It was at that moment that Moses finally agreed to go, and it was at that moment, the *midrash* says that God revealed Godself to Aaron, and told him to go out and meet his brother in the desert.[5] God said to Moses, "he [Aaron] is setting out to meet you; and when he sees you, he will be happy in his heart." In the identical instant, both brothers set out excitedly to meet each other, looking forward to being reunited in their purpose after so many years apart.

It would seem, therefore, that these two brothers had at long last broken the trend of brothers being angry, suspicious, and hateful towards one another. Finally, the two brothers were able to rejoice in each other's blessings; Aaron rejoiced in Moses's leadership of the nation, and Moses rejoiced in Aaron's being chosen to serve as the religious leader of the nation. I would add to this the idea that both brothers also rejoiced in their mutual sibling, their sister Miriam, who was the third member of the triumvirate team that led the nation in the wilderness. It was through her merits that the nation received water during the forty years in the desert, and who led the women in praising God after the parting of the Red Sea.

Alluding to verse 29 of our reading, R. Simeon ben Yohai said that the heart that was happy at his brother's greatness would be privileged to wear the breastplate bearing the names of the sons of Israel over his heart when he entered the sanctuary.[6]

Each of us has different talents and different roles to play. God urges us to support each other and celebrate the successes of the other, without being envious. Indeed, the *midrash* quotes this well-known verse from the Psalms: *Hiney mah tov u'mah nayim shevet achim gam yachad!* "Behold, how good and how pleasant it is for brothers to dwell together in unity!" [Psalm 133:1]

HINDSIGHT IS 2020

We are Each Holy to God

This *aliyah* completes the description of the eight garments that the *cohen gadol* was required to wear when serving in the *mishkan*. The first garment he donned himself; for the purpose of modesty, he wore a pair of linen breeches [28:42]. He was assisted by other priests in putting on the remaining seven items: *ephod* (robe that serves as an undergarment) [28:31]; *avnet* (girdle) [28:39]; *choshen* (breastplate); *me'il* (blue robe); *kutonet* (coat of fine linen) [28:39]; *mitznefet* (turban) [28:37]; and *tzitz* (engraved plate) [28:36].

The *tzitz* was a gold plate tied to the front of the turban. On it were engraved the words "holy to God." Aaron was unable to see this while he was wearing it and, therefore, it could not possibly have been intended for his own benefit. Rather, it was for the benefit of the people. As they saw him entering the Tabernacle wearing these words on his forehead, they would know that he was going to attain atonement for each of them. Additionally, I think the inscription was for the benefit of God. As Aaron stood before the Holy of Holies once each year on Yom Kippur interceding for the nation, he reminded God of the holiness of the people. Aaron and the nation were set apart as holy to God by God.

Imagine how Aaron must have felt as he was dressed in his priestly garments. It started out by putting those breeches on one leg at a time, just like the rest of us. As he gradually added the *ephod*, the *avnet*, the *me'il*, the *choshen*, the *kutonet*, and, finally, the *mitznefet* with that magnificent *tzitz* tied onto it, he was transformed. With each subsequent article of clothing he donned, more of his own personality was diminished as he no doubt became increasingly aware of the awesome responsibility literally being placed upon him as he represented the people of Israel and stood before God to intercede and secure their pardons. The fact that he could not see that inscription "holy to God" on the *tzitz* probably discouraged him from thinking of himself as too important. He was there to remind God that the people were holy.

Just yesterday we passed a very sad milestone in our country: more than 500,000—half a million—people have died from COVID-19. The number is incomprehensible to us, representing a figure more than the total deaths in World War I, World War II, and the Vietnam War combined. We find it difficult to wrap our heads around the number. But rather than concentrate on the number, we cannot lose sight of the fact that each one of those souls was an individual, each one was created in the image of God, each one is "holy to God." We need to make sure that they are not forgotten and that we hold their memories dear. And in memory of them all we must pledge ourselves anew to do everything in our power to bring this pandemic under control, to keep ourselves and those around us healthy and safe.

FOURTH ALIYAH: EXODUS 29:1–18
WEDNESDAY, FEBRUARY 24, 2021

Dressing for Spiritual Success

This *aliyah* outlines the procedure for consecrating Aaron and his sons to serve as priests now that their holy garments have been described. Since they were to serve as the initiators, the first generation to serve as priests, a special ritual was required to set them apart as the religious leaders of the nation. This very visual display was no doubt for the benefit of both the priests and the people for whom they would perform the sacrifices.

The discussion begins with God's instructions to take three animals for sacrifices [29:1]: "take a young bull from the herd and two rams." Many commentators point to the fact that the first animal to be brought was a young bull. Rashi says that this bull was "to atone appropriately for the sin of the Golden Calf."[7] (Others say that the three animals being offered as sacrifices represent the three patriarchs.) Aaron needed to be keenly aware of what he had done in building the idol for the people to worship even as his brother was on the mountain receiving the tablets of the Ten Commandments. The Baal haTurim points out that the word *lekach* (take) used here appears in only one other verse in the entire *Tanakh:* "Take his garment for he has become a guarantor for a stranger" [Proverbs 20:16].[8] Relating the two verses to each other, he says that this shows that God commanded that Aaron's defiled garments, the ones he had worn when making the Golden Calf, be stripped from him.

Following this, we see these instructions: "Lead Aaron and his sons up to the entrance of the Tent of Meeting and wash them with water" [29:4]. All the commentators agree that what is referred to here is a total bodily immersion in water: a *mikveh.* Such an immersion was performed for purification purposes for anyone who had become unclean in any way. It marked a demarcation between states of being: washing away the old, impure person and allowing the newly cleansed soul to emerge.

Today, a *mikveh* is used for two main purposes: for women who observe the laws of *niddah* and immerse after each monthly menstrual cycle, and for those who have chosen to convert to Judaism. It is also customary for brides (and sometimes grooms, as well) to visit the *mikveh* on the morning of their wedding. In recent years, many people have come to use immersion in a *mikveh* to mark any major life-changing status, developing beautiful contemporary rituals to mark such occasions as the loss of a pregnancy, or the end of a marriage, or moving to a new home, or starting a new job. When I attended rabbinical school at the Jewish Theological Seminary, we went as a class to the *mikvah* to mark the beginning of our rabbinic studies, and again at the culmination, the day before our ordination. Both were truly moving experiences.

It is only after Aaron has been stripped of his old garments and undergone total immersion that he is adorned in the uniform of the *cohen gadol.*

All of this is for the benefit of not just Aaron and his sons, but for the people, as well. Though they had urged Aaron to make a god for them, he bore his own guilt for actually having done so. The people needed to see two things. First, they needed to see Aaron's example that, even though—or maybe especially because—he was a leader of the nation, he needed to seek atonement for his own sin before he could serve the nation as the *cohen gadol.* Second, the people needed to see that, despite the gravity of the sin which he had committed, Aaron could be forgiven and receive atonement from God. How much more so would they be able to be reconciled with God if they truly sought it?

Aaron's priestly uniform also carries a message for the people. The clothing that Aaron and his sons are commanded to wear when officiating in the *mishkan* is an important symbol. They are not to officiate in their priestly capacity unless they are wearing their Divinely ordained vestments. The only way that they can be in the proper mindset for discharging the duties of their office is to be wearing the appropriate attire. These days, when so many of us are participating in services virtually, I have heard from more than a few people about how they like to sit at services in their den or living room, comfortable in their jeans or pajamas, coffee cup in hand.

At the same time, we at my home synagogue, the North Shore Jewish Center, are once again starting this coming Shabbat morning to have services in person in addition to online. I will have to make a conscious decision about what to wear, not because I am concerned about impressing the others, but because I acknowledge that I will be participating in a holy experience.

When we stand before God, wearing the proper clothing puts us in the right frame of mind. We realize that we need to show respect for our Creator as we rise to sing God's praises. We realize that this prayer experience is different from the rest of our day. This time and space is *kadosh*—holy—to God. And that is true whether we are in the synagogue sanctuary, or our living room, office, or den.

FIFTH ALIYAH: EXODUS 29:19–37
THURSDAY, FEBRUARY 25, 2021

Claim Your Crown

This section continues to lay out the details of the ceremony of consecration of Aaron and his sons for the priesthood. The rams are slaughtered and some of the blood is smeared on the right ear, the right thumb, and the right big toe of Aaron and each of his sons [29:20]. The singling out of these parts of the body are symbolic of the idea that they are to listen to the commandments of God and direct their actions accordingly. The blood is then to be sprinkled on the altar and on the special garments of the priesthood worn by Aaron and his sons, making them holy [29:21]. These vestments were never to be worn by anyone but Aaron and his sons, and Aaron and his sons were never to serve in the *mishkan* unless they wore these clothes. The parts of the offering that are to be consecrated are designated to come "from that which was Aaron's and from that which was his sons" [29:27]. The Baal haTurim explains that it was on Aaron's merit that his sons were anointed as *cohenim*.[9] He bases this statement on the following Talmudic passage:

> Rabbi Yoḥanan said: There were three crowns on the sacred
> vessels in the Temple: The crown of the altar, and of the Ark, and
> of the table . . . . The crown of the altar symbolized the crown of
> priesthood; Aaron was deserving and took it, and the priesthood
> continues exclusively through his descendants. The crown of
> the table symbolized the abundance and blessing associated
> with the crown of kingship; David was deserving and took it for
> himself and his descendants after him. The crown of the Ark
> symbolized the crown of Torah; it is still sitting and waiting to
> be acquired, and anyone who wishes to take it may come and
> take it and be crowned with the crown of Torah . . . . the strength
> of the other crowns is derived from the crown of Torah, which is
> greater than them all. [*BT Yoma 72B:6*]

Aaron's sons became *cohenim* only on his merit because they were descended from him. Similarly, David's descendants became kings only on his merit because they were descended from him. The crown of Torah, however, does not belong exclusively to one family. It can be acquired by any person—and not just the sons—in every generation. Sometimes people are envious of the *cohenim* who receive preferential recognition in the synagogue. And who wouldn't want to wear the crown of royalty? And yet, here we are told that the crown of Torah is greater than either one of these, and it is available to us all. Every one of us has the right to claim this crown for ourselves. Torah comes to us in many ways: through private study, through listening to sermons, through (online) classes that are in abundance these days and accessible to us all, and even through endeavoring to teach what we ourselves have learned, sharing our own Torah that we have acquired with others. The crown of Torah is waiting there for each of us. How do you/will you go about claiming it for yourself? And how do you/will you help others to also claim it for themselves? There is no greater pursuit for us to undertake than this.

SIXTH ALIYAH: EXODUS 29:38–46
FRIDAY, FEBRUARY 26, 2021

I Will Meet You There

Here we read of the daily offerings that were to be made on the altar: two lambs—one in the morning and one in the evening—along with flour, oil, and wine. This was commanded in perpetuity as an offering of thanks to God [29:38-42]. Abarbanel explains that the lamb offered in the morning was to thank God for the gift of Torah, which was given as morning dawned [19:16]; and the lamb which was given in the evening was to thank God for the gift of the exodus from Egypt, which came about when they offered the Passover sacrifice in the evening [12:6].[10] Today, of course, these have been replaced by the *shacharit* and the *ma'ariv* services.

The sacrifices are to be offered at the door of the Tabernacle, where God makes this promise: "there I will meet with you, and there I will speak with you" [29:42]. The first "you" in this sentence is the second person plural object pronoun, and the second [to] "you" has a second person singular object suffix. God promises daily to interact with the nation in just the same way that the interaction occurred at Sinai: meeting the assembled people all at once, while simultaneously speaking with each person there individually. Each person heard exactly the message that (s)he needed to hear. This promise is no less binding today when we gather together to offer prayers of praise and thanks to God, regardless of whether we are physically together in the sanctuary or virtually together on Zoom. God speaks to us all collectively when we gather to pray or study and at the same time, God promises to give each of us the individualized comfort and support we need.

Finally, God reiterates the promise made at the beginning of this *parashah*: "I will abide among [within] them" [29:46]. And this is the reason why we were brought out of Egypt, that God might abide in our midst, for that is where God desires to be.

SEVENTH ALIYAH: EXODUS 30:1–10
WRITTEN FOR SHABBAT, SATURDAY, FEBRUARY 27, 2021

Take a Deep Whiff

This *aliyah* finishes up with the description of the altar of incense. The specifics are similar to those of the sacrificial altar: "It shall be a cubit long and a cubit wide—it shall be square" [30:2]. Like the first altar, this one, too, is commanded to be perfectly square. It is, however, considerably smaller than the first altar. With length and width of 1 cubit, it is approximately 1.5 feet by 1.5 feet with a flat top for burning the incense on. This was to be placed in front of the *parochet* (the curtain) that was in front of the ark. What was the purpose of the incense that was burned on this altar? Rambam says that the sweet smell of the incense was used to mitigate the foul aroma emanating from the animals that were being sacrificed on the outer altar.[11] Others say that the cloud of smoke that it created actually shielded Aaron from seeing the Divine presence in the *keruvim* above the ark when he entered the Holy of Holies.[12] Sforno says that the incense was meant to symbolize the souls of the sacrificed animals returning to God, and that the purpose of the incense was to welcome the presence of God after the sacrifices had been accepted, both morning and evening.[13,14] Still, other commentators say that the smoke of the incense is symbolic of the prayers of the people rising up to God. In any event, it seems clear that the sweet smell of the incense was pleasing to God.

Aaron was to burn the incense both morning and evening as he tended the lamps. And so, we have come full circle: as Aaron cleaned out the lamps in the manner that was discussed in the beginning of the *parashah*, cleaning out each one and inserting a new wick and new oil to rekindle the lamps, the incense was also burned.

The lights each morning and evening were rekindled from the wick from the western lamp which had not burned out. The kindling flame of the old wick was held against the new wick until it began to burn on its own. In a similar fashion, those of us who teach and share Torah endeavor to light the flame of Torah in others. Our hope is that the flame will thrive, and be transferred in a similar fashion, from one generation to the next. May the flame of Torah study, whose fragrance is pleasing to God, continue to be ignited and reignited as each new generation claims the Torah for itself.

Take a deep whiff—the odor is pleasant.

Parashat Ki Tissa

FIRST ALIYAH: EXODUS 30:11–31:17
SUNDAY, FEBRUARY 28, 2021

Where Do We Go From Here?

This passage begins with the instructions for a census to be taken of the men of Israel from age twenty and upward. Each is to bring a half shekel as an offering towards the Tabernacle [30:11-16] and in this way, the counting will be done indirectly. After the final amount had been tallied up, all that Moses (or anyone else) had to do was double the total number of *shekalim* collected to get the total number of men in the congregation. The Baal haTurim offers a beautiful short little *drash* on one word in this section: the word *v'natnu* (and each shall pay) [30:12].[1] A better translation of this word is "they shall give." In Hebrew, the word is *venatnu*, וְנָתְנוּ—a palindrome, reading the same both backwards and forwards. A closer look shows that this is not only true of the letters, but also of the *trop* markings (the notes for chanting):

$$\text{וְנָ֛תְנֻ֗ו}$$

Most words have only one note on them, while this word has two, as can be seen above. The two notes, the *kadma* and the *geresh*, usually come together in a pair, and are mirror images of each other, resembling an apostrophe and a backwards apostrophe. Thus, the word is even a palindrome in terms of its cantillation marks! This *kadma geresh* combination, which appears above the word, draws the listener upwards as well, as the Torah reader chants a sequence of rising notes. According to the Baal haTurim, the message here is that whatever we give freely will come back to us. There is nothing that we will miss out on as a result of our giving. Those of us who give freely from the heart will be rewarded in kind.

Continuing in the reading, we see how God instructs Moses to set up a pedestal for the priests to use for washing before going in to serve in the Tabernacle [30:17-21]. Next, instructions are given for the ingredients of a holy anointing oil to be used for all the accoutrements of the Tabernacle [30:22-29]. Aaron and his sons are also to be anointed with this oil and no one is to use it for any mundane purpose, nor is anyone to attempt to duplicate this oil for themselves [30:30-33]. The ingredients are also given for a special perfume that is to be made for placing in front of the ark in the Holy of Holies [30:34-38]. This, too, is not to duplicated by anyone for personal or mundane purposes.

Next, God speaks about Bezalel, who is designated to oversee the construction of the Tabernacle and its furnishings because he has been filled with both the wisdom and the artistic skills to oversee this most holy of construction projects [31:1-5]. Oholiab, designated as his assistant, and everyone else who will be assisting in the construction will have their hearts filled with the wisdom needed to complete their important task [31:6-11].

This very long reading finishes up with a reminder of the importance of the observance of the Sabbath [31:12-17]. *Shabbat* is designated as a sign of the covenant between God and Israel and is a remembrance of the fact that God created the world in six days and rested on the seventh day. We are called upon to do the same and are told that anyone who violates the Sabbath by performing work on it will be cut off from the nation. All of this is mentioned now because the people are to understand that, as important as the construction of the *mishkan* may be, it is not more important than the Sabbath, and work on it must cease on the seventh day. It is from here that the rabbis derived the thirty-nine categories of work that are designated as forbidden activities on *Shabbat*. Any activity that was involved in the construction of the *mishkan* is prohibited on *Shabbat*.

However, this entire discussion of *Shabbat* begins with a small but significant word: *ach* (nevertheless, however) [31:13]. This word usually indicates that something is being excluded. Several commentators indicate that the exclusion here comes in the case where life is endangered. In that case, one is not only permitted, but commanded, to violate the laws of *Shabbat*. Saving a life, *pikuach nefesh,* is a *mitzvah* that takes precedence over all others.

> . . . Our sages . . . state that it is permitted to violate the Sabbath
> legislation for the sake of a sick person if the sick person's life
> would be endangered unless the Sabbath were violated for his
> sake. Any situation in which a life is at stake overrides the

Sabbath prohibitions. This is what the Torah hinted at when it introduced this piece of legislation with the restrictive word [*ach*], "however." The word simply means that situations may arise which override the legislation about to be recorded . . . . for the sake of such sick people one may violate more than one Sabbath if the patient has not recovered in the interval. [*Or HaChaim*][2]

It is based partially on this and other similar passages that the leaders of the CJLS (Committee on Jewish Laws and Standards) of the Conservative Movement wrestled with finding ways to deal with the period during this past year when our synagogues had to close their doors because we were all in danger. Being able to use computers, tablets, and phones on the Sabbath would be forbidden in "normal" times. *Ach* (nevertheless) when it is the only way for us to be able to join our prayers together on Shabbat, bringing us out of our isolation, a ruling was made which made these things possible.[3]

As we begin to emerge from our cocoons and return to in-person worship services, the questions that we will have to answer are: Where do we go from here? How do we determine when we will be able to return to normal? And does that mean going back to the way things were before the pandemic? And, if not, then in what ways, if any, will these exceptions be permitted to continue going forward?

SECOND ALIYAH: EXODUS 31:18–33:11
MONDAY, MARCH 1, 2021

Whose People Are We, Anyway?

This very long *aliyah* tells the infamous story of the Golden Calf. Most of us are familiar with the story in which the people became impatient waiting for Moses to come back down from the mountain, where he had gone to meet with God. When they asked Aaron to make a god for them to worship, he told them to give him their gold, which he melted down and made a calf. The people brought offerings and celebrated. Meanwhile, up on the mountain, God told Moses what was going on down below, and advised him to get on down there. God wanted to destroy the people and Moses talked him out of it. Moses came down carrying the two tablets inscribed with the Ten Commandments. When he saw what was going on, he became angry and threw down the tablets, smashing them. Moses burned the calf, put the ashes in the water, and forced the people to drink it. At Moses' orders, the Levites went through the camp, slaying all those who had participated in the worship of the Golden Calf, and three thousand men lost their lives. Moses went back up to the mountain to meet God and seek atonement for the people. Moses constructed the *mishkan*, where he went to speak with God in the Holy of Holies. The length of this reading (forty-seven verses!) is due to the fact that the Levites did not participate in the worship of the Golden Calf. Therefore, the Torah reading is split up so that the entire incident of the calf is recounted in this second, or Levi, *aliyah*.

Having said all that, I did notice several interesting things going on here. The first question I would ask is: whose people are they anyway? Throughout the reading, there are references to "the people" nineteen times. The progression is interesting to note: *ha-am* (the people) appears four times: [33:1(2X),3,6]. *Amo* (his people) appears three times: God to Moses [33:7] and Moses to God [33:11,12]. *Ha-am hazeh* (this people) appears once: referring to God [33:12].

First, the nation is referred to in the generic term, the people. Next, there are possessive pronouns attached to them. Once God apprises Moses of what is taking place at the bottom of the mountain, a heated discussion takes place between the two of them where each seems to want to disown the people, referring to them as your people, and God still seems detached from his people. The relationship becomes more generic as Moses and Aaron talk about this people, finally reverting to the people. All this stands in stark contrast to the earlier chapters of the book of Exodus in which God referred to the nation as "my people" no less than fourteen times!

Another question one might ask based on this *aliyah* is who was responsible for bringing the nation out of Egypt? This is addressed seven times:

- In verse 1, the people say it was Moses.
- In verse 4, the people say it was the calf (as a stand-in for God).
- In verse 7, God says it was Moses.
- In verse 8, the people say it was the calf (as a stand-in for God).
- In verse 11, Moses says it was God.
- In verse 23, the people say it was Moses.
- In verse 1, God says it was Moses.

Here, both Moses and the calf receive more credit for the deliverance from Egypt than God; even God gives Moses the credit. Only Moses, refusing to take the credit, attributes the redemption to God! This also stands in contrast with the many times in the Torah in which God reminds us that it was God who brought us out of the land of Egypt!

All of this demonstrates just how much the incident of the Golden Calf had a disruptive and destructive effect on the relationship between God and the nation of Israel. Idol worship, like infidelity in a (new) marriage, caused a rift in the covenantal relationship. At the exact moment that should have been the climactic moment, the culminating moment in forging this new relationship, the people lost faith and became unfaithful. We will see that this mistake had long-term consequences. In the immediate situation, three thousand men were lost. Additionally, the trust in the relationship had been broken and would not be repaired easily.

Most of us do not worship golden idols these days. Yet there isn't one of us that doesn't have some thing or things that we allow to stand in the way of our spiritual lives. Work? Family? Exercise? Recreational activities? Money? Possessions? Add your own.

If you examine this list, you will see that most of these things are not inherently problematic or immoral; the difficulty arises when we put them before our spiritual health.

Perhaps my thoughts have helped you to understand how hurtful these things can be to God. In relationship to the Divine, they can each take on the status of an extramarital affair, each of them can be construed as the cause of infidelity.

So, we all need to challenge ourselves: do you want God to be able to refer to you as "my people?" If so, are you willing to put aside your personal idols?

Only you have the power to decide how you will answer these questions.

THIRD ALIYAH: EXODUS 33:12–16
TUESDAY, MARCH 2, 2021

Lead the Way, God

Continuing the theme of the previous reading, this very short (five verses) reading, which is completely comprised of Moses speaking to God, contains four references to the nation.

In the first reference [33:12], Moses quotes God as saying to him, "lead this people forward." God designates the nation using the term of specificity, but not a term of possessiveness. In God's language, this nation, which throughout the book of Exodus has lovingly been claimed as God's own unique, singular people, belongs to no one.

Moses, however, is having none of that. In the remainder of the reading, he refers to the nation three times, reminding God each time that they are

"Your people." In verse 13, Moses seems to turn God's language right back at God: *"this nation is Your people"* (emphasis added is mine). It is as if he is saying to God: "Don't refer to the people impersonally; this people that you speak of is Your people, whom You have chosen and set apart for Yourself." Furthermore, Moses insists that he will not lead the people from this place as God has instructed him to do unless God not only goes with them but leads the way.

When we share a relationship of intimacy with God, we have the right to demand that God travel with us and lovingly give us guidance through the words of Torah.

In these next several months, as the nation and the world try to navigate the way to a post-pandemic world, the journey will include a great deal of uncertainty. What will that world look like? And what pace is safe to get there? How will it affect our home life, our work life, our school life, and our religious life? Will our synagogue look the same as it did before COVID? More than likely, there will be some permanent changes in every aspect of our world. We look to our medical professionals and government officials for guidance on how to proceed. And we must also turn to God and say, "We will not go forward unless You, oh God, go before us and lead the way . . ."

[Note: as it turned out, things were looking up in February 2021 and continued trending that way for several months. However, as the end of 2021 approached, a new surge in cases due to the Omicron variant of COVID-19 caused many places to institute vaccine and mask mandates. As of mid-February 2022, the United States once again appeared to be moving towards an endemic, rather than a pandemic, status with regard to the coronavirus.]

FOURTH ALIYAH: EXODUS 33:17–23
WEDNESDAY, MARCH 3, 2021

God's *Tefilin*

Following up on the previous *aliyah*, God promised Moses to grant his request, leading him and the nation on their journey. Moses, expressing a desire for more intimacy with the Divine, begs to be shown God's glory. God's answer is that God will go before Moses and show him goodness. However, Moses is told that he, like every other human being, may not see the face of God and live.

God continues to address Moses with one of the most beautiful anthropomorphisms in the entire Torah, promising to shield him in a cleft of the

HINDSIGHT IS 2020

rock, covering him with God's hand to protect him as the presence of God passes by. In the final verse of the section [33:23], God says that Moses will see God's back. Ramban explains this in terms of the alternate creation story, which teaches that human beings were originally created as one single human being, with both masculine and feminine attributes, and two faces facing out in opposite directions. Following this idea, he says that Moses was able to see God's rear-facing (i.e., feminine) face.[4]

Rashi and several other commentators take a different direction, explaining that, as Moses saw God's back, he actually was able to see God's *tefilin*:

> What did Moses see? . . . This teaches that the Holy One, Blessed be He, Who, as mentioned above, wears phylacteries, showed him the knot of the phylacteries of His head, which is worn on the back of the head. [*BT Berakhot 7a:33*]

> . . . it is taught in a *baraita* that . . . This is a reference to the phylacteries of the head, upon which the name of God is written, as they demonstrate to all that the name of God is called upon the Jewish people . . . . the Holy One, Blessed be He, showed Moses the knot of the phylacteries of the head. [*BT Menachot 35b:8*]

This idea, though of course not factually accurate, suggests a harmonious symbiotic relationship between God and man. Just as we wear *tefilin* as a sign of the covenant relationship between us and God, so, too, does God, according to this *midrash*. Our *tefilin* contain parchments with the four passages of the Torah that speak of a sign that we are commanded to wear between our eyes. The straps encircle our head like a royal diadem, anchored in place by the knot at the nape of the neck in the shape of the letter *dalet*, whose numerical value is four. If that is truly the case, we may wonder, what is contained in God's metaphorical *tefilin*, which Moses is given the privilege of seeing? Most sages say that the following verse can be found there: "And who is like Your people Israel, a unique nation on Earth, whom God went and redeemed as His people, winning renown for Himself and doing great and marvelous deeds for them [and] for Your land . . ." [*2 Samuel 7:23*].

Thus, God's *tefilin* are a mirror image of our own, containing a verse of praise for our nation. Just as our *tefilin*, placed on our bodies, express our love of God, so, too, do God's *tefilin*, placed on God's metaphorical body, express God's love for us. That is exactly what God wishes for Moses to see.

God's *Tallit*

Now it was time to replace the broken set of tablets. God told Moses to carve a new set out of stone and bring them up onto the mountain where God would once again carve the words of the Ten Commandments. Before doing so, the Divine Presence came down on the mountain, and "stood" with Moses, proclaiming what we call the Thirteen Attributes of God: "The LORD! the LORD! a God compassionate and gracious, slow to anger, abounding in kindness and faithfulness, . . . extending kindness to the thousandth generation, forgiving iniquity, transgression, and sin" [34:6-7].

The text is ambiguous as to whether it was God or Moses who declared the Divine attributes that affect forgiveness when we seek it. Most commentators believe that actually it was Moses who extolled God's virtues. He began by calling out God's sacred name *Adonai* two times, as if making sure to gain the attention of God. Rashi, quoting the Talmud (see below) says that Moses declaims the Divine name twice to demonstrate God's mercy: one is for the time before an individual sins, and one is for the time after (s)he sins and repents.[5] Thus, true repentance can restore our relationship with God.

Moses then goes on to list the other attributes of God that affect our forgiveness: [God is] compassionate, gracious, slow to anger, abounding in kindness and faithfulness, forgiving all manner of sins.

According to our liturgy, these verses are recited three times before the open ark on each of our three major holidays, and multiple times over the course of the High Holidays. For me personally, I find them to be one of the most moving parts of the service.

In the previous reading, we learned about God's *tefillin*. Here the Talmud talks about God's *tallit*:

> . . . The verse teaches that the Holy One, Blessed be He, wrapped Himself in a prayer shawl like a prayer leader and showed Moses the structure of the order of the prayer. He said to him: Whenever the Jewish people sin, let them act before Me in accordance with this order. Let the prayer leader wrap himself in a prayer shawl and publicly recite the thirteen attributes of mercy, and I will forgive them. [*BT Rosh Hashanah 17B:5*]

The verse continues: "The Lord, the Lord," and it should be understood as follows: I am He before a person sins, and I am

He after a person sins and performs repentance, as God does not recall for him his first sins, since He is always "God, merciful and gracious." [*BT Rosh Hashanah 17B:6*]

Rav Yehuda said: A covenant was made with the thirteen attributes that they will not return empty-handed, meaning that if one mentions them, he will certainly be answered, as it is stated in this regard: "Behold, I make a covenant" [Exodus 34:10]. [*BT Rosh Hashanah 17B:7*]

God serves as an example, not only showing us how to pray, but joining with us as we do so. All of this tells us that God truly desires our repentance, because God truly wants to be able to forgive us.

God's desire is to restore the relationship that we fractured by sinning. The generation of the Exodus, as we have seen in this *parashah*, committed one of the most egregious of sins, engaging in the idol worship of the Golden Calf. And yet, in the end, due to Moses' intercession on their behalf, God was able to extend forgiveness to the nation. This was followed by the construction of the *mishkan*, a place where God came and dwelt among (within) them.

If the nation at Sinai could receive forgiveness for this monumental sin, how much more so are we able to seek and receive atonement, calling on the Thirteen Attributes of Divine Forgiveness.

SIXTH ALIYAH: EXODUS 34:10–26
FRIDAY, MARCH 5, 2021

One God and No Other

At the end of the previous *aliyah*, Moses had entreated God to go forward with the nation, traveling in their midst. God's answer here is to reiterate the covenant relationship, promising to perform wonders that the world has never seen before, for the people of Israel and not for the other nations. The Israelites must witness all the wonderful deeds that God would bring about for their benefit. A covenant comes with promises and requirements. The immediate promise made by God here is to drive out the nations that are now living in the land that God has promised to Israel.

Next come the requirements. First, God issues several negative commandments [34:14-17], beginning with a prohibition on worshipping any other gods. Next, they are not to make a covenant with the inhabitants of the land and are not to intermarry with the inhabitants of the land. Finally, and probably most importantly in terms of what has just happened to precipitate all of this, they are not to make any molten images. These are all "thou shalt nots." All these things would pull them away from their relationship with God, Who is, as pointed out, a jealous God.

But telling them what not to do was not enough. The worship of God cannot be defined only in terms of avoiding the practices of others. We now encounter a section of positive commandments, the "thou shalts" of a relationship with God [34:18-23]:

- Observe the Feast of Unleavened Bread (*Pesach*).
- Redeem the firstborn of your animals, as well as your firstborn sons.
- Cease from working every seventh day (i.e., observe Shabbat).
- Observe the Feast of Weeks (Shavuot).
- Three times a year, all males are to appear before the Lord (in Jerusalem on *Pesach*, Shavuot, and Sukkot).

Once again, a promise is made by God to drive all the nations out of their territory. This is followed by a few more "thou shalt nots:" the blood of the sacrifice is not to be offered with anything leavened, the Passover Sacrifice is not to be left until morning, a kid is not to be boiled in its mother's milk.

I couldn't help but notice that the number of verses devoted to the foreign practices we are to avoid is far less than the verses devoted to the positive requirements of a relationship with God. There has to be a clear distinction between the two. This is demonstrated in verse 14: "for you must not worship any other god, because the LORD, whose name is Impassioned, is an impassioned God." The word for "other," *acher*, appears in the Torah scroll with an enlarged letter *resh* at the end. This is done to call attention to the fact that it is indeed a *resh* and not a *daled*, two letters that are very similar in appearance and often confused. But if it were a *daled*, then the word would be *echad* (one). If that were the case, the verse would have read "for you must not worship the one god." Heaven forbid!

This is in direct contradistinction to the familiar first verse of the *Shema:* "Hear, oh Israel, the Lord our God, the Lord is One" [Deuteronomy 6:4]. Here the word *echad* (one) appears in the Torah with an enlarged *dalet,* calling attention to the fact that that is indeed a *dalet*, and not a *resh*. For if it were a *resh*, then the word would have been, *acher* (other).

These two verses with their enlarged final letters are, on the one hand, opposites of each other, but partners with each other at the same time. Just like the verses of this *aliyah,* they warn us not to worship a foreign god, and at the same time exhort us to worship the One God.

To live a life of a covenanted relationship with God is to make conscious decisions. It is not enough to avoid those things which would pull us away from God. That might keep us from sinning, but it wouldn't necessarily draw us closer to knowing God. The conscious observance of a life of prayer and *mitzvot* will accomplish that.

We must not only walk away from sin, but we must also walk towards God. And when we do, just like God's promise to Moses at the very beginning of this *aliyah,* God promises to walk with us.

SEVENTH ALIYAH: EXODUS 34:27–35
WRITTEN FOR SHABBAT, SATURDAY, MARCH 6, 2021

A Divine Mask Mandate

In this last *aliyah* of *parashat* Ki Tissa, we read how Moses spent another forty days and nights on the mountain communing with God. The second set of tablets was engraved with the words of the Ten Commandments, just like the first. This time, as he descended the mountain bearing the Tablets, we are told that his face was shining from his encounter with God. At first, Moses himself was unaware of this phenomenon [34:29].

By bestowing this physical, supernatural change to Moses' appearance, God made it clear to the nation that he, Moses, was the one chosen by God to lead the nation, not the calf. The calf had also been shiny due to its gold content but Moses' face was shiny because he had been imbued with the spirit of God.

The people, however, were frightened of Moses' new appearance. They were afraid to come near him [34:30]. Moses first spoke with Aaron and all the chieftains, then afterward assembled the people so that he could address the nation, telling them everything that God had told him. And when he was done, he covered his face with a veil [34:33]. Why did he do this? Because he knew that the people were frightened of his face and would not come near him. Whenever he went into the *mishkan,* however, to talk with God, he removed the veil as he did not need to wear it in the private space where he entered God's presence.

When he came out again, the same scenario would repeat itself: the people would be frightened by his appearance, so he would place the veil back on his face once again. This veil that Moses wore on his face most of the time was clearly not for his own benefit. It was for the benefit of the others around him, who were afraid to come too close to him.

Moses always had to cover his face when he was with people, in much the same way that we have been called upon to cover our faces for the last year. The masks that we have been asked to wear, unlike Moses' mask, have been for our own benefit, our own health and safety, as much as for others. Now that many of us have been vaccinated, we have been told that we can safely gather with others who are vaccinated without our masks. Yet, when we go out into the public, whether it be to a store, a gym, a school, a restaurant, or a synagogue, we are asked to wear our masks, not for our own benefit, but rather for the benefit of the others around us. God-willing, with more and more people being vaccinated, we will make it to a time when we can do away with the masks. But if we want to make it to that time, we need to be like Moses. You can take your mask off when you are alone inside, but when you go outside in the presence of others, for the sake of everyone else, keep it on, please!

Parashat Vayakhel

FIRST ALIYAH: EXODUS 35:1–20
SUNDAY, MARCH 7, 2021

Resting and Renewing Our Souls

Now that Moses had returned with the second set of tablets (intact!), he turned his attention to instructing the people about preparing for the construction of the *mishkan* and its accoutrements. But first he took time to remind them once again about the observance of *Shabbat*: work is permitted for six days, but the seventh is to be a day of complete rest, holy to God. Two warnings accompany this instruction: whoever does any work on the seventh day should be put to death, and no one is to light a fire on the sabbath. The sages are all in agreement that these exhortations are strategically placed here, just before the section on the construction of the *mishkan*. The message that is meant to be conveyed is that, as important as the Tabernacle might be, even its construction does not override the *Shabbat*. All manner of work must cease on the Sabbath, even work on the building of the sanctuary. Therefore, we will see that it is from this idea that the rabbis derived the list of thirty-nine categories of *melachah* (work) that are prohibited on *Shabbat*: any task which was involved in any way in building the Tabernacle becomes, by inference, prohibited on *Shabbat*.

We also notice that we are told from the outset that Moses convened "the whole Israelite community" [35:1]. This phrase is used to convey to us the message that everyone was included here, both the men and the women. We will see this identical phrase used twice more in this reading: in verse 4 when Moses transitions from instructions regarding *Shabbat* to instructions regarding the gathering and collecting of the supplies needed for the construction of the *mishkan*, and again at the very end in verse 20, when we are informed that the entire community left Moses' presence when he was done giving them all these instructions. Thus, the women along with the men received the instructions about the Sabbath. The women along with the men were instructed to bring gifts for the building of the Tabernacle and the women left together with the men after they had received all these instructions.

The men and women came together in partnership to hear the instructions of Moses. The Baal haTurim explains that, since we are told that Moses gathered everyone to hear about Shabbat, we should understand that everyone is to be gathered together for public discourses on the Torah on Shabbat. He goes on to quote a beautiful *midrash*:

> "The Torah complained before God, 'Master of the Universe, when
> Israel will enter the land and this one will run to his vineyard and that
> one will run to his field, what will become of me?' God replied, 'I have a
> mate for you by the name of [*Shabbat*], . . . for on it they are free from
> their labors and thus are able to engage in studying your words.'"[1]

Therefore, the Baal haTurim goes on to explain that it is incumbent upon us to teach the people God's statutes and Torah.

This implies that one of the very reasons for the existence of *Shabbat* is to provide a time for us to be able to study Torah. Many of us get so wrapped up in the cares and concerns of our daily lives that we don't/can't find time during the week to study Torah. This is exactly why we must take advantage of the opportunity that is provided to us to do so by the fact that we are called upon to refrain from work on the seventh day. When we attend *Shabbat* services, either in person or virtually, we hear the words of the weekly *parashah* in Hebrew, and we receive words of teaching from the rabbi in English. We are, of course, encouraged to expand upon that by further study, either on our own or with others.

Just as the men and women came together in partnership to hear the words of Moses, and together left his presence when he was done speaking, so, too, do we all come together to celebrate the partnership of Shabbat and Torah.

SECOND ALIYAH: EXODUS 35:21–29
MONDAY, MARCH 8, 2021

We Come Bearing Gifts

Here we read of the response of the people to Moses' instructions regarding donations for the construction of the *mishkan*. We see that the people were

HINDSIGHT IS 2020

very generous: everyone whose heart moved him/her freely gave of their possessions, their time, and their creative efforts towards the building of the Tabernacle.

Note that in verse 22 we once again see specific mention of both men and women: "Men and women, all whose hearts moved them, all who would make an elevation offering of gold to the LORD, came bringing brooches, earrings, rings, and pendants—gold objects of all kinds."

We know from *parashat Tetzaveh* that copious amounts of gold were needed for the ark, the altar, and other objects in the *mishkan*. In response to Moses' instructions, the gold jewelry requested here is brought and given willingly by members of both genders. Contrast this with the following verse from last week's *parashah Ki Tissa*, regarding the Golden Calf: "Aaron said to them, 'Take off the gold rings that are on the ears of your wives, your sons, and your daughters, and bring them to me'" [32:2]. The wording indicates that Aaron spoke specifically to the men here, instructing them to take the gold jewelry from (literally off of) their wives and children. Rashi, citing *Midrash Tanchuma, Ki Tissa 21*, says that this was a delay tactic on Aaron's part because he thought that the women would be reluctant to give up their jewelry, and hoped that that would stall things long enough for Moses to return from the mountain. However, his plan backfired:

> . . . They (the men), however, did not wait until the women and children made up their minds but they took the ornaments off themselves (. . . they took off the pendants which were in their ears; there is no reference to the pendants belonging to the women).[2]

This tells us that the women did not participate in the incident of the Golden Calf. Not only did they not give up their jewelry, but the men did not even take it from them! This, of course, explains why the women still had jewelry in their possession to donate in our present reading for the construction of the *mishkan*.

Further, we learn in *Midrash Pirkei Eleazer* that because the women refused to participate in the building of the Golden Calf, God rewarded them with a special day on which they specifically celebrate: Rosh Chodesh.[3] This day, the beginning of each month, which we still mark today as a day for women to rest and celebrate, was set aside by God as recompense for having made the right decision. Because women refused to contribute to the worship of the gilded idol, we have been given a special day to worship the One true God once each month.

Today, many women's groups, including the sisterhood of my own synagogue, mark the day by gathering, either in person or virtually, to study together, sing together, worship together. Often, the topic of study is specifically a topic of interest to women.

Our reading here concludes with another verse specifically mentioning both the men and women: "Thus the Israelites, all the men and women whose hearts moved them to bring anything for the work that the LORD, through Moses, had commanded to be done, brought it as a freewill offering to the LORD" [35:29]. Abarbanel comments on this verse, saying that it is not a repetition of a previous verse or thought. Rather, he says, it comes to make clear the idea that they all, both women and men, brought their gifts for the purpose of serving God, and not for show.[4]

Today, we are not called upon to bring gold to the synagogue. We are still called upon, however, to bring our gifts to the service of God, be they material gifts, or gifts of our time and service.

And so, we each must ask ourselves: what gifts can I/will I bring? And can I bring them willingly, offering them as gifts from my heart? We are called to do this today, in 2021, amid an ongoing pandemic, no less—perhaps even more—than the generation of the Exodus who brought their gifts to Moses.

THIRD ALIYAH: EXODUS 35:30–36:7
MONDAY, MARCH 8, 2021

Choosing a Leader

Here we read how God designated Bezalel to oversee the design and construction of the *mishkan*. Bezalel, whose name means "in the shadow of God," is the grandson of Hur and great-grandson of Miriam. He receives merit, therefore, through his lineage since Miriam was a prophet and the sister of both Aaron and Moses. Additionally, Hur, it is said, had tried (unsuccessfully) to stop the people from sinning with the Golden Calf and for his efforts was rewarded by having Bezalel as his grandson. Together with his designated assistant Oholiav, Bezalel was imbued with a divine spirit [35:31] and all the skills and abilities they needed to oversee this most important project: designing work in precious metals, cutting stones, carving wood, embroidering and weaving linens, and one extremely important skill, the ability to give directions [35:34]. Several of the commentators point out that possessing great knowledge does not necessarily give one the ability to transmit that knowledge: "There are many great scholars whose wisdom is locked up in their hearts due to their inability to transmit it successfully to outsiders.

The ability to teach is a great gift, and this is why the Torah testifies that [God] granted this gift to Betzalel."[5] Those of us who have spent our lives in education can especially appreciate this statement. Who among us cannot recall classes with teachers who were poorly suited to the profession, as well as with those who demonstrated a strong ability to inspire us to learn. Both extremes live for a long time in our memory.

Before we learn any of these things about Bezalel, however, we learn in the very first verse that Moses announced his appointment to the entire nation: "And Moses said to the Israelites: See, the LORD has singled out by name Bezalel, son of Uri son of Hur, of the tribe of Judah" [35:30]. The reason for this pronouncement, as we see in this Talmudic passage, is that a communal leader should not be appointed without first consulting the people:

> . . . Rabbi Yitzḥak said: One may only appoint a leader over a community if he consults with the community and they agree to the appointment . . . The Lord said to Moses: Moses, is Bezalel a suitable appointment in your eyes? Moses said to Him: Master of the universe, if he is a suitable appointment in Your eyes, then all the more so in my eyes. The Holy One, Blessed be He, said to him: Nevertheless, go and tell Israel and ask their opinion. Moses went and said to Israel: Is Bezalel suitable in your eyes? They said to him: If he is suitable in the eyes of the Holy One, Blessed be He, and in your eyes, all the more so he is suitable in our eyes. [Berakhot 55a:11]

Here we see that God insisted on consulting Moses and the people before announcing Bezalel's appointment. The people had a say in choosing their leader. At each step along the way, the question was, "is Bezalel a suitable man for the job?"

We ourselves have recently been through a tumultuous election in this country. Record numbers of people came out to participate in the democratic process of choosing our president. At each step along the way, we had to ask ourselves the same question: is my candidate a suitable man for the job? Now that the decision has been made, and verified, and endorsed, we owe it to ourselves and our new president to support him and work together with him for the good of the country, no less than the people of Israel came together to support the appointment of Bezalel, and to support him in his mission.

Tell Me Again

There's one in every crowd: the person who takes f-o-r-e-v-e-r to tell a story: embellishing it, getting sidetracked, repeating him/herself. We listen impatiently, wanting to practically pull the words out of his/her mouth. It can wear on our nerves.

But what if that person is only a child? Better yet, a child who happens to be related to you? Several of my grandsons can take a very long time telling a story, embellishing it, getting sidetracked, repeating themselves. And in each case, the adults in their lives, their parents, and grandparents, can hang on every word, thinking how cute they are. Perception is important: we indulge the cute little person who displays the same traits that we would find very irritating in an adult. Why? Simply because we love the child, and every word that comes out of his/her mouth!

In this *aliyah* we read the precise details of the activity of the people as they constructed the *mishkan* according to instructions. Not only do the details seem lengthy and tedious, but by this point we realize that we have encountered this topic, the construction of the *mishkan* and all its furnishings, with all its very specific details, more than once before. Ramban points out that the details of the construction of the Tabernacle are repeated in the Torah no less than five times![6] He says that this is an effective and distinctive way to say that God took pleasure in the work that the people were doing in constructing God's sanctuary, and therefore mentions it these many times in the Torah, to multiply the reward of those involved in the completion of the project. He then continues:

> . . . that which they said in the *midrash*, "The conversation of the fathers' servants is [more precious to] the Holy One, blessed be He, than the Torah of [their descendants]; as behold the section about Eliezer (the servant of Abraham) is two or three pages."[7]

This, of course, refers to Abraham's servant Eliezer retelling in painstaking detail the story of his encounter with Rebecca at the well to her family members. But every word is recorded in the Torah, and we read (and reread) this story, and indeed all the stories in the Torah every year as we return to the cycle of Torah readings again and again.

Our conversations about Torah are, as the *midrash* tells us, important to God, Who takes delight in listening to them, just as I delight in listening to the stories of my grandsons. Let us continue to delight the *Kadosh Baruch Hu* by speaking words of Torah at every opportunity that we have.

FIFTH ALIYAH: EXODUS 36:20–37:16
TUESDAY, MARCH 9, 2021

Does Your Inside Match Your Outside?

This *aliyah* begins with the painstaking details of the construction of the outside walls of the *mishkan*: the planks, the bars, the curtains. Moving to the inside of the tent, the description begins with the most important item: the ark. Whereas the rest of the items were constructed by multiple people, we are told here that one person alone constructed the ark, Bezalel himself [37:1]. Ramban says that this is because he had been endowed with the divine spirit and understood precisely how God wished for it to be created.[8] He created it according to God's directions, with all three imperfect dimensions: 2.5 x 1.5 x 1.5 cubits. We are also told that he overlaid (covered) it with pure gold, inside and out [37:2]. Rabbeinu Bahya explains:

> "A Midrashic [Tanchuma Vayakhel 7] approach concerning the words: . . . Rabbi Chanina of Tzippori said that he [Betzalel] actually made three arks, two of gold and one of acacia wood. He inserted the wooden one into the golden outer one; then he inserted the inner golden one into the wooden one . . . . He understood the wording of the Torah to mean that although the wood of the Ark was totally enclosed, invisible, it was to be accorded honor seeing that the Torah is contained within it."[9]

So, the vision here is of three separate arks nesting inside of each other like Russian dolls; the outermost and innermost were made of gold, surrounding the inner one, which was made of wood. The ark was intended to be the repository of the tablets containing the Ten Commandments (both sets), above which would rest the *Shekhinah* sheltered by the wings of the two golden cherubim. Therefore, the ark, the wooden part, was completely lined with gold and covered with pure gold. Both its inside and its outside needed to be pure because its contents were holy.

Today, despite the best efforts of Indiana Jones, we no longer know where the ark rests. However, each of us individually is like an ark, with a precious soul resting within our bodies. Therefore, we, like the ark, must be pure on both the inside and the outside. Only we ourselves know what lies within our hearts, and whether it matches the image that we project to others on the outside world. God calls us to a life of observance of the *mitzvot*. While it is true that our world and others around us can benefit from that observance even if the motivation may not be pure, how much more so can that happen when our motivation matches our actions. God demands of us not only pure actions, but a pure heart, as well, motivating and driving those actions. This must be the standard to which we aspire.

SIXTH ALIYAH: EXODUS 37:17–29
TUESDAY, MARCH 9, 2021

Keep the Candles Burning

A major part of this *aliyah* is spent on describing the construction of the *menorah* for the *mishkan* [37:17-24], followed by a few verses talking about the incense altar [37:25-28], and one verse that mentions the incense itself and the aromatic oils [37:29]. The *menorah* was by far the most intricate of the items that needed to be created for placement inside the Tabernacle, with its six branches, each containing three cups shaped like almond blossoms, along with calyxes and stems, and four more of these on the main center stem, along with the seven lamps. Additionally, the entire *menorah* was to be formed from one single piece of pure gold. It is understandable that Moses was somewhat confused about this item and felt rather inadequate and insecure about its creation. God instructed that it was to be made from pure gold that is *miksheh* (hammered work). This Hebrew word, however, is apparently related to the word *kasheh*, which means "hard" or "difficult." This shows us that Moses had difficulty with this item. There are two midrashim told about this:

> . . . When Moses ascended Sinai, the Holy One was showing
> him on the mountain how he would make the Tabernacle. When
> he showed him the making of the menorah, Moses found it
> difficult . . . The Holy One said to him: See, I am making it
> before you. What did the Holy One do? He showed him white
> fire, [red fire,] black fire, and green fire. Then from them he
> made the menorah, its bowls, its pomegranates, its blossoms,
> and the six branches. Then he said to him . . . This is the

making of the menorah. When the Holy One showed him with the finger, he nevertheless found it difficult. What did the Holy One do? He engraved it on his hand. He said to him: Go down and make it just as I have engraved it on your hand.] *Midrash Tanchuma Buber Shemini 11:1*][10]

As a retired teacher, this *midrash* brought a smile to my face. It reminded me of all those high school students I encountered over the years who found it too difficult to memorize the formulas and facts they needed to know for their math tests and instead wrote them on the inside of their hands, thinking that I would not notice them trying to cheat on their tests! On the other hand (no pun intended), there were also the students who were too lazy to find a piece of paper or their assignment pads to write down their homework and instead just wrote it on their hands.

In this instance, Moses was the student of God who didn't have enough confidence in himself to remember what he saw, but also was not able to carry anything else with him, as he was carrying the second set of tablets when he descended from the mountain. Therefore, the *midrash* tells us that it was God Who inscribed the instructions on Moses' hand so that he could neither forget nor lose them!

In this second *midrash*, God takes a much more direct role in the construction of the menorah:

> ... Moses struggled ... with the design of the Menorah ... until [God] showed him with a finger ... "This is how the Menorah was made: it was hammered work [*miksha*] of gold" ... which is to say how hard [*kasha*] it is to make, since Moses became weary on account of it. When he struggled, [God] said to Moses: take a talent of gold and throw it in the fire and take it out, and it will be formed on its own ... Moses took the talent [of gold] and threw it in the fire. Moses said, "Master of the Universe, behold the talent is in the fire. Whatever you wish, so shall it be done." The Menorah immediately came out made according to its design, ... And who made it? [God]. Therefore, [God] said to Moses: If you are careful to light [it] before me, I will protect your souls from every evil thing, since souls are compared to a candle, as it says. "the candle of Adonai is the soul of a person" [Proverbs 20:27] [*Bamidbar Rabbah 15:2*][111]

Here God instructs Moses to throw the gold into the fire, and the menorah comes out completely formed. This *midrash* is God's answer to the incident of the Golden Calf, where we were told that Aaron recounted to Moses that he had thrown all the gold into the fire, and out popped this calf, completely formed [32:24]! God constructs the menorah for Moses with a caveat: if the people will see to its lighting, then God will protect their souls, which God compares to candles. The light of a candle can be strong and burn brightly, but it can also be blown out by a sudden gust of wind or burn out if its wick is too short and left unattended.

We no longer have the menorah to light, yet we do have the candle of our souls. God asks us to light these candles through prayer, observance of the *mitzvot*, and study of Torah, and to tend to the flame, keeping it burning. And, in return, God makes a promise to watch over and protect our souls.

SEVENTH ALIYAH: EXODUS 38:1–20
WEDNESDAY, MARCH 10, 2021

What Do You See When You Look in the Mirror?

Here we read of the construction of the altar for burnt offerings with its square shape. We also read about the horns of the altar, as well as all the utensils used to tend the altar, the netting, the rings, and the poles used for carrying the altar when traveling in the desert [38:1-7]. Next, we are told of the laver, or basin, for washing: "He made the laver of copper and its stand of copper, from the mirrors of the women who performed tasks at the entrance of the Tent of Meeting" [38:8].

According to Sarna, many women in the ancient Near East used hand mirrors. The reflective part was usually made of molten copper or bronze, and Egypt was the land most known for their construction.[12] If that was the case, that would explain how so many Israelite women had such an item in their possession. No doubt, they came with the spoils taken from the Egyptians on the night the nation went out from Egypt. There are several different stories told by the sages about these mirrors. Rashi cites a *midrash*:

— The Israelit[e] women possessed mirrors of copper into
which they used to look when they adorned themselves.
Even these did they not hesitate to bring as a contribution
towards the Tabernacle. Now Moses was about to reject them
since they were made to pander to their vanity, but the Holy
One, blessed be He, said to him, "Accept them; these are dearer
to Me than all the other contributions, because through them

the women reared those huge hosts in Egypt!" For when their husbands were tired through the crushing labor they used to bring them food and drink and induced them to eat. Then they would take the mirrors, and each gazed at herself in her mirror together with her husband, saying endearingly to him, "See, I am handsomer than you!" Thus, they awakened their husbands' affection and subsequently became the mothers of many children . . . [*Midrash Tunchuma, Pekudei* 9][13]

Had the women not been so persistent in enticing their husbands after they returned exhausted from the backbreaking labors of slavery, they would have had very few children, and the next generation would have been so small that there may not have been enough people to stand at Sinai and receive the Torah. No doubt the continuation of the nation was extremely important, yet this *midrash* still relegates the women to the usual, "traditional" role of babymakers.

Ibn Ezra, on the other hand, describes these mirrors, and their owners, a little differently:

. . . It was usual for women then as now to beautify themselves in front of a mirror in the morning. But there were some pious women who renounced worldly vanities and donated their copper mirrors for the making of the holy vessels. These women would gather every day near the entrance to the Tent of Meeting to pray and receive instruction in the commandments.[14]

According to this interpretation, we learn that women could be pious, wishing to be involved in a life of prayer and Torah study. However, these women were able to donate their mirrors because they had "renounced worldly vanities," going completely to the other extreme. Sforno expresses a similar sentiment:

. . . approaching this holy domain was intended to show that they wanted to hear the words of the living [God] . . . . this was an acceptable practice . . . "anyone who wanted to seek out the Lord would go out to the Tent of Meeting." The women who had donated these mirrors indicated that they had overcome their sense of vanity, they considered jewelry and the need for it a human weakness. Moreover, they knew that the time when these mirrors had been of constructive use was past.[15]

It seems that women were only vain and interested in their physical experience, or totally ascetic, devoted so strongly to a closer relationship with God that they were completely uninterested in their physical appearance. There was no middle ground, no happy medium. I have problems with both extremes.

Then, there are the thoughts of Chizkuni:

> . . . assembled at the entrance of the Tent of meeting." They [the women who had given up their mirrors] did so in order to pray and recite the praises of the Almighty as near to the sacred compound as was allowable for ordinary Israelites who were ritually pure. They also wished to receive the blessings by the priests and Levites.[16]

The women in Chizkuni's vision had a true sense of spirituality, wishing to be as close to the Tabernacle as anyone else, to participate through prayer and praise, and to receive the blessings that came from that participation. These women had given up their mirrors not because they had given up on vanity, but rather because they wished to make a contribution to the Tabernacle. Like many Jewish women today, these women had a foot in each world—one in the spiritual, one in the secular. These women sought equal participation with their male counterparts, no less than today's women who are rabbis, cantors, Torah readers, daveners, teachers, and lay leaders, as well as all those who devote time to Torah study. Let us continue to follow their example.

Parashat Pekudei

FIRST ALIYAH: LEVITICUS 38:21–39:1
WEDNESDAY, MARCH 10, 2021

Counting to One Hundred

In this *aliyah*, we read about the inventory that was taken of all the items brought by the people for the construction of the Tabernacle. The first items listed were the precious metals of gold and silver. The silver was collected through the census, where each man between the ages of twenty and sixty was required to give a half-shekel. The total amount collected was one hundred talents (a talent equaled three thousand shekels) and one thousand seven hundred seventy five shekels. The one hundred talents of silver were designated for the one hundred sockets of the sanctuary [38:27]. These sockets held together the framework of the *mishkan* upon which the cloths and curtains were suspended. According to Ibn Ezra, "the whole Tabernacle would stand on the sockets that were made from this silver."[1] The significance of this is explained further in this Musar text:

> . . . The number one hundred is important both allegorically and
> halachically: . . . everyone is duty bound to recite one hundred
> [*brachot* (blessings)], daily . . . Kabbalists have described the
> "higher" world as consisting of one hundred "gates." Each "gate"
> is to be perceived as a fountain of blessings. . . . When the
> Tabernacle had one hundred silver sockets . . . they symbolized
> these one hundred sources of blessings. Every single . . . socket,
> was a . . . receptacle (for heavenly blessing). [*Shenei Luchot
> HaBerit, Torah Shebikhtav, Toldot, Torah Ohr 1*][2]

I have mentioned this idea before, that we are supposed to recite one hundred blessings a day, which will keep us focused on all the good that we receive from God in our daily lives. For many of us, this number is not quite a reality yet. Rather, it is something towards which we strive. The striving itself raises our consciousness of the presence of God both in our lives and in the world around us and should foster within us a sense of humility and gratitude. The Musar quoted above equates the one hundred blessings with the one hundred sockets of the Tabernacle. Just as the whole Tabernacle stood on these silver sockets, so, too, do our lives stand on these one hundred blessings. The sockets were small but oh so important, as they held together the very framework of the *mishkan*. In much the same way, each blessing taken by itself is small, but taken together, they are the framework that holds everything together in our daily lives.

So, whatever number you're up to, try adding a few more blessings each day. Besides the blessings of the three daily services, we have blessings for every different kind of food we eat, blessings for seeing things like rainbows or other miracles of nature, blessings for momentous occasions (like receiving a vaccination for COVID-19!), blessings for performing *mitzvot*. Look online for a website that gives a list of blessings. If you look hard enough, you'll find a blessing for just about anything you could think of.

Can you meet the challenge?

SECOND ALIYAH: EXODUS 39:2–21
THURSDAY, MARCH 11, 2021

Following God's Blueprint

These next two *aliyot* are devoted to the creation of Aaron's priestly garments. Here we read about the ephod, the shoulder pieces, and the breastplate. One thing that stands out is that three times [39:5,7,21] in this *aliyah* we encounter the phrase, "just as God had commanded Moses." We are left with no doubt that the garments of the *cohen gadol* met with God's approval since they exhibited no deviation from what God had instructed Moses to make.

It is interesting to note that this phrase appears a total of forty-one times in the entire *Tanakh;* thirty-eight of those are in the Torah. Of those, fourteen, more than one-third of the total occurrences, appear in these last two chapters of the book of Shemot, and none of them appeared in the previous chapters that discussed the construction of the *mishkan* and its furnishings. And so we might ask ourselves why this phrase occurs so frequently here. The answer is addressed in the following *midrash*:

> . . . Why is it stated so many times: According to all, the Lord commanded Moses . . . Because the Israelites criticized Moses at the time they strove to erect the Tabernacle but could not do so. They said: "Perhaps the Holy One, blessed be He, told Moses some simple thing to do to erect the Tabernacle, and (thus) Moses alone is responsible for all this difficulty." Therefore, the Holy One, blessed be He, said: Since you have criticized him, I will attach My name to whatever I command him. Thus, it is written: According to all the Lord commanded Moses. [*Midrash Tanchuma, Pekudei 11:9*][3]

This implies that Moses was being rewarded by God with the repeated statement of this endorsement. Because Moses had been talked about multiple times by others, who blamed him for the difficulties they encountered in constructing the *mishkan*, God needed to state again and again the Divine endorsement of the one chosen by God to lead the people. The Zohar takes a different approach:

> . . . While the Tabernacle represented the Jewish people, Moses, as its leader could "be on the same wavelength" as [God] concerning it. Seeing that Moses was not a priest, he could not be expected to be on the same "wavelength" as the priests, so that he required to be instructed in the details of how and from what materials the priestly garments were to be made.
> Only after Moses had divested himself of all aspects of ego, individualism, was he able to know exactly how the priestly garments were to be made and from which materials. [*Kedushat Levi, Exodus, Tetzaveh 3*][4]

This tells us more about Moses. He related easily to the details about the construction of the physical space and was able to effectively transmit them to those responsible for carrying them out. But when it came to the priestly garments, there may have been some envy on his part of the leadership role that had been assigned to his brother Aaron. That, of course, would have clouded his thinking and, if he were not fully invested in creating the priestly garments for Aaron and his sons, then perhaps the workmanship might have been shoddy. Therefore, the Zohar explains, the fact that these garments were created perfectly according to God's plan is evidence that

Moses was able to overcome his personal issues, recognizing that the Divine needs supersede his own. It was for this reason that God continually pointed out here that everything was done exactly according to God's plan as it was revealed to Moses.

Moses's experience is an example for us all that we, too, need to recognize the Divine plan for our lives and the world, recognizing that the needs of others often take precedence over our own.

THIRD ALIYAH: EXODUS 39:22–32
THURSDAY, MARCH 11, 2021

Postponing Joy

Here we read about the robe for the ephod, with its bells and pomegranates on its hem, the tunics for Aaron and his sons, the headdress, and the linen breeches, the sashes, and the *tzitz* for Aaron's headdress. Throughout the description, we read our familiar phrase, "just as God had commanded Moses," an additional three times. Finally, we are told, 'Thus was completed all the work of the Tabernacle of the Tent of Meeting. The Israelites did so; just as the LORD had commanded Moses, so they did'" [39:32]. This comes to tell us that every member of the nation of Israel participated in some way in the construction of the *mishkan*, even if it was only through their material contributions. Many also participated in the actual construction. Several commentators indicate that we know the exact date on the Hebrew calendar when this completion took place, and it is a familiar date:

> "thus was completed all the work;" according to our sages the
> work was completed on the twenty-fifth day in the month
> of Kislev, the day we commence to celebrate the festival of
> Chanukkah. [*Chizkuni*]⁵

The Baal haTurim elaborates on this, citing a *midrash* from Pesikta Rabbati 6:5: the *mishkan* was indeed completed on the twenty-fifth of Kislev.⁶ However, since God wished for its inauguration to take place in the month containing Isaac's birthday (since it is through the merit of Isaac that the *Shekhinah* rests on the *mishkan*), it was delayed until the month of Nisan, thus depriving the month of Kislev of this great celebration. Later, in the time of the Maccabees, the Temple was rededicated, celebrating the miracle of Chanukah on the twenty-fifth of Kislev. This was God's way of compensating the month of Kislev for having given up the celebration and gone without it for so many years.

For the past year, we have had to give up on so many celebrations. All our holidays were held in muted commemorations that took place over Zoom (if at all), and many had solitary celebrations. Major lifecycle events, too, were rescheduled or reimagined; *bar* and *bat mitzvahs* took place via the internet, or with a very limited number of attendees in the synagogue. Others postponed weddings in the hopes that things would be better in a year's time. As many of us are receiving our vaccinations, we arestarting to feel hope, and some of us are starting to feel impatient, anxious to be able to celebrate again. As difficult as it is, we need to be smart and wait a little longer. But just think! Oh, how truly joyous and wonderful will be all our celebrations when we are able to have them again! And that, my friends, will be our reward for having been deprived of them for this past year.

Oh, soon. Let it be soon . . .

FOURTH ALIYAH: EXODUS 39:33–43
FRIDAY, MARCH 12, 2021

Do Good Work

Here we read how the nation presented to Moses the finished project: the Tabernacle and all its furnishings. All the items that went into the construction of the tent itself, the furniture and all the items contained within it, as well as the garments that were to be worn by the High Priest and the other priests, are listed here yet again, down to the last detail [9:33-41]. Once more we are told that this was all completed according to all that God had commanded Moses: "Just as the LORD had commanded Moses, so the Israelites had done all the work" [9:42]. However, we do notice something unusual in the second part of this verse. Here, the word used to represent the work that the people had completed is *avodah*, instead of the more commonly used word, *melachah*. This second word, which is used in verse 43 to refer to what the people had completed, is also the word which is used when we talk about the thirty-nine categories of work that are forbidden on Shabbat, so designated precisely because they were involved in the construction of the *mishkan*. The word *avodah*, however, is used in the Torah specifically to refer to the religious work performed by the *cohenim* and the *leviim* in the *mishkan*; it implies religious work, service to God. So, why the unusual word usage here? This question was addressed by Rabbeinu Bahya:

. . . We would have expected the Torah to write [*kol melachah*] instead of [*kol ha'avodah*]. The Torah, however, wanted to remind us that all work performed for the building of the Tabernacle was equivalent in spiritual value to service in the Sanctuary, [*avodah*], i.e., something sacred, holy. Just as the expression [avodah] is always used in connection with directly serving the Lord, so this [the construction of the *mishkan*], too, was directly serving the Lord. [*Rabbeinu Bahya*][7]

With this thought in mind, let us return to the idea that for each of us, our body, specifically our *neshama*, or soul, has taken the place of the Tabernacle and the Temple. Let us also call to mind our verse from *parashat Terumah*: "Make me a sanctuary and I will dwell among [inside] you" [25:8]. God calls upon each one of us to be involved in the construction of our own sanctuary, preparing a space there for the *Shekhinah* to dwell. That is done through prayer and contemplation, and through the observance of *mitzvot*, an ongoing project of perfecting the soul that has been placed within us. That process is truly a process of *avodah*, of holy, spiritual work, of worship.

In the last verse of this reading, we see that Moses, upon seeing all that the people had done, according to God's command, was moved to bless the people. The Torah does not give us the text of that blessing. Rashi, along with several other sources, says that the blessing consisted of these words: "May it be the will of God that His Shechinah rest upon the work of your hands."[8] May we, the inheritors of the Torah delivered to us by the hand of Moses, be recipients of the same blessing in our holy endeavors.

FIFTH ALIYAH: EXODUS 40:1–16
FRIDAY, MARCH 12, 2021

Fasting Not Allowed

In this *aliyah*, we read about Moses setting up the *mishkan*; the first item to be placed inside is the ark, because it is the most important. Following that, the table and its furnishings, the lampstands, the incense altar, the altar of burnt offering, the laver are all put into place [40:1-8]. Next, everything is to be anointed with oil [40:9-11], and Aaron and his sons are to be washed and anointed in preparation for serving in the priesthood [40:12-15]. Now, we are told that Moses did everything that God had told him to do [40:16], following God's instructions just as the people did.

HINDSIGHT IS 2020

And when did all of this happen? The Torah tells us that it occurred "On the first day of the first month" [40:1]. This, of course leads to some debate amongst the rabbis: what month was referred to as the first, Nisan or Tishrei? Nisan, occurring in the spring, is the month during which *Pesach* falls; Tishrei, occurring in the fall, is the month during which Rosh HaShanah occurs. The vernal or the autumnal equinox? Which is it?

In the fall, with the beginning of the High Holidays, we officially change the year on the Jewish calendar. And yet, we are told that the new year really begins with Nisan, when, according to Gersonides, "the sun moves closer to inhabited areas, plants and trees are renewed, and all life rejoices."[9] Most commentators agree that Moses erected the Tabernacle for the first time on Rosh Chodesh Nisan. This corresponded to the eighth day of ordination of the priests. Prior to this, for the first seven days of the ceremony of ordination, say the sages, Moses was assembling, disassembling, and reassembling the *mishkan* every day, anywhere from one to three times a day, depending on the commentator! Regardless of how many times they say he did this, the idea was for him to demonstrate to the *leviim* what the procedure was for disassembling and reassembling the Tabernacle. All of this, because, after this first official day, the *mishkan* became their official responsibility, and Moses never again had to be involved in setting it up.

This Talmudic text expands on the idea that this final dedication occurred on the first of Nisan:

> And why do we not fast in the month of Nisan? Because on the
> first of Nisan the Tabernacle was erected . . . and twelve princes
> offered their sacrifices during [the first] twelve days, a day for
> each tribe . . . and everyone held a festival on his day. Between the
> twelfth of Nisan and the fifteenth, on which Passover begins, only
> two days intervene; therefore they, too, are regarded as festival days.
> The Passover ending on the twenty-first (in the land of Israel) or on
> the twenty-second (in the Diaspora), only eight or nine days of the
> month remain. As by far the greater part of the month was made
> up of festival days, the entire month is treated as a festival season
> in which fasting is prohibited. Furthermore, in the time to come,
> the Sanctuary will be rebuilt in Nisan. [*BT Soferim* 21:2][10]

This year (5781), the first day of Nisan falls on Sunday, March 14. For those of you who have been following along since I first began these *drashot*, this is a significant date. This Shabbat, tomorrow, marks the end of a full yearly cycle of Torah readings. The next day, Sunday, is the first of Nisan— and the annual cycle of Torah readings will begin again.

It has been an amazing journey together with you studying the Torah in this Time of Pandemic. I hope that my words have brought you some support and sustenance during the dark, difficult, and uncertain days of this past year. May this new month of Nisan, a month in which we have no fasting, a month in which we celebrate the Feast of Freedom, bring blessings to us all!

SIXTH ALIYAH: EXODUS 40:17–27
WRITTEN FOR SATURDAY, SHABBAT, MARCH 13, 2021

Censoring God's Book?

This *aliyah* recounts the procedure followed by Moses in erecting the Tabernacle. First, he formed the framework, using the sockets, boards, bars, and pillars. Next, he spread out the various layers of curtains and coverings. Subsequently he moved to the interior of the Tabernacle, where he first placed the ark, with the tablets containing the Ten Commandments deposited inside of it. Next, he placed the veil that cordoned off the Holy of Holies, and placed the table in front of the ark, with the bread on the table [40:17-23]. He put the lampstand in its place, lit the lamps, placed the golden altar, and burned incense. Throughout this eleven-verse passage, we read the phrase, "just as God had commanded Moses," no less than five times! The Baal HaTurim addressed this: the phrase is repeated in this passage after the mention of every specific item that had been created for the Tabernacle. This, he says, contrasts with the words from last week's *parashah, Ki Tissa*, when, in response to the fact that God wanted to destroy the nation and start over again with Moses in response to the incident of the Golden Calf, Moses had said the following to God: "Now, if You will forgive their sin [well and good]; but if not, erase me from the record which You have written!"[11] [32:32].

Instead of erasing Moses's name from the book, God did just the opposite, mentioning his name multiple times, again and again!

Have you ever tried to read a text that was censored or redacted? We're tempted to try to read through and decipher it but try as we might, we are unable to discern what lies underneath the thick black lines. Instead, the remaining text takes on a totally different meaning, sometimes unintelligible, sounding like so much gibberish with gaping holes.

Now, think of our Torah text. With only the exception of the book of *Bereshit*, Genesis, we would be left with just such a text if God had actually taken Moses at his word and removed his name from the book. Very little would make any sense. Moses is tied to the people of Israel for all time.

To be sure, it certainly is true that none of us has gained or will gain the stature of Moses Rabbeinu. Nevertheless, the world would still be left with big, gaping holes in the narrative of it if any one of us were to be erased. The text of God's book would be left with indelible stains on it, for each individual soul is as important to God as that of Moses.

In the past year, we have heard so much controversy over the dueling philosophies of Black Lives Matter, Blue Lives Matter, White Lives Matter, and the "always inclusive" All Lives Matter. In truth, to our Creator, no qualifier is needed: lives matter, period. Yours matters no more or less than mine and mine no more or less than yours, or that of the next person. When someone asks you for help because (s)he is hurting or in pain, look him/her in the eyes and see beyond to the soul of the person that lies inside. Together, we fill the pages of God's book. Let us unite in a quest to make sure that there are no lines of censorship in that book.

SEVENTH ALIYAH: EXODUS 40:28–38
WRITTEN FOR SHABBAT, SATURDAY, MARCH 13, 2021

For Both the Pandemic and Our Torah Study—
the End or Just the Beginning?

And here we are—Moving In Day! The Tabernacle has been completed, the tent has been set up, all the furnishings have been installed. The priests who will serve there have been properly attired and anointed. The first burnt offering and meal offering have been offered. We read one final time (for the book of Shemot) that Moses did this according to all that God had commanded him [40:29]. When Moses finished the work, "the cloud covered the Tent of Meeting, and the Presence of the LORD filled the Tabernacle" [40:34].

According to Abarbanel, the Presence of the Lord refers both to a light that the people could see inside this cloud, as well as to the *Shekhinah*, the indwelling spirit of the Divine.[12] Additionally, he says that this was not a cloud like any that we are familiar with; this cloud had been specially created on the first day of creation, then hidden away until now.

A similar experience had occurred at Sinai: "When Moses had ascended the mountain, the cloud covered the mountain. The Presence of the LORD abode on Mt. Sinai, and the cloud hid it for six days. On the seventh day, He called to Moses from the midst of the cloud. Now the Presence of the LORD appeared in the sight of the Israelites as a consuming fire on the top of the mountain. Moses went inside the cloud and ascended the mountain; and Moses remained on the mountain forty days and forty nights" [24:15-18].

Then the people had been frightened by what they saw and heard. They sent Moses as their ambassador to meet with God on the mountain and come back and report to them. So much has happened in these sixteen chapters since then. The nation has been transformed. They have sinned and been reconciled with their God. We know that this pattern will repeat itself again and again as they journey into and through the desert. Now, however, the presence of God is not on the mountain, removed from them. Instead, it rests on a tent that travels in the midst of them. And the people are ready to journey forward together with the *Shekhinah*, the Presence of God accompanying them and leading the way.

We, too, have been transformed by the events of this past year. It was just a year ago, on March 11, 2020, when our world shut down due to a pandemic. And nothing about our lives has remained exactly the same as it was before. It was a very frightening time one year ago. With synagogues shut down, many of us felt as though our primary access to the Divine Presence had been closed. We looked for alternatives.

It was then that Rabbi Aaron Benson asked me what I could offer to our synagogue's congregation to help navigate these uncharted waters. In response, I began writing this cycle of Torah commentaries, seven on each *parashah*. The calendar dictated that I begin with the book and *parashah* of Vayikra. Today, with this last *aliyah* of Shemot, I have completed the entire cycle of Torah readings, fifty-four *parashiot*, for a total of three hundred seventy-eight *drashot*. Many, though not all, have been reflective of the strange and difficult times in which we live: a pandemic, social and political unrest, a contentious election, and the fallout from all these things individually and collectively. I know that I have learned a lot this year through this process, and sometimes it wasn't easy. I've challenged myself. For those of you who journeyed along with me for all or any part of this year, *todah rabah*. I hope that I have challenged and inspired you to continue Torah study on your own.

As the light appears at the end of this very long tunnel, and we gradually emerge from our pandemic-induced cocoons, let us go on from here in the Presence of God, confidently walking together with the Divine.

With this *Aliyah*, we have concluded the study of the book of *Shemot*, Exodus, and of our year-long journey through the Torah.

חֲזַק חֲזַק וְנִתְחַזֵּק!

EPILOGUE

There's Got to Be a Morning After[1]

So much has happened since the arrival of the coronavirus.

It has been over three years since we first heard the words "COVID-19." Two and a half years since I received my first two doses of the vaccine designed to protect me from it. Eight months since I actually contracted the virus.

Perhaps you may remember the 1972 movie *The Poseidon Adventure*.[2] Part of the mega-disaster movie genre so popular at the time, it tells the story of a cruise ship making its final voyage on New Year's Eve, traveling from New York City to Athens. In the middle of the Atlantic crossing, the captain receives word of an underwater earthquake that has produced a tsunami that is headed directly toward the ship. Unable to move out of the path of impending disaster, the ship is turned completely upside down by the giant wave, effectively killing or trapping everyone on board. A small ragtag group of survivors wends their way through a treacherous path to the vessel's outer hull, near the propellor, which is at this point out of the water. Encountering one obstacle after another, the group of ten is gradually diminished to six by the time they reach their destination and the rescuers who cut through the hull in response to their banging, finally delivering them to safety in the light of day.

I remember seeing this movie in college.

It was the Academy Award-winning theme song from this movie, titled "The Morning After," that got me to thinking about it recently. The song describes the experience of weathering a storm together with others through a difficult and dangerous night, holding on in the hope of finding the warmth and safety of the sunshine that awaits in the morning.

The hopeful message conveyed by the phrase, *There's got to be a morning after* of the lyrics is unmistakable; these words are intended to bolster the resolve of the fictional characters on the Poseidon who are fighting to survive the disaster that was thrust upon them unexpectedly (in the movie, the unsuspecting revelers heard the song when it was sung by an entertainer at the New Year's Eve Party shortly before the wave hit the boat). But it speaks allegorically, as well, to anyone facing extraordinary circumstances.

While the disaster on the Poseidon was imagined, the entire global community had a true-to-life, yet unimaginable disaster thrust upon us unexpectedly in early 2020. Like the fictional passengers on the Poseideon, we also had our lives turned upside-down with very little advance warning. Many did not survive. Many who did survive were scarred physically and/or emotionally.

As I write this, the world seems to be returning at last to much of the way it was before the pandemic. Many, though far from all, people are returning to the workplace. Students have returned to their classrooms. By and large, mask mandates have been lifted. Many still choose to wear them, but the number seems to dwindle daily. Eager to see others once again in person instead of on a computer screen, congregants are returning to synagogue services, and many happily attend social gatherings once more.

While the virus and its many variants are still with us, this year did not see a huge January surge in the number of cases. On May 11, President Biden declared that the public health emergency of the pandemic was over. Things appear to be returning to "normal" or at least settling in to a "new normal."

And yet . . .

It would be inaccurate at best to say that we have arrived at this time unscathed. The political divide that predated and was exacerbated by the pandemic continues to plague our country. The social unrest and outrage that was unleashed in the wake of the murder of George Floyd is, unfortunately, also still with us. The number of mass shootings, which had seemed to wane somewhat during 2020, now seems to be higher than ever, outpacing the number of days in the year. Schoolchildren whose education suffered when they were mandated to study from home via Zoom are still trying to get caught up from a lost year. Many who survived the pandemic physically have been scarred by depression and other forms of mental illness.

And to date, over one million Americans have lost their lives to COVID-19. The national emergency is over, yet people continue to contract the virus. For many, though, symptoms are mild and are compared to a common cold. Still, no one can say for sure that we will not experience pandemic status once again.

On the other hand, it would also be inaccurate to say that there were not some good things that came out of the coronavirus years. The forced isolation gave many of us time to do things we had never been able to find the time to do before. We found more time to spend with our family members. Many of us took better care of our physical health. Longing to be outdoors, we walked, jogged, ran, swam, and biked our way to new destinations. Our national parks saw such a surge in attendance that many required advance reservations for timed attendance slots that quickly filled up. Three years ago, I began my practice of walking three to five (and sometimes more) miles each day. Most days it's just a roundabout excursion through my neighborhood, but I also explored many destinations both near and far that I had never previously visited or even been aware of.

We read more, studied more, and prayed and meditated more, improving our mental health. As mentioned previously in this book, I began a practice in 2020 of going out onto my backyard deck (which just happens to face east) to daven *shacharit* each morning. This, too, was originally born out of a desire to be outside of the confines of my house. I continue this practice to this day, only abandoning it if there is rain or snow falling. I can hear the sounds of birds just about every day; only their numbers and species vary as the seasons change. Some days I hear neighbors' dogs barking or squirrels scampering through the trees. Yes, some days I also hear the sounds of school buses or the garbage truck, and I always know when someone in the neighborhood is getting a new roof installed on their house. These, too, are the sounds of life continuing on. I have witnessed three full cycles of the trees budding, blooming, shedding their leaves, and waiting dormant to begin again. Some mornings the air is very still. On others, the breeze turns the pages of my *siddur* before I am ready to do so myself. Some mornings are cloudy, and others require me to wear my sunglasses as I turn my face to the east. The signs of nature that surround me keep me focused on the One who is the object of my prayers.

And then there is Zoom, which allows us to connect with people literally all over the world at the same time. Through our computer screens, we were able to work at our jobs, worship together, "attend" school, consult with our doctors. The world of information literally opened up for us as we were able to watch or attend classes on a myriad of topics at any time of the day. Now we can have programs with speakers from anywhere in the world without having to pay to bring them into town. That technological genie is not going back in the bottle.

Indeed, it was COVID-19 that gave me the inspiration and the opportunity to write this book.

As much as I love studying and writing, I love even more to be able to inspire others by sharing what I have learned. For the last two years, I have taught a weekly online Zoom class for Women's League for Conservative Judaism. Most recently, we have studied the book of *Mishle*, Proverbs. About a month ago, I came across this verse: "For surely there is a future, and your hope will not be cut off" [Proverbs 23:18].

In the Hebrew text of this verse, the word translated as "future" is not the word *atid*, the word most often used to designate a time beyond the present. Instead, the word is *acharit*, literally, "a [time] after." It was this message of hope expressed in this verse, and this word specifically, that led me to think about that song directed at the fictional passengers of an upended cruise ship. With these words of encouragement, Solomon exhorts his child, and by extension all of us, the readers, to maintain hope in the promise of a better time awaiting us—a "morning after," if you will. But how?

How does one remain hopeful? What imparts the strength to endure, to deal with adversity? Solomon elaborates in the next chapter of *Mishle*: "My son, eat honey, because it is good; and the honeycomb, which is sweet to your palate. Know that wisdom is such to your soul; when you have found it, then there will be a future, and your hope will not be cut off" [Proverbs 24:13-14].

Wisdom, says Solomon, holds the key to weathering the storms of adversity. This Wisdom, a recurring theme in the book of Proverbs, comes from the study of Torah. Solomon compares it to honey: just as honey is sweet and good for physical health, so is Wisdom sweet and good for nourishing the soul. Honey imparts immediate sweetness when we taste it, and the honeycomb gives lasting sweetness to the palate. The Wisdom of Torah study is also sweet when we acquire it, but has a greater, lasting effect when we turn it and turn it again, making it our own. Having the freedom to ask difficult questions and wrestle with the answers has provided me with spiritual sustenance for the greater part of my adult life. Indeed, it was my pursuit of meaningful answers that sustained me through what was probably the darkest period of my life some forty years ago, ultimately leading me to seek conversion to Judaism. (I am writing about that story in my next book.) It was only natural, then, that I would turn to Torah study for comfort and sustenance when faced with a global pandemic and a scarcity of physical human contact. Just as I knew that the Wisdom of the Torah would provide me with much-needed solace to weather the storm of COVID-19, so too, did I believe that others would find it comforting, as well. It was that belief that led me to embark on what turned out to be a year-long project that resulted in the words found on these pages.

I hope, dear readers, that you have drawn some inspiration from my writings.

One thing that the pandemic has brought home very clearly is that ultimately, we do not have complete control of our own destiny, no matter how much we may think that we do. What we can control is our response to adversity.

There is so much Wisdom to be acquired, not only in the words of the Torah itself, but in all the commentaries that have been written, both ancient and contemporary. That is only the tip of the iceberg; there are also the other two parts of the *Tanakh*: the Prophets and the Writings. Beyond that are the texts of the Mishnah, the Talmud, the various Midrashim, and so much more.

With so much available to us, surely, we must acknowledge that there is, indeed, a bright and beautiful morning after.

AFTERWORD

My book was just about ready to go to publication. The final edits were done. I finished on a positive note—the Morning After. Everything was getting better—right?

When I wrote this book, the subtitle was "Torah Lessons for A Turbulent Time." I vacillated between using the words "Turbulent Time" and "Turbulent Year," ultimately deciding on the former. In light of the events of the past few days, I find my decision fortuitous. The year from March 2020 through March 2021, was indeed a turbulent year. We were embattled with an unseen, inanimate enemy—COVID 19—and had little to no control over our fates. Additionally, we found ourselves confronted by foes of human making: social unrest and political unrest. This book chronicles that year. This book was initially written to offer some spiritual guidance for navigating that most difficult of years. Yet the decision to publish my writings after that year was done with the realization that it could possibly offer some insight and guidance for navigating in a post-pandemic world as well.

The turbulence of 2020 pales in comparison to that which we are currently experiencing. Today is the fifth day since the horrific events of the attack perpetrated by Hamas terrorists on innocent citizens of Israel. With each day, we learn more details of the levels of depravity that were committed. I read the updates online and watch the news reports on television. Indeed, as I am writing this, an hour-long special report is playing in the background. And each day I reach a point where I need to turn the television off because I simply cannot take any more.

And I wonder—how can this be?

I was born in the 1950s into a non-Jewish household. I knew nothing about the Holocaust until I first learned of it in a high school History class.

Years later, as my interest in Judaism grew, I read and studied everything I could get my hands on regarding Jewish belief, practice, and history. That included educating myself on the events of the Shoah, and cultivating a love for the State of Israel. I traveled to Israel for the first time in 1996, spending three weeks as a volunteer on an IDF base near Tel Aviv, doing menial tasks that freed the soldiers to be able to do more important things. Since then, I have been back four additional times; the last of these was in 2016, when I spent a full semester of my rabbinic studies living in Jerusalem.

Like many other thousands of Jewish parents, I taught my children about the Holocaust, and I also taught them to love Israel. When each of them was sixteen years old, I put them on a plane with other Jewish teenagers destined for Poland. Together with their adult guides, they spent ten days in Poland, visiting the sites of concentration camps and the Warsaw Ghetto. From there they flew to Israel, where they were taken directly to the Kotel, the Wall, in Jerusalem after landing. The message was clear to them: we have a Jewish homeland now, a place where we can be safe, a place where we can be shielded from the horrors of anti-Semitism. Like me, my children developed a love for Israel. And, like me, they came to understand the atrocities of the Holocaust— from the vantage point of history. It couldn't ever happen again, right?

In the last five days, we—the worldwide Jewish community—indeed, the world—have been relieved of that naïve notion. We have learned of complete families, complete kibbutzim that were brutally murdered: shot, burned alive, decapitated. Young and old alike. Adults and children—babies. Soldiers. Innocent people in the streets and in their homes. And, reminiscent of the atrocities at Babi Yar, over 250 young people attending an outdoor concert rounded up and gunned down in a forest. And all of this took place in our beloved Israel. Like the modern-day inheritors of the Nazi ideology, the Hamas terrorists, it seems, have no line of depravity that they will not cross in their stated mission of killing not just Israelis, but Jews.

To be sure, I have known about anti-Semitism, even experienced it first-hand several times. But now I have witnessed pure unadulterated, unfiltered, baseless hatred in real time. It is no longer a purely intellectual experience for me. It is real. I saw a video of a 12-year-old boy being taken captive by the terrorists; his mother, who was speaking to him on the phone when they broke into the home, heard him pleading with them not to take him because he is too young. I watched that video and thought of my own grandson who turned 12 just two weeks ago and I pray that he and my other grandchildren can be shielded from all of this.

We all are touched in multiple ways by the atrocities we have learned of. Indeed, these last days have been more turbulent than the year during which I wrote this book. Our reactions are often visceral and overwhelming.

It is early yet. The situation promises to get much worse before it gets better. And yet we must not allow ourselves to be crippled by what we have witnessed or to lose our faith.

Judaism tells us to turn to our holy scriptures at all times, but especially in times of trouble. Study of the Torah, Mishnah, and Talmud have bolstered our faith for thousands of years. It is where I turn now for solace and comfort. It is my hope that my writings from the turbulent year of 2020-2021 will offer some comfort now as we face the turbulent year of 2023-2024. To myself. And to you, my dear readers. It's hard to imagine it now, but I pray that we will find our way through to a new morning after.

Comfort my people, comfort them, says your God. [Isaiah 40:1]

ACKNOWLEDGMENTS

This, my first book, has come about with the support and encouragement of so many people. I will try to recognize them all.

Most importantly—my family.

To my husband Raymond, who has been by my side for over 50 years since we first met: We've truly been through many major life changes together. Still, I'm fairly certain that supporting your wife through five years of rabbinical school was not what you envisioned for retirement. You have continued to encourage me as I reinvent myself in a new career as a rabbi, and now a third as an author. These last few years, the initial writing and multiple revisions of this book have taken huge amounts of my time. And every time I encountered technological issues and was ready to throw the computer through the nearest wall or window, you were there to calm me down and fix the problem. I truly could not have done this without you. For this and all the myriad other things you do for me, there are not enough words to express my gratitude. I thank you and I love you.

To my children Jessica and Ben, who have known from a very young age that your mother marches to no one's drumbeat but her own: from the time that you were able to understand it, I told you both the story of how our family came to be Jewish though both Dad and I were raised in Christian households. You know that the early mistakes we made and the difficulties we faced as a result of those poor decisions have made me a much stronger person. I've always striven to be a good role model for you both, even though my many involvements, including the time spent on writing this book, have taken away much family time over the years. The most important lesson I have always hoped to convey is to be yourself and think for yourself. Never let anyone take away your right to do so. And if you have dreams, pursue them. Though you are very different from each other, you have grown into adults with families of your own, and you are both secure in your identity. I am so very proud of you both and love you very much.

To the people brought into my life by my children, to Daniel and to Mara: thank you for your love and support as well. Daniel, only you can call me Rabbi Mom Cella, a unique appellation that expresses the *kavod* that comes with my rabbinic title, and, more importantly, the affection that comes with being your mother-in-law. While others think it is "cute", I see it as expressing both respect and love. Thank you for that and for helping to ensure that the legacy of our family is passed down to the next generation as well. Mara, you are so much like me—strong and determined to follow your dream. I thank you for the many times you were able to offer support when I was feeling down or overwhelmed—especially when you talked me out of quitting my rabbinic studies after that time when I left my backpack on the train during my first year. I hope that I have been able to offer you the same support and encouragement as I have striven to fulfill that promise I made to your mother.

To my four beautiful grandsons Jackson, Rory, Tal, and Ezra, and to my two "bonus" grandchildren Ilan and Doriya: you are my legacy. You are my reasons for doing the things I do. I hope that you will come to understand and respect the values of Judaism that have shaped my life, and that you will be guided by them in your lives as well. My prayer is for all of you to grow up to be kind, ethical people, and that you will each leave your own special mark on this world. I hope that you will be able to proudly say, "My grandmother is a rabbi," and "my grandmother wrote a book," and, most importantly, "my Savta loves me very much."

To my parents, who instilled in me a strong love of family, and were role models for living a life that is guided by the values of faith: Though I chose a different life path than the one in which you raised me, I nevertheless feel that I am following your strong examples. Dad, you never could tolerate hypocrisy; consequently, I have always striven to be sincere in my faith and observance. Mom, the devotion that you always had to the church is something that I have endeavored to duplicate in the synagogue. And I couldn't have asked for a better example of what it means to be a strong, independent woman, and a leader among one's peers. I thank you both for instilling in me a love of learning from a very young age; it has served me well throughout my life, both on my journey to Judaism, and in my rabbinic studies. Though neither one of you lived to see my more recent accomplishment, I'd like to think that you would have been happy to brag about your daughter the rabbi, and your daughter the author. You might have even liked to read this book!

To my sisters and brothers, Bet, Barbara, Robert, and Arthur: though we are scattered from New York to Florida, we are still that rare group of adult siblings who genuinely like each other, and always have a good time when we are together. Though I have chosen a different path in life, you have been my strongest supporters, and I know that you are genuinely proud of my accomplishments. Bet and Barbara, you are my biggest cheerleaders, singing my praises to anyone who's willing to listen. Barbara, you lived with me and Raymond during the first five months that I was working on this book. Though it took a long time to compose each day's entry, you always respectfully gave me my space. Rob and Artie, you are the best two "little" brothers anyone could ask for. I love you all.

Next, my NSJC family.

First and foremost, a huge thank you to Rabbi Aaron Benson. You were the person who first gave me the opportunity to begin to write the series of daily emails that ultimately became this book. What was meant to help bolster the members of the congregation during the isolation brought on by the pandemic ultimately became therapeutic for me as well. My writing improved as the year went on and continued to bolster my self-confidence. When I started with Leviticus we had no idea how long this would last. By the time we got to Exodus, we had returned to the sanctuary for good. Yet when I said that I had come so far with this project that I wanted to see it through to completion, you agreed, and continued to send out the emails on my behalf. And when I had completed the entire annual cycle of writings, you invited me to mark the occasion by teaching at the Siyyum Bechor, the Fast of the Firstborn. Thank you for your continued support and for allowing me to have this awesome experience.

To the members of the NSJC congregation—long before this project began, you have supported and encouraged me in my growth as a Jew. When the Cella family first came to the synagogue over forty years ago, you welcomed us with open arms. You marveled at our story and claimed us as your own, involving us in every aspect of synagogue life. You built me up and encouraged me to go to rabbinical school. And though you had always known me as just Margie, you now greet me as Rabbi. And when I started writing these emails, you sent me emails in return, asking questions and giving me your feedback. I value your friendship and encouragement more than you can know.

There are so many of you that I call friends it would be difficult to list you all. Please know how much I appreciate you all. There are a few in particular whom I must mention by name.

Ann Helfgott and David Kessler—you have been our friends since we first met forty years ago. We have raised our children together, celebrated holidays, weddings, and bar and bat mitzvahs together. Ann, we have studied together and worked together to increase women's participation in the services. You believed in me when I didn't believe in myself. When I told you that I thought rabbinical school was just a pipe dream, you told me that you could see yourself attending my ordination. And when I needed private tutoring in Talmud in order to be able to take the first year class at the Seminary, you spent a summer working with me, giving me the foundation I needed to ultimately take five classes in Talmud. Thank you so much for all this and more.

Nancy Gold—in addition to being my friend, you are perhaps my biggest advocate. When my completed manuscript needed its first proofreading, you agreed to do it for me. For all the time you spent going through it—not once, but twice—I thank and appreciate you from the bottom of my heart. And I will never view a semi-colon the same way again! I am privileged to call you my friend and I treasure your steadfast support.

Hilary and David Kramer—what can I say? You were the first NSJC family to invite us to your home and we soon became fast friends. We put our children on a bus together and sent them to Solomon Schechter. Who would have predicted that one day we would become *machatunim*, and now share grandchildren together? Our friendship became a family connection. Your support through it all has been invaluable.

Amy Russell—thank you so much for creating a beautiful website for me. Your expertise , as well as your friendship and encouragement, is greatly appreciated.

To Rabbi Moshe Edelman, I owe a huge debt of gratitude. You didn't turn me away when I told you I wanted to discuss a formal conversion to Judaism for a family of four. Instead, you agreed to work with us. After you brought us to the *mikveh*, you encouraged the members of the Congregation to accept us. And you did so much to inspire my personal growth as a Jew, encouraging me to study and to learn new skills such as reading Torah and Megillah. And you were the first person to publicly state that you thought that I belonged in the rabbinical school at the Jewish Theological Seminary. Your confidence in my abilities nearly blew me away. I carried with me the memory of your statement—though it would take a full twenty-five years before I finally submitted my application. And in my senior year you not only recommended me as a rabbinical candidate to Congregation Agudas Israel in Newburgh, but you also volunteered to share the pulpit with me. It was then that I knew we had come full circle. It is an understatement to say that this book would not have been possible if you hadn't seen that spark in me so long ago and kept it alive for so many years. You are still one of my biggest advocates and I cannot thank you enough.

To the teachers at JTS who offered me encouragement and helped me to believe in myself during all those many times of self-doubt—I offer you immeasurable gratitude. I would not have made it to ordination without you. Though I cannot list you all by name, there are two members of the Bible Department who stand out as having the greatest impact on me. David Marcus, I can hardly look at a biblical text without considering the Masoretic notes as you taught me to do in every one of the five classes I took with you. Benjamin Sommer, I can hardly look at a biblical text without parsing each sentence, especially the verbs, just as you taught me to do in every one of the five classes I took with you. At various points in the writing of this book I leaned on the skills that I learned in both of your classrooms. My love of text study was nurtured and increased by your influence, and for that I thank you both.

Next, my Women's League for Conservative Judaism family—thank you all for the love and support you have given and continue to show me since I began working for you as an educator. Your enthusiasm inspires me to keep learning so that I can keep teaching. And I know many of you have been waiting anxiously for the publication of this book. While I thank you all, there are 2 specific people within the organization whom I must thank. During a Zoom meeting regarding an upcoming Torah Fund program at which I would be the keynote speaker, I mentioned to Marjorie Fourmann and Cheryl Wasserman that I had written a book. They asked if I had a publisher yet. When I said that I did not, Cheryl offered to connect me with her friend who is a publisher, and that is how I came to meet Emily Barosse at Bold Story Press. Thank you, Cheryl, for that serendipitous introduction.

So, finally, to Emily and your entire staff, thank you for believing in me and helping to make this book a reality.

—Rabbi Margie Cella
October, 2023

APPENDIX A
List of Commentators

Abarbanel, Yitchak ben Yuhudah, 1437-1508, Portugal

Baal HaTurim, R. Yaakov ben Ra'ash, Rabbeinu Asher, c. 1269-c. 1343,
Toledo and Castile

Gersonides, R. Levi ben Gershom (Ralbag), 1288-1344, France

Hizkuni, R. Hezekiah ben Manoah, thirteenth century France

Ibn Ezra, (R. Avraham ben Meir Ibn Ezra), c. 1089 (92)-c. 1164 (67), Spain

Kimhi, Solomon ben Nissim Yosef David, nineteenth century Turkey

Leibowitz, Nehama, 1905-1997, Israel

Luzzatto, Moshe Chaim (RamChal), 1707-1746, Italy

Onkelos, c. 35-120, Roman Empire

Or HaChaim, Chaim Ibn Attar, 1696-1743, Morocco

Ramban, R. Moshe ben Nachman (Nahmanides), 1195-1270, Spain

Rashbam, R. Shmuel ben Meir, c. 1085-c. 1158, France

Rashi, R. Shlomo Yitzchaki, 1040-1105, France

APPENDIX B
Glossary of Hebrew Terms

adam   man; a human being; humankind.

Akedah   the story of Abraham (almost) sacrificing his son Isaac at God's command.

aliyah   literally "going up." One of the seven sections of each weekly Torah portion, so named because for each one a congregant is called up to [stand at] the Torah.

amidah   from the verb *"omed,"* meaning to stand. This is the central part of each service; one stands in prayer as if standing before God.

Aramaic   vernacular semitic language of the Jews of Babylonia; it is the language in which the Talmud is written.

aron kodesh   literally "holy ark." This was the structure in which the Torah and the tablets were stored. In the modern synagogue, it is the structure housing the synagogue's Torah scrolls.

arvit   the evening prayer service.

Av   the fifth month of the Hebrew calendar; it usually falls in the summer.

avnet   the girdle worn by the high priest.

avodah   the religious work performed by the priests and Levites in the Tabernacle.

barchu   meaning "let us bless," this is the official call to prayer in both the morning and evening services.

bayit, batim   literally "house, houses." This refers to the box(es) on the arm and head tefilin that contain miniature hand-written scrolls.

birkat cohenim   the priestly blessing given by the cohenim at the end of each holiday service.

birkat hamazon   grace after meals.

bracha (brachot)   blessing (blessings) recited before observing a commandment, eating a food, or engaging in a specific activity.

cahuna   title of priesthood passed down to all the male descendants of Aaron.

chametz   any food made from the five grains (wheat, barley, rye, spelt, oats) which Jews are forbidden to eat during Passover.

chol hamoed   the intermediate days of the festivals of Sukkot and Passover.

choshen   the breastplate worn by the high priest.

chumash, chumashim   book(s) containing the text of the five books of the Torah in both Hebrew and English.

chuppah   canopy under which a wedding ceremony takes place.

cohen, cohenim   priest(s), male descendants of Aaron.

cohen gadol   high priest.

daven, davening   pray(ing) with intention.

drashah   a sermon.

dugma   a role model or example.

d'var Torah   words of Torah shared with others in either spoken or written form.

Elul   the twelfth month of the Hebrew calendar; it usually occurs in the fall.

ephod   apron worn by the high priest.

eretz   land or country.

erev   evening.

etrog   a fragrant yellow citron fruit used during the morning service for the holiday of Sukkot.

gabbai, gabbaiim   individual(s) involved in the running of the synagogue service; one of two people whose responsibility is to correct the Torah readers.

Gemora   the part of the Talmud comprising rabbinical commentary on the Mishna.

gematria   Hebrew numerology.

glatt   literally meaning "smooth," particularly when applied to the lungs of a kosher animal. This is a stricter system of kosher observance (of meat).

hagbah   lifting the Torah scroll to display it to the congregation after the public reading.

haggadah   book of songs, stories, and prayers used for the Passover seder.

halachah   Jewish law.

ha-motzi   blessing recited over bread.

heckscher   symbol of kosher certification.

hiphil   Hebrew verb tense indicating causative action.

ish   a man.

kaddish   Aramaic prayer separating parts of the service; there is both a full and a half kaddish, and a mourner's kaddish that is recited by mourners during their period of mourning and on the anniversary of a death.

kamatz   Hebrew vowel that is shaped like a capital letter "T" and makes an "ah" sound.

kapporet   cloth covering of the ark in the Tabernacle.

kashrut   system of Jewish dietary laws.

keruvim   angelic shaped beings; depictions of a pair of these were placed above the ark in the Tabernacle.

keshet   a bow such as an archer's bow; a rainbow.

kavod   honor, respect.

kol demamah   the still small voice (of God).

kutonet   coat of fine linen worn by the high priest.

Levi, Leviim   member(s) of the tribe of Levi who were assigned to assist the priests in the operation of the Taberncale.

leyn   to chant Torah with the appropriate cantillation notes.

lulav   a palm frond; bundle of a palm, two willow branches, and three myrtle branches waved during the morning service on Sukkot.

ma'ariv   the evening prayer service.

mamzer   person born from an adulterous or incestuous relationship.

Megillah   scroll containing the Book of Esther that is read on Purim.

me'il   blue robe worn by the high priest.

melachah   the thirty-nine categories of work prohibited on the sabbath because they were part of the construction of the Tabernacle.

midrash   biblical interpretation or exegesis.

mikvah   ritual bath.

minchah   the afternoon prayer service.

mishkan   Tabernacle; the portable tent used for worship in the desert.

Mishna   first written collection of the Oral Torah; redacted in the third century CE. Together with the gemora, it comprises the text of the Talmud.

mitznefet   turban worn by the high priest.

mitzvah, mitzvot   commandment(s).

musaf   additional prayer service following the morning service on Shabbat and holidays.

narrishkeit   foolishness.

nazir   one who takes on a vow not to cut his/her hair, drink any wine or grape juice, and not to have any contact with the dead for a specified period of time.

nefesh   the soul or non-physical essence of a human being.

nekudot   vowels; in Hebrew, these are not letters, but rather symbols attached to the letters.

niddah   a woman who is experiencing a discharge of blood, most commonly through menstruation, or who has experienced the discharge but has not yet immersed in a ritual bath. The immersion takes place seven days after the last date of seeing blood. During this time, she is forbidden from physical contact with her husband.

Nisan   the first month of the Hebrew calendar; it occurs in the spring, and is the month during which the festival of Passover occurs.

olam habah   the world to come; the afterlife.

omer   a dry measure of grain; an omer of grain was commanded to be brought on forty-nine consecutive days beginning with the second day of Passover, followed the next day by the holiday of Shavuot; this seven-week period of semi-mourning is also referred to as "the Omer".

parasha   one of the fifty-four weekly portions of the Torah text.

Pesach   Passover, the spring holiday celebrating the liberation of Israel from Egypt.

peyes   sidelocks; men of the ultra-Orthodox sects do not shave the hair in front of their ears, allowing it to grow very long.

pidyon shevuyim   ransoming the captives; it is an obligation to free any Jew who has been kidnapped, captured, or imprisoned unjustly.

pikuah nefesh   saving a life; one of the primary commandments, it takes precedence over all but three commandments: refraining from murder, idolatry, or acts of sexual immorality.

Ploni, Plonit   Hebrew equivalent of John Doe, Jane Doe.

Purim   holiday celebrating the deliverance of the Jews of Persia from the vizier Haman who had plotted to have them all killed; the story is told in the biblical book of Esther.

sefer   book.

shacharit   the morning prayer service.

shaliach tzibur   the individual who leads the congregational prayers.

shalshelet   a rare Hebrew cantillation note that occurs only four times in the entire Torah; it is sung in a very distinct pattern, trilling both up and then down three times.

Shavuot   holiday celebrated in late spring at the culmination of the seven-week period of the counting of the omer commencing on the second day of Passover; it commemorates the giving of the Torah at Mt. Sinai.

shekel, shekalim   Biblical silver coin; unit of currency in modern Israel.

Shekhinah (Shechinah)   the indwelling presence of God; sometimes referred to as the feminine presence of God, it was believed to dwell in the Holy of Holies in the Tabernacle and later the Temple.

Shema   fundamental prayer in Judaism expressing a belief in the one God; Jews are obligated to recite it twice each day, in the morning and the evening.

Shemini Atzeret   the Eighth Day of Assembly; a holiday that is celebrated after the holiday of Sukkot in the fall.

shevarim   one of the three notes blown on a shofar. Consists of three short blasts.

shiksa   pejorative Yiddish word for a non-Jewish woman.

shin   the twenty-first letter of the Hebrew alphabet: שׁ.

shiva   the seven-day period of mourning following the death of an immediate relative.

shloshim   literally thirty; this is the total time for mourning all immediate relatives other than parents (who are mourned for eleven months).

shmittah   sabbatical year; the last year in every seven-year cycle when no crops are planted.

siddur, siddurim   prayer books(s).

Siyyum Bechor   celebration of the completion of the study of a tractate of Talmud held on the morning of the day before Passover to free those who are firstborn from the obligation to fast on that day.

sofer   Hebrew scribe; one who handwrites Torah scrolls and other sacred documents.

sotah   a woman suspected by her husband of adultery.

sukkah   a portable structure in which Jews eat and sleep during the seven days of the fall holiday of Sukkot.

Sukkot   seven day fall holiday commemorating the final harvest; observance includes dwelling in a *sukkah*, and waving a lulav and etrog during the morning service.

tallit, tallitot   prayer shawl(s).

Tanakh   the Jewish bible, consisting of three parts: Torah, Neviim (Prophets), and Ketuvim (Writings).

Targum   a translation of the Tanakh from Hebrew to Aramaic.

taryag   Hebrew word that has no meaning but whose numerical value in *gematria* is 613, so the commandments in the Torah are referred to as the *Taryag Mitzvot.*

techelet   a blue dye used for one of the eight strings, or *tzitzit.*

tekiah   one of the three notes played on the shofar, it is one single long blast.

tefilin   sometimes called phylacteries, these are two small leather boxes, one worn on the head with two long straps hanging down, the other worn on the bicep with a single long strap that is wound around the forearm and hand, during prayers on weekday mornings.

tefilin shel rosh   tefilin worn on the head.

tefilin shel yad   tefilin worn on the arm (hand).

teruah   one of the three notes blown on the shofar. Consists of nine short staccato blasts.

tikkun   literally "repair." Also, the book that is used by a Torah reader when preparing a reading.

Tikkun Olam   repairing the world. Refers to social justice actions designed to make the world a better place; it is an obligation incumbent on all Jews to repair the world in some way.

Tisha B'Av   the Ninth Day of the Hebrew Month of Av, which is the fifth month on the Hebrew calendar. This day, which falls in the summer, commemorates many tragedies which have historically befallen the Jewish people on that day, including the destruction of both the first Temple by the Babylonians in 586 BCE and the second Temple by the Romans in 70 CE.

Tishrei   the seventh month of the Hebrew calendar; occurring in the fall, it is the month during which Rosh HaShanah falls.

tochecha   the sections of admonition in the Torah text from the twenty-sixth chapter of Leviticus and twenty-eighth chapter of Deuteronomy; they outline the consequences for a failure to observe God's commandments.

tohu va-vohu   unformed and void; a biblical phrase used to describe the condition of the raw materials of Creation just before God began with the creation of light.

Tu B'Av   the fifteenth day of the month of Av, which falls during the summer. It is a day that celebrates love.

Tu B'Shvat   the fifteenth day of the Hebrew month of Sh'vat, the fifth month of the Hebrew calendar; occurring in the winter, it commemorates the New Year of the Trees.

tzara'at   a disease of uncleanness manifested by white patches in the skin, hair or beard.

tzitz   golden plate worn by the high priest on his turban; on it were engraved the words, *"Kodesh l'Adonai,"* meaning Holy to God.

APPENDIX C
Endnotes

Note: All passages from the Babylonian Talmud (indicated as *BT*) are from the website, Sefaria (https://www.sefaria.org/texts). The text used is the William Davidson edition of the Talmud with translation and commentary by Rabbi Adin Steinsalz z"l. Parts of the text in **bold lettering** are the original Talmud text, and those not in bold are R. Steinsalz' commentary.

BOOK OF VAYIKRA

Parashat Vayikra

1 *Baal HaTurim Chumash*, Davis Edition, Mesorah Publications, Ltd., 4401 Second Ave., Brooklyn, NY 11232, 2000 Vayikra, pg. 1020-1021
2 Carasik, *The Commentators Bible, The Ruben JPS Miqraot Gedolot*, JPS, 2009, Vayikra, Leviticus, p. 15
3 *ibid.*, p. 29
4 www.jtsa.edu/torah/the-jewish-lost-and-found/

Parashat Tzav

1 Carasik, p. 34
2 *ibid.*, p. 34
3 www.sefaria.org/Leviticus.6.2?lang=bi&with=all&lang2=en
4 Carasik, p. 36
5 www.sefaria.org/Pirkei_DeRabbi_Eliezer.53.3?lang=bi&with=all&lang2=en
6 Carasik, p. 35
7 *ibid.*, p. 41
8 *Biblia Hebraica Stuttgartensia*, K. Elliger and W. Rudolph Editors, Deutsche Bibelgesellschaft Stuttgart, 1983, page 353
9 aishdas.org/toratemet/en_pamphlet9.html
10 *Biblia Hebraica Stuttgartensia*, page 169
11 Carasik, p. 104
12 *ibid.*, p. 54

Parashat Shemini

1 *Baal HaTurim Chumash*, pg. 1080
2 Carasik, p. 56
3 Leonard Nimoy, *Star Trek, The Original Series*, Paramount, 1969
4 www.sefaria.org/Leviticus.9.23?lang=bi&with=Rashi&lang2=en
5 Larry David, 2000
6 www.sefaria.org/Leviticus.10.2?lang=bi&with=Rashi&lang2=en
7 *ibid*
8 *Baal HaTurim Chumash*, p. 1089-1090
9 Carasik, p. 64
10 www.sefaria.org/Leviticus.10.16?lang=bi&with=Or%20HaChaim&lang2=en
11 Sly and the Family Stone, lyrics by Sylvester Stewart, I Want to Take You Higher, Stand!, 1969

Parashat Tazria

1 *Baal HaTurim Chumash*, p. 1115
2 *ibid.*, p. 1114
3 Carasik, p. 87
4 Stephen Colbert, The Late Show With Stephen Colbert, www.cbs.com/shows/the-late-show-with-stephen-colbert/, title of a popular segment during the pandemic
5 Carasik, p. 89
6 See Me Feel Me Touch Me Heal Me, The Who, lyrics by Peter Townsend and Dennis Blandfor, Tommy, 1969
7 *Baal HaTurim Chumash*, p. 1127
8 Every Breath You Take, The Police, lyrics by Gordon Sumner, Synchronicity, 1983
9 *Baal HaTurim Chumash*, p. 113
10 Carasik, p. 96
11 *ibid.*, p. 99

Parashat Metzora

1 Carasik, p. 101
2 *ibid.*, p. 102
3 *Baal HaTurim Chumash*, p. 1143
4 Carasik, p. 104
5 www.sefaria.org/Kav_HaYashar.50.2
6 www.sefaria.org/Mishnah_Negaim.12.5?lang=bi&with=all&lang2=en
7 *Baal HaTurim Chumash*, p. 1146-1147
8 Carasik, p. 112
9 Baruch A. Levine, *The JPS Torah Commentary, Leviticus*, page 94
10 Carasik, p. 114
11 Levine, p. 98

Parashat Acharei Mot

1 *Baal HaTurim Chumash*, p. 1169
2 www.sefaria.org/Leviticus.16.21?lang=bi&with=Chizkuni&lang2=en
3 Carasik, p. 126
4 Levine, p. 113
5 *Midnight Cowboy,* Directed by John Schlesinger. Dustin Hoffman, 1969
6 Levine, p. 123
7 Carasik, p. 140

Parashat Kedoshim

1 Carasik, p. 140
2 *ibid.*, p. 144
3 www.mediaite.com/tv/msnbcs-stephanie-ruhle-breaks-down-over-a-deaf
-grocery-clerk-unable-to-read-lips-due-to-covid-masks/
4 Levine, p. 134
5 Carasik, p. 157
6 *Baal HaTurim Chumash*, p. 1209
7 Carasik, p. 159

Parashat Emor

1 Levine, p. 141
2 Dueling Banjos, written by Arthur "Guitar Boogie" Smith and Don Reno for the
movie *Deliverance*, Warner Brothers, 1972
3 Levine, p. 160
4 Carasik, p. 188
5 *ibid.*, p. 191

Parashat Behar

1 Carasik, p. 203
2 *ibid.*, p. 208
3 www.sefaria.org/Mishneh_Torah%2C_Sabbatical_Year_and_the_Jubilee.11.3
4 Carasik, p. 212
5 www.sefaria.org/Mishneh_Torah%2C_Slaves.1.6
6 Levine, p. 179
7 www.sefaria.org/Leviticus.25.55

Parashat Bechukkotai

1 www.sefaria.org/Sifra%2C_Bechukotai%2C_Chapter_2.4
2 Leviticus 26:21 with Rashi (sefaria.org)
3 Carasik, p. 225
4 *Baal HaTurim Chumash*, p. 1305
5 *ibid.*, p. 1313

BOOK OF BAMIDBAR

Parashat Bamidbar

1 Carasik, *The Commentators' Bible, The Ruben JPS Miqraot Gedolot*, JPS,
2009, Numbers, p. 4
2 *Baal HaTurim Chumash*, Davis Edition, Mesorah Publications, Ltd., 4401 Second
Ave., Brooklyn, NY 11232, 2000, Bamidbar, p. 1363
3 Carasik, p. 13
4 *ibid.*, p. 16
5 *ibid.*, p. 19

Parashat Naso

1 Carasik, p. 28
2 *ibid.*, p. 29
3 *Baal HaTurim Chumash*, p. 1397
4 https://medium.com/@rabbijustus/ger-tzedek-the-righteous-convert-956edd4ab7
5 Jacob Milgrom, *The JPS Torah Commentary, Numbers*,
The Jewish Publication Society, 1989, p. 51

6 www.sefaria.org/Numbers.7.12

7 Carasik., p. 46

8 *ibid.*, p. 47

9 *Baal HaTurim Chumash*, p. 1428-1429

10 www.sefaria.org/Numbers.7.48

11 Carasik., p. 54

Parashat Behaalotecha

1 *Baal HaTurim Chumash*, p. 1445

2 Carasik, p. 57

3 *ibid.*, p. 58

4 *ibid.*, p. 59

5 *Baal HaTurim Chumash, Vayikra*, p. 1450-1451

6 *ibid.*, p. 1451

7 Carasik, p. 59

8 www.sefaria.org/Mekhilta_d'Rabbi_Yishmael.12.17

9 Carasik, p. 66

10 *ibid,* p. 68

11 *ibid,* p. 85

12 *Baal HaTurim Chumash*, p. 1499

13 Carasik, p. 84-85

Parashat Shelach Lecha

1 www.sefaria.org/Midrash_Tanchuma%2C_Vayakhel.8.2

2 Carasik, p. 110

Parashat Korach

1 Carasik, p. 116

2 *Baal HaTurim Chumash*, p. 1568

Parashat Chukkat

1 Carasik, p. 138

2 Carasik, p. 143-144

3 www.sefaria.org/Numbers.20.12

4 Carasik, p. 148

5 *ibid.*, p. 149

6 Carasik, p. 151

7 *Baal HaTurim Chumash*, p. 1604-1605

8 Carasik, p. 158

Parashat Balak

1 Jacob Milgrom, p. 187

2 Carasik, p 168

3 *ibid.*, p. 169

4 Carasik, p. 176

5 *ibid.*, p. 177

6 *ibid.*, p. 178

7 *ibid.*, p. 178-179

8 *ibid.*, p. 183

Parashat Pinchas

1 *Baal HaTurim Chumash*, p. 1679
2 Carasik, p. 196
3 *ibid.*, p. 205
4 Milgrom, p. 232
5 "Stay (Just a Little Bit Longer) Lyrics." Lyrics.com. STANDS4 LLC, 2022. Web. 18 Apr. 2022. https://www.lyrics.com/lyric/25931335/Maurice+Williams+%26+the+Zodiacs.

Parashat Mattot

1 Nehama Leibowitz, *Studies in Bamidbar (Numbers)*, World Zionist Organization, Jerusalem, 1980, page 376
2 *ibid.*, page 377-378
3 *Baal HaTurim Chumash, Vayikra*, pages 1726

Parashat Masei

1 Ya Gotta Have Heart, Damn Yankees, lyrics by James Komack, Nathaniel Frey, Albert Linville, and Russ Brown, soundtrack album, 1958
2 Elton John, lyrics by Elton John and Bernie Taupin, Elton John, 1970
3 www.sefaria.org/Numbers.34.17?ven=The_Contemporary_Torah,_Jewish_Publication_Society

BOOK OF DEVARIM

Parashat Devarim

1 Carasik, *The Commentators' Bible, Deuteronomy*, p. 10
2 William Shatner, Star Trek, 1966, https://genius.com/Star-trek-star-trek-opening-lyrics
3 www.sefaria.org/Sifrei_Bamidbar.10.34
4 Jeffrey H. Tigay, *JPS Torah Commentary, Deuteronomy*, p. 20
5 This Land Is Your Land, words and music by Woodie Guthrie, 1940 and 1944
6 Carasik, p. 17
7 *ibid.*, p. 20
8 *ibid.*, p. 23

Parashat Vaetchanan

1 www.sefaria.org/Deuteronomy.4.2
2 Carasik, p. 38

Parashat Ekev

1 Carasik, p. 62
2 *ibid.*, p. 65
3 *Baal HaTurim Chumash*, p. 1929
4 Carasik, p. 73
5 *ibid.*, p. 75
6 *ibid.*, p. 80

Parashat Re'Eh

1 Carasik, p. 82
2 *ibid.*, p. 84
3 *ibid.*, p. 90

Parashat Shoftim

1 Carasik, p. 114
2 Tigay, p. 161
3 www.sefaria.org/Deuteronomy.16.201
4 www.sefaria.org/Rambam_Introduction_to_the_Mishnah.14.6
5 Carasik, p. 122
6 *Back to the Future*, Paramount Pictures, 1985, www.imdb.com/title/tt0088763
7 Carasik, p. 126
8 *Baal HaTurim Chumash*, p. 2025
9 Tigay, p. 177
10 Carasik, p. 136
11 *ibid.*, p. 140

Parashat Ki Tetzei

1 Carasik, p. 142–143
2 *ibid.*, p. 148–149
3 https://www.youtube.com/watch?v=D01t7v8Kg2Y&feature=youtu.be

Parashat Ki Tavo

1 Carasik, p. 177
2 *ibid.*, page 179
3 www.sefaria.org/Mishnah_Middot.3.4?ven=Mishnah_Yomit_by_Dr._Joshua_Kulp
4 www.sefaria.org/Midrash_Tanchuma%2C_Ki_Tavo.4.1
5 Carasik, p. 182

Parashat Nitzavim

1 www.sefaria.org/Deuteronomy.29.14?ven=The_Contemporary_Torah,
   Targum Jerusalem
2 www.sefaria.org/Deuteronomy.29.14?ven=The_Contemporary_Torah,
   Targum Jonathan
3 www.sefaria.org/Deuteronomy.29.14?ven=The_Contemporary_Torah,
   Midrash Tanchuma Pikudei 3:4
4 Carasik, p. 197
5 Tigay, p. 278
6 *Baal HaTurim Chumash*, p. 2159
7 Carasik, p. 204
8 *ibid.*, p. 205

Parashat Vayelech

1 www.sefaria.org/Deuteronomy.31.2, Rashi
2 Carasik, p. 207
3 www.lyrics.com/lyric/3468387/Rodgers+%26+Hammerstein/
   You%27ll+Never+Walk+Alone>
4 Tigay, p. 290
5 Carasik, p. 208

Parashat Ha-azinu

1 Carasik, p. 215
2 *ibid.* page 216
3 *ibid.* page 219
4 www.sefaria.org/Deuteronomy.32.7?lang=bi&with=Bekhor%20Shor&lang2=en
5 www.sefaria.org/Deuteronomy.32.10?lang=bi&with=Rabbeinu%20Bahya&lang2=en

6   Carasik, p. 220

7   www.sefaria.org/Deuteronomy.32.11?lang=bi&with=Rashi&lang2=en

8   Carasik, p. 221

9   *ibid.* page 223

10 Tigay, p. 307

11 Carasik, p. 224-225

12 *ibid.* page 228

13 www.sefaria.org/Kiddushin.70b.15?lang=bi&with=Tosafot&lang2=en

14 Carasik, p. 232

15 *ibid.* page 234

Parashat V'Zot HaBrachah

1   *Baal HaTurim Chumash*, p. 2213

2   www.sefaria.org/Deuteronomy.33.19?lang=bi&with=Rashi&lang2=en

3   Carasik, p. 251

4   www.sefaria.org/Deuteronomy.33.24?lang=bi&with=Rashi&lang2=en

5   Carasik, p. 253

6   www.sefaria.org/Tractate_Derekh_Eretz_Zuta.1.18?lang=bi&with=all&lang2=en, accessed October 7, 2020

BOOK OF BERESHIT

Parashat Bereshit

1   www.sefaria.org/Genesis.1.27?lang=bi&with=Commentary&lang2=en

2   Carasik, *The Commentators' Bible, Genesis*, p. 35

3   *ibid.*, p. 50-51

Parashat Noach

1   Carasik, p. 71

2   Nahum Sarna, *JPS Torah Commentary, Genesis*, p. 54

3   Carasik, p. 89

4   *ibid.*, p. 91

5   Nahum Sarna, p. 65

6   Carasik, p. 102

Parashat Lech Lecha

1   Henny Youngman, https://en.wikipedia.org/wiki/Henny_Youngman, accessed October 26, 2020

2   www.sefaria.org/Sefer_HaYashar_(midrash)%2C_Book_of_Genesis%2C_Lech_Lecha.5?

3   Sarna, p. 379

4   Gilad Shalit - Wikipedia

Parashat Vayera

1   Carasik, p. 152

2   www.sefaria.org/Pirkei_DeRabbi_Eliezer.25.8?lang=bi&with=all&lang2=en

3   Neil Sedaka, lyrics by Neil Sedaka and Howard Greenfield, Tuneweaver, 1975

4   Carasik, p. 168

5   *ibid.*, p. 175

6   Be Our Guest, lyrics by Ewan McGregor, Beauty and the Beast Soundtrack, 2017

7   www.sefaria.org/Midrash_Tehillim.110.1?lang=bi

8   www.sefaria.org/Pirkei_DeRabbi_Eliezer.31.10?lang=bi&with=all&lang2=en

Parashat Chaye Sarah

1 www.sefaria.org/Rabbeinu_Bahya%2C_Bereshit.23.1.8?lang=bi
2 www.sefaria.org/Ein_Yaakov%2C_Bava_Batra.1.41?lang=bi
3 www.sefaria.org/Genesis.24.1?lang=bi&with=Ramban&lang2=en
4 www.sefaria.org/Genesis.24.1?lang=bi&with=Rabbeinu%20Bahya&lang2=en
5 www.sefaria.org/Genesis.24.1?lang=bi&with=Rashi&lang2=en
6 Carasik, p. 218
7 *ibid.*, p. 219
8 *ibid.*, p. 223

Parashat Toldot

1 www.sefaria.org/Genesis.25.21?lang=bi&with=Rashi&lang2=en
2 www.sefaria.org/Genesis.25.21?lang=bi&with=Ruth%20Rabbah&lang2=en
3 www.sefaria.org/Genesis.25.22?lang=bi&with=Tur%20HaAroch&lang2=en
4 www.sefaria.org/Genesis.26.19?lang=bi&with=Radak&lang2=en
5 Sarna, p. 187
6 *ibid.*, p. 193

Parashat Vayetzei

1 Stairway to Heaven, Led Zeppelin, lyrics by Robert Plant and James Patrick (Jimmy Page), Led Zeppelin, 1971
2 *Baal HaTurim Chumash*, p. 251
3 Eight is Enough, ABC, American Comedy-Drama television series, 1977-1981
4 Carasik, p. 262
5 *ibid.*, p. 263
6 https://happydays.fandom.com/wiki/%22Sit_On_It%22
7 Carasik, p. 278
8 www.sefaria.org/Genesis.31.19?lang=bi&with=Rabbeinu%20Chananel&lang2=en
9 www.sefaria.org/Pesachim.3a.12?lang=bi&with=all&lang2=en

Parashat Vayishlach

1 *Baal HaTurim Chumash*, p. 292
2 Carasik, p. 290
3 www.sefaria.org/Genesis.32.8?lang=bi&with=Daat%20Zkenim&lang2=en
4 www.sefaria.org/Genesis.32.23?lang=bi&with=Rashi&lang2=en
5 www.sefaria.org/Genesis.32.23?lang=bi&with=Radak&lang2=en
6 www.sefaria.org/Genesis.32.23?lang=bi&with=Siftei%20Chakhamim&lang2=en
7 www.sefaria.org/Genesis.33.4?lang=bi&with=Radak&lang2=en
8 www.sefaria.org/Genesis.33.4?lang=bi&with=Bereishit%20Rabbah&lang2=en
9 www.sefaria.org/Sifrei_Bamidbar.69.2?lang=bi
10 Sarna, p. 230
11 *ibid.*, p. 236
12 Carasik, p. 311
13 *ibid.*, p. 323
14 www.sefaria.org/Genesis.36.24?lang=bi&with=Chizkuni&lang2=en

Parashat Vayeshev

1 Carasik, p. 330
2 https://en.wikipedia.org/wiki/Joseph_and_the_Amazing_Technicolor_Dreamcoat, Music by Andrew Lloyd Weber, Book and lyrics by Tim Rice
3 Carasik, p. 331
4 www.last.fm/music/The+Smothers+Brothers/_/Mom+Always+Liked+You+Best

5   *Baal HaTurim Chumash*, p. 344-345

6   Carasik, p. 335

7   *ibid.*, p. 336-337

8   Sarna, p. 262

9   Carasik, p. 357

Parashat Miketz

1   https://nosweatshakespeare.com/quotes/famous/to-sleep-perchance-to-dream/, Shakespeare, Hamlet

2   https://en.wikipedia.org/wiki/I_Dreamed_a_Dream, Les Miserables

3   Carasik, p. 367

4   Sarna, p. 367

5   www.sefaria.org/Pirkei_DeRabbi_Eliezer.38.1?ven

6   Walk Like An Egyptian, The Bangles, lyrics by Liam Sternberg, Different Light, 1986

Parashat Vayigash

1   *Baal HaTurim*, p. 415

2   Carasik, p. 397

3   *Baal HaTurim*, p. 421

4   Carasik, p. 399

5   www.sefaria.org/Sefer_HaYashar_(midrash)%2C_Book_of_Genesis%2C _Vayigash.1?lang=bi

6   Carasik, p. 406

Parashat Vayechi

1   www.sefaria.org/Genesis.47.28?lang=bi&with=Chizkuni&lang2=en

2   www.sefaria.org/Genesis.47.28?lang=bi&with=Or%20HaChaim&lang2=en

3   www.sefaria.org/Genesis.47.28?lang=bi&with=Radak&lang2=en

4   www.sefaria.org/Genesis.47.28?lang=bi&with=Tur%20HaAroch&lang2=en

5   *Baal HaTurim*, p. 443

6   Carasik, p. 414

7   Carasik, p. 426

8   www.sefaria.org/Genesis.49.13?lang=bi&with=Rashi&lang2=en

9   www.sefaria.org/Genesis.49.14?lang=bi&with=Rashbam&lang2=en

10   www.sefaria.org/Jerusalem_Talmud_Horayot.2.5.5?lang=bi&with=all&lang2=en

11   Carasik, p. 447

12   *ibid.*, p. 447

BOOK OF SHEMOT

Parashat Shemot

1   *Baal HaTurim Chumash, Shemot*, p. 514

2   Carasik, *The Commentators' Bible, Exodus*, p. 4

3   Nahum Sarna, *JPS Torah Commentary, Exodus*, p. 9

4   Carasik, p. 8-9

5   www.sefaria.org/Exodus.2.11?lang=bi&with=Rashi&lang2=en

6   www.sefaria.org/Shemot_Rabbah.1.26?lang=bi&with=all&lang2=en

7   Carasik, p. 20

8   *ibid.*, p. 21

9   www.sefaria.org/Shemot_Rabbah.1.26?lang=bi&with=all&lang2=en

10   Carasik, p. 27

11   Burton L. Visotzky, translator, ed., *The Midrash on Proverbs*, Yale University Press, 1992, p. 111

Parashat Vaera

1 *Baal HaTurim Chumash*, p. 571
2 Sarna, p. 42
3 Carasik, p. 59
4 *ibid.*, p. 60

Parashat Bo

1 Carasik, p. 65
2 *Baal HaTurim Chumash*, p. 612
3 Reach Out In the Darkness, Friend and Lover, lyrics by Jim Post, Reach Out of the Darkness, 1968
4 Signs, Five Man Electric Band, lyrics by Les Emmerson, Good-Byes and Butterflies, 1971
5 Carasik, p. 81
6 R. Yitzchak Ginsburgh, *The Alef-Beit: Jewish Thought Revealed through the Hebrew Letters*, Jason Aronson, Inc., Northvale, NJ, c. 1991, p. 125
7 Carasik, p. 90
8 *ibid.*, p. 91
9 www.sefaria.org/Exodus.12.42?lang=bi&with=Kli%20Yakar&lang2=en

Parashat Beshallach

1 www.sefaria.org/Ein_Yaakov%2C_Sotah.1.9?lang=bi&with=all&lang2=en
2 www.sefaria.org/Mishnah_Sotah.1.9?lang=bi&with=all&lang2=en
3 *Baal HaTurim Chumash*, p. 665-666
4 Carasik, p. 121
5 *Baal HaTurim Chumash*, p. 687
6 www.fao.org/hunger/en/
7 www.feedingtexas.org/learn/what-is-food-insecurity/
8 www.healthaffairs.org/doi/10.1377/hlthaff.2015.0645
9 Carasik, p. 123
10 *Baal HaTurim Chumash*, p. 689
11 www.sefaria.org/Bamidbar_Rabbah.15.24?lang=bi
12 www.sefaria.org/Legends_of_the_Jews.3.1.91?lang=bi&with=all&lang2=en
13 www.sefaria.org/Midrash_Tanchuma_Buber%2C_Yitro.17.1?lang=bi

Parashat Yitro

1 www.sefaria.org/Exodus.18.5?lang=bi&with=Rashi&lang2=en
2 www.sefaria.org/Exodus.18.25?lang=bi&with=Ibn%20Ezra&lang2=en
3 www.sefaria.org/Exodus.18.25?lang=bi&with=Chizkuni&lang2=en
4 Carasik, p. 143
5 *ibid.*, p. 145
6 *ibid.*, p. 146-147
7 www.sefaria.org/Exodus.19.4?lang=bi&with=Rabbeinu%20Bahya&lang2=en
8 www.sefaria.org/Exodus.19.4?lang=bi&with=Or%20HaChaim&lang2=en
9 www.chabad.org/parashahh/article_cdo/aid/4305087/jewish/The-Clouds-of-Glory -What-Were-They.htm#footnote8a4305087
10 www.sefaria.org/Pirkei_DeRabbi_Eliezer.31.11?lang=bi&with=all&lang2=en
11 http://www.jstor.org/stable/1205494., Revelation at Sinai in the Hebrew Bible and Jewish Theology, Benjamin D. Sommer, *The Journal of Religion*, Vol. 79, No. 3 (July, 1999), p. 422-451
12 *Baal HaTurim Chumash*, p. 751
13 https://www.sefaria.org/Pirkei_Avot.3.6?ven=Mishnah_Yomit_by_Dr._Joshua_ Kulp&lang=en,

Parashat Mishpatim

1 Carasik, *The Commentators' Bible, Exodus*, p. 177
2 https://www.sefaria.org/Kitzur_Shulchan_Arukh.192.3?lang=bi&with=all&lang2=en, accessed February 7, 2021
3 *Baal HaTurim Chumash*, p. 787
4 Sarna, p. 142
5 www.sefaria.org/Exodus.23.3?lang=bi&with=Or%20HaChaim&lang2=en
6 https://blogs.library.duke.edu/rubenstein/2015/01/14/jewish-voices-selma-montgomery-march/
7 https://minimalistquotes.com/frederick-douglass-quote-23333/
8 *Baal HaTurim Chumash*, p. 800
9 www.sefaria.org/Pirkei_Avot.6.2?lang=bi&with=all&lang2=en

Parashat Terumah

1 www.sefaria.org/Midrash_Tanchuma%2C_Terumah.3.3?lang=bi&with=all&lang2=en
2 *Baal HaTurim Chumash*, p. 815
3 www.sefaria.org/Exodus.25.22?lang=bi&with=Sifra&lang2=en
4 www.sefaria.org/Exodus.26.8?lang=bi&with=Midrash%20Tanchuma&lang2=en
5 www.sefaria.org/Pesikta_Rabbati.20.1?lang=bi&with=all&lang2=en
6 Carasik, p. 234
7 Scribing the Tabernacle: A Visual Midrash Embedded in the Torah Scroll - TheTorah.com
8 www.sefaria.org/Daat_Zkenim_on_Exodus.27.1.1?lang=bi&with=all&lang2=en
9 www.sefaria.org/Exodus.27.1?lang=bi&with=Rabbeinu%20Bahya&lang2=en
10 Carasik, p. 235

Parashat Tetzaveh

1 Light My Fire, The Doors, lyrics by Rolf Soja, Jim Morrison, Peter Zentner, John Paul Densmore, Robert A Krieger, Raymond D Manzarek, The Doors, 1
2 *Baal HaTurim Chumash*, p. 849
3 *ibid.*, p. 856
4 www.sefaria.org/Midrash_Tanchuma%2C_Shemot.27.1?lang=en
5 www.sefaria.org/Midrash_Tanchuma%2C_Shemot.27.3?lang=bi&with=all&lang2=en
6 www.sefaria.org/Midrash_Tanchuma%2C_Shemot.24.1?lang=bi&with=Lexicon&lang2=en
7 Carasik, p. 255
8 *Baal HaTurim Chumash*, p. 865
9 *ibid.*, p. 871
10 Carasik, p. 262
11 Nahum Sarna, p. 194
12 *ibid.*, p. 193
13 Carasik, p. 264
14 www.sefaria.org/Exodus.29.45?lang=bi&with=Sforno&lang2=en

Parashat Ki Tissa

1 *Baal HaTurim Chumash*, p. 883
2 www.sefaria.org/Exodus.31.13?lang=bi&with=Or%20HaChaim&lang2=en
3 www.rabbinicalassembly.org/story/cjls-guidance-remote-minyanim-time-COVID-19
4 Carasik, p. 300
5 *ibid.*, p. 302

Parashat Vayakhel

1 *Baal HaTurim Chumash*, p. 930-931
2 www.sefaria.org/Exodus.32.2?lang=bi&with=Rashi&lang2=en
3 www.sefaria.org/Exodus.32.2?lang=bi&with=Pirkei%20DeRabbi%20 Eliezer&lang2=en
4 Carasik, p. 318
5 www.sefaria.org/Exodus.35.34?lang=bi&with=Or%20HaChaim&lang2=en
6 Carasik, p. 320
7 www.sefaria.org/Exodus.36.8?lang=bi&with=Ramban&lang2=en
8 Carasik, p. 322
9 www.sefaria.org/Rabbeinu_Bahya%2C_Shemot.37.1.4?lang=bi&with=Lexicon &lang2=en
10 www.sefaria.org/Midrash_Tanchuma%2C_Shmini.11.1?lang=bi&with=all &lang2=en
11 www.sefaria.org/Bamidbar_Rabbah.15.4?lang=bi&with=all&lang2=en
12 Nahum Sarna, p. 230
13 www.sefaria.org/Rashi_on_Exodus.38.8.1?lang=bi&lookup3A&with=Lexicon &lang2=en
14 www.sefaria.org/Exodus.38.8?lang=bi&with=Ibn%20Ezra&lang2=en
15 www.sefaria.org/Exodus.38.8?lang=bi&with=Sforno&lang2=en
16 www.sefaria.org/Exodus.38.8?lang=bi&with=Chizkuni&lang2=en

Parashat Pekudei

1 Carasik, p. 328
2 www.sefaria.org/Exodus.38.27?lang=bi&with=Shenei%20Luchot%20 HaBerit&lang2=en
3 www.sefaria.org/Midrash_Tanchuma%2C_Pekudei.11.9?lang=bi&with=all &lang2=en
4 www.sefaria.org/Kedushat_Levi%2C_Exodus%2C_Tetzaveh.6?lang=bi&with =Lexicon&lang2=en
5 www.sefaria.org/Exodus.39.32?lang=bi&with=Chizkuni&lang2=en
6 *Baal HaTurim Chumash*, p. 970
7 www.sefaria.org/Exodus.39.42?lang=bi&with=Rabbeinu%20Bahya&lang2=en
8 www.sefaria.org/Exodus.39.43?lang=bi&with=Rashi&lang2=en
9 Carasik, p. 333
10 www.sefaria.org/Exodus.40.2?lang=bi&with=Tractate%20Soferim&lang2=en,
11 *Baal HaTurim Chumash*, p. 979
12 Carasik, p. 337

EPILOGUE

1 The Morning After, Maureen McGovern, lyrics by Al Kasha and Joel Hirschhorn, The Morning After, 1973
2 *The Poseidon Adventure* (1972) - Turner Classic Movies (tcm.com), The Poseidon Adventure, Twentieth Century Fox Film Corp., December, 1972

ABOUT THE AUTHOR

Rabbi Margie Cella received rabbinic ordination and an MA degree in Bible from the Jewish Theological Seminary of America upon completion of her studies in 2019, after having retired from her first career as a high school mathematics teacher in 2014. She also holds an MA degree in Liberal Studies from SUNY at Stony Brook and a BS degree in mathematics from Hofstra University. She is a member of the Rabbinical Assembly and the New York Board of Rabbis.

She is currently the rabbi of the Jewish Center of the Moriches in Center Moriches, NY, as well as an educator for the Women's League for Conservative Judaism.

This is Rabbi Cella's first book, reflecting her love of biblical exegesis, and her desire to inspire others to delve into the mysteries of the Torah.

She lives in Port Jefferson Station, NY, where she and her husband Raymond are surrounded by the love of their children and grandchildren.

ABOUT BOLD STORY PRESS

Bold Story Press is a curated, woman-owned hybrid publishing company with a mission of publishing well-written stories by women. If your book is chosen for publication, our team of expert editors and designers will work with you to publish a professionally edited and designed book. Every woman has a story to tell. If you have written yours and want to explore publishing with Bold Story Press, contact us at https://boldstorypress.com.

**BOLD
STORY
PRESS**

The Bold Story Press logo, designed by Grace Arsenault, was inspired by the nom de plume, or pen name, a sad necessity at one time for female authors who wanted to publish. The woman's face hidden in the quill is the profile of Virginia Woolf, who, in addition to being an early feminist writer, founded and ran her own publishing company, Hogarth Press.

Made in the USA
Middletown, DE
18 November 2023

42861174R00351